Proof of Causation in Tort Law

Causation is a foundational concep
compensation, a claimant must demonstrate that the defendant
was a cause of the injury suffered in order for compensation to be
awarded. Proof of Causation in Tort Law provides a critical,
comparative and theoretical analysis of the general proof rules of
causation underlying the tort laws of England, Germany and
France, as well as the exceptional departures from these rules
which each system has made. Exploring the different approaches
to uncertainty over causation in tort law, Sandy Steel defends the
justifiability of some of these exceptions, and categorises and
examines the kinds of exceptional rules suggested by the case law
and literature. Critically engaged with both the theoretical
literature and current legal doctrine, this book will be of interest
to private law scholars, judges and legal practitioners.

SANDY STEEL is an associate professor of law at the University of
Oxford, and a fellow of Wadham College. He was previously a
lecturer in law at King's College London. His work has been cited
by the UK Supreme Court and the High Court of Australia. In
2013, he was a visiting scholar at the Westfälische Wilhelms-
Universität Münster. His other books include *Great Debates in
Jurisprudence* (co-authored with Nick McBride, 2014) and *The
Structure of Tort Law* (a translation of Nils Jansen's *Die Struktur des
Haftungsrechts*, forthcoming).

CAMBRIDGE STUDIES IN INTERNATIONAL AND COMPARATIVE LAW

Established in 1946, this series produces high-quality scholarship in the fields of public and private international law and comparative law. Although these are distinct legal sub-disciplines, developments since 1946 confirm their interrelations.

Comparative law is increasingly used as a tool in the making of law at national, regional, and international levels. Private international law is now often affected by international conventions, and the issues faced by classical conflicts rules are frequently dealt with by substantive harmonisation of law under international auspices. Mixed international arbitrations, especially those involving state economic activity, raise mixed questions of public and private international law, while in many fields (such as the protection of human rights and democratic standards, investment guarantees and international criminal law) international and national systems interact. National constitutional arrangements relating to 'foreign affairs', and to the implementation of international norms, are a focus of attention.

The series welcomes works of a theoretical or interdisciplinary character, and those focusing on the new approaches to international or comparative law or conflicts of law. Studies of particular institutions or problems are equally welcome, as are translations of the best work published in other languages.

General Editors   James Crawford SC FBA
                         Whewell Professor of International Law, Faculty of Law,
                         University of Cambridge
                         John S. Bell FBA
                         Professor of Law, Faculty of Law, University of Cambridge

A list of books in the series can be found at the end of this volume.

Proof of Causation in Tort Law

Sandy Steel

CAMBRIDGE
UNIVERSITY PRESS

CAMBRIDGE
UNIVERSITY PRESS

University Printing House, Cambridge CB2 8BS, United Kingdom

One Liberty Plaza, 20th Floor, New York, NY 10006, USA

477 Williamstown Road, Port Melbourne, VIC 3207, Australia

4843/24, 2nd Floor, Ansari Road, Daryaganj, Delhi - 110002, India

79 Anson Road, #06-04/06, Singapore 079906

Cambridge University Press is part of the University of Cambridge.

It furthers the University's mission by disseminating knowledge in the pursuit of education, learning and research at the highest international levels of excellence.

www.cambridge.org
Information on this title: www.cambridge.org/9781107679856

First published 2015
First paperback edition 2017

A catalogue record for this publication is available from the British Library

Library of Congress Cataloging in Publication data
Steel, Sandy, author.
Proof of causation in tort law / Sandy Steel.
    pages   cm. – (Cambridge studies in international and comparative law)
Includes bibliographical references and index.
ISBN 978-1-107-04910-9 (Hardback) – ISBN 978-1-107-67985-6 (pbk.)
1. Proximate cause (Law)–Great Britain.   2. Proximate cause (Law)–Germany.
3. Proximate cause (Law)–France.   4. Torts–Great Britain.   5. Torts–Germany.
6. Torts–France.   I. Title.
K579.C34S74 2015
346.03–dc23   2015000386

ISBN   978-1-107-04910-9   Hardback
ISBN   978-1-107-67985-6   Paperback

Contents

France

England and Scotland

Australia

Canada

USA

Elsewhere

Introduction

Proof of causation: three types of problem

No proof of causation, no compensation. The general proof rule in perhaps every system of tort law is that the claimant must prove that the relevant aspect of the defendant's conduct was a cause of its injury in order to obtain substantial compensatory damages in respect of that injury.[1] And yet, almost equally universally, legal systems have made exceptions to this rule. This has allowed claimants to succeed either in full or partially, without proof that the defendant's conduct was a cause of their injury.[2]

This book is about the general proof rule and the exceptions that have been made to it.[3] At the outset, it is important to be clear that the book is not principally concerned with the analysis of the concept of causation. Questions about the *nature* of causation arise even when all of the facts are in. The focus of this book is on what the law of tort does and should do in situations where there is evidential *uncertainty* relative to some standard of proof as to whether the phenomenon of interest caused the outcome of interest. This inquiry only gets off the ground once we have decided upon what it is we are seeking to prove, that is, once we have decided upon what it means for something to cause something else.[4]

The aim of the book is to offer analysis and normative critique of the general and exceptional rules, concentrating on English, German, and French tort law, but comparisons will also be made with certain other

---

[1] See Chapter 1, 37–43. The terminology of 'injury', 'loss', and 'damage' is discussed therein: 40–41.

[2] See Chapters 4–6.   [3] The general rules are defined in Chapter 2.

[4] As it is possible, however, to elide (with ensuing confusion) conceptual issues as to the nature of causation with the question of what proof rules should govern the causal issue between the parties, it will be necessary to say something of the boundary between the two later. See Chapter 1, 16–37 and Chapter 5, 239–246.

common law systems.[5] The inquiry is prompted by the many difficult problems to which these rules have given rise. These problems are of three kinds: conceptual problems, problems of consistency, and normative problems.

The main *conceptual* problem in relation to the general rule concerns what is meant by 'proof' of causation. All of the systems examined here refer to an idea of 'probability' in the formulations of their standards of proof. English law requires proof on the balance of probabilities. What, however, is the nature of the probabilistic element in standards of proof? This question arises here because courts are often faced with statistical evidence of causation. The conceptual difficulty is in understanding the extent to which such evidence, and probabilistic evidence more generally, is capable of satisfying legal standards of proof either itself or in combination with other evidence.[6] Some courts have found that statistical evidence on its own is not sufficiently 'individualised' or 'particular' to the case at hand. But the sense in which this is so is often obscure.

Exceptional rules also raise conceptual problems. When legal systems depart from the general proof of causation rule, there are a number of ways of conceptualising this. It may be considered a reversal of the burden of proof. It may be a reduction in the standard of proof. It may be a shift from a threshold, all-or-nothing, system, whereby a person only recovers damages upon proving certain facts to a threshold probability and then recovers in full, to a non-threshold, proportionate system, whereby a person recovers in proportion to the probability of the facts (or some mixture). In the face of uncertainty over causation, some systems even claim to be altering the nature of the concept of causation, or the very basis upon which a person is liable to another in tort law, in order to allow claims to succeed.[7] Properly taxonomising different exceptions is not a mere conceptual obsession. Without a clear understanding of the nature of exceptional rules, we cannot hope to develop the law in a consistent way or to assess its merit.

The main problem of *consistency* is raised by the recognition of exceptional rules alongside the general rule. Here the question is whether any exceptional rule can rationally be contained within narrow limits or whether it undermines insistence upon the general rule *in any case*. For example, is it possible to create a localised system of proportionate

---

[5] The other comparisons are principally with Canada (see Chapter 4) and the United States (see Chapters 4–6).

[6] See Chapter 2.   [7] See Chapter 4, 166–167; Chapter 5, 225ff.

liability without undermining the threshold, all-or-nothing, general regime? The history of the development of exceptional rules in each system is marked by examples of an exceptional rule being created, its potential radically to undermine the general rule then being recognised, before, finally, it is subject to some apparently arbitrary limitation.[8] Some have argued that there is a kind of necessity to this history, and that only arbitrary limitations can *ever* be found once the initial departure from the general rule is made.[9] This book argues, on the contrary, that principled exceptions can be made, even if all systems have imposed arbitrary restrictions upon their current exceptional rules.[10] At any rate, it is a pressing question for all systems whether (and how) their exceptional rules can be rationalised consistently with their commitment to applying the general rule.

The general and exceptional rules give rise to two connected *normative* problems. First, there is the question of whether the general rule can be justified. The universal recognition of (some form of) exceptional rule(s) challenges the normative foundations of the general rule. Perhaps it is misguided. Perhaps the burden of proof on causation ought quite generally to be upon defendants. Perhaps uncertainty over causation should always be reflected simply by damages proportionate to the probability of causation, rather than by a threshold, all-or-nothing rule. Second, there is the question of whether, if the general rule can be justified, its justifications either positively suggest or leave open the possibility of exceptional rules being created (and, if so, what the scope of such rules should be). If one thought, for example, that the general rule were justified as efficient only in situations in which defendants cannot reliably predict that claimants could not prove causation against them, this might provide (an incentives-based) reason to create exceptional rules in situations where proof of causation is predictably and recurrently impossible.[11]

The book's argument

This book argues that the common law's version of the general rule – the requirement that the claimant prove that the relevant aspect of the defendant's conduct was a cause of its injury on the balance of

---

[8] See, especially, Chapter 5, 237–239.
[9] J. Morgan, 'Causation, Politics and Law: the English – and Scottish – Asbestos Saga', 63.
[10] See Chapter 4, 174–197.   [11] See Chapter 3, 135–137.

probabilities in order to obtain compensatory damages in respect of that injury – is generally justified.[12]

It is also argued, however, that a set of exceptions to this rule can be justified. The argument is that these exceptions should primarily be governed by the following principles:

> *Reliance upon wrongful conduct principle.* A defendant is not permitted to rely upon another's wrongful conduct in order to avoid a liability to pay damages, which would otherwise arise against that defendant, where that has the effect of depriving a person, whose injury would not have occurred had no-one behaved wrongfully in relation to that person, of any right to compensation in respect of that injury.[13]
>
> *Prevented claim principle.* If D1 has either wrongfully injured C or wrongfully prevented C from recovering damages for a wrongful injury caused by D2, C should recover damages from D1, even if C is unable to establish whether D1 wrongfully caused the injury or prevented C's recovery from D2.[14]
>
> *Proven causation principle.* If the evidence shows that D has wrongfully caused x per cent of the injuries within a group of persons, each of whom has suffered an injury which may have been caused by D, but none of whom can establish on the balance of probability that D's wrongful conduct was a cause of their injury, D should be liable either (a) to each member for x per cent of each member's losses or (b) to contribute in the entirety of the amount of loss it has caused to a court held fund from which members may claim proportionate shares, to the extent that this does not more likely than not require D to pay for more loss than D has wrongfully caused.[15]

The fundamental justification of the first principle is tort law's concern to ensure that a person is not deprived of a right to compensation in respect of an injury which would not have occurred had no one behaved wrongfully in relation to that person. The fundamental justification of the other principles is that requiring the defendant to pay compensation is in fact the best way to enforce its secondary moral duty of corrective justice in the special circumstances to which these principles apply. For example, suppose that D1 and D2 have each caused an injury to C1 and C2, but it cannot be determined whether C1's injury was caused by D1 or D2 nor whether C2's injury was caused by D1 or D2. Here, it is more consistent with each defendant's secondary moral duty

---

[12] See Chapter 3.   [13] See Chapter 4, 189–192.

[14] See Chapter 4, 175–185. The *reliance upon wrongful conduct principle* is partly justified by the *prevented claim principle*, but it is broader than the latter principle.

[15] See Chapter 6, 357–359.

to pay compensation to require them to pay damages into a fund to be dispersed to their victims than to deny liability. These principles justify liability, it will be argued, in what will be termed the indeterminate defendant situation, the claimant indeterminacy situation, and complex variants of these situations.[16] In short, the book only countenances exceptional rules being created in circumstances where either the defendant has in fact wrongfully caused injury or the claimant has been the victim of an injury that would not have occurred without wrongful conduct.[17]

Beyond these principles and these situations, the book argues, legal systems should not go. It thus rejects, for example, a reversal of the burden of proof on causation where the defendant has behaved with gross fault, a general reversal of the burden of proof, and proposals to abandon an all-or-nothing system of proof in favour of a system of proportional, probabilistic liability in relation to causation. It also rejects the award of substantial compensatory damages purely in respect of a lost chance, which is sometimes (incorrectly) termed a proportional liability.[18]

Even if the specific arguments of the book are not accepted, it also aims, more modestly, to present the conceptual and normative issues at stake more clearly than before, partly by drawing upon tort theory and the theory of the law of evidence, and partly through critically sifting the normative repository which the case law and legal literature of different legal systems provide. In this way, it will at least show some responses to causal uncertainty in tort law to be dead ends.

Causal uncertainty: its nature and sources

The kinds of causal uncertainty faced by tort law can be classified in different ways for different purposes. It will be helpful straight away to introduce two particular classifications of causal uncertainty which are commonly found in legal doctrine and legal literature and will be discussed later in the book.[19] These are the distinction between uncertainty over *general* and *specific* causation and the distinction between *factual* and *scientific* uncertainty. Both of these, broadly, draw distinctions

---

[16] See Chapters 4, 5, and 6.

[17] These are stated here as necessary, not sufficient, conditions of an exceptional rule being created. These necessary conditions follow from applying only the three principles stated.

[18] See Chapter 6.   [19] See Chapter 2, 67ff.

as to the *nature* of the uncertainty faced by the law. A third taxonomy, which distinguishes causal uncertainty by reference to the *source* of the uncertainty, is then introduced.

Uncertainty over general and specific causation

Causal uncertainty in tort law is often said to relate either to *general* causation or to *specific* causation.[20] The former concerns uncertainty over whether c can cause e (Can smoking cause cancer?). The latter concerns uncertainty over whether c caused e on a specific occasion (Did smoking cause John's cancer?). In essence, there is a broad distinction between cases where our uncertainty extends to ignorance over whether c can ever cause e and cases where our uncertainty is simply over whether c caused e on a specific occasion.

Some nuances of the general–specific distinction are explored later.[21] Two points should, however, be borne in mind now. First, one should avoid the impression that general causation is of any interest to tort law except in so far as it affects the fact-finder's judgement on specific causation. Tort law's primary concern is whether the alleged cause actually caused the outcome in the case before the court, not whether it can generally do so. Second, it must be emphasised that uncertainty over general causation is not wholly distinct from uncertainty over specific causation. In so far as we are uncertain about the former, we may be uncertain about the latter. And, conversely, in so far as a claimant has provided evidence that c can cause e in circumstances similar to its own, the claimant has already adduced *some* evidence that c did cause e.[22]

Factual and scientific causal uncertainty

Courts and legal academics often distinguish – with various purposes in mind – between 'factual' and 'scientific' uncertainty over causation.[23] Without more, this is an unsatisfactory distinction. Scientific uncertainty is just uncertainty over facts. However, the distinction can be used in ways which make it possible to attach some sense to it.

First, it may be used to isolate a set of typical problems that may arise when courts are faced with technical evidence of causation, presented by experts – evidence which will relate to areas of knowledge going beyond

---

[20] See, for example, L. Khoury, *Uncertain Causation in Medical Liability*, 49–50.
[21] See Chapter 2, 67ff.   [22] See Chapter 2, 94ff.
[23] See, for example, L. Röckrath, *Kausalität, Wahrscheinlichkeit und Haftung*, 213; L. Khoury, *Uncertain Causation*, 47–8.

common general knowledge.[24] These include uncertainty as to the probative force of *statistical* evidence, uncertainty arising from *disagreement* between scientific experts over the existence of a causal relationship, and uncertainty over the *reliability* of scientific evidence.[25]

Second, the distinction may also be used simply to refer to the difference between uncertainty over *general* causation and *specific* causation. Sciences, it might be said, are in the business of discovering causal generalisations or laws; they are not in the business of discovering whether a particular element of one of those generalisations was instantiated at a particular time.[26] This might be generally true, though some sciences are concerned with whether a particular fact was instantiated on a particular occasion, for example, forensic sciences such as ballistics.

Even in so far as a distinction between factual and scientific uncertainty can be said to refer to some conceptually robust, or even pragmatically robust, distinction, any attempt to rely upon it for some normative purpose, as some courts have done, must be thoroughly scrutinised.[27]

Causal uncertainty by source

It is possible to classify causal uncertainty by reference to typical causes of it. To say that *c* is a cause of causal uncertainty is, roughly, to say that without *c*, we would know or have greater understanding of the causal facts and normally we would know the causal facts were it not for *c*.

Time

The passage of time is a cause of causal uncertainty. Memories fade, records are lost, and people die. Suppose C used a drug forty years ago which only now materialises in injury, and that drug was manufactured by different manufacturers at the time it was ingested.[28] Uncertainty may arise over the identity of the manufacturer because C or C's pharmacist or doctor no longer has a record or recollection of the manufacturer. Had less time elapsed, this may well have been otherwise.

---

[24] See, using it in this sense, L. Khoury, *Uncertain Causation*, 47.

[25] This is not, of course, to claim that these types of problem require reasoning which is not continuous with general inductive reasoning. See D. Dwyer, *The Judicial Assessment of Expert Evidence*.

[26] See, emphasising the role of science in coming to know causal generalisations, R. Wright, 'The NESS Account of Natural Causation: A Response to Criticisms', 289.

[27] See Chapter 5, 237–238; 282–285.

[28] As in *Sindell* v. *Abbott Laboratories* (1980) 26 Cal 3d 588. See Chapter 4, 165–168.

Multiplicity of possible causes

If there is only one possible cause of an effect, then it is obviously easier to determine whether the defendant's conduct brought about the effect than if there are multiple possible causes of that effect. So the multiplicity of causes of an effect may lead to causal uncertainty.

Similarity of possible causes

If there are different circumstances (different causally sufficient sets of conditions) which can bring about e, and those circumstances operate in a similar way to bring about e, this often causes uncertainty as to which set of circumstances actually caused e. The classic example of this situation is where two or more hunters negligently fire in the direction of the claimant, at the same time, using identical bullets, and the claimant suffers injury from one bullet. The similarity of the causal process by which any of the hunters could have brought about the claimant's injury is one significant reason why we are uncertain about which hunter did so.[29]

Unobservability of causation

Many causal processes are directly observable.[30] Burnings, breakings, smashings, liftings are all such. But many causal processes (mechanisms) produce their effects behind closed doors. Most obviously, many mechanisms which bring about disease occur within the human body. One reason why it is difficult to attribute the causation of a mesothelioma (an asbestos-induced cancer) to a particular exposure to asbestos is the unobservability of the mechanism by which asbestos produces mesothelioma.

Absence of mechanistic knowledge

More generally, our absence of knowledge about a causal mechanism can create uncertainty. Sometimes we may be very confident that c can cause e, yet understand little about the mechanism, as is the case with asbestos and mesothelioma.[31] If we want to discern whether c rather than any other number of potential causes of e actually caused e, we often need information about the mechanism by which c does this. For example, if we know that a mechanism operates by leaving a certain residue on a person's lung, then this may be crucial evidence in earmarking c as a

---

[29] See Chapter 4, 161–165; 170–174.   [30] See Chapter 2, 67.   [31] See Chapter 5, 266ff.

cause. The consequence of not having such knowledge is that it is often only possible to speak in terms of statistical probabilities as to whether c was a cause of e.[32]

Counterfactual nature of causation

Assessing whether c was a cause of e often, possibly always, involves answering a counterfactual question: had c not occurred would e have occurred?[33] It is often said that the hypothetical nature of such a question creates uncertainty.[34] This is not as obvious as it may seem. Many hypotheticals (counterfactuals) are evidentially straightforward: 'would I have won Wimbledon if I had entered last year?' or 'would I have donated money to Oxfam if I had known they used it all to buy champagne?'

However, if we accept that it is generally easier to gain evidence as to observable events, we should also accept that it is generally more difficult to assess counterfactuals. It is not possible to observe whatever it is that makes a counterfactual true. We do not *observe* what would have happened, only what did happen.

Indeterminism and randomness

Indeterminism leads to causal uncertainty.[35] A world is indeterministic in so far as its state at one time does not entail (by virtue of physical laws) its state at another time.[36] If we imagine a world which is exactly the same in all respects at t, it is possible that the world will develop in different ways after t if that world is indeterministic. If our world is indeterministic, then there is an ineliminable uncertainty built into its fabric, because if a process is indeterministic, we could never *in principle* be sure how it would have developed (knowing all the facts will not help). In so far as we are concerned with an indeterministic process, we must talk in terms of probability.

In reality, we have little idea which, if any, aspects of our world are deterministic or indeterministic.[37] Many events seem to be undetermined (such as which lottery ball will appear next or human decisions). But there is always the possibility that some hidden difference between initial conditions explains a difference in outcomes. Nonetheless, we

---

[32] See Chapter 2, 62.   [33] See Chapter 1, 16–17.

[34] See, for example, R. Strassfeld, 'If. . . : Counterfactuals in the Law', 348–52 (discussing 'counterfactual dread').

[35] See, G. Mäsch, *Chance und Schaden*, 19–20.

[36] See C. Hoefer, 'Causal Determinism', section I.   [37] See Chapter 6, 351, n 224.

may sensibly say that many events display *randomness*, where randomness consists in variation of outcomes despite extremely similar initial conditions. This randomness means that we do not have specific evidence how a certain process would have developed on a specific occasion; again, the only evidence is probabilistic.

Human agency

Human beings can create causal uncertainty. Suppose that C is negligently shot by either D1 or D2. D1 and D2 use different kinds of bullets and the bullet which missed C cannot be found. A surgeon, told that the bullet lodged in C's body is essential evidence, carelessly misplaces it. Had the surgeon not behaved in that way, we would know which of D1 or D2 negligently injured C.

Cost

Sometimes we do not have causal knowledge because it is very expensive to obtain. For example, in the Canadian case of *Letnik* v. *Municipality of Metropolitan Toronto*, the claimant's ship suffered minor damage as a result of the defendant's negligence.[38] The ship unexpectedly sank two weeks later. The cost of raising the ship would have been somewhere between $324,000 and $890,000 (while the ship was itself valued at around $450,000). If the ship had been raised, it would in all likelihood have been possible to ascertain whether the initial collision, resulting from the defendant's negligence, had caused the ship to sink.

Tort law

In this book, 'tort law' refers primarily to the bodies of law which provide persons with remedies which respond to breaches of legal duties owed to them by other persons, where those duties are owed independently of contracts between them or declarations of trusts. Analytically, if X breaches a duty owed to Y, X also violates Y's legal rights. Conversely, whenever Y's legal rights are violated by X, X must have breached a legal duty owed to Y.[39] One could equally, then, describe the subject matter of this book as the bodies of law which provide remedies to persons that

---

[38] (1988) 44 CLT 69.

[39] At least on a plausible Hohfeldian analysis of legal rights and duties: see W. Hohfeld, 'Some Fundamental Legal Conceptions as Applied in Judicial Reasoning'. For similar views, R. Stevens, *Torts and Rights*, 2; E. Descheemaeker, *The Division of Wrongs*, 22.

respond to the invasion of legal rights those persons enjoy independently of contract and independently of the declaration of a trust.

The intention is thus to discuss the bodies of law referred to under the labels 'tort law', 'responsabilité civile extracontractuelle', and 'Deliktsrecht'. What holds these bodies of law together, beyond the labels, is the analytical and structural centrality of the idea that liability responds to the breach of a legal duty owed by one person to another, independently of a contract between the parties or a declaration of trust.[40] Call such a duty a 'basic duty' (or in rights-based terms, a 'basic right').[41] To the extent that is true, however, the body of law designated by the labels is somewhat arbitrarily distinguished from structurally similar bodies of law in each system and thus also excluded from any comparison between systems based upon these labels. Equitable wrongdoing, for example, is not treated as part of the English law of tort.[42] And if one focuses upon responsabilité civile extracontractuelle, one excludes the cognate body of law applicable to public bodies in France (responsabilité administrative). Comparisons with these structurally similar areas are limited in the present study.

The central notion of a breach of a basic duty is problematic in another respect. It excludes certain strict liabilities which are traditionally thought to fall within tort law in England and France. At least in some situations covered in books on tort law, the law is not imposing a primary legal duty not to cause injury through some activity, but only a legal liability to pay damages if loss is caused.[43] This is true, for example, of liability for damage caused by defective products under the Consumer Protection Act 1987.[44] Nonetheless, English tort law textbooks almost universally discuss liability under this Act.[45] Similarly, in

[40] See, for English law, N. McBride and R. Bagshaw, Tort Law, 4th edition, ch 1; for German law, G. Wagner, 'Commentary on §823 BGB' in Münchener Kommentar zum BGB, 5th edition, [12]; for French law, E. Descheemaeker, The Division of Wrongs, 17, especially n. 8 and 170ff; J. Halpérin, 'French Legal Doctrine', 79.

[41] See, N. McBride and R. Bagshaw, Tort Law, 4th edition, 2.

[42] See, pointing out this problem, E. Descheemaeker, The Division of Wrongs, 30. For example, knowing receipt of property held under a Treuhand (a contractual agreement to hold property on behalf of another) would fall within §826 BGB (a tort law provision).

[43] For a useful caution against rejecting an analysis of some strict liabilities in terms of primary legal duties, see J. Gardner, 'Some Rule-of-law Anxieties about Strict Liability in Private Law'; see also, P. Birks, 'The Concept of a Civil Wrong', 42.

[44] For reasons set out in N. McBride and R. Bagshaw, Tort Law, 4th edition, 397, especially n. 50.

[45] See, for example, S. Deakin, A. Johnston, B. Markesinis, Markesinis and Deakin's Tort Law, 7th edition, ch 20; J. Murphy and C. Witting, Street on Torts, 13th edition, ch 15; M. Lunney and K. Oliphant, Tort Law: Text and Materials, 5th edition, 572ff.

French law, Article 1384 of the Civil Code is interpreted as imposing strict liability for loss caused by things of which one is the keeper, yet it is not clear that this liability is to be understood as liability for the breach of a duty.[46] In German law, the predominant view is that strict liability is not part of the law of *delict (Deliktsrecht)*, though delict and strict liability are said to fall within the broader term *Haftungsrecht* – 'liability law'.[47] The focus of the book is upon wrong-based liabilities, but strict liabilities arising in respect of loss caused by human conduct which are conventionally treated alongside wrong-based causes of action also receive some attention.

The role of comparative law

The book principally compares English, French, and German law. The focus of the comparison is upon the content of the legal rules and reasons given for those rules by judges and scholars in each system. The systems were chosen because each system has developed both extensive case law and doctrinal literature on proof of causation. There are three main reasons for the comparative aspect of this study.

First, it is likely that legal systems can learn from each other's approaches to the three kinds of causal proof problem identified above. This might consist either of finding better justifications for existing rules, of realising that reform is necessary and what shape it might take, or it might consist simply in the process of engagement itself. For example, each system has faced the question of how rationally to limit exceptions to the general rule that the claimant must prove causation. As we shall see, each offers answers that, while similar in some respects, diverge considerably. By considering the justifications offered by other systems, there is at least some likelihood that each system may be able to better rationalise its own approach or to avoid the potential dangers of alternatives.

---

[46] It might be thought that the same could be said of Article 1382: 'Tout fait quelconque de l'homme, qui cause à autrui un dommage, oblige celui par la faute duquel il est arrivé à le réparer'. This speaks only of a secondary duty to repair, not a primary duty not to injure by fault. However, as Descheemaeker points out, the notion of a primary obligation/duty is implicit in one dominant conception of *fault* under Article 1382. E. Descheemaeker, *The Division of Wrongs*, 17, n. 8.

[47] See N. Jansen, *Die Struktur des Haftungsrechts*, 31. See also G. Wagner, 'Comparative Tort Law', defining strict liability (too narrowly) as 'liability which is not based on the infringement of a duty', 1029.

Second, the English law on proof of causation is, in several respects, problematic, as shown later in the book.[48] There are few defenders of certain key aspects of it. It may therefore be particularly helpful for the English lawyer to consider alternative approaches which have been developed over time in other systems.

Third, comparing the reasoning and results in legal systems can assist in a wider process of 'reflective equilibrium'. Reflective equilibrium is a method in normative ethics of attempting to subsume one's moral intuitions or judgements about particular cases within some wider framework of principle, ultimately setting aside those intuitions which cannot be satisfactorily reconciled with a principle, or set of principles, which has wide explanatory power of particular instances.[49] One reaches 'reflective equilibrium' when one reaches an acceptable consistency among one's beliefs about particular cases and overarching principles. To the extent that, say, an English lawyer has a firm conviction as to the moral validity of some principle, the fact that the same principle has been explicitly rejected by German Courts gives at least some reason to pause and consider whether the conviction should be as firmly held. If comparative law can assist in this way, it can assist in coming to informed, robust views about the normative issues identified in this Introduction.

The structure of the book

The book is structured as follows. Chapter 1 briefly sets out, as necessary preliminary to consideration of the proof rules of causation, the substantive understanding of causation in each system, and the legal roles that the concept of causation plays.

Chapter 2 then describes the general proof rules of causation in each system: the general burden and standard of proof. It considers the nature of the probabilistic aspect to standards of proof – comparing the different standards in each system – the processes of reasoning and types of evidence by which fact finders arrive at judgments of causation, and specific problems involved in the application of these general rules.

Chapter 3 examines the normative foundations of the general rule that the claimant prove causation to a particular standard of proof. It considers consequentialist and non-consequentialist justifications for this

---

[48] See Chapters 5 and 6. Even its creators have been critical of it: see Lord Hoffmann, 'Fairchild and After', especially at 65–6.

[49] See, generally, N. Daniels, 'Reflective Equilibrium'.

requirement. It argues that strong justification is needed to depart from the rule that the claimant must prove causation on the balance of probability.

Chapter 4 begins the analysis of existing departures from the requirement that the claimant must prove causation to the legal system's requisite standard of proof. It is concerned with liability in situations of 'defendant indeterminacy' and complex variants of this situation. That is: it is concerned with the liability of defendants in situations in which the claimant cannot prove which of a number of defendants, each of whom has behaved wrongfully in relation to it, were a cause of its injury to the requisite standard of proof, where it is proven that at least one defendant did wrongfully injure the claimant. It argues that an exception to the general rule can be justified in situations like this and that this exception is normatively distinctive – it does not entail wide-ranging further exceptions.

Chapter 5 moves beyond the situation of defendant indeterminacy to situations where the claimant cannot prove that its injury was due to a tort, and yet legal systems hold defendants who may have caused the injury liable in full. It argues that the justifications for doing so, where the defendant has not been proven to have caused wrongful injury, do not withstand scrutiny.

Chapter 6 is concerned with the same types of case as Chapter 5, but in which systems have not imposed *full* liability, but only a probabilistic, proportionate liability. Different species of probabilistic liability are distinguished and the complex law in each system is analysed. It is argued that, while individuals do have interests in chances of good things and thus that the loss of a chance can be described as a genuine 'loss', individuals' interests in chances are insufficiently powerful to generate freestanding legal rights that those chances not be destroyed and that the extent of damages awarded for lost chances should be minimal. However, it is suggested that a version of the *proven causation principle* may generate proportional liability in cases where defendants have been proven to have wrongfully caused injury to unidentified claimants.

Chapter 7 summarises the main conclusions.

1 Causal concepts and causal questions in tort law

This book takes as its subject the proof rules of causation in tort law: the legal rules which determine what judges must do in tort cases when there is uncertainty about the empirical causal truth.[1] But to know when there is uncertainty about causation (rather than something else), it is necessary to know what causation is, or, at least, what causation is from tort law's perspective. So, the first part of this chapter describes tort law's understanding of causation.

This first part will be limited to setting out the causal concepts recognised by each system, the application of which may be faced with empirical uncertainty. The reason for this limitation is simply that our principal concern is with the legal treatment of empirical uncertainty over causation.[2] In general, when one moves beyond the aspects of the concept of causation described in the different systems as the 'factual' or 'natural' aspects of the concept, the only uncertainty one faces over causation is conceptual or normative, not empirical.[3] So, the causal concepts described in this chapter are those typically categorised as relating to 'factual' or 'natural' causation.[4]

The second part of the chapter explains the different roles the concept of causation plays in substantive tort law rules and how it relates to other legal concepts in those rules. This is of importance, first, because

---

[1] For further detail on what a proof rule is, see Chapter 2.

[2] See Introduction, 7–10, for a catalogue of the sources of empirical uncertainty.

[3] For example, if one accepts that causal chains are broken by 'free, deliberate, and informed' actions (for this view, see H.L.A. Hart and T. Honoré, *Causation in the Law*, 2nd edition, 41–4 and *passim*), one might be uncertain as to whether a certain act should be classified as truly 'free' for this purpose. This is a *conceptual* uncertainty.

[4] For the designation of these causal concepts as 'factual' or 'natural' aspects of the causal inquiry, see, for example, A. Spickhoff, *Folgenzurechnung im Schadensersatzrecht*, 12–19; J. Stapleton, 'Factual Causation', 468.

different proof rules apply depending on the stage of the legal inquiry at which causation is involved[5] and, second, because it will assist in delimiting what constitutes a causal question, rather than some other question relevant to liability.

Causal concepts in tort law

English, German, and French tort law each recognise that if c and e are specific distinct events or states of affairs, and c and e have occurred, c was a cause of e, if and only if:

(a) e would not have occurred had c not occurred *or*
(b) c contributed to the production of e
     (i)   The core case of contribution in each system is where c plays a positive role in the causal process by which e occurs.

(a) is the 'but-for' test of causation and is briefly explained first. (b) refers to the causal concept which is employed by each system – though not termed by each system as the concept of 'contribution' – when it accepts that c was a cause of e even where it is known that e would have occurred regardless of c or where it is not established that e would not have occurred without c.[6] The existence and nature of this causal concept is illustrated in the second and third sections of this part of the book through discussion of the legal analysis of situations of 'causal redundancy': cases where c is accepted to be a cause despite being known to fail the but-for test.[7] The fourth section examines some attempts to analyse the concept of contribution in order further to clarify the substantive subject matter of this book. The final section summarises the main conclusions.

The but-for or conditio sine qua non test

The primary test of causation recognised by each system's tort law is the but-for or conditio sine qua non test.[8] According to the but-for test, c is a

---

[5] See Chapter 2.
[6] That is: where it is not established to the requisite standard of proof that e would not have occurred without c and it is held, *according to the orthodox standard of proof*, that c was a cause of e.
[7] The helpful terminology of 'causal redundancy' is used by philosophers of causation to refer to the genus of cases where c caused e despite e not being counterfactually dependent upon c. See, for example, L. Paul and N. Hall, *Causation: a User's Guide*, ch 3.
[8] See, generally, B. Winiger, H. Koziol, B. Koch and R. Zimmermann, *Digest of Natural Causation*, 99; C. van Dam, *European Tort Law*, first edition, 310: 'all jurisdictions apply the conditio sine qua non test'. England: L. Khoury, *Uncertain Causation in Medical Liability*, 21.

cause of e if e would not have occurred had c not occurred. So a defendant's negligent failure to provide a safety harness to an employee is a cause of the employee's death if the provision of the harness would have prevented the employee's death.[9] Normally, the but-for test is formulated not merely as a sufficient condition of causation (as above), but also as a necessary one.[10] However, as we shall see, each system accepts that causation can exist even when the but-for test is not satisfied; hence it is more appropriate to formulate the test as a sufficient condition.

The but-for test simply asks whether e would have occurred if c had not. Whether this is true of c and e depends crucially upon how c, e, and the world in which c is imagined not to occur are described.[11] The but-for test, or any other test of causation, does not itself fully determine the relevant description of c and e. This depends upon the legal rule at issue. For example, in the tort of negligence the issue is whether D's *negligent driving* was a but-for cause of C's injury not whether D's *driving* was a but-for cause of C's injury. The appropriate description of c is thus 'D's negligence', not 'D's conduct'.[12]

The description of the counterfactual world to be considered in determining whether e would have occurred without c is similarly determined by reference to the legal rule in question. The general rule, in cases where one is concerned with the causal connection between wrongful conduct and an outcome, is that one imagines a world exactly similar to the actual world except that the defendant behaves non-wrongfully.[13] So, in the last example one imagines a world exactly similar to the actual world until c, except that *Driver* conforms to his legal duty of care: that is, drives non-negligently.

USA: *Restatement of the Law (Third) Torts: Liability for Physical and Emotional Harm*, §26 (subject to §27); R. Wright, 'Causation in Tort Law', 1775; D. Robertson, 'The Common Sense of Cause in Fact', 1768; D. Fischer, 'Insufficient Causes', 279. Germany: H. Kötz and G. Wagner, *Deliktsrecht*, 11th edition [186]; H. Lange and G. Schiemann, *Schadensersatz*, 79 (a 'Faustregel'). France: S. Galand-Carval, 'Causation in French Tort Law', 53. See also: *Principles of European Tort Law*, Art. 3:101.

[9] *McWilliams* v. *Sir William Arrol & Co. Ltd* [1962] UKHL 3.

[10] See, for example, *McWilliams* v. *Sir William Arrol & Co. Ltd* [1962] UKHL 3, 7: "...if the accident would have happened in just the same way whether or not I fulfilled my duty, it is obvious that my failure to fulfil my duty cannot have caused or contributed to it".

[11] See J. Stapleton, 'Unnecessary Causes', 42–3.

[12] See, for example, *Phethean-Hubble* v. *Coles* [2012] EWCA Civ 349, [47].

[13] The matter is a little more complex. In English law, one imagines, in constructing the hypothetical comparator, that D minimally complied with D's legal duty in the circumstances *unless* D would actually have done more than the minimum in conforming to their duty. See *Robbins* v. *London Borough of Bexley* [2013] EWCA Civ 1233. See further, S. Steel, 'Defining Causal Counterfactuals in Negligence'.

Contribution: pre-emption

A first situation in which c can be said to be a cause of e despite failing the but-for test (and so a case where c could only be said to have 'contributed' in our terminology) is where c is a pre-emptive cause of e.[14] A pre-emptive cause is one which produces an effect in such a way as to prevent a different factor (or factors) from producing the effect, where that different factor, if it had run to completion, would have been sufficient[15] to cause e at the same time, or within a short space of time. Consider:

> Assassins. Assassin A plants a bomb at 14.30, timed to explode beside Victim at 15.00. Assassin B replaces the bomb at 14.35 with his own, identical, bomb, also programmed to explode at 15.00. The latter bomb explodes, killing Victim.

Assassin B is a cause of Victim's death even though the death would have happened at exactly the same time anyway: B pre-empted A. Of course, such cases are rare: often it will be possible to say that the effect would not have occurred *when* it did but-for the pre-empting factor or that *this specific event* (e.g. death *at a certain time*) would not have occurred. It follows that many, but not all, cases of pre-emption can be brought within the but-for test (i) without the need to treat them separately as cases of contribution.[16]

Nonetheless, there are cases in each system where the causal status of a pre-empting factor has been recognised, to the exclusion of the pre-empted factor, without reliance upon the but-for test. In *Steel* v. *Joy*, the claimant was the victim of an accident caused by D1 in December 1996 and the victim of an accident caused by D2 in March 1999. The first accident was held to have caused the acceleration of a pre-existing spinal problem – even though the problem would have been accelerated, to the same extent, by D2's accident anyway. D1's tort could nonetheless

---

[14] For discussions of pre-emption, see L. Paul and N. Hall, *Causation*, 70–143; R. Wright, 'Causation in Tort Law' 1794–8; J. Stapleton, 'Choosing what we mean by "Causation" in the Law' 451–3 (who is, however, sceptical that there is a causal problem for the law in pre-emption cases).

[15] It should be assumed, unless otherwise stated, that whenever the word 'sufficient' is used that this means 'sufficient in combination with other factors'.

[16] Wright denies the legitimacy of this qualification of the but-for test (see his 'The NESS Account of Natural Causation: A Response to Criticisms', 292–4). To this, one may reply *ad hominem* that his own account of causation (on which, see p. 26) needs to define precisely *when* an effect occurs if it is to be successful in pre-emption cases. Cf. J. Stapleton, 'Choosing what we mean by "Causation" in the Law', 451–3.

be said to be a cause of losses that would have happened anyway due to D2's tort. Lord Justice Dyson said: 'It is true that, but for the first accident, the second accident would have caused the same damage as the first accident. But that is irrelevant.'[17] Similarly, in the famous New Hampshire case of *Dillon* v. *Twin State*, a boy fell from a bridge, doomed to die, but was electrocuted by a negligently placed cable as he fell.[18] It was plain that the boy died from electrocution even if his death, guaranteed by his hurtling toward the ground, would have happened anyway.[19] The impression given by these cases is that the causal status of the pre-empting factor can be established without the but-for test being satisfied.

The phenomenon of contribution by pre-emption is explicitly recognised in German law. Such cases are doctrinally denoted as concerning 'hypothetical causation' (*hypothetische Kausalität*). The idea behind the terminology is that while one factor actually caused the effect, the other (pre-empted) factor only *would have* caused the effect (hypothetical causation). The factor which *would have* caused the effect, but actually did not, is usually termed the 'reserve' or 'substitute' cause.[20] The BGH has appealed to the idea that the 'actual' causal relationship between the pre-empting factor and the effect is not affected by what *would* have happened. By implication, then, causation is established in these cases without the but-for test.[21]

---

[17] *Steel* v. *Joy* [2004] EWCA Civ 576, at [70]. See, similarly, *Performance Cars Ltd* v. *Abraham* [1962] QB 33. For a structurally identical case to *Performance Cars*, also involving damage to a car in German law, with the same result, see: BGH NJW-RR 2009, 1030, especially at 1031, [25]. Nothing turns here, *for the causal question* of whether the pre-empting cause was indeed causative, upon whether the pre-empted factor was tortious or non-tortious. That goes to the separate question of damages. See, further, p. 42.

[18] *Dillon* v. *Twin State Gas & Electric Co.* (1932) 85 NH 449 (*Dillon*).

[19] *Dillon*, 457: '...he died from electrocution'. The court considers various hypothetical inquiries as relevant to the issue of damages in respect of the death, but not causation of the death (*Dillon*, 456–7).

[20] For example, G. Schiemann, 'Commentary on §249 BGB' *in Staudinger BGB*, 2005 edition, [93]; H. Oetker 'Commentary on §249 BGB' in *Münchener Kommentar zum BGB*, 6th edition, [207]. A subspecies of hypothetical causation is 'overtaking causation' (*überholende Kausalität*). This term is usually reserved for situations in which the pre-empted factor was already in existence when the pre-empting factor (the 'overtaking' cause) caused the effect. See M. Gebauer, *Hypothetische Kausalität*, 5.

[21] BGHZ 104, 356, NJW 1988, 3265, 3266: 'Daß der durch das haftungsbegründende Ereignis real bewirkte Schaden später durch einen anderen Umstand (die Reserveursache) ebenfalls herbeigeführt worden wäre, kann an der Kausalität der realen Ursache nichts ändern'.

Contribution in overdetermined situations

The only other situation in which c may be a cause of e despite not meeting the but-for test is where c contributes to the production of e where e is overdetermined.[22] A cause, c, contributes to the production of an overdetermined effect, e, wherever it plays an unnecessary, but causal, role in bringing about e, and the effect was brought about at the same time by other causes which were sufficient, independently of, or jointly with, c, to bring e about at that time.[23] The crux of the difference to pre-emption cases, then, is that the reason why c is not a but-for cause in overdetermination situations is due to the existence of other *actual causes* of e. In each of the following cases A causally contributes to the effect despite failing the but-for test:[24]

> *Two Hunters. Hunter A* and *Hunter B* each, independently, negligently fire towards *V*. *V* is struck in the head by both bullets simultaneously. *V* dies.
>
> *Votes. Director A, Director B* and *Director C* each negligently vote to manufacture a dangerous product. A simple majority carries the vote. The vote is carried.

These cases tend to be distinguished in the literature.[25] The first is said to involve unnecessary, sufficient causes, while the latter is said to involve

---

[22] Why is this the only other situation beyond pre-emption? Because there are only two ways in which causes can be unnecessary for their effects. They are unnecessary only if some other sufficient factors are on the scene and these factors will either be non-causes (pre-emption) or causes (overdetermination). Notice that the problem for causal analysis raised by overdetermination situations is not an *epistemic* problem. It is not that we do not *know* which factor or factors were causative of the result. We *know* that both hunters caused V's death and each vote was a cause of the passing of the motion in the examples below in the text (what we *may* lack is an analysis). Cf. S. Green, *Causation in Negligence*, 67, who non-standardly claims that the 'very issue' in overdetermination cases is that we do not know which factor was actually causative. This leads Green to treat genuine cases of empirical uncertainty, such as where only one bullet struck V, but we cannot determine which, as overdetermination cases (73, 85). This occludes an important moral difference between these types of case, namely, that in the empirical uncertainty type, *only one defendant* has actually played a causal role in V's death. To the extent that we agree with Green, however, that there is a genuine uncertainty over whether each hunter was a cause in *Two Hunters*, this uncertainty is *conceptual,* not evidential, albeit there is some plausibility in treating conceptual and evidential uncertainty in analogous ways. See Chapter 4, 189–191.

[23] More formally: an effect is overdetermined if and only if: (i) at least one of the causes of the effect, C, is not necessary for its occurrence at the time it occurred; (ii) the effect was also caused by other factors [D, E, F, etc.]; (iii) the other factors were sufficient, independently or jointly with C, to cause the effect at the time it occurred.

[24] Admittedly, there are some doubters about whether the unnecessary contributors to overdetermination situations are causes. See, notoriously, D. Lewis, 'Causation', 567 n. 12.

[25] See, for example, J. Stapleton, 'Factual Causation', 473–5.

unnecessary and insufficient causes.[26] This is tolerable so long as it is realised that 'sufficiency' is being used to mean: 'sufficient, holding fixed the non-salient causes of e in the circumstances'. It does not literally mean: 'individually sufficient' in the sense of 'sufficient absent all other causes of e'. Nothing individually suffices, in this latter sense, to produce anything else; arsonists only cause fires by dint of oxygen in the air. In this way of speaking, then, overdetermination cases either involve unnecessary, independently sufficient causes *or* unnecessary, insufficient causes *or* a combination of these two (e.g. one unnecessary, insufficient cause and one independently sufficient cause[27]).[28]

Such cases are not only philosophical fantasies.[29] Each system has developed more or less tentative answers to them. English law is probably committed to the possibility of a factor being a cause in an overdetermination situation. In relation to independent sufficiency cases, this is so for two reasons. First, there are decisions in which reasoning assumes that c can cause e in this kind of situation. In *Baker* v. *Willoughby*, the claimant's leg was tortiously injured by D1 in 1964. In 1967, his leg was tortiously injured by D2 and was amputated.[30] It was held that D1 and D2 were *both* causes of C's 'present disability' after 1967.[31] D1 was a cause of this despite the fact that it would have occurred anyway after 1967 due to D2's tort and D2 was a cause despite the fact that D1's tort was independently sufficient for the disability. Each tort was independently sufficient for (part of) the disability after 1967. Second, there are dicta, and extensive academic consensus, to the effect that each factor could be said to be a cause in an independent sufficiency situation.[32]

It has also been recognised in English law that there can be causation in insufficient cause cases. Clear examples are cases involving human decisions, where common law systems have generally accepted that a *reason* can causally influence a person's decision to do something even

---

[26] Ibid.

[27] This last situation is sometimes termed one of 'asymmetric' overdetermination: see, for example, M. Moore, *Causation and Responsibility*, 489–90.

[28] See also S. Green, *Causation in Negligence*, 61–2.

[29] For general philosophical discussion, see H.L.A Hart and T. Honoré, *Causation in the Law*, 2nd edition, 122–5; M. Moore, *Causation and Responsibility*, 411–25. L. Paul and N. Hall, *Causation*, ch 3.

[30] *Baker* v. *Willoughby* [1970] AC 467.   [31] See *Baker*, 492 (Lord Reid).

[32] *Kuwait Airways Corporation* v. *Iraq Airways Co (Nos 4 and 5)* [2002] 2 AC 883 at [74] (Lord Nicholls); *Orient-Express Hotels Ltd* v. *Assicurazioni General SpA* [2010] EWHC 1186 at [33] (Hamblen J); *Greenwich Millennium Village Ltd* v. *Essex Services Group Plc* [2013] EWHC 3059, [174] (Coulson J); *Huyton SA* v. *Peter Cremer GmbH* [1999] 1 Lloyd's Rep 620, 636 (Mance J); *March* v. *E & M H Stramare Pty Ltd* (1991) 171 CLR 506, 516 (Mason CJ); *Chappel* v. *Hart* (1998) 195 CLR 232, 282–3. J. Stapleton, 'Factual Causation', 474.

if it is neither a necessary nor independently sufficient factor.[33] The phenomenon has also been implicitly recognised in the context of cases involving purely physical processes (cases not involving the causal influence of reasons upon behaviour). Consider, for example, *Bailey v. Ministry of Defence*.[34] The defendant's negligently inattentive medical care had added to severe muscular weakness on the part of the claimant, who was already weakened by the effect of a non-tortious surgical operation. In her weakened state she was unable to cough, aspirated her own vomit, and as a result suffered a heart attack and severe brain damage. It was impossible to say on the balance of probability whether her injuries would not have occurred if the defendant had taken care. Nonetheless, the Court of Appeal held that the defendant's negligence was, on the balance of probability, a cause of the injury.

This was on the basis of the finding of the trial judge, Foskett J, that the negligence 'contributed materially to the overall weakness and it was the overall weakness that caused the aspiration'.[35] The claimant in *Bailey* succeeded on the causal issue, then, because it could at least be shown on the balance of probability that the defendant's negligence contributed to the injury in a similar way to the way that an individual vote contributed to the passage of the vote in *Voting*.[36] Even if the pre-existing weakness was independently sufficient to cause the injury (like the other two votes in *Voting*), nonetheless the defendant at least made an unnecessary, insufficient, contribution to it. It must be emphasised that the claim here is simply that *one* way in which the language of 'material contribution' is used in English law is to capture unnecessary causal contributions to an effect.[37]

---

[33] *Barton v. Armstrong* [1976] AC 104; *Henville v. Walker* (2001) 206 CLR 459, 493 (McHugh J).

[34] [2008] EWCA Civ 883, [2009] 1 WLR 1052. This interpretation of *Bailey* was suggested in S. Steel and D. Ibbetson, 'More Grief on Uncertain Causation in Tort', 454–5, 458.

[35] [2007] EWHC 2913 at [60].

[36] If this is not clear, consider a different analogy. *Unwanted Car*: A and B pushed a car off a bridge at 15.00. If B had not pushed, the car would have fallen off at 15.00 due to A's push anyway. Here B contributes to the car's fall. The additional weakness in *Bailey* was known to have played a role similar to the additional force of B's push in *Unwanted Car*.

[37] See Chapter 5 at p. 240 for other uses. The position in American tort laws is similar. For recognition of causation in sufficient cause cases, see: *Anderson v. Minneapolis, St Paul & Sault Ste Marie Railway Co.* (1920) 146 Minn 430, 440–1; *Basko v. Sterling Drug Inc* (1969) 416 F 2d 417, 429 (2nd Circuit, applying Connecticut law); *Callahan v. Cardinal Glennon Hospital* (1993) 863 SW 2d 852, 862 (Missouri Sup Ct); *Sanders v. American Body Armor & Equipment Inc* (1995) 652 So 2d 883, 884–5 (Florida CA); *Restatement Torts (Third): Liability for Physical and Emotional Harm*, §27. For insufficient cause cases, see: *Warren v. Pankhurst* (1904) 92 NYS 725; *Tidal Oil Co v. Pease* (1931) 5 P 2d 389 (Oklahoma); *Boim v. Holy Land Foundation for Relief and Development* (2008) 549 F 3d 685, 697–9 (7th Circuit); *Paroline v.*

German law also clearly accepts causation in independent sufficiency cases. This is an established doctrinal category: it is a case of duplicative or double causation (*Doppelkausalität*).[38] The BGH recently described this category of case as follows:

If an injury has been caused by several, simultaneously or concurrently effective, events, each of which would have been sufficient on its own to produce the entire injury, then, according to the case law of this court, each event is to be classed as a cause of the injury, as a matter of law, even though none satisfies the *conditio sine qua non* test.[39]

The position in relation to insufficient cause cases is less clear. German *criminal* law has faced situations similar to *Votes*. In a decision of 1990, the BGH held each of the members of a company board which failed to recall a dangerous product from the market criminally responsible for the injuries caused by the product.[40] It was held that each board member could be said to be a cause of the injury, even though it may have been the case that, had the defendant conformed to its own duty to take available steps to recall the product – for instance, by voting in favour of its being recalled – the other board members would still have refused to recall the product.[41] Here each defendant was said to be causal, despite their conduct being neither necessary nor sufficient for the injuries. There is some support among doctrinal writers for a similar solution in tort law.[42]

The position in French law on causal overdetermination is obscure. The leading textbooks on tort do not discuss the problem.[43] Quézel-Ambrunaz's recent monograph on causation claims (citing no decisions) that causation would 'indisputably' be found in independent sufficiency cases.[44] It may be that the rarity of true overdetermination cases is such that the problem has simply not arisen for judicial decision.[45]

United States 701 F 3d 749 (Supreme Court, 2014); see generally, D. Fischer, 'Insufficient Causes', 284–6.

[38] See generally, L. Röckrath, *Kausalität, Wahrscheinlichkeit, und Haftung*, 39–40.

[39] BGH NJW 2013, 2018. See also, for example, BGH 17.12.2013, VI ZR 211/12, [50].

[40] See BGH NJW 1990, 2560, 2566. Where the defendant had participated in a common decision not to recall the product, their liability was also justified on the grounds of (non-causal) accessorial liability. See also, BGH NJW 2003, 522, 526.

[41] Ibid., 2566.   [42] See L. Röckrath, *Kausalität*, 43–4.

[43] It is not mentioned, for instance, in the latest 4th edition of G. Viney, P. Jourdain, S. Carval, *Les conditions de la responsabilité*.

[44] C. Quézel-Ambrunaz, *Essai sur la causalité en droit de la responsabilité civile*, 605.

[45] It may be that a precise application of the but-for test has dealt with cases which approximate overdetermination cases (i.e. by describing the injury with precision). This approach has been proposed in French criminal law: see Quézel-Ambrunaz, *Essai*, 42–3.

Pre-emption, overdetermination, and omissions

English and German tort law seem to differ in relation to whether an *omission* can be a cause despite failing the but-for test. In German law, the BGH has recently stated, in a claim in tort for the failure to inform a patient of the risks of an operation allegedly resulting in injury, that:

> An omission is *only* causative of an injury if duty-conforming behaviour would have prevented the injury's occurrence.[46]

This logically rules out the possibility of omissive pre-emption or omissive overdetermination. The position in criminal law seems, however, to be different.[47]

English law seems to recognise the possibility that an omission may play a causal, but non-necessary, role in the production of an outcome where the omission leads to the existence of an element in a positive causal process which brought about the outcome. This seems to underpin the causal judgment in *Bailey*, where but-for D's negligence there would have been less of the physical process (the weakness) which led to C's injury.[48]

However, it is not clear whether English law recognises the possibility of omissive conduct being a cause in other situations where the but-for test is not satisfied. Consider, for example, *McWilliams* v. *Sir William Arrol & Co.*[49] Here D negligently failed to provide V, D's employee, with a safety harness to wear while V was working at height. V fell and died. V's estate argued that D's negligent failure to provide a safety harness was causative of C's death. This was rejected because it was clear that the but-for test was not satisfied: V would not have worn a safety harness had it been provided and thus would have fallen to his death in any event.

It might be that *McWilliams* shows that English law accepts that an omission can only be causative, if the but-for test is not satisfied, where the omission leads to the existence of an element in the positive causal process by which C's injury occurred. This would reconcile *McWilliams* and *Bailey*: both are omissions cases, but in *Bailey* D's wrongful conduct led to the existence of an additional physical element in the process by which C's injury occurred. By contrast, in *McWilliams* the physical process by which V died would have been exactly the same had D provided a harness.

The correctness of this analysis depends upon how English law would treat cases like the following:

---

[46] BGH 7.2.2012, VI ZR 63/11, [10] (emphasis added).   [47] See Note 81.   [48] See Note 36.
[49] [1962] UKHL 3.

Unheated seeds. C's seeds need to be heated between 12.00 and 1.00 in order not to deteriorate physically. D1 negligently fails to press the switch to turn on the heating system at 12.00. Simultaneously, but independently, D2 negligently fails to turn on the power supply to the heating system. The seeds are not heated and deteriorate.

This case is, in one sense, structurally similar to *Two Hunters*: two independent events occur which are each sufficient to bring about the outcome which occurred. In neither case is the but-for test satisfied in relation to D1 and D2 individually, since had either defendant behaved nonnegligently the injury would still have occurred. The difference is that in *Unheated seeds* it cannot be said that each defendant is necessary for the existence of a positive element in the process by which the injury occurred. The seeds would have been destroyed in exactly the same way had D1 conformed to its duty. Consequently, *Unheated seeds* would fall outside both *McWilliams* (the but-for test is not satisfied) and *Bailey* (neither defendant provided part of the physical process by which the injury occurred). It seems likely that English law would hold each defendant liable in full here, but it is not clear what the causal analysis of this situation would be.[50]

The analysis of causation beyond the but-for test

A factor is a cause, then, if and only if it satisfies the but-for test or if it contributes to the occurrence of the effect.[51] Can, however, something more illuminating be said by way of general analysis of what it is for *c* to be a cause where *c* does not satisfy the but-for test? Such an analysis is important for this inquiry into proof of causation for two reasons. First, it is impossible to understand what it is to *prove* causation, and what evidence might assist in doing so, without understanding what causation is. Second, it cannot properly be determined whether a rule ought to be classified as establishing an exception to proof of causation until that concept is clarified.

This section considers analyses of causation which aim to account for the possibility of pre-emption and overdetermination and so to model more precisely when *c* is a cause of *e*. The argument is that a revised version of the necessary element of a sufficient set (NESS) analysis of causation provides the best available analysis of causal pre-emption and overdetermination.

---

[50] See pp. 43–45.

[51] Clearly, this is not a reductive definition of causation. Indeed, even the but-for test does not provide a *reductive* analysis of causation. See J. Schaffer, 'Counterfactuals, Causal Independence and Conceptual Circularity', 307–8.

The NESS analysis of causation

In the legal literature,[52] Richard Wright has offered an analysis of causation which, in his view, avoids the limitations of the but-for test by adequately modelling judgements about pre-emption and overdetermination.[53]

Wright provides the following account of what it is for c to be a cause of e:[54]

> NESS: c contributed to e if and only if c was a member of a set of conditions which actually existed prior to e, which were sufficient for e, and which would not have been sufficient for e without c.

The basic idea here is this: the but-for test is a test of necessity.[55] This is why it reaches the incorrect conclusions about (certain) pre-emption and (all) overdetermination cases: a cause in those cases is *not* necessary for the effect: the effect would have occurred anyway. A natural suggestion, then, is to model causation not (only) as necessity, but as sufficiency: c is a cause of e if c is in some sense *sufficient* for e.

Since no single event is sufficient in itself to produce an effect, as Wright recognises, the analysis needs to be that c is a cause of e if c is a member of a set of factors which, together, are sufficient for e.[56] Moreover, one also needs to say that only *non-redundant* parts of a sufficient set count: only factors which are *necessary*[57] for the sufficiency of a

---

[52] Similar accounts of causation have been developed outside of legal philosophy. See J. Bennett, *Events and their Names* 52ff. Wright's account builds on the account in H.L.A. Hart and T. Honoré, *Causation in the Law*, 2nd edition, 112–13 and that in J.L. Mackie, *The Cement of the Universe: a Study of Causation*, ch 3. This family of 'sufficiency-based' accounts of causation has seen something of a revival in recent philosophical work, see M. Strevens, 'Mackie Remixed'; M. Baumgartner, 'A Regularity Theoretic Approach to Actual Causation'; L. Paul and N. Hall, *Causation*, 43, 57–8, 72–5.

[53] For a useful introduction to NESS, see C. Miller, 'NESS for Beginners'.

[54] See R. Wright, 'Causation in Tort Law', 1790.

[55] It is a test of 'necessity' in the sense that it implies that if c had not occurred, e would not have occurred (which means, roughly in the closest possible world(s)... in which c did not occur, e did not occur). See, for disambiguation of concepts of necessity in this context, J.J. Thomson, 'Some Reflections on Hart and Honoré, Causation in the Law', 145–6. The terminology of 'weak' and 'strong' necessity is best avoided. It is used in different ways by different people. Compare Thomson's usage with R. Wright, 'The NESS Account of Natural Causation: a Response to Criticisms', 286ff.

[56] Strictly, there *are* analyses of 'sufficiency' which allow that one factor can be individually sufficient for an effect. These are not relevant here.

[57] The meaning of 'necessity' here is not strictly the same as that expressed by the but-for test. According to Wright, c is necessary for the sufficiency of a set for e if, without c, the causal law linking c events and e events would be incomplete or invalid. See R. Wright, 'Acts and Omissions', 297; R. Wright, 'The NESS Account of Natural Causation', 291.

set count as causes.[58] If [firing a bullet in the direction of V] is sufficient for V's death, then so too is the set [firing a bullet in the direction of V *and* wearing a yellow shirt]. However, wearing a yellow shirt played no role in V's death. Thus, the set must be restricted to members *necessary* for its sufficiency to produce the death.

Finally, we need to specify more precisely the sense of 'sufficiency' here. According to Wright, a set of factors is sufficient for an effect if the actual occurrence of those factors, given the causal laws of nature, entails the instantaneous occurrence of the effect.[59] A causal law has the form: 'if [a,b,c...] occur, then, always, and, instantaneously, [e]'.[60] So c counts as a cause of e in virtue of the fact that 'c' and 'e' can be viewed as particular instantiations of a causal law which states that if c (and a whole host of other positive and negative conditions) occurs, then e occurs.

If a causal law has the form: if [a,b,c], then *instantaneously*, [e], and for a specific factor to be causally involved in an outcome is for the specific factor and outcome to occur in the way described by the causal law, then Wright's analysis is, without modification, untenable.[61] If D fires a bullet at t and this strikes and kills C at t+2, D's *firing* the bullet did *not* suffice for C's death according to Wright's definition of 'sufficiency'. The death was not *instantaneously* entailed by the bullet's being fired.

To make Wright's definition of sufficiency plausible, one needs to add that the firing of the bullet suffices for some other event or state of

---

[58] Wright (now) restricts the 'necessity' aspect of his analysis to the formulation of the relevant causal laws – a causal law only includes abstract conditions which are necessary to entail the result – and requires only, in analysing singular instances of causation, that c be 'part' of the instantiation of the relevant causal law. This modification seems to be introduced in order to deal with complex asymmetric overdetermination cases, such as those discussed in R. Bagshaw, 'Causing the Behaviour of Others', 372. See further, p. 29.

[59] This definition of sufficiency in terms of *causal* laws gives rise to a charge of circularity – causation is being defined in terms of sufficiency and sufficiency is being defined in terms of causal notions. See, for example, R. Fumerton and K. Kress, 'Causation and the Law: Preemption, Lawful Sufficiency, and Causal Sufficiency', 101–2. The charge is ultimately true, but the circularity need not render the analysis vacuous. If the mere fact that an account of causation were *non-reductive* were to render it vacuous, then the but-for analysis would be vacuous, since we already need causal knowledge to apply it (how else are we to know what would have happened had c not occurred, except by relying upon causal laws and generalisations?). But the but-for test, though it cannot deal with causal redundancy cases, is not *vacuous*. See further, on this, M. Strevens, 'Mackie Remixed', 20–4.

[60] R. Wright, 'The NESS Account of Natural Causation', 289.

[61] Wright recognises this point and the modification needed: see R. Wright, 'The NESS Account of Natural Causation', 291.

affairs before the death where that event (or an event for which that event suffices) itself suffices for the death. In other words, a factor is a cause of an outcome if it suffices in Wright's sense or if it is connected by a chain of intermediate sufficient factors to the outcome.

Wright denotes any factor which satisfies the above definition as a 'NESS' factor: it is a factor which is a necessary element for the sufficiency of a set of conditions sufficient for the occurrence of the effect.

To see how Wright's NESS analysis deals with straightforward cases of overdetermination, consider again:

> *Two hunters. Hunter A* and *Hunter B* each, independently, negligently fire towards *V*. *V* is struck in the head by both bullets simultaneously and dies.

Here each hunter's firing is sufficient (actually: is sufficient for the existence of an intermediate event [or series of events] sufficient for the death) for the victim's death in combination with a number of background factors (e.g. the position of the victim, the absence of deflecting wind, and so on). And we can construct a set of actual factors in this situation in which each hunter is *necessary* for the sufficiency of that set. Consider *Hunter A*. The set is (crudely): [*Hunter A* fires, the victim is in proximity, the bullet is travelling at a certain speed, the wind does not deflect the bullet, the victim is struck, etc.] This set of factors is sufficient for the victim's death and would not be sufficient without *Hunter A's* firing. This is because the causal laws are (let us suppose) such that if a bullet is fired in this way, at this time, towards such a victim, and the victim is struck in the head, the victim dies. Thus *Hunter A* is a cause of the death. The same can be said of *Hunter B* and tested in the same way.[62]

The following sections consider objections to the NESS analysis, some of which force us to revise it in certain ways.

NESS: False negatives

It might be claimed that the NESS analysis fails to detect genuine causal relationships in some circumstances: it gives rise to false negatives. Consider:[63]

---

[62] The NESS analysis of *Votes* is as follows: each vote can be grouped as part of *a* sufficient set along with one other vote. The vote is *necessary* for the sufficiency of that set (the outcome would not be entailed by that set if the vote was not present). Hence, each vote is a cause of the decision.

[63] For a similar example, see R. Bagshaw, 'Causing the Behavior of Others and Other Causal Mixtures', 368.

Resignation. Paul decides to leave his job. His decision was influenced by his poor salary, but mainly by his being harassed by his manager.

Suppose that even had Paul been better paid, he would still have left his job due to the harassment. Nonetheless, it seems conceptually possible in these circumstances that Paul's decision could have been caused *both* by his harassment and his poor salary. On the face of it, the NESS analysis cannot explain this because there is no sufficient set to which the fact of Paul's being poorly paid belongs as a necessary factor for its sufficiency.[64] While it may be possible in other circumstances to 'disaggregate' the other sufficient cause, such that the decision could be grouped as a necessary element of some set, which includes part of that, disaggregated, sufficient cause, this is not possible here. This objection is overstated. We can describe a divisible mechanism by which Paul's reasons for leaving his job operate: plausibly, Paul's decision is only made once the reasons for the decision have a certain *weight* or *strength*. It is then possible to construct a sufficient set of this property of the reasons – their weight – which includes the poor salary reason, and whose weight is only sufficient when it includes that reason. More generally, in applying the test 'one can ignore the actual individuation of units or degrees of a property that actual objects present in the particular situation happen to possess'.[65]

NESS: *False positives*

It has been argued that the NESS analysis also finds causal relationships where none exist.[66] This objection is correct in relation to the NESS analysis presented by Wright. The most convincing argument for this is that if the NESS analysis finds that D2's negligence was a cause of the injury in the following case, then it is committed to finding that an employer's negligence was causative of the injury in cases such as *McWilliams* – involving a failure to provide a safety harness to an employee who would never have worn the harness. Yet, holding that the provision of a harness which would have made no difference

---

[64] The move discussed in Note 58 may also assist here.

[65] M. Moore, *Causation and Responsibility*, 490.

[66] See, for example, R. Stevens, *Torts and Rights*, 142–3. Some would add here that the NESS analysis falsely treats pre-empted conditions as causes. See R. Fumerton and K. Kress, 'Causation and the Law: Preemption, Lawful Sufficiency, and Causal Sufficiency', 100–2; M. Moore, *Causation and Responsibility*, 491–5. The better view that NESS (or a close surrogate) can avoid this is well explained in M. Strevens, 'Mackie Remixed', 10–19.

to the occurrence, or process of occurrence, of the injury seems problematic. Here is the case:

> *Defective brakes.* D1 negligently fails to repair the brakes of D2's car, rendering those brakes useless. While driving the car, D2 negligently fails to depress the brakes until it is too late, when approaching C. The car collides with, and injures, C. [67]

Here Wright claims that the NESS analysis leads to the conclusion that D2 pre-empts D1.[68] This is, on the face of it, incorrect.[69] D2's failure to brake is only conceivably part of a set sufficient to produce the collision if that set includes the car, moving at speed, which D2 was driving. Failing to press brakes in the abstract will not produce an injury. If that is true, it is far from obvious that one can set aside the fact that the car's brakes were *actually* defective when one attempts to construct a sufficient set of conditions for the outcome which includes the failure to brake. The failure to use the brakes was a failure to use *the brakes in question.* The significance of this is that it is impossible to say that the failure to brake was *necessary* for the sufficiency of any actual set of antecedent conditions. If the failure to brake is removed from the set, the set will still be sufficient to produce the injury, because the brakes were defective. Thus D2's failure to brake is not a cause.

Now consider the following possible reply. The reply claims that the failure to brake is indeed *necessary* for the sufficiency of an antecedent set, since one can 'set aside' the fact the car's brakes were defective in constructing a set which includes the failure to brake. The reason is that the relevant causal law covering this situation need not mention the fact that the car in question's brakes were defective. The law might run: 'if an object moving at a certain speed at point Q is not subject to a countervailing force at t, it will reach the point P at $t + n$'. The failure to brake is an instantiation of the part of the law which requires that the object 'is not subject to a countervailing force at t'. In other words, the causal law simply requires, abstractly, that there be an *absence* of 'countervailing forces' at a certain time, and the failure to brake is such

---

[67] The facts are based upon *Saunders System Birmingham Co.* v. *Adams* (1928) 117 So 72 (Alabama).

[68] Wright's analysis here bears negligible relation to the NESS analysis itself. Instead, he relies upon a distinct theory of 'causal priority' between omissions: R. Wright, 'Acts and Omissions as Positive and Negative Causes', 290–2. For penetrating criticism, see D. Fischer, 'Causation in Fact in Omissions Cases', 1357–64; J. Stapleton, 'Choosing what we mean by "Causation" in the Law', 477–9.

[69] See also A. Beever, *Rediscovering the Law of Negligence,* 424–5.

an absence. If successful, however, this reply leads to the conclusion that *both* D1 and D2 are causes, since D1's failure to repair the brakes equally leads to the absence of a countervailing mechanism and so equally instantiates part of the covering causal law.

If we then accepted that *both* D1 and D2 are causes of the injury in *Defective brakes*,[70] we are confronted with the following problem. If we accept that D2's failure to brake in *Defective brakes* was a cause, what prevents the employer's negligence in *McWilliams* being classed as a cause?[71] If we apply the NESS analysis directly to the facts of *McWilliams*, once again, the result depends upon a difficult issue of set construction. The non-existence of a harness of a certain kind upon a person falling from a height is ceteris paribus sufficient to produce their death. Was the failure to provide the harness a NESS of its non-existence upon V? The non-provision of a harness to a person at t is sufficient, given other conditions, for that person not to be wearing a harness. But was the non-provision a *necessary* element of this sufficient set? If we include V's disposition not to wear the harness in the set, then the failure to provide it was not necessary, and is thus not causative of V's injury. But if we take the same 'abstract' approach to set construction that is required to generate the result that D2 was a cause in *Defective brakes*, and thus 'set aside' V's disposition not to wear the harness, we reach the result that D's failure was indeed causative.

Hence, the NESS analysis is confronted with this problem: if it accepts causation by D2 in *Defective brakes*, it will be difficult to deny causation by the employer in *McWilliams*. Yet a finding of causation in *McWilliams* seems counterintuitive. This conclusion was reached because an 'abstract' approach to set construction was adopted in *Defective brakes* – an approach which somehow blotted out the fact that the brakes in question were defective.[72] It therefore seems preferable, *contra* Wright, to adopt a more concrete approach to set construction which rejects causation by D2 in *Defective brakes*.

Now the following objection may arise. If we reject causation by D2 in *Defective brakes*, are we not also compelled to reject causation by D1

---

[70] Note that it would not follow that both should be *liable*. D1 might argue that the injury was a coincidence of his negligence. On this non-causal limitation on liability, see R. Wright, 'The Grounds and Extent of Legal Responsibility', 1479ff; R. Bagshaw, 'Causing the Behaviour of Others and Other Causal Mixtures', 377.

[71] See, similarly, D. Fischer, 'Causation in Fact in Omissions Cases', 1357; J. Stapleton, 'Choosing what we mean by "Causation" in the Law', 478–9.

[72] For a similar point that if it suffices for causation that *c* is necessary for *e*, if *the situation had been different* (i.e. if the brakes had been in working order), one generates spurious causation, see C. Sartorio, 'How to be Responsible for Something without Causing it', 321–2.

in that case? If so, then neither D1 nor D2 is a cause. It might then be argued that one should bite the smaller bullet and accept causation by D2 in *Defective brakes*, and therefore causation in *McWilliams*, since failure to do so leads to the even more counterintuitive result that neither D1 nor D2 is a cause in *Defective brakes*.

Here is a response. On reflection it is not particularly counterintuitive that neither D1 nor D2 is *individually* a cause of the injury in *Defective brakes*.[73] Neither omission itself made a difference to whether the injury occurred. Nor did either omission, individually, significantly alter the causal process by which the injury occurred. Had the brakes been depressed, the car would still have continued at the same speed towards C. The same is true had the brakes been operational. In either event there would have been a positive force of the same magnitude hurtling towards the claimant. It may then be preferable to say that D1 and D2 are *jointly* causes in *Defective brakes*. More precisely, it is the complex state of affairs of 'its neither being the case that the brakes were repaired or that they were pressed', which is a cause of the injury.[74] This does justice to the view that the injury in *Defective brakes* was not without causes at the time it occurred *and* avoids the conclusion that there was causation by the negligent employer in *McWilliams*.

NESS: Incompleteness

The 'sufficiency' in the NESS analysis is a kind of nomological sufficiency – it concerns laws of nature.[75] Moreover, as Wright presents it, it is concerned only with physical causal laws.[76] An important objection is that some, arguably causal, relationships do not involve 'laws of nature'.[77] For

---

[73] See also J. Stapleton, 'An "Extended But-for" Test for the Causal Relation in the Law of Obligations', text at notes 87-91. S. Green, *Causation in Negligence*, 76 argues that D2 alone is a cause on the basis that the risk created by D1 by not repairing the brakes did not materialize – the brakes were never used. Here are two doubts about this. First, suppose a modified *Defective Brakes* where D2 drives off and, just prior to approaching C, discovers that the brakes are utterly useless. Knowing this, and unable to do anything else, D2 does not press the brakes. It is very implausible that D2's not pressing brakes, which he knows to be defunct, was a cause of the crash here (if it was, why not say that a failure to wear a red shirt was a cause, too?). But if that is so, how can the result be different simply because D2 is ignorant of the status of the brakes? Second, whether a particular risk actually materialized in injury depends upon whether the risk actually caused the injury. Appeals to risk to settle the factual causal issue beg the question.

[74] Cf. H. Spector, 'The MMTS Analysis of Causation', 354–6.

[75] See for the restriction to *causal* laws of nature, Note 59.

[76] See 'The NESS Account of Natural Causation', 309–11.

[77] For further discussion of determinism, see Chapter 6, 314–315.

example, in *Votes*, the rule that two votes are sufficient to carry the motion is not a *law of nature*, yet it plays an important role in our judgement that each vote plays a causal role in the carrying of the motion. To account for such cases, the NESS analysis needs to be extended to include factors which are necessary for the sufficiency of the satisfaction of some rule's requirements. More generally, we might describe this sufficiency as 'normative sufficiency' – sufficiency according to some relevant set of rules or standards.[78]

Conclusions on the NESS analysis of contribution
The main virtue of the NESS analysis is its ability to illuminate and accurately identify what it is for *c* to be a cause of *e* across most cases of causal pre-emption and overdetermination. It suffers, however, from two defects: (1) it generates false positives if an abstract process of set construction is adopted, and (2) it cannot account for causal processes not strictly involving laws of nature. The remedies for (1) and (2) have already been suggested and can be summarised as follows.

Revised NESS: *c* counts as a cause of *e* if it is necessary for the sufficiency of a concretely specified set sufficient for *e*, where sufficiency may be determined both by physical laws of nature and by the requirement of a rule or set of rules.

Alternative analyses of contribution

Some other suggestions for modelling our judgements of causation in pre-emption and overdetermination cases are analytically inferior to the revised NESS analysis.[79]
    Consider:

But-for with precise description of effect and manner of occurrence: c contributes to e iff had c not occurred, e would not have occurred at exactly the time and in the manner in which it did.[80]

---

[78] The analysis may need to be extended yet further to include causal generalisations about human decisions if human behaviour is not governed by causal *laws*. See T. Honoré, 'Necessary and Sufficient Conditions in Tort Law', 381–385.

[79] This is not to say that the analyses in the text may not be more *forensically* friendly or easier for use as heuristics. Stapleton's analysis of causation (see, p. 35) provides us with a very reliable heuristic for determining causation, which avoids recourse to the complex issues of set construction involved in the revised NESS analysis.

[80] In German scholarship, this is sometimes referred to as *Die Lehre vom Erfolg in seiner konkreter Gestalt* (the doctrine of the effect in its concrete form): see generally L. Röckrath, *Kausalität*, 21–3.

In *Two Hunters*, it might be argued that the death would not have occurred *in the same way* had *each* hunter not fired and thus each is a cause. This generates false positives. A person who is shot by a pink bullet would not have died in the same way had the bullet not been pink but the colour of the bullet is causally irrelevant. One could object that the colour of the bullet is not *part* of the way in which the person died. But this already requires us to have a way of separating out which part of the history of an event is causally relevant to it and which part is not. This analysis provides no assistance in that regard.

> *But-for with grouping*: c contributes to e iff c is one of a group of conditions, C, where if C had not occurred, e would not have occurred, where it is not true that if a smaller part of C had not occurred, then e would not have occurred.[81]

Consider *Two Hunters*. It is true that had both hunters not fired, then the death would not have occurred, and it is not true if only one hunter had fired that the effect would not have occurred.[82] Hence, both are causes under this analysis. The problem with this account is that, unmodified, it counts pre-empted factors as causes. Consider *Assassins*: had neither assassin planted a bomb, the explosion would never have occurred. Hence both are causes. But only one assassin is a cause. So this account needs to build in an additional negative requirement that no member of the group was pre-empted by another factor. In analysing which factor pre-empted which, this account will likely need to rely upon the notion of sufficiency, with one factor being genuinely causally sufficient, while the other is not. It will then very much resemble the NESS analysis in substance.

---

[81] This is the formal structure of Stapleton's 'targeted but-for test' (which she now rejects). See J. Stapleton, 'Unpacking "Causation"', 175–6. For discussion of similar analyses, see L. Paul and N. Hall, *Causation*, 77–9, 112–16, 121–4. For legal examples of a similar approach of modifying the relevant counterfactual (in criminal law): BGHSt 48, 77, 94; on which, I. Puppe, Commentary to §13 StGB, in Kindhäuser/Neumann/Paeffgen, (eds), *Strafgesetzbuch*, [122]. See also S. Green, *Causation in Negligence*, 13-14, whose approach, geared to the tort of negligence, defines C as 'conduct in breach of a duty of care' and then asks whether any specific breach was 'operative' when the claimant's injury occurred. This avoids the objection in the text, but it is open to doubt whether the concept of a breach being 'operative' can be elucidated without recourse to NESS or some other substantive causal analysis.

[82] This last qualification – that no subset of the group is necessary for the effect is necessary to exclude adding in causally irrelevant details to the group. See G. Graßhoff and M. May, 'Causal Regularities'.

Stapleton's but-for test: c is a cause of e iff had c not occurred, e would not have occurred *or* there would not have been an actual contribution to an element of the positive requirements for the existence of e.[83]

The idea here is that a cause either makes a difference to whether the effect occurs or whether *a certain aspect of the process* by which the effect occurred occurs. For Stapleton, only factors which made a difference to the existence of a *positive* aspect of the process are causes. The 'requirements for e' for the existence of an effect can be thought of as a 'recipe' for producing the effect in the circumstances as they occurred.[84] The recipe can, but need not be, framed in terms of physical laws of nature. It may also include, for example, the requirements for the validity of a will. 'Requirements' are either positive or negative. For example, the positive requirements of the phenomenon for a billiard ball to move include force on the billiard ball and the negative requirements for this include the absence of equally countervailing force.

The main divergence between the revised NESS analysis and Stapleton's test is that the latter requires that c be necessary for some 'positive' aspect of the requirements for c, while the NESS analysis makes no such restriction. Why does Stapleton's test require that c made a difference only to *positive* requirements for the existence of e? There seem to be two reasons. First, it is intuitively appealing that causes must make a difference in some positive way.[85] In this way causes 'leave a trace' on the world. In *Defective brakes*, neither defendant's negligence individually makes a difference either to whether the injury occurs or to the positive process (the movement of the car towards the victim) by which the injury occurs. In short, failing to press broken brakes is simply irrelevant to any aspect of the production of the outcome. Second, Stapleton argues that the law ought to select the causal relation which requires that the defendant at least made a difference to the positive occurrence of the phenomenon because this reflects a concern for individual responsibility.[86] One is only responsible in relation to outcomes to whose occurrence one (individually) made a *difference*.

Both of Stapleton's arguments can be criticised. First, the argument from 'making a (positive) difference' sometimes leads to counterintuitive results. Consider:

---

[83] See J. Stapleton, 'An "Extended But-for" Test for the Causal Relation in the Law of Obligations', text at notes 81–2.
[84] Cf. T. Honoré, 'Necessary and Sufficient Conditions in Tort Law', 375, 385.
[85] See J. Stapleton, 'An "Extended But-for" Test for the Causal Relation', text at notes 101–2.
[86] Ibid.

Redundant bodyguard. A, B's bodyguard, shoots and kills assassin, C, who was about to shoot and kill B. Had A not done so, D would have.[87]

Intuitively, it is A who saves B's life: A is a cause of B's life being saved. Stapleton's analysis reaches the contrary result. The positive requirements for B's continued existence include, for example, the continued beating of B's heart and flow of B's blood. But there is, on the face of it, no positive requirement or element of such a requirement for whose existence A's shot is necessary, since D would have acted to save B in any event. To avoid this problem, one would need to treat the 'shooting of the bodyguard' as a positive requirement for saving B's life. This is still insufficient, however, since A's shot is not necessary for the existence of this positive requirement. To resolve this problem, one needs to say that c is a cause if c provides a NESS condition for the existence of a positive element in the positive requirements for e. A's shot is such a NESS condition for the death of C.

This revision will not reach the intuitively correct result in other cases, however. Suppose that for a fire prevention system to prevent a fire from destroying a building Engineer A must press a switch at 1pm and, independently, Engineer B must press a switch at 1pm. The switches operate by closing different parts of an electrical circuit. Both fail to do so and the fire destroys the building. Neither A nor B is necessary for the existence of the positive requirements for the burning down of the building (namely, for the existence of the fire or some element of the fire). Yet, it seems perfectly reasonable to describe both failures as causes.[88] The NESS analysis reaches this result on the assumption that the different aspects of the circuit can be grouped into different sufficient sets.

Second, the argument from individual responsibility is also open to doubt. In *Redundant bodyguard*, intuitively A, not D, deserves the credit for saving B's life. This is presumably in virtue of the fact that A rather than D is indeed *responsible* for the saving of B's life.

Stapleton's view nonetheless provides an analytically workable sufficient condition for when c is a cause of e. It neatly captures, without the complexity and uncertainty of constructing a NESS set, the sense in which the defendant's conduct is causative in cases such as *Bailey* and

---

[87] The example is based upon that in N. Hall, 'Two Concepts of Causation', 271–2.
[88] See, similarly, H.L.A. Hart and T. Honoré, *Causation in the Law*, 2nd edition, 128.

Resignation.[89] Moreover, it provides reasonable guidance in delimiting the boundaries of causal relationships: the less that D's wrongful conduct alters the process or mechanism by which C's injury occurs, the less likely it is that we can say that it was a cause of the injury. Where the revised NESS analysis would be needlessly complex, the book draws upon Stapleton's account.

Conclusion

Each system recognises the but-for test as a sufficient condition of natural causation, but not a necessary one. Each system also recognises a broader concept of causation. This broader concept was illustrated by the legal treatment of the two logically possible ways in which c may cause e despite failing the but-for test: contribution by pre-emption and contribution to an overdetermined effect.

It was then suggested that the central cases of contribution by pre-emption and by overdetermination in each system involve situations where c played a positive role in the production of e. The extent to which c may contribute to e, where c is an omission is unclear. German law seems to require that if c is an omission, that c was a but-for cause of e. English law allows that an omission may be causative if it results in the existence of a positive element of the causal process by which e occurred. Finally, it was suggested that the better view is that contribution can reasonably be modelled by reference to a revised NESS analysis.

The main consequence of this section's analysis for this book's inquiry into the legal treatment of empirical uncertainty over causation is simply that a decision-maker's uncertainty over causation will involve uncertainty as to the existence of facts relevant to the question of whether c was a but-for factor for e or over whether c contributed to the production of e. The latter, in turn, will involve uncertainty either over whether c was necessary for the sufficiency of a set of factors concretely sufficient for the existence of e or whether c formed part of the positive causal process for e.

Causal questions in tort law

Causal questions arise at four different stages of the legal analysis in each system's tort law:

---

[89] See p. 29.

(i) *Causation as establishing the infringement of a right and any liability arising in response to the infringement alone (wrong-constituting causation)*: a causal connection between the defendant's conduct or some aspect of that conduct and the claimant's injury or some other state of affairs may be required for the defendant to commit certain torts or to fulfil certain causes of action.

(ii) *Causation as determining the extent of consequential liability in respect of a wrong or cause of action (consequential-liability causation)*: if the claimant has established that the defendant has committed a wrong and then seeks to recover compensatory damages in respect of losses which are not part of the definition of that wrong, it must be shown that these are 'consequential' losses. This minimally requires that the wrong be a cause of those losses. Here the causal connection is between the 'wrong' and (further) 'loss'. Similarly, so far as gain-based damages can be recovered in respect of a wrong, the wrong must be a cause of the gains.

(iii) *Causation as an element of a defence*: a causal connection is required in order to make out certain defences. For instance, the defence of contributory negligence requires that the claimant's negligence be a cause of its injury.[90]

(iv) *Causation as establishing secondary responsibility for a wrong*: it may be that certain forms of secondary responsibility for wrongdoing in tort law embed a causal requirement. For instance, accessorial liability arguably requires that the accessory have contributed to the wrong.[91]

The first section of this part elaborates upon (i) and (ii), which form the primary subject matter of the book. It first describes wrong-constituting causation and establishes that causation of either injury or some non-injurious state of affairs is required as a matter of wrong-constituting causation for all torts. It then explains the role of causation in determining the availability and extent of, principally, compensatory liability, distinguishing the role of causation from that of other concepts. It will be seen that causation between the defendant's conduct and a loss is a virtually exceptionless requirement for the availability of compensatory damages in respect of that loss. The second section argues, however, that there are narrow situations in which tort law imposes liability without requiring causation. It will be argued later that these situations are of significance in connection with liability under circumstances of empirical uncertainty.[92]

---

[90] See, for example, 254 BGB. Contributory negligence is not strictly a defence in German law, but part of the law of damages.

[91] For discussion of this issue, see P. Davies, 'Complicity', 275ff.

[92] See Chapter 4, 189–192.

Causation as constituting the legal wrong or establishing the cause of action

To varying degrees, each system recognises a distinction between causation of outcomes relevant to constituting a wrong or establishing a cause of action and causation of outcomes relevant to the scope of consequential liability in respect of an established wrong or cause of action. This is most prominent in German law, which distinguishes between liability-establishing causation (*haftungsbegründende Kausalität*) and liability-fulfilling causation (*haftungsausfüllende Kausalität*).[93] The former concerns the causal connection between the defendant's conduct and the initial infringement of the claimant's right.[94] The latter concerns the causal connection between the established infringement of the claimant's right and loss in respect of which compensation is claimed.[95] English law speaks of causation of the 'gist' of the tort as opposed to causation of consequential losses.[96] The 'gist' of the tort is included in a description of the primary duty imposed by the tort – not so, consequential losses.[97] The distinction is least prominent in French law, which tends not explicitly to define the content of primary rights and duties in terms of invasions of particular interests.[98]

Causation of an outcome is a necessary constitutive element of virtually all torts. The causal element is either explicit or implicit. It may relate either to an injurious outcome or a non-injurious outcome. The central tort provisions or causes of action in each system explicitly or implicitly require that the defendant caused an *injurious* outcome for the tort to have been committed:

Article 1382 Code Civil

Tout fait quelconque de l'homme, qui cause à autrui un dommage, oblige celui par la faute duquel il est arrivé à le réparer.

If a person causes damage to another through their fault, that person is under a duty to compensate the other in respect of it.

---

[93] See, for example, H. Oetker in *Münchener Kommentar zum BGB*, §249 BGB, [105]; B. Winiger, H. Koziol, B. Koch and R. Zimmermann, *Essential Cases on Natural Causation*, 593.

[94] H. Oetker in *Münchener Kommentar zum BGB*, §249 BGB, [105].   [95] Ibid.

[96] See, for example, J. Stapleton, 'The Gist of Negligence Part I: Minimum Actionable Damage'.

[97] See, further, R. Stevens, 'Rights and Other Things', 118–19.

[98] Cf. E. Descheemaeker, *The Division of Wrongs*, 154–8.

823 I BGB

Wer vorsätzlich oder fahrlässig das Leben, den Körper, die Gesundheit, die Freiheit, das Eigentum oder ein sonstiges Recht eines anderen widerrechtlich verletzt, ist dem anderen zum Ersatz des daraus entstehenden Schadens verpflichtet.

If a person intentionally or negligently unlawfully injures the life, body, health, freedom, property or some other specific right of another, that person is under a duty to compensate for the loss resulting from the injury.

The tort of negligence

A person commits the tort of negligence only if they owed the claimant a duty of care not to cause the type of injury suffered and the breach of that duty was a cause of the injury suffered.

All of the French and German tort provisions use the words 'to cause' (all of Articles 1382 – 1386 CC) 'to injure' (*verletzen*, 823 I, II BGB) or 'to inflict' (*zufügen*, §§824 – 827 BGB) and concern injurious outcomes. In the common law, but theoretically not in France or Germany, it is possible to commit a tort without being a cause of what is normally considered an injurious outcome. Torts are committed simply by walking upon another's land without their consent or by the non-consensual stroking of a person's hair while they are asleep. Nonetheless, even these torts actionable *per se* involve causation of an (non-injurious) outcome – be it interference with exclusive possession or the occurrence of force upon another person.[99]

There are two elements of wrong-constituting causation (apart from the causal relationship itself) – the conduct element and the outcome element. In torts constituted by injurious outcomes, the outcome which constitutes the tort will be referred to in what follows as an 'injury'.[100] All injurious outcomes will also be denoted as 'losses'. There is relative

---

[99] See, similarly, M. Moore, *Causation and Responsibility*, 19. But cf. P. Cane, *Responsibility in Law and Morality*, 115. It is not surprising that proof of wrong-constituting causation is rarely treated as a separate issue in such torts since a finding of causation follows *analytically* from the fact that the defendant engaged in the wrongful action – be it 'imprisoning', 'touching' or 'entering'. These are *causal* verbs. The fact that the non-injurious outcome would have occurred had the defendant not engaged in the wrongful action may be relevant, however, to *consequential liability* causation. See *Lumba* v. *Secretary of State for the Home Department* [2011] 1 AC 245, [95] (Lord Dyson).

[100] The use of the terms 'loss', 'damage', 'injury', and 'harm' is somewhat unstable in the common law. Cf. E. Descheemaeker, *The Division of Wrongs*, 229.

uniformity in relation to which losses may count as injuries for the purposes of wrong-constituting causation. A person *may* suffer injury in each system where:[101]

(a) they undergo a physical change in their person or property which affects their well-being or reduces the property's value or
(b) they suffer a reduction of financial assets or non-receipt of financial value which they either had prior to the injurious event or would have had or
(c) they are deprived of their freedom or
(d) they suffer experientially or
(e) they lose a valuable chance.

The *conduct* element in the wrong-constituting part of the causal inquiry, however, varies significantly. In negligence-based torts, Anglo-American and French law require that the negligent aspect of the defendant's conduct be a cause of the injury.[102] Under §823 I BGB, German tort law only requires that the defendant's *act* be a cause of the claimant's injury in order to establish the infringement of the claimant's right (except where the claimant's tortious right is concurrently protected by a contract).[103] If the negligent aspect of the defendant's conduct was not also a cause, this is relevant as a *defence* to liability (*Einwand rechtmäßigen Alternativverhaltens*).[104] So, if D negligently collides with C while negligently driving at 80, D will be said to have infringed C's right to bodily integrity under §823 I BGB. It will then fall to D to prove, *as a defence*, that had D been driving at a non-negligent speed, the injury would still have occurred.[105]

If a person has established wrong-constituting causation, it is not necessarily the case that they are entitled to an award of compensatory damages. This will only be the case if the tort is constituted by the causation of an *injurious* outcome and if the conduct is also a *legally relevant* cause of that outcome within the scope of the defendant's responsibility (and no defences are proved).[106] Similarly, the fact that

---

[101] See generally B. Winiger, H. Koziol, B. Koch, R. Zimmermann, *Digest of European Tort Law: Essential Cases on Damage*.

[102] See, for example, J. Stapleton, 'Factual Causation', 478: 'the formulation of breach ... sets up what needs to be proved in the factual cause step of legal analysis'.

[103] See, on this qualification, Chapter 2, 57.

[104] H. Oetker, in *Münchener Kommentar zum BGB*, §249 BGB, [210]; C. Grechenig and A. Stremitzer, 'Der Einwand Rechtmäßigen Alternativverhaltens – Rechtsvergleich, Ökonomische Analyse und Implikationen für die Proportionalhaftung', 339–45.

[105] G. Mäsch, *Chance und Schaden*, 23. See, for example, OLG Düsseldorf, 14.1.2008, I-1U79/06.

[106] For a recent account of the additional requirements of *legal* causation, beyond natural causation, see S. Steel, 'Causation in Tort and Crime: Unity or Divergence?' See generally, H.L.A. Hart and T. Honoré, *Causation in the law*, 2nd edition, ch 6.

the tort has been a cause of a gain to the defendant will not itself entitle the claimant to restitution of that gain: this will depend upon whether the claimant's infringed legal right entitled it to the gains made through its wrongful infringement and normally upon whether the gain would have been made even had the defendant acted non-wrongfully.[107]

Causation determining the extent of liability

The question of whether an established tort has been a cause of (further) loss is a question of consequential-liability causation. Causation is, of course, only one determinant of the extent of liability for consequential losses: it determines whether a loss is 'consequential' in the minimal, natural-causal sense. It is important not to confuse this causal determinant of liability with non-causal determinants. These non-causal determinants might generally be called 'scope of responsibility' doctrines. Consider the following two general rules recognised by each system, which are sometimes treated in common law systems as 'causal' rules:[108]

> *No better off rule*: If D's tort is a cause of C's loss of earnings for the next x years, but that loss of earnings would have occurred in any event for that period due to a non-tortious event, C cannot recover those earnings from D.[109]

> *No worse off due to multiple torts rule*: If D1's tort is a cause of C's loss of earnings for the next x years, but that loss of earnings would have occurred in any event due to D2's committing a tort against C, C can nonetheless recover the loss of earnings from D1 for that x year period.[110]

These two rules can apply to situations which are causally identical – situations where a tort is a cause of some further loss and some other independent event would have or did also cause that loss – and yet

---

[107] See A. Burrows, *The Law of Restitution*, 3rd edition, 625, ch 24.

[108] See, for example, J. Murphy, C. Witting, *Street on Torts*, 13th edition, 176–7; W. Rogers, *Winfield & Jolowicz Tort*, 18th edition, 315–16. For their statement as non-causal rules, see, emphasising the distinction between issues of natural causation and damages, J. Stapleton, 'Cause in Fact and the Scope of Liability for Consequences' 394, 412–15; M. Stiggelbout, 'The Case of 'Losses in any Event': a Question of Duty, Cause, or Damages', 563–5; M. Green, 'The Intersection of Factual Causation and Damages', 680, passim; J. Stapleton, 'Unnecessary Causes', 58–61. In German law, these are accepted to be rules about the extent of damages, not causation: H. Lange and G. Schiemann, *Schadensersatz*, (2003) §4 XII 1; M. Gebauer, *Hypothetische Kausalität*, 8.

[109] *Jobling* v. *Associated Dairies Ltd* [1982] AC 794.

[110] *Baker* v. *Willoughby* [1970] AC 467. For German law, see M. Gebauer, *Hypothetische Kausalität*, 386ff. The French position is unclear.

different conclusions as to liability are reached depending on whether the subsequent event is tortious or non-tortious. It is difficult to believe that the (factual) causal status of a tort in respect of some loss can vary depending upon the legal quality of some act in the future. It follows that these rules cannot be based solely upon causal considerations.

Non-causal liability

The virtually universal rule is that the claimant is not entitled to any compensatory damages from the defendant in respect of a loss unless the defendant's tort has been a cause of it.[111] There may, however, be two types of exception to this rule in English law.[112]

Wrongful omissions rendered causally redundant by other wrongful conduct

Consider *Wright* v. *Cambridge Medical Group*.[113] In this case, the defendant doctor negligently failed to refer the claimant, whose proximal femur was being attacked by a bacterial infection, to hospital for treatment on 15 April. She was later referred to hospital on 17 April, at which time the infection was treated ineffectively. She ultimately sustained permanent damage to her hip. The doctor argued that had he not been negligent, and had referred her to hospital on 15 April, the claimant would in any event have been treated negligently by the hospital doctors and would have suffered the injury regardless. The Court of Appeal found for the claimant and rejected the trial judge's factual finding that the injury would have occurred in any event because the hospital would have treated the claimant negligently.[114] Rather, it could be presumed that the hospital would have treated the claimant *non-negligently*, had she been referred on 15 April. On the assumption that she would have been treated non-negligently, it was held that the claimant had established on the balance of probability that but-for the defendant's negligence, she would not have suffered the injury.

---

[111] G. Mäsch, *Chance und Schaden*, 12 (a 'universally valid principle'); C. Quézel-Ambrunaz, *Essai sur la Causalité en Droit de la Responsabilité Civile*, 2; B. Winiger, H. Koziol, B. Koch, R. Zimmermann, *Essential Cases on Natural Causation*, 99.

[112] For one other, much criticised, narrow exception in German law, covering the situation where an agency entrusted with protecting certain intellectual property rights recovers damages in respect of the costs of measures geared towards protecting against future infringements unconnected with the specific infringement, see H. Oetker in *Münchener Kommentar zum BGB*, §249 BGB, [206]. C recovers against the tortfeasor for the expense of adopting the measures, despite the fact that C would have taken them in any event.

[113] [2011] EWCA Civ 669; [2011] Med LR 496. [114] Ibid., [79]; [91]; [124].

Lord Neuberger MR and Lord Justice Elias also held, however, that the defendant could not, as a matter of law, rely upon the fact (had it been one) that the hospital doctors would have been negligent to avoid a finding of causation.[115] Thus, even if the defendant had shown that, had he not been negligent, the claimant would have suffered her injury in any event as a result of the hypothetical negligence of the hospital doctors, he would nonetheless be held liable. Two reasons were given for this: (1) the defendant should not be permitted to rely upon the wrong, even if hypothetical, committed by another person; (2) in those circumstances, the defendant's negligence would have deprived the claimant of the opportunity of suing the hospital for the negligence it would have committed against the claimant.[116]

How ought we to characterise the liability of the doctor in the situation where, had the doctor not been negligent, the claimant's physical injury would have occurred in any event due to the hypothetical negligence of a third party? There are four possibilities:

1. The liability is *causal* since the but-for test is satisfied but with a modified counterfactual. We ask: what would have happened had neither the defendant nor anyone else behaved wrongfully in relation to the claimant? If that counterfactual is applied, the but-for test is satisfied in relation to the defendant.
2. The liability is *causal* on the ground that, even if the but-for test is not satisfied, the defendant's negligence *contributed* to the physical injury.
3. The liability is *causal* since the defendant's negligence has been a but-for cause of the *different loss* – namely, the loss of the right to sue the hospital for its negligence.
4. The liability is *non-causal*: the defendant is held liable for the physical injury despite it not being the case that the defendant is a cause of the physical injury.

The first characterisation, (1), is problematic. Although the selection of the appropriate counterfactual for the purposes of applying the but-for test may be influenced by normative considerations which have nothing to do with the concept of causation itself, the law does not usually select counterfactuals which are inconsistent with any plausible causal analysis of the facts. If we applied the counterfactual in (1) to other cases, we would reach manifestly incorrect results. For example, if we applied it to the *Assassins* example,[117] we would reach the incorrect result that *both* assassins were causal. This points against (1). In any event, (1) does not

---

[115] Ibid., [61]; [98].   [116] Ibid., [57]–[58]; [98].   [117] See p. 18.

reflect Elias LJ's understanding: liability was being imposed where '[the] negligence has not in fact caused or contributed to the injury'.[118] This also suggests that (2) is implausible. An independent argument for that conclusion is that the court did not limit its suggestion that liability would be imposed to situations where D's negligence could be said to have provided a positive aspect of the mechanism by which C's injury occurred.[119]

Finally, if (3) were correct, it would be difficult to explain why Elias LJ described the liability as 'exceptional'.[120] If (3) were correct, D's negligence would straightforwardly be a cause of the loss in respect of which C is recovering damages. This tends to suggest that (4) is the best characterisation of the hypothetical liability situation discussed in Wright and so the liability in that situation is non-causal.

Wholly de minimis causal contributions

In the Votes example, each vote's contribution to the passing of the motion could be said to be a non-minimal one. But suppose a modified Votes example, Votes* where there are 1000 votes in favour of the motion and only 100 are required to pass the motion. There is an intuitive sense in which each vote in Votes* is a less significant cause than each vote in Votes. There are two respects in which this is so. First, in Votes*, each vote is much farther from being necessary to change the outcome of the vote than in Votes. In order for an individual vote to be necessary to change the outcome in the former, it would have had to have been the case that 900 voted differently, whereas in the latter, it would only have to have been the case that 1 voted differently. Second, in Votes*, each vote is farther from being sufficient to carry the motion than in Votes: 2 votes are sufficient in the latter, whereas 100 are sufficient in the former.

---

[118] Ibid., [98]. Cf., however, the description of Kay LJ in the similar case of Gouldsmith v. Mid Staffordshire General Hospitals NHS Trust [2007] EWCA Civ 397, [44]: 'alternative route to proving causation'.

[119] On the facts of Wright itself, it was clear on the balance of probability that the defendant's negligence had been at least a but-for cause of the earlier occurrence of the permanent injury or had materially contributed to it: Wright [73] (Lord Neuberger).

[120] Wright, [98]. There is another reason for doubting that (3) is correct. Depriving another of a claim for damages is prima facie to cause a purely economic loss, which would typically fall beyond the scope of the doctor's duty of care. Even if it may be permissible to treat interference with the ability to enforce an existing right to compensation in respect of a physical injury as sufficiently similar to interference with a person's physical integrity itself so as to avoid this objection, this seems more difficult to justify where the defendant has merely failed to allow such a right to come into existence. See further Chapter 4, 175ff.

Now suppose that there are 100 defendants each of whom independently adds the same amount of pollution to a river or contributes in some way to obstruct a public right of way, where no defendant's contribution is either necessary or sufficient to constitute a nuisance, and where some relatively small number of contributions would suffice in the circumstances to constitute a nuisance. Here it is arguable that even if each contribution is (equally) very distant (in the sense described above) from being either necessary or sufficient for the existence of a nuisance, that each defendant is nonetheless potentially liable.[121] Strictly, if this is true, this is not an *entirely* non-causal liability, since each defendant has still made a contribution to the existence of the nuisance. However, the greater the number of the defendants, and the fewer that are required for the existence of the nuisance, the less plausible it is to say that each defendant *materially* contributes to it. Liability in such cases, then, would depart from the requirement of *material* contribution.

Conclusion

In claims for compensatory damages in respect of a loss, the claimant must establish that the defendant's wrongful conduct was a cause of it. In torts constituted by injurious outcomes, the claimant will have already established causation of a loss in virtue of establishing wrong-constituting causation. In torts actionable per se, the claimant will only receive substantial compensatory damages by establishing as a matter of consequential-liability causation that the tort was a cause of loss.

It is virtually never the case that a claimant will receive compensatory damages for a loss when it is known that the defendant was not a cause of the loss or when it is impossible to say, for reasons independent of empirical uncertainty, that the defendant was a cause of the loss. Nonetheless, this may be so where C has suffered an injury which would not have occurred had no-one behaved wrongfully in relation to C, but no defendant's wrongful conduct, which risked injury to C, is a but-for factor or contribution to C's injury.

---

[121] Cf. *Lambton* v. *Mellish* [1894] 3 Ch. 163, 165–66.

2 Proof of causation: general rules

Having described the substantive law of causation in Chapter 1, this chapter describes the general rules regulating evidential uncertainty over causation.[1] Three important types of rule are described: rules concerning the burden of proof, rules concerning the standard of proof, and what are here termed probabilistic liability rules.[2] A clear understanding of these rules is indispensable to the discussion, in later chapters, of the ways in which systems have departed from them.

The chapter is divided into three parts. The first describes the general burden of proof, standard of proof, and probabilistic liability rules on causation in each system. The second examines more precisely the meaning of 'probability' employed by these rules. This is of considerable importance in determining what must be demonstrated in order to satisfy the general rules. The third part describes the reasoning processes by which courts arrive at factual conclusions about causation and the roles which different kinds of evidence play in those reasoning processes. Its focus is upon the nature and role of inferential reasoning and statistical evidence.

---

[1] The rules described are 'general' in the sense that they are considered by each system to be the default rules which apply in every civil case.

[2] Chapter 6 contains a fuller discussion of probabilistic liability rules. Some discussion of them is necessary here, however, since probabilistic liability is a general rule in relation to some causal questions in English law.

The general burdens of proof, standards of proof, and probabilistic liability rules in each system

The burden of proof

The expression 'burden of proof' is used in different senses.[3] The *legal* or *objective* burden of proof (*objective Beweislast, risque de la preuve*) is recognised by each system as a distinct rule, which determines the party that loses on a factual issue when the factfinder cannot determine to the requisite standard of proof whether the factual claim is true or not.[4] The party bearing the burden of proof loses the factual point entirely in such a situation. The burden of proof is thus an *all-or-nothing* rule in that the party who loses the point loses it *entirely*. The essence of the legal burden of proof, then, is that it determines who loses a factual issue entirely in situations where proof is impossible according to the standard of proof. In the common law, this will be either where the evidence is equally balanced or where there is insufficient evidence to form a judgement on the balance of probability. In France and Germany, this will be where the judge cannot be convinced of the truth or falsity of the factual claim.[5]

Each system accepts, as a general principle, that the burden of proof rests with the claimant in relation to the factual elements of their claim which belong to the 'cause of action' or which 'establish' the claimant's legal right against the defendant.[6] The burden of proof for defences or 'right-negating' facts (as it is put in German writing[7]) rests with the defendant. This is described by each system as a fundamental rule underpinned by strong considerations of justice and public policy.[8]

---

[3] R. Cross and C. Tapper, *Cross and Tapper on Evidence* 12th edition 120–127.

[4] H. Ahrens, 'Die Verteilung der Beweislast', 11; A. Porat and A. Stein, *Tort Liability under Uncertainty*, 16 n. 2; R. Cross and C. Tapper, *Cross and Tapper on Evidence*, 120; C. Quézel-Ambrunaz, *Essai sur la causalité en droit de la responsabilité civile*, 253; H. Mazeaud, L. Mazeaud, and J. Mazeaud, *Traité Théorique et Pratique de la Responsabilité Civile Délictuelle et Contractuelle Tome II*, 6th edition, 801.

[5] See further pp. 53–60.

[6] H. Ahrens, 'Die Verteilung der Beweislast', 17; C. Quézel-Ambrunaz, *Essai sur la causalité en droit de la responsabilité civile*, 252; R. Béraud, 'Quelques difficultés de preuve de la responsabilité délictuelle'. In Germany, this principle was considered so obvious as to be excluded from the text of the BGB: H. Prütting, *Gegenwartsprobleme der Beweislast*, 266.

[7] See, for example, H Prütting, *Gegenwartsprobleme der Beweislast*, 111–13.

[8] 'It is an ancient rule founded on considerations of good sense, and it should not be departed from without strong reasons': *Joseph Constantine Steamship Line Ltd* v. *Imperial Smelting Corporation Ltd* [1942] AC 154, 174 (Viscount Maugham). Similarly: H. Ahrens, 'Die Verteilung der Beweislast', 17; E. Karner, 'The Function of the Burden of Proof in Tort Law', 70 (underpinned by 'fundamental fairness considerations').

As natural causation is a substantive element of the cause of action in common law, as well as French and German tort claims for substantial compensatory damages, it follows that the claimant bears the burden of proof with respect to it.[9]

To be distinguished[10] from the legal burden of proof are the burden of producing evidence (*subjective Beweislast, Beweisführungslast, charge de la preuve*); the burden of pleading certain facts (*objective Behauptungslast*); and the evidential burden of proof (*konkrete Beweisführungslast*).[11] The former two burdens generally follow the allocation of the legal burden of proof: the party who will lose if the facts are not shown to the requisite standard must plead those facts and adduce evidence to support them.[12] The evidential burden is held by the party who, at a given point in a trial, will lose the case unless it makes a further factual submission, because the judge is, at that point, convinced of the other party's case. Consequently, this burden may shift to and fro, between the parties, throughout the proceedings. This alternation occurs all the while the legal burden of proof remains in its original (pre-trial) position.

Standards of proof

Legal standards of proof describe the degree of proof at which a factfinder must take a fact to be established for the purposes of some legal process. If a proposition meets the standard of proof, it is accepted as true.

Each system makes the application of a certain standard of proof contingent upon a certain kind of factual question being at issue. How different kinds of factual question are distinguished for this purpose varies from system to system. In loose terms, there is a distinction in terms of standard of proof rules between questions going to *establish*

---

[9] *Bonnington Castings v. Wardlaw* [1956] AC 613, 625; *Snell v. Farrell* [1990] 2 SCR 311, 321; *Chappel v. Hart* (1998) 195 CLR 232, 273; D. Dobbs, R. Keeton and D. Owen, *Prosser & Keeton on Torts*, 5th edition, 243; K. Barker, P. Cane, M. Lunney, and F. Trindade, *The Law of Torts in Australia*, 5th edition, 532; L. Khoury, *Uncertain Causation in Medical Liability*, 31; H. Oetker, 'Commentary on §249 BGB' in *Münchener Kommentar zum BGB*, 6th edition, [103]; H. Mazeaud, L. Mazeaud, and J. Mazeaud, *Traité théorique et pratique de la responsabilité civile délictuelle et contractuelle Tome II*, 6th edition, 808.

[10] These distinctions are not always made in French doctrinal writing. See, however, E. Karner, 'The Function of the Burden of Proof in Tort Law', 69.

[11] For these distinctions in German law: H. Prütting, 'Commentary on §286 ZPO' 97–103; U. Foerste, 'Commentary on §286 ZPO' in *Musielak zum ZPO*, 10th edition, 32–3. For the common law: L. Khoury, *Uncertain Causation in Medical Liility*, 30.

[12] E. Karner, 'The Function of the Burden of Proof in Tort Law', 71. In this way the party is incentivised to produce evidence if it will lose the case on the legal burden of proof.

liability and questions going to determining the *extent* of liability. The former generally attract standard of proof rules in each system, while the latter either attract proportional liability rules or less strict standards of proof.

More precisely, there are two principal distinctions. In English law, there is a distinction between questions of *past fact* and questions about the *future*. The general rule is that wrong-constituting causation is a question of past fact which attracts the standard of proof described in the section on English law. Future questions, in so far as they concern consequential liability causation, are subject to proportional liability rules. In German law, there is a distinction in the standards of proof between wrong-constituting causation and consequential-liability causation. French law applies a strict standard of proof to establishing liability but allows considerable discretion in the assessment of the extent of it. All of this requires some elaboration.

English law

Wrong-constituting causation: the balance of probability
In the common law, the general rule is that past facts in civil cases must be proven on the 'balance of probability' or on the 'preponderance of the evidence'. The general rule is that wrong-constituting causation is a question of past fact and so must be proven to this standard.[13]

The predominant formulation of the balance of probability rule (henceforth 'the BPR') in England, Canada, and the United States, is that a factual proposition p should be taken to be true whenever it is more probable than not that p.[14] As a directive to the factfinder, this

---

[13] See Note 9.

[14] *Miller* v. *Ministry of Pensions* [1947] 2 All ER 372, 374 (Denning J): 'the evidence is such that a tribunal can say "we think it more probable than not"'; *Davies* v. *Taylor* [1974] AC 207, 219 (Lord Simon): 'the concept of proof on a balance of probabilities. . .can be restated as the burden of showing odds of at least 51 to 49 that such-and-such has taken place'; *Nulty* v. *Milton Keynes Borough Council* [2013] EWCA Civ 15, [37] (Toulson LJ): 'In deciding a question of past fact the court will, of course, give the answer which it believes is more likely to be (more probably) the right answer than the wrong answer'; *F H* v. *McDougall* [2008] 3 SCR 41: the BPR requires a '51% probability' at [43]; F. O'Mally et al. (eds) *Federal Jury Practice and Instructions*, §166.51: 'To "establish by a preponderance of the evidence" means to prove that something is more likely so than not so. In other words, a preponderance of the evidence in the case means such evidence as. . .produces in your minds belief that what is sought to be proved is more likely true than not true'. For this formulation in the literature see, for example, A. Beever, *Rediscovering the Law of Negligence*, 481; R. Brown, 'The Possibility of "Inference Causation": Inferring Cause-in-fact and the Nature of Legal Fact-finding' 19; R. Goldberg, 'Using Scientific Evidence to Resolve Causation Problems', 150.

formulation of the BPR requires that the factfinder find that p just whenever they are persuaded that p is more probable than not.[15]

The legal consequences of proof of wrong-constituting causation on the balance of probability

If the defendant's wrongful conduct is found to have caused the claimant's injury on the BPR, the court acts as if that fact were true. It follows that no discount is made in the assessment of damages for any probability that the defendant did not cause the injury.[16] Thus it is said that the BPR, like the burden of proof, is an *all-or-nothing* rule: by establishing that the defendant is more likely than not a cause of the damage, full recovery is obtained, while no damages will be awarded if the causal claim is not established to that standard.[17] For example, if it is shown on the BPR that the claimant would not have gone ahead with an operation had she been informed of a certain risk, which then instantiated, no discount will be made in the assessment of damages for any chance that she would have.[18]

---

[15] This might seem trivial, but the predominant Australian formulation of the BPR differs in requiring that the judge find that p just whenever the factfinder is actually persuaded that p, albeit that the factfinder's conviction that p need not be very strong. See *Briginshaw* v. *Briginshaw* [1938] HCA 34, (1938) 60 CLR 336. 'The truth is that, when the law requires the proof of any fact, the tribunal must feel an actual persuasion of its occurrence or existence before it can be found. It cannot be found as a result of a mere mechanical comparison of probabilities independently of any belief in its reality.' In *Seltsam* v. *McGuinness* [2000] NSWCA 29, [136], Spiegelman CJ described this as the 'predominant position in Australian case law'. Cf. C. Sappadeen and P. Vines, *Fleming's Law of Torts*, 357, where the BPR is said 'sometimes' to involve actual persuasion. The difference in the formulations is that, under the English law view, the 'probability' in the BPR is part of the *content* of what the factfinder must be persuaded. In the Australian formulation, the 'probability' in the BPR is a measure of the *strength* of the factfinder's being persuaded that p. The following analysis focuses upon the English law formulation of the BPR.

[16] *Hotson* v. *East Berkshire Health Authority* [1987] 1 AC 750, 783 (Lord Bridge) 793 (Lord Ackner): 'Such a finding [of causation on the BPR] does not permit any discounting – to do so would be to propound a wholly new doctrine which has no support in principle or authority'. In agreement: L. Khoury, *Uncertain Causation in Medical Liability*, 36; R. Stevens, *Torts and Rights*, 52; L. Klar, *Tort Law* 4th edition, 453 n 121; D. Nolan, 'Causation and the Goals of Tort Law', 185; K. Barker, P. Cane, M. Lunney, and F. Trindade, *The Law of Torts in Australia*, 5th edition, 538 n. 27. See also *Cabral* v. *Gupta* [1993] 1 WWR 648 (Manitoba, CA).

[17] For example, V. Black, 'Decision Causation', 318.

[18] There was no suggestion of such a discount on such facts in *Chester* v. *Afshar* [2005] 1 AC 134. There are some *dicta* in *Chappel* v. *Hart* (1998) HCA 55 (e.g. at [19] per Gaudron J) which could be misinterpreted in this way, however.

Consequential-liability causation

In English law, the general rule is that the question of whether a tort has caused a loss is decided on the BPR if the loss is claimed to have occurred in the past.[19] However, the BPR does not apply in relation to determining the *extent* of loss caused by the tort, where determining the extent of the loss caused involves asking questions about what will happen or would have happened in the future (post-trial) had the tort not occurred.[20] These are questions of 'quantification' or 'the assessment of damages', traditionally contrasted with questions of causation of 'damage' or 'injury'.

The classic statement of the proof rules applicable to quantification is Lord Diplock's in *Mallett v. McMonagle*:

> The role of the court in making an assessment of damages which depends upon its view as to what will be and what would have been is to be contrasted with its ordinary function in civil actions of determining what was. In deter-mining what did happen in the past a court decides on the balance of prob-abilities. Anything that is more probable than not it treats as certain. But in assessing damages which depend upon its view as to what will happen in the future or would have happened in the future if something had not happened in the past, the court must make an estimate as to what are the chances that a particular thing will or would have happened and reflect those chances, whether they are more or less than even, in the amount of damages which it awards.[21]

Smith v. Leech Brain provides a helpful illustration.[22] The claimant was negligently struck on the lip by a piece of hot metal. This triggered a cancer. The tort was established on the BPR when the negligence caused the lip injury. The question of whether the lip injury was a cause of the cancer was determined on the BPR. The court then made a discount in assessing damages for the 5 per cent chance that the cancer would have been triggered anyway. This discount did not reflect uncertainty over whether the cancer was caused by the lip injury. Rather it reflected the separate possibility that the consequential losses caused by the lip injury would have occurred anyway at some point in the future.

---

[19] *Thorp v. Sharp* [2007] EWCA Civ 1433; *Lay v. Cambridgeshire and Peterborough Mental Health Partnership NHS Trust* [2013] EWCA Civ 436 (QB) at [4].

[20] The position is the same in Canada and Australia, often with citation to the leading English case discussed in the text. For Canada, see S. Waddams, 'Damages: Assessment of Uncertainties'; L. Klar, *Tort Law*, 4th edition, 461. For Australia: see H. Luntz, 'Loss of a Chance in Medical Negligence', 15. The position in many US states is unclear according to D. Fischer, 'Tort Recovery for Loss of a Chance', 638.

[21] *Mallett v. McMonagle* [1970] AC 166, 176.   [22] [1962] 2 QB 405.

English (and Commonwealth) law could thus be described as operating a bifurcated system of proof of causation. The first stage, which concerns questions of wrong-constituting causation, and questions of consequential-liability causation involving past losses, requires the claimant to meet a threshold probability: the balance of probability. The second stage, which concerns questions as to whether the tort will cause a loss in the future or what would have happened in the future had the tort not occurred, requires the court to award damages in proportion to the chance that the loss will occur and reflect the chance that the loss would have occurred anyway.[23] The second stage thus involves a kind of proportional liability: the extent of liability is proportional to the chance of the claimant being worse off; no *finding* is made as to the truth or falsity of this issue. The question of whether this bifurcation in proof rules is normatively defensible is taken up in Chapter 6.[24]

German law

Wrong-constituting causation: §286 ZPO

German law divides the standard of proof applicable to questions of natural causation between liability-grounding causation (*haftungsbegründende Kausalität*) and liability-fulfilling causation (*haftungsausfüllende Kausalität*).[25] The first concerns the causal link between the defendant's conduct and the initial infringement of the interest protected by the claimant's legal right. Here §286 ZPO (*Zivilprozessordnung* – Code of Civil Procedure) governs the situation. According to this provision, the judge must decide whether the factual claim is to be adjudged true or false according to their conviction (*nach freier Überzeugung*).[26] The judge must be personally *convinced* of the truth of the claim.[27] Precisely *how* convinced the judge must be of the truth of the claim does not emerge directly from §286 ZPO. The BGH has, however, stated that the judge

---

[23] Cf. *Doyle* v. *Wallace* [1998] PIQR Q146.   [24] Chapter 6, 324–5; 364–365.

[25] BGH NJW 2008, 1381. See H. Oetker, Commentary on §249 BGB, 2012, [105].

[26] Broadly, the point of the provision was to free courts from formalistic methods of proof. The legislative history of the earlier §§259, 260 CPO is set out in G. Wagner, 'Proportionalhaftung für ärztliche Behandlungsfehler de lege lata', 460–1.

[27] C. Katzenmeier, 'Beweismaßreduzierung und probabilistische Proportionalhaftung', 192. M. Brinkmann, *Das Beweismaß im Zivilprozess aus rechtsvergleichender Ansicht*, 42 suggests that the concept of conviction in §286 ZPO is influenced by Kant's discussion of it in the *Critique of Pure Reason*. See further A. Chignell, 'Belief in Kant', 331.

should have 'a level of certainty which silences doubts for practical purposes even if not eliminating them fully'.[28]

§286 ZPO and the balance of probability

Three features of §286 ZPO, and the BGH's statement of what it requires, stand out in comparison to the common law. The first is §286 ZPO's primary focus upon the state of mind of the judge. While the predominant formulation of the BPR in the common law refers more objectively to the 'balance of probability', §286 ZPO seems to frame the standard of proof entirely around whether the judge is personally convinced of the truth. The second is the requirement that the judge be convinced of the *truth* of p rather than that the judge be convinced that p is *more probably true* than not. The requirement is being convinced of the truth, not of the probable truth. The third is that the standard of proof is apparently higher than the BPR. To be convinced that something is more probably true than not is not to have a 'level of certainty which silences doubts for practical purposes'.[29]

The first and second contrasts are less stark than this. First, it is accepted that the judge's conviction in the truth or falsity of the claim must not be based upon a deductive fallacy or flout basic principles of inductive reasoning.[30] An irrationally formed belief in the truth or falsity of the claim can therefore be challenged. It is accurate, therefore, to say that §286 ZPO requires that the judge be convinced of p on rational grounds – *mere* personal conviction does not suffice.

Second, even if conviction that p is more probably true than not is insufficient, probability still has a role in determining when the judge should be convinced that p is true. The nature of this role is disputed.[31] Two points may be made. First, in explaining what constitutes 'a level of certainty which silences doubts for practical purposes', the courts do use

---

[28] The judge must '[sich] mit einem für das praktische Leben brauchbaren Grad von Gewißheit begnügen, der den Zweifeln Schweigen gebietet, ohne sie völlig auszuschließen': BGHZ 53, 245, 256 (the Anastasia case). The formulation has been repeated by the BGH many times: NJW 1989, 2948; NJW 2000, 953; NJW 2008, 1381.

[29] Indeed, the balance of probability standard is explicitly distinguished from the requisite, higher, standard in some decisions: see, for example, AG Brandenburg, 18 July 2014, 31 C 147/12, [31].

[30] C. Katzenmeier, 'Beweismaßreduzierung und probabilistische Proportionalhaftung', 195; G. Mäsch, *Chance und Schaden*, 373.

[31] For an overview of different theories of the relationship between §286 ZPO and probability, see C. Katzenmeier, 'Beweismaßreduzierung und probabilistische Proportionalhaftung', 192–6.

the language of probability.[32] Thus, on a number of occasions the BGH has distinguished the applicable standard of proof under §286 ZPO from 'a probability close to certainty' on the ground this is too high a level of probability and less is required.[33] Second, some influential evidence scholars accept that it may be rational for the judge to be convinced of p when p has a sufficiently high probability. One version of this view holds that being convinced of p is only ever really to be convinced that p is (very) highly probable.[34] So when the law requires the judge to be convinced of p, it can only reasonably be interpreted as requiring one be convinced that p is very highly probable.[35] Another version holds that one may legitimately come to be convinced of p if p is highly probable.[36]

The third contrast – that the standard of proof under §286 ZPO is higher than the BPR – does have merit. As we observed above, the BGH has distinguished the §286 ZPO from a 'probability close to certainty'. There is some divergence as to what this lower level of probability is, though it is clearly beyond a mere balance of probability. In one medical negligence case where the claimant's chances of being healed, had he been non-negligently treated, were 'not clearly above 90%', this was insufficient.[37] However, other cases have allowed a probability of 80 per cent in respect of liability-grounding causation to suffice and still others have spoken of a need (only) to have greater than a 70 per cent probability.[38] Consequently, the claim that German courts apply the common law 'beyond reasonable doubt' standard in all civil cases seems untenable.[39]

---

[32] For example, OLG Hamm 29 March 2000, 13 U 99/99; OLG Hamm 18 March 2002, 6 U 115/ 01. For a catalogue of judicial formulations of the standard of proof involving probability (and in relation to causation): H. Weber, *Der Kausalitätsbeweis im Zivilprozeß*, 48.

[33] BGH NJW 1989, 2948, 2949; BGH NJW 2003, 1116, 1117.

[34] C. Katzenmeier, 'Beweismaßreduzierung und probabilistische Proportionalhaftung', 194, citing H. Musielak, *Die Grundlagen der Beweislast im Zivilprozeß*, 105–19.

[35] Ibid.

[36] This is Katzenmeier's own view in C. Katzenmeier, 'Beweismaßreduzierung und probabilistische Proportionalhaftung', 195–6.

[37] OLG Hamm VersR 2000, 325. Similarly: OLG Koblenz, 12 March 2014, 5 U 640/13, [20] (10 per cent probability that injury would have occurred anyway with no negligence prevented finding of causation under §286 ZPO). Cf., accepting a 90 per cent probability (as stated by an expert) as sufficient, OLG Hamm, 18 January 2014. 26 U 30/12.

[38] OLG Koblenz NJW 2000, 3435, 3437 (80 per cent is enough); OLG Frankfurt, reported in BGH NJW 1999, 860, 861. G. Mäsch, *Chance und Schaden* 374, considers the former decision to be an exception. But there are other cases allowing even a 70 per cent probability to suffice: OLG Koblenz VersR 2000, 219; OLG Rostock OLG-NL 2004, 146.

[39] Cf. K. Clermont and E. Sherwin, 'A Comparative View of Standards of Proof', 250 (their analysis is based upon French law, but they infer that this is the position in continental

Consequential-liability causation: §287 ZPO

§287 ZPO[40] states that 'whether a damage exists and the extent of the damage or of a compensable interest' is to be decided by the court 'at its free discretion taking into account all the circumstances'.[41] The clear effect of this provision is the imposition of less stringent requirements of proof than under §286 ZPO for factual questions to which it applies.[42] This is generally said to involve a reduction in the standard of proof.[43] A number of formulations of this lower standard exists, varying between something akin to the balance of probability and a higher probability: preponderant probability (*überwiegende Wahrscheinlichkeit*),[44] substantial probability, (*erhebliche Wahrscheinlichkeit*),[45] high probability (*höhere Wahrscheinlichkeit*).[46] The basic position is essentially that the court must make a reasonable *estimation* (*Schätzung*) of the extent of the loss. These formulations are attempts to precisify the more general idea of reasonable estimation.[47]

The precise division of labour between §286 ZPO and §287 ZPO in respect of natural causation questions has been the subject of dispute. Present orthodoxy draws the distinction between liability-grounding and liability-fulfilling causation.[48] Thus in delictual claims under §823 I BGB, the causal link between the defendant's conduct and the initial infringement of the claimant's right (liability-grounding causation) must be shown according to the higher standard of §286 ZPO,[49] while

Europe). Their position is justly criticised by M. Brinkmann, *Das Beweismaß im Zivilprozess aus rechtsvergleichender Ansicht*, 41ff.

[40] What is said here with respect to the lower standard of proof applies also to §252 2 BGB, which has a similar evidential function as §287 ZPO for consequential losses:
H. Großerichter, *Hypothetischer Geschehensverlauf und Schadensfestellung*, 184: 'zwischen denen [§252 2 BGB and §287 ZPO] in der Praxis kaum differenziert wird'.

[41] This is §287 ZPO, sentence 1.

[42] H. Prutting, Commentary on §287 ZPO in *Münchener Kommentar zum ZPO*, 4th edition, 2013, [3].

[43] Ibid. See also U. Foerste, Commentary on §287 ZPO in *Musielak Kommentar zum ZPO*, 10th edition, 2013, [1].

[44] H. Prutting, above, [17], [36].

[45] For example, H. Großerichter, *Hypothetischer Geschehensverlauf und Schadensfestellung*, 67.

[46] For this and other formulations, see OLG München NJW 2011, 396. See also BGH NJW 2003, 1116; BGH NJW 2004, 777; BGH NJW 2008, 1381.

[47] Note the titles of leading articles on §287 ZPO: W. Henckel, 'Grenzen richterlicher Schadensschätzung'; H. Arens, 'Dogmatik und Praxis der Schadensschätzung'.

[48] G. Wagner, 'Proportionalhaftung', 457–8; G. Mäsch, *Chance und Schaden*, 378. This division between §286 and §287 ZPO between the concepts of *Haftungsbegründung* and *Haftungsausfüllung* originates in BGH NJW 1952, 301, 302. For the historical development: B. Maassen, *Beweismaßprobleme im Schadensersatzprozeß*, 91ff.

[49] BGH NJW 2004, 777; BGH NJW 2008, 1381.

consequential losses are assessed under §287 ZPO. It further follows that in contractual claims and claims for breach of statutory duty (§823 II BGB), where the simple breach of a legal duty gives rise to the liability,[50] all causal questions are subject to the lighter §287 ZPO regime.[51] Importantly, however, where contractual duties are aimed at protecting the interests protected in §823 I BGB, the causal link between the breach of the contractual duty and the initial infringement of the right must be shown according to §286 ZPO.[52]

This is of significant importance. Claims for medical negligence are predominantly based upon contractual liability in German law. Since contractual liability (as in English law) is established merely upon breach of duty, it can be argued that §287 ZPO should apply to the causal issue. But this is not accepted. The causal aspect of such a contractual claim falls within the tort proof regime and attracts the stricter §286 ZPO standard. This is to avoid the apparent arbitrariness that a contractual claim in respect of medical negligence would be subject to a lighter proof standard than a delictual one in respect of natural causation; §286 ZPO also applies here.[53] The result is that persons suing for breaches of contracts protecting purely economic interests are subject to a standard of proof on causation approximating the BPR standard, while those suing for breaches of contracts protecting one of the interests under §823 I BGB (like bodily integrity) are subject to the stricter §286 ZPO in respect of causation of the initial injury. It may also be noted that since many common law tort claims in relation to pure economic loss will be analysed in contractual terms in German law, §287 ZPO brings German law substantially closer to the common law so far as proof of causation is concerned.[54]

Where §287 ZPO does apply, the BGH has drawn a distinction between cases concerning loss of earnings in which a specific future hypothetical

---

[50] G. Wagner, 'Proportionalhaftung', 463.

[51] Ibid., 461. As Wagner argues, however, the simple wording of §287 ZPO ('whether a damage exists') makes a strong case for placing uncertainty over the causal link between D's wrongful conduct and the initial infringement of C's right under §823 I BGB within its scope.

[52] BGH NJW 1987, 705, 706. Thus a medical negligence claimant must prove natural causation to a higher standard (§286 ZPO) than a legal malpractice claimant, since the latter's claim will be for a pure economic loss not recognised under §823 I BGB (§287 ZPO).

[53] G. Mäsch, Chance und Schaden, 383. But ultimately the arbitrariness is pervasive, as Note 52 shows.

[54] For the broader contract law: B. Markesinis, H. Unberath, and A. Johnston, The German Law of Contract, 89ff; B. Markesinis and H. Unberath, The German Law of Torts, 265ff.

course of events is shown to a substantial probability and cases in which it is *merely* estimated (*abgeschätzt*).[55] In the former set, certain pre-tort facts exist (*Anknüpfungstatsachen*) which allow the judge to be convinced that a certain course of events would probably have occurred. In the latter, the number of alternative courses of events makes a prediction of what specifically would have happened impossible, such that one may only estimate what would have happened (sometimes by taking an average amount of possible loss of earnings suffered or the lowest amount of the alternative possible courses of events).

The claim to be merely 'estimating' as opposed to accepting 'proof' of the extent of loss is most often evident in two categories of case: those involving severe injuries to young children and cases where there is no usual course of events to take as a reference point for how matters would have turned out.[56] This looser approach is justified by the BGH, in the case of injured children, with the reasoning that the defendant is 'responsible' for the fact that proof is so difficult, as injury to the child occurs at such an early stage of its life.[57] However, the boundary between the looser approach of 'estimation' and 'proof' is a porous one. For example, in a case where a 12-year-old schoolchild was injured, the court allowed full recovery in the amount of the salary he would have obtained from the age of 25, had he first passed a test which only 25 per cent of candidates pass and then another test which only 20 per cent of candidates pass.[58] The court claims to predict what would have happened in the child's life by reference to *Anknüpfungstatsachen* – including, for example, the employment history of its parents and siblings.[59]

Whether a specific consequential loss has been suffered is, in principle, an all-or-nothing question under §287 ZPO. This follows from the understanding of this provision as lowering the standard of proof. On this understanding, there is no room for an award of damages in proportion to the probability that a loss would have been avoided but for the tort.[60] Nonetheless, some recent decisions of the BGH seem to hold that

---

[55] BGH NJW 2011, 1145, 1146–7. (note Schiemann). This analysis is supported by H. Großerichter, *Hypothetischer Geschehensverlauf und Schadensfestellung*, 187ff.

[56] H. Großerichter, ibid., 187–8.

[57] BGH NJW 2011, 1148. See also: OLG Karlsruhe VersR 1989, 1102.

[58] OLG Köln NJW 1972, 59.   [59] See also, more recently, BGH NJW 2011, 1148.

[60] G. Mäsch, *Chance und Schaden*, 144. Some authors make a distinction in how §287 ZPO should apply between questions of quantum and questions relating to the causal link between an initial damage and further individual types of damage; it is argued that while the causal link between the initial damage and further damage cannot be 'estimated', the mere extent of quantum can be. A similar distinction exists in English

it is possible to make a discount in the award of damages in proportion to the chance that certain consequential financial losses would have occurred without the tort.[61] Each of these cases has involved a set of facts where a concrete assessment of what would have happened absent the tort has been thought impossible (in the sense that there is not a sufficient factual basis to infer what would have happened absent the tort to a substantial probability). So in cases where the courts describe what they are doing as merely providing a reasonable 'estimation' of the loss, there is a tendency to mirror the common law approach of taking into account the chances that loss would have occurred anyway and reflecting that in the amount of damages.[62] This is a novel development. Orthodoxy, in relation to awards of damages, is all-or-nothing.

French law

Liability-grounding causation: intime conviction

The Code Civil contains no provision governing the standard of proof in civil cases. Article 427 I of the Code of Criminal Procedure states that the general rule in *criminal* cases is that the judge must decide whether the facts have been established according to his or her 'intime conviction' – a firm conviction. French authors generally hold that the judge must decide according to her *intime conviction* in civil cases, too.[63] Thus, as in German law, the standard of proof is defined by reference to the judge being subjectively convinced in the truth or falsity of the claim.

The necessary strength of this conviction is, similarly, divergently expressed. Most authors begin their presentation of proof requirements generally, and natural causation in particular, by stating that in theory the defendant must be shown *certainly* to have caused the claimant's injury.[64] This is immediately qualified with the statement that absolute certainty is unobtainable and something to the effect that 'une certaine souplesse dans l'appréciation de la preuve du lien

---

law, where not all consequential liability questions attract the proportional liability approach; questions of past fact, even if liability is established, do not. See H. Stoll, 'Haftungsverlagerung durch Beweisrechtliche Mittel', 194.

[61] BGH NJW 1998, 1633, 1634 (noting that '[v]erbleibende Risiken können. . .gegebenenfalls auch gewisse Abschläge rechtfertigen [in the award of damages]'); NJW-RR 1999, 1039 = VersR 2000, 233; NJW 2000, 3287; BGH NJW 2011, 1148.

[62] For a case where the claimant receives nothing, having received a 100 per cent award in a lower court: BGH NJW 2011, 1145.

[63] L. Khoury, *Uncertain Causation in Medical Liability*, 37, n 147.

[64] For example, C. Quézel-Ambrunaz, *Essai sur la causalité en droit de la responsabilité civile*, 253, who contrasts it with the BPR.

causal' is permissible.[65] Moreover, doctrinal writers often contrast the level of strength necessary in criminal and civil cases, with a lower strength being permissible in the latter.[66] It has thus been stated that 'in practice, a very high probability will suffice'.[67] Or, slightly differently, where it is very probable that the defendant's conduct has caused the damage, the judge can rationally reach an *intime conviction* that this occurred.[68]

Consequential-liability causation

There is no strict division, in proof terms, between matters going to liability and matters going to the quantification of loss.[69] The claimant can only recover for losses which certainly have or will flow from the defendant's wrong. This is the requirement of *dommage certain*.[70] The requirement is, however, applied with some looseness. First, the trial judge (*juge du fond*) has what is known as the *pouvoir souverain d'appréciation du dommage* ('unfettered discretion'). This provides a considerable discretion in the assessment of damages: so long as the judge justifies the conclusion that some loss exists, the amount of the loss is unlikely to be scrutinised by appellate courts.[71] Second, in respect of future losses, which will of course be difficult to prove to a certainty, the claimant may succeed in showing that the defendant has caused the lost chance of, for example, advancing to a certain career.[72] It should be noted, however, that quantification of lost earnings is not always made on a loss of a chance basis. Although the specific course of events absent the defendant's wrong will not be demonstrable to a certainty, it will often be possible to say – to a high probability – that the claimant would *at least* have earned a certain

---

[65] Ibid.

[66] E. Poisson-Drocourt, 'Note under Cass Civ 2e 15 December 1980', 456;
C. Quézel-Ambrunaz, *Essai sur la causalité en droit de la responsabilité civile*, 253, n. 3. Cf.
K. Clermont and E. Sherwin, 'A Comparative View of Standards of Proof', 250.

[67] L. Khoury, *Uncertain Causation in Medical Liability*, 38.

[68] T. Fossier and F. Lévêque, 'Le "presque vrai" et le "pas tout à fait faux": probabilités et décision juridictionnelle', [7], who distinguish classical and frequentist probability from probability in the sense of 'croyance dans la force d'une hypothèse', [21].

[69] There has, however, been a tendency towards 'standardised' damages assessment in personal injury cases: Y. Lambert-Faivre and S. Porchy-Simon, *Droit du dommage corporel*, 7th edition, 28–9.

[70] Ibid. 77–9.

[71] H. Großerichter, *Hypothetischer Geschehensverlauf*, 91; Y. Lambert-Faivre and S. Porchy-Simon, *Droit du dommage corporel*, 26.

[72] For example, Cass Civ 2e, 27 February 1985, RTDC 1986, 117 (note Huet).

amount of income.[73] This is generally recoverable in full without discount for the risk that the loss is not attributable to the defendant's conduct.[74]

The meaning of probability and standards of proof

The description of the standards of proof in each system has made reference to the concept of 'probability'. This reference is ambiguous since the concept of probability can receive different interpretations.[75] This section suggests that, in general, the relevant concept is what may be termed 'evidential probability'.[76] Evidential probability is a function of (1) the extent to which a body of evidence supports a proposition and (2) the specificity of the evidence in relation to the proposition. In relation to the BPR, this means that the BPR requires that the (factfinder believe that the) evidence points more towards p than not-p or, equivalently, there must be more of an evidential *case* for p than not-p, where the evidence is sufficiently specific to the case at hand. This section is principally concerned with (1). The significance of (2) – the specificity dimension of evidential probability – will be explained in connection with the probative force of statistical evidence.

The following discussion will clarify the concept of 'evidential probability' by distinguishing it from other concepts of probability and establish that the BPR involves evidential probability. This discussion will also serve as a basis for the discussion of the probabilistic concept of loss of a chance in Chapter 5. It is useful to begin by distinguishing evidential probability from other understandings of the concept of probability.[77]

---

[73] H. Großerichter, *Hypothetischer Geschehensverlauf*, 98. As in English law, this may be ascertained by reference to generalised statistical tables (although these are not binding upon the court): ibid. 85.

[74] For example, Cass Civ 2e, 16 January 1985, Bull Civ II No. 13 (striking down the appeal court's discount).

[75] See generally, for example, A. Hajek, 'Interpretations of Probability'.

[76] The idea that there is a concept of probability which measures the support of a body of evidence for a hypothesis is developed at length in L.J. Cohen, *The Probable and the Provable*. He dubs it 'inductive probability'. The position in the text remains uncommitted to whether Cohen's axiomatisation of this concept is correct. It may be that the notion of 'evidential support' can ultimately be given a (Bayesian) analysis conforming to the standard probability axioms. For similar views, see A. Stein, *Foundations of Evidence Law*, ch. 3; T. Fossier and F. Lévêque, 'Le "presque vrai" et le "pas tout à fait faux": probabilites et decision juridictionnelle', [7].

[77] This presentation is much influenced by Hajek, 'Interpretations of Probability'.

(1) *Classical probability.*[78] According to the classical theory of probability, the probability of an event's occurring or having occurred is the ratio of the possibilities in which the event occurs to the total number of possibilities, on the assumption that each possibility is equally probable. Hence the probability of rolling a six with a fair die is 1/6. In determining whether the possibilities are equiprobable, a 'principle of indifference' is relied upon.[79] According to such a principle, if one has no evidence supporting one possibility more than another, each possibility is equally probable (or: one should *assign* each an equal probability).

The classical probability that an event occurred may be relevant to the inquiry of whether the evidence satisfies the BPR or suffices to ground a rational conviction in the truth of the claim. But the BPR or the conviction-based standards cannot *require* that the factfinder believe that the classical probability of the proposition is greater than 0.5. In most cases, factfinders do not, and cannot, partition the factual claims at issue into ratios of equiprobable possibilities and yet the BPR can be satisfied.

(2) *Frequentist (or statistical) probability.* Frequentist theories of probability come in different forms.[80] Each defines the probability of an event as the frequency of that event within a certain reference class of events. *Actual frequentism* holds that the probability of an event is the amount of times that event actually occurs within a reference class. Such probabilities are sometimes also referred to as *statistical probabilities*. If the class is infinite, the probability is the limit frequency. *Hypothetical frequentism* holds that the probability of an event is the number of times that the event would occur if a given number of trials of the event were to take place (often, an infinite number).

Again, while frequentist probabilities may be relevant to the inquiry of whether the evidence satisfies the BPR, the BPR cannot be understood as requiring that the frequentist probability of p is greater than 0.5.[81] This is mainly because in many cases judges reason to a conclusion on the BPR without it being possible to consider such reasoning as an attempt to ascertain the frequentist probability of the conclusion. For example, the judicial assessment of whether a witness is telling the truth on the balance of probability is not purely, if at all, an exercise in determining how frequently this witness (or similar witnesses) tells the truth.[82]

---

[78] Ibid., section 3.1.

[79] The coinage is Keynes': see J. Keynes, *A Treatise on Probability*, 41–64. For an overview of the principle and its problems, see Hajek, 'Interpretations of Probability', section 3.1.

[80] See A. Hajek, '"Mises Redux" – Redux: Fifteen Arguments against Finite Frequentism', 211–2.

[81] R. Allen and A. Stein, 'Evidence, Probability, and the Burden of Proof', 567 assumes this is the dominant approach to the interpretation of the BPR.

[82] For a similar conclusion: L.J. Cohen, *The Probable and the Provable*, 88; M. Redmayne, 'Objective Probability and the Assessment of Evidence', 278.

(3) *Degrees of confidence.* The probability that p can be understood as the degree of confidence which a person has in p.[83]

Philosophers tend to speak of 'degrees of confidence' as an attitude one can have towards a proposition which is neither outright belief nor outright disbelief.[84] For example, Alice might simply be *unsure* (to greater or lesser extent) whether Bill will turn up for dinner, without actually believing that he will or that he will not.[85]

The simplest version of this view states that the BPR requires that the factfinder have a degree of confidence greater than 0.5 in p. This view has gained a fair amount of support in the philosophically oriented evidence literature among those would adopt a probabilistic interpretation of the BPR.[86] This is because of the view's broader scope, and hence greater descriptive plausibility as an understanding of the BPR, than the preceding conceptions: one might have a degree of confidence in relation to virtually any proposition which might arise in litigation.[87]

There are at least two principal objections to this unadorned version of the degree of confidence view. The first is its subjectivity: if the probability that p is *simply* a person's degree of confidence in p, then it appears that there cannot be rational disagreement about the probability that p.[88] There is no rational inconsistency in my having a high degree of confidence in p and your having a low degree of confidence in p, just as there is no rational inconsistency in my asserting 'I am very cold' and your asserting 'I am a little cold'. A major descriptive problem, then, is

---

[83] Cf. A. Hajek, 'Interpretations of Probability', section 3.3.1: 'We may characterize *subjectivism*...with the slogan "Probability is degree of belief"'.

[84] See, for example, R. Wedgwood, 'Outright Belief', 309–10. Alternative terms are 'credences' or 'degrees of belief'. The terminology can be confusing, however, as some hold that there can be degrees of *outright* belief (one can believe p, *tout court*, more or less strongly), which differ from simple degrees of belief, for example, E. Zardini, 'Luminosity and Vagueness', 386–7. For the view that the BPR involves a certain strength of *outright* belief: H.L. Ho, *Philosophy of Evidence Law*, 124–51; R. Wright, 'Proving Causation: Probability versus Belief'.

[85] Of course, as a matter of psychological reality, people do not have *precise* degrees of confidence (such as 0.5653627) in propositions.

[86] See, for example, D. Kaye, 'The Paradox of the Gatecrasher and Other Stories', 105–10; S. Gold, 'Causation in Toxic Torts', 382–3.

[87] H.L. Ho, *Philosophy of Evidence Law*, 117–18.

[88] As pointed out by, for example, L.J. Cohen, 'Subjective Probability and the Paradox of the Gatecrasher', 629–30. For instance, there would be nothing irrational in assigning a 0.99 probability to the proposition that one's cat has secretly proven the Riemann hypothesis, so long as one assigned a 0.01 probability to its negation.

that factfinders *do* appear to disagree rationally about the probabilities of facts in litigation.

The second objection is that the typical formulation of the BPR identified earlier is not straightforwardly understandable in terms of degrees of confidence.[89] The statement 'I am persuaded that p is more probable than not' does not mean the same as 'I am surer that p is true than not true'. The former claims an objectivity that the latter does not claim.

> (4) *Propensity.*[90] Propensity interpretations of probability typically hold that the probability of an event refers to the disposition of a set of conditions to produce that event. Such a view might hold that, for example, the probability that a coin will land heads is an inherent metaphysical property of the coin. It seems impossible that this understanding of probability, tied as it is to the inherent dispositions of physical entities, is broad enough to capture the range of propositions to which the law attaches probabilistic assessments.

The concept of 'probability' in the BPR or the conviction-based standards of proof cannot, then, be identified with the classical theory, the frequentist theory, the degree of confidence theory or the propensity theory. This may give rise to scepticism that the BPR embeds an idea of probability at all. Yet ordinary thought recognises another concept of probability. This concept is a measure of the extent to which evidence supports a hypothesis. As Williamson has written: 'Given a...hypothesis h, we can intelligibly ask: how probable is h on present evidence? We are asking how much the evidence tells for or against the hypothesis. We are not asking what the objective physical chance or frequency of truth h has'.[91]

This concept is implicit in the recent formulation of the BPR in the English Court of Appeal in *Nulty* v. *Milton Keynes Borough Council*:

> The civil "balance of probability" test means no less and no more than that the court must be satisfied on rational and objective grounds that the case for believing that the suggested means of causation occurred is stronger than the case for not so believing.[92]

The basic concept here is one of 'evidential support' or 'evidential case'. In so far as German courts accept that a very high probability may suffice for 'conviction' under §286 ZPO, it is likely that this refers also to

---

[89] See p. 50.   [90] A. Hajek, 'Interpretations of Probability', section 3.5.

[91] T. Williamson, *Knowledge and its Limits*, 209.

[92] [2013] 1 WLR 1183, [2013] EWCA Civ 15, at [35].

evidential probability.[93] That is suggested by the fact that conviction must be based upon rational and objective grounds.[94] This implies that the probabilities in question must track the evidence.

Three points need to be made about evidential probability. First, the evidential probability that p should, plausibly, be influenced by the relevant frequentist probability and (in appropriate contexts) the classical probability that p. The case for p is stronger if there is a very high frequentist probability that p. The point made earlier was only that it cannot be *reduced* to these.[95]

Second, it is not clear whether the concept of evidential probability, as it is understood in the law, can be shown to obey all of the standard mathematical axioms of probability.[96] Cohen identified a number of possible difficulties in this regard.[97] First, the negation rule – that $P(notA) = 1 - P(A)$ – implies that if 1000 attend a stadium and only 499 pay the admission fee, the probability that a person did not pay is 0.501. But, Cohen argued, this would not satisfy the BPR. Hence, the concept of probability in the BPR does not conform to a standard mathematical probability axiom.[98] Cohen is probably correct about the law.[99] However, it is not clear whether this shows that the negation rule has no application under the BPR. It may only demonstrate that a statistical probability cannot be equated with an evidential probability. Second, Cohen argued that the understanding of probability in the BPR does not seem to obey the conjunction rule for independent events: $P(A \text{ and } B) = P(A) \times P(B)$. Suppose a cause of action consists of elements A, B, C, where these elements are independent. If a claimant proves $P(A) = 0.6$, $P(B) = 0.6$ and $P(C) = 0.6$, then the conjunction rule implies that $P(A \text{ and } B \text{ and } C) = 0.216$. Consequently, though the claimant has proven each element to a probability greater than 0.5, the probability of the case is less than 0.5. But, Cohen argued, the law does not require the claimant to prove the global case is greater than 0.5, only each element.[100] Hence, again, the BPR fails to conform to the standard probability axioms. The force of the argument is blunted in so far as it will often be the case that the elements are not independent (e.g. negligence and causation are not

[93] See pp. 54–59.   [94] Ibid.   [95] See further p.85ff.

[96] For example, that the probability of an event's occurrence and the probability of its non-occurrence sum to 1; that probability of independent events both occurring is given by the multiplication of the probability of each event occurring.

[97] L.J. Cohen, *The Probable and the Provable*, chs 5–10.

[98] L.J. Cohen, *The Probable and the Provable*, 74–81.   [99] See p.85ff.

[100] L.J. Cohen, *The Probable and the Provable*, 65–7 (citing no authority).

stochastically independent).[101] Moreover, the legal position is not as clear as Cohen claims.[102]

Third, the measurement of evidential probability is inherently vague. It is difficult to state precisely the extent to which evidence supports p more than not-p. The imprecision in a concept is not necessarily reason to doubt its validity, however.

Proving causation according to the general rules

This part analyses how courts reason to the conclusion that causation is established according to the governing standard of proof. First, it argues that virtually all conclusions that x was a cause of y involve inferential reasoning. Second, it seeks to delineate the role which different kinds of evidence play in inferences about causation. Evidence is categorised as either 'general evidence' or 'case-specific evidence'. The final section analyses at greater length disputed questions concerning the inference of causation.

Inference

Inference is the activity of extrapolating information from other information. It is either deductive or inductive.[103] A deductive inference from p and q to r requires that p and q logically entail the truth of r. Inductive inference from p and q to r is fallible: p and q provide evidence for r but do not logically entail r. Examples of inductive inference include the inference that the next observed raven will be black from the fact that previously observed ravens have been black or the inference that Sally is upset from the fact that her eyes are watery.

There is a sense in which all of our conclusions about matters of fact involve inductive inference.[104] On coming to believe that the cat is on the mat from seeing the cat there, one could be said to infer that the cat is there from the fact of one's experience and the fact that one's perceptual capacities are generally effective. Normally, however, evidence scholars

---

[101] Cf., however, ibid., 61–2.

[102] See D. Nance, 'A Comment on the Supposed Paradoxes of a Mathematical Interpretation of the Logic of Trials'. For a persuasive critique of Cohen's arguments about conjunction in relation to witness testimony, see P. Dawid, 'The Difficulty about Conjunction'.

[103] For simplicity, 'abductive' inference is treated as species of inductive inference here on the basis that it also involves fallible inferences. Abductive inference is inference from p and q to r on the basis that r would best explain p and q. The inference about Sally in the text is abductive. On 'abduction', see T. Anderson, D. Schum, and W. Twining, *Analysis of evidence*, 56–8.

[104] See, ibid., 100–1; 262–3.

distinguish between conclusions based upon 'direct' and 'indirect' evidence, where conclusions based upon the latter, but not the former, require inferential reasoning.[105] The standard example of direct evidence is eyewitness testimony or video footage.[106] Yet even conclusions based upon such evidence can be said to involve inference: one infers the factual conclusion from the eyewitness testimony in conjunction with the facts that the witness appears to be honest and has good eyesight.

This is not to deny that there can be direct, in the sense of 'perceptual', evidence of causation. People perceive things being caused to happen all the time (e.g. I saw Laura break the vase).[107] But, in the tort context, such cases are largely restricted to cases involving the initiation of visible physical forces by human agents or other relatively large phenomena. In many cases – for example, involving the initiation of a disease – causation cannot practically be observed. More fundamentally, it is often the case that *in principle* there can be no direct evidence of causation. To the extent that our judgement that x was a cause of y depends upon the answer to the counterfactual question 'would y not have occurred had x not occurred?', our judgement cannot be perceptual. One does not observe what would have happened but only what did. This is a feature even of simple cases. One does not *observe* whether D's negligently driving at 80 rather than lawfully, at 60, was a cause of the accident; this needs to be tested by a counterfactual.[108]

The components of causal inference

To reach the conclusion, according to the standard of proof, that x was or was not a cause of y, then, factfinders rely upon inference. This section explores the forms of reasoning and evidence used in making causal inferences. The following each plays a role: (i) general reasoning and evidence and (ii) case-specific evidence.

---

[105] See, for example, J. Murphy, *Murphy on Evidence*, 4th edition, 18; R. Emson, *Evidence*, 6–7.

[106] See, for example, T. Anderson et al., *The Analysis of Evidence*, 382.

[107] E. Anscombe, 'Causality and Determination', 69. 'As surely as we learned to call people by name and to report from seeing it that the cat is on the table, we also learned to report from seeing it that someone drunk up the milk, or that the dog made a funny noise, or that things were cut or broken by the things that cut and broke them...[Hume] confidently challenged us to "produce an instance wherein the efficacy is plainly discoverable by the mind, and its operations obvious to our consciousness or sensation". Nothing easier: is cutting, is drinking, is purring not efficacy?'

[108] Cf. Lord Macmillan's remark in *Jones* v. *Great Western Railway Co.* (1930) 47 TLR 39, 45: 'The attribution of an occurrence to a cause is, I take it, always a matter of inference'. For other emphases on the inferential nature of proof of causation: R. Brown, 'Inferring Cause in Fact', 102–4; K. Abraham, 'Self-proving Causation'.

General reasoning and evidence

'General reasoning and evidence' refers here to general propositions about the world and evidence whose truth would not be expected to vary with the truth or falsity of the claims at issue in an individual piece of litigation. It is useful to distinguish three forms: natural laws, generalisations, and causal mechanisms.

Natural laws include, for example, Newtonian laws of motion.[109] Such natural laws are relied upon in simple cases involving the motion of large physical processes. For example, they are applied (normally by experts) in determining whether a car would have decelerated in time to avoid a collision or whether a properly fitted banister would have been able to sustain the weight of a falling man.[110]

The most pertinent generalisations are *causal generalisations*.[111] They have the form: 'X causes Y to occur with a certain frequency'. For example: 'Confidence causes success'; 'Throwing a fair die causes a six to occur 1/6 of the time'; 'Non-stressful situations do not normally cause experienced drivers to panic'. Statistical evidence that X causes Y to occur in Z per cent of cases is a kind of causal generalisation.

Whenever we seek to identify what would have happened absent some factor, the use of generalisations is practically inevitable.[112] Suppose we are trying to ascertain whether a person would have made an investment if their financial adviser had not failed to advise of its high risks. If that person produced an e-mail left with the adviser just prior to the transaction strongly emphasising the need for low risk, this would *ceteris paribus* be highly probative that the person would not have gone ahead if properly advised. But even this reasoning would implicitly rely upon a generalisation to the effect that people normally do not change their mind in a short period of time having given a matter serious thought.

---

[109] The role of laws in causal inference is acknowledged by, for example, H.L.A. Hart and T. Honoré, *Causation in the Law*, 2nd edition, 14–15; R. Wright, 'Proving Causation: Probability versus Belief', 205.

[110] As in *McGee* v. *RJK Building Services Ltd*, 2013 SLT 428.

[111] Hart and Honoré refer to the idea of causal generalisations in the text as 'causal apophthegms', to distinguish them from statements of invariable sequence. See H.L.A. Hart and T. Honoré, *Causation in the Law*, 2nd edition, 48. The notion is more precisely stated in R. Wright, 'Causation, Responsibility, Risk', at 1052–3.

[112] H.L.A. Hart and T. Honoré, *Causation in the Law*, 2nd edition, 16, 47, 408; R. Wright, 'Causation in Tort Law', 1807. Cf. *Sienkiewicz* v. *Greif (UK) Ltd* [2011] UKSC 10, [7] (Lord Phillips): 'Where the court is concerned with a speculative question – "what would have happened but for a particular intervention" it is likely to need to have regard to what normally happens'.

A third kind of general evidence is evidence about causal mechanisms. A causal mechanism is the process by which a cause brings about an effect.[113] For example, arsenic causes death by the intermediate process of dehydration. Causal generalisations simply tell us *that* X causes Y, without telling us *how* X causes Y. It is possible that we have knowledge of a causal generalisation without understanding the underlying mechanism. For example, it is known that asbestos exposure causes mesothelioma but the underlying mechanism is not well understood. Causal inference in a specific case is facilitated when our understanding of mechanisms underpinning causal generalisations is more refined. This is again illustrated by asbestos-mesothelioma cases. If we had more refined knowledge of the mechanism here, it might be possible to conclude that all, or only certain, exposures play a role in the generation of the mesothelioma.[114]

The sources of general evidence: scientific evidence of causation

How do factfinders gain knowledge of what can cause what in cases where the causal generalisation is not common knowledge? Here are some examples of this sort of case: whether a child's acute lymphatic leukaemia could be caused by her father's pre-conception occupational exposure to ionising radiation at a nuclear power plant;[115] whether an anti-nausea drug prescribed to pregnant women could cause birth defects in their children;[116] whether a Hepatitis B vaccine could cause multiple sclerosis.[117]

In such cases, the factfinder must rely upon expert scientific evidence of general causation; the failure to adduce such evidence will therefore almost always be fatal to the claimant's case on the causal issue.[118] The kinds of scientific study relevant to establishing that a factor can cause an effect are experiments and observational studies.[119] The classic form

---

[113] The precise content of the concept of a 'causal mechanism' is controversial. See P. Illari and J. Williamson, 'What is a Mechanism?', 119 for different analyses.

[114] The utility of mechanistic causal knowledge is emphasised by M. Green, 'The Future of Proportional Liability', 374.

[115] *Reay* v. *British Nuclear Fuels Plc* [1994] 5 Med LR 1. See further, R. Goldberg, *Causation and Risk in the Law of Torts*, 93–4 and L. Khoury, *Uncertain Causation in Medical Liability*, 49–50.

[116] *Daubert* v. *Merrell Dow Pharmaceuticals Inc.* (1993) 509 US 579.

[117] Cass Civ 1e, 22 May 2008, D.2008.1928.

[118] R. Wright, 'Proving Causation: Probability versus Belief', 205; L. Khoury, *Uncertain Causation in Medical Liability*, 48–9. See, for example, *Kay's Tutor* v. *Ayrshire and Arran Health Board*, 1987 SC (HL) 145, 168.

[119] P. Dawid, 'The Role of Scientific and Statistical Evidence in Assessing Causality', 135–7. For more technical detail on RCTs, see M. Hernan and J. Robins, *Causal Inference*, chapter 2.

of causal inference experiment is a randomised controlled trial (RCT).[120] An RCT is designed such that a factor is applied to a target population and not applied to a control population, where the target population and control population are believed not to differ in any way causally relevant to the effect being tested for, except that the target population has been exposed to the factor.[121] To assist in ensuring that the populations do not differ in any respect causally relevant to the outcome other than exposure to the factor, randomising processes are used.[122] For example, selected individuals may be randomly assigned to the target or the control population. RCTs are powerful in causal inference because, assuming that the study has been designed and carried out correctly, alternative, non-causal, explanations of an association (due to bias, or confounding, or, if the study is large enough, chance) between the factor and the outcome can be ruled out.[123]

In practice, evidence of the injurious causal effect of a factor upon humans based upon RCTs is not available (often for the obvious reason that there are moral reasons against such trials).[124] The main forms of scientific evidence adduced in this connection[125] are thus likely to be observational studies of humans – principally, epidemiological studies – and experimental studies on animals or cells – principally, toxicological studies.[126]

Epidemiology is the study of the incidence and causal determinants of disease.[127] It is an observational science in the sense that it does not perform experiments that directly apply the potentially causative factor to a population but rather collects data about existing exposures or cases of disease. The ultimate aim of epidemiological studies is to determine

[120] Ibid., 135–6, also describing the RCT as 'the most important medical advance' of the twentieth century.

[121] Ibid., 136. See also the helpful brief summary in N. Cartwright, 'Are RCTs the Gold Standard?', 15–17.

[122] Ibid.

[123] See J. Hill, J. Reiter, and E. Zanutto, 'A Comparison of Experimental and Observational Data Analyses', 49.

[124] P. Dawid, 'The Role of Scientific and Statistical Evidence in Assessing Causality', 137.

[125] In the context of consequential-liability causation, other forms of scientific evidence may be adduced: actuarial evidence, or economic models.

[126] While epidemiology and toxicology are both concerned with determining whether certain substances have injurious causal properties, toxicology proceeds principally by experimentation (usually on animals and cell samples). See B. Goldstein and M. Henefin, 'Reference Guide on Toxicology', 635–9.

[127] K. Rothman, *Epidemiology: an Introduction*, 2nd edition, 1. Helpful general descriptions of epidemiology in a legal context include: M. Green, 'The Future of Proportional Liability: the Lessons of the Toxic Substance Causation', 375ff; C. McIvor, 'The Use of Epidemiological Evidence in UK Tort Law'.

whether there is any association between a factor and a disease and to determine whether the association is causal. There are different kinds of study.[128] The principal types are cohort studies and case-control studies.[129] A cohort study compares the incidence of disease in exposed and unexposed ('control') groups. A case-control study compares the frequency of exposure to a factor in groups with a disease and groups without the disease. As with RCTs, the study design aims to compare groups which are causally similar to each other apart from exposure to the factor. But this aim is hindered, in observational studies, by the inability to control who is exposed to the factor and who is not. Moreover, a variety of additional difficulties surrounding the reliability of data collection in observational studies arise.[130] The inference from an observed association between a factor and a disease to the conclusion that this association is *causal* is thus significantly dependent upon the extent to which the study design and study analysis has taken into account the possibility of bias and confounding factors. Much of the interpretation of epidemiological studies is concerned with testing whether there are alternative explanations of an observed association other than a causal one.[131]

The first step in causal inference based upon an epidemiological study is to determine whether there is indeed an association between the factor and the disease that is unlikely to be down to chance or bias, and to measure the strength of any association. This strength may be measured in different ways. A typical measure is the relative risk (RR).[132] This is calculated by dividing the number of cases of disease in the exposed population by the number of cases of disease in the unexposed population. If the RR = 1, there is the same number of cases of disease in the exposed versus the unexposed population; this provides no positive evidence of causation. Conversely, there is no specific RR > 1 at which an association is automatically deemed to be causal. Rather, the move from an observed association of a particular strength to a claim about causation involves the exercise of judgement.

There are well-known considerations taken into account by epidemiologists in making the move from an observed association to a claim about causation.[133] The medical statistician Austin Bradford Hill set these out in a famous article:[134]

---

[128] See generally, K. Rothman, S. Greenland, and T Lash, *Modern Epidemiology* 3rd edition, chapter 6.

[129] Ibid 94–95; Chapters 7 and 8.   [130] Ibid, e.g. 111.   [131] Ibid, 25–29.

[132] For a much more technically nuanced and detailed introduction, see, ibid, 52ff.

[133] Ibid, 26–29.

[134] A.B. Hill, 'The Environment and Disease: Association or Causation?'.

(1) *The strength of the association*. This refers to the extent of the increased incidence of the disease among the exposed population compared to the incidence in the unexposed population (i.e. the extent of the RR). In this regard Hill refers to the RR of 9–10 of lung cancer for smokers compared to non-smokers and the 200-fold increase of incidence of scrotal cancer in chimney sweeps compared to workers not exposed to tar or mineral oils.[135]

(2) *Consistency*. This refers to whether different studies, conducted by different scientists in different places, at different times, evidence the same or similar results.

(3) *Specificity*. If the association is only observed in specific individuals at specific places and for a specific type of disease, this is an indication of causality.

(4) *Temporal precedence*. The observed potential cause must come before the observed effect in time. This is the only Hill consideration which can be considered a necessary condition of an inference of causation.

(5) *Biological gradient* (or *dose–response relationship*). If the rate of the disease varies in proportion to the level of exposure to the factor, this is an indication of causal connection.

(6) *Biological plausibility*. If there is a plausible underlying biological explanation of the association, this is a further indication of causal connection.

(7) *Coherence*. A consideration somewhat overlapping (6) is that a causal interpretation of the association should not conflict fundamentally with known facts about the biology of the disease in question.

(8) *Experiment*. If the potentially causative factor is eliminated or removed in part from the environment, and the incidence of disease is reduced, this provides support for a causal claim.

(9) *Analogy*. If a similar factor to the one being investigated causes a similar disease to the one with which the factor is associated, this gives some support to a causal claim.

Epidemiological evidence is frequently relied upon in establishing general causation in each system[136] and the 'Hill criteria' have been referred to approvingly by courts.[137] Four points about these criteria are in order. First, none, apart from (4), is a necessary condition of inferring – to any

---

[135] Ibid., 295.

[136] For example, Cass Civ 1, 5 April 2005, Bull civ 2005 I 173, RTDC 2005, 607 (obs Jourdain) (epidemiological evidence relied upon to establish that a hypertension drug could cause Lyell's syndrome); CA (admin) Paris, 19 March 2008, no 06NC01598 (absence of statistical association between radioactive exposure and thyroid cancer evidence of absence of causal connection).

[137] See *Ministry of Defence* v. *Wood* [2011] EWCA Civ 792, [61]; *XYZ* v. *Schering Health Care Ltd* [2002] EWHC 1420, [301]; *Reay* v. *British Nuclear Fuels Plc* [1994] Env 320, 341. For the United States, see the cases cited in *Restatement (Third) Torts* §28, 441.

standard of proof – that the association is causal (as Hill recognised).[138] Thus it may be that there is a low RR and yet the association is causal – Hill himself gives the example that relatively few people who are exposed to rat urine develop Weil's disease.[139] Or it may be that one compelling study could be sufficient grounds to infer causation.[140] Second, as the authors of the chapter on epidemiology in the US Reference Manual on Scientific Evidence write: 'There is no formula or algorithm that can be used to assess whether causal inference is appropriate based on these [Hill's] guidelines'.[141] Third, though it is true that the more that each individual consideration is satisfied, the more probable the causal hypothesis, it is not necessarily the case that the absence of evidence satisfying a particular consideration positively reduces the probability of a causal hypothesis. That is, the absence of evidence that *p* is not always evidence that *not-p*.[142] So, evidently, the mere fact that only one study has been conducted is not itself evidence against a causal hypothesis. Conversely, if multiple reliable studies, *involving similar exposures to the one at issue in the case,* find no association, this is some evidence against a causal inference.[143] Fourth, it should be borne in mind that an inference of causation need only be made on the BPR or to a high probability – to the extent that scientists insist upon a higher standard of proof, this needs to be taken into account in determining whether the evidence suffices for the governing legal standard.[144] A concrete

---

[138] See A.B. Hill, 'The Environment and Disease: Association or Causation', 299: 'None of my nine viewpoints...can be required as a *sine qua non*'. Though this is erroneous in relation to (4).

[139] A.B. Hill, 'The Environment and Disease: Association or Causation?', 296, observing that 'We must not be too ready to dismiss a cause-effect hypothesis merely on the grounds that the observed association is slight'. See also K. Rothman and S. Greenland, 'Causation and Causal Inference in Epidemiology', 148 giving the examples of passive smoking and lung cancer, and smoking and cardiovascular disease as weak associations that are causal.

[140] Ibid., 297, giving the example of one convincing study of a nickel refinery showing an association with nose and lung cancer.

[141] M. Green, M. Freedman, and L. Gordis, 'Reference Guide on Epidemiology', 600.

[142] This is emphasised by C. Cranor, *Toxic Torts*, 243–4.

[143] Ibid., 245, n. 145. See also *Conde v. Velsicol Chemical Co.* (1994) 24 F 2d 809, where the court acknowledged the evidential force of the fact that: 'Nineteen epidemiological studies in humans have found little evidence of long-term adverse health effects from chlordane doses hundreds of times higher than those [claimants] were subject to under a worst-case'.

[144] This has often been judicially recognised. See, for example, *Dingley v. Chief Constable Strathclyde Police* 1998 SC 548, 603 (Lord Prosser) and 2000 SC (HL) 77, 89 (Lord Hope); *Sienkiewicz v. Greif (UK) Ltd* [2011] UKSC 10, [9] (Lord Phillips); *Ministry of Defence v. Wood* [2011] EWCA Civ 792, [76].

consequence of this is that even results which do not have a very high level of statistical significance may still have enough force to lead to an inference on a lower standard of proof.[145]

Since even observational studies demonstrating a statistical association may often not yet exist in relation to some potentially causal factors, the question arises whether claimants will inevitably fail if they cannot adduce statistical evidence of an association. There does not appear to be such a requirement in English law.[146] As a matter of principle, it has convincingly been argued that statistical evidence is not necessary to establish general causation on the BPR.[147] First, our knowledge of similar causal mechanisms may assist in (largely) non-statistical causal inference. For example, experimental studies on animals or *in vitro* studies on cells may assist in determining that an agent can cause a particular disease in a human being. If the mechanism by which an agent causes a disease in an animal is understood, it may be possible to extrapolate from such a study to the likely effect of the agent upon human beings. Needless to say, this depends upon the plausibility of the comparison of the biological processes in the animal to the human being.[148] Here, then, the causal

---

[145] See, for example, the evidence relied upon in *Ministry of Defence* v. *Wood* [2011] EWCA Civ 792 at [64].

[146] See *Ministry of Defence* v. *Wood* [2011] EWCA Civ 792, [61] (Smith LJ). However, Smith LJ's view that the Hill criteria may be considered without epidemiologic evidence of an association is controversial. Hill himself writes (Note 138, at 295) that he is considering the situation where 'our observations reveal an association between two variables, perfectly clear-cut and beyond what we would care to attribute to the play of chance'. Many US courts have not insisted upon the existence of epidemiological evidence demonstrating an association. According to the *Restatement (Third) Torts*, 443: 'A quite substantial body of case law...rejects an epidemiologic threshold for sufficient proof of general causation' (listing many cases). See, recently, the important decision in *Milward* v. *Acuity Specialty Products Group Inc.*, (2011) 639 F 3d 11, 24 (disavowing the necessity of statistical evidence). See also: *Landrigan* v. *Celotex Corporation*, (1992) 127 NJ 404, 419: 'a relative risk of 2.0 is not so much a password to a finding of causation as one piece of evidence among others'; *Minnesota Mining and Manufacturing* v. *Atterbury* (1998) 978 SW 2d 183, 198: '[t]here is no requirement in a toxic tort case that a party must have reliable evidence of a relative risk of 2.0 or greater'. Compare, for example, *Blum* v. *Merrell Dow Pharmaceuticals Inc.*, 705 A 2d 1314, 1323 (Pa 1997): 'Replicated epidemiological studies consistently finding a strong association are necessary to establish causation'. See further M. Green, 'Pessimism about *Milward*', 51, n. 57.

[147] C. Cranor, *Toxic Torts*, 122–3, 268–70; S. Haack, 'Proving Causation: The Atomism of *Daubert* and the Holism of Warrant', 278.

[148] That animal studies may be important evidence was recognised in *Reay* v. *British Nuclear Fuels Plc* [1994] Env 320. For discussion of the conditions under which such evidence will be relevant: C. Cranor, *Toxic Torts*, 105–11.

inference is based primarily upon an *analogy* with the causal properties of a similar biological system.[149]

Second, it seems arguable that general causation can be inferred on the basis of a single case, or a small number of cases.[150] Certainly, the fallacy of *post hoc ergo propter hoc* lurks nearby here. It is true that the *mere fact* that *y* temporally succeeded *x* cannot itself suffice as proof of causation.[151] However, in some cases, temporal proximity of potential cause and effect, an observed dose–response relationship between them, and the exclusion of other known causal factors for the effect in the circumstances may be enough to conclude that the factor was causal, even if there are no known prior cases of such a causal relationship. Such rare cases show the need for caution in conceiving of general causation and specific causation as entirely distinct inquiries. In a rare case, general causation is established by what actually happened in the case at hand.

Case-specific evidence
Case-specific evidence describes evidence concerning litigated events, the presence of which one would expect to vary depending on the details of the case at hand.[152] General evidence and claims about causal mechanisms are true independently of what happened in the particular case at hand. It will remain true that smoking causes 80 per cent of all cases of lung cancer regardless of whether it caused it in this particular case. Case-specific evidence, on the other hand, is evidence of *x*, which, to varying degrees of probability, we would not expect to be available unless *x* occurred.

Case-specific evidence assists in causal inference in at least two ways. First, it might be relevant to determining whether a causal generalisation

---

[149] For an early example of this reasoning, see *Roe* v. *Minister of Health* [1954] 2 QB 66, 70, where McNair J's conclusion that the injection of phenol into the patient's theca caused paralysis was made on the basis of 'the observed effects of phenol in other circumstances and the known effects of other toxic substances on the contents of the theca itself'.

[150] For real examples of causal inference without formal statistical evidence, see C. Cranor, *Toxic Torts*, chapter 4.

[151] See, for example, OLG Hamm 2003, NJW-RR 2003, 1382 (rejecting a causal link between an injection against Hepatitis B and a child's blindness where the 'only circumstance supporting causation between the injection and the blindness was the temporal relationship'); *Dingley* v. *The Chief Constable, Strathclyde Police* 1998 SC 648, 604 (Lord Prosser): 'the mere fact that on one occasion B happened after A (and perhaps very quickly after A) would not, in the absence of other indications, lead one easily to conclude that B was caused by A'.

[152] The notion of 'case-specific' evidence is controversial. The question is taken up at p. 94ff.

is applicable to the facts at hand. The generalisation 'Passive smoking causes cancer in 51 per cent of cases where the victim lives with a smoker' is only applicable if the victim did indeed suffer cancer and did indeed live with a smoker. Or if we are trying to determine whether an earlier diagnosis would have made a difference to the progression of a patient's cancer, and we have good evidence that earlier diagnosis makes a difference in 80 per cent of cases where the patient's cancer was of a particular size, case-specific evidence (e.g. a scan result) would relate to the size of the patient's cancer. Second, case-specific evidence might be relevant to determining whether a particular causal mechanism has been instantiated in the particular case.

The inferential process

How, then, is general and case-specific evidence used to generate an inference that x was a cause of y in this specific instance to the requisite standard of proof?

In all cases, it should be remembered, the question which the inferential process is aiming at answering to the standard of proof is the specific causation one: was x a cause of y in this case? It may seem that, in order to answer this question, as a matter of logic, factfinders should begin by asking the general causation question – *can x cause y*? However, in many cases, the general causation question is not posed, but assumed. This is because, in many cases, the answer is obvious.[153] There is no need to ask whether failure to pay attention while driving *can* cause an accident.

The typical inferential process followed can usefully be distinguished, then, depending upon whether general causation is a live issue. Where it is, the process tends to follow a 'top-down' structure. The focus first falls upon general scientific evidence purporting to establish that the factor at issue can cause the injury.[154] Then it is questioned whether the individual case can be subsumed within the proposition established by the general scientific evidence, by comparing the scientific evidence with the features of the individual case. The clearest example of this is the practice of some US courts of splitting general causation into a separate hearing from specific causation.[155]

---

[153] H.L.A. Hart and T. Honoré, *Causation in the Law*, 15 2nd edition: 'the effects of impacts, blows, gross mechanical movements...are so deeply embedded in our whole outlook on nature that we scarcely think of them as separate elements in causal statements'.

[154] Cf. L. Khoury, *Uncertain Causation in Medical Liability*, 49: 'This level of inquiry normally involves minimal reference to the facts of the case'.

[155] See, for example, *Milward*, referenced in n. 146.

In cases where general causation is established, general evidence and case-specific evidence tend to be considered together. Of course, to the extent that causal inference always involves considering causal generalisations (or natural laws), case-specific evidence is always being subsumed within a general proposition. Nonetheless, this process is frequently more implicit in cases where general causation is established (consider the example of the e-mail message and advice given earlier).

A useful example of this synergistic interplay of general and case-specific evidence is provided by *McGlone* v. *Glasgow Greater Health Board*.[156] The pursuer had a hysterectomy in 2008 as a radical treatment option for an invasive adenocarcinoma of the cervix. She alleged that had the defendant's doctors not negligently failed properly to interpret her test results in 2005 and 2006, she would have received further tests leading to an earlier diagnosis of cancer, and that a more conservative treatment option would have been undertaken successfully. Her claim was successful. The causation question depended upon a variety of counterfactuals:[157]

(1) Had the defendant interpreted the test result properly in 2005 or 2006, would the claimant have been referred for further tests?
(2) Would those tests have led to a diagnosis of cancer?
(3) Would a less radical treatment option have been undertaken?
(4) How would the pursuer have responded to that treatment?

The bulk of the judge's analysis focused upon (3). The answer depended upon both general and case-specific evidence. The general evidence (agreed upon by the experts) was to the effect that if a person has a tumour of diameter greater than 2 cm, there are considerable risks that not removing the uterus will fail to remove the cancer and that this treatment would not be advised.[158] This raised the question of what size the pursuer's tumour would have been in early 2006 when she ought to have been diagnosed with cancer. This question depended upon the case-specific evidence concerning the size of the tumour when it was removed in 2008, the case-specific evidence concerning the pursuer's symptoms in 2005 and 2006, and the general data that are known about the growth rates of tumours.[159] The general data consisted partly of generalisations concerning the likely advancement of a tumour given certain symptoms, and explicit statistical evidence. The latter comprised of the observed growth rates of tumours in 730 cases.[160] This general data was applied by

---

[156] [2011] CSOH 63.   [157] Ibid., [3] (framed in slightly different terms).   [158] Ibid., [15].
[159] Ibid., [38]–[39]; [49]–[57].   [160] Ibid., [38].

the pursuer's expert to the case-specific evidence relating to the size of the tumour and the symptoms.

Ultimately, the judge rejected the calculation upon which this was based because the expert had taken the mean growth rate of a variety of tumours originating in different locations in the body as the basis of the calculation. Had the statistical evidence related to the mean growth rate of adenocarcinomas originating in the cervix, the evidence would likely have been accepted as probative.[161] The judge rested his decision that the tumour was likely less than 2 cm in diameter on the case-specific evidence concerning the pursuer's symptoms and the generalisations associated with them. Thus the fact that the pursuer had episodes of odourless vaginal discharge in late 2005 was only present in persons with cancer in approximately fewer than 4 per cent of cases according to one expert. More importantly, the judge accepted that the colposcopy tests which the pursuer had in late 2005 would have revealed a tumour of greater than 1 cm diameter if there had been one.[162] This, in turn, was based upon the general evidence that 98 per cent of tumours originate in an area which would be visible to a colposcopy test.[163] Here, then, case-specific and general evidence operate in synergy.

It has been suggested that, at an abstract level, the process of causal inference described here can be considered as involving inference to best explanation (IBE).[164] The claim is that what guides inference is whether the claimant's causal hypothesis or the defendant's causal hypothesis *better explains* the evidence. Suppose that factfinder arrives home to find the cheese she left on the kitchen counter has small bite marks on the side of it, she hears scratching noises, and traces of cheese are visible near a small hole in the wall. Hypothesis: factfinder has a mouse in her house. This plausibly explains the evidence and alternative explanations (e.g. her neighbour needed some cheese and broke into the house) are less plausible.

The basic idea behind IBE is that there are criteria for what constitutes a better explanation that are not explicitly *probabilistic*, but which nonetheless lead us to the probable truth.[165] In short, if a hypothesis better

---

[161] Ibid., [47]–[48].   [162] Ibid., [59].   [163] Ibid., [60].

[164] See R. Brown, 'The Possibility of "Inference Causation"'. See, for explanations of IBE, for example, M. Pardo and R. Allen, 'Juridical Proof and Best Explanation', 227–33; L. Laudan, 'Strange Bedfellows: Inference to the Best Explanation and the Criminal Standard of Proof', 295–6.

[165] As Lipton points out, if IBE simply said that we infer the *likeliest* explanation, it would be close to trivial. Rather, IBE has to offer an account of explanatory considerations which are not directly based upon the likelihood of the conclusion being true: 'Inference to the Best Explanation is an advance only if it reveals more about inference than that it is

explains the evidence, it is more likely to be true than alternative, less explanatory hypotheses. Explanatory virtue is a proxy for probability. These explanatory criteria are generally said to include the extent to which the hypothesis explains more and different kinds of evidence (*consilience*); the *simplicity* of the explanation, understood as measuring the number and kind of assumptions underpinning it; the extent to which the hypothesis *coheres* with background beliefs; and the extent to which the hypothesis is *ad hoc*.[166]

IBE certainly seems to play a role in the way judges infer causation. For instance, the Hill considerations could plausibly be considered as explanatory criteria for causal inference. The more that a hypothesis satisfies the Hill criteria, the better is the explanation that the hypothesis is *causal*. And judges do make reference to explanatory criteria. In *McGlone*, for example, Lord Tyre said: 'A single explanation for a pattern of symptoms should...be preferred to a multiplicity of explanations for each symptom viewed individually'.[167] More generally, judges refer to the 'consistency' of a causal hypothesis with the evidence. For example, in *Corbett* v. *Cumbria Kart Racing Club*, the defendant's hypothesis that the claimant's head injuries were caused by a collision with a barrier, rather than the negligently parked nearby ambulance, was not consistent with the extent of the claimant's injuries.[168] Finally, in some cases, a causal hypothesis is accepted on the basis that it can provide the only plausible explanation of the fact that the claimant suffered the injury.

Nonetheless, the the descriptive adequacy of the IBE model of causal inference is, in my view, overplayed. There are two reasons for this. First, the more that judges directly reason with probabilistic evidence (including causal generalisations, which are implicitly probabilistic, as well as explicitly statistical evidence), the less accurate the IBE model. This is because the IBE model claims that factfinders reach conclusions about probability *indirectly*, by using explanatory criteria. But, quite clearly, direct considerations of the probability of a causal hypothesis (on the basis of statistical evidence) are not infrequent. Of course, IBE proponents could criticise such use – but, in purely descriptive terms, explanatory considerations

---

often inference to the likeliest cause. It should show how likeliness is determined (at least in part) by explanatory considerations'. See P. Lipton, *Inference to the Best Explanation*, 63.

[166] As M. Pardo and R. Allen, 'Juridical Proof and Best Explanation', observe, 230: 'There is no formula for combining such criteria; rather each criterion is a standard which must be weighed against the others'.

[167] *McGlone*, [57].   [168] [2013] EWHC 1362, [35]–[37].

sit alongside directly probabilistic considerations. Second, the IBE model is highly abstract. It may be more helpful (because slightly less abstract) to conceive of the task of causal inference as involving the subsumption of case-specific evidence within the framework of, principally, laws, causal generalisations and mechanistic knowledge. The more that a causal hypothesis is supported by these, the more probable it is.

The boundaries of causal inference under the general rules

This section deals with important boundary questions in causal inference. These are boundary questions in that they raise the issue of where proof according to the standard of proof ends and exceptional departures from proof begin. The first concerns proof of causation by reference to general evidence – evidence, for example, that 'X is typically the cause of Y in these circumstances'. The second concerns the role of proof that a factor increased the risk of the result which occurred. The third is whether statistical evidence can suffice to prove causation. These questions are closely connected in so far as they each concern the role of predominantly general indirect evidence of causation.

Proof by generalisation

The extent to which predominantly general evidence can satisfy the standard of proof is controversial. There is an intuitive, if difficult precisely to formulate, point at which evidence is too general and does not speak enough to the case at hand. This issue is treated in detail below, in relation to statistical evidence.[169] The point of this section is simply to observe that evidence which courts accept as probative of causation is often of a predominantly general character and could be re-described as explicitly statistical in nature.

This is salient in the German doctrine of 'prima facie proof' (*Anscheins-beweis*).[170] According to this doctrine, the claimant may prove causation under §286 ZPO indirectly by first establishing that the defendant's conduct *typically* leads to the injury suffered (the requirement of a *typische Geschehensablauf*).[171] If the claimant makes this out, then it falls to the defendant (by way of an evidential burden) to show a serious possibility (*ernsthaft Möglichkeit*) of another (atypical) chain of events in the concrete

---

[169] See further, p. 85ff.

[170] See generally, H. Prütting, 'Commentary on §286 ZPO', [48]–[79] in *Münchener Kommentar zum ZPO*, 4th edition 2013; D. Leipold, 'Commentary on §286 ZPO', [128]–[186]; C. Katzenmeier, *Arzthaftung*, 429–39.

[171] For a recent judicial exposition: BGH NJW 2010, 1072.

circumstances.[172] So, if the claimant falls down an icy, negligently untreated staircase, there will be a presumption that this was caused by the failure to de-ice it.[173] Proof here consists primarily of the general causal proposition that icy staircases typically cause people to slip and the absence of case-specific evidence to the contrary.

Such reasoning is also found in English law. For example, in *Levicom* v. *Linklaters*, Jacob LJ stated that '[w]hen a solicitor gives advice that his client has a strong case to start litigation rather than settle and the client then does just that, the normal inference is that the advice is causative'.[174] The generalisation here is that *in the normal course of events* confidently-worded advice from an expert causes clients to act in accordance with the advice. The normal inference is rebuttable – the defendant may adduce evidence that this was not the normal case – but, without more, an inference of causation is made out on the BPR. Another example is *Whitehead* v. *Bruce*.[175] The Court of Appeal approved the trial judge's conclusion that D2 would not have swerved off road, injuring C, had D1 overtaken a parked car more quickly with the observation that it 'accords with human experience' that 'naturally' people form a better impression of the speed of oncoming vehicles when they have greater time to do so.[176]

The proof-of-fault analogue of this reasoning is the maxim *res ipsa loquitur* ('the thing speaks for itself'). If the injury suffered would not normally occur without fault, and the defendant does not point to an alternative plausible explanation consistent with non-fault, then the claimant succeeds on the fault issue. In English law this is recognised to rest upon an inference made in accordance with the BPR that the

---

[172] See D. Leipold, 'Commentary on §286 ZPO', [138]–[141]. This is *not* a shift in the legal burden of proof: the defendant does not need to prove the absence of natural causation to the §286 ZPO standard: ibid.

[173] OLG Frankfurt VersR 1980, 50.

[174] [2010] PNLR 29, [284]. See, similarly, the Court of Appeal's acceptance (by a majority) of the fact that 'most' specialist treatment centres would have treated the claimant in a certain way had she been referred to one as proof on the balance of probability that she would have been treated in that way: *Gouldsmith* v. *Mid Staffordshire General Hospitals NHS Trust* [2007] EWCA Civ 397.

[175] [2013] EWCA Civ 229, [33].

[176] Ibid. See also *Drake* v. *Harbour* [2008] EWCA Civ 25, [28] (Toulson LJ): 'where a claimant proves both that a defendant was negligent and that loss ensued which was of a kind likely to have resulted from such negligence, this will ordinarily be enough to enable a court to infer that it was probably so caused, even if the claimant is unable to prove positively the precise mechanism'. It was emphasised that this is not a rule of law and 'the court must consider any alternative theories of causation advanced by the defendant before reaching its conclusion', ibid.

defendant was at fault.[177] The same is true of inferences drawn by reference to an applicable causal generalisation. In these circumstances, the court is simply drawing an inference based upon the evidence available to it.[178]

The role of proof of increased risk in inference

The question here is 'what role does proof that a factor, which occurred, increased the risk of the injury suffered play in *inferring* that the factor was a cause of the injury suffered according to the standard of proof?'[179]

What does it mean to say that x increased the risk of y? A risk is a probability of a bad outcome occurring in the future.[180] The basic meaning is therefore that x increased the probability of y occurring in the circumstances. As we have seen, 'probability' can be cashed out in different ways. Sometimes risk is understood by reference to a frequentist analysis. Sometimes, as when we say, 'there is a risk of rain', we are arguably relying upon a notion of evidential probability, meaning something like 'the available evidence supports to some degree the proposition that it will rain'. Sometimes, we may be referring in some way to a physical propensity of a situation.

Typically, however, when we claim that x *increased the risk of* y, we are referring to more than simply the extent to which the occurrence of x increases the evidential probability that y will occur. For example, if I watch a video of a football match from 1975, which I have not seen before, and the result of which I do not know, it would be odd if, half way through the video when team A is losing 1–0 to team B, to say that team A is *at risk* of losing. Although the evidence may greater support the claim that team A will lose the game, it seems inapposite to say *there is a risk* of team A losing.[181] There are two reasons for this. First, the events are not really happening. Risks obtain in relation to actual events. Second, at the time the 'risk' is assessed, it is clear that the result is fully

---

[177] *Lloyde* v. *West Midlands Gas Board* [1971] 1 WLR 749, 755; *Ratcliff* v. *Plymouth & Torbay Area Health Authority* [1998] PIQR 170, 186. The same is true in Canadian law: *Fontaine* v. *Loewen Estate* [1996] 9 WWR 305 at [83].

[178] This was emphasised in *Drake*, referenced in n. 176, at [28].

[179] More precisely, the issue discussed is: *in so far as courts claim to be engaged in an inferential process*, what role does proof of increase in risk play in that process? The issue is not the role of increase in risk as a *substitute* for proof of causation according to the standard of proof. This kind of exceptional rule is discussed at length in Chapters 4–6.

[180] S. Perry, 'Risk, Harm, Interests and Rights', 190: 'A risk is a chance or probability of a bad outcome'.

[181] See C. List and M. Pivato, 'Emergent Chance'.

determined and that the result could be ascertained easily (just fast-forward). Does this mean that talk of 'risk' where the outcome is determined is misguided? That would seem overly narrow.[182] If a gunman is firing recklessly in the direction of a crowd, but ultimately does not strike any of the crowd, it would still be acceptable to say that the gunman increased the risk of injury to the crowd, even if an unthinkably precise ballistics analysis could have been done at the time of firing of each bullet demonstrating that each was destined to miss. If this is true, then we do use the notion of risk even in deterministic contexts. The boundary line between cases where, because knowledge is available to determine the outcome ex-ante (as in the video example), talk of 'risk' seems inappropriate and cases where the knowledge is theoretically available ex-ante but practically impossible to obtain (as in the reckless gunman example) will not always be clear.[183]

Whatever the precise analysis of the concept of probability embedded in the concept of risk, merely to prove the occurrence of a factor which increases the risk of a result by some amount and that the result has occurred is not sufficient (in the sense that such proof does not, ipso facto, entitle the claimant to success on the causal issue) to prove that the factor was a cause of the result on the BPR or to a higher standard of proof. This is widely recognised.[184] That mere proof of some amount of increase in risk is insufficient is precisely why various acknowledged exceptions to the standard of proof on causation in each system are built upon accepting proof of an increased risk *in lieu of*, or as *fictionally* satisfying, the standard of proof.[185] The reason is obvious: that a factor has increased the risk of a result is consistent with there being other higher, or equally high, risk factors present, which are equally or more likely to have caused the result. The proof by causal generalisation cases can be considered as meeting this point – in those cases the causal generalisation is so strong that the risk imposed by the factor at issue is considerable, with the effect that, absent specific evidence of other

---

[182] See, similarly, T. Handfield and A. Wilson, 'Chance and Context', 39: 'gambling games will remain paradigm games of chance, however fundamental physics should turn out'.

[183] For an attempt to precisify the notion of 'available' knowledge, see T. Handfield, *A Philosophical Guide to Chance*, 23–9.

[184] *AB* v. *Ministry of Defence* [2013] 1 AC 78, [85] (Lord Mance), [98] (Lord Phillips); *Sanderson* v. *Hull* [2008] EWCA Civ 1211 [52] ('trite law'); *Clough* v. *First Choice* [2006] PIQR 22, [44], [48]; UKSC; *Restatement (Third) Torts: Liability for Physical and Emotional Harm*, 432–3.

[185] See Chapters 4–6.

causes, an inference of causation can be made in accordance with the standard of proof.[186]

However, proof that the defendant's wrongful conduct increased the risk of the injury which the claimant suffered can and does play a legitimate role in causal inference, in so far as it is conceived as a strand of a causal inference after which other potential risk sources are ruled out as less probable than the one in question. Thus, French courts often employ this line of reasoning ('presumption by elimination'): the factor in question is presumed to have caused the injury if it has been shown to have increased the risk of it and alternative known risk sources of the injury are ruled out. For example, in the *Laboratoire Servier* decision, the claimant, who suffered from pulmonary hypertension, succeeded against the manufacturer of the drug Isomeride upon adducing epidemiological evidence that the drug was a risk factor ('facteur favorisant') for this injury and that other individual risk factors for the injury could be ruled out.[187]

The point at which reliance upon the proof of an increased risk shifts from a legitimate intermediate step in a larger inferential process to an outright departure from the standard of proof depends upon two factors. First, it depends upon the *extent* of the increase in risk. As we have seen, if the increased risk of the injury suffered is high, this may licence an inference absent contrary evidence. Second, it depends upon the extent to which other risk sources are convincingly ruled out as less probable than the factor alleged to be causal. There is a difficult line to be drawn between absence of evidence of other causal factors and evidence that those factors did not cause the effect. The more that there are *known* additional risk factors for an outcome, which have not been ruled out,

---

[186] Some Canadian cases which rely upon the idea of a 'material increase in risk' in drawing a causal inference have emphasised that the risk must be considerable: 'the breach of duty contemplated must be such that the risk it creates is of a magnitude that would prompt one to say about the risk that "it is so unreasonable that injury is more likely to occur than not"': *Nowsco Well Service Ltd* v. *Canadian Propane Gas & Oil Ltd* (1981) 122 DLR (3rd) 228, 246, cited by L. Khoury, *Uncertain Causation*, 216. See, similarly, the famous Louisiana case, where the Court found that the negligent failure to light a staircase was a cause of the claimant's fall, *Reynolds* v. *Texas & Pacific Railway Co.* (1885) 37 La Ann 694, 697–8: 'where the negligence of the defendant *greatly multiplies the chances* of accident to the plaintiff ... the mere possibility that it might have happened without the negligence is not sufficient to break the chain of cause and effect' (emphasis added).

[187] Cass Civ 1e, 24 January 2006, no.02–16.648: JurisData no. 2006-031776, JCP G 2006, II, 10082 (note Grynbaum), RTDC 2006, 323 (obs Jourdain). For this reasoning in a case involving asbestos cancer case: CA Caen, 20 November 2001, JCP G 2003 II 10045.

the less plausible the inference. Clear instances of where the courts in each system have departed from the orthodox standard of proof are discussed in Chapter 5.

Proof by statistical evidence

The position as to whether purely statistical evidence may suffice to prove that x was a cause of y on a particular occasion varies across England, France, and Germany. In no system is the position entirely free from doubt.[188]

England

The current position in English law appears to be as follows. Statistical evidence, alone, is capable of satisfying the BPR in relation to causation if: (i) it is established, on the BPR, that the factor at issue, F, *can* cause the phenomenon of interest, P, (general causation is established); (ii) the statistical evidence is based upon population(s) whose objects are sufficiently similar to the events in the litigation; (iii) the statistical evidence is based upon sound statistical methodology; (iv) the statistical evidence is that F more than doubles the risk of P due to other factors; (v) the statistical evidence is sensitive to what is known about the causal mechanism between F and P.

These propositions emerge from a series of cases dealing with what has come to be called the 'doubling the risk' method of proving that x was a cause of y on the BPR. This is first mentioned, judicially, in *XYZ Ltd v. Schering Health Care Ltd*.[189] The causal issue in this case was whether the ingestion of a third generation of oral contraceptive pills manufactured by the defendant was a cause of the claimants' cardiovascular injuries (venousthromboembolisms [VTE]). Mackay J said this:

If factor X increases the risk of condition Y by more than 2 when compared with factor Z it can then be said, of a group of say 100 with both exposure to factor X and the condition, that as a matter of probability more than 50 would not have suffered Y without being exposed to X.[190]

The simple logic here is this: if there are only two factors, X and Z, which could have caused condition Y, and X increases the risk of Y more than Z does, then X is more probably the cause of Y if Y has occurred. Mackay J's statement must be read subject to the proviso that factor X and factor

---

[188] For Australian law, see *Amaca Pty Ltd* v. *Ellis* [2010] HCA 5, [62].
[189] [2002] EWHC 1420.   [190] [2002] EWHC 1420 at [21].

Z are the only two risk sources of condition Y or, more generally, that factor X more than doubles the risk due to all other risk sources. To see this, suppose that Alice ingests drug A and this carries a risk of a blood clot of 1/100. If Alice also ingests drug B, this increases the risk of a blood clot to 2.1/100. But if Alice is already subject to a pre-existing risk of a blood clot of 75/100, independently of drug A and drug B, then, if Alice suffers a blood clot, this pre-existing risk source is obviously more statistically probable to have caused it than either drug A or drug B. Ultimately, in *XYZ*, Mackay J came to the conclusion that the pill did not increase the risk of VTE beyond the pre-existing risk of VTE. However, the judge made clear that, had the risk been doubled, the inference of specific causation could only be completed if he were convinced on the balance of probability that the contraceptive pill could cause the VTE. This was not itself settled by the doubling of the risk due to the pill.[191]

The 'doubling of statistical risk' logic was approved by the Court of Appeal in *Novartis (Grimsby) Ltd* v. *Cookson*.[192] The causal issue in that case was whether an employee's bladder cancer had been caused by his employer's negligently exposing him to certain carcinogenic dust during the manufacture of dyestuffs between 1964 and 1980 or whether it had been caused by his smoking – both of which can cause cancer due to the amine content. That both, rather than either individually, might have caused the cancer seems to have been set aside. The trial judge had found, on the basis of expert evidence, that 70–75 per cent of the total risk had resulted from negligent occupational exposure and had found that it had therefore been a cause of the cancer. In the Court of Appeal approved this reasoning on the basis that: 'In terms of risk, if occupational exposure more than doubles the risk due to smoking, it must, as a matter of logic, be probable that the disease was caused by the former.'[193]

This approach was applied most recently at first instance in *Jones* v. *Secretary of State for Energy and Climate Change*.[194] The judgment concerned the cases of eight lead claimants in group litigation of 250 claimants. Each claimed damages in respect of respiratory diseases or various types of cancer, which they alleged had been caused by negligent exposure to carcinogenic dust or fumes at their workplace – the Phurnacite plant in Wales. Three of the lead claimants suffered from lung cancer. Swift

---

[191] Ibid., [344]. The important fact that the doubling of risk 'test' is only applicable where general causation is established is not always emphasized by its critics. Cf S. Green, *Causation in Negligence*, 114–5.

[192] [2007] EWCA Civ 1261.   [193] Ibid., [74] (Smith LJ).   [194] [2012] EWHC 2936.

J accepted that the level of exposure to the carcinogens at the plant experienced by each claimant more than doubled their risk of suffering lung cancer and that this would licence the inference that such exposure had caused each claimant to develop lung cancer.[195] Two points should be made here. First, the conclusion that there had been more than a doubling of risk of lung cancer due to exposure was made on the basis of *individualised* estimates of the level of exposure of each claimant.[196] Second, the more than doubling of statistical risk conclusion was based upon well-respected epidemiological evidence demonstrating an increased risk in plant workers in the USA due to exposure to coke oven emissions.[197] These risks were not exactly the same as those faced by workers in the Phurnacite plant but they were 'the closest match available'.[198] These parts of the judge's reasoning tend to support the propositions made above concerning the need for similar (though not – the impossible – identical) populations, and sound statistical studies.

Finally, there is at least one case supporting the proposition that if the classical probability that *x* caused *y* is greater than 0.5 that causation can be established. In the *Creutzfeldt-Jakob Disease Litigation, Group A and C Plaintiffs*,[199] the claimants had developed Creutzfeldt Jakob Syndrome (CJD) by receiving an injection of human growth hormone. Claimants had received some injections prior to 1 July 1977 (the 'cut off date'), which were non-tortiously administered by the defendant, and some afterwards which were. It was accepted that CJD was caused by a single injection but that 'there is no scientific method of establishing whether that dose was given before or after [1 July 1977]'.[200] Morland J held that if a claimant could show that he or she had more injections after the cut-off date than before, then he or she would succeed in showing on the BPR that the CJD had been tortiously caused by the defendant. This is not a conclusion based upon a frequentist probability stating how many times the injury occurs among a group of people given a certain exposure. Rather, it is based upon the ratio of equal possibilities favouring causation by the tortious agent against the total number of equal possibilities of causation: it is a classical probability.

These cases remain good law. Nonetheless, there is reason to be uncertain whether English law will remain in its current position. The use of solely statistical evidence to establish causation in an individual case was criticised by four members of the Supreme Court in *Sienkiewicz* v. *Greif UK Ltd*, a case concerning proof of specific causation of mesothelioma due to

---

[195] Ibid., section 8, [63].   [196] Ibid., section 8, [63].   [197] Ibid., section 8, [63].
[198] Ibid., section 8, [3].   [199] (2000) 54 BMLR 100.   [200] Ibid. 101.

asbestos exposure.[201] The *obiter* statements of Lord Rodger,[202] Lady Hale,[203] Lord Mance,[204] and Lord Kerr[205] were sceptical of such use. Lord Phillips and Lord Dyson thought that, under conditions akin to those mentioned above, purely statistical evidence could be probative on the BPR.[206] Lord Dyson also would perhaps insist upon a *high* statistical probability being shown.[207]

Of the sceptical judges, only Lord Rodger asserted that statistical evidence could *never* prove the individual case. The basis of his view, asserted more or less on the basis of conceptual intuition,[208] was that statistical evidence, on its own, could only satisfy the judge, on the balance of probability, *that probably the defendant caused the injury*; it could not satisfy the judge, on the balance of probability, *that the defendant caused the injury*. His Lordship did not consider the contrary authorities mentioned above.

The basis of the other judges' objections is less clear. Lady Hale seemed to argue that the statistical evidence only allowed one to assert *ex-ante* that there was an increased *risk* that an event will occur but that it says nothing or little about the *probability* of what happened in the past.[209] This is difficult to accept. If I believe (rationally) that my lottery ticket is highly unlikely to win one second before the draw is made, surely I ought, if I have gained no further information, to think that it is unlikely that I have won one second after the draw has been made. By contrast, Lord Mance's objection seems not to have been that statistical evidence is less probative than other evidence, but rather that – as a matter of morality – the courts should not 'treat people and even companies as statistics'.[210] This claim is considered below.[211]

Sienkiewicz also offers support for the final condition (v) stated above: the statistical probability of causation must be sensitive to what is known about the causal mechanism at issue.[212] The details of the mechanism by which asbestos exposure induces mesothelioma are unclear.

---

[201] [2011] UKSC 10. For detailed discussion, see Chapter 5, 233–234.
[202] Ibid., [153], [156].   [203] Ibid., [170], [172].   [204] Ibid., [190].   [205] Ibid., [204]–[206].
[206] Ibid., [93], [96]–[102] (Lord Phillips), [222] (Lord Dyson).   [207] Ibid., [222].
[208] Ibid., [156]. His Lordship cited S. Gold, 'Causation in Toxic Torts: Burdens of Proof, Standards of Persuasion, and Statistical Evidence', at 382–4, where the author distinguishes 'belief probability' and 'fact probability'. Gold's views are problematic as he assumes that the BPR requires the judge to have a certain degree of confidence. See, for objections to that view, pp. 63–64.
[209] *Sienkiewicz*, [170].   [210] Ibid., [190].   [211] See p. 96.
[212] See *Sienkiewicz*, [90]–[93], where Lord Phillips remarks upon the need to consider the relevant causal mechanism when applying statistical reasoning. For a clear explanation of the relevance of knowledge over the causal mechanism, J. Stapleton, 'Factual Causation, Mesothelioma and Statistical Validity', 223–4.

It may be that most of the fibres during a certain period together cause the mesothelioma. Or it may be that only some of the fibres during a certain period cause the mesothelioma, others being causally inert. Suppose D1 negligently exposed C to asbestos between 1960 and 1962, then D2 negligently exposed C to asbestos between 1962 and 1966. Suppose further that the level of exposure in the first period increases the risk of mesothelioma by 10 per cent and that in the second period it increases the risk by 20 per cent. What is the statistical probability that D2's negligence caused the mesothelioma? It might seem that the probability is 66 per cent (D2's exposure represents 2/3 of the total risk, assuming there are no other risk sources). But this would underestimate the probability of causation. It does not take into account the possibility that the mechanism is cumulative, with each exposure contributing to the mesothelioma. What can be said is that P(D2 is causal) is *at least* 66 per cent.[213]

Germany

Under §286 ZPO, the judge must be convinced of the *truth* of the causal claim at issue. Courts typically contrast this with conviction in a *probability* of truth: 'the standard of proof is conviction of the truth ... it does not suffice that the judge is convinced of a probability that something is true, even a high probability'.[214] In order to determine whether a high statistical probability could suffice under §286 ZPO, one must, then, understand the relationship between conviction in the truth, conviction in the probability of truth, and statistical probability. As Weber has written, this relationship is 'deeply unclear'.[215]

Some decisions suggest that a high probability of *p* should *suffice for* or *provide an adequate foundation for* conviction that *p*.[216] This position is also reflected in the fact that it is permissible for the judge to be convinced of *p* even if expert testimony only speaks in terms of a high probability that

---

[213] For an explanation as to why probabilities of specific causation generated by epidemiological evidence should *always* be expressed as inequalities, see A. Broadbent, 'Epidemiological Evidence in Proof of Specific Causation', 255–60. One important reason is that epidemiological evidence measures the *difference* that an agent makes to the incidence of a negative outcome. But not all causes make a difference to whether an outcome occurs or not (some only affect the manner of its occurrence). So there is a persistent possibility of *underestimating* the probability of specific causation.

[214] OLG Celle, 18 July 2012, 4 U 122/10, [23].   [215] H. Weber, *Kausalitätsbeweis*, 28.

[216] OLG Hamm, 18 January 2014, 26 U 30/12; BGH 16.4.2013, VI ZR 44/12, [7] ('objective probability considerations...can provide a sound basis...for the formation of conviction in the facts'). See the earlier cases listed by Weber, *Kausalitätsbeweis*, 29, n. 80.

p.[217] But often it is difficult to discern what the nature of the 'probability' is in judicial statements that a high probability should suffice for conviction in the truth. It is doubtful that these statements always refer to a *statistical* probability, since in some cases where the statements are made there is no statistical evidence at issue.[218] Even in cases where a quantified probability is discussed and accepted as probative, this often simply reflects the language used in the expert testimony, which may reflect an overall judgement as to evidential support for causation, rather than a report of a statistical probability.[219]

It is arguable, however, that a very high statistical or classical probability that p could suffice to ground conviction that p. Consider a modified CJD case, where 999 injections were given after the breach date and 1 injection prior. Would this 0.999 probability of tortious causation suffice? This level and kind of probability is acceptable as sufficient basis for a conviction that p in paternity cases involving statistical DNA evidence, at least where there is some other evidence of paternity (e.g. there was some evidence of a relationship between the mother and alleged father).[220] Some authors nonetheless insist that the move from acceptance that p is very highly statistically probable to conviction that p actually occurred is an illicit one. The basic objection is that evidence that, say, 90 out of 100 people respond effectively to a drug is not evidence that *this individual* would have responded effectively. Consequently, it cannot give rise to a conviction that the individual would have so responded.[221]

France

The French position is unclear. On the one hand, it is possible to find decisions where a very high statistical probability (above 90 per cent) has sufficed. Thus, where the claimant haemophiliac contracted HIV after blood transfusions received in hospital as a result of a car accident caused by the defendant, it sufficed to prove that *those* transfusions were causative, rather than transfusions received prior to the accident, that the statistical probability of causation was between 93 per cent and 95.35 per cent.[222] These figures were based on the fact that the claimant had

[217] BGH NJW 1994, 801; OLG Celle, 18 July 2012, 4 U 122/10, [23].

[218] See H. Weber, *Kausalitätsbeweis*, 30–4.

[219] As, probably, in OLG Celle, 18 July 2012, 4 U 122/10.

[220] BGH 3.5.2006, XII ZR 195/03, [39].   [221] H. Weber, *Kausalitätsbeweis*, 36.

[222] CA Dijon, 16 May 1991, D.1993.242 (note Kerckhove), affirmed by Cass Civ 1e, 17 February 1993, Bull Civ 1993 I 80. The case is discussed in L. Khoury, *Uncertain Causation in Medical Liability*, 180–1.

received at least 168,000 units of Factor VII and 20 units of blood during his hospitalisation, but only 8190 units of Factor VII as treatment for his haemophilia since the discovery of the HIV epidemic in France, as well as the different (less risky) provenance of the earlier transfusions.

On the other hand, a high statistical probability has implicitly been rejected in other cases as insufficient. Where a claimant proved that one of two manufacturers of a defective drug caused its injury, and that one manufacturer had a 97.7 per cent share of the market at the time the drug was ingested, this did not suffice to prove that the manufacturer's product caused the injury.[223] Perhaps this case can be distinguished from the HIV case on the basis that the statistical evidence here is relatively unspecific to the case at hand in that it referred to the national market. By contrast, the statistical evidence in the HIV case was more tailored to the facts of the case at hand.

The United States

The probative force of statistical evidence has been extensively considered in US jurisprudence and literature and merits brief consideration. The position is varied.[224] There are well-known statements in, typically, earlier cases that a classical probability of greater than 0.5 or a statistical probability of greater than 50 per cent is not sufficient to prove a fact in a particular case:

Quantitative probability...is only the greater chance. It is not proof, nor even probative evidence, of the proposition to be proved. That in one throw of the dice there is a quantitative probability, or greater chance, that a less number of spots than sixes will fall uppermost is no evidence whatever that in a given throw such was the actual result. Without something more, the actual result of the throw would still be utterly unknown. The slightest real evidence that sixes did in fact fall uppermost would outweigh all the probability otherwise.[225]

[T]hat colored automobiles made in the current year outnumber black ones would not warrant a finding that an undescribed automobile of the current year is colored and not black ...[226]

In this vein, the famous Massachusetts case *Smith* v. *Rapid Transit* held that the fact that the claimant's car had been forced off the road by a bus

---

[223] CA Paris, 26 September 2012, no10/18297, D.2012.2859.
[224] D. Enoch and T. Fisher, "Sense and "Sensitivity": Epistemic and Instrumental Approaches to Statistical Evidence', 561, describe it as 'incoherent'. See, similarly, J. Koehler, 'When do Courts Think Base Rate Statistics are Relevant', 373.
[225] *Day* v. *Boston and Maine Railroad* (1902) 52 A 771, 774.
[226] *Sargent* v. *Massachusetts Accident Company* (1940) 29 NE 2d 825, 827.

on a street on which the defendant bus company had a franchise, and ran a bus route, did not prove on the BPR that the bus was owned by the defendant; it only proved (at most) that the 'mathematical chances somewhat favour the proposition'.[227] The basis of these views was that the BPR requires that the factfinder *believe* that *p* actually occurred not merely that *probably p* and that this sort of general evidence could not generate a belief that *p* actually occurred.[228]

However, the law is now more dappled than these statements alone would suggest.[229] First, there are some cases accepting the probative force of statistical evidence on its own, particularly where the evidence implies a high statistical probability. In *Kaminsky* v. *Hertz*, the Michigan Court of Appeals held that Hertz should be presumed to be the owner of a truck that had caused an accident on the basis of testimony that the truck had a Hertz logo and that Hertz owned 90 per cent of the yellow trucks bearing a Hertz logo.[230] It has even been questioned under Massachusetts law – the birthplace of *Smith* v. *Rapid Transit* – whether a high statistical probability of causation might well satisfy the BPR.[231]

Second, a considerable number of states accept that statistical probabilities generated by reliable epidemiological evidence of causation may satisfy the BPR.[232] These states accept that a claimant may be able to show specific causation if it is demonstrated that the defendant has wrongfully doubled the risk of the injury it has suffered.[233] This is

---

[227] (1945) 317 Mass 469, 470. In fact, there was more evidence in *Smith*: the defendant was the only bus company licensed by the city to run a bus route there and there was a bus scheduled to run close to the time at which the claimant was injured. As F. Schauer, *Profiles, Probabilities, and Stereotypes*, 81, points out, the hypothetical examples based upon *Smith*, which mention only the relative number of buses in the town, make the problem of purely statistical evidence 'analytically crisper'.

[228] See, for example, *Sargent*, at 827.

[229] Cf. *Galvin* v. *Eli Lilly* (2007) 488 F 3d 1026 (CA, District of Columbia Circuit), describing the case law on statistical evidence as 'mixed', 1034–5.

[230] (1979) 288 NW 2d 426 (CA, Michigan). See, similarly, *Kramer* v. *Weedhopper of Utah Inc.* (1986) 490 NE 2d 104 (CA, Illinois), where the fact that Weedhopper bought 90 per cent of its bolts from Lawrence and 10 per cent from Hughes licensed the inference that the bolt in the Weedhopper airplane kit that injured the claimant came from Lawrence.

[231] *Spencer* v. *Baxter International Inc. & Others* (2001) 163 F Supp 2d 74, 88, n. 7.

[232] For example, *Manko* v. *United States*, 636 F Supp 1419 (WD Mont 1986); *Maiorana* v. *National Gypsum Co. (In Re Joint E & S District Asbestos Litigation)* 872 F Supp 1014, 1027 (SDNY 1993); *Merrell Dow Pharmaceuticals Inc.* v. *Havner* (1997) 953 SW 2d 706, 717–18; *Daubert* v. *Merrell Dow Pharmaceuticals Inc.* (1995) 43 F 3d 1311, 1314, 1320; *In Re Silicone Gel Breast Implants* (2004) 318 F Supp 2d 879, 893–4.

[233] These developments are usefully discussed by S. Haack, 'Risky Business: Statistical Proof of Individual Causation'.

subject to three provisos. First, the claimant must have established *general causation* on the BPR.[234] Second, the claimant must show sufficient 'fit' between its case and those underlying the (reliable) statistical study relied upon.[235] Third, the epidemiological evidence must be reliably founded on scientific methodology.[236]

Although some have argued that in these cases US courts are fictionally equating a statistical probability with proof under the BPR for policy reasons,[237] this is not generally how such reasoning is conceptualised. Two lines of reasoning tend to undergird the judicial acceptance of purely statistical evidence. First, it is argued that all evidence is fundamentally statistical in nature.[238] The claim here is that even intuitively 'case-specific' evidence supports a hypothesis only in a statistical way. For example, if an eyewitness attests that a bus of a particular colour ran over the claimant, this testimony supports the hypothesis only in so far as the witness is reliable, and this reliability is constituted or measured by the number of times the witness would correctly identify the colour of the bus under testing. So if the witness identifies correctly 80 per cent of the time, then, on this argument, her evidence suggests there is an 80 per cent statistical probability that the bus had that colour.[239] Second, it has been pointed out that some statistical probabilities are intuitively highly probative, especially when they are based upon particular facets of the case at hand.[240] Similarly, it has been noted that the rejection of purely statistical evidence as sufficient sits uneasily with the weight (albeit, non-determinative, weight) attached to statistical DNA evidence in criminal trials under a more stringent standard of proof.[241]

---

[234] See, for example, *Havner*, referenced in Note 232, 717–18; *In Re Silicone Gel Breast Implants*, referenced in Note 232, 893–4.

[235] See ibid. and S. Gold, 'The More we Know, the Less Intelligent we are? – How Genomic Information Should and Should not, Change Toxic Tort Doctrine', 381.

[236] See generally *Restatement (Third) Torts: Liability for Physical and Emotional Harm*, §28 comment c and Reporters' Notes thereon.

[237] Cf. Lord Rodger's comments on *Havner*, referenced in Note 232, in *Sienkiewicz* [154].

[238] *In re Agent Orange Product Liability* (1984) 597 F Supp 740, 835 (Weinstein J); *Howard* v. *Wal-Mart* (1998) 160 F 3d 358, 358 (Posner J); *US* v. *Veysey* (2003) 334 F 3d 600, 605–6 (Posner J).

[239] Cf. L. Tribe, 'Trial by Mathematics: Precision and Ritual in the Legal Process' (1971) 84 *Harvard Law Review* 1329, n. 2: 'all factual evidence is ultimately "statistical"'. Similarly: A. Stein, *Foundations of Evidence Law*, 206.

[240] *Hart* v. *Secretary of the Department of Health and Human Services* (2004) 60 Fed Ct 598, 607–8 (distinguishing between probative force of more and less general statistics).

[241] For example, *US* v. *Veysey*, above, 605–6.

Statistical evidence: analysis

Should statistical probabilities of causation greater than 50 per cent be enough to satisfy the BPR on specific causation?

Some preliminaries are in order. First, this is a question about *specific* causation, which assumes that there is plausible evidence of general causation (though *part* of that evidence may also be the statistical evidence relied upon at the specific causation stage). Second, this is a question about *reliable* statistical probabilities. For instance, no one would accept that an epidemiological study based upon an extremely small number of cases would generate reliable statistical probabilities of causation.

It is suggested that, subject to these conditions, and subject to the considerations concerning the 'weight' of the probabilities in question set out below, statistical evidence is capable of proving specific causation on the BPR. There are two simple, but powerful positive arguments in favour of this. The first is that the BPR requires the evidence, on balance, to favour a finding of causation. If there is a reliable frequentist or classical probability favouring a finding, then there is better evidential reason to believe in causation than not. This is not to commit the fallacy of equivocating 'evidential' and 'statistical probability' but is rather to accept that statistical probability influences evidential probability.[242] The second is that statistical probabilities are guides to the truth and the law is fundamentally concerned with assigning liability according to the truth.[243]

Why, then, is there opposition to accepting purely statistical proof of specific causation? The central objection of principle in the literature is that the acceptance of purely statistical evidence leads one to accept liability in counterintuitive situations. The following are favourites:[244]

Blue Bus

Victim, who is colour-blind, is run over by a bus in a town. There are 100 buses in the town. Of these, Blue Bus Company owns sixty blue buses and Red Bus Company owns forty red buses. The only witness to the accident is Victim. Should the 60 per cent statistical probability that the bus was

---

[242] Cf. S. Haack, 'Risky Business', who states that the 'key argument' for the sufficiency of statistical evidence is a 'fallacy of equivocation', 27.

[243] Similar arguments are found in A. Broadbent, 'Epidemiological Evidence in Proof of Specific Causation', 269–72; A. Pundik, 'The Epistemology of Statistical Evidence', 132–4.

[244] For a useful presentation of these hypotheticals, see M. Redmayne, 'Exploring the Proof Paradoxes', 281–3.

blue suffice to establish under the BPR that one of Blue Bus Company's buses caused Victim's injury?[245]

Rodeo

1000 people attend a rodeo. 501 people do not, however, pay their admission fee. The rest do. Is each person liable in trespass to land on the basis of the greater than 50 per cent statistical probability that each trespassed?[246]

Market Share

Drug Company A manufactured 90 per cent of a defective batch of drugs produced in the USA in 1965. Drug Company B manufactured the other 10 per cent of defective drugs. The drug can cause cancer. Victim's mother ingests a defective drug in 1965. In 1985, the drug causes Victim's cancer. Should Drug Company A be held liable, under the BPR, for causing injury to Victim through manufacture of a defective drug?[247]

Two Hunters, Different Pellets

Two hunters independently go on a hunting trip in the woods. Hunter 1 has twenty-five pellets in his gun. Hunter 2 has five pellets. Each negligently fires simultaneously in the direction of victim, who is occluded behind a tree. All bullets from each gun are fired at once. Should Hunter 1's negligence be said, given only these facts, to be causative on the BPR?[248]

There is widespread consensus that it is *prima facie* intuitively troublesome to impose liability in these cases and that this difficulty arises due to the statistical nature of the evidence involved.[249]

Various accounts of why these instances of liability based upon purely statistical evidence seem problematic have been proposed. Perhaps the least convincing is the claim that the availability of only statistical evidence may itself be evidence against the party adducing that evidence. The claim is that the inability to find other evidence on causation itself may lower the probability of the case of the person adducing the evidence.[250] This is a valuable observation. But it will hardly do *in general*. First, in cases where we have no reason to expect the party to adduce further evidence, it need not lower the probability of their case on causation – and one can imagine modifications of *Blue Bus* to this effect.

---

[245] Inspired by *Smith* v. *Rapid Transit*, Referenced at Note 227.

[246] See L.J. Cohen, *The Probable and the Provable*, 75–6.

[247] Based upon *Sindell* v. *Abbott Laboratories* (1980) 26 Cal 3d 588. See further Chapter 4, 165ff.

[248] Based upon *Summers* v. *Tice* (1947) 33 Cal 2d 80, as modified by J.J. Thomson, 'Liability and Individualized Evidence', 201.

[249] See M. Redmayne, 'Exploring the Proof Paradoxes', 281, referring to an 'overwhelming intuition'.

[250] See D.H. Kaye, 'The Paradox of the Gatecrasher and Other Stories', 106–7. For similar objections to this view, see P. Tillers, *Probability and Inference in the Law of Evidence*, 30–1.

Second, there is no reason to think the failure to adduce further evidence would always lower the probability below the level required by the BPR. Third, it is not clear why the absence of further evidence would always reduce the probability only against the party adducing that evidence; the failure of the other party to adduce such evidence might cancel out any such inference. The claim that allowing purely statistical evidence to satisfy the BPR would reduce incentives to produce further evidence of causation is similarly problematic.[251] It may well be true. But it will not explain why the intuition that liability is problematic remains in cases where it would be impossible to adduce further, non-statistical, evidence.

Another type of explanation focuses upon moral considerations pertaining to the individual parties involved.[252] According to Wasserman, the moral problem is 'the reliance upon others' conduct ... to infer [the defendant's] commission of a wrongful act. We object to this inference because it ignores the defendant's capacity to diverge from his associates...thereby demeaning his individuality and autonomy'.[253] There are at least two problems here. First, to say that 70 per cent of people with certain characteristics behave in a certain way under certain circumstances is not to say of any such individual that they *could* not have behaved in that way. It need not imply that there is a causally deterministic explanation for why 70 per cent of people behave in such a way. So the claim that acceptance of purely statistical evidence undermines or demeans their *autonomy*, understood as capacity to choose from a set of options, is difficult. Second, the autonomy-based view has difficulty explaining the difficulty one feels about allowing proof purely on the basis of statistical evidence in *Two Hunters*, *Market Share*, and *Blue Bus*. The inference of causation in these cases is not an inference based (primarily) upon what other people have done, but either upon what the defendant has done or, in *Blue Bus*, upon the relative proportions of buses in the town. In so far as there is an objection from autonomy, it seems considerably weaker where the inference is based upon the defendant's own conduct.[254]

---

[251] For example, D.H. Kaye, 'The Paradox of the Gatecrasher and Other Stories', 106.

[252] A distinction is typically drawn between 'epistemic' and 'moral' objections to statistical evidence. (See, for example, H.L. Ho, *Philosophy of Evidence Law*, 138–41). This is helpful but it should, of course, be borne in mind that there are moral objections to using bad (i.e. epistemically deficient) evidence (though not all epistemic deficiencies may be relevant here).

[253] D. Wasserman, 'The Morality of Statistical Proof and the Risk of Mistaken Liability' 942–3.

[254] For further objections, see A. Pundik, 'Statistical Evidence and Individual Litigants', 315–23. The objection also seems weaker in relation to purely legal persons.

Another moral consideration, which does have some force in explaining the difficulties with liability in *Rodeo*, is that if the rodeo owner sued all 1000 attendees for £n damages she would obtain £499n too much. We *know* in *Rodeo* that we will make a mistake as to the extent of recovery that a specific person (the owner) should obtain. This is unlike the usual case where, though we know that, in the long run, we will make mistakes in the assignment of liability, we do not know who, specifically, will wrongly profit from this. This also applies to versions of *Market Share* and *Blue Bus*, where there is more than one claim brought and there is recurrently only statistical evidence available to adjudicate it. But the problem with this explanation is that it does not capture the intuitive sense that there is something different about statistical evidence itself – the problem is not so much in the consequences of accepting purely statistical evidence; it resides in the nature of the evidence itself and its probative capacity.

Finally, then, there are explanations of the intuitive reaction to the cases which do relate specifically to epistemological considerations. It has been claimed that purely statistical evidence cannot generate a *belief* that p occurred but only a belief that *probably p* occurred.[255] This has plausibility. Suppose I have entered a lottery with one million tickets. After the numbers have been drawn, I may have a very high degree of confidence that my lottery ticket has lost (999,999/1,000,000) and yet I probably would not say: 'I believe that my lottery ticket has lost'. Many argue that this attitude is rational and that denying it leads to paradoxical results.[256] If I believe that my ticket has lost, then I ought to believe of every individual ticket that it has lost, and, since I ought to believe the logical consequences of my beliefs, I ought to believe that no ticket has won. But this contradicts my knowledge that one ticket will have won.[257] The difficulty with this view is simply that, whatever the normative plausibility of requiring the factfinder to *believe* that p, the BPR, as predominantly stated, only requires the factfinder to believe it *more probably not that p*.[258] So even if purely

---

[255] See p. 88. This is the line in J.J. Thomson, 'Liability and Individualized Evidence'; H.L. Ho, *Philosophy of Evidence Law*, 140–2; L. Buchak, 'Belief, credence, and norms'.

[256] Cf. H.L. Ho, *Philosophy of Evidence Law*, 133–4. The paradox in the text – the 'lottery paradox' – derives from H. Kyburg, *Probability and the Logic of Rational Belief*, 197.

[257] See generally, J. Hawthorne, *Knowledge and Lotteries*.

[258] Cf. H.L. Ho, *Philosophy of Evidence Law*, 122–4, who objects to this interpretation on the ground that the factfinder can *never* be shown to be incorrect if, *at the time of making the decision*, the evidential probability was greater than 0.5, even if *later*, compelling new evidence arises – because it is still true that the evidential probability at the time of the

statistical evidence cannot generate a belief that *p* occurred, it may generate a belief that more probably than not *p* occurred. However, this argument does have substantial force in relation to the French and German standards of proof, which probably do require an outright *belief that p*.

There are two epistemological considerations which do seem to have some purchase. The first concerns the *generality* of statistical evidence. Many people explain their judgements about these cases by referring to the idea that somehow statistical evidence does not speak to the particular case at hand – but only to the general course of things.[259] Now, it has rightly been pointed out that the distinction between 'general' and 'case-specific' evidence is vague.[260] And it is possible that the general–specific distinction is used to capture different ways in which statistical evidence is thought to differ from non-statistical evidence. Nonetheless, there does seem to be an important distinction between different kinds of evidence in terms of its capturing more or fewer features of the case at hand. Suppose in *Blue Bus* we had evidence that sixty blue buses and forty red buses passed through the street on which victim was injured in the nearest two hours to the time of the accident. Although the statistical probability remains the same, the reference class 'number of blue buses passing through the accident zone at the time' seems more appropriately *specific* to the facts than the reference class 'number of blue buses in the town'. The reference class is more specific because it takes into account more factors of the situation at hand which might be thought to alter the statistical probability of causation. The probability is, quite simply, based upon more evidence. This way of understanding the levels of generality which a probability might possess is sometimes expressed as the 'weight' of the probability – the more that the probability takes into account features of the case at hand which might affect the probability estimate, the greater its *weight*.[261]

A second kind of epistemological consideration is the *sensitivity of the evidence to the truth* of the proposition for which that evidence is adduced

decision was greater than 0.5. There is no real problem here. There is nothing problematic about the law saying: 'the decision was in accordance with the BPR, on the evidential base at the time of the decision. However, since new, better, evidence has arisen which makes it unlikely that D is liable, the decision can no longer stand'.

[259] See M. Redmayne, 'Exploring the Proof Paradoxes', 284.

[260] A. Pundik, 'What is Wrong with Statistical Evidence? The attempts to establish an epistemic deficiency', 482–3.

[261] A. Stein, *Foundations of Evidence Law*, 69–70. The idea probably originates in J. Keynes, *A Treatise on Probability*.

to support.[262] Suppose in *Blue Bus* that one comes to believe that it was indeed a blue bus that ran over the victim, on the basis of the statistical evidence. If, in fact, one were wrong about that, because a red bus was causative, it would remain true that there are sixty blue buses to forty red buses in the town. In this sense, one's evidence does not vary with the truth of the proposition which it supports: even if the proposition were false, one's evidence would remain the same. Suppose, however, that one had eyewitness testimony that the bus was blue, and the witness was tested to be reliable 60 out of 100 times under the same identification conditions. Here, one's evidence, probably, *would* vary if the bus were not blue. One probably would have different evidence (different testimony) if the bus were red. This seems to capture another aspect of what counts as 'specific' evidence and what counts as 'general'. Specific evidence is that which we would expect to be sensitive to the truth of what actually happened.

We can now state three possible responses to these problematic cases in relation to the issue of sufficiency of statistical evidence:

(1)   The problematic cases constitute a *reductio* of the claim that statistical evidence is sufficient to prove specific causation because they show that accepting statistical evidence on its own logically entails absurd results.

(2)   The problematic cases demonstrate that *certain kinds* of statistical evidence do not alone suffice to prove specific causation.

(3)   The problematic cases are not problematic at all. The explanations adduced to differentiate the evidence therein do not convince.

It is suggested that the appropriate response is (2). The main problem with the evidence in *Blue Bus, Rodeo*, and *Market Share* is that it is too *unspecific* in the sense of lacking in sufficient weight. In *Blue Bus*, this is because there are many variables that could affect the statistical probability of causation that the mere relative numbers of buses in the town does not take into account. How many buses of each company were around the vicinity of the accident at the time? How many accidents was each company involved in over the past year? How are drivers from each firm recruited?[263] The evidential base on which the statistical probability is based is simply too thin. The same is true of *Rodeo*, where

---

[262]   This idea is usefully discussed in A. Broadbent, 'Epidemiological Evidence', 264–5; D. Enoch, L. Spectre, and T. Fisher, 'Statistical Evidence, Sensitivity, and the Legal Value of Knowledge'.

[263]   The distinction between 'likelihood' and 'prevalence' drawn in *Garner* v. *Salford City Council* [2013] EWHC 1573 [25]–[26] reflects the distinction between probabilities with weight and abstract probabilities with little weight.

the relative numbers of gatecrashers to fee-payers says little about the propensity of an individual to trespass.

Similarly, in *Market Share*, the statistical probability could obviously be affected significantly by the relative number of drugs bought by the dispensing pharmacist in the victim's local area. It seems that *Two Hunters* is different. Here the probability is relatively weighty. The number of bullets negligently fired towards the victim at the time of the accident provides a reasonable estimate of the probability of causation. This is because we do not have reason to think that one set of bullets is likely to have a special causal potency not shared by the other bullets (unlike the obvious skewing effect which a different distribution of cabs in the town at the time of accident would have on the probability). Of course, we can construct more refined reference classes in *Two Hunters*: how many of Hunter 1's bullets compared to Hunter 2's were approaching victim's body less than three milliseconds before impact?[264] This would be an even weightier probability of causation. The claim here, however, is only that the probability in *Two Hunters* seems to have greater weight than that in *Market Share, Rodeo*, and *Blue Bus*. If the diagnosis of these problematic cases is that the statistical probabilities do not have enough specificity to the case at hand – in the sense that they do not take into account enough probability-influencing features of the case at hand – then statistical evidence should be sufficient to prove causation when those probabilities do have sufficient weight. Hence (2) seems the correct response.

The obvious objection, however, is that the *sensitivity to the truth* consideration points in the direction of (1). Suppose we have *Market Share** where we know only that the pharmacist who dispensed the drug to the victim had bought sixty boxes of drugs from Company A and forty from Company B. The 60 per cent statistical probability of causation is weightier than the general market share data. But there remains a sense in which the evidence is 'unspecific'. The sensitivity consideration seems to capture this: the evidence would be the same regardless of whether Company A or Company B caused the injury. If the problem cases are problematic because the evidence lacks sensitivity, then this would appear to rule out the possibility that statistical evidence could ever itself suffice to prove specific causation because such evidence lacks sensitivity.

---

[264] Equally, if we continue to partition the reference class, we would reach the partition where one bullet has probability 1 and the rest 0. Given our limited knowledge, the search for more refined partitions has to be called off at some point.

The objection can be met. The response is that it is puzzling why the law should be concerned with the sensitivity to the truth consideration. Some philosophers adduce sensitivity (or a version of sensitivity) as a possible necessary condition of a philosophical analysis of knowledge. The claim is that for one to *know* that p on the basis of certain evidence, that evidence must be sensitive to the truth of p – it is not enough that it makes p very highly statistically probable. Even granting this, it is not clear why the *law of tort* ought to be concerned about sensitivity. Following (reliable) statistical evidence makes courts more likely to arrive at the truth and so improves accuracy. So long as the statistical probability estimate takes into account enough features of the case at hand, it is not clear what complaint litigants (or others) could have. As Enoch and Fisher ask: '...why should the law of evidence care about knowledge or epistemology more generally? It should care, undoubtedly, about truth or the avoidance of error. But why is it important that courts base their findings on knowledge?'[265]

Conclusions

This chapter has described the general proof rules governing natural causation in each system. The main conclusions are as follows.

First, the burden of proof in each system is a legal rule, which determines how the court must proceed in situations where the truth or falsity of a factual claim cannot be determined according to the standard of proof. It should now be clear that there are two general ways in which this may arise. The first is where the evidential base is too thin to arrive at a conclusion on the balance of probability or to a higher probability. The second, specific to the common law, is where the evidential probabilities are equally balanced.

Second, the standard of proof on wrong-constituting causation in the common law requires that the factfinder be persuaded of a probability: that causation is more probable than not. This was interpreted as an evidentially constrained probability – a probability that varies depending on the support which evidence provides for a hypothesis.

---

[265] This is not to say that the law should *only* be concerned with accuracy. If a court rejects the victim's claim in *Blue Bus*, it is more likely than not incorrect. So the insistence that the probability be based upon a sufficient degree of *weight* is probably not accuracy-maximising. But if we think that it is important that our probability judgements be based upon sufficient evidence, we ought nonetheless to endorse some kind of *weight* restriction.

The German and French standards of proof on wrong-constituting causation are framed in terms which require the judge not to be convinced that the defendant probably caused the claimant's injury, but to be convinced that the defendant actually did cause the claimant's injury.

The extent to which there are differences between the wrong-constituting standards of proof depends upon how one interprets what each system means by 'probability', and how one understands the relationship between that concept of probability and 'conviction'. In so far as each accepts that a statistical probability alone can satisfy the standard of proof, the difference between them is in substance quantitative, not qualitative – the French and German standard simply requires a *higher* statistical probability. To the extent that French law and German law reject a high statistical probability as sufficient, the difference is both qualitative and quantitative. The qualitative difference is the requirement that the judge be convinced of what actually occurred, which is what precludes the sufficiency of statistical probabilities.

These differences should of course be considered in context. The lower standard of proof under §287 ZPO applies to some causal questions which would be considered to be wrong-constituting in the common law and thus generates a similar standard of proof in respect of those questions. Thus in claims for pure economic loss involving a special relationship between the defendant and the claimant, there would normally be a contract in German law, with the result that liability is established simply upon breach of the contract and the causal question falls under the less stringent §287 ZPO. Moreover, we shall see that French and German law apply significantly wider exceptional rules in relation to wrong-constituting causation than in English law.

Third, reasoning to causal conclusions is inferential. The nature and process of causal inference was described. It was shown that both general reasoning and evidence and case-specific evidence operate together in the inferential process. This process often involves inferences to the best explanation as well as direct assessments of the statistical probability of causation.

Fourth, three issues concerning the boundaries of legitimate inferences of causation were considered. It was argued that predominantly general evidence has been accepted as probative of causation in each system. Then it was shown that proof of a mere increase in risk does not suffice to prove causation according to the BPR or a higher standard of proof, but that it may nonetheless play a preliminary role in inferring causation. It was shown that English law currently accepts statistical evidence alone as probative of specific causation under certain conditions. Finally, it was argued that this is the correct position, in the common law, so long as the statistical evidence has sufficient specificity to the case at hand.

3   Justifying proof of causation

The aim of this chapter is to offer a limited defence of the rule that the claimant must prove causation on the balance of probability (and not to a greater or lesser standard) in order to be entitled to compensatory damages. The argument is divided into two stages.

The first stage adduces reasons why *as a matter of substantive law* causation matters to establishing compensatory liability. The reason for beginning with justifying causation as a matter of substantive law is that causation's role in the substantive law partly determines which proof rules should govern it.[1] For example, if a causal connection between the defendant's wrongful conduct and injury were normatively crucial to establishing that the claimant had been the victim of a wrong (and so forms part of the cause of action), then one would normally expect the claimant to have to prove this. The argument is that the justification of requiring causation lies principally in the importance of responsibility to the assignment of liability. In particular, without the sense of responsibility described, it is difficult to identify the rational source of a duty of compensation.

The second stage directly addresses the justification of the *proof rules* of causation in light of this conclusion. It suggests that the justification of the rule that the claimant prove causation on the balance of probability rests upon a number of considerations. First, there is a moral asymmetry

---

[1] Similarly, if, for example, absence of causation were properly characterised as a 'defence', this would generally be thought to entail that the defendant should prove its absence. More generally, the importance of causation to liability is crucial in assessing the 'cost' of a false positive (finding defendant liable without their having caused the claimant's injury) which is, in turn, relevant to choice of proof rule governing causation. See A. Porat and A. Stein, *Tort Liability under Uncertainty*, 10–1; H. Stoll, 'Haftungsverlagerung durch beweisrechtliche Mittel'; V. Wahrendorf, *Die Prinzipien der Beweislast im Haftungsrecht*, 18: 'Die Beweislastentscheidung kann [deshalb] nur unter Einbeziehung der Haftungsprinzipien...sinnvoll getroffen werden.'

in false positives and false negatives over causation. Second, the defendant ought to be considered to have a limited right not to be falsely declared a wrongdoer. Third, though there is a moral asymmetry in false positives and false negatives, the asymmetry is not substantial; this favours the balance of probability rule over a higher standard of proof. Fourth, the all-or-nothing quality of the balance of probability has significant advantages over a rule which proportions liability to the probability of the claim.

Causation and liabilities to compensate between individuals

Why, if at all, should the existence of a causal relationship between some aspect of A's conduct and a loss suffered by B matter to establishing that A ought to compensate B in respect of that loss? The first section of this part considers and rejects some non-consequentialist answers. The second section then defends another non-consequentialist account.[2] It will be useful to state the outline of the argument here:

(1) If there is no causal relationship between A's conduct and B's loss, then generally there is no morally significant sense in which A is responsible for B's loss.
(2) If there is no morally significant sense in which A is responsible for B's loss, then A generally does not owe B a moral duty to compensate for that loss.
(3) If B does not owe A a moral duty to compensate for A's loss, then it would be unjust to impose a legal liability upon B to compensate for A's loss.

Call this the 'responsibility account'. The third section of this part shows that holding persons legally liable only for the outcomes they cause is only likely to be generally welfare-maximising if some dubious empirical assumptions are made.

Justifications of causation as a requirement of legal liabilities of compensation

It might seem odd to ask why the law should insist upon causation as a requirement of liabilities to compensation between individuals.[3]

---

[2] It suffices to say that the account is non-consequentialist in the sense that it suggests there is strong reason to require causation even before the consequences of doing so are taken into account.

[3] Cf. *Snell* v. *Farrell* [1990] 2 SCR 311, 326: 'Causation is an expression of the relationship that must be found to exist between the tortious act of the wrongdoer and the injury to the victim in order to justify compensation of the latter out of the pocket of the former'.

The natural question is: what rational alternatives could one imagine to requiring that A was a cause of B's loss in order to render A liable to pay compensation to B? But there are candidates for relationships which might sit alongside causation as non-causal generators of liabilities to compensate. Consider the following candidate principles:

> *Risk liability*: If A unreasonably increases the risk of injury to B and
>   B suffers such an injury, A may legitimately be called upon to compen-
>   sate B for that injury, even if it is known that A did not cause B's injury.
> *Accessorial liability*: If A assists, procures, or agrees with C to commit a
>   wrong against B, A may legitimately be called upon to compensate B.
> *Vicarious liability*: If A bears a suitable relationship to C, and C wrongs B in a
>   manner connected with that relationship, A may legitimately be called
>   upon to compensate B, even if it is known that A did not cause B's injury.

Only the *risk liability* principle would render causation entirely redundant as a source of liabilities to compensation. The validity of *vicarious liability* or *accessorial liability* would not render causation redundant, since the wrongs to which they apply may require causal elements.

In what follows, the argument focuses upon showing that *risk liability*, the most wide-ranging threat to the importance of causation, is incorrect. The basic reason will be that *risk liability* is inconsistent with the role that responsibility (in a sense to be defined) should play in ascribing legal liability. It will be suggested that even if *vicarious liability* is a valid non-causal reason for liability that this does not undermine the general moral necessity of causation.

To make the discussion more manageable, it will be helpful to consider an example:

> *Accident*. A and C are driving alongside each other towards a crossroad
> at the top of a hill. The traffic light at the crossroad is just about to turn
> red but each is driving at such a speed that they cannot stop in time.
> Each decides to accelerate through. Not far over the crest of the hill,
> B is crossing a pedestrian crossing at a green light. A is unable to brake
> in time and seriously injures B. C manages to swerve away from the
> accident, just missing B in the process.[4]

Both A and C have unreasonably risked injury to B, but only A has unreasonably caused injury to B. The reason for considering this example is to assess whether B ought to be able to recover damages from

---

[4] For discussion of a similar example, see J. Waldron, 'Moments of Carelessness and Massive Loss', 387.

C for the loss caused only by A. If causation is necessary to B's entitlement to damages for his injury from another individual, then the answer
must be no. Most people's strong intuition seems to be just this – only
A should be liable to compensate B's loss (among private individuals)
because C caused B no injury.[5] If this intuition is justified, it will be
shown that the main contender for generating a liability to compensate
between individuals – culpable risk-creation – can be ruled out.

Freedom of action

Judith Jarvis Thomson once argued that causation is necessary for liability because requiring A to compensate B for loss A did not cause interferes too greatly with B's freedom of action.[6] Her argument was as
follows. Suppose (1) B intentionally caused B's own injury for B's own
purposes and A had absolutely no causal connection to it. A owes B no
compensation – even if A was doing something highly culpable like
deliberately throwing bricks at B.[7] Now suppose (2) that B has been
injured *somehow* – either by B himself or by C or D or by natural causes,
but not by A. Thomson's argument is that, in (2), nothing *about A* has
changed from (1) which 'rule[s] out [B]'s injury had the history described
in (1), and therefore nothing true of [A] which rules out that [B] should
bear his own costs'.[8]

The argument is problematic on two grounds. First, even if nothing has
changed about A in (2), we might plausibly think that changes in facts
about B are relevant. The argument provides no reason for thinking that
the liability-fixing facts are entirely based upon facts about A (what if B is
entirely faultless and A is highly culpable?). Second, suppose we appeal
directly to the idea of A's 'freedom of action' as a basis for requiring that
A has *caused* B's loss. By freedom of action, Thomson meant:

...freedom to plan on action in the future, for such ends as one chooses oneself.
We take it that persons are entitled to a certain "moral space" in which to assess
possible ends, make choices, and then work for the means to achieve those ends.[9]

This general notion provides no reason for drawing the boundaries of A's
freedom of action at causation. We might think each person should only
enjoy freedom to act without negligence and that if A had negligently

---

[5] S. Kagan, 'Causation, Liability, and Internalism', 41: 'Almost all of us believe that it
matters who caused the damage'; M. Moore, *Causation and Responsibility*, 29: '"[c]ausation
matters" seems a pretty good candidate for a first principle of morality'.
[6] J.J. Thomson, 'Remarks on Causation and Liability'.   [7] Ibid., 110.   [8] Ibid.
[9] Ibid., 108.

risked B the injury B suffered then A ought to compensate B. After all, it may be thought that there is little value in protecting A's freedom to behave negligently without bearing any costs.

Causation as essential to wrongdoing

It might be suggested in *Accident* that C ought not to be legally liable to B in respect of B's loss because C has committed no moral wrong, or no moral wrong that is the appropriate subject of legal recognition, against B. If true, this would answer the objection to Thomson's account by providing a principled explanation of where C's freedom of action runs out. It runs out at the point where C's action *wrongs* B.

On the former possibility – that C has committed no moral wrong against B – the claim would be that C's culpable risk-creation is not itself a wrong in relation to B.[10] It seems implausible that we do not owe other people any moral duties not carelessly to risk them serious injuries by our actions. Such duties seem closely to follow on the heels of, and to derive from, duties not to inflict injury. But, more importantly, even if this were true, it does not appear to be the explanation (for the intuition) why B should not be able to recover compensation from C. Even if we were willing to say that C had committed a wrong against B simply in virtue of unreasonably increasing B's risk of injury, it would *still* seem odd to say that B had a moral entitlement to compensation from C in respect of the injury it actually suffered.

The defender of the wrongdoing-centred justification might object that, even if culpable risk-creation is itself a wrong in relation to the person risked injury, if that person is claiming compensation for an injury suffered, they must show that the suffering of the injury itself constituted a wrong against them. On this view, although B has been wronged by C in *Accident*, B's suffering injury was not itself *part* of any wrong committed against B by C. The difficulty with this objection is that it would provide us with no reason for insisting upon a causal relationship between a wrong and 'consequential' loss, since consequential losses will (by definition) not be the subject of a wrong against the victim. Yet there seems to be (almost) as much reason to insist upon causation between a wrong and a subsequent loss as there is to insist upon a causal relationship between conduct and some initial injury if compensation is to be obtained for that subsequent loss.

---

[10] This claim is defended by E. Weinrib, *The Idea of Private Law*, 157–8. But cf. E. Weinrib, *Corrective Justice*, 44.

Causation as morally particularising A and B

Holding C liable to B in *Accident* for a loss which C has not caused B may seem arbitrary in the sense that doing so singles out B and C from other potential claimants and defendants without sufficient reason.[11] On the one hand, the question arises why C is being singled out over someone else who did not cause the injury. On the other hand, one might wonder why B should benefit from C, rather than some other victim of injury who was also not caused injury by C. While causation singles out A and B in a morally significant way, there seems to be nothing marking out B and C.

But, of course, there *is* some kind of relationship between B and C and something which marks C out beyond other potential loss-bearers.[12] C has behaved negligently *in relation to B* and has risked the kind of injury which B suffered. The question is why this relationship does not mark C out as someone who could justly be called upon to compensate B. A deeper explanation is needed as to why culpable risk-creation cannot serve the morally particularising function of causation.

The responsibility account of causation's role in generating duties to compensate

The deeper explanation of why culpable risk-creation is not enough to generate a moral duty to compensate between individuals, and therefore an answer to why C should not be liable to B, is that C is not *responsible* for B's injury.[13] Responsibility has many senses, so some distinctions are necessary.[14] First, the claim that causation grounds responsibility is obviously about *moral* responsibility, not *legal* responsibility (we are looking for an explanation of why C should not be *legally* responsible, so it would be circular simply to claim that C is not legally responsible). Second, we are not referring to the idea of moral responsibility as capacity – what Gardner calls 'basic responsibility'[15] – a person is responsible in that sense if they have an ability to respond to reasons. Third, we are not talking about responsibility as causal responsibility – no explanatory progress has been made if we say that causation matters to liability

---

[11] See E. Weinrib, 'Causation and Wrongdoing', 414–16.

[12] As others have noted, for example, J. Coleman, 'Property, Wrongfulness and the Duty to Compensate', 452.

[13] For versions of this answer, see, for example, A. Ripstein, *Equality, Responsibility, and the Law*, 72–4; J. Coleman, 'Doing away with Tort Law', 1165–6; P. Cane, *Responsibility in Law and Morality*, 136–41.

[14] See H.L.A. Hart, *Punishment and Responsibility*, 211–30.

[15] J. Gardner, 'The Mark of Responsibility', 182–5.

because causal responsibility matters. Fourth, we are not talking about the 'forward-looking' sense of responsibility, which refers to the idea of one's being under a duty to see to it that something occurs (e.g. 'the referee's responsibility to draw the match to a close').

The notion of responsibility involved in the claim that culpably risking an outcome is not itself to be responsible for that outcome is the notion of responsibility as 'answerability' or 'accountability': the idea is that, if A is responsible for an outcome in this sense, A can be appropriately required to explain why A brought the outcome about. We can call this *outcome responsibility*.[16] This notion of responsibility requires more than mere factual causation of injury. It also imports some notion of the injury flowing from *actual conduct* (rather than a mere muscle spasm) and its being to some extent avoidable, perhaps by being sufficiently foreseeable. C is not morally responsible, in this sense, for B's injury in *Accident*. Being responsible for an outcome in this sense requires an agent to bear some relation to that outcome which goes beyond risk-creation otherwise the outcome is simply not tied to the existence of the agent. This is just a basic truth about outcome responsibility.

Why think that *outcome responsibility* underlies our intuitive judgement about C, rather than, simply and trivially, that C is not *causally* responsible? One reason is that outcome responsibility explains our intuitive judgements about other cases of liability – for instance, that C should not be liable to B if A used C's hand to strike B without C's knowledge. The next section provides a further reason.

Responsibility and moral liabilities or duties to compensate

If outcome responsibility requires, minimally, factual causation, why should liability to compensate rest upon outcome responsibility? This section establishes that without C's being responsible for B's injury, C has no moral duty to compensate B for that injury. The focus will again be on the case of culpable risk-creation. The argument will show that C's culpably risking B's injury in *Accident* does not generate a moral duty to compensate for that injury.[17]

So: why does C not have a moral duty to pay B damages? It is difficult to see where such a duty could come from. If C is to be under such a duty, it

---

[16] The term 'outcome responsibility' to refer to the responsibility described in the text was coined by T. Honoré, 'Responsibility and Luck: The Moral Basis of Strict Liability'.

[17] In fact, even if one rejects the overall point that absence of outcome responsibility is what justifies the absence of liability in C, this section provides an independent argument against C's liability.

must surely arise somehow from C's unreasonably risking injury to B. Yet the best understanding of how duties of compensation typically arise from a person's behaving in a certain way in relation to another person is that those duties are a rational reflection of the person's primary duty to behave in a certain way. The breach of one's primary duty to behave in a certain way gives rise to a duty to make the world as if the breach had never occurred. This secondary duty is a duty of *corrective* justice (CJ) simply in so far as it concerns the undoing of a 'transaction' (the wrong) between the parties.[18] The now familiar explanation of the origin of this duty is just a truth about reasons: conform to reason (conform to your duty not to commit the wrong) or come as close as you can.[19] Coming as close as one can requires one to do the next best thing to the wrong never having occurred. If the wrong has caused loss, this means compensation: putting the party in the position it would have been had the wrong never occurred. But if there is no causal link between the wrong and a loss, either because C has suffered no loss or because the loss C has suffered is not causally connected to D's conduct, then one cannot speak of undoing the wrong as a justification for compensation. The very idea of 'undoing' the wrong involves imagining a counterfactual where the wrong did not occur. If the claimant's loss is not causally connected to the defendant's conduct, then it will not be subtracted from the world where the wrong did not occur.[20] So even if we accept that C's conduct constitutes a moral wrong in relation to B, it simply cannot count as next-best-conformity to C's duty for C to compensate B.[21] In the world in which C's wrong never occurred, B is still injured.[22]

---

[18] Cf. J. Gardner, 'What is Tort Law for? Part 1: The Place of Corrective Justice' for the fullest development of this view.

[19] Ibid. 28ff.

[20] Most corrective justice (and related) theories include a requirement of causation of loss: cf., for example, N. Jansen, *Die Struktur des Haftungsrechts*, 132 n. 302.

[21] McCarthy defends the claim that causation is not necessary to create a duty to compensate by reference to defendant indeterminacy cases (on which, see Chapter 4). But he concedes that if the evidence to attribute causation to a particular individual were available, that this should determine the liability issue. This is consistent with the argument here, which is only seeking to establish that there is a strong moral reason not to impose liability where causation is known not to exist. The question of what degree of belief we should have before finding a defendant to have been causative or whether we should make proof-based exceptions is a distinct question, taken up below. See D. McCarthy, 'Liability and Risk', 244–7.

[22] Tadros suggests that attempters (people who wrongfully risk, but do not cause, harm) should be liable in respect of the 'security resources' they divert from the prevention of crime. The state spends valuable resources in detecting and preventing those who risk harm to others, with the result (according to Tadros) that the diversion causes less

Liabilities to compensate beyond responsibility?

If not a duty of corrective justice arising as next-best conformity to the breach of a primary duty of conduct, from where else could B's duty to repair come?[23] A natural suggestion is that some norm of *distributive* justice mandates that C pay B damages.[24] Distributive justice can plausibly impose duties upon people to alleviate losses for which they are not responsible.[25]

The risk liability principle

Consider again:

> *Risk liability principle*: If A unreasonably increases the risk of an injury to B and B suffers such an injury, A may legitimately be called upon to compensate B for that injury, even if it is known that A did not cause B's injury.

It might be argued that *risk liability* can be justified on distributive grounds, even if A is not responsible for B's injury. It is suggested that the risk liability principle, as formulated, cannot be defended on such grounds.

A first argument for *risk liability* is that it would ensure that persons of equal blameworthiness are subject to the same liability. Since only luck differentiates A and C in *Accident*, it seems that they are of equal blameworthiness.[26] Why would we want to ensure that persons of equal blameworthiness are subject to the same liability? The reason seems to be that if two persons are equally blameworthy, they equally deserve

---

   people who actually cause harm from being prevented from doing so. Cf. V. Tadros, 'Obligations and Outcomes' 186–8. Even if it were successful, this argument would not justify paying compensation to the victim in particular.

[23] Cf. J. Coleman, *The Practice of Principle*, 32: '*Someone* does not incur a second-order duty of repair unless he has failed to discharge some first-order duty.' Note that B's being outcome responsible for A's loss may also give us a *distributive* reason to shift the loss from B to A. See J. Gardner, 'What is Tort Law for? Part 2. The Place of Distributive Justice', 348–9.

[24] Cf. the moral luck critics described by M. Moore, *Causation and Responsibility*, ch 2.

[25] J. Coleman, 'Tort Law and Tort Theory', 198: 'Many duties of distributive justice require coming to the aid of others to alleviate misfortunes for which one is not causally, or otherwise, responsible'.

[26] Cf. C. Schroeder, 'Corrective Justice, Liability for Increasing Risks', 465. For the terminology of 'moral luck', see B. Williams, 'Moral Luck'. For recent doubts as to the existence of moral luck, see D. Parfit, *On What Matters: Volume one*, 157. For helpful exposition of Schroeder's views, see A. Ripstein and B. Zipursky, 'Corrective Justice in an Age of Mass Torts'. See also T. Handfield and T. Pisciotta, 'Is the Risk-Liability Theory Compatible with Negligence Law?'

sanction. If one is distributing liability according to deserved sanction, it is unjust not to sanction equally persons of equal desert. If, however, this is the reason, then there is no reason why C should pay B in *Accident*, rather than some other person. We could impose a similar hardship on C without B being involved at all: this would equally ensure that C is as equally sanctioned as A. Moreover, if we required C to pay B, it seems that other victims of loss would have a legitimate complaint that B is being unjustly favoured over them. If the only concern is to sanction C on the grounds of his blameworthiness, then it is unclear why B's hardship should be favoured over that of others.

In short, the giving effect to the concern for C's desert is quite independent of any particular person's need for compensation. Thus, when construed as attempting to achieve equal deserts among persons who have behaved culpably, *risk liability* cannot justify the existence of moral liability or duty in C owed to B in particular.[27]

A second argument for *risk liability*, instead of focussing upon seeing to it that wrongful risk-takers each get what they deserve, might try to focus simply upon the 'localized'[28] distributive justice between the two parties: the person who has carelessly risked injury to the victim and the victim of an injury that was not caused by that risky behaviour. Could it not be said that *as between these two people*, it is fairer for the careless risk-taker to bear the loss, even though he did not cause it, than for the victim to receive nothing?

A standard objection to this is that it is unjustifiable to limit the potential loss-bearers to the careless risk-taker alone – why should others not be brought within this distributive scheme?[29] If the question is one of distributive justice, why single out the person who has culpably risked, but not caused, the injury among other potential loss-bearers (for example: other, more culpable, persons)? A more fundamental objection, however, is that it is not obvious that *simply* in virtue of being blameworthy that one should bear the costs of harm to others as a matter of distributive justice. Suppose that one is deciding whether to confer a benefit on D or E, and D is (overall) more blameworthy in respect of some action. Suppose, however that D has been sanctioned in relation to that blameworthiness. Is there now any further reason as a

---

[27] Cf. E. Weinrib, *The Idea of Private Law*, 114–44; P. Cane, 'Corrective Justice and Correlativity in Private Law', 484.
[28] S. Perry, 'The Moral Foundations of Tort Law', 461.
[29] For an explanation of this standard objection to localised distributive justice, see J. Gardner, 'What is Tort Law For? Part 2. The Place of Distributive Justice', 348.

matter of distributive justice to favour E over D? It seems not. Apart from blameworthiness' contribution to someone's desert (and thereby their deserving sanction), it is not clear that blameworthiness makes some *further* contribution to distributive justice. Finally, it is again the case that C's blameworthiness at any rate hardly justifies B being singled out as the beneficiary of a distributive scheme which holds that the blameworthy should pay the costs of the injured – perhaps there are those whose hardships are far greater than B's who should come first in the distributive queue.

A third argument for *risk liability* might be that risk imposers benefit from their unreasonable risk impositions and that these benefits should be disgorged. To justify liability in A to B, it would at least be necessary that A's unreasonable risk imposition constituted a wrong in relation to B. This is controversial. The more fundamental problems, however, are that much of the time momentary acts of negligence do not give rise to benefits and that such benefits as do arise would only plausibly justify liability to the extent of the benefit, rather than the extent of loss suffered.

It should be observed that nothing argued here requires us to say that it would be illegitimate to require monetary contributions to compensation funds from certain risk imposers. For instance, suppose that the state taxes cigarettes partly to fund compensation schemes for those suffering cancer attributable to passive smoking. Surely those who smoke and thereby impose risks on others could have no objection to such a tax. Part of the justification is that each individual smoker contributes to uncertainty over which smoker (or smokers) are causally responsible for individuals' cancers. But such a tax could even be justified if it were proven that an individual smoker was not a cause of any person's cancer. Part of the justification for the tax in such a circumstance would be the benefit derived from such risk impositions. None of this means, however, that any individual smoker is under a moral liability *to another* individual smoker.

Other non-causal bases of liability?

The upshot of the argument so far is that more than culpable risk creation is necessary to generate a moral liability to compensate for loss between individuals. This still leaves open the possibility that outcome responsibility (and so, causation) is not necessary to generate such a liability.

Vicarious liability stands as a potential example of liability for loss one did not cause. Of course, one may question whether vicarious liability can truly be justified. In so far as it can be justified, it is suggested, it is not inconsistent with the general moral necessity of causation. First, in virtually all cases of vicarious liability recognised in the law, it will be possible to say that the person vicariously liable was at least a factual cause of the wrong for which they are held vicariously liable. In many cases, it will also be possible to say, additionally, that the person vicariously liable is outcome responsible for the victim's loss. It is a reasonably foreseeable cost of continuing certain enterprises that they will give rise to at least certain forms of wrongdoing. Second, it may be that, in many cases, the rules on vicarious liability are justified as rules for attributing certain actions to collective entities. On that view, the collective is indeed outcome responsible for the harm. Third, even in so far as justified vicarious liability is liability without causation or without outcome responsibility, the existence of such liability would not support the idea that causation is not normally necessary for liability.

The proposition that justifiable accessorial liability to compensate requires causality cannot be defended here. However, there is a strong argument that, with an appropriately broad understanding of causation, which goes beyond a simple but-for analysis, the moral responsibility of accomplices is causal, since an accomplice needs to exert some actual influence upon the primary wrongdoer's conduct.[30]

Legal liability and responsibility

If it is true that causation matters to the existence of moral liabilities to compensate between individuals, why should legal liability to compensate depend upon the existence of moral liabilities to compensate? One reason is simply that if A is not morally liable to compensate B then it would seem to violate A's right to be free of coercion by the state to impose a legal liability upon A to do so.[31] If there is no moral ground for A's being liable to compensate B, it is difficult to see by what right the state could force A to compensate B.

Does A really have a legitimate complaint, however, if A is held liable to B in circumstances where, though A is not morally liable to B, A could legitimately be called upon to contribute to a fund to compensate victims of harm? For instance, suppose that A could legitimately be made legally liable to pay a tax for imposing risks of cancer upon others through

---

[30] See J. Gardner, 'Complicity and Causality', 128. On the explanation of the non-causal liabilities identified in Chapter 1, see Chapter 4, 189–192.

[31] On this moral right, see C. Wellman, 'The Rights Forfeiture Theory of Punishment', 372–3.

passive smoking, even if those risks have not materialised due to A's smoking. Would it be unjust for A to be required to compensate a *specific* victim of cancer caused by the effect of passive smoking? It seems so. A can legitimately complain that A is being unjustly singled out when, if the compensation scheme has not been created, other risk imposers are not being required to contribute. If this is correct, it provides strong reason not to impose tort liability upon individuals only on the ground that those individuals could legitimately be subjected to liability through other means.

This much is recognised by those who would institutionalise a version of risk liability. Schroeder and Coleman have proposed versions of this principle.[32] For both, the risk principle operates by extracting some payment from those who wrongfully increase the risk of injury, which is then allocated to a central fund or pool.[33] People who are wrongfully risked injury, and who suffer injury as a result, then make claims from this central fund rather than their injurers.[34] In this scheme, then, the culpable risk-creator pays into a central fund from which claimants seek compensation rather than individuals seeking compensation from another particular individual.

Consequentialist justifications of causation as an element of liability

The core of consequentialist theories of morality is that the right action is the action which maximises the good.[35] So far the only consequentialist theories of tort law have been developed by legal economists. The version of consequentialism most associated with legal economists is the idea of wealth-maximisation: the good to be maximised is 'wealth'.[36] The only remotely plausible version of that view considers wealth to be an instrumental proxy for maximising what is truly valuable

---

[32] J. Coleman, *Risks and Wrongs*, 306–18.

[33] For a parallel suggestion that persons convicted of criminal offences, if given fair warning, fund disability welfare schemes: M. Otsuka, *Libertarianism without Inequality*, ch 2.

[34] J. Coleman, *Risks and Wrongs*, 306–18.

[35] Cf. C. Brown, 'Consequentialize This', 751: 'The non-negotiable core of consequentialism... is the claim that an action is right, or permissible, iff it maximizes the good'.

[36] Posner initially proposed wealth-maximisation as superior to utilitarianism – seemingly because of problems with interpersonal comparisons of utility. Now he thinks that wealth-maximisation cannot be given philosophical defence but is somehow pragmatically useful: R. Posner, 'Wealth Maximisation and Tort Law: a Philosophical Inquiry', 111.

(e.g. welfare, fewer rights violations). Such an instrumentalist-proxy view is still problematic: it is often simply assumed without argument that maximising wealth will maximise, say, welfare.[37] In what follows, I will discuss wealth-maximising theories of the requirement of causation under the assumption that they can be translated into *welfare-maximising* terms.[38] The argument will be that a requirement of causation can be supported in the tort of negligence on welfare-maximising grounds if there is regular judicial over-estimation of the standard of care, and causation can be reliably ascertained, but that there is slender empirical basis for such a claim. The conclusion is that existing consequentialist analyses support a causal requirement only in the tort of negligence, and only if a questionable empirical assumption is made.

Causation and economic analysis

The starting point of legal economic analysis is that the aim of liability rules is to minimise the sum of the cost of precautions and expected loss.[39] The incidence of liability is to be tailored so as to incentivise people to take efficient precautions against the occurrence of loss. Quite simply, liability rules should incentivise people to take all and only those precautions whose (expected) cost is outweighed by their (expected) benefit.

It is relatively straightforward – in theory – to justify a causal requirement in strict liability regimes on such a basis. Suppose that a paint manufacturer cannot avoid manufacturing 1 defective paint can per 100. The defective can causes 100,000 in damage to the walls to which it is applied. Damage to walls can also occur through natural causes, costing 50,000. If the firm manufactures 100 paint cans, rationally it should stop manufacturing if its profits are less than 100,000. So long as the firm makes greater than 100,000 in profits per 100 cans (and enough profits to cover its manufacturing costs, etc.) then it would be wealth-maximising for it to continue. If, however, the firm is held liable for the additional 50,000 in damage, which it did not cause, then it may be

---

[37] R. Dworkin, 'Is Wealth a Value' 205–19. For a more sophisticated consequentialist view, see L. Kaplow and S. Shavell, *Fairness versus Welfare*.

[38] Welfare is often defined in terms of fully informed preferences. But this is problematic. See Chapter 6, 340–2 for a discussion and rejection of this concept of welfare in the context of the value of chance.

[39] H. Schäfer and C. Ott, *Lehruch der ökonomischen Analyse des Zivilrechts*, 158; C. Grechenig and A. Stremitzer, 'Der Einwand rechtmäßigen Alternativverhaltens – Rechtsvergleich, ökonomische Analyse und Implicationen für die Proportionalhaftung', 357.

deterred from beneficial activity. If the firm makes 140,000 in profits, it is wealth-maximising, but if it had to compensate for the 50,000 it would be rationally deterred from this wealth-maximising activity.[40]

It is often observed that any incentive-based picture has particular difficulty in justifying a requirement of causation under a negligence rule.[41] While requiring defendants to pay for all and only the injuries caused by their inefficient conduct does create incentives to behave efficiently, it would seem to provide a stronger incentive to behave efficiently if defendants were sanctioned simply for their inefficient behaviour. This would not result in over-deterrence: defendants need only behave efficiently to avoid liability.[42] And although this would likely cause extra administrative expense, it would also remove the costly process of determining causation in individual cases. A system which allowed claims to be brought by claimants who were risked injury and *suffered* that injury against defendants who had behaved inefficiently might well provide a better incentive to behave efficiently, while also reducing overall administrative costs.[43]

Indeed, early economic accounts generally did not build the requirement of causation into their models of negligence liability.[44] When the issue was more fully considered, most legal economists accepted that causation is superfluous under a negligence rule. Liability beyond the amount of the loss caused, or without a causal link between the inefficient behaviour and any loss would simply serve to increase incentives to take the requisite level of care (and not a more onerous, inefficient one).[45]

More recently, however, it has been claimed that a requirement of causation is wealth-maximising in a world in which judges overestimate the standard of care in negligence.[46] The basic idea is that if the standard

---

[40] See S. Shavell, 'Causation and Tort Liability', 211.

[41] R. Wright, 'Actual Causation vs. Probabilistic Linkage: the Bane of Economic Analysis', 440–1; J. Oberdiek, 'Philosophical Issues in Tort Law', 741.

[42] A. Stremitzer, 'Negligence-Based Proportional Liability', 33: 'As every injurer can avoid liability simply by meeting his duty of care and very high sanctions would certainly motivate him to do so, compliance would be perfect and the sanctions would never need to be implemented'.

[43] Cf. R. Wright, 'Actual Causation', 438.

[44] An exception: G. Calabresi, 'Concerning Cause and the Law of Torts', 85. For criticism of Calabresi, see R. Wright, 'Actual Causation', 441.

[45] M. Kahan, 'Causation and Incentives to Take Care under the Negligence Rule', 431; cited approvingly by C. Grechenig and A. Stremitzer, 'Einwand', 360. Cf. S. Shavell, 'Economic Analysis of Accident Law', 61.

[46] For a very clear exposition of this line of thought: C. Grechenig and A. Stremitzer, 'Einwand', 358–9; K. Hylton, 'Causation in Tort Law: A Reconsideration', 107–112. For a

of care is set at an inefficient level (i.e. the costs of taking the precautions are greater than the benefits) and injurers are held liable for *all* damage, which even the inefficient level would not have prevented, they have greater incentive to conform to the inefficient standard than they would have if they were liable *only* for the damage which would not have occurred had the inefficient standard been conformed to. 'Thus, if there is a causal requirement, injurers are more likely to continue to follow the efficient standard rather than the incorrect, inefficient, standard'. This can be illustrated by an example. Suppose an owner is deciding whether to deepen a concrete wall under its factory to prevent the seepage of noxious chemicals into the foundations of surrounding houses. Currently, the wall is of 1 metre (m) depth. The cost per metre one builds underground is £1.5 million (ml). P stands for 'probability'. The damage if the noxious chemicals escape at any depth underground is £100 million (ml).

Depth underground	P(Chemicals escaping at that depth)	Damage on escape
1–2m	2%	100ml
2–3m	1%	100ml
3–4m	1%	100ml

It would be efficient for the owner to extend the wall to 2m in depth since this would reduce the expected damage by 2ml at a cost of 1.5ml. However, it would not be efficient to build a further metre to 3m since this would cost 1.5ml with a reduced cost of only 1ml. Suppose, however, that a court mistakenly sets the legally required depth at 3m. How will the owner behave? If the claimant must show causation, then the owner will still be incentivised to take optimal care. This is because the owner will only be liable for escapes which a 3m depth would have prevented. The probability of a 2–3m escape is however only 1 per cent and thus the cost of the precautions (1.5m) *still* outweighs this expected liability.[47] How will the owner behave if claimants need not prove that a 3m wall would have prevented their damage? If the claimant wins whenever the

slightly less technical presentation, see R. Cooter and A. Porat, *Getting Incentives Right*, 20–5.

[47] Stremitzer seems to think that the potential injurer will *always* continue to take reasonable care where there is judicial overestimation of the standard of care. That seems incorrect, however: the effects of overestimation are merely reduced, not eliminated. See K. Hylton, 'Causation in Tort Law: A Reconsideration', 110–112.

defendant has not built to 3m, regardless of whether building at that level would have made a difference to the outcome, then the defendant is incentivised to take inefficient precautions, since there is now an expected liability of 2m and a cost of 1.5m.[48]

This is a strained account, which rests upon rather uncertain empirical claims about the regularity of judicial over-estimation of the standard of care. The empirical basis of these claims is sometimes said to be hindsight bias:[49] 'the tendency for people who have outcome knowledge (hindsight) to overestimate the probability that they would have assigned to this particular outcome in foresight'.[50] Perhaps this leads judges to overestimate the probability with which an event occurs in a certain situation, given that it has occurred. Sometimes it is said to arise from lack of information or a general 'better safe than sorry' mindset.[51]

Beyond its being empirically unsubstantiated in which contexts and to what extent this tendency exists, there are at least three further reasons why this is an unsatisfactory account. First, it may be more efficient to encourage judicial awareness of biases in assessing the ex-ante probability of outcomes rather than to insist upon a causal requirement. Second, this account could hardly claim to justify a causal requirement *generally*. In contexts where we can be confident that judges are not overestimating the standard of care, the justification falls away. So, for example, this account would seem to support the following legal rule: if a potential injurer falls significantly below the efficient standard of care, the injurer should be liable, but if the injurer has only slightly fallen below the efficient standard, the injurer should only be liable if causation is proven. The reason is that presumably we can trust the courts to identify a standard setting out *clear* cases of inefficient conduct, even if the courts cannot be trusted to identify the perfectly optimal standard. In such cases, there is little reason to insist upon causation. Third, relatedly, this account will not apply to intentional torts. What reason is there, on this account, for instance, in insisting upon a causal connection between harassment and loss in order for there to be recovery in respect of that

---

[48] Furthermore, Shavell claims: 'the administrative costs of the liability system are reduced because the volume of cases is lowered owing to the causation requirement': S. Shavell, 'Economic Analysis of Accident Law', 62–3.

[49] Cf. L. Klöhn, 'Wertende Kausalität im Spiegel von Rechtsvergleichung, Rechtsdogmatik und Rechtsökonomik', 478, referring to hindsight-bias, and A. Stremitzer, 'Negligence-Based Proportional Liability', 36.

[50] J. Koehler, 'Decision Making and the Law: Truth Barriers', 11.

[51] A. Tabbach, 'Causation, (Dis)continuity, and Incentives to Choose Levels of Care and Activity under the Negligence Rule', 140.

loss? Assuming that harassment is generally inefficient behaviour, har-assers can easily assure themselves of being free of liability by simply not engaging in repeated forms of certain conduct with certain intentions.

So it seems clear that, even if we accept that lack of information, hindsight bias, and a 'better safe than sorry' mindset do lead to judicial overestimation of the standard of care, economic analysis would require causation only in simple negligence cases.[52] To that extent there would be no conflict with the non-consequentialist responsibility account. But a conflict between the accounts does arise in so far as the economic analysis suggests that it would be efficient to dispense with a causal requirement in cases of gross negligence (or in relation to liability for higher levels of culpability). That being the case, one needs to decide whether the expected gains in efficiency are sufficient to outweigh the defendant's moral right to be free of liability unless it is morally liable to the other party.

Justifying the proof rules for causation

If the responsibility account is correct, then there is a strong moral reason for defendants not to be liable when they have not caused the claimant's injury. This moral reason is that liability forces the defendant to do what it has no moral duty to do in relation to the claimant and so, in that sense, illegitimately interferes with the defendant's freedom. Nothing *directly* follows from this, so far as the proof requirements of causation are concerned. But the moral reason not to find non-causative defendants liable in damages is clearly relevant to the choice of proof rules. The moral cost of finding someone liable who is not morally responsible must be taken into account in determining the level of belief factfinders should have before assigning liability, just as the grave injust-ice of convicting an innocent person should be taken into account in determining the required standard of proof in criminal cases.

This part begins by assessing non-consequentialist justifications of the general burden and standard of proof. As Chapter 2 demonstrated, there is a difference in the standard of proof on causation between common law jurisdictions and France and Germany. The argument will be that the general common law rule is superior to a general reversal of the

---

[52] All of this is assuming that whether A caused B's injury can be reliably determined by courts. For the analysis where causation cannot be reliably determined, see pp. 136–137.

burden of proof, the higher French/German standard, and a general non-threshold (proportionate) rule.

The second section of this part then introduces some consequentialist analyses of proof rules of causation. These analyses will be assessed more fully in Chapters 5 and 6.

The burden of proof

Why should the claimant lose where there is a perfect equality of probability between its allegations and the defendant's allegations (the common law) or why should the claimant lose where it cannot be demonstrated to any probability whether the defendant caused its injury (the common law, France, and Germany)? Familiar justifications of the general rule that the claimant bears the burden of proof for elements of its cause of action are typically laconic: 'ei incumbit probatio qui dicit, non qui negat' – 'he who asserts must prove'.[53] This is no justification at all; it is assertion without more.[54] Often, the proposition is simply considered to be self-evident.[55]

The significance of the status quo: acts and omissions

A more informative, if loose, thought is that the claimant is seeking to upset the *status quo* in so far as it seeks certain remedies against the defendant.[56] The *status quo* certainly seems to have some moral significance.[57] Suppose you are driving a train which is hurtling towards *Twin A*, who is tied to the track. It is not possible to stop the train, but it is possible to divert it to another track, on which *Twin B* is tied. Many people think you ought not to switch.

Part of the explanation of this is that it is generally thought worse to inflict an injury upon an individual than to fail to aid an individual from an equal injury.[58] In imposing a duty to compensate, where it is not

---

[53] D.22.3.2 (Paulus).

[54] Cf. G. Fletcher, *Rethinking Criminal Law*, 523: '[s]ophisticated common-law scholars despair of finding a coherent theory to explain the system's burden of persuasion practices'.

[55] I. Giesen, 'The Reversal of the Burden of Proof in the Principles of European Tort Law: A comparison with Dutch tort law and civil procedure rules', 24 ('[the general rule] is followed everywhere and is considered self-evident').

[56] H. Ahrens, 'Die Verteilung der Beweislast', 30; A. Porat and A. Stein, *Tort Liability under Uncertainty*, 38.

[57] See generally, C. Sartorio 'Moral Inertia'.

[58] Cf. ibid., 118. Some psychological studies seem to establish that litigants often view the state of affairs prior to litigation as the status quo by reference to which they judge 'gains' and 'losses'. People tend to see winning litigation as making a 'gain' and losing it

merited by the real facts, the court is inflicting a harm upon the defendant. In failing to impose a duty to compensate, where it ought to be imposed, if the truth were known, the court is failing to aid the claimant. There is therefore a slight moral asymmetry, from the internal perspective of the fact-finder deciding the case, between false positives and false negatives. This is plausibly a partial justification why, when the probability of the parties allegations are equal on causation, the claimant loses.[59]

An obvious objection looms, however. Surely it is irrational to think *generally* that a false positive is worse than a false negative: it depends. For instance, if the defendant is very rich and the claimant is very poor, then it might be thought that a false negative is much worse than a false positive. The difficulty with this suggestion is that it introduces normative considerations into the determination of evidential rules, which are arguably irrelevant at the level of the substantive law. In so far as the content of the primary rights and obligations in tort law is wealth-independent, in the sense that the existence and stringency of the parties' rights and obligations is normally independent of their relative wealth, it is inconsistent for the law of evidence to operate on entirely different considerations.

Thus, in so far as one defends a moral asymmetry as between false positives and false negatives, one cannot mean that a false positive is always harder to bear for the defendant. That is patently false. Rather, the idea must be that greater 'moral harm' or (non-distributive) *injustice* would be inflicted by a false positive than a false negative.[60] In determining what constitutes moral harm one is restricted (at least as a matter of consistency) to the types of moral consideration relevant to determining the substantive norms of liability. If so, it becomes more plausible to find an asymmetry in moral harm between false positives and negatives given

---

as a 'loss'. There is substantial evidence that people prefer avoiding losses to making gains (relative to the status quo) even where these are of relatively similar amounts. This is known as a 'framing' bias. Thus Zamir and Ritov suggest: 'The same negative outcome will typically be perceived as worse when it is the result of action rather than inaction, and a positive outcome will be seen as more gratifying when it is the result of action rather than of inaction. Faced with uncertainty, people who are loss averse thus have a bias toward omissions': 'Loss Aversion, Omission Bias, and the Burden of Proof in Civil Litigation', 166.

[59] This is supported by A. Porat and A. Stein, *Tort Liability under Uncertainty*, 38. Only a partial justification, since this explanation cannot explain why C does not bear the burden of proof for the absence of defences.

[60] Cf. R. Dworkin, *A Matter of Principle*, 89.

the prominence of the substantive act/omission distinction. Nonetheless, this does suggest that in so far as distributive considerations *are* justifiably prominent in the reasons why the defendant is liable (for example, the greater ability of the defendant to bear the loss), then the general burden of proof may be less justifiable by reference to a general moral asymmetry in false positives and false negatives.

Civility

A further reason why the claimant bears the burden of proof is based upon a principle set out by Nance: the principle of civility.[61] The basic idea is that an entailment of our duty to respect others is to presume that they have complied with 'serious social obligations'.[62] Consequently, where proof, at least on the balance of probabilities, that the defendant has breached a serious obligation is unavailable, this presumption requires a decision in favour of the defendant. The principle of civility works reasonably well at identifying which allegations must be shown by which party in a civil case. It explains, for example, why the *defendant* bears the burden of proof of showing that the claimant was behaving illegally if it is to benefit from that defence in the common law.

Nance does not explore in much detail the normative foundations of this principle. One justification is that the defendant has a moral right not to be defamed. The basis of this right is possibly the important interest an individual has in social relations; defamatory statements can lead to damaging social exclusion or tarnishing of valuable relationships.[63] Quite simply, people have an important interest in avoiding the social stigma of being publicly declared a wrongdoer. Another ground for the right not to be defamed is that my interest in freedom demands that I am not called upon to clear my name simply by the allegation of another person.[64] Of course, neither of these fairly loose underpinnings states a precise probability threshold at which the defendant loses the protection of the right. But the former gives some reason to prefer a false negative over a false positive. And it seems to render the right not to be defamed empty of content if, in cases where it is impossible to say

---

[61] D. Nance, 'Civility and the Burden of Proof'. For discussion of the idea: A. Stein, *The Foundations of Evidence Law*, 222 and H. Ho, *The Philosophy of Evidence Law*, 226. Cf. H. Prütting, *Gegenwartsprobleme der Beweislast*, 278. who speaks of relying upon the 'Richtigkeit und Vernünftigkeit' of the *status quo*.

[62] D. Nance, 'Civility and the Burden of Proof', 653.

[63] See D. Howarth, 'Libel: Its Purpose and Reform', 849–52.

[64] See A. Ripstein, *Force and Freedom*, 51–2.

whether the allegation is true, or not even probably true, I am nonethe-less found to be a wrongdoer.

The principle of civility certainly has some weight. But talk of 'stigma' and 'defamation' in relation to causation may seem misguided. While it may be plausible to think that defendants ought to be protected against a finding (without adequate substantiation) that they behaved culpably, a finding that they *caused* injury is morally neutral. This is, of course, disputable.[65] To the extent that our legal and moral duties involve duties not to *cause* injury, then causation is wrongful or constitutes the wrong.[66] That causation forms an element of the duty breached in many torts is certainly a widespread assumption.[67]

Freedom, responsibility, and casum sentiit dominus

At the risk of replacing one opaque Latin maxim with another, there is a sense in which the starting point in a liberal society is *casum sentiit dominus*: the default position is that the loss is mine to bear *unless* it is another's responsibility. Conversely, the default position is that I have a right to freedom unless I am responsible for your loss.[68] If one is attempting to pray in aid of the coercive apparatus of the state against another free individual, where the only basis of that other's liability is their responsibility, this responsibility must be positively shown. If it is impossible to show, or equally probable as not, their responsibility is simply not implicated. It is hardly consistent with my general right to freedom that I am held liable where it is equally probable as not that I am responsible for the claimant's loss. In other words, in a liberal society, one ought not to presume that another private individual is responsible rather than not.[69]

---

[65] Cf., disputing it, J. Gardner, 'Obligations and Outcomes' and J. Gardner, 'The Wrongdoing that Gets Results'.

[66] This raises a further question as to whether the principle of civility protects us from unsubstantiated allegations of socially recognised wrongdoing or allegations of wrongdoing *tout court*.

[67] For a strong defence of a contrary view in negligence, see N. McBride, 'Duties of Care: do they Really Exist?'

[68] Cf. J. Rawls, *Justice as Fairness*, 44: 'there is a general presumption against imposing legal and other restrictions on conduct without sufficient reason'.

[69] A. Stein, *Foundations of Evidence Law*, 222 argues that the claimant ought to bear the burden of proof for legal elements which 'benefit' the claimant, while the defendant bears the burden of proof for legal elements which 'benefit' the defendant. For him, this is a requirement of 'equality' (219). If the claimant bore the burden of proof for all elements of a case, then the risk of error which the burden of proof distributes would systematically favour defendants. Consequently, a distribution of the burden of proof

A framework

Under certain assumptions, the considerations discussed so far offer reasonably strong justification for the orthodox allocation of the burden of proof on causation. First, there is the general moral asymmetry between false positives and false negatives. Second, if one allows that there are wrongs with a constitutive causal element, then it can be said that civility requires presuming compliance, rather than breach, in situations of equipoise or impossibility of proof. In this sense, the law of tort can be said to embody a presumption of innocence:[70] if causing damage is an element of the wrong, then the law should not presume that the defendant has committed that wrong *unless* that claim is *at least* more probably true than not. Third, if the burden of proof on causation is not with the claimant, the defendant is held liable without it being shown even probably true that he committed a wrong against the claimant in wrongs with a constitutive causal element, and without it being shown that the defendant is responsible for the loss in other situations. If such a wrong or such responsibility is the very basis of the defendant's liability, it is odd that the defendant loses without either being shown at least more probably to have occurred than not.[71] It may finally be noted here that the justifications offered for the orthodox position are offered against the background that neither of the parties is meaningfully responsible for the inability to determine the causal issue.[72]

The framework of principles described suffers from a significant omission. In so far as any tort causes of action are not based upon breach of a duty, there is no reason why civility should demand a presumption that the defendant did not perform the action which generates the liability. Furthermore, *if* some types of strict liability are justified partly by

---

between different legal categories – those pertaining to the cause of action and those not – is necessary to distribute the risk in a more equal fashion. The difficulty with this account is that it provides no explanation of why certain claims 'benefit' the claimant while others 'benefit' the defendant. The fact that the claimant has not been contributorily negligent 'benefits' the claimant, yet the defendant bears the burden of proof in respect of it. The problem is that equality (on Stein's account) only requires that the burden of proof be distributed equally between categories of claim; it does not dictate which categories belong to which party.

[70] This presumption is approved in the civil context in *Joseph Constantine Shipping Ltd* v. *Imperial Smelting Corp. Ltd* [1942] AC 154, 194 (Lord Wright). For further discussion of it in English law: J. Stone, 'Burden of Proof and the Judicial Process'. See, similarly, A. Beever, *Rediscovering the Law of Negligence*, 447.

[71] For similar reasoning: J. Stone, 'The Burden of Proof and the Judicial Process', 270.

[72] The force of the qualifier 'meaningfully' is discussed in Chapter 5, 276–282.

notions of fair loss distribution – including the notion that one person is better able to bear the loss than another – it might be thought that a false negative is generally worse than a false positive. The substantive law 'allows' this judgement to be made, since the substantive law is itself based upon such a consideration. This issue can be left open here. The general point is that there may be greater room for re-allocation of the burden of proof where considerations of loss distribution are licensed by the normative underpinning of the substantive law.[73]

The standard of proof

A number of authors have convincingly drawn links between the balance of probability rule (the p>0.5 rule[74]), the treatment of the parties as equals, and the importance of truth in adjudication.[75] The equality claim is that the rule best expresses the idea that a false positive is as equally regrettable as a false negative. Even if we accept that this is not strictly true because of the partial asymmetry between acts and omissions, it remains reasonable to think that there is an approximate equality between the parties' interests. So if one party's case is only a bit more probable than the other's, then it is legitimate to favour that party's interest. To insist upon a higher standard of say, p > 0.75 would be to favour defendants' interests against false positives too much over claimants' interests against false negatives. And, conversely, a lower standard would privilege claimants too much. As soon as one party's case becomes more probable than not, it is legitimate to favour that party.

A second subsidiary equality-related virtue of the rule is that it is generally unbiased in the sense that there is generally (though this is ultimately an empirical question[76]) no reason to expect a greater incidence of false positives than false negatives. Sometimes claimants will succeed where they ought not and conversely. This will generally be true

---

[73] See, briefly, pp. 285–286.

[74] This is purely for shorthand; it refers to the propositions developed in Chapter 2 on the balance of probability rule. It is not being assumed that the sense of probability here conforms to mathematical probability axioms.

[75] D. Hamer, 'The Civil Standard of Proof Uncertainty: Probability, Belief and Justice', 509; A. Porat and A. Stein, Tort Liability under Uncertainty, 37; M. Geistfeld, 'The Doctrinal Unity of Alternative Liability and Market-share Liability', 461–2.

[76] As emphasised by D. Kaye, 'The Error of Equal Error Rates', 4. The fact that a relatively equal number of false positives and false negatives may be expected is clearly not a reason in itself to adopt a certain proof rule: tossing a fair coin would achieve the same distribution but this would neither treat the individual parties with sufficient respect nor would it sufficiently pursue truth.

where the probabilities vary randomly from case to case. For example, one might hazard the guess that the probability that the defendant caused the claimant's damage in some traffic accident cases will be greater than a half, and in others it will not be; there will not generally be a cluster of cases at either end of the spectrum.[77]

The connection of the balance of probability rule with truth is two-fold. First, and quite simply, in so far as a legal system endorses a lesser standard of proof, it holds people liable while considering it more likely to be true that they should not be liable for the claimant's injury. Intuitively, there is a significant moral difference between saying to a litigant: 'You are liable even though we think it is more likely not to be the case that you are liable' and 'You are liable because we think it is more likely to be true than not that you are liable'. Since the defendant's obligation to pay damages is only objectively triggered by its being the case in the world that it caused the claimant's loss, there is good reason that standards of proof should aim more towards truth than not. Second, the balance of probability rule minimises the expected number of errors (false positives and false negatives).[78] The simple point here is that 'judges will maximise the total number of correct decisions by treating their best chances of arriving at the factually correct result as decisive'.[79]

So the balance of probability rule has strong justification in the ideas of approximate equality and truth-seeking.[80] If this is correct, it follows that the higher standard of proof in German and French law is problematic.[81] To bolster this conclusion, it will be helpful to consider the criticisms of the balance of probability rule made by some German scholars.[82] There are two recurring criticisms of the common law position. First, it is claimed that since a decision in favour of the claimant is

---

[77] For the effect of base-rates on the distribution of errors: L. Laudan, *Truth, Error and the Criminal Law*, ch 3.

[78] See, for example, D. Hamer, 'Probabilistic Standards of Proof: Their Complements and the Errors that are Expected to Flow from Them'.

[79] A. Porat and A. Stein, *Tort Liability under Uncertainty*, 18.

[80] Cf. H. Ho, *Philosophy of Evidence Law*, 171; this is not to deny that values other than 'truth' are relevant as Ho also makes clear (78ff).

[81] It must be remembered, however, that the difference between the two standards is not as stark as has sometimes been claimed. See Chapter 2, 53–59.

[82] A number of German scholars have however supported the balance of probability rule on normative grounds: see, for example, G. Kegel, 'Der Individualanscheinsbeweis und die Verteilung der Beweislast nach überwiegender Wahrscheinlichkeit'. Kegel appeals to the idea that under conditions of uncertainty, it is better to hold for the party with more probable right than the other (344). See, similarly, R. Motsch, *Vom rechtsgenügenden Beweis*, 248.

only truly justified when the facts *actually* exist which are necessary and sufficient for the claim, the defendant has a *right* only to be found liable in such circumstances.[83] From this it is said to follow that a decision more probably correct than not is not enough: courts must insist upon higher standards of approximation to the truth – a very high probability, at the least.[84] The difficulty with this argument is that it does not take into account the claimant's corresponding 'right' not to lose, when the facts actually hold. The question is how these rights or interests are to be balanced. Nor does it explain why a lower standard of proof, closer to the balance of probability, is acceptable under §287 ZPO.[85] Second, some have rejected the claim that the balance of probability rule maximises the number of correct decisions. Katzenmeier argues that the uncertainty over all estimations of the probability of the parties' individual claims in civil cases, and the difficulty in arriving at the global probability of a party's case, makes the minimisation of error claim (empirically) untenable.[86] This might be true, but it does not follow that the court ought not to act upon what it takes to be its best chances of arriving at the truth.

Proportional liability rules

Why should one adopt a burden of proof rule and a standard of proof rule rather than a rule which awards liability in damages in proportion to the probability of the claimant's allegation? Porat and Stein argue that a thorough-going commitment to equality in the design of rules of proof should generate a rule where each party is successful to the extent of the probability of their allegation.[87] This can be taken as both a challenge to the burden of proof and the standard of proof. In burden of proof cases, where there is a perfect equipoise between the parties'

---

[83] G. Mäsch, *Chance und Schaden*, 129.   [84] Ibid.

[85] See, on this provision, Chapter 2, 56–59.

[86] C. Katzenmeier, 'Beweismaßreduzierung und probabilistische Proportionalhaftung', 213, with references to others rehearsing this criticism.

[87] A. Porat and A. Stein, *Tort Liability under Uncertainty*, refers to this as the 'ideal implementation of the equality principle', 38. This idea is of considerable vintage. Pascal and Fermat (and Cardano) thought that the appropriate distribution of the stakes in an interrupted game of chance was according to the probability of reaching the relevant number of 'points' (determined at the time of interruption), upon which the parties agreed. See A. Hald, *A History of Probability and Statistics and Their Use before 1750*, ch 5. Leibniz seems to be one of the first to suggest applying such a rule in *litigation*. See N. Rescher, 'Leibniz, Keynes, and the Rabbis on a Problem of Distributive Justice'. For a similar, more recent, treatment inspired by this idea: J. Coons, 'Approaches to Court Imposed Compromise – the Uses of Doubt and Reason', 755–60, 778.

allegations on this view, the claimant ought to succeed in proportion to the 50 per cent probability that the defendant caused its damage, rather than failing entirely. And in cases where one party's allegations are more probable than the other's, the balance of probability rule is both too generous and too severe: where the claimant's allegation is only just more probable than not, the claimant recovers all of its damage. If the allegation is less than more probable than not, the claim totally fails. If, however, a purely probabilistic approach were taken then the claimant would recover damages to the extent of the probability that the defendant was liable in damages.[88]

There is indeed an intuitive sense in which the *burden of proof* seems to treat the parties unequally. Where the parties' allegations are of perfectly equal probabilistic strength, on the face of it, there is as much reason for the defendant to lose as the claimant to win. However, this does not yet entail proportional to the probability liability (PL), however. Why not give each party the 50 per cent chance of winning (by tossing a coin)? There are potential answers to this question; the point is only that the answer is not wholly determined by a commitment to equality. Most importantly, in any event, as we argued above, there is an asymmetry between false positives and false negatives such that the *apparent* equality in the parties' claim is indeed only apparent.

It is less obvious why the balance of probability rule should be thought to be inferior in terms of equality compared to PL. What notion of equality do Porat and Stein have in mind? It seems that their implicit premise is something like this: 'the strength (in justice) of parties' claims varies completely in proportion to their probabilistic likelihood'.[89] So if the probability of each party's allegation is 50 per cent, then both have an equal claim to the good. But if one party's allegation is 51 per cent, and the other 49 per cent, then the other's claim is greater – *but only to the extent of* 1 per cent.

There are at least four basic objections to this view. First, courts should attempt to ascertain the truth because the defendant's obligation is only triggered by the facts. That is, they should try to ascertain the truth, and, recognising that certainty is not available, set thresholds at which evidence should be taken to be true.

The reason truth matters is simple. The defendant's obligation to pay damages is only triggered by his actually having caused the claimant's loss. The defendant is only objectively under a moral obligation to compensate

---

[88] See further Chapter 6, 356–367.   [89] Cf. J. Broome, *Weighing Goods*, 95.

if it has actually caused the loss. And whatever the causal truth is, it is all or nothing: the defendant either caused the damage or it did not.[90] Setting a standard of proof recognises that it is the defendant's actually having caused the claimant's injury which matters.

It does not follow that because the defendant's obligation is only objectively triggered by his actually having caused the loss that the court must be *certain* that the defendant caused it. I may only objectively be permitted to harm another person if they are actually posing a threat to my life, but it may still be permissible, relative to the evidence, for me to harm them if I reasonably believe there is a strong probability that they are imminently about to harm me. But if I harm someone in self-defence who actually was posing no threat to me, even though I reasonably believed that they were, I wrong them. Similarly, though it is not object-ively permissible to impose liability upon me when I have not caused the claimant's injury, it may be permissible to do so when there is a certain probability, less than a certainty, that I have caused the injury.

A second objection is that there is plausibly a threshold of probability below which one must not impose liability upon the defendant. To make the defendant liable below a certain threshold of belief in their actually being liable is like recklessly risking them harm. The analogy between acting under reasonable ignorance in self-defence and judicial decision-making under uncertainty may be pressed further here. Con-sider *Kill or Don't Kill*. Suppose that you can intervene to save A from what appears to be a very serious wrongful attack by B, but *only* by killing B. One is, however, uncertain as to whether B is the one who is wrongfully attacking A. In this case, there is surely a threshold degree of belief below which it is impermissible to inflict any injury whatso-ever upon B. If only killing B will prevent A's death, then either one kills B or not. If one's degree of belief as to whether it is indeed B who is the attacker falls below a certain level, then it is impermissible to harm B at all. It would be absurd to think that if one's degree of belief fell below a certain level, that it would be permissible to harm B to a lesser extent.[91]

---

[90] Even if it is meaningful to speak of 'causal potency' and so c can be more or less a cause of e, the notion of causal potency here is not a probabilistic one.

[91] The idea that there is deontological constraint against harming people when one's belief that they are liable to be harmed falls below a certain level is challenged by F. Jackson and M. Smith, 'Absolutist Moral Theories and Uncertainty', 280. Their objection is to my mind defused by R. Aboodi, A. Borer, and D. Enoch, 'Deontology, Individualism, Uncertainty: A Reply to Jackson and Smith'.

The question is to what extent tort litigation is like *Kill or Don't Kill*.[92] That is: is there a level of belief below which it is not permissible to inflict *any* liability upon the defendant? Proponents of PL (proportionists) say there is not. Rather, it is permissible to make a defendant pay in a situation where there is, say, an 80 per cent probability that it did not cause the loss. In such a situation, the defendant pays 20 per cent of the claimant's loss. In principle, for proportionists, there is no threshold probability below which it is impermissible to hold the defendant liable.[93]

There certainly seem to be some situations in which tort litigation is like *Kill or Don't Kill*.[94] Suppose that there is a 0.3 probability that D was negligent and a 0.8 probability that D's negligence caused C's loss. Let us assume the conjunction rule applies such that there is a 0.24 probability that D is liable. A thorough-going proportionist should say that it is fairer to allow C to recover 0.24 of C's loss here. But most people would, I think, consider it deeply unjust to impose liability (of any significant amount) upon someone in respect of whom there was a 70 per cent chance that they behaved without fault (in a situation where only fault-based liability is just). There seems to be a threshold probability below which it is simply not fair to hold people liable on the basis that they were negligent when negligence is (substantively) required for their liability to be just.

Admittedly, it is difficult to prove that there is such a threshold in relation to causation. It suffices to say for the moment that there seems to be considerable injustice in holding a person liable (in any amount) when you strongly believe (e.g. $p > 0.7$) they did not cause any loss. This amounts to saying: 'although I know that you only actually have a duty to pay compensation when you have caused harm, and so you ought only to be liable if you caused the claimant's injury, and although I have very strong grounds for believing that you did not cause the claimant's injury, you are nonetheless liable in respect of it'. It is hard to believe that this is consistent with the defendant's general right to be free unless it is responsible for another's injury.

---

[92] Of course, there is an obvious distinction between the two in that any amount of taking from the defendant is always going to benefit the claimant in tort litigation, whereas only one specific action can be performed against B to save A in *Kill or Don't Kill*.

[93] There may, of course, be reasons of efficiency for a threshold to oust speculative claims.

[94] Virtually everyone accepts that criminal punishment is like this. Punishment in proportion to the probability, with no threshold of beyond reasonable doubt, is morally diabolical. Alas, not everyone thinks this: T. Fisher 'Conviction without Conviction'.

A third objection is that while proportionism makes sense with divisible goods, it does not make sense with indivisible goods. Suppose that a new heart will more probably work with *Twin A* than *Twin B*, both of whom urgently need a transplant. It would obviously make no sense to give each a proportionate share (!). It might make sense to give each a chance of having the heart in proportion to the size that the heart transplant would be successful (by tossing a biased coin). But that situation needs an all-or-nothing rule.

Clearly tort litigation is quite different. In the *Twins* case, necessarily no justice will be done if the good is divided – or at least, it is certain that more injustice will be done if the good is divided.[95] But the divisibility of damages awards means that PL can always *potentially* achieve some justice, though it will *certainly* always also lead to injustice (since it is certain always to make a mistake – be it a partial false positive or a partial false negative).

Nonetheless, there is a clear sense in which the benefits and burdens distributed by tort law – legal rights to the enforcement of one's moral right to corrective justice (and correlative legal duties) – are indivisible. If I do not have a duty of corrective justice, I owe nothing at all. If I do have a duty of corrective justice, then in principle, I owe full reparation, subject to countervailing distributive considerations (e.g. the claimant's contributory negligence).[96] Attempting to enforce the rights and duties in corrective justice is necessarily an all-or-nothing exercise, since those rights and duties simply are all-or-nothing. Although the strength of the parties' claims might vary according to their probabilistic strength, they are claims either to the legal enforcement of a moral duty (subject to defences), which itself requires full compensation or claims to the legal finding that one is not under a moral duty to make correction, that one has *no obligation whatsoever*. The moral reality which legal rights and duties of corrective justice track is all-or-nothing.

But surely one can conform *more* or *less* to one's duties of corrective justice? If one owes £10 in compensation, then paying £8 is more conformant than paying £5. This is true. But to say that someone should pay 50 per cent damages if the probability that they caused harm is 50 per cent rather than nothing is not because this will do *more* corrective justice. It might do, but it might not. The increasing probabilistic

---

[95] Perhaps there is a residual injustice in the *Twins* case, such that the loser should be compensated to the extent of the difference between the strength of his claim and that of the other twin.

[96] Cf. J. Gardner, 'What is Tort Law for? Part 2. The Role of Distributive Justice'.

strength of the parties' entitlement is an increasing entitlement to everything or nothing. The more probable my case, the greater my claim to a finding that I am owed a duty of corrective justice. In short, there is a difference between being entitled to a proportion of x, and one's entitlement to x increasing proportionately to the probability of one's being entitled to x.

A fourth objection is that adopting a system of proportional liability generally leads to more expected injustice (departures from the true rights and obligations of the parties) than a PL regime.[97] Under a PL regime, the total amount of expected injustice is greater than that under BPR.[98] To see this, suppose that the probability of the claimant's (C) having been injured by the defendant (D) is p and the probability that this is not the case is $1\text{-}p$. Suppose further that we decide to award damages in proportion to the probability of the claimant's case on causation. Finally, suppose, for simplicity, that the value of C's claim is 1. If C is awarded damages in proportion to p, then the amount by which C is short-changed if C's claim is true is $(1\text{-}p) \times 1 = 1 - p$. Similarly, the amount by which D overpays if C's claim is not true is $p \times 1 = p$. The total expected amount of departure from the true rights and obligations of the parties is then as follows:

(Probability of getting it wrong as against the claimant x amount of departure from claimant's entitlement (short-changing)) + (Probability of getting it wrong as against the defendant x amount of departure from the defendant's obligation (over-charging))

Total expected injustice value (TEIV): $p(1 - p) + (1 - p)p = 2p - 2p^2 = 2p(1 - p)$

Now suppose that the claimant's case is more probable than not ($0.5 < p < 1$). If we operated a simple all-or-nothing rule where $p>0.5$, then the expected injustice value would be $(1 - p) \times 1 = 1 - p$. This value will always be less than under *TEIV* where $p>0.5$ (since we are at least multiplying $(1 - p)$ by greater than 1 under *TEIV*). The fact that PL produces greater expected total injustice is not decisive against it, any more than the fact that a rule is not welfare-maximising is decisive against it.[99] But it does weaken the claim that PL is somehow a

---

[97] The situations in which this may not be so are briefly discussed in Chapter 6, 356–360.

[98] See D.H. Kaye, 'The limits of the Preponderance of the Evidence Standard: Justifiably Naked Statistical Evidence and Multiple Causation'.

[99] It should also be noted that while PL leads to greater overall expected injustice than the BPR, it does lead to a smaller expected amount of *large* errors: see N. Orloff and J. Stedinger, 'A Framework for Evaluating the Preponderance-of-the-evidence Standard of Proof', 1165–6.

'second-best' attempt to achieve corrective justice, since it leads to a greater total amount of departure from corrective justice than the $p > 0.5$ rule.[100]

We have offered four considerations against a general proportional liability rule. First, courts should attempt to seek the truth because the facts actually trigger the defendant's obligation. Second, defendants probably have a right not to be risked harm below a threshold degree of probability of their being liable. Third, the rights and duties in tort law are themselves all-or-nothing. Fourth, PL generally leads to greater expected injustice than the BPR.

Consequentialist justifications of the burden and standard of proof

The standard economic justification for the burden of proof is simply that it saves enforcement costs. If the social cost of an error is assumed to be equal between claimants and defendants, and if there is no reason for believing the claimant's case over the defendant's, then it is better simply to save on the costs of enforcement as well as the costs of calculating damages and any transaction costs involved in performance.[101]

As to the standard of proof, the BPR is said to be generally sound. The rule is allegedly a sound mid-position: it encourages private individuals to bring suit by granting them full damages where their allegations are more probable than not – thus allowing litigation to promote deterrence – while also discouraging frivolous over-use of the licence to sue, which would supposedly be the effect of a general probabilistic liability regime without a threshold probability requirement.[102]

A second virtue of the BPR is that it minimises the overall amount of expected loss from wrongful transfers (false positives or false negatives) as compared to other decision rules.[103] This is the same point, with the same proof, as the one we laid out above when comparing BPR with PL in relation to expected total injustice. From an economic perspective, this virtue is somewhat limited, or at least unclear, however. The analysis does not take into account the effect of the BPR or PL on optimal incentives.

---

[100] For the claim that proportional liability may be a second-best implementation of corrective justice in certain circumstances, see R. Wright, 'Liability for Possible Wrongs', 1326.

[101] R. Posner, *Economic Analysis of Law*, 7th edition, 647.

[102] A. Porat and A. Stein, *Tort Liability under Uncertainty*, 29–34. A quite different efficiency-based explanation of its general soundness is given by S. Leshem and G. Miller, 'All-or-nothing versus Proportionate Damages'.

[103] D.H. Kaye, 'The Limits of the Preponderance of the Evidence Standard: Justifiably Naked Statistical Evidence and Multiple Causation', 500.

But the burden of proof and the BPR are often considered to be efficient only in situations where they do not give rise to pervasive gaps in incentives concerning primary behaviour. Two situations can be identified where there is at least *prima facie* plausibility that the BPR gives rise to a problem of underdeterrence. The first is where it is predictable by the defendant that the ex-post (at the time of the litigation) probability of causation if he behaves negligently will be less than 0.5.[104] The claim is often made in the context of medical treatment.[105] The suggestion is that patients typically face antecedent risks of developing the loss in respect of which they are seeking compensation which are above 50 per cent (or significantly high such that the ex-post probability of causation is less than 50 per cent). As an illustration, Porat develops a somewhat idealised example in which the average ex-ante probability of survival in a hospital accident and emergency ward is 30 per cent. In such cases, it is said, doctors have no incentive to behave carefully.

The second situation is one in which the defendant can predict that there will be impossibility of proof as opposed to measurable probabilities ex-post. That is to say, the defendant can predict that there will be a burden of proof situation in relation to causation at the time of the litigation. The result again is that the defendant is provided ex-ante with no incentive by the law of tort to take the efficient level of care. A potential example is asbestos exposure in relation to mesothelioma. It may be predictable ex-ante that the probability of causation ex-post *in respect of mesothelioma* will be unascertainable. So the unifying feature of these situations is the ex-ante predictable inability of claimants to prove causation on the balance of probability.[106]

The solution to this problem of underdeterrence is sometimes said to be proportional liability.[107] Again, in a world in which judges (or regulators) do not overestimate the required standard of care, and in which

---

[104] For a clear account of such situations, see A. Porat, 'Misalignments in Tort Law', 82, 108.

[105] See Chapter 5 at 217–218; 237–239; 253; 257–260; and Chapter 6 at 338 for such claims in a variety of other contexts.

[106] There are thus similar problems here as with judgment proof defendants: cf. L. Klöhn, 'Wertende Kausalität im Spiegel von Rechtsvergleichung, Rechtsdogmatik und Rechtsökonomik', 455.

[107] Cf., for example, C. Grechenig and A. Stremitzer, 'Der Einwand rechtmäßigen Alternativverhaltens – Rechtsvergleich, ökonomische Analyse und Implikationen für die Proportionalhaftung'.

causation of injury could be determined ex-post with certainty, there would in principle be no reason to have proportional liability here, rather than full liability.[108] However, in so far as such over-estimation occurs, imposing full liability would re-introduce the problem of over-deterrence, which the introduction of the causation requirement is intended to reduce.[109]

There are two kinds of question one needs to ask about such a proposal. First, is it empirically convincing? Second, if it is, should the inefficiency of the BPR lead us to reject it, given the non-consequentialist considerations which support it? The first question clearly cannot be asked in the abstract. Whether defendants can reliably predict ex-ante that causal proof ex-post will be impossible and whether that leads them, or some number of them, not to adhere to legally required standards of conduct clearly depends upon a variety of factual circumstances. These issues are addressed in Chapter 5.

Conclusions

The aim has been to offer a limited defence of the rule that the claimant prove causation on the balance of probability. The argument can be summarised as follows. Causation is generally necessary for responsibility. Liability should be based upon responsibility because this responsibility is what creates a moral liability in the defendant to compensate the claimant. Without such a liability, the claimant forces the defendant to do something he has no duty to do, and so interferes with his general right to freedom.

The claimant bears the burden of proof on causation because: (i) a false positive on causation is slightly more unjust than a false negative, (ii) the defendant has a claim not to be designated as a wrongdoer without this at least being more likely to be true than not, (iii) the default position is that the defendant is free to pursue his own ends unless he is responsible for another's injury. The balance of probability rule is prima facie superior to the higher standard of proof in French and German law because it is more representative of the approximate equality of the parties' interests against false positives and false negatives. The rule is also prima facie superior to a non-threshold, proportionate rule, for the four reasons described.

---

[108] See pp. 118–119.
[109] See A. Stremitzer, 'Negligence-Based Proportional Liability', 36ff.

The main challenge described here to this basic position is the consequentialist one that reliably predictable causal uncertainty leads to underdeterrence. Later chapters address this challenge. The non-consequentialist considerations set out here help to see this problem in a clearer light, as a conflict between a constraint upon using defendants as a means to promote general welfare and the demands of welfare.

4   Defendant indeterminacy: full liability and proportional liability

This chapter begins the examination of departures from the general proof of causation rules. Its central subject is that of rules which allow a claimant to obtain full or partial compensatory damages from a defendant despite its not being shown to the requisite standard of proof that the defendant was a cause of the claimant's injury where:

(1) The claimant is proven, according to the standard proof, to have suffered an injury as a result of a tort;

(2) there are a number of persons each of whom has, independently of the others, behaved in such a way that they may have been a cause of the claimant's injury;

(3) each such person would be liable in damages to the claimant if their conduct were proven to be a cause of the claimant's injury;

(4) it is impossible to determine according to the standard of proof whether any such person has been a cause of the claimant's injury, though it is proven that at least one has been a cause of the claimant's injury.

Situations to which such rules are applied are termed here situations of 'defendant indeterminacy' or cases involving the 'indeterminate defendant problem'. As this suggests, the central difficulty in such cases is identifying *which* defendant(s) was a cause of the claimant's injury. Here is a classic example:

> *Two hunters.* D1, D2, and C are on a hunting trip. D1 and D2 negligently fire in the direction of C. One bullet strikes C but it cannot be determined, due to the simultaneity of the shots, and the similarity of the bullets used, which of D1 and D2 caused C's injury.

Two variants of this central situation are also discussed. The first can be called the 'extent of loss' variant. This occurs where the claimant has suffered *multiple* injuries as a result of distinct torts, where these injuries have caused losses of different extent, but it cannot be determined which person, among a group of persons, each of whom could have been a tortious cause of any of the claimant's injuries, caused which injury. This encompasses two situations: where the injuries inflicted are of different, *known*, extents (e.g. one eye injury and one leg injury); where the injuries inflicted are of different, *unknown*, extents (each defendant has caused some part of a divisible injury, but it cannot be determined precisely how much is attributable to each defendant).

The second variant can be called the 'causative defendants' variant. This occurs where there are a number of persons, each of whom is shown, according to the standard of proof, to have been a tortious cause of injury to *someone*, where that person may be the claimant, but this cannot be determined according to the standard of proof, though it is known that the claimant has been the victim of a compensable tort at the hands of one of the persons. For example, suppose that C1 and C2 have ingested defective drugs manufactured by D1 and D2 and that D1 and D2 have each certainly caused injury to one of C1 and C2, but it cannot be determined which of D1 and D2 caused which claimant's injury.

These rules are dealt with first for two reasons. First, a rule permitting recovery under defendant indeterminacy is the earliest recognised departure from proof of causation in the common law and France and Germany.[1] Consequently, and especially in France and Germany, defendant indeterminacy rules are considered a core form of exceptional rule and other rules are often conceived of as extensions of this basic core case.[2] A proper understanding of the legal doctrine in these countries thus moves out, as it were, from the case of defendant indeterminacy. Second, it will be suggested that if liability cannot be justified in these situations, especially the causative defendants variant, it will become significantly more difficult to justify in situations where the defendant has not been shown to have caused the claimant's injury to the requisite standard of proof and the injury was possibly caused by entirely non-tortious causes. These cases might thus be said to have a justificatory priority over other exceptional rules.

This chapter first provides an analysis of the development of the modern form of such rules in each system which recognises them. This discussion focuses upon the scope, conceptualisation, and justifications offered for these doctrines. Second, the justifications offered for each

---

[1] See pp. 141–142; 161–162; 170–171; 155–156.   [2] Ibid.

exceptional doctrine in the cases and legal literature are critically analysed. It will be argued that some of the justifications for liability fail but
that an exceptional rule applicable to the central defendant indeterminacy situation and its variants can be justified. The chapter concludes by
setting out the form that a defendant indeterminacy rule should take.

Germany: §830 I 2 BGB

The German Civil Code (the *Bürgerliches Gesetzbuch* – BGB) contains a
provision which creates full liability in cases of defendant indeterminacy, §830 I 2 BGB. The context and basic import of this provision are
introduced first. Second, the nature of the liability under that provision
is discussed. Third, the requirements for the application of §830 I 2 BGB
are explained in more detail; the aim of this discussion is to explore the
extent to which the scope of the provision follows from a particular
principle or set of principles.

Introduction to §830 I 2 BGB

§830 I BGB provides as follows:[3]

1 If several persons (*mehrere*) have caused injury through a jointly
undertaken delict, each person is liable for the injury. 2 The same applies
where it cannot be established which of several participants (*Beteiligten*)
has caused the injury by his act.

This inspiration for this provision is traceable through nineteenth-
century German case law to Roman law.[4] The Roman jurists had discussed a case where it was unclear which wrongful actor had killed a
slave, where each had inflicted blows upon the slave, and had held that
each person would nonetheless be liable for the slave's killing.[5]
Nineteenth-century courts often cited these Roman texts to justify liability in cases involving brawls where the causative defendant among a

---

[3] 'Haben mehrere durch eine gemeinschaftlich begangene unerlaubte Handlung einen
Schaden verursacht, so ist jeder für den Schaden verantwortlich. Das Gleiche gilt, wenn
sich nicht ermitteln lässt, wer von mehreren Beteiligten den Schaden durch seine
Handlung verursacht hat'.

[4] C. Kruse, *Alternative Kausalität*, 4ff, 136ff.

[5] D.9.2.51.1 (Julian); D.9.2.11.2 (Ulpian). On balance, these texts do deal with true
defendant indeterminacy situations. See, for a defence of that view, J. Kortmann, 'Ab alio
ictu(s): Misconceptions about Julian's View on Causation'. For further discussion of them:
Fairchild v. *Glenhaven Funeral Services* [2003] 1 AC 32, 113ff (Lord Rodger); C. Kruse,
Alternative Kausalität, 9ff. Cf. B. Sirks, 'The Delictual Origin, Penal Nature, and
Reipersecutory Object of the *actio damni iniuriae legis Aquiliae*', 336 n. 111.

group of attackers could not be identified.[6] This type of situation (along with cases where the *extent* of a defendant's known contribution to damage was unascertainable[7]) was the core example of a situation to which the rule given by the BGB draft commissions should apply.[8] Although there are ambiguous overtones of accessorial liability in the cases involving brawls, the discussions of the draft §830 I 2 BGB make clear that the provision is intended to apply to cases where the defendants have *not* acted in common.[9] These discussions also suggest that the concept of a participant (*Beteiligter*) does not imply any kind of relationship between the potentially causative defendants.[10] The final text of §830 I BGB, however, leaves the differentiation between a rule of accessorial liability, which is the subject of the first sentence of the provision, from a rule dealing solely with defendant indeterminacy in the second sentence, to implication.[11]

Despite these ambiguities, the situations to which §830 I 2 BGB will apply are, by and large, clear. Six conditions must be established:

(1) It must be the case that more than one person has acted, each person independently[12] of the other, in such a way that each person's conduct increases the risk of injury to the claimant.[13]

---

[6] Amstgericht Celle, SeuffArch 27 (1873), 40 no. 28; RGZ 1 89 (1879); RG JW 1886, 153 no. 34 (1886); RGZ 23, 158 (1879).

[7] Cf. especially von Kübel's draft: discussed in T. Mehring, *Beteiligung und Rechtswidrigkeit bei §830 I 2 BGB*, 21–3; C. Kruse, *Alternative Kausalität*, 150ff.

[8] T. Mehring, *Beteiligung und Rechtswidrigkeit*, 24; C. Kruse, *Alternative Kausalität*, 155.

[9] Cf. §714 of the first draft, which explicitly distinguishes where defendants have acted 'nicht gemeinsam': T. Mehring, *Beteiligung und Rechtswidrigkeit*, 17.

[10] The concept was added at a late stage in the drafting proceedings without any suggestion that it changed previous references simply to 'mehrere': T. Mehring, *Beteiligung und Rechtswidrigkeit*, 25. It may be that the concept was intended to refer to the case of *Anteilszweifel*. See p.143.

[11] C. Kruse, *Alternative Kausalität*, 154: it is to be implied 'from systematic considerations' (*aus der Systematik*).

[12] Older cases concerning §830 I 2 BGB *had* insisted upon a particular 'objective' relationship existing between the defendants' possibly causative activities (the requirement of 'unity of process' (*einheitlicher Lebensvorgang*)): RGZ 58, 357, 361; 96, 224, 226; BGHZ 25, 271, 274; 33, 286, 291; 55; 86, 93, 95. There is virtual unanimity in the literature that this requirement is no longer necessary. See, for example, F. Bydlinski, 'Aktuelle Streitfragen um die alternative Kausalität', 11ff; M. Bauer, 'Die Problematik gesamtschuldnerischer Haftung trotz ungeklärter Verursachung', 7; T. Mehring, *Beteiligung und Rechtswidrigkeit*, 49–52; L. Röckrath, *Kausalität, Wahrscheinlichkeit, und Haftung*, 152; G. Wagner, 'Commentary on §830 I 2 BGB', [59]. Compare the insistence of a single agent in English law: see pp. 233–235.

[13] Strictly *mere* risk is not enough: See pp. 150–151.

(2) Either (a) the risk-increasing conduct of only one such person was a cause of the claimant's injury or (b) the risk-increasing conduct of some such persons caused the claimant's damage.

(3) Each person's conduct may have caused the entirety of the claimant's damage.

(4) Either (a) it is not possible to determine which person(s) caused the damage or (b) it is not possible to determine the extent of the damage caused by each person.

(5) Apart from proof of natural causation, the claimant has satisfied the other conditions of a cause of action against each person.[14]

(6) The claimant must not be able to establish that any individual person, against whom it seeks to rely upon §830 I 2 BGB, was a wrongful cause of its injury.

These conditions envisage two distinct kinds of situation. The first involves a doubt entirely as to the causal author of the injury (*Urheberszweifel*). For example, the claimant has been struck by one bullet and it cannot be determined whether it came from D1 or D2's gun. Assuming D1 and D2 would be liable if causation were shown against them, each is liable in full, jointly and severally, under §830 I 2 BGB. The second situation involves a doubt as to the *extent* of injuries caused by a defendant (*Anteilszweifel*) (the first variant mentioned above[15]). Suppose that the claimant has been struck by two bullets, one from D1 and one from D2. One bullet caused a small injury, evaluated at £1000. The other caused extraordinary injuries, evaluated at £150,000. It is impossible to determine whose bullet caused which injury. Each defendant is individually certainly liable for £1000 on ordinary principles. By virtue of §830 I 2 BGB, each would also be jointly and severally liable for £149,000.

The nature of liability under §830 I 2 BGB

The legal nature of liability under §830 I 2 BGB is disputed. On the one hand, the BGH has sometimes described it as a cause of action.[16] On the other, it has been described as a proof rule: a reversal of the burden of proof.[17]

The better view is that §830 I 2 BGB creates a reversal of the legal burden of proof. First, there is a close convergence in function between §830 I 2 BGB and a burden of proof rule. §830 I 2 BGB determines what the

---

[14] BGH NJW 1971, 506, 508ff. See C. Eberl-Borges, 'Commentary on §830 I 2 BGB', [67]; G. Wagner, 'Commentary on §830 I 2 BGB', [44].

[15] See p.139.

[16] BGH NJW 1976, 1934, 1935; BGH NJW 1979, 544 ('im Interesse Geschädigten neue abgewandelte Haftungtatbestände'); BGH NJW 1994, 932, 934.

[17] Earlier BGH decisions favoured this formulation: BGH NJW 1971, 506, 507; BGH NJW 1957, 1834.

court must do in certain circumstances where the causal issue cannot be determined according to the standard of proof. Second, the application of §830 I 2 BGB is parasitic upon proof that each defendant fulfils some cause of action (except for the element of causation); conceiving of it as a burden of proof rule captures this parasitic nature. Certainly, this is not conclusive – one could capture these features by treating §830 I 2 BGB as a *sui generis* liability rule. Analytical parsimony is served, however, if one locates §830 I 2 BGB within the framework of burden of proof rules.

Bydlinski objects that the burden of proof view leads to a paradox: despite its being known (in a two-defendant case) that only one defendant has caused the damage, both are taken to have caused the damage.[18] There is nothing paradoxical about this. The court is not *asserting* that both defendants caused the damage; it is merely acting, fictionally, *as if* both did.[19]

The rationalisation of the requirements for the application of §830 I 2 BGB

The requirement that the claimant be the victim of a tort caused by at least one of a number of persons each of whom may have caused the injury by a tort

It follows from conditions (1)–(5) that the claimant must have a complete cause of action against at least one of a group of persons (against which being, of course, unknown) each of whom has behaved wrongfully in relation to it. That is: according to the relevant substantive norms of the law of tort, the claimant ought to be compensated by at least one of an identified group of persons (*festehende Ersatzberechtigung*). Therefore, §830 I 2 BGB does not apply to cases where the claimant's damage may have been caused entirely by non-tortious causes (for example, a pre-existing illness) or by the claimant's negligence.[20]

---

[18] F. Bydlinski, 'Aktuelle Streitfragen', 8 ('abwegig'). The point is also made by H. Koziol, *Grundfragen des Schadenersatzrechts*, 142.

[19] Cf. Wagner's (compatible) view that §830 I 2 BGB, [37]–[38] operates first by reducing the standard of proof on natural causation whereupon the burden of proof falls upon each defendant to demonstrate that it did not cause the claimant's damage: G. Wagner, 'Commentary on §830 I 2 BGB'.

[20] BGH NJW 1973, 993, 994. Most authors accept that *de lege lata* §830 I 2 BGB does not apply to such cases: for example, C. Eberl-Borges, 'Commentary on §830 I 2 BGB', [83]; L. Röckrath, *Kausalität*, 179; G. Wagner, 'Commentary on §830 I 2 BGB' 46. G. Mäsch, Chance und Schaden,136 ('ganz überwiegende Meinung'). Cf K. Larenz and C. Canaris, *Lehrbuch des Schuldrechts*, 13th edition 1994, §82 II 3b, 578, describing the restriction of liability as 'unverdienten Glücksfall' (undeserved fortune) for the defendant, and denying such a restriction *de lege lata*. Cf. the earlier (now rejected) decision in OLG Celle NJW 1950, 951,

The main legal arguments for this exclusion are based upon the text of the provision itself, legislative intention as ascertained from the draft materials, and the place of §830 I 2 BGB within the structure of the law.

First, the textual argument is that §830 I 2 BGB only refers to liability where it is uncertain which participant's *conduct (Handlung)* has caused the injury. This excludes natural events. Moreover, if 'conduct' were interpreted as including *non-tortious* conduct, then an indefensible distinction would be created between injury potentially caused by non-tortious conduct, and injury potentially caused by non-tortious natural events.[21] Hence, the restriction to cases where wrongful conduct was a cause of the injury.

Second, the BGB draft commissions focused only upon cases, paradigmatically, brawls involving a number of people striking the victim, where it was clear that the injury was caused by a wrongful event and this requirement was almost explicit in their formulations of the scope of the provision.[22]

Third, the structural argument is that the application of the rule to a case where the claimant's injury is not proven to have been the result of a wrongful cause would be to undo the *general* rule that the claimant bears the burden of proof, which clearly cannot have been the intention of the legislator.[23] §830 I 2 BGB is an *exceptional* rule.[24]

These are points of statutory interpretation. The requirement that the claimant have a cause of action against at least one person has also been defended on normative grounds. The main argument is simply one of fairness. The claim is that it is more just to allow the claimant to succeed (rather than to receive no compensation from any defendant) against a defendant, who is not proven according to the standard of proof to have been a cause of its injury, *only* where the claimant is known to be entitled, according to the substantive law of tort, to compensation from

---

which had apportioned liability under §254 BGB in a case where the injury had potentially been caused by the claimant's contributory negligence.

[21] F. Bydlinski, 'Aktuelle Streitfragen', 22.

[22] See T. Mehring, *Beteiligung und Rechtswidrigkeit bei §830 I 2 BGB*, 22–4, especially 23, n. 22. Moreover, the Roman texts on which the nineteenth-century case law was built only concerned such cases. See pp. 141–142. The nineteenth-century cases and discussion are all of this form: see C. Krüse, *Alternative Kausalität*, 140–9.

[23] BGH NJW 1973, 993, 994: 'Hier mu[ss] es vielmehr bei der Regel bleiben, da[ss] der Kläger die Voraussetzungen seines Anspruchs voll zu beweisen hat'. See also, spelling out the supposed unravelling of the general proof rule, OLG Bamberg 24.6.2003, 5 U 21/02, NZV 2004, 30.

[24] G. Spindler, 'Commentary on §830 I 2 BGB' [18] ('eng begrenzten Ausnahmefall').

a defendant.[25] On this view, what makes the claimant's claim in a defendant indeterminacy situation normatively distinctive, so as to disapply the general burden of proof, is that the claimant is *known* to be entitled to damages (and each defendant may have been a tortious cause of the claimant's injury). The defendant's general interest in not being held liable absent proof of causation to the standard of proof is said to be outweighed by the certainty of doing an injustice to the claimant.[26]

This argument has been criticised on a number of grounds. First, it has been said to rest merely upon an ad-hoc judgment of fairness that cannot be derived from foundational principles.[27] Second, it is claimed to be arbitrary that a defendant's liability to a claimant depends upon whether *another* defendant, for whom the former defendant is not responsible, behaved wrongfully or not.[28] Third, the fact that the claimant has a cause of action against *a* defendant is said to make no normative difference in relation to each defendant individually.[29] The same point is that the fact that the claimant has a cause of action against at least one of a group of defendants has no normative significance unless there is a legitimate reason to treat the defendants as a collective.[30]

Such criticisms have had little impact upon the law itself. This is probably because those who make them tend to argue against the limitation of §830 I 2 BGB to situations where the claimant's injury has been caused by a tort and instead propose a general system of liability in proportion to the probability that a defendant was a cause of the claimant's injury (regardless of whether the injury may have been caused by a

---

[25] See BGH NJW 1971, 506, 509 (§830 I 2 BGB is based upon 'an idea of fairness' (*Billigkeitsgedanke*)); BGH NJW 1973, 993, 994 (describing the argument in the text); OLG München Vers 2012, 1267, [27], 'Es erscheint gerechter, jedem nachweislich Beteiligten zuzumuten, im Einzelfall den Entlastungsbeweis zur Widerlegung der hier normierten Kausalitätsvermutung bezüglich seiner eigenen Handlungen zu führen, als dem unzweifelhaft Geschädigten den positiven Nachweis für die Folgen der Handlungen gerade des in Anspruch Genommenen'; T. Mehring, *Beteiligung und Rechtswidrigkeit bei §830 I 2 BGB*, 47; C. Eberl-Borges, 'Commentary to §830 I 2 BGB', 2012, [68]; J. Häger, 'Kausalität bei Massenschäden', 405; G. Spindler, 'Kausalität im Zivil- und Wirtschaftrecht', 310. This account is particularly emphasised by C. Eberl-Borges, '§830 BGB und die Gefährdungshaftung', 508–11. It is also reflected in the conditions for the application of other statutory exceptional rules which are modelled on §830 I 2 BGB: see §§6, 7 of the UmweltHG and §84 2 AMG. On these, see L. Röckrath, *Kausalität, Wahrscheinlichkeit, und Haftung*, 185.

[26] C. Eberl-Borges, '§830 BGB und die Gefährdungshaftung', 510–11.

[27] L. Röckrath, *Kausalität, Wahrscheinlichkeit, und Haftung*, 187, 214.

[28] F. Bydlinski, 'Aktuelle Streitfragen um die alternative Kausalität', 9.

[29] See L. Röckrath, *Kausalität, Wahrscheinlichkeit, und Haftung*, 214.   [30] Ibid.

non-wrongful event or not).[31] The problem is that if §830 I 2 BGB were applied to cases involving potential non-tortious causation, there would be no available legal mechanism by which *full* liability could be avoided, since §830 I 2 BGB creates liability in solidum.[32] Some have attempted to avoid this conclusion by arguing that liability could be apportioned by analogy to the code provision on contributory negligence (§254 BGB).[33] The insuperable problem with such arguments is that the existence of a potential non-tortious cause simply does not involve the allegation that the claimant has failed to take appropriate care.[34]

The application of §830 I 2 BGB to strict liability

Textually, §830 I 2 BGB appears to be restricted to delictual causes of action. The first sentence of §830 I 1 BGB refers to the common undertaking of 'unerlaubte Handlung' – unlawful or delictual conduct – and imposes joint and several liability for damage caused by it. The second sentence imposes the same rule where it cannot be established which of several participants has caused the injury by his act. We might therefore interpret the second sentence to imply that §830 I 2 BGB applies to causes of action involving 'unerlaubte Handlung' – that is, unlawful conduct. And indeed it has been accepted that §830 I 2 BGB applies to all delictual causes of action.[35] However, decisions of the Reichsgericht and earlier views in the literature supported this as a *restrictive condition* for the application of §830 I 2 BGB.[36] Apart from the textual argument, as well as the fact that all references in the pre-Codification discussions involved defendants acting with fault, this view rested upon the idea that the attribution of fault to the defendants is critical to the justification of the rule in §830 I 2 BGB.[37]

A restriction to fault-based causes of action has, however, been rejected both by the BGH and by most doctrinal writers.[38] The crux of the reasoning to this conclusion is that whatever feature of the situation which could justify §830 I 2 BGB in fault-based causes of action is also

---

[31] For example, F. Bydlinski, 'Haftungsgrund und Zufall als alternative mögliche Schadensursachen'; L. Röckrath, *Kausalität, Wahrscheinlichkeit, und Haftung*. These arguments are addressed in Chapter 6.

[32] G. Wagner, 'Commentary on §830 I 2 BGB', [35]–[38].

[33] Notably, F, Bydlinski, *Probleme der Schadensverursachung*, 87, and see also his work cited in Note 32.

[34] See T. Mehring, *Beteiligung*, 108.

[35] See L. Röckrath, *Kausalität*, 147; C. Eberl-Borges, '§830 BGB und die Gefährdungshaftung' 504; G. Wagner, 'Commentary on §830 I 2 BGB', [39].

[36] See RGZ 67, 260, 261; RGZ 102, 316, 319.   [37] Ibid.

[38] See, for example, BGH NJW 1957, 1834, 1835; BGH NJW 1979, 544, 545. See, especially, C. Eberl-Borges, '§830 BGB', 508ff.

present in strict liability causes of action.[39] If one asks 'How *could* fault justify the rule?', the answer cannot be that the fault of one defendant justifies shifting the burden of proof, since the general position is that the claimant must prove causation in addition to fault. If one then asks 'What else, then, differentiates the indeterminate defendant situation from the general case?', the answer is 'The presence of another defendant who has behaved wrongfully.' The claim is that the *only* normative difference this makes to the situation is that it allows one to know that the claimant has a cause of action against one of the defendants. Thus, the reasoning relies upon the central justification of §830 I 2 BGB being the fact of the claimant's having a demonstrated right to damages and only failing for want of ability to identify the causative defendant – and this clearly does not depend upon the nature of the causes of action at stake.[40]

Ultimately, this argument is questionable, since the addition of another *wrongdoer* might be thought to have some other normative significance. For example, it could be thought that allowing the causative defendant to escape liability by relying upon another's *wrongdoing* is particularly problematic.[41] Hence, the premise that the *only* normative significance of an additional wrongful defendant is the ability to know that the claimant has a right to damages against someone is attackable.

The expansion of §830 I 2 BGB to strict liability causes of action nonetheless shows that the accepted normative kernel of §830 I 2 BGB is the idea that the claimant ought not to fail in a claim for damages *where it has a demonstrated right to damages* as against one of those who have possibly caused its loss, simply where it is impossible to identify the causative defendant from those who may have caused the loss. This feature can exist regardless of whether the cause of action is fault-based or not.

The inapplicability of §830 I 2 BGB where the claimant can prove causation against one defendant[42]

§830 I 2 BGB does not apply in the following type of situation:[43]

> C is negligently struck by D1's vehicle. As a result of this, C is left on the road and negligently struck by D2's vehicle. It is not possible to

[39] See C. Eberl-Borges, '§830 BGB', 508–11.

[40] Nor does it matter if one potentially causative defendant is only liable under a strict liability cause of action, while the other is liable under a fault-based cause of action: BGHZ 101, 106.

[41] See pp. 189–192.   [42] Condition (6), p. 143.

[43] See, generally, C. Eberl-Borges, 'Commentary on §830 I 2 BGB' [93]–[97].

determine whether the injuries that C suffered, or part thereof, would not have occurred had D2's vehicle not struck C.[44]

Here D1 would be liable for all of C's injuries on the basis that it is proven to have directly caused them or it was proven to be a legally responsible cause of the injuries inflicted by D2. The issue then is whether D2 is *also* liable even though it cannot be proven that D2 was a cause of the injuries or some identifiable part of them.

Initially, the BGH did apply §830 I 2 BGB in such cases, holding D1 and D2 liable in full.[45] The Court argued, first, that the victim had a substantial interest in making out such a claim where D1 was untraceable or insolvent.[46] Second, it argued that the rule by virtue of which D1 was responsible for the action of D2 (the law on adequate causation) was intended to protect the victim. It should not therefore *worsen* the victim's legal standing, by depriving C of the benefit of §830 I 2 BGB.[47]

The Court shifted position firmly in a decision of 1978.[48] First, it stated that since D1 was known to be a cause of all of the claimant's injuries, it could not be said that it could not be determined *whose* conduct caused the claimant's injury, as required by the wording of §830 I 2 BGB. Mere uncertainty over whether *another* person was a cause of the injury did not engage the provision.[49] Second, the fact that the claimant had a 'substantial interest' in having a claim against another person in the event of insolvency or untraceability was not a strong enough consideration to justify extending the scope of a provision exceptionally imposing liability without proof of causation.[50] The provision was not designed to protect claimants from insolvency risks, which are faced by *all* claimants, but only the specific difficulty that the claimant has no legal entitlement against anyone in the event that multiple persons act wrongfully against it.[51]

The Court distinguished the following type of case:[52]

---

[44] The facts of BGH NJW 1961, 263. Compare the facts of *Fitzgerald v Lane* [1987] 1 QB 781, discussed p. 233 and p. 234 n 199.

[45] As in BGH NJW 1961, 263 itself, and BGH NJW 1971, 506.

[46] BGH NJW 1971 506, 507.   [47] Ibid., 507–8.

[48] BGH NJW 1979, 544. The shift had begun earlier in BGH NJW 1976, 1934. The Court in the 1978 decision cited J. Gernhuber, 'Haftung bei alternativer Kausalität', which had made the arguments in the text, and emphasised the 'subsidiarity' of §830 I 2 BGB. See ibid., 148–9. Cf., defending the original position, W. Brehm, 'Zur Haftung bei alternativer Kausalität' and E. Deutsch, 'Die dem Geschädigten nachteilige Adäquanz: Zur einschränkenden Auslegung des §830 I 2 BGB durch den BGH'.

[49] Ibid., 545.   [50] Ibid., 546.   [51] Ibid.

[52] Ibid. The example (*Kanalschachtbeispiel*) was first given in BGH NJW 1976, 1934.

D1 negligently fails to close a drain hole. C is negligently knocked into the drain by either D2 or D3 – both of whom have behaved negligently – and suffers serious injuries, but it cannot be determined which of D2 or D3 was causative of the injuries.

Here §830 I 2 BGB would probably apply in relation to D2 and D3, even though C has a claim against D1.[53] In relation to D2 and D3, it is true that it cannot be determined which of the two was a cause of the injury. In relation to that pair, it is true that C is certainly denied an entitlement that it otherwise would have if §830 I 2 BGB were not applied. That is not so in the simpler type of case above.

The BGH's current position is consistent with the accepted normative kernel of §830 I 2 BGB. In the first type of case above, it is not true that denying the application §830 I 2 BGB will certainly deny the claimant a legal entitlement that it otherwise would have if the facts were known.[54]

The requirement of concrete endangerment (konkrete Gefährlichkeit)

In the statement of conditions (1)–(6), it was stated that each defendant must have risked the claimant the injury that it has suffered. Strictly, it would seem that more than mere increase of risk is required. The defendant's conduct must have concretely endangered the claimant (the requirement of konkrete Gefährlichkeit).[55]

The idea is difficult to define and is best explained by an example.[56] Suppose that an unidentified car collides with the claimant's car. The cars of D1–D6 were observed in the vicinity of the accident. This alone would probably not be enough to show that each car concretely endangered the claimant.[57] Or suppose that, in breach of a strict statutory duty, a person lit a cigarette in a forest and a forest fire occurred. It has been argued that this would not be enough to show that the smoking concretely risked the forest fire.[58]

---

[53] Ibid. In agreement: C. Eberl-Borges, 'Commentary on §830 I 2 BGB', [100].

[54] See, similarly, A. Quentin, Kausalität und deliktische Haftungsbegründung, 192.

[55] The idea seems to emerge in the work of Bydlinski. See F. Bydlinski, 'Haftung bei alternativer Kausalität', 12. It is precisified in H. Koziol, Haftpflichtrecht I, 1973, 52. See further, F. Bydlinski in his 'Aktuelle Streitfragen', 25, 33. See, generally, describing this requirement: K. Larenz and C. Canaris, Lehrbuch, §82 II 2 c; C. Eberl-Borges, 'Commentary on §830 I 2 BGB', [91], [114]–[115]; L. Röckrath, Kausalität, Wahrscheinlichkeit, Haftung, 152–6.

[56] Cf. G. Spindler, 'Kausalität im Zivil- und Wirtschaftrecht', 307, describing the idea as still largely unclear.

[57] See C. Eberl-Borges, 'Commentary on §830 I 2 BGB', [91].

[58] L. Röckrath, Kausalität, Wahrscheinlichkeit, Haftung, 153.

On the other side of the line, suppose that three horses belonging to the defendant escape from a field. An accident occurs 800 metres away between a horse and a car. More than three horses were observed to be present near the accident. On these facts, the OLG Köln said that the defendant's three horses had concretely endangered the victim in virtue of their escape and their temporal and spatial proximity to the accident.[59] In another case, three drunken people were raucously dancing on a table in the Erfurt cathedral square. One fell off the table and injured the claimant, though it could not be determined which. Here it was held that each was liable under §830 I 2 BGB.[60] Finally, in a case where D1 and D2 kept eight sheep in an electrically fenced pen, and of these, D1 had two black sheep, and D2 had one black sheep, it was held that §830 I 2 BGB applied so as to hold both liable where one black sheep (of unknown ownership) escaped the pen and injured a nearby person.[61]

Two justifications tend to be adduced for this requirement. First, there is a particular concern as to unbounded liability under §830 I 2 BGB as applied to *strict liability* causes of action, because the class of potentially liable people is not narrowed down by fault.[62] For example, if an accident occurs on the road, it should not be enough to engage §830 I 2 BGB that the cars of D1–D6 were observed to be present near the time of the accident. Second, there is a moral concern for individual defendants that their liability is not based upon a probability which is very low or insufficiently *weighty*.[63]

Defendant indeterminacy variants

Extent of loss variant
As discussed above, §830 I 2 BGB also applies in cases where each defendant has wrongfully caused an injury to the claimant but it cannot be determined which defendant caused which injury. Suppose that one bullet strikes C in the arm and one bullet strikes C in the leg and it cannot be determined which of D1 and D2 caused which injury. Suppose that the arm injury causes £x pain and suffering and the leg injury

---

[59] OLG Köln NZV 1990, 351, 352. The same was (*a fortiori*) true where a person was injured by a horse in a field in which four horses belonging to different owners grazed and it was impossible to tell which caused the injury: OLG Koblenz VersR 2013, 328.

[60] LG Erfurt, 26 July 2013, 10 O 1141/11.   [61] OLG München Vers 2012, 1267.

[62] Indeed, some authors claim the requirement is automatically satisfied in fault-based claims: see C. Eberl-Borges, 'Commentary on §830 I 2 BGB', [90]–[91].

[63] L. Röckrath, *Kausalität*, 153.

causes a further £2x. Here each D is known at least to have caused £x pain and suffering and will be straightforwardly liable for that. It is possible that each caused an additional £x pain and suffering. Here §830 I 2 BGB will render each jointly and severally liable in respect of that £x.

The analysis in cases of *unknown* extents is different. Suppose that C has been caused an injury by multiple defendants, which, if the facts were known, could be divided up into component segments according to the causal contribution to that injury by each defendant, but it cannot be determined how much each defendant has contributed, though it is known that each defendant did not cause the entirety of the injury. Here, unlike in the previous examples, the loss caused by each segment of the injury cannot be identified without identifying the causal contribution made to the total injury by each defendant. In German law the court will attempt to estimate the loss caused by each defendant under §287 ZPO.[64] §830 I 2 BGB probably cannot be applied unless there are distinct injuries of ascertainable extents.

Causative defendants variant

Causative defendant type defendant indeterminacy problems do not seem to have arisen before German courts. But they have been much discussed. It will be helpful to consider the simple hypothetical case described by Häger:[65]

> *Two cars.* C1's car and C2's car, which are almost identical, are destroyed by the wrongful conduct of either D1 or D2. D1 is known to have wrongfully destroyed one car and the same is true of D2. It cannot be determined which D destroyed which car.

On the face of it, §830 I 2 BGB applies. Each of C1 and C2 can say that they have suffered injury due to wrongful conduct and it cannot be determined which of a number of wrongdoers caused that injury. More needs to be known to determine whether each of D1 and D2 concretely endangered each C's car. If, for example, each D had placed an explosive device under each car, and only one device went off, then each D would have endangered each car. The difficulty is that if §830 I 2 BGB is applied, and each defendant is sued by each claimant, then each D is liable for *more* than it is known to have caused. It is unclear how this difficulty would be avoided.

---

[64] L. Röckrath, *Kausalität*, 158–9.   [65] J. Häger, 'Kausalität bei Massenschäden', 410ff.

In more realistic cases, such as where multiple drug manufacturers manufacture generic, defective, drugs, each causing injury to at least one claimant, though it cannot be determined which, the claim will face the difficulty that each manufacturer must have concretely endangered the claimant. The mere placement of a defective drug on the national market would not do.[66]

France: faute collective, garde en commun, reversal of the burden of proof

The Code Civil contains no counterpart to §830 I 2 BGB, nor do the Roman texts which informed the codification of the latter seem to have played a significant a role in French law.[67] The first part of this section describes the initial rejection of an exceptional doctrine in cases of defendant indeterminacy in French law. The second part then traces the shift which occurs in the middle of the twentieth century towards liability in solidum. The third part demonstrates that the modern law recognises a reversal of the burden of proof in such cases.

Defendant indeterminacy: initial rejection

While a number of early post-Code decisions dealt liberally with claimants who could show that more than one wrongdoer had caused them *some* damage, though of unascertainable extent, there do not appear to be any cases dealing with core indeterminate wrongdoer situations until much later in the nineteenth century.[68] The dominant trend of decisions, almost always involving hunting accidents, from that period until the middle of the twentieth century is towards rejection of such claims.[69]

---

[66] Supportive of the application of §830 I 2 BGB are: T. Bodewig, 'Probleme alternative Kausalität bei Massenschäden'; L. Röckrath, *Kausalität*, 160ff; J. Häger, 'Kausalität bei Massenschäden', 410ff (where the *Two cars* example is found). Cf. C. Eberl-Borges, 'Commentary on §830 I 2 BGB', [114]–[116].

[67] A modified *actio de effusis vel dejectis*, which would have dealt with the very specific defendant indeterminacy situation arising where something fell from a block of apartments and it could not be determined from which, was initially included in drafts of the Code Civil but was later excised. See E. Descheemaeker, *The Division of Wrongs*, 134.

[68] For a clear example of the unknown extent variant: Cass 8 November 1836, Jur Gén 1836.1.411. For similar decisions: F. Chabas, *L'influence de la pluralité de causes sur le droit à la réparation*, 42ff.

[69] Tribunal de la Seine, 8 January 1912, D.1912.II.312; Cour de Douai, 13 October 1930, Gaz Pal 1930 II 702; Cour de Paris, 24 January 1931, Gaz Pal 1931 I 486 (not raised by the facts in this case, but affirming the principle); Cass Civ 1e, 29 September 1941, Gaz Pal 1941 II

A typical illustration is the decision of the tribunal de la Seine, 9 January 1912.[70] A team of footballers decided to have a game in the street, near some offices, before proceeding to their practice ground. One of them accidentally kicked the ball through a window, injuring the claimant; it did not emerge which player kicked the ball. The court held that each player had been at fault in deciding to play in the street, but that *this* common fault was not causative of the claimant's injury. Rather the decision to play in the street merely formed part of the background circumstances; the *cause directe* was the negligent play of one individual. Given the necessity of demonstrating individual causation, the claim failed. A note below the decision observes that while this may seem particularly 'rigorous', the solution must be approved as 'conforming to the accepted general principles of civil liability'.[71]

Courts also rejected claims where, for example, two hunters negligently fired towards the claimant and only one bullet struck the latter. Thus, a decision of the Cour d'Appel d'Orléans from 17 January 1949 involved the simultaneous negligent fire of multiple bullets by two hunters towards an accompanying child, who was struck multiple times in the eye and arm. Despite the infliction of multiple injuries, the case is not simply a question of the *quantum* of damage caused by each, since the multiple wounds may have originated in only one of the hunters, who fired many times. Even in the face of a severe injury to a child, the court held for the negligent defendants. The decision reads simply as straightforward application of general principles:

> ... it is not enough that each was at fault; it is also necessary that a direct relation of cause and effect exist between the fault of each person and the damage; as a result, if it is impossible to determine the causative fault, none of them should be held liable.[72]

The same court would remark in a later decision that, even in a case where each defendant has been at fault, to hold a non-causative defendant liable would be to occasion 'une iniquité flagrante' and thus it could not be 'sérieusement soutenu qu'il n'incombe pas à la victime de prouver

---

437; Chambre des Requêtes, 20 February 1946, D.1947.J.222 (note Théry); Cour d'Appel d'Orléans 17 January 1949, D.1949.J.502 (note Ripert); Cour d'Appel Orléans, 5 March 1952, Gaz. Pal. 1952 I 351. For an early exception: Cour d'Appel Pau, RTDC 1912 966 (obs Demogue).

[70] D.1912.II.312.

[71] Ibid.; cf. R. Demogue, *Traité des Obligations en Général Tomes III–IV*, 223–4.   [72] Note 69.

le caractère causal de l'intervention'.[73] One can see in this a rejection of the equal injustice of false positives and false negatives in respect of causation. The preference is in respect of the latter.

Defendant indeterminacy: the shift towards liability in solidum

Professors Jourdain and Viney suggest that a shift occurs in the decisions of the courts beginning in the middle of the twentieth century, in response to doctrinal arguments, towards liability in solidum in cases of defendant indeterminacy.[74] The nature of the shift is said to lie in the application of two doctrines: *faute collective* and *garde en commun*. The former doctrine attributes fault to a group of persons and claims that this group fault is causative of the claimant's damage. The latter notion is a strict liability analogue. Article 1384 as interpreted by the courts imposes strict liability upon the keeper of a thing which has caused damage.[75] The doctrine of *garde en commun* attributes the status of *keeper* to a *group* of persons. Viney and Jourdain claim that these doctrines are applied to cases where the legal rules invoked do not explain the result reached in that they are applied only selectively, only where there is defendant indeterminacy and not where the causative defendant is known.[76]

This account is broadly accurate, although some refinements are helpful. It is true that there are decisions which give ground to believe that the courts are straining the *faute collective* doctrine to reach a desired result.[77] Thus in a hunting accident case, where twelve hunters fired (each of them negligently) at the same time (a celebratory shot after the hunt), with one bullet striking the claimant, ten of the hunters were held liable *in solidum*. Two of the twelve hunters could prove that they did not cause the damage and so were not held liable: one had used a different calibre of bullets to the others; and one had fired in a different direction.[78] On the *faute collective* theory, all twelve ought to have been held

---

[73] Cour d'Appel Orléans, 5 March 1952, Gaz. Pal. 1952 I 351.
[74] G. Viney and P. Jourdain, *Les Conditions de la Responsabilité*, 3rd edition 239.
[75] For an overview of the law on article 1384, see F. Werro, 'Liability for Harm Caused by Things'.
[76] G. Viney and P. Jourdain, *Les Conditions de la Responsabilité*, 243–4.
[77] See Cass Civ 2e, 10 January 1973, RTDC 1973, 773 (obs Durry); Cass Civ 2e, 19 May 1976, JCP 1978.II.18773 (note Dejean de la Bâtie); RTDC 1977, 129 (obs Durry); Cass Civ 2e, 4 May 1988, Bull Civ II no.102, RTDC 1988, 769 (obs Jourdain).
[78] See the case in the above note. Cf, A. Bénabent, *Droit Civil: Les Obligations*, 12th edition 401 (agreeing with Viney and Jourdain's analysis on this point). Cf, M. Fabre-Magnan, *Droit Des Obligations: Tome 2*, 12th edition 198 (explaining *faute collective* in a non-fictional way).

liable. Yet it is important to note that a significant strand of doctrinal writing *did* endorse the theory that all twelve ought to be liable. Durry observed that this decision had undermined the doctrine of *faute collective*, which was particularly problematic, since without it one is holding defendants liable without their having causally contributed to the damage.[79] Moreover, a number of other decisions employ the notion of *faute collective* in ways which embody a plausible notion of accessorial liability.[80] It is not true that *faute collective* is *always* employed as an 'explication[s] inventée[s] *a posteriori*'[81] to justify liability in the indeterminate wrongdoer situation.

However, there is significant evidence that French courts from the 1950s were generating liability in solidum in cases of defendant indeterminacy where the connection between the defendants plays no plausible role in the judges' justification for their decision. In addition to the case of the twelve hunters, there are cases where the judges themselves hint that the real justification for the liability is not the relationship between the defendants. Thus, in a case where a child was injured during a group game by a stone negligently thrown by an unidentifiable child, the court held that it was necessary to hold that each child was liable under the *faute collective* doctrine since 'to hold otherwise would deprive the victim of any right to compensation' and would allow those in analogous situations who come together and commit acts of negligence to exonerate themselves very easily – simply by pointing to the presence of another.[82] The attribution of the acts of the unidentified child to the other negligent children is justified, then, by considerations of compensation and perhaps an inchoate deterrence argument.[83]

Similarly, there are a number of decisions where the legal analysis is patently strained in order to generate liability in cases where the

---

[79] G. Durry, Note on Cass Civ 2e, 19 May 1976. Similarly, H. Aberkane, 'Du dommage causé par une personne indeterminée dans un group determiné de personnes' had defended liability of the entire group. See, similarly: E. Poisson-Drocourt, 'Note under Cass Civ 2e 15 December 1980', 456. Cf. the Court of Appeal judgment (Cour d'Orléans, 15 October 1974, referred to in JCP.II.18773, 1978) in the case of the twelve hunters, which holds each liable on the basis that each participated in the causative *faute commune*.

[80] Cour d'Appel Riom, 12 January 1885, D.1885.II.133. Cf. however, Cass Civ 2e, 10 January 1973, RTDC 1973 773 (obs Durry); Cass Civ 2e, 2 April 1997, no. 95-14428, cited by M. Fabre-Magnan, *Droit civil*, 2nd edition 199. For an analysis of the relationship between accessorial liability in criminal law and the civil law doctrine of *faute collective*: A. Galia-Beauchesne, 'Note under Cass Crim, 19 May 1978', 3.

[81] G. Viney and P. Jourdain, *Les Conditions de la Responsabilité*, 3rd edition 244.

[82] Cour d'Appel Aix, 6 June 1950, JCP 1950.II.5736 (note Rodière).

[83] Cf. Cass Civ 2e, 4 May 1988, JCP.1988.IV.238, RTDC 1988, 769 (obs Jourdain).

claimant is unable to point to a causative defendant. Thus, where two hunters have simultaneously fired bullets and one has struck the claimant, courts have applied article 1384, which requires that a thing have escaped from human control and have caused damage to the claimant, on the ground that each hunter had guardianship over the *gerbe de plombs*. That is: the simultaneous firing of each bullet creates a unique object travelling towards the claimant, *une chose*, for the purposes of article 1384 – 'a shower' of bullets, over which *each* hunter has guardianship.[84] In one case, two hunters had fired simultaneously and one bullet struck a farm worker on a nearby field. There was no possibility of a *faute collective* analysis: neither had encouraged the other to fire at the time,[85] nor had they organised themselves in a negligent formation,[86] nor had they previously agreed to fire at that point in time,[87] nor were their individual actions negligent. Even, then, in a case where there is no possibility of *faute collective*, the court arrives at the conclusion of liability in solidum by means of the obvious fiction of the *gerbe unique*. Despite extensive criticism of the reasoning, this solution is still accepted by the Cour de Cassation.[88]

Finally, there are some rare cases which do not rest in any way upon *faute collective* reasoning or the fiction of *garde en commun*. The first appears to be a decision of the Cour de Grenoble.[89] Again, the case involves a hunting accident where two hunters negligently fire at the claimant and it is not possible to determine which bullet has struck. The court begins with the recognition that the notion of a 'gerbe unique' has been subject to criticism and proceeds to offer the following solution. While it is not possible to say of each defendant that it has caused the

---

[84] Devised initially by CA Angers, 13 November 1957, D.1957.721; JCP 1957 II 10339. A similar fiction is that each hunter has control over the other hunters' guns: JCP 1957. II.10308 (note Savatier). For discussion of the obvious artifice: H. Aberkane in D.1960.365; H. Mazeaud and L. Mazeaud, 'Tir simultané par plusieurs chasseurs', 480; D. Mayer, 'La "garde" en commun', 197.

[85] For this as a (sufficient) condition of *faute collective*: Cass Civ 1e, 5 June 1957, D.1957.493 (note Savatier): 'excitation mutuelle'.

[86] For this as a (sufficient) condition of *faute collective*: Cass Civ 2e, 18 May 1955, D.1955, 520; J Demarez, *L'indemnisation du dommage occasionné par un membre inconnu d'un groupe determiné*, 200–1.

[87] For this as a (sufficient) condition of *faute collective*: E. Poisson-Drocourt, 'Note', 457; P. Esmein in JCP.1957.II.10205.

[88] Cass Civ 2e, 15 December 1980, D.1981.455 (note Poisson-Drocourt).

[89] Cour de Grenoble, 5 May 1952, D.1963.137 (note Azard). The idea of a cause of action for negligent destruction of a cause of action under Article 1382 CC was already suggested by the *arretiste* to an old decision of the Cour de Besançon, 19 May 1882, D.1882, 2, 245. This is the first suggestion of this idea this author has encountered.

claimant's physical injury, it is possible to say that each defendant has *either* caused the physical injury or the inability to prove the causality of the other defendant for the physical injury. The inability to prove an otherwise complete claim constitutes a damage for the purposes of Article 1382 CC. And though which defendant has caused the physical injury and which the inability to prove the case against that defendant is (*ex hypothesi*) unknown, it suffices that one of these bases of liability is certainly attributable to each defendant. On this account, the pre-existing relationship between the hunters has no direct significance in the account of liability.

The Cour de Grenoble decision was cited (almost *verbatim*) and followed in a slightly different case where the claimant had been struck by two bullets, which either came (in each case, negligently) solely from D1, solely from D2 or one from D1 and one from D2.[90] Notice that the judgment *begins* by noting the 'paradox' that 'the increase in the number of persons who fired, and therefore of the danger, corresponds to a complete evaporation of liability', before then endorsing the reasoning that a cause of action must exist under Article 1382 CC against both defendants, either by negligent causation of physical injury or by negligent causation of the impossibility of advancing an established legal right. The idea that the negligent causation of the inability to prove an established legal right was approved by the Cour de Cassation in 1961 in a case where the operator of an ice rink failed to make inquiries as to the identity of a customer who negligently injured another customer, while the latter was taken to hospital.[91] Subsequently, however, this form of reasoning appears to have fallen somewhat into abeyance.[92]

The modern law: a reversal of the burden of proof

Perhaps in recognition of these earlier developments, it emerges from recent decisions of the Court of Cassation that French law recognises a principle applicable to the indeterminate wrongdoer situation, *distinct* from that of *faute collective* and *garde en commun*, which involves a reversal of the burden of proof on the issue of causation. In two decisions of the

---

[90] Cour d'Appel Riom, 5 February 1964, JCP 1964.II.13640 (note Esmein).
[91] Cass Civ 1e, 8 February 1961, JCP 1961.4.413. The case is discussed by J. Demarez, *L'indemnisation du dommage*, 140.
[92] A recent, extensive, account of responses to situations of defendant indeterminacy surprisingly fails to mention it: C. Quézel-Ambrunaz, 'La fiction de la causalité alternative'.

Cour de Cassation from 24 September 2009,[93] the claimants were women, both of whom suffered from a type of adenocarcinoma, which they attributed to the ingestion of diethylstimbesterol (DES) by their mothers during pregnancy. Both joined the only two firms which manufactured the drug in France during the pregnancy, one of which had a 90 per cent share of the market at the time of manufacture.[94] Where, as in the second case, the hurdle of showing that the cancer was caused by DES could be surmounted, the Court relieved the claimant of showing which of the two defendants' negligently[95] manufactured products had been causative of her cancer, which was almost impossible[96] given the thirty to forty year latency period of the drug. Rather: '[il] appartenait...à chacun des laboratoires de prouver que son produit n'était pas à l'origine du dommage'.[97]

The *motifs* of the decisions are particularly brief. Nonetheless, these decisions are most unlikely to be invocations of the *faute collective* doctrine[98] for four reasons. First, this doctrine is explicitly conceived as an evidential rule – a reversal of the burden of proof on causation. This preserves the logical possibility that a defendant may exonerate itself.[99] This would not be the case under *faute collective*, since each defendant's participation in the collective fault would be a cause of the damage. Second, the facts of the case are significantly beyond the factual situations to which *faute collective* has been applied: there existed no spatial proximity between the defendants; there was no antecedent agreement between them to undertake the activity giving rise to the damage; and it would be difficult to say that each encouraged the other to manufacture the drug without appropriate testing.[100]

---

[93] Cass Civ 1e, 24 September 2009, no. 08–10.081, JurisData no. 2009-049535; Cass Civ 1e, 24 September 2009, no. 08–16.305, JurisData no. 2009-049537; JCP G. 2009, no.41, 304 (obs Mistretta); JCP G. 2009, no.44, 18 (note Hocquet-Berg); RTDC, 2010, 111 (obs Jourdain); D.2010.51 (obs Brun).

[94] This illustrates that a high statistical probability of causation is not enough to satisfy the general standard of proof. Earlier decisions are not uniform on this point, however: CA Pau, 16 Jan 2002, RG 00/00926 (causation found against one defendant on basis of high statistical likelihood); Cass Civ 1e, 8 April 1986, D.1987.Jur.73 (obs Huet) (no liability).

[95] Previous decisions had found manufacturers of DES to be at fault, for example, Cass Civ 1e, 7 March 2006, RTDC 2006, 565.

[96] Cf. C. Radé, RCA.2010.no.4, 17: 'sera en pratique impossible à établir'.

[97] Approved by Cass Civ 1e, 28 January 2010 N°: 08-18837.

[98] The court may have been influenced by the *Avant-projet Catala*, whose proposed Article 1348 creates an identical rule. Moreover the note to the proposed text mentions drug manufacturers. Cf. also: Art. 3:103 PETL; DCFR 4:103.

[99] C. Quézel-Ambrunaz, 'La fiction de la causalité alternative' considers it to be a 'fiction' of causation.

[100] Similarly: RTDC 2010, 113 (obs Jourdain); RCA no. 11, November 2009 étude 15 (Radé).

Third, some of the more recent rulings of the Cour de Cassation have spoken against the fictional application or straining of *faute collective*.[101] Fourth, many authors, critical of the (at times) fictional nature of *faute collective* and *garde en commun* had previously spoken of the need for a legal presumption of causation in situations of defendant indeterminacy.[102]

While the juridical conceptualisation of this rule no longer itself implies some relationship between the defendants, its scope is obscure.[103] Even if one may assume that the recent DES decisions are in some sense a culmination of (the virtually uncontested[104]) evaluations already immanent in the previous *faute collective* case law, the reasoning used to explicate those evaluations was itself various. Thus, there is the (largely ignored) explanation of the Cour de Grenoble, which relies upon the cause of action for the destruction of a cause of action. Additionally, there is the very often expressed argument that the claimant ought not to be legally disadvantaged by the fact that more than one defendant has acted (wrongfully) towards it.[105] This argument is thought to follow from 'la plus élémentaire équité',[106] 'bon sens'[107] or 'une impérieuse exigence de justice'.[108] Third, there is the argument that defendants may avoid their obligations too easily,

---

[101] Cass Civ 1e, 23 November 2004, no. 03–16.865.

[102] For example, G. Ripert, 'Note on Cour d'Orléans, 17 January 1949'; N. Déjean de la Bâtie, 'Note under Cass Civ 3ᵉ, 19 May 1976'; P. Jourdain, 'Un recul de la responsabilité "in solidum" des membres d'un groupe de personnes', 770; P. LeTourneau, *Droit de la responsabilité et des contrats*, 7th edition [1724].

[103] Cf. the later decision applying the rule to uncertainty with six potentially causative defendants: Cass Civ 1e, 17 June 2010, no. 09–67.011, JCP G, no.36, 870 (note Gout); RCA, no.10, 2010 (comm.259 Radé).

[104] All of the following support liability in solidum in situations of defendant indeterminacy, without placing emphasis upon the defendants' relationship with each other: G. Ripert, 'Note'; R. Béraud, 'Quelque difficultés de preuve de la responsabilité délictuelle'; I. Postacioglu, 'Les faits simultanés et le problème de la responsabilité'; P. Esmein, 'Note under Cour d'Appel Riom, 5 February 1964'; R. Schmelck, 'Note under Cass Civ 2e, 11 February 1966'; N. Déjean de la Bâtie, 'Note'; E. Poisson-Drocourt, 'Note'; P. Jourdain, 'Un recul de la responsabilité'. Cf. the earlier, hostile, doctrine: H. Mazeaud and L. Mazeaud, 'Impossibilité d'identifier parmi les membres d'un groupe l'auteur de la faute dommageable'.

[105] Almost all of the pieces cited in the above note make this argument.

[106] Cour d'Appeal Riom, 5 February 1964, JCP 1964.II.13640 (note Esmein).

[107] R. Béraud, 'Quelque difficultés'; E. Poisson-Drocourt, 'Note', 455: 'En équité, par contre, la solution peut paraitre souhaitable. La pluralité d'auteurs possibles du dommage ne devrait pas réduire les chances de la victime d'être indemisée'.

[108] N. Déjean de la Batie, 'Note under Cass Civ 3ᵉ, 19 May 1976'. See also, especially, G. Ripert, 'Note on Cour d'Orléans, 17 January 1949'.

simply by pointing to the presence of other defendants.[109] Fourth, there is the (related) argument that to deny liability in certain situations where the impossibility of determining the causative defendant is recurrent is to deny compensation to a large number of persons who ought to be compensated.[110] Fifth, some have reasoned simply that as between negligent defendants and innocent claimants, the burden of proof on causation ought to rest with the former.[111] Sixth, the fact that the claimant's burden of proof is 'impossible' to discharge has been suggested as a justification for altering that burden.[112] These arguments and different combinations of these arguments will lead to rules of different scope.

The United States: alternative liability and market share liability

Defendant indeterminacy

Many US states recognise what is known as 'alternative liability'.[113] The doctrine derives from the decision of Californian Supreme Court in *Summers* v. *Tice*.[114] In that case, two hunters negligently fired a shot in the direction of the claimant with the result that the claimant was struck in the eye and lip. It was impossible to tell which hunter's shot resulted in the (main) eye injury: both hunters used the same type of shotgun with the same size of bullets. The court held that the burden of proof on the issue of which of the two hunters caused the eye injury was shifted to the defendants.[115]

Three lines of reasoning were offered for this reversal. The court noted the 'relative position of the parties and the results that would flow if plaintiff was required to pin the injury on one of the defendants only':[116] an innocent claimant is left without compensation, while negligent defendants, one of whose conduct has caused the harm, are exonerated. In assessing the 'relative position' of the parties, it also

---

[109] Cour d'Appel Aix, 6 June 1950, JCP 1950.II.5736 (note Rodière).
[110] R. Schmelk, 'Note under Cass Civ 2e, 11 Feburary 1966'.
[111] N. Déjean de la Bâtie, 'Note under Cass Civ 3e, 19 May 1976'.
[112] P. Esmein, 'Note under Cour d'appel Riom, 5 February 1964'.
[113] The misleading (liability is joint and several; causation is (in some cases) alternative) phrase 'alternative liability' was coined by R. Keeton, D. Dobbs, and D. Owen (eds), *Prosser & Keeton on Torts*, 271. Perhaps Prosser was aware of the German phrase *alternative Kausalität*.
[114] 33 Cal 2d 80; 199 P 2d 1 (1948). Cf the earlier *Anderson* v. *Maloney* 111 Or 84 (1924), which, like the early French decisions, reads as an application of orthodox proof rules.
[115] Strictly the case is one of unknown extents. Ibid., 86.   [116] Ibid.

seemed relevant that the defendants had created the conditions of uncertainty: 'The injured party *has been placed by the defendants* in the unfair position of pointing to which defendant caused the harm'.[117] Second, the court pointed to the greater ability of defendants generally to point to which defendant caused the injury. This rested upon the earlier *res ipsa loquitur* case *Ybarra v. Spangard*[118] where the burden of adducing exonerating evidence on negligence and (effectively) caus-ation was placed upon all the medical staff associated with an operation in which the unconscious claimant had suffered a shoulder injury: such a burden was justified by the disparity in access to evidence as to what happened while the claimant was unconscious. Finally, there existed the same reasons of 'policy and justice', which shift the burden to independent tortfeasors who have caused *some* damage to apportion it among themselves.[119]

As Dobbs observes: '[t]he opinion in *Summers* did not spell out the reasons for this extraordinary liability in any precise way ...'.[120] The argument based upon the relative positions of the parties is little more than an appeal to intuitive unfairness (however alluring it may be). Moreover, the court's reliance upon the earlier decision in *Ybarra* is strained: the defendants did not have better access to means of proof.[121] It might be said that *Summers* is *a fortiori Ybarra* since all the possible causes were wrongful in the former. Yet, given the *Ybarra* production of evidence rationale does not apply, this would be to assume that there is some other good reason to depart from orthodox proof of causation principles. There is thus some justice in the only reasoned (entire) rejec-tion of alternative liability, by the Supreme Court of Oregon, which observes that 'none of the cases or commentaries presents a rigorous analysis of why it is "fair" to impose joint liability without a preponder-ance of proof of causation'.[122]

Nonetheless, the burden-shifting rule was adopted by the Second and Third Restatements of Torts.[123] The former locates the justification in 'the injustice of permitting proved wrongdoers, who among them have inflicted an injury upon the entirely innocent plaintiff, to escape liability merely because the nature of their conduct and the resulting harm has

---

[117] Ibid. (emphasis added).   [118] 154 P 2d 687 (1944).   [119] *Summers*, at 88.

[120] D. Dobbs, *The Law of Torts*, 427.

[121] The court in *Sindell v. Abbott Laboratories* 607 P 2d 924, 929 (Cal 1980) made this point.

[122] *Senn v. Merrell-Dow Pharmaceutical Inc.* 751 P 2d 215, 222 (Oregon, 1988).

[123] *Restatement (Second) Torts*, §433B, subsection (3); *The Restatement (Third) Torts: Liability for Physical and Emotional Harm* §28 (b).

made it difficult or impossible to prove which of them has caused the harm'.[124] The Third Restatement makes clear that the rule applies only where the claimant cannot show which of a set of defendants, which contains the defendant who caused its injury, and who have *all behaved wrongfully*, caused its harm.[125] Further, it notes that all reported cases employing the doctrine involved conduct by defendants which was roughly simultaneous; imposing substantially the same level of risk of harm; and where all defendants were joined, though suggesting that modification might be necessary where those features are absent.[126]

These features have rarely been departed from in states which accept this form of liability.[127] Thus, the current doctrine requires that: (1) the cause of the harm must be shown to be one of a group of defendants who have all behaved wrongfully;[128] (2) all defendants must be joined in the action;[129] (3) in products liability cases exposure to the product manufactured by the defendants must be shown[130] and generally some further 'connection' between the defendants' conduct and the claimant's injury showing that the risk of harm posed by the defendants was not too remote;[131] (4) some courts require the defendants' conduct to be simultaneous.[132] Finally, it is unclear whether contributory negligence will affect the availability of alternative liability, since there is virtually no authority in point.[133]

---

[124] Ibid. The Restatement (Third) is almost identical although it speaks of the preference of placing the 'risk of error' on 'culpable defendants': §28 comment *f*.

[125] A necessary condition for the application of the doctrine for courts which accept it, for example, *Goldman* v. *Johns-Manville Sales Corp*, 514 NE 2d 691, 697 (Ohio, 1987); *Clift* v. *Nelson*, 25 Wn App 607, 610; 608 P 2d 647 (1980).

[126] *Restatement (Third) Torts*, §28 comment *k*.

[127] Only two states have explicitly rejected the alternative liability doctrine *tout court* since the Second Restatement: *Leuer* v. *Johnson* 450 NW 2d 363 (Minn CA 1990) and the Oregon case cited in Note 122.

[128] *Restatement (Third) of Torts*, §28, comment *j*.

[129] This requirement emerged largely through rejection of the application of Restatement §433B in DES litigation where not all defendants were joined: *Sindell* v. *Abbott Laboratories* 607 P 2d 924, 931 (Cal 1980); *Hymowitz* v. *Eli Lilly & Co.*, 539 NE 2d 1069 (NY 1989).

[130] *Restatement (Third) Torts* §28, comment *j* and *Reporters'* Note to comment *j*.   [131] Ibid.

[132] For example, *Smith* v. *Cutter Biological Inc.* 823 P 2d 717 (Hawaii, 1991). None of the decisions provides explanation for the simultaneity requirement. Cf. *Restatement (Third)* §28, comment *k*.

[133] *Restatement (Third) Torts*, §28, comment *o*.

If the rationale for the *Summers* doctrine is that stated by the Restatement, a number of these restrictions are questionable.[134] The requirement of joinder seems unnecessary if the claimant can show that all possible causes of its injury are wrongful without joinder. The simultaneity requirement is arbitrary if the claimant still cannot prove natural causation (through no fault of its own) where the defendants have acted non-simultaneously. Nor is it obvious what normative role is being played by the 'connection' which must obtain between the defendants' conduct and the injury. Comment *j* to §28 of the Third Restatement observes that the connection in *Summers* was 'quite tight, regardless of the actual causal relationship' since '[b]oth defendants were physically present, fired their guns in the direction of the plaintiff, and by doing so created an imminent risk to the plaintiff'. The requirement is similar to that of *concrete endangerment* in German law.[135] It may have at least two functions. On the one hand, it avoids too great a number of defendants being at risk of suit. On the other hand, it may be that the requirement is motivated by the general worry over non-specific statistical evidence: the reason for such a close connection is possibly that at some undefined point alternative liability becomes unfair because the probability that the defendant has caused the harm becomes conjectural or without any weight.[136]

Defendant indeterminacy variants

Extent of loss variant

In *unknown extent* cases, several states accept a rule whereby each defendant is liable for the totality of the claimant's losses, unless it can prove to a reasonable probability the extent of its contribution to those losses. The burden of proof to apportion the extent of the loss caused is, then, upon the defendants who have wrongfully caused *some* loss. For example, in *Landers* v. *East Texas Salt Water Disposal Co.*, each defendant had negligently polluted the claimant's lake with salt water and oil, killing his fish, but it could not be determined how much injury had been caused by

---

[134] 'The litany of limits on the rule has not been fully explained': D. Dobbs, *The Law of Torts*, 429. For a recent attempt at doctrinal rationalisation, see M. Geistfeld, 'The Doctrinal Unity of Alternative Liability and Market Share Liability'.

[135] See pp.150–151.

[136] *Senn* v. *Merrell-Dow Pharms. Inc.*, 751 P 2d 215, 222 (1988). Cf. D. Fischer, 'Products Liability – An Analysis of Market Share', 1634; R. Wright, 'Liability for possible wrongs: causation, statistical probability and the burden of proof', 1325; *Hymowitz*, referenced in Note 129, at 1074.

each defendant.[137] Each defendant was held liable for the total injury, since each could not identify to a 'reasonable certainty' how much injury it had caused.[138] The basis for this was that it is less unjust for each wrongful defendant to pay for more than it caused than it is for the claimant to fail entirely.[139]

Causative defendants variant

In *Sindell* v. *Abbott Laboratories*,[140] the claimant led a class action against manufacturers of diethylstilbestrol (DES), alleging *inter alia* that they had negligently marketed DES as a miscarriage preventative and had failed to test its safety properly.[141] The claimant suffered injuries which could be shown to be caused by DES but it was not possible, due to the passage of time (the cancer has a minimum latency period of 10 or 12 years from ingestion[142]) and the generic nature of the drug, to identify the manufacturer of the drug ingested by the claimant's mother. The claimant's case proceeded against ten defendants of whom, it was claimed, five or six represented 90 per cent of the market when her mother ingested the drug[143] – earlier in the proceedings one defendant had exculpated itself on the basis that it had not manufactured the drug during that period. Given each defendant's share in the market, it was known that *each* had wrongfully caused injury *to some claimants*. Moreover, it was also known that the claimant had wrongfully suffered injury as a result of one such defendant. Hence, this was a causative defendant variant of the defendant indeterminacy problem.

The court created a rule that required the claimant to join in the litigation defendants who represented a 'substantial share' in the relevant drug market. Each of these defendants would bear the burden of proof as to causation. Failure to show that their product did not cause the claimant's injury would result in liability based upon the manufacturer's market share. That is: if D enjoyed a market share of 10 per cent, and C suffered $n loss, then D's liability is 10 per cent of $n.[144]

This liability was justified by a number of considerations. The court relied partly upon the same broad fairness argument made in *Summers* v.

---

[137] (1952) 248 SW 2d 731 (Texas Sup Ct).   [138] Ibid., 734.

[139] Ibid. For a summary of the law in other states, see D. Robertson, 'Causation in the Restatement (Third) of Torts: Three Arguable Mistakes', 1014–16.

[140] (1980) 26 Cal 3d 588; 607 P 2d 924.

[141] Cf. A. Bernstein, 'Hymowitz v Eli Lilly & Co.: Markets of Mothers', 157.

[142] *Sindell*, 594.   [143] Ibid., 612.

[144] The *national* market at the time of the ingestion A. Twerski, 'Market Share – a Tale of Two Centuries', 870.

Tice that as between an innocent claimant and wrongful defendants, the latter should bear the risk of uncertainty.[145] The court refused to apply *Summers* itself for the reason that the probability of any individual defendant having caused the injury was minimal, given that only 10 defendants were joined out of a number of greater than 200 defendants who manufactured the drug during the period.[146] It was also noted that the claimant was not 'at fault' for there being no evidence and that though the lack of evidence was not 'attributable' to the defendants, their conduct played a 'significant role' in creating the unavailability of proof.[147] The court also observed that the defendants could better bear the costs of the injuries and that their liability would result in increased deterrence.

Perhaps most importantly, the court stated that the measure of the liability (according to market share) would lead to the position that 'each manufacturer's liability would approximate its responsibility for the injuries caused by its own products'.[148] To illustrate, suppose 10,000 cancers were caused by DES and that each cancer caused $x in losses. Each DES drug has equal likelihood of causing the cancer. If D had a 30 per cent share in the market which produced the drugs, it can reasonably be assumed that 30 per cent of the cancers are attributable to D. Thus, D ought to pay, in total, $3,000x. If each cancer victim is allowed to sue D for 30 per cent of its losses, then D's liability will match the total loss it has caused: $10,000 \times 0.3 \times \$x = \$3,000x$.[149]

A number of courts followed *Sindell* in holding that defendants who had manufactured DES were liable in damages despite (nearly all) claimants not being able to prove the identity of their injurer on the preponderance of the evidence. Most conceived of this an exception to the general proof rules.[150] Some courts, however, claimed to be re-configuring the *substantive* law by holding that the basis of the defendant's liability was *simply* that it had culpably risked harm to the claimant

---

[145] *Sindell*, 611.   [146] Ibid.   [147] Ibid.

[148] Ibid., 612. It was clarified in *Brown* v. *Superior Court* 751 P 2d 470, 485–7 (Cal 1988) that the defendant's liability was *restricted* to its market share.

[149] For this reason, it is unclear why a substantial share of the market needs to be joined: R. Bush, 'Between Two Worlds: the Shift from Individual to Group Responsibility in the Law of Causation of Injury', 1485; A. Porat and A. Stein, *Tort Liability under Uncertainty*, 62, n. 15.

[150] Cf. *Collins* v. *Eli Lilly & Co* 342 NW 2d 37 (Wisconsin Sup Ct 1984) (applying a mixture of burden of proof principles and apportionment (ibid. 53)). The more recent decision in *Thomas (Gramling)* v. *Mallett* 701 NW 2d 523 (Wisc, 2005) applies *Collins* to a case where the prospects of exculpation are virtually nil due to the inability to pinpoint the relevant time during which the possibly causal lead paint was marketed (cf. *Sindell*).

(without treating that *risk* as a type of harm). *Hymowitz* v. *Eli Lilly & Co.* is the famous example.[151] The court held that a defendant would not be allowed to avoid liability by producing evidence that it did not injure the particular claimant – for example, by showing that it manufactured some memorably shaped pills or sold only to certain pharmacists.[152] The court reasoned that since it was imposing liability based upon *culpability*, it was 'mere fortuit[y]' for the defendant to exculpate itself on the chance availability of disproof in an individual case.[153] This consideration led Coleman to understand *Hymowitz* as creating a localised fault pool, institutionalising a limited version of the risk liability principle described in Chapter 3.[154] This is problematic since a necessary condition of contribution to the pool is having wrongfully caused damage *to someone*. Moreover, the refusal to allow the defendant to show that it did not cause a particular claimant's damage is consistent with the goal of tailoring the defendant's liability to the defendant's aggregate wrongfully *caused* loss.[155]

Despite some academic support for more liberal proportionate liability generally,[156] and especially in mass tort situations,[157] market share liability is of very limited application. While courts are fairly equally spread on the question of whether to accept a variant of market share,[158] there is virtual unanimity that the doctrine cannot be applied to situations where the risks posed by defendants' conduct are not uniform. The doctrinal expression of this idea is the requirement of 'fungibility'.[159] Thus, courts have refused expansion of the doctrine to asbestos litigation,[160] where claimants can be exposed to an immense variety of

---

[151] 539 NE 2d 1069 (NY 1989).

[152] Ibid., 1078; except by showing that it did not manufacture the drug during the relevant period, at 1078, n. 2.

[153] Ibid.   [154] J. Coleman, *Risks and Wrongs*, 405–6. See pp.112–114.

[155] R. Wright, 'Liability for Possible Wrongs', 1324ff.

[156] G. Robinson, 'Multiple Causation in Tort Law: Reflections on the DES Cases', 769 (arguing for general causal apportionment based upon probabilistic conception of causation).

[157] For example, D. Rosenberg, 'The Causal Connection in Mass Exposure Cases: a Public Law Vision of the Tort System'.

[158] On the split in courts, see A. Rostron, 'Beyond Market Share Liability: a Theory of Proportionate Share Liability for Non-Fungible Products', 170, n. 103.

[159] A. Rostron, 'Beyond Market Share Liability', 163–6.

[160] Among many, see, for example, *Blackston* v. *Shook & Fletcher Insulation Co.* 764 F 2d 1480, 1483 (market share unfair because products 'differ in degrees of harmfulness') (11th Cir, 1985); *Rutherford* v. *Owens-Illinois* 941 P 2d 1203 (Cal 1997). For an exception: *Wheeler* v. *Raybestos-Mannhatan* 11 Cal Rptr 2d 109 (Cal CA 1992) (at 111).

asbestos-containing products posing different risks of harm;[161] in blood product litigation;[162] and in lead paint products litigation.[163] The principal line of reasoning in these cases is that unless the risks involved in each manufacturer's product are the same, then market share liability will be unworkable and a crude approximation of the losses wrongfully caused by an individual defendant. Thus the Third Restatement observes: '...there is virtually no case support for a *risk-adjusted* market-share theory'.[164]

England

Defendant indeterminacy

English law has never had a set of legal rules addressed exclusively to the situation of defendant indeterminacy. However, the English position merits brief attention here, since it was a case – *Fairchild* v. *Glenhaven Funeral Services Ltd*[165] – treated as one of defendant indeterminacy which re-founded a significant part of the law relating to exceptional causal proof doctrines. Further, some of the arguments relied upon therein relate exclusively to such a situation. The genesis and current scope of the broader rule of which *Fairchild* is an instance are explained in the next chapter.

In *Fairchild*, each victim claimant had been exposed to asbestos for varying periods of time, by different employers all in breach of duty to the claimant, and had contracted mesothelioma. While it is clear that mesothelioma is caused by asbestos exposure, it was assumed in *Fairchild* that scientific knowledge at present cannot determine the precise mechanism by which the cancer is triggered: the condition may be caused by a single or few fibres,[166] or there may be a large threshold of fibres involved[167] and it is known that once contracted the cancer is not exacerbated by further exposure. The House of Lords proceeded upon the basis that this scientific uncertainty precluded attribution of causal responsibility to a specific defendant on the balance of probabilities: the claimants' mesothelioma may have eventuated from a specific fibre of one defendant or more than one defendant could be causally involved

---

[161] A good example is *Mullen* v. *Armstrong World Indus., Inc.*, 246 Cal Rptr 32 (Cal CA 1988).

[162] *Doe* v. *Cutter Biological* 852 F Supp 909, 914 (Idaho, 1994) (different risks).

[163] *Skipworth* v. *Lead Paint Industries Association* 690 A 2d 169 (Philadelphia, 1997).

[164] §28, comment *o*; emphasis added.   [165] [2003] 1 AC 32.

[166] A helpful judicial exposition of the latest medical evidence, which suggests that a large number of fibres are involved in the mechanism, is found in *Employers' Liability "Trigger" Litigation* [2009] 2 All ER 26, [103]–[113] (Burton J).

[167] *Fairchild*, 43 (Lord Bingham).

through a cumulative mechanism: it was not possible to say which was more probable though, trivially, exposure could be said to increase the risk of suffering mesothelioma. Further, it was assumed that background exposure could be discounted such that all possible sources of asbestos were wrongful.[168]

In these circumstances, the defendants were unanimously held liable for the entire damage; apportionment was not addressed.[169] The reasoning of their Lordships varied. Three arguments may be identified. First, it was unfair that if only one defendant had breached a duty to the claimant, there would have been recovery, but because there were multiple defendants in breach of duty, the claimant could not recover because he could not point to the causative one;[170] second, there was the (*Summers*-like) consideration that as between those in breach of duty and one who has suffered serious harm through a breach of duty in circumstances where it is impossible to identify the causative party, injustice to the defendants is outweighed by injustice to the claimant;[171] third, if there were no liability, the defendants would be at liberty to ignore their duty of care without sanction.[172]

Although the third argument may apply in any case where the defendant can reasonably predict that it will not be subject to liability because of recurrent impossibility in the proof of causation,[173] the first two arguments are directed at the defendant indeterminacy situation. Subsequent developments in English law, which expand its set of doctrines beyond the defendant indeterminacy situation, have necessarily placed less emphasis upon them. Nonetheless, given that the central arguments for the decision in *Fairchild* apply to it, it is relatively clear that English law would find each defendant liable in a *Summers* v. *Tice* situation, where the claimant has proven that its injury was caused by wrongful conduct.[174]

---

[168] Ibid. 43.   [169] *Fairchild*, 68 (Lord Bingham); 95 (Lord Hutton) 97 (Lord Rodger).

[170] Ibid. 44 (Lord Bingham); 78 (Lord Hutton).

[171] Ibid. 67 (Lord Bingham); 69–70 (Lord Nicholls); 75 (Lord Hutton); 112 (Lord Rodger).

[172] Ibid. 69 (Lord Bingham), 74 (Lord Hoffmann), 112 (Lord Rodger).

[173] See further, Chapter 5, 269ff.

[174] See *Heneghan* v. *Manchester Dry Docks Ltd* [2014] EWHC 4190, which applies *Fairchild* to what is probably a defendant indeterminacy situation involving several negligent defendants. On this case, see further S. Steel, 'On When *Fairchild* Applies' and Chapter 5, 233–235. Liability is, however, proportional to the probability of causation: see *Heneghan*, and Chapter 5, 231–233. The decision in *Summers* v. *Tice* was approvingly cited in *Fairchild* [39] (Lord Nicholls); see also at [164] (Lord Rodger). It is also notable that Lord Phillips in *Sienkiewicz* v. *Greif UK Ltd* [2011] UKSC 10, [2011] 2 WLR 523 at [105] described a hypothetical

Defendant indeterminacy variants

Extent of loss variant

In *unknown extent* cases, English law adopts a liberal approach to determining how much loss each defendant has caused. The approach is liberal in the sense that the claimant is not required to identify with great precision the extent of the defendant's contribution.[175] Strictly, if the amount caused by each defendant cannot be ascertained even roughly, the claimant loses entirely, since it bears the burden of proof. It is, however, difficult to envisage such cases.

Causative defendants variant

The causative defendants situation has not arisen in English law.

Canada

Canadian law recognises liability in solidum in cases of defendant indeterminacy.[176] The leading case is *Cook* v. *Lewis*, where one of the two defendant hunters' negligent shots struck the claimant who was beyond them in the bushes.[177] The majority judgment cautiously adopted the reasons (without elaborating precisely which) of the court in *Summers*,[178] holding that while the general rule was that where C establishes that his injury is caused by the negligence of either A or B, but has not shown which, C must fail, 'special circumstances' may demand an exception to the rule.[179] They stated that if the jury had been unable to pin down causation to a specific hunter 'both defendants should have been held liable'.[180]

In contrast to the majority, Rand J provided an argument similar to that of the Cour de Grenoble[181] in order to shift the burden of proof on

situation structurally similar to *Summers* v. *Tice* (injury caused by a tort, but unknown by whom) as one to which the *Fairchild* exception would apply. *Fairchild* itself is not precisely analogous to *Summers* since in *Fairchild* there was a possibility that more than one defendant had contributed to the injury for which the claimant sought compensation, whereas in *Summers*, only one of the two defendants had caused the claimant's eye injury. In one respect, this makes *Fairchild* an even stronger case for liability than *Summers*, since there is a higher probability that each defendant was causative. See also *Zurich Insurance Plc* v. *International Energy Group Ltd* [2015] UKSC 33 [127].

[175] See *Holtby* v. *Brigham & Cowan (Hull) Ltd* [2000] 3 All ER 421, 429 (Stuart-Smith LJ). See further, Chapter 5, 243–246.

[176] L. Klar, *Tort Law*, 3rd edition 2008, 455; A. Linden, *Canadian Tort Law*, 7th edition 2002, 116–18.

[177] [1951] SCR 830 (*Cook*). For a searching discussion of *Cook*, favouring the result, see G. Williams, 'Case Comment on Cook v Lewis'.

[178] *Cook*, 842.   [179] Ibid., 840.   [180] Ibid., 842.   [181] See pp.157–158.

natural causation onto the defendants. The argument sought to render the defendants *responsible* for the impossibility of proof: '[the defendants] violated not only the victim's substantive right to security, but...also culpably impaired [his] remedial right of establishing liability' by confusing their acts with the 'environmental conditions'. The latter violation was not too remote a consequence of their negligent conduct since it was a 'direct' consequence within the then applicable *Re Polemis* rule of remoteness.[182] Both Rand J and the majority, however, agreed upon the necessity of there being an impossibility of proof: if the jury had only failed to make proper findings on which defendant caused the injury then the special rule would not apply.[183] Subsequent cases have made use of Rand J's reasoning in perhaps unexpected ways.[184] In *Lange v. Bennett*, the claimant carelessly got in the line of fire during a hunting accident. The Court stated that the claimant 'must be taken to have known that he might have been struck by a shot fired by either of them and it would be difficult to say in such circumstances which [defendant] fired the shot that struck him'.[185] That being the case, the facts did not constitute the 'special circumstances' required by *Cook*.

Though *Cook v. Lewis* has scarcely been applied,[186] it was confirmed by the Supreme Court in *Resurfice Corp.* v. *Hanke* to be part of Canadian law's approach to 'exceptions to the basic "but for test"'.[187] Somewhat confusing substantive concepts of causation with doctrines relating to the proof of causation, these situations were classed as applications of a 'material contribution test' of causation.[188] This test was said to apply so that 'liability may be imposed'[189] despite the absence of proof of but-for causation, where two conditions are met: (1) where it is 'impossible', due to factors outside the claimant's control (the court gave the current

---

[182] [1921] 3 KB 560.

[183] The rejection of its application in *Joseph Brant Memorial Hospital* v. *Koziol* [1978] 1 SCR 491 is based upon the failure to show that all possible causes were through defendants' negligence: ibid. 500–1. Similarly: *Kolesar* v. *Jeffries* (1977) 2 CCLT 170 (SCC); *Snell* v. *Farrell* (1990) 2 SCR 311, 326–8.

[184] Cf. the expansive use of this reasoning in: *Dorschell* v. *City of Cambridge* (1980) 117 DLR 3d 630, 635: 'breach [of] its duty to the plaintiff to keep the sidewalk clear of ice and snow has impaired the plaintiff's opportunity of proving liability'.

[185] *Lange* v. *Bennett* [1964] 1 OR 233, 237.

[186] It was applied in *Woodward* v. *Begbie* [1962] OR 60.

[187] *Resurfice* v. *Hanke* [2007] 1 SCR 333. It had also been approved in *Hollis* v. *Dow Corning Corp* [1995] 4 SCR 634, 639–40. For discussion of *Resurfice*: D. Cheifetz and V. Black, 'Through the Looking Glass, Darkly: Resurfice v Hanke'.

[188] *Resurfice*, [24] (McLachlin CJ).   [189] Ibid., [25].

limits of scientific knowledge as an example[190]) for the claimant to prove the defendant's negligence was a but-for cause of her injury; (2) where it is clear the defendant was in breach of duty to the claimant, thereby exposing it to an unreasonable risk of injury; and it has suffered an injury of the type risked.[191] Such exceptions were justified on the basis that 'it would offend basic notions of fairness and justice to deny liability by applying a "but for" approach'.[192]

The Court gave *Cook* as an example of 'one situation' where this exceptional rule can be applied. However, the two criteria justifying the application of an exceptional rule pointed to a wider rule; the Court did not require that the claimant have been the victim of a compensable tort. This was also possibly suggested by the second example given by the *Resurfice* court of an exceptional situation: *Walker Estate* v. *York Finch General Hospital*.[193] The causal issue in that case was whether X, a blood donor, would have donated his HIV infected blood, which infected the claimant, had the defendant blood provider (the Canadian Red Cross Society) non-negligently screened X. Though it was accepted that on the balance of probability X would not have donated his blood, the Supreme Court reasoned, *obiter*, that 'it may be difficult or impossible to prove hypothetically what the donor would have done' and stated that the claimant needed only to prove a 'material contribution'.[194]

This could be understood in three ways. First, it could be understood to mean that the claimant needed only to prove a 'contribution' in the sense described in Chapter 1 – namely, that D's negligence was a NESS condition of the result. This would be a conceptual enlargement of the

---

[190] The Ontario Supreme Court had used the absence of scientific impossibility as a reason to deny applying *Resurfice*: *Tompkins* v. *Home Depot Holding Inc.* 2009 CanLII 2.

[191] *Resurfice* [25]–[26].

[192] Ibid. The influence of *Fairchild*, though not cited by the Court, is apparent here. The reference to the limits of scientific knowledge; increase in risk; and 'basic notions of fairness and justice' has clear affinities with the *Fairchild* rule. D. Cheifetz and V. Black, 'Through the Looking Glass', 252 also suggest that *Resurfice* may have been implicitly accepting *Fairchild*. Similarly, *Cottrelle* v. *Gerrard* (2003) 67 OR (3d) 737 had hinted at a link between the 'material contribution' approach to cases where but-for causation is 'unworkable' [30]. (The material contribution approach to causation was first established in Canada in *Athey* v. *Leonati* [1996] 3 SCR 458 as encompassing cases where the but-for test of causation is deemed 'unworkable' [15]. Unworkable was undefined.) *Cottrelle* stated that cases of unworkability were linked by 'it [being] impossible to determine the precise cause of the injury' [30]. For a pre-*Clements* comparison of English and Canadian law here, see M. Tse, 'Tests for Factual Causation'.

[193] [2001] 1 SCR 647.   [194] Ibid., [88].

but-for test. Second, it could be understood to be creating what would more transparently be called a 'material contribution to risk' rule, whereby D's negligence *may* have been a but-for or contribution cause to the result, but this cannot be determined on the balance of probability, yet nonetheless the defendant will be held liable. Third, it could be understood to be creating a rule according to which D is not permitted to rely upon the hypothetical negligence of the donor in order to avoid a finding of but-for causation. The first reading is probably correct, yet the *Resurfice* court appears to have adopted the second reading.[195] According to that second reading, the primary question is simply whether proof of causation on the balance of probability is impossible – there is no focus on whether the claimant has proven that their injury was caused by wrongful conduct, as in *Cook*.

Cases subsequent to *Resurfice* seemed to confirm that Canadian law was shifting from an exceptional rule solely covering defendant indeterminacy to a rule encompassing situations involving potential non-tortious causation. The crucial question in the application of *Resurfice* was not whether the claimant had been the victim of a wrong, but rather whether there was sufficient 'impossibility of proof' (the first requirement laid down in *Resurfice*).[196] The limits of the principle were therefore determined by the extent to which proof on the balance of probability was treated as 'impossible'.

The post-*Resurfice* Supreme Court decision in *Clements* v. *Clements* has now closed off this development and returned the ambit of Canadian law's exceptional departures from proof of causation on the balance of probability to the defendant indeterminacy situation.[197]

Clements itself was a simple case: the causal issue was whether the defendant's negligent speeding was a but-for cause, on the balance of probability, of his losing control and injuring the claimant, or whether the injury would have occurred anyway due to the fact that his motorcycle tire had burst. At first instance, the trial judge had held this question to be insusceptible of proof on the balance of probability, and had held the defendant liable under the *Resurfice* 'impossibility of proof' exception.[198]

---

[195] See ibid.

[196] *Zazelenchuk* v. *Kumleben* [2007] AJ No 1500 (CA); *Bohun* v. *Segal* (2008) 289 DLR (4th) 614 [53]-[55]. Cf. *Fullowka* v. *Royal Oak Ventures Inc* 2008 NWTCA 9 (no impossibility of proof) upheld by the SC: [2010] 1 SCR 132.

[197] *Clements* v. *Clements*, 2012 SCC 32.   [198] *Clements* v. *Clements*, 2009 BCSC 112.

In a restatement of Canadian proof of causation law with which all Justices agreed, McLachlin CJ emphasised that 'impossibility of proof' alone was not a suitable criterion for determining whether a departure from proof on the balance of probability should be made in respect to causation.[199] In effect, allowing claimants to succeed whenever proof of causation is impossible is to reverse the legal burden of proof in all cases.[200] Rather, for an exception to be made, it had to be impossible to prove causation on the balance of probability on the specific ground that each of a number of negligent defendants, one or more of whom has in fact been a cause of the claimant's injury, can 'point the finger at the other'.[201]

In such circumstances, 'the underlying goals of the law of negligence' were met by making an exception to proof on the BPR:[202] 'compensation' is achieved, 'fairness' is satisfied because the claimant is entitled to compensation under the law of tort and each defendant may have been a wrongful cause of its injury, and 'deterrence' is furthered. Moreover, it was claimed, these goals were achieved consistently with 'corrective justice' because: 'the plaintiff has shown that she is in a correlative relationship of doer and sufferer *with the group of defendants as a whole*'.[203]

It would seem that the *dicta* in *Walker Estate* are now to be rationalised as holding that a negligent defendant is not permitted to 'point the finger' at a person's *hypothetical negligence* – the negligence that an HIV-infected donor would commit were it to give blood, having been warned of the risks of so doing – in order to avoid a finding of but-for causation. It should be observed that the rule in *Walker Estate* is conceptually distinct from the defendant indeterminacy rule in *Cook* – even if the two share a similar normative justification.[204] The *Walker Estate* rule also applies where all the facts are known – even if it were shown that the donor *would* have negligently given blood, the claimant is still entitled to damages from the defendant screening organisation – whereas *Cook* is a rule applicable only under conditions of evidential *uncertainty* as to the identity of the wrongdoer.

Justifications for liability under defendant indeterminacy: analysis

Can liability in the core defendant indeterminacy situation and its variants be justified? This section argues that it can. Two principal forms of justification for liability in cases of defendant indeterminacy can be distilled from

---

[199] *Clements* (SC), [35]–[38].   [200] Ibid., [37].   [201] *Clements*, [39].   [202] Ibid. [42].
[203] *Clements*, [41].   [204] See Chapter 1, 43–44.

the systems studied. The first form is characterised by the attempt to demonstrate that, contrary to appearances, each defendant has violated the claimant's rights in such a way as to give rise to a claim for substantial damages. The general strategy of such arguments is to show that each defendant has either caused the claimant's injury *or* has caused the claimant to be unable successfully to sue in respect of that injury. The second form of justification is a direct appeal to *fairness*. Two versions of the fairness argument are typically found: one appeals to *relative injustice* and the other appeals to the *reliance upon another person's wrongdoing*.

It will be argued that the first form of justification is not successful in relation to the core defendant indeterminacy situation or its variants if it is construed as a claim about the current law. This is principally for the reason that, in most cases, causing another person to lose the ability to sue another person in respect of an injury is to inflict a remote, and purely economic, loss. However, it is argued that a normative version of this argument, which departs in certain respects from the existing law in at least England and Germany, is successful. Second, it is argued that a different form of the first justification, which holds each defendant responsible for failing to authorise another person to act on its behalf, is successful in relation to the causative defendant variant of the defendant indeterminacy situation. Third, it is argued that the two fairness arguments together plausibly justify liability in the core defendant indeterminacy cases and their variants and that these justifications do not spill over into cases where the claimant's injury has been potentially been caused entirely by non-tortious causes.

Justifying defendant indeterminacy by showing that each defendant has wrongfully caused the claimant injury

Liability for wrongfully causing the inability to establish a claim in tort

A justification advanced by some French courts,[205] and by various authors,[206] for liability in cases of defendant indeterminacy is that it is shown to the requisite standard of proof that each defendant is straightforwardly liable in tort *or* that it has caused the claimant to be unable to

---

[205] See pp. 157–158. This is also one way of reading Rand J's judgment in *Cook* v. *Lewis*; see p.171.

[206] I. Postacioglu, 'Les faits simultanés'. In Anglo-American-Canadian law: A. Porat and A. Stein, *Tort Liability under Uncertainty*, 162 (their views are discussed in more detail in Chapter 5, 276–282); A. Beever, *Rediscovering the Law of Negligence*, 462–5. In German law: T. Weckerle, *Die deliktische Verantwortlichkeit mehrerer*, 124ff.

establish a claim in tort. To illustrate this argument, let us take a simple (and paradigmatic) case:

> *Two Hunters, Evidential Uncertainty.* D1 and D2, each on separate hunting trips in the same wood, negligently fire towards C. One bullet strikes C, causing C physical injury. Due to the identical guns and calibre of bullets used, it is not possible to determine which bullet struck C.

The argument proceeds as follows. Either it is the case that D1 has negligently physically injured C and D2's negligent firing has prevented it being known that D1 has damaged C *or* it is the case that D2 has caused C's physical injury and D1 prevented it being known that D2 has caused the physical injury. In both possibilities, then, each defendant has either caused physical injury or the inability to prove the cause of a physical injury with the result that no compensation in respect of it is obtained. Consequently, since each defendant is liable for the damage on either possibility, D1 and D2 are liable in solidum. In the Cour de Grenoble case, this conclusion is generated by the claim that causing the inability to prove the case against the other defendant is itself to cause an actionable loss.[207] The value of the latter claim is the value of the claim for physical injury which has been destroyed. Although it cannot be determined which defendant is liable for which loss, it can be said that both are at least liable in the same amount. Call this the 'prevented claim theory' in virtue of the fact that the ground of one defendant's liability is that it has prevented the success of the claim against the other defendant. The term 'primary claim' is used to refer to the claim in respect of the physical injury itself. The term 'prevention claim' is used to refer to the claim whose ground is that the defendant has prevented a claim against the other defendant.

Prevented claim theory: the unadorned version
What can be called the 'unadorned' version of the prevented claim theory – the version just presented – suffers from four difficulties.[208] These concern: (1) the nature of the loss suffered by the claimant in the prevention claim; (2) the remoteness of the type of loss suffered in the prevention claim; (3) the insolvency or untraceability of one or more defendants; and (4) the paradoxical implications of the theory. The aim

---

[207] See p.157.
[208] See further N.J. McBride and S. Steel, 'Suing for the Loss of the Right to Sue: Why *Wright* is Wrong', 33-9.

here is ultimately to vindicate the prevented claim theory. First, however, these problems are explained, before a more defensible version of the prevented claim theory, which addresses almost all of the problems with the unadorned theory, is introduced.

The nature of the loss

Preventing a person from being able to sue another for damages (without physically injuring them or their property) is *prima facie* to cause that person a purely economic loss: the defendant prevents the claimant receiving the monetary damages it would otherwise have received.[209] Common law systems are generally described as adopting a restrictive or generally exclusionary approach to negligent infliction of this form of loss.[210] The German position is structurally similar: economic loss is not itself one of the interests explicitly protected under §823 I BGB. In these systems, the recovery of pure economic losses in tort outside of situations where one party has assumed responsibility to another in respect of a task is relatively rare.[211] Even in French law, which is more expansive in respect of purely economic losses, it has been suggested that careless destruction of another's legal case would not in general constitute *fault*.[212] There is, then, a difficulty with the legal justification of the prevented claim theory, in view of the general position on pure economic loss.[213] More precisely, the difficulty is that one does not have a legal right, outside of special relationships, that others not intentionally or negligently inflict merely economic loss upon one.[214]

Remoteness

Even if each defendant in *Two Hunters* could be said either to be a cause of the injury or a cause of the inability to claim in respect of the injury, the latter is *prima facie* a *remote* consequence of the negligence.

---

[209] See D. Robertson, 'The Common Sense of Cause-In-Fact', 1787; R. Stevens, *Torts and Rights*, 140; T. Keren-Paz, 'Risks and Wrongs' Account of Corrective Justice', 103.

[210] See, for example, A. Bernstein, 'Keep it Simple: an Explanation of the Rule of No Recovery for Pure Economic Loss', 773; C. van Dam, *European Tort Law*, 1st edition 711.

[211] C. van Dam, *European Tort Law*, 711; N. Jansen, 'Developing Legal Doctrine: Fault in the German Law of Delict', 107–9.

[212] G. Viney and P. Jourdain, *Les Conditions de la Responsabilité*, 3rd edition 245. Admittedly, it may be possible to generate liability under Article 1384 CC, which does not require fault.

[213] This legal objection to the prevented cause of action theory was made early on by L. Traeger, *Der Kausalbegriff im Straf- und Zivilrecht*, 291. It is echoed by later scholars. See, for example, L. Röckrath, *Kausalität*, 184.

[214] R. Stevens, *Torts and Rights*, 21–3.

First, the risk which eventuates is not one of the risks which make the conduct negligent in the first place. In German law this is expressed by the idea that the injury must be within the protective purpose of the norm breached (*Schutzzweck der Norm*).[215] For example, that the *Fairchild* defendant's conduct risks the claimant's inability to prove its case plays no role in the reasons why its conduct is negligent: it is neither necessary nor sufficient for that conduct's being negligent. Even if somehow it were possible to identify causative defendants in mesothelioma cases, the defendant's conduct would still be negligent in that it unreasonably risks physical injury. And it is difficult to say that it is a necessary element of a sufficient set of reasons sufficient for the negligence of the conduct.[216] Second, the preclusion of the ability to sue another person for negligent injury is arguably not a reasonably foreseeable consequence of negligently firing in, for example, *Two Hunters, Evidential Uncertainty*.[217]

Insolvent or untraceable defendants

Suppose in *Two Hunters, Evidential Uncertainty* that D1 is bankrupt. If D2 has caused the claim against D1 to fail, D2 has caused the loss of a valueless claim. Consequently, D2 should not be liable for substantial damages. Hence, the prevented claim theory would only be able to justify liability in a case where all defendants are solvent. The law in each jurisdiction does not, however, *require* that D1 and D2 be solvent in order for C to have a cause of action against both. Of course, the law may be open to challenge on this point. At the least, the prevented claim theory is in need of further defence or revision on this point.

Paradox

A premise of the prevented claim theory is that one defendant has prevented the claimant from being able to recover damages in respect of the infringement of its primary right by the other defendant. But this premise seems to be contradicted by the fact that, if the prevented claim theory is successful, the claimant can after all sue the defendant who caused the physical injury. Thus, it turns out that no claim has been prevented after all. But, if the claimant has not been deprived of a claim, then the basis of the defendants' liability collapses. If so, then the claimant cannot sue either defendant, and therefore has been deprived

---

[215] B. Markesinis and H. Unberath, *The German Law of Torts*, 107–8.

[216] For this way of analysing the 'harm within the risk' test, see M. Moore, *Causation and Responsibility*: Chapters 7–10.

[217] Cf., however, Rand J in *Cook* [1951] SCR 830, 834.

of a claim. Then it follows that the claimant *can* sue both defendants. But if it *can* sue both, then it has not been deprived of a claim against the defendant who caused the physical injury. It seems that the law is propelled into an infinite regress here.[218]

Multiple defendants?

The prevented claim theory could seem to have a further limitation in that it may only apply in a case involving two defendants, while the law in each jurisdiction does not limit the application of the defendant indeterminacy rules to two defendant cases.[219] Suppose *Two Hunters, Evidential Uncertainty*, where three hunters fire negligently and only one bullet has struck. An objection to the liability of each hunter (D1, D2, D3) runs as follows:

(1) Either D1, D2, or D3 has caused the physical injury.
(2) In the case where D1 has caused the physical injury, either D2 has caused the inability to show that D1 caused the injury and D3 has caused no injury, or D3 has caused the inability to show D1 has caused the injury and D2 has caused no injury.

Thus, unlike in *Two Hunters*, there is a possible situation for each defendant in which that defendant appears to have caused no injury. However, this problem is illusory. First, it can be argued that the loss of the claim against D1 is causally overdetermined by the actions of D2 and D3: each is a cause of the loss of the claim. Second, it is possible to say in (2) that D3 has caused the loss of a claim against D1 and D2, which C would otherwise have had: D3 has prevented the prevention claim against D2.[220] Assuming that the claim against D1 is a valuable one, D2 would be liable in full, and therefore the destruction of the claim against D2 is destruction of a valuable claim. This analysis could be extended recursively to *n* defendants (tortuously). The increased number of defendants *does* seem to intensify the remoteness problem, however. The prolix causal route by which the defendant causes loss to the claimant becomes less and less foreseeable the more defendants are added.

Prevented claim theory: answering the objections

There are, then, four principal objections to the unadorned theory: that the loss is purely economic, too remote, that the theory does not cover

---

[218] The objection (described as a 'circularity' problem) is made by R. Stevens, *Torts and Rights*, 150.

[219] See, for this objection, J. Stapleton, 'Review of Porat and Stein', 311.

[220] This argument is made by A. Beever, *Rediscovering*, 463–4.

the insolvency situation, and that it leads to paradoxical implications. It is now argued that the first two objections can be addressed by a more nuanced version of the prevented claim theory. The basic strategy involves justifying a normative approximation of infliction of physical injury to prevention of a claim in respect of that injury such that wrongful infliction of one can be assimilated to wrongful infliction of the other. Here I draw upon and refine an argument offered by Beever that the claimant's secondary right to damages in respect of an injury is a normative equivalent to its (primary) right to bodily integrity. Then I offer tentative solutions to the insolvency and paradox problems, but concede one important limitation to the solution given.

Beever: interference with the right to bodily integrity

Beever[221] claims that the defendant who does not cause the physical injury itself in *Two Hunters* nonetheless violates the claimant's 'right to bodily integrity' by preventing the claimant from obtaining compensatory damages in respect of the violation of their bodily integrity by another person.[222] What appears to be merely economic loss is in fact, on his account, an infringement of the claimant's right to *bodily integrity*. Moreover, since each defendant has acted negligently *in relation to the claimant's bodily integrity*, the loss is not too remote.

The argument (as I reconstruct it) is as follows: (1) the claimant's legal right to damages in respect of an invasion of its bodily integrity is the normative equivalent of its legal right to be physically uninjured by negligence in the first place;[223] (2) violating the normative equivalent to one's right to bodily integrity is itself to violate that right; therefore (3) injuring the normative equivalent of the claimant's right to bodily integrity violates that right.

Premises (1) and (2) are plausible so long as they are not too strongly put. The claimant's 'right to bodily integrity' is *simply* the legal right that others not (inter alia) negligently cause them (reasonably foreseeable) physical injury by their action. It is not *analytically* identical to the legal right to compensation for the violation of that right. The legal right that others not negligently cause one physical injury is held against the whole world, while the legal right to damages is held only

---

[221] A. Beever, *Rediscovering*, 459–65.
[222] A. Beever, *Rediscovering*, 460: 'in acting as he did, the defendant who did not hit the claimant nevertheless violated the claimant's right to bodily integrity'.
[223] See *Rediscovering*, 462–4. See also E. Weinrib, *Corrective Justice*, 87ff.

against the person who violates the former right. The legal right to compensation is sometimes assignable, whereas the right not to be physically injured is not.

It is nonetheless true that there is a significant normative continuity between primary and secondary rights.[224] Given this close normative continuity, there is some plausibility both in treating each defendant's negligence in relation to the claimant's actual bodily integrity as negligence in relation to this normative 'stand in' or substitute for the primary right and in treating the causation of interference with the claimant's secondary right as *similar* to causing of physical injury itself.

Here are two further arguments for the normative equiparation of interference with the claimant's secondary right to compensation and its right to bodily integrity in this context so as to avoid the pure economic loss and remoteness objections. First, the effect of the deprivation of the claim is not simply that C did not obtain money, but that the injustice that the money would have served to correct went uncorrected. This provides an additional reason to favour the claim.[225] Second, the remoteness objection seems particularly weak in this context since the defendant is only being asked to pay the same amount of damages as they would have been liable to pay had their conduct actually resulted in the very thing which their conduct risked. Each defendant in *Two Hunters, Evidential Uncertainty* is only being required to pay for *an amount* of losses which one would reasonably expect to occur as a result of their negligence.

---

[224] Cf. *Wright* v. *Cambridge Medical Group* [2011] EWCA Civ 669, [30]: 'an award of damages for clinical negligence is, in a sense, the legal equivalent of proper clinical treatment' (Lord Neuberger). That the prevention of the claim for the physical injury is non-remote is also supported by the decision in *Haxton* v. *Phillips Electronics Ltd* [2014] EWCA Civ 4, where C argued that D's negligently causing her to suffer mesothelioma reduced her life expectancy and thereby reduced the extent of her claim for loss of dependency under the Fatal Accidents Act 1976 in respect of the death of her husband (which had also been caused by D's negligence). This loss was held to be non-remote (ibid., [23]).

[225] Another version of the prevented claim theory might simply hold that people should enjoy *a right that others not negligently cause one an economic loss affecting one's physical interests by negligently endangering those physical interests*. This would require some modification of English law: *Murphy* v. *Brentwood District Council* [1991] 1 AC 398. This change would, however, be desirable. There is considerable moral force in the claim that causing a person an economic loss, where the money would have been used to ameliorate the person's health, is indirectly to interfere with the claimant's general interest in physical integrity. See, similarly, E. Voyiakis, 'The Great Illusion: Tort Law and Exposure to Danger of Physical Harm', 925.

Vindicating prevented claim theory

Beever does not address the insolvency or paradox problems. In relation to the former, he asserts that 'the liability of the party who did not shoot the claimant [in *Two Hunters*] is in no way parasitic on the liability of the party who did shoot the claimant'.[226] Yet if the basis of one defendant's liability is that it has interfered with C's right to bodily integrity *by precluding that right being enforced against another defendant*, it is, on the face of it, highly relevant in assessing damages that this preclusion made the claimant *no worse off* (if the other defendant was insolvent, the claim would have been valueless).[227]

Here, then, is a tentative response to the insolvency problem. If the preventing defendant is said to have prevented a judgment being entered against the other defendant for having caused the physical injury, then this remains true even if that defendant is insolvent. If, given the normative continuity between primary and secondary rights and the fact that remoteness objections have less force in this type of situation, it is legitimate to treat this interference with the claimant's secondary right as 'in effect' an invasion of its primary right, then each defendant can be said to have either caused the claimant's physical injury or done something normatively highly similar to having caused the physical injury. In other words, it is just as if the preventing defendant had negligently caused physical injury itself. Both then are jointly and severally liable in respect of the physical injury.

The paradox objection can be defused by more precisely specifying the claim that the claimant has been prevented from pursuing. If the claim which the claimant is given under the prevented claim theory against the defendant who caused the physical injury is *different* to the claim that it was deprived of against that defendant by the other defendant, then the paradox does not arise. The paradox only arises because it seems that the result of applying the theory is that the claimant is not deprived of a claim against the defendant who caused the physical injury after all – since it can sue both defendants. And it is true that the claimant is not deprived of 'a' claim against that defendant. But the prevented claim theory does not assert this: it asserts that the claimant was deprived of its ordinary physical injury claim (which would have been available on the balance of probability) against the causative defendant. The claimant *has*

---

[226] A. Beever, *Rediscovering*, 462.   [227] Chapter 1, 42.

lost *this* claim. The claim arising from the prevented claim theory is not the *same* claim as the one of which the defendant deprived the claimant.[228]

It might still be objected by each defendant that, although it is true that one of them did indeed deprive the claimant of a claim which it would not regain by the application of the prevented claim theory, this deprivation made the claimant *no worse off*. This is because the claimant still has a claim for damages *in respect* of the physical injury against the causative defendant, even if it is not the same claim as it would have had. But in order to make this argument, each defendant will need to rely upon its own wrongful conduct or the wrongful conduct of the other defendant(s). To that extent, the prevented claim theory and the reliance upon wrongdoing argument discussed later are not entirely distinct.

Conclusions on prevented claim theory

The prevented claim theory has three principal virtues. First, it explains the relationship between the exceptional rule of liability in solidum in cases of defendant indeterminacy in a clear way: the exceptional rule, in fact, conforms to the general rules of proof. Second, it appears to give more precise content to the often expressed idea[229] that, as a matter of justice, the claimant ought not to be legally worse off by the addition of wrongdoers. Third, it provides relatively clear boundaries to the scope of any 'exceptional' doctrine: each defendant must have acted in relation to the claimant in a way which would generate a claim for the injury suffered, were causation of that injury proven against them, and it must be that the wrongful conduct of each has either been a cause of the injury or has prevented a claim arising in respect of that injury. However, even the more nuanced prevented claim theory only safely justifies liability in cases where all defendants are solvent and traceable. Moreover, in order to avoid the paradox objection it needs to rely upon the reliance upon wrongdoing argument discussed later in this section.

Liability for wrongfully failing to authorise another to pay damages on one's behalf

Consider again the following causative defendant variant, suggested by Häger:

---

[228] The claims are different because the grounds of the claims are different.
[229] See, e.g. p.160.

Two Cars D1 and D2 wrongfully, independently, destroy the cars of C1 and C2. It is impossible to determine whether D1 or D2 damaged C1 or C2's car.[230]

On the face of it, each claimant should fail: neither can prove which defendant caused its injury on the balance of probability. Intuitively, this is extremely unjust. Here is an argument why both should succeed under certain conditions. Both D1 and D2 owe a moral duty to compensate one of C1 and C2 in virtue of the fact that each has wrongfully caused injury to one of them. D1 and D2, acting separately, cannot fulfil this duty. What should they do?[231] It hardly seems consistent with D1's knowledge that he owes a duty to compensate to one of C1 or C2 to do nothing.[232] Rather, D1 and D2 should make an agreement whereby each authorises the other to act on the other's behalf. In this way, each can be sure that he is compensating *his* victim because either he, or someone whom he has authorised, is paying the compensation. Liability in *Two Cars* is thus justifiable as premised on what the defendants actually have a duty to do.

This argument only works to the extent that each car is of the same value and to the extent that the defendants are all solvent. If the cars have different values, each is liable for the maximum amount both have caused on the balance of probability: each defendant has a duty to make an agreement at least in respect of that amount. In respect of any further amount, or in the event that one defendant is insolvent, the claim must be justified in some other way.

Fairness

A characteristic of the development of justifications for liability in situations of defendant indeterminacy is the emphasis upon argument from broad notions of fairness. These can be categorised as follows. On the one

---

[230] See p. 152.
[231] For this argument in the context of similar problems in the morality of self-defence, see V. Tadros, *The Ends of Harm*, 192–5. See further S. Steel, 'Justifying Exceptions to Proof of Causation in Tort Law' for a detailed treatment of this argument.
[232] Cf. the obligation of the finder of some unknown other person's property: *Parker* v. *British Airways Board* [1982] QB 1004, 1017: 'A person having a finder's rights has an obligation to take such measures as in all the circumstances are reasonable to acquaint the true owner of the finding'.

hand, there is an argument from *relative injustice* (RI).[233] This argument purports to justify the departure from the general proof rules on the grounds of the greater injustice of the consequences of there being no liability relative to a rule of liability. Forms of this argument are found in the French and German literature, in the majority opinions in *Cook*, in *Fairchild*, and in the American Restatements. On the other hand, there is an argument which appeals more to the fact that the defendant is relying upon another's wrong to evade liability (RW). These are considered in turn.

Relative injustice

Consider, again, *Two Hunters, Evidential Uncertainty*. RI focuses directly upon the idea that it is 'more unjust'[234] to allow the claimant, who has been the victim of a legal wrong, to receive no damages in such a case than to impose liability in damages upon one defendant who has not caused the claimant's injury.[235] This is the situation, since it is certain that an injustice will be inflicted upon the non-causative defendant if liability is imposed upon both defendants, and if no liability is imposed upon either, then it is certain that liability will fail to be imposed where justice demands it be imposed. In other terms, a false positive or a false negative is inevitable. RI claims that this false negative is more unjust than a false positive.[236]

The main consideration in support of this RI claim is the one emphasised particularly in German law – that the claimant is known, as a matter of justice, to be entitled to compensation.[237] It has been argued that, in light of this, there is a 100 per cent chance of injustice from the

---

[233] D. Nolan, 'Causation and the Goals of Tort Law' calls these arguments from 'equity', 174. Cf. J. Stapleton, 'Lords a'leaping Evidentiary Gaps' who refers to the 'justice argument', 289, 288ff.

[234] J. Fleming, 'Probabilistic Causation in Tort Law', 665, speaks of the 'equities' as different between the claimant and defendants. J. Stapleton, 'Lords a'leaping Evidentiary Gaps', 289, notes that 'it might be said that the injustice to the victim in applying the orthodox common law was very great'.

[235] Cf. A. Porat and A. Stein, *Tort Liability under Uncertainty*, 134: '...is it really possible to compare two distinct injustices from the corrective injustice perspective?...There seems to be no satisfactory answer to these questions'. We need a theory of how to rank departures from perfect justice. For this crucial point: T. Keren-Paz, 'Risks and Wrongs Account of Corrective Justice', 103.

[236] For a particularly clear exposition of this argument: *Vasquez v. Alameda* 49 Cal 2d 674, 682 (Cal 1958) (Traynor J).

[237] See also, for example, A. Ripstein and B. Zipursky, 'Corrective Justice in an Age of Mass Torts', 242; C. Eberl-Borges, Commentary on §830 BGB '§830 BGB', 509

claimant's perspective, while each defendant is only exposed to a 50 per cent chance of injustice.[238] Hence, it is permissible to favour C's interests. The initial problem with this argument is that from the perspective of one of the defendants there is a 100 per cent chance of injustice. On the face of it, it seems implausible to claim that the claimant's interest in receiving compensation is more important simply because there is a 100 per cent chance of injustice falling upon an *identified* person (while the causally innocent D is *unidentifiable*).

But this difference is crucial. In denying liability, the court must knowingly impose a 100 per cent risk of injustice upon a particular individual. In imposing liability the court can only say to each individual defendant that it is imposing a 50 per cent risk of injustice upon that defendant. In the former case, the risk imposition is targeted at one individual. In the latter case, the risk imposition is distributed across individuals. This distribution seems fairer than one placing all 100 per cent risk upon the claimant. This argument will also apply where there is more than one defendant. If there are three defendants, there is 66.6 per cent risk of injustice against each, while it remains true that there is a 100 per cent risk of injustice against the claimant.

The objection from relational injustice

It will be objected that, if one considers the claimant in relation to each defendant individually, there is only a 50 per cent risk of injustice to the claimant and a 50 per cent risk of injustice to the defendant, and thus no reason to favour the claimant over the defendant.[239] This is because injustice in tort law, on this view, must be considered as a relation between individual persons.[240] Injustice consists only in the breach of an obligation owed by a particular individual to another particular individual. If we consider C in relation to D1 alone, there is only a 50 per cent chance that a finding of no liability will result in D1 not being held liable for the breach of an obligation D1 owed to C.

This objection is confused. It is one thing to say that the legal rights and duties in tort law are rights and duties owed by and to particular individuals. That is the sense in which these rights and duties are relational. It is another to say that each individual has a legal entitlement to have their case considered by a judge in isolation from its consequences upon other cases. If C, D1, and D2 are before the court, the court knows

---

[238] G. Williams, 'Case Comment on Cook v Lewis', 351ff.
[239] See A. Beever, *Rediscovering*, 457–8.   [240] Ibid., 457.

that there is a 100 per cent chance of a *relational* injustice being committed against C – there is a 100 per cent chance that the person before the court who owes damages *to C* will not pay them – if there is no liability and a 50 per cent chance of committing an injustice against each D if liability is imposed. This does not involve treating the defendants as if they were a collective, each responsible for the actions of the other. It simply involves the judge taking into account the consequences of a finding of liability upon the parties.

The objection from insolvency or untraceability

Suppose that, in *Two Hunters, Evidential Uncertainty*, one defendant is insolvent. The effect of the RI argument here depends upon what exactly the injustice to the claimant in a finding of no liability consists in. If the injustice to the claimant consists in the court's refusing to make an order that the defendant pay damages, when it is known that the claimant is entitled to such an order against someone, then there remains a 100 per cent risk of injustice to the claimant, compared to a 50 per cent risk that the solvent defendant is subject to a legal duty to compensate to which it ought not to be subject. If, however, the injustice to the claimant is understood as 'being denied compensation, which it would actually have obtained had the facts been known, for the violation of its right', then there is only a 50 per cent risk of injustice to the claimant, compared to a 50 per cent risk of injustice to the solvent defendant. There would then, on the face of it, be no reason to favour the claimant over the defendant.

The better view is that the injustice consists in the denial of the existence of the claimant's entitlement by the court, rather than the satisfaction of the entitlement.[241] What, intuitively, seems particularly problematic about the defendant indeterminacy situation is that the multiple wrongful acts of defendants lead to a situation where the claimant's otherwise existing legal right to compensation evaporates. The normative difficulty is not the general one, faced by all claimants, of an entitlement not being *satisfied* due to insolvency.

If this is incorrect, it may still be plausible that a 50 per cent risk of injustice to a defendant who has wrongfully imposed a risk upon the claimant is preferable to a 50 per cent risk that a person, who is known

---

[241] This is reflected in German law's refusal to apply §830 I 2 BGB simply to generate a cause of action due to the insolvency of the defendant who is known to have been a cause of the injury. See pp. 148–149.

to have been caused injury by wrongful conduct, does not receive compensation that they otherwise would have received from the wrongdoer. The 50 per cent chance of doing justice to an innocent claimant who has been the victim of injury caused by a wrong is preferable to the 50 per cent risk of injustice to the defendant that wrongfully risked injury to the claimant.

Two objections may be made to this. If it is correct, it undermines the burden of proof on causation in every case. Normally, if there is a 50 per cent chance of doing justice to the claimant and a 50 per cent chance of doing an injustice to the defendant, the claimant loses. That is a consequence of the general burden of proof. The response to this objection is that the injustice which there is a chance of committing against the defendant in the defendant indeterminacy situation is of a different kind to injustice which there is a chance of committing against the defendant in the usual burden of proof situation. In the defendant indeterminacy situation, the injustice consists in holding the defendant liable for an injury caused by another's tort, while in the usual situation it consists in holding the defendant liable for an injury caused entirely by non-wrongful causes.

It may again be objected that it makes no difference to the injustice to the causally innocent defendant whether it is incorrectly held liable for injury caused by another's tort or for a non-wrongfully caused injury. It is true that in both cases the claimant obtains damages from the defendant which it was not entitled to receive from that defendant. A claimant wrongfully injured by D1 has no more claim against D2, who is not causally responsible for that injury, than a claimant who has been caused injury by entirely non-wrongful causes does against D2. Nonetheless, it does not seem unreasonable that tort law should have more concern for those who have suffered injury as a result of wrongdoing compared to those who have suffered it non-wrongfully.[242] As Weinrib once wrote: '[t]here seems to be a significant leap between making whole a plaintiff who has suffered a tortious injury and allowing recovery to one whose injury might not otherwise fail within the scope of tort law'.[243]

---

[242] This will be denied by those who insist upon injustice consisting in and being exhausted by the relationship between the individual parties.

[243] E. Weinrib, 'A Step Forward in Factual Causation', 525.

The second objection is that, in the tort of negligence at least, the legal wrong consists in negligence causing injury and thus a merely negligent defendant is 'entirely innocent' from a rights-based perspective – it has committed no legal wrong.[244]

It is suggested that this objection is probably incorrect.[245] A defendant who negligently risks physical injury to the claimant has committed a legal (and moral) wrong against the claimant. There are two reasons for this. First, it is commonplace for judges to say that the defendant has breached its legal duty of care but has caused no injury. This only makes sense if the defendant's duty can be specified independently of the causation of injury. Second, this is not inconsistent with the proposition that damage is the 'gist' of the action in negligence. It could plausibly be said that the law imposes two duties: a duty not unreasonably to risk physical injury and a duty not unreasonably to risk physical injury and thereby cause physical injury, with both having to be breached before compensation is due.[246]

In summary, the main response to the solvency problem has to be that the injustice to the claimant consists in the court's refusing to make an order for damages, rather than the failure of the claimant to *receive* damages. If this response fails, the RI argument is in difficulty. Even if the secondary response made above is successful in *Two Hunters* – namely, that a 50 per cent risk of injustice against a wronged claimant should be preferred to a 50 per cent risk of injustice against a wrongful defendant – this response will not work in cases where there are more insolvent defendants than solvent defendants. In such cases there will be a greater risk of injustice against an individual defendant than against the individual claimant.

Reliance upon another's wrongful conduct

A second form of fairness argument appeals to analogies with other areas of the law of tort where a person is prevented from relying upon the wrongdoing of another in order to avoid a liability to pay

---

[244] D. Nolan, 'Causation and the Goals of Tort Law', 175; A. Beever, *Rediscovering*, 446.

[245] See generally N. McBride, 'Duties of Care – Do They Really Exist?'.

[246] Although Weinrib has denied that risk imposition is itself wrongful, he refers, inconsistently, to unreasonable risk impositions as injustices. See E. Weinrib, *Corrective Justice*, 44. Cf. E. Weinrib, *The Idea of Private Law*, 157–8.

compensatory damages.[247] Consider the following case, which is in important respects analogous to *Two Hunters*:

> *Drug.* D1 negligently fails to include a warning on the packaging of a drug directing medical professionals not to administer the drug to persons using certain other medication. D2, doctor, administers the drug to C, negligently failing to check for any warnings on the packaging. C suffers injury due to a toxic combination of medications.

Neither defendant can be said to be a but-for cause here because each can argue that C's injury would have happened anyway. English law would nonetheless probably hold each defendant liable in full in this case, preventing each defendant from relying upon another's wrongful conduct to avoid a liability which would otherwise have arisen.[248] This result follows even if it is unclear (on conceptual, rather than evidential, grounds) whether one ought to hold that each D is a cause of C's injury because of the difficulties of arguing that either defendant materially contributed to the injury or was a NESS cause of it. Nonetheless, it is difficult to dispute the fairness of this result. It is better to hold each negligent defendant who has risked injury to the claimant liable although neither individually can be said to be a cause of the injury than not to award compensation to the victim whose injury would not have occurred had no-one behaved wrongfully. Here, then, two negligent defendants are made liable in order to compensate a claimant who would not have suffered an injury had no-one behaved wrongfully in relation to it.

The similarity between this case and the defendant indeterminacy case is that neither defendant can be shown to be a cause of the claimant's injury on the balance of probability (albeit on conceptual, rather than

---

[247] See, drawing an analogy with the doctrines described in Chapter 1 at pp.43–46, J. Morgan, 'Lost Causes in the House of Lords', 280–1 (tentatively); M. Geistfeld, 'The Doctrinal Unity of Alternative Liability and Market Share Liability', 116–20; N. McBride and S. Steel, 'Suing for the Loss of the Right to Sue', 31–2; S. Steel, 'Causation in English Tort Law: Still Wrong After All These Years', 260-3.

[248] Chapter 1, 43–44. Those who will insist that each defendant's negligence is in fact causative in *Drug* (or that only one of the two is actually causative) are invited to consider the other cases discussed under non-causal liability in Chapter 1, 43–46 as instances of the principle defended in the text. Moreover, even if one or both defendants can be successfully analysed as causative in *Drug*, it will remain true that no individual defendant has rendered the claimant *worse off*, a further requirement of liability. At this point, if the defendant is to be held liable in damages, it will then be necessary to rely upon the principle defended here – namely, that the defendant cannot rely upon another's wrongdoing to avoid a liability which would otherwise arise where that will have the effect of depriving a person of a right to compensation for an injury which would not have occurred had no-one behaved wrongfully in relation to that person.

evidential, grounds in *Drug*) and that imposing no liability would leave a claimant, who would not have suffered injury had no-one behaved wrongfully in relation to it, without any compensation for its loss. A narrow formulation of the principle underlying this result would plausibly be that a defendant is not permitted to rely upon another's wrongful conduct in order to avoid a liability to pay damages, which would otherwise arise against the defendant, where that has the effect of depriving a person whose injury would not have occurred had no-one behaved wrongfully of a right to compensation. This would, quite simply, be deeply unfair.

There is certainly a leap in moving from this situation to the indeterminate wrongdoer case. In *Drug,* it can said of *each* defendant that, had one defendant not been negligent, the other would straightforwardly be liable. In this way, a clear sense can be given to the notion that each defendant is relying upon the other's wrongful conduct to evade liability. This is not so in *Two Hunters*, where it cannot be said of each defendant individually that, had the other not behaved wrongfully, it would have been liable – that is unknown. All that is true of *Two Hunters* is that the *causative defendant* is relying upon the wrongful risking of the other defendant in order to evade liability. In relation to that unidentified defendant, a no-liability result would be to allow the causative defendant to rely upon the wrong of another. In itself, this is not a particularly powerful argument for burdening the non-causative defendant.

Nonetheless, the liability of both defendants in *Two Hunters* can be considered an extension of the principle of fairness underlying the result in cases like *Drug*.[249] The extended principle is that each defendant who has wrongfully risked injury to the claimant is precluded from pointing to the wrongful conduct of another defendant, where, if that same argument were open to the other defendant, the victim of an injury which would not have occurred but-for wrongful conduct, would have no legal entitlement to compensation in relation to that injury.

There is, of course, an element of bootstrapping about this claim and this analogy. It could be objected that the basis of liability in cases like *Drug* is itself obscure and so the analogy sheds more darkness than light. Nonetheless, to the extent that the liability in *Two Hunters* is supported by our convictions of fairness in other similar cases, it gains support. That is plausibly the case. As we have seen in Chapter 1, in the discussion of non-causal liabilities, the law is generally averse to

---

[249] Cf. M. Geistfeld, 'The Doctrinal Unity of Alternative Liability', 116.

allowing the mere multiplicity of wrongful actors to have the effect of depriving a person whose injury would not have occurred had no one behaved wrongfully in relation to them to extinguish that person's right to compensation.[250]

Further issues

Application to strict liability

If the strict liability cause of action in question is wrong-based (i.e. is constituted by the breach of a legal duty), and that wrong has been established as against each defendant, all of the arguments made above apply.[251] Thus, if the foundations of the claimant's house have been damaged by one of two wrongful emanations from the neighbouring land either of D1 or D2, each of which may have caused the injury, each should be liable in respect of that injury in the tort of private nuisance.

The more difficult case is where the strict liability cause of action is either constituted by a wrong which consists in the causation of injury, and no defendant has behaved wrongfully in relation to the claimant, or the cause of action is not based upon a wrong. For example, suppose it cannot be determined which of two defective products, each manufactured by a different manufacturer, injured the claimant. The Consumer Protection Act 1987 does not impose a primary legal duty upon a manufacturer. It only imposes a liability in the event that certain injuries are caused by a defective product.[252] Here, therefore, it cannot be said that the causative defendant is relying upon another's *wrong* – the manufacture of a defective product need not itself be legally wrongful. The prevented claim theory does not apply directly since it relies upon a normative similarity between primary and secondary rights. The problem here is that there is no primary *right*.

However, the relative injustice argument still applies: it remains the case that a 100 per cent risk of a false positive is being placed upon the claimant if no liability is imposed, compared to lesser risks to defendants, if liability is imposed. This may alone be enough to justify liability.

---

[250] Our moral intuitions gain support by their coherence with others, on one plausible view. See R. Dworkin, *Justice for Hedgehogs*, ch 1.

[251] This gains support from the fact that, in English law, the rule in Fairchild was held to be applicable to a case where common law negligence could not be made out, but only the breach of certain statutory duties: see *McDonald v. National Grid Electricity Transmission Plc* [2014] UKSC 53, [128].

[252] N. McBride and R. Bagshaw, *Tort Law*, 4th edition, 381.

This position is also supported by the fact that French, German, and US law each apply their defendant indeterminacy rules to strict liability causes of action.

A predominance of tortious potential causes to non-tortious potential causes

Suppose a variation on *Two Hunters*, where only one hunter fires negligently, the other non-negligently. On these facts, none of the arguments would generate the conclusion that the negligent hunter should be held liable. But suppose a further variation where there are three hunters, two of whom fire negligently in the direction of the claimant, and one fires non-negligently. Here there is a two-thirds probability that the claimant has been the victim of a wrong, but not the certainty which has generally been supposed in the discussion.[253] However, there should still be liability in this case since the prevented claim argument still works, and so too the relative injustice argument. Indeed, both arguments apply wherever there are a greater number of potential tortious causes to potential non-tortious causes (so long as that accurately reflects the greater probability of tortious causation to non-tortious causation).[254]

The conceptualisation of the defendant indeterminacy doctrines

In cases to which the prevented claim theory applies, liability can be conceived of as simply requiring each defendant to compensate for the injury it has caused. To the extent it does not apply, liability could be considered as based on a reversal of the burden of proof or as a distinct liability rule. The disadvantage of the former is that it raises the question of whether, in a three defendant case, each defendant could exculpate itself by pointing to the one-third classical probability that it does not cause the injury. This probability has insufficient weight to

---

[253] In *Burks* v. *Abbott Laboratories* (2013) 917 F Supp 2d 902, it was held that a claimant would succeed under *Summers* v. *Tice* if it could prove *on the preponderance of the evidence* that its injury was due to a tortious cause.

[254] The possibilities under the prevented claim theory, with two negligent defendants and one non-negligent are: [D1 cause of physical injury, D2 prevents claim against D1, D3 (non-tortious) prevents claim against D2], [D2 cause of physical injury, D1 prevents claim against D2, D3 (non-tortious) prevents claim against D1], [D3 causes injury, D2 cause of lack of knowledge over this, D1 also a cause of lack of knowledge]. In two of three possible states of the world (thus on the balance of probability), D1 and D2 are liable.

satisfy the BPR, but to avoid this issue it may be better to frame the rule simply as a distinct rule of liability.

Full and proportional liability

Of the systems under study, only English law would apply proportional liability in the *core* defendant indeterminacy situation (in all cases except those involving mesothelioma[255]) – each defendant being held liable in proportion to the abstract probability that they were a cause of the injury; French and German law (as well as US and Canadian law) hold each defendant liable in full, jointly and severally – each defendant then must seek contribution *inter se*.

The prevented claim theory convincingly justifies joint and several full liability in each defendant where all defendants are solvent. This follows from the fact that each defendant is either liable for directly causing the physical injury or for indirectly preventing its repair. The value of these claims ought to be the same if both defendants are solvent.[256] In the, practically significant, event of the insolvency of one defendant, the prevented claim theory becomes problematic and may not justify *any* liability.

The relative injustice argument is indifferent between full, joint and several, liability and proportional liability in cases where the defendants are solvent – this is because, where each defendant is solvent, each will, in effect, be liable proportionately to the probability, after seeking contribution from the other solvent defendant. The practically significant situation is again insolvency. Consider again, *Two Hunters*, where one defendant is insolvent. There is a 100 per cent risk of the injustice that the claimant is wrongly denied an entitlement to full compensation (say 100 units) if no liability is found, and a 50 per cent risk of the injustice that the solvent defendant is wrongly subject to full liability (100 units), when it in fact owes nothing, if the defendant is held liable in full. Under proportional liability, there is the same 100 per cent risk of injustice of amount 100 to the claimant if neither defendant is held liable, while there would be a 50 per cent risk of injustice of amount 50 to the solvent defendant if it were held proportionally liable. Proportional liability would therefore reduce the expected *extent* of the injustice to the defendant in situations of insolvency. Moreover, it would not increase the

---

[255] See further Chapter 5, 221ff.

[256] See, for a slight wrinkle with that claim, N. McBride and S. Steel, 'Suing for the Loss of the Right to Sue', 38.

overall expected amount of injustice compared to an all-or-nothing rule (as proportional liability normally does[257]): this remains the same. Under an all-or-nothing rule, there is a 50 per cent risk of an injustice of 100 to the defendant, and no risk of an injustice to the claimant if the defendant is held liable in full; under a proportional liability rule, there is a 50 per cent risk of injustice of amount 50 to both parties if the defendant is held liable.

The reliance upon wrongdoing argument has been applied to generate full liability in the analogous cases, though this is not logically entailed by that argument.[258]

The main argument for proportional liability is as follows. The normative starting point is that a defendant ought not to be liable unless a causal case is proven against him. Putting aside the prevented claim theory, which does conform to that principle, and looking only to the reliance upon another's wrong argument, a departure is being made from that starting point in favour of the claimant. Consequently, there ought to be some 'trade-off' to each defendant, to reflect the infringement of the defendant's general right to be free from liability absent proof of causation. This argument is all the more appealing given that it does not increase the expected amount of injustice as proportional liability normally does.

Defendant indeterminacy variants

Extent of loss variant

Suppose that C has been the victim of two tortiously caused injuries, each caused by either D1 or D2, one injury has caused loss amounting to 1,000, and one has caused additional loss amounting to 10,000, and each defendant may have caused and each defendant may have caused either injury.

Under the prevented claim theory, each D should be liable jointly and severally for 11,000. Each has either caused 1,000 injury or prevented the claim in respect of the 1,000 and each has either caused the 10,000 injury or prevented the claim in respect of the 10,000 injury. Hence, each is liable for 11,000 – on the assumption of solvency of all defendants.

Under the relative injustice argument, in respect of the 10,000, there is a 100 per cent chance of injustice to the claimant if neither is held liable, and a 50 per cent chance of injustice in respect of each defendant if liability is awarded. However, there is a 100 per cent chance of injustice against each defendant if each is additionally held jointly and severally

---

[257] See Chapter 3, 134–136.   [258] See Chapter 1, 43ff.

liable in respect of the 1,000 – we know that each did not cause 11,000 of loss. Hence, each should be liable jointly and severally only for 10,000. The same result follows under the reliance upon wrongdoing argument, upon the assumption that this argument is qualified by the principle that the defendant should not be held liable for injury it is individually known not to have caused.

In a case involving *unknown extents* of tortiously caused loss, where it is known that each defendant could not have caused the *whole*, it would again be more unjust certainly to inflict a total injustice upon the claimant than to risk imposing too great a liability upon each defendant. The court must apportion liability.

Causative defendant variant

In causative defendant variants, like *Two Cars*, each defendant should be liable in full for wrongful failure to authorise the other defendant to pay damages on its behalf, if all defendants are solvent and it is impossible for each defendant to conform to its secondary duty due to the impossibility of determining its victim according to the standard of proof.

This argument, as well as the prevented claim theory, also applies in relation to structurally identical cases such as the DES cases. There is also a powerful relative injustice argument in such cases for holding each defendant proportionally liable. Suppose that D1 had a 90 per cent share of the market in DES and D2 had a 10 per cent share of the market. Suppose further that there are 100 victims of DES, of which we would expect 90 to have been caused by D1 and 10 by D2. Under the BPR, there is a 100 per cent chance of 100 injustices (of amount, £100, say), since no individual claimant can prove causation against a particular defendant. Under a PL rule, the expected injustice would be far less. Suppose all 100 claimants sue D1. Ninety will receive £10 less than they should. Ten will receive £10 too much. Suppose all 100 claimants also sue D2. Ninety will receive £10 too much and ten will receive £90 too little. The total expected injustice under PL, then, is £2800.

Conclusions

The last part of this chapter has argued that it is possible to carve out an exceptional departure from the burden of proof that is rationally limited to the defendant indeterminacy situation and its variants. The strongest cases are those in which all defendants are traceable and solvent. Here it is possible to rely upon the combined force of the prevented claim theory, the relative injustice argument, and the reliance upon another's wrongdoing argument. In cases where there is an insolvent defendant, probably only the last two arguments may be relied upon.

It is suggested that this position also gains support from comparative considerations. English, German, French, the law of most US states, and Canadian law all support liability in the core defendant indeterminacy situation. As a mere head-count of jurisdictions, this is, of course, insignificant. More significant is that the result, in the core situation, has gained general acceptance in different legal traditions. Nor could it be argued that this convergence is a product of these systems unreflectively adopting the Roman law solution. It is true that §830 I 2 BGB was significantly influenced by Roman law, and the citation of the Roman texts in the nineteenth-century German case law was generally made without much normative analysis (though the Roman position was accepted to be demanded by fairness to the claimant).[259] However, the US and Canadian position seems to have developed independently of this. There is, then, a convergence on the normative justifiability of an exceptional rule in the core defendant indeterminacy situation among different legal traditions, none of which has reached that position by reasoning that is clearly flawed in some respect.

---

[259] See C. Kruse, *Alternative Kausalität*, 143–9.

5 Full liability beyond defendant indeterminacy

The extent of convergence around liability in defendant indeterminacy situations described in the last chapter is matched only by the extent of divergence in the nature of departures from the general proof of causation rules beyond those situations. This chapter and the next examine such rules. This chapter considers those which allow the claimant to recover *full* damages in respect of an injury against a defendant, where it is not demonstrated to the requisite standard of proof that the defendant's wrongful conduct was a cause of the claimant's injury, and it is not demonstrated to the requisite standard of proof that the claimant's injury was caused by wrongful conduct.

The focus of the analysis is on the following type of case:

> *Simple uncertainty*: C's injury may have been caused entirely by non-wrongful causes or D's wrongful conduct may have been a cause of the injury. If C's injury has been caused by wrongful conduct, it will have been D's wrongful conduct, and if D's wrongful conduct has caused injury, it will have been C's injury.

It will be useful to have descriptions of more complex types of case, which will also be discussed in this and the next chapter:

> *Claimant indeterminacy*: D has behaved wrongfully in relation to C1, C2...Cn. It is known according to the standard of proof that D has wrongfully injured at least one of C1-Cn, each of whom has suffered similar injuries, but it is not known which. The claimants not injured by D have suffered injury non-wrongfully. This is the mirror image of defendant indeterminacy.
>
> *Claimant and defendant indeterminacy*: D1, D2 ... Dn each behaved wrongfully in relation to C1, C2 ... Cn. It is known according to the standard of proof that at least one D has wrongfully injured one of

C1-C*n*, each of whom has suffered similar injuries, but it is not known which D or which C. The claimants not injured by the wrongful conduct of one D have suffered injury non-wrongfully.

Claimant and defendant indeterminacy, causative variant: D1, D2 ... D*n* have each wrongfully caused injury to at least one of C1-C*n*, where some number of C1-C*n* have also suffered injuries non-wrongfully, but it cannot be determined which D has caused which C's injury.

It will emerge that the approach of legal systems in this domain has been inconsistent. Each system has recognised exceptional rules in one context, for reasons which would equally apply in other contexts, but these rules are either not applied in those other contexts, or an *ad hoc* limitation is placed upon the rule, simply in order to limit its field of application.

The chapter is organised into two main parts. The first part examines the mechanisms by which full liability is achieved in each system. These are considered as rules which are best conceived *either* as reversals in the burden of proof, or as rules which are functionally equivalent to reversals in the burden of proof, reductions in the standard of proof as to causation, and presumptions of causation. The second part of the chapter critically analyses the justifications for such rules. It argues that the only valid justification is one which appeals to the defendant's responsibility for the evidential uncertainty over causation. It offers a narrow account of the circumstances in which that justification holds.

Germany

More than either French or English law, German tort law is characterised by a complex system of evidential doctrines, ranging (sometimes uncertainly) from reversals of the burden of proof to reductions in the standard of proof on causation.[1] Three major situations in which the burden of proof is reversed are discussed first. Second, the arguable reduction in the standard of proof which occurs through the use of *prima facie* proof is considered.

---

[1] See H. Stoll, 'Haftungsverlagerung durch beweisrechtliche Mittel', 146–7, 161–73. See for further examples of reversals of the burden of proof: §§831–834. These provisions are concerned with *inter alia* the liability of employers, keepers of animals, and parents. Where (wrongful) causation of injury by an employee, animal or child is proven, the burden falls to the defendant to prove that the injury did not occur through failure to take reasonable care on their part.

Reversing the burden of proof on causation

Reversal of the burden of proof for gross breaches of duty in the medical context

German law contains an exceptional rule that applies almost exclusively to the liability of medical professionals. If the defendant professional has committed a gross error in the delivery of treatment, it falls to the professional to prove to the standard of §286 ZPO[2] that its error was not a cause of the claimant's injury.[3] This rule first emerged in the case law of the Reichsgericht.[4] Although that court had emphasised the basic principle that the claimant bears the burden of proof on causation, this rule itself was located in *fairness* (*Billigkeit*) and was therefore subject to flexibility.[5] This flexibility was realised in a decision of 1940, where the court held that the burden of proof would shift to a doctor who had consciously or with reckless indifference (*leichtfertiger Gleichgültigkeit*) created a risk of injury to its patient, where that risk may have caused the claimant's injury.[6] The reversal of the burden of proof was grounded in a 'just balancing of the interests of the parties in the particular case at hand'.[7]

This rule was then explicitly taken up and developed by the BGH,[8] and has now been codified in the Patients' Rights Statute.[9] Much of the case law is concerned with the definition of the concept of a *gross* treatment error. In this regard, the general progression (in line with the increasingly objective understanding of the fault concept[10]) has been from the subjectively-orientated formulation of the Reichsgericht toward an objective conception. The latter had gestured towards the intentional or reckless creation of a risk, whereas the BGH from the middle of the

---

[2] See, generally on §286 ZPO, Chapter 2, 53ff.

[3] BGH NJW 2005 427; BGH NJW 2004, 2011. See, extensively, C. Katzenmeier, *Arzthaftung*, 439ff.

[4] A. Hausch, *Der grobe Behandlungsfehler in der gerichtlichen Praxis*,18ff; R. Seifert, *Ärztlicher Behandlungsfehler und schicksalhafter Verlauf*, 108.

[5] A. Hausch, *Der grobe Behandlungsfehler*, 18.

[6] RG Warn Rspr 1941, No.14, 29, 32 (with reference to an unpublished decision of 1937). For an overview of the early cases, see C. Katzenmeier, *Arzthaftung*, 439–40; T. Riegger, *Die historische Entwicklung der Arzthaftung*, 127.

[7] Ibid., 32: 'gerechte Interessenabwägung im Einzelfall'.

[8] BGH NJW 1956, 1835, VersR 1956, 499. For the early decisions of the BGH: A. Hausch, *Der grobe Behandlungsfehler*, 26ff.

[9] §630h (5) BGB, incorporating the Gesetz zur Verbesserung der Rechte von Patientinnen und Patienten, passed by the Bundestag in November 2012.

[10] N. Jansen, 'Developing Legal Doctrine: Fault in the German Law of Delict', 117–18.

1960s has required simply a gross or severe error (*grober oder schwerer Behandlungsfehler*).[11] This is a more objective conception in so far as it connotes only the (fundamental) divergence from medically accepted standards of conduct.[12] Typical formulations of the level of divergence necessary are that the erroneous conduct must be 'no longer comprehensible' from the perspective of medical standards of training and knowledge[13] or that the conduct must be contrary to 'elementary' standards of treatment or medical knowledge.[14] Such an error may take a number of forms, relating to the various elements of 'treatment', understood broadly: for example, errors in diagnosis or failures to perform tests (*Befunderhebungsfehler*) come within the doctrine.[15]

The doctrine is limited by three further requirements. First, the connection between the defendant's gross breach of duty and the injury must not be 'wholly improbable' (*ganz unwahrscheinlich*).[16] Logically, this is simply an expression of the high standard of proof (§286 ZPO) to which the defendant is subject in its negative claim that it did not cause the claimant's injury.[17] Second, the injury which has occurred must be within the risk which made the defendant's conduct *grossly* erroneous in order for the burden of proof to be reversed.[18] Thus, if a doctor fails to inform a patient who has decided to leave hospital of risks A, B, and C, and risk C (the risk of a minor infection occurring) materialises, the burden of proof will not be reversed unless the failure to advise of risk C was a gross breach of duty – or part of what made the conduct a gross breach of duty; if the failure to advise of risks A and B was what made the conduct grossly erroneous, rather than the failure to advise of risk C, then the burden of proof will not be reversed as to whether the doctor's gross negligence led to the materialisation of risk C.[19] Third, the reversal

---

[11] BGH NJW 1965, 345, 346; BGH NJW 1967, 1508; BGH NJW 1970, 1230.

[12] C. Katzenmeier, *Arzthaftung*, 440.   [13] BGH NJW 1983, 2080, 2081.

[14] BGH NJW 1986, 1540, 1541; BGH NJW 1997, 798, 799.

[15] C. Katzenmeier, 'Verschärfung der Berufshaftung durch Beweisrecht – der grobe Behandlungsfehler', 913; E. Deutsch and A. Spickhoff, *Medizinrecht*, 6th edition, 2008, 333ff.

[16] BGH NJW 2008, 1304; BGH NJW 2004, 2011, 2013 (äußerst unwahrscheinlich).

[17] A. Spickhoff, *Folgenzurechnung in Schadensersatzrecht*, 2346; G. Mäsch, *Chance und Schaden*, 58, describing it as 'überflüssig'. Nonetheless it is understood as a distinct requirement: BGH NJW 2004, 2011, 2013.

[18] BGH NJW 1981, 2513.

[19] These were the facts and result in the BGH NJW 1981, 2513. This limitation has, however, been thrown into doubt by the decision of the BGH in BGH NJW 2012, 2653, MedR 2013, 365. The premature claimant baby was intubated after birth. The defendant doctor negligently continued to operate the artificial breathing equipment at too strong

applies only to 'primary damage'. Primary damage is that potentially immediately caused by the defendant's negligence, whereas secondary damage is that potentially caused by the primary damage. How this distinction is drawn in practice is somewhat unstable.[20]

Reversal of the burden of proof for gross breach of duty beyond the medical context

While the core application of the reversal of the burden of proof based upon the grossness of the defendant's breach of duty has been in medical cases, it has very occasionally been stretched beyond this context. The BGH held that a swimming instructor who failed to supervise the deceased had to show that his failure to supervise had not been causative of his drowning.[21] The court held that the defendant's conduct amounted to a gross breach of his professional duty and, recalling the 1940 Reichsgericht formulation, that 'the basic principles of fairness and of justly weighing the parties' interests' compel an alteration in the burden of proof.[22] This demand of fairness seems to extend only to cases where the defendant's duty is to safeguard the life or bodily integrity of the claimant since, subsequently, the reverse burden has been rejected in the context of liability for grossly negligent legal advice, partly for the reason that the lawyer's duty is not directed towards the protection of life, but only of economic interests.[23]

---

a level and this led to the child becoming hyperventilated. This was grossly negligent because hyperventilation was known to risk serious injury to the baby's lungs. The child, however, suffered from a brain injury, not injury to the lungs. At the time of the treatment, it was not known that hyperventilation risked brain injury. Hence, the risk which occurred was not one which made the conduct grossly negligent. Nonetheless, the BGH reversed the burden of proof on causation, unconvincingly distinguishing the earlier decision on the ground that it had concerned two distinct breaches of duty (the duty to inform of risks A and B, and the duty to inform of risk C), while the present case only concerned one breach of duty. For an attempt to rationalise the decisions on other grounds, see M. Finn, 'Anmerkung zu BGH, Urt v.19.6.2012 – VI ZR 77/11', 367–8.

[20]   G. Mäsch, *Chance und Schaden*, 60–1.   [21]   BGH NJW 1962, 959.

[22]   Ibid. 959. In BGHZ 61, 118, the court explains that the rule applies generally to breaches of professional duties which have as their object the 'protection of another from risks to their life and body'.

[23]   BGH NJW 1988, 200, 203. See also BGH NJW 1994, 3295, 3297, where it is claimed that gross breaches of lawyers' duties do not generally increase the risk of injury to the claimant to the same degree as gross breaches of treatment duties. See generally, G. Mäsch, *Chance und Schaden*, 117–18. The restriction is criticised by K. Heinemann, 'Baustein anwaltlicher Berufshaftung: die Beweislast', 2352; W. Teske, 'Note on BGH 9.6.1994', 474. Cf. OLG Köln 22.08.2007, Beck RS 2008, 09246, describing the doctrine as subject to a restrictive interpretation because it has an 'exceptional nature' (*Ausnahmecharakter*); as well as incorrectly suggesting that it is specific to the medical area.

The reversal of the burden of proof has also been rejected, however, in cases of gross breaches of failures to warn of the dangers of products, or to recall a dangerous product, where these breaches of duty *have* risked physical injury.[24] In a recent decision, the BGH reasoned that the breach of a duty to fail to recall a dangerous drug from the market would not engage the reversal of the burden of proof because, unlike gross breaches of doctors' duties, such a breach of duty does not cause there to be a particular difficulty for the claimant to prove that the defendant's conduct was a cause of its injury.[25] It is, however, difficult to understand why the failure to supervise a swimming pool properly is a cause of uncertainty over causation but the failure to recall a dangerous drug is not. It may have been that the court was hesitant to extend the application of a doctrinally controversial, judge-made rule, which, at the time of the decision had no basis in the BGB.

Doctrinal rationalisation and critique of the rule

The justification typically offered by the BGH for the reversal of the burden of proof is that the *grossness* of the defendant's breach of duty has made the ability to prove causation especially difficult for the claimant.[26]

This is justly criticised on the basis that the grossness of the error does not necessarily cause proof of causation to be more difficult than in a case of simple (i.e. non-gross) negligence.[27] While it may be that the grossness of the defendant's error has made causal proof more difficult than usual, this is not true in every case. Indeed, often the grossness of the error will make proof of causation *easier* to establish, since the grossness of the error may lead to such a substantial increase in risk to

---

[24] BGH NJW 1992, 560; BGH NJW-RR 2010, 1331. For criticism of the reasoning of the latter decision, see B. Ballhausen, 'Anwendung der Beweislastumkehr nach den für die Arzthaftung entwickelten Grundsätzen bei einem groben Behandlungsfehler im Rahmen der Arzneimittelhaftung'.

[25] BGH NJW-RR 2010, 1331.

[26] BGH NJW 1983, 333; BGH NJW 1988, 2949; BGH NJW 1996, 1589. In substance, this is the justification relied upon in the most recent cases: BGH NJW-RR 2010, 1331; BGH NJW 2005, 427.

[27] See, for example, G. Mäsch, *Chance und Schaden*, 35ff; C. Ehlgen, *Probabilistische Proportionalhaftung und Haftung für den Verlust von Chancen*, 169–75; C. Katzenmeier, 'Verschärfung', 916; H. Lange and G. Schiemann, *Handbuch des Schuldrechts: Schadensersatz*, 3rd edition, 2003, 168.

the claimant that this could justify an inference that the high risk source was causative of the claimant's injury.[28]

A further problem is that in many cases it is meaningless to ask whether the grossness of the error caused proof to be particularly difficult. For example, suppose the defendant doctor has failed to take basic hygiene precautions when administering an injection – a gross error.[29] It is not clear how one should test whether that gross error led to greater difficulty over proof of causation. It would be incoherent to ask – supposing that this error had been merely negligent, would proof of causation have been easier? If the error committed is grossly negligent, one cannot imagine its being merely negligent. It seems that one would have to imagine some alternative course of merely negligent events. But it is far from clear how one could non-arbitrarily select such a course of events (there will often be multiple ways of behaving *merely* negligently).

Another justification for the reversal, offered principally by doctrinal authors, but at one point also by the BGH, is that gross errors expose persons to a substantially increased risk of injury.[30] It is unclear precisely how the proponents of this justification understand it to justify the reversal of the burden of proof. It seems to be offered simply as a more precise, albeit still broad, reason why it is fair to reverse the burden of proof.[31]

A further justification, usually offered in conjunction with the 'increase in risk' justification, is that the 'the course of events (*der Geschehensablauf*) can generally be controlled by adherence to elementary professional standards of care'.[32] This, again, seems to be offered as a way of precisifying a simple appeal to fairness. If 'course of events' refers to 'the claimant's suffering an injury', the claim is problematic.

---

[28] H. Fleischer, 'Schadensersatz für verlorene Chancen im Vertrags-und Deliktsrecht', 773; G. Mäsch, *Chance und Schaden*, 36.

[29] Cf., for such facts, BGH NJW 2008, 1304.

[30] BGH NJW 1971, 241, 243; C. Katzenmeier, *Arzthaftung*, 465; C. Katzenmeier, 'Verschärfung', 917; A. Spickhoff, *Folgenzurechnung*, 75; C. Ehlgen, *Probabilistische Proportionalhaftung*, 335.

[31] This is conceded by C Ehlgen *Probabilistische Proportionalhaftung*, 336. It should be noted that the reasoning cannot be that the substantial increase in the risk of injury should justify an *inference* of causation. First, this is simply not the argument presented by Katzenmeier, its main proponent: see the references in Note 15. Second, this reasoning would not justify the reversal of the burden of proof in cases where it is reversed although the gross error imposes much less risk than the patient's pre-existing risk of succumbing to their injuries. For such a case, see OLG Hamm VersR 1999, 622.

[32] C. Ehlgen, *Probabilistische Proportionalhaftung*, 336, drawing upon the work of Katzenmeier cited in Note 15.

As Schiemann observes, if we are uncertain about whether the defendant's negligence was a cause of the claimant's injury, there will be
uncertainty as to whether the claimant's injury could have been avoided
by proper treatment.[33] In addition, there seems to be little basis for the
claim that the claimant's injury or injuries of that type could *generally*
have been avoided if the gross error had not occurred. This depends
entirely upon the claimant's pre-existing condition.

A final, fairness-based, argument is that the defendant's gross breach
of duty is a particularly severe breach of the trust placed in the professional, who has assured the claimant that they will take reasonable
care.[34]

Some authors have offered an alternative, consequentialist, justification for the rule.[35] As explained in Chapter 3, economic theories justify
the causal requirement of liability, in negligence, largely on the basis
of an observation about the effects of uncertainty over the relevant
standard of care.[36] Spindler observes that such uncertainty – uncertainty
over what the standard of care requires – does not obtain in cases
involving gross errors: since they involve very basic mistakes, the level
of care required is knowable *ex-ante* by those engaging in the relevant
activity and unlikely to be mistaken by the court.[37] Thus, in principle,
the reason to insist upon proof of causation simply falls away. One
problem with this argument, however, in so far as one construes this
as an attempt to rationalise the current law, is that it would justify an
absolute liability rule in cases of *grober Behandlungsfehler*, yet the law only
imposes a reversal of the burden of proof. This is not entirely fatal, since
the high standard of proof under §286 ZPO does make proof that the
error was not causative very difficult, particularly in the medical context. Another difficulty is that there is no justification for limiting the
doctrine to duties protecting physical injury: in other areas, there is the
possibility of breaching clear, determinate, elementary standards of care.

There are three principal justifications offered, then, for the *grobe
Behandlungsfehler* rule.[38] The first is the fairness argument that in cases
of gross breach of duties to take care to protect physical safety, where

---

[33] G. Schiemann, 'Kausalitätsprobleme bei der Arzthaftung', 1169.
[34] C. Ehlgen, *Probabilistische Proportionalhaftung*, 336.
[35] L. Röckrath, *Kausalität*, 205ff; G. Spindler, 'Kausalität im Zivil-und Wirtschaftrecht', 302.
[36] See p. 117ff.   [37] G. Spindler, 'Kausalität', 302.
[38] Some authors have also appealed to *Waffengleichheit* (equality of arms in the civil trial)
based upon Art 3 GG. This is unconvincing for the reasons given in G. Mäsch, *Chance und
Schaden*, 39ff.

the defendant has substantially increased the risk of injury, and severely breached the trust placed in the proper performance of their duties, it is preferable that the defendant bear the risk of non-persuasion on causation. The second is that the defendant's grossly wrongful conduct has made it more difficult to prove causation. The third is the economic justification. Despite its loose formulation,[39] the problems with the second and third of these make the first the most plausible.

Reversal of the burden of proof for causing causal uncertainty

The main justification currently offered by the BGH for the *grober Behandlungsfehler* (GB) rule is, as we have seen, that the grossness of the breach of duty causes it to be more difficult for the claimant to prove causation than a non-gross breach of duty. The legal claim is that causation of uncertainty justifies the rule. This section discusses other legal rules which also attach legal consequences to the causation of uncertainty, including causation of uncertainty over causation. In some cases, the legal consequence is a reversal of the burden of proof.

The most general such doctrine is that of 'destruction of proof' (*Beweisvereitelung*). Such a general doctrine is not explicitly mentioned either by the ZPO or the BGB, though some scattered provisions of the ZPO attach procedural consequences to the intentional destruction of specific kinds of proof (e.g. documents).[40] Nonetheless, it is largely undisputed among courts and doctrinal writers that a general doctrine does exist.[41] The legal nature, conditions of application, and legal consequences of the doctrine are, however, disputed.[42]

In general terms, it can be said that the doctrine applies where an object of proof (*Beweisobjekt*) is intentionally or negligently destroyed, or its ability to assist in proof diminished, by the action or omission of another person, in breach of a duty so not to act or omit, where the intention or negligence relates not only to the destruction of the object, but also to the fact that object would be used to prove a proposition in litigation.[43]

---

[39] This aspect of the justification is harshly criticised by G. Mäsch, *Chance und Schaden*, 44ff.

[40] For example, §444 ZPO.

[41] Cf. H. Weber, *Kausalitätsbeweis*, 211. In 1977 there was a proposal made by the Ministry of Justice to alter §286 ZPO to include a provision on *Beweisvereitelung*. It would have read: 'If the party has, with fault, breached a duty to produce, maintain or otherwise not to damage the usefulness of an item of proof, the court may reverse the burden of proof on causation'. See D. Fröhlich, *Die Beweisvereitelung im Zivilprozess*, 6, n. 41.

[42] Ibid., 211.   [43] D. Fröhlich, *Die Beweisvereitelung*, 191–2.

A decision of the BGH from 16.4.1955 provides a helpful illustration.[44] The defendant doctor left a piece of swab in the claimant's body after an operation. This necessitated a second operation, where the swab was removed and the defendant disposed of it. Without knowing the material from which it was made or its size, the claimant could not prove that the defendant had been at fault in leaving the swab in his body or that this had been the cause of severe pain after the first operation. The court, without explaining the legal basis of its holding,[45] held that, upon finding the swab during the second operation, the doctor ought to have realised that the claimant might have relied upon it in a claim for damages against him, and that nature and size of the swab would have been significant to that litigation.[46]

The following are situations in which the courts have recognised legal duties whose purpose is *partly* to protect evidence.[47] Though they are from the medical context, the reasoning used to justify such duties is general in character. At a general level, it will emerge that these duties normally only arise between parties with some pre-existing relationship, which does not exist primarily to protect the other party's evidential situation, but where the duty arising from the relationship can be said partly to serve the purpose of recording or maintaining evidence. The courts have, then, rejected the existence of a freestanding legal right, arising independent of contract, to protect another's evidential situation; the significance of the fact that a person has caused uncertainty is, instead, parasitic upon the breach of other legal duties, where part of the purpose of those duties can be said to preserve evidence.

Doctors' duties to maintain documentation of treatment (*Dokumentationsfehler*)[48]

In two decisions from 1978, the BGH first recognised that doctors owe legal duties to patients to maintain appropriate records of treatment.[49]

---

[44] BGH VersR 1955, 344.

[45] Cf. D. Fröhlich, *Die Beweisvereitelung*, 9–10, noting the failure of the case law clearly to describe the legal basis for the general *Beweisvereitelung* doctrine.

[46] Ibid., 345.

[47] See, noting the uncertain doctrinal relationship between *Beweisvereitelung* and the rules discussed in the following text, Y. Harder, *Die Beweisfigur des Befunderhebungs-und Befundsicherungsfehlers im Arzthaftungsprozess nach der Rechtsprechung des BGH und Instanzgerichte*, 19.

[48] See, generally, E. Deutsch and A. Spickhoff, *Medizinrecht*, 6th edition, 2008, 328–30.

[49] BGH NJW 1978, 1681; BGH NJW 1978, 2337. On the previous law, see A. Hausch, 'Vom therapierenden zum dokumentierenden Arzt', n 4.

This duty was said to be justified as an entailment of the duty to care for the patient's health: one must keep adequate records since this is necessary for appropriate (future) treatment.[50]

The court reasoned in the originating 1978 decision that while the duty to maintain appropriate documentation was justified as a requirement for proper treatment of the patient's illness, the breach of the duty could not be 'without consequence' when it came to the proof rules applicable in a later claim for damages.[51] This, in turn, was justified on the basis that the doctor owes a duty to account (*Rechenschaftspflicht*) for the process of the treatment by analogy to the (legally recognised) duty to account of a person who manages the finances of another.[52] The purpose of this duty is to allow adequate monitoring of the use of funds and to allow legal claims in the event of maladministration.[53] The patient stands in a similar relationship, on this argument, so far as the administration of treatment goes, to the doctor. In a later case, the BGH also observed that duties of documentation serve to protect the patient's personality rights (*Persönlichkeitsrecht*).[54]

The court has since clarified, however, that the duty of documentation only exists to the extent that the documentation is medically necessary for the treatment of the patient.[55] Thus, the duty to account for the course of treatment or the 'personality rights' of the patient do not justify a broader duty to maintain documents, going beyond that which is medically necessary. This throws some doubt on the correctness of the decision in the 1955 case involving the lost swab, where the duty to maintain the swab probably could not be justified as *medically* necessary.

Both 1978 decisions left open the precise evidential response to the failure to maintain appropriate documentation, leaving it to judicial discretion (based upon fairness in the particular case) whether to reverse the burden of proof or merely to lower the standard of proof in respect of some factual claim.[56] The scope of any reversal or reduction in the standard of proof was broadly formulated, however, seeming to cover both the issue of whether the treatment was negligent and also whether the negligence was a cause of the patient's injury.[57]

---

[50] BGH NJW 1978, 2337.   [51] BGH NJW 1978, 2337, 2338.   [52] BGH NJW 1978, 2337.

[53] Y. Harder, *Die Beweisfigur*, 18.   [54] BGH NJW 1987, 1482.

[55] See BGH NJW 1993, 2375: 'Documentation which is not medically necessary is also not legally required, and so the failure to maintain such documentation does not attract any consequences as a matter of the law of proof'.

[56] BGH NJW 1978, 2337.

[57] See A. Hausch, 'Vom therapierenden zum dokumentierenden Arzt', text at n. 13–15.

Subsequent decisions restricted this broad rule. In a BGH decision from 9.11.1982, the claimant suffered from serious debilitating complications after a sterilisation operation.[58] She alleged that these were due to operation or post-operative care being negligently carried out. No records concerning the operation itself or the post-operative care (except the kind of medication used) were found to exist. The BGH accepted that the breach of the duty to maintain documentation of treatment could result in 'reductions in the requirements of proof, up to and including a reversal of the burden of proof'.[59] However, ordering the case to be re-tried, it emphasised that:

...the breach of the duty to maintain documentation is not itself a cause of action. It may only lead to a reduction in the proof requirements in relation to the proof of negligent treatment – the proof of which has been made more difficult by the failure to document. However, it remains a requirement that the claimant prove that negligent treatment comes seriously into consideration as a cause of the injury for which damages are sought.[60]

This seems to restrict the consequences of failure to maintain documentation of treatment to proof of *negligence*, rather than causation.[61] This is borne out by more recent decisions of the BGH, which tend to restrict the failure-to-maintain-adequate-documentation doctrine to proof of fault.[62] Moreover, the current position of the BGH in cases where the occurrence of a procedure is not recorded in the patient's documents is not to reverse the burden of proof, but to establish a rebuttable presumption that the procedure was not in fact carried out.[63] In relation to proof of causation, the most that can be said is that there is still a tendency in some lower courts to adopt a liberal approach to proof of causation, where necessary

---

[58] BGH VersR 1983, 151, 152.   [59] Ibid., 152.

[60] Ibid., 152: '... die unterlassene Dokumentation nicht selbst eine Anspruchsgrundlage bildet. Sie kann nur dazu führen, dass dem Patienten der durch sie erschwerte Beweis eines behaupteten Behandlungsfehlers erleichtert wird. Damit bleibt es aber Voraussetzung des Anspruchs, dass ein schuldhafter Behandlungsfehler als Ursache des auszugleichenden Schadens ernstlich in Betracht kommt'.

[61] It is interpreted thus by A. Hausch, 'Vom therapierenden zum dokumentierenden Arzt', text at n 19.

[62] See, for example, BGH NJW 1993, 2375, 2377: 'As a matter of principle, it [the breach of the duty make documentation] does not lead to a reversal of the burden of proof in respect of causation'; BGH NJW 1989, 2949. See also, for example, OLG Karlsruhe, 12.12.2012, 7 U 176/11.

[63] M. Stauch, *The Law of Medical Negligence in England and Germany*, 69.

documentation of the treatment, which would likely provide causally relevant information, is absent.[64]

Doctors' duties to undertake tests and to retain undertaken test results

Although the consequences of the breach of the duty to maintain documentation of treatment (*Dokumentationsfehler* (DF)) seem to be restricted to proof of fault, two closely related doctrines continue to have significance for proof of causation.[65] These are: the failure to perform a test (*Befunderhebungsfehler* (BEF)), and the failure to retain the results of an undertaken test (*Befundsicherungsfehler* (BSF)).

In a decision from 21 September 1982, the BGH held that a reversal in the burden of proof on causation could follow the failure to perform a test (BEF).[66] In that case, a patient died from a lung embolism one day after suffering a loss of circulation. After the loss of circulation, the treating doctor had failed to make elementary tests in order to understand the cause of this development; this itself was negligent treatment. The court stated that where the doctor had failed to take 'elementary'[67] tests such that the most important information about the course of the treatment was missing, the burden of proof on causation should be reversed. The reasoning behind this decision is a logical extension of the *grobe Behandlungsfehler* rule. The court observed that even errors in treatment *which do not qualify as gross* can make understanding the causal relation between the defendant's treatment error and the claimant's injury more difficult.[68] Moreover, it made no difference that the aspect of the defendant's conduct which was alleged to have been a cause of the patient's death – the failure to make a proper assessment of the cause of the loss of circulation and react accordingly – was itself the cause of uncertainty over causation.[69] This reversal of the burden of proof was subsequently extended to the failure to *retain* the results of an undertaken test (which might be seen as re-introducing a narrower DF doctrine by other means).[70]

The justification for reversing the burden of proof in each case was said to reside in the fact that the doctors' duty to undertake, and maintain the results of, tests to establish the nature of a patient's condition is

---

[64] See A. Hausch, above, text at n. 24–38.   [65] The first decisions draw parallels to DF.
[66] BGH NJW 1983, 333.   [67] BGH NJW 1983, 333, 334.   [68] Ibid., 334.
[69] Ibid., 335. Compare the swab case described on p. 207.
[70] See, for example, BGH NJW 1988, 2949. For more detailed discussion of the development of the BEF and BSF rules, see Y. Harder, *Beweisfigur*, 35–43.

partly directed towards protecting the patient's evidential situation in litigation.[71] However, the court acknowledges, somewhat straining to justify the rule, that:

The duty, arising out of the doctor-patient relationship, to undertake tests to establish the nature of the patient's illness indeed serves *in the first instance* a therapeutic aim. But it also serves, as with the duty to maintain documentation, to preserve the personality rights of the patient, to whom an account of the course of the treatment is owed. Certainly, this duty does not directly serve to protect the patient in the event of a future claim for damages. But if, as a matter of substantive law, there is a duty to undertake a test, and if an account of the treatment is owed, then the breach of this duty cannot be ignored in any later litigation.[72]

Mirroring the initial breadth, and subsequent restriction, of the DF doctrine, the scope of application of the reversal of the burden of proof for BEF or BSF has also been significantly restricted. This initially involved essentially reducing the legal response to a BEF or BSF to the reduction of the standard of proof on causation – the burden of proof would only be reversed if causation were 'sufficiently probable'.[73] In a decision of 13 February 1996, the BGH restricted the reversal of the burden of proof even further.[74] The claimant presented himself at the defendant's medical practice with pains in his chest. The latter performed an ECG and sent the claimant home. Shortly after, the claimant suffered a heart attack. It was claimed that the defendant had failed to react appropriately to the results of the ECG by immediately hospitalising him. The results of the ECG were lost. The court stated that, in itself, the negligent failure to retain the test result at most gave rise to a *presumption* that the test result required positive steps to be taken by the defendant if this was 'sufficiently probable' (*Vorliegen einer 'hinreichender Wahrscheinlichkeit'*). It remained for the claimant to demonstrate causation of the failure to react appropriately to the test for the heart attack.[75] If, however, the claimant could show that the failure to react appropriately itself constituted a gross breach of duty, then the burden of proof would be reversed on the causal issue of whether the hospitalisation would have made any difference.

The import of this decision is that the failure to undertake a test or maintain its results will only generate a *presumption* as to content of the test. It then falls to the claimant to demonstrate causation according

---

[71] BGH NJW 1987, 1482.   [72] Ibid., 1483 (emphasis added).
[73] BGH NJW 1988, 2949, 2951.   [74] BGH NJW 1996, 1589.   [75] Ibid., 1590.

to §286 ZPO. However, in seeking to demonstrate causation, the claimant can rely upon the GB rule.[76] The corollary is that the burden of proof on causation in cases of failures to maintain test results (BSF) or failures to perform a test (BEF) will only be reversed where the doctor:[77]

(1) negligently (for reasons relating to the possible effects upon the claimant's health) failed to carry out a test (or failed to preserve it),

(2) that the test had it been taken (or preserved) would probably have revealed (or did reveal) a result which needed some medical treatment, and

(3) that failure to react to the probable result of the test would (or did) constitute a *grobe Behandlungsfehler*.

To illustrate, suppose that C visits a doctor, D, with a head injury. D negligently fails to perform a certain test, which would probably have revealed the need for immediate surgery. C suffers from a brain haemorrhage. It is unclear whether, had the test been performed, any treatment would have prevented the brain injury. In such a case, the burden of proof will be reversed as to whether non-negligent treatment would have prevented the brain injury because the failure to react to such a test result would be grossly negligent.[78]

In summary, the current law recognises that doctors owe certain duties to create or maintain certain information-storing items in the interests of caring for patients' health. While the primary purpose of such duties is acknowledged to be therapeutic, it is accepted that such duties also serve in part to maintain the claimant's evidential situation in the event of litigation.[79] There are, however, no freestanding duties imposed upon doctors to preserve evidence – such duties only exist to the extent that the doctor's primary duty to care for the patient's health requires that information be maintained. The evidential consequences of breaching such a duty are limited. While the original response was a reversal of the burden of proof, the current position is to lower the standard of proof in relation to what the claimant alleges the information-storing item would have shown.

---

[76] See Y. Harder, *Beweisfigur*, 44–5.

[77] See Y. Harder, *Beweisfigur*, 44ff; M. Stauch, *The Law of Medical Negligence in England and Germany*, 86–7.

[78] See, for criticism of this curious rule, H. Helbron, *Entwicklungen und Fehlentwicklungen im Arzthaftungsrecht*, 59ff.

[79] BGH NJW 1987, 1482, 1483.

Duties to preserve evidence beyond the medical context

There have been attempts to extend duties to maintain evidence beyond the medical context. The attempt has been unsuccessful in relation to legal advice; lawyers do not owe duties to their clients to maintain documentation of the advisory process itself.[80] A duty to maintain documentation can in principle arise, however, in the course of a contractual relationship as an aspect of the duty of good faith under §242 BGB.[81]

Certain statutory duties have also been interpreted as imposing a duty, part of whose purpose is to preserve evidence for the purposes of litigation. Thus, the duty regularly to monitor and take readings of the water supply under §8 of the Drinking Water Ordinance (*Trinkwasserverordnung*), in order to ensure that the mandated level of nitrates under §3 was not surpassed, was so interpreted by the BGH in a decision from 25 January 1983.[82] The claimant sued in tort for breach of that statute under §823 II BGB, alleging that the defendant had negligently failed to take readings of the water supply and that the increased levels of nitrates in the water she had ingested had caused her brain damage at birth. Had the defendant conformed to its duty to monitor the water supply, it would have been possible to determine accurately the level of nitrates in the water at that time. As matters stood, it was only possible to infer that the increased levels of nitrate found at a later date would also have been present at the earlier time at which the claimant ingested the water. The court held that the burden of proof on the question of whether the nitrate level was greater than the statutory level was on the defendant, because part of the purpose of the defendant's duty was 'to protect a party bearing the burden of proof [on this question] in later litigation'.[83]

It is difficult to find instances of this reasoning beyond the context of contractual relationships and specific statutory duties part of whose purpose is to maintain information. In a claim under §823 I BGB, the OLG Bamberg rejected the application of the *Beweisvereitelung* doctrine where the defendant driver had accidently collided with a moped, and the moped driver died of his injuries. Although the defendant had deprived the claimant estate of the moped driver's evidence – by killing him – this did not justify a reversal of the burden of proof on the issue of whether the defendant had been at fault. The court gave the reason

---

[80] BGH NJW 2006, 429. See A. Jungk, 'Grundsätze und manche Ausnahme: Beweislastfragen im Regressprozess', 143.
[81] As explained in BGH NJW 2008, 371. [82] BGH NJW 1983, 2935. [83] Ibid., 2937.

that the destruction of proof doctrine does not apply where the event which caused the uncertainty is the one in respect of which the claimant is also seeking to hold the defendant responsible. A more convincing[84] reason is that the defendant did not breach any duty that was geared in part towards protecting the claimant's evidential situation.

Reversal of the burden of proof where the defendant has infringed the claimant's right by contributing to an injury

If the defendant's wrongful conduct has been shown, according to §286 ZPO, to have contributed (in the sense of Chapter 1[85]) to the claimant's injury, the claimant is entitled to full compensation in respect of that injury, unless the defendant can demonstrate that the injury would have occurred even if the defendant had behaved non-wrongfully.[86] This is a question of 'hypothetical causation' (*hypothetische Kausalität*) or an issue of the 'defence of lawful alternative conduct' (*Der Einwand rechtmäßigen Alternativverhaltens*).[87] The rule, then, is that the defendant bears the burden of proof for this question.[88] If the defendant is to avoid liability, it must prove that the claimant's injury would have occurred anyway. The standard of proof is generally said to be §287 ZPO.[89] The justification generally given for the rule is that the defendant is raising a *defence* to liability and the normal rule is that the burden of proof for a defence lies with the defendant.[90]

The rule can be illustrated by a decision of the BGH from 1980.[91] The claimant erroneously received an injection in his radial artery, instead

---

[84] This is unconvincing as the law in relation to doctors' duties to maintain documentation does not impose such a restriction. It is often the case that the failure to perform a test is relied upon both as the cause of uncertainty over causation, and as the conduct for which the defendant is being held responsible.

[85] See Chapter 1, 23–25.

[86] This question will not arise if the only way in which the loss would have occurred anyway is due to another's wrongful conduct: the defendant cannot rely upon this: M. Gebauer, *Hypothetische Kausalität*, 188.

[87] Following M. Gebauer, *Hypothetische Kausalität*, 4–6. For a brief history of the different terminology, see C. Grechenig and A. Stremitzer, 'Der Einwand rechtmäßigen Alternativverhaltens', 339

[88] BGH NJW 1959, 2299; BGH NJW 1967, 551; BGH NJW 1972, 1515; BGH NJW 1981, 628, 630; BGH NJW 2009, 993, 994. See also H. Oetker, 'Commentary on §249 BGB', in *Münchener Kommentar zum BGB*, 6th edition, [218].

[89] P. Hanau, *Die Kausalität der Pflichtwidrigkeit*, 138ff; H. Lange and G. Schiemann, *Handbuch des Schuldrechts: Schadensersatz*, 198, 209. Cf. M. Stauch, *The Law of Medical Negligence in England and Germany*, 125.

[90] H. Oetker, 'Commentary on §249 BGB', [218]; H. Großerichter, *Hypothetischer Geschehensverlauf*, 56.

[91] BGH NJW 1981, 628.

of in one of his veins. As a result, two of his fingers needed to be amputated. The injection was given in two doses in quick succession: the first dose was taken to be non-tortious; the second dose was negligently given (after the claimant had cried out in pain from the first dose, the second dose became negligent). The court held that there was no question that the second (greater) dose had been causative of the destruction of the tissue cumulatively with the first dose. There remained the question, however, whether the first dose was nonetheless sufficient to cause the tissue destruction itself. Clearly distinguishing the natural causal issue from the issue of whether the injury would have occurred in any event, the court held that the burden of proof for this latter question lay with the defendant:

> ...whilst the causality of the conduct alleged of the defendant for the damage is for the claimant to prove, it is for the defendant, according to the dominant view, to prove the facts which make out the *defence* that the damage would have occurred anyway due to a legally relevant hypothetical cause.[92]

The extent to which the claimant bears the burden of proof depends crucially, then, upon the concept of contribution. The easier it is for the claimant to prove a contribution to the injury, the more often that the defendant will bear the burden of proof on the question of whether the injury would have occurred in any event in order to avoid liability. As we observed in Chapter 1, the BGH's current position appears to be that it is not possible to contribute by omission.[93] If the defendant's wrongful conduct consists in an omission, the claimant must therefore prove that the injury would not have occurred had the defendant behaved non-wrongfully.[94] If, however, the claimant can prove that the defendant's positive wrongful act (as in the double injection case described above) contributed to the injury, the defendant must prove that the injury would have occurred in any event to avoid liability.

Breach of doctors' duties to inform
The rule that the burden of proof for hypothetical causation rests with the defendant has been applied so as to reverse the burden of proof in cases involving a breach of a duty to inform as to the risks of medical treatment. The reasoning is as follows. If a doctor breaches the duty to inform, the operation performed becomes unlawful (*rechtswidrig*).[95]

---

[92] BGH NJW 1981, 628, 630 (emphasis added).   [93] See Chapter 1, 24.

[94] BGH 7.12.2012, VersR 2012, 491, 492; MedR 2012, 456. See R. Baur, 'Anmerkung on BGH 7.12.2012'.

[95] See M. Stauch, *The Law of Medical Negligence in England and Germany*, 117.

Further, it is accepted that any (even beneficial) incision constitutes a bodily injury (*Körperverletzung*) under §823 I BGB.[96] Thus, if an operation is performed without the required consent and one of the risks with respect to which the patient ought to have been informed instantiates during the operation, then the doctor is *prima facie* liable in respect of that injury under §823 I BGB, since the doctor has unlawfully infringed the claimant's bodily integrity, and this infringement led to further injury. To avoid liability, the doctor then bears the burden of proof to show that the patient would have consented, if the risk had been disclosed, to the actual operation which occurred, and that the injury which occurred during the operation would have occurred in any event.[97]

The BGH stated that this proof – proof that the claimant would have consented in any event – must be subject to strict requirements so that 'the patient's right to be informed is not undermined'.[98] However, if the defendant demonstrates that the claimant would have been 'objectively unreasonable'[99] in refusing the operation when aware of its risks, then an evidential burden falls upon the claimant to demonstrate that she personally would have faced a real conflict in deciding whether to have the operation or not (*echte Entscheidungskonflikt*).[100] This is, however, a relatively easy burden to discharge; the claimant need only make 'plausible' that she would have faced a significant dilemma.[101]

The courts have clearly evinced a particular concern to protect the patient's right to an informed decision over a course of treatment. Originally, the plea that the patient would have consented to the operation that took place, if properly informed, was absolutely not permitted.[102] The BGH has argued that there is simply no certainty to be had in cases as to how a patient would have decided: proof to a very high probability is generally impossible, and consequently, in order to ensure adequate protection of the claimant's right to be informed, it is

---

[96] C. Katzenmeier, *Arzthaftung*, 111ff.

[97] The doctor may also avoid liability by proving that the injury or loss would have occurred anyway through some event unrelated to the operation: BGH NJW 2005, 2072.

[98] BGH NJW 1998, 2734.

[99] Note that this 'reasonable patient' is only used in order to shift the evidential burden to C; the causal inquiry is in substance a *personalised* one, which looks to the personal characteristics of C: BGH NJW 1984, 1397, 1399.

[100] C. Katzenmeier, *Arzthaftung*, 349. A. Laufs, C. Katzenmeier, V. Lipp, *Arztrecht*, [64] treat this as an application of §286 ZPO.

[101] G. Mäsch, *Chance und Schaden*, 73 is perhaps too strong in stating that C will win so long as her claim is not 'absurd'.

[102] G. Schiemann, 'Commentary on §249 BGB', 114.

preferable that the defendant bear the risk of proof being impossible.[103] Here then, the consequentialist consideration of incentivising defendants to conform to their duties to inform – to uphold a particularly valuable interest of the claimant – is partly what justifies the reversal of the burden of proof.[104]

The BGH has recently thrown the application of the reversal of the burden of proof for hypothetical causation in this context into doubt.[105] It reasoned that, if a wrongful omission is only causative of an injury if the injury would not have occurred, then breaches of duties to inform (omissions) can only be causative of injury if that injury would not have occurred had the duty been fulfilled. Hence, there is no room for the defence of hypothetical causation in this context: the defence, and so the reversal of the burden of proof, is only engaged after the claimant has proven that the defendant's wrongful conduct has been causative of its injury.[106] This is a radical departure from the previous law. Some lower courts have followed suit;[107] others have not.[108]

Breach of other duties to inform

The BGH recognises a reversal of the burden of proof on causation of injury where a contractual duty to inform has been breached by certain kinds of advisor.[109] These include investment advisors,[110] stockbrokers,[111] and insurance brokers.[112] Although the statements of principle in these decisions are broad – 'a person who breaches a contractual or pre-contractual duty to inform another bears the burden of proof to show that the loss would have occurred even if they had conformed to their duty'[113] – the reversal is not applied to lawyers or accountants.[114] In relation to the latter, there is only a prima facie presumption that advice would have been heeded if that advice would have revealed only one reasonable course of action.[115] Similarly, the non-contractual tortious duty to warn of the dangers of products does

---

[103] BGH NJW 1991, 1543, 1544.   [104] M. Gebauer, *Hypothetische Kausalität*, 342–3.
[105] BGH VersR 2012, 491.   [106] Ibid., 492.   [107] OLG Köln MedR 2013, 47.
[108] OLG Karlsruhe, 12.12.2012, 7 U 176/11; LG Wiesbaden, 20.6.2013, 9 O 294/10.
[109] See, generally, C. Canaris 'Die Vermutung "auflkärungsrichtigen Verhaltens" und ihre grundlagen'. Canaris argues that the law here can justified as applying the reversal of the burden of proof for 'hypothetical causation' on the basis that the breach of the duty to inform *contributes* to the loss as it actually occurred.
[110] BGH 8.5.2012, NJW 2012, 2427.   [111] BGH NJW 1994, 512.
[112] BGH NJW 1985, 2595.   [113] BGH NJW 2012, 2427.   [114] BGH NJW 2012, 2435.
[115] Ibid. See also A. Jungk, 'Grundsätze', 144. This was at one point criticised by the BGH as inconsistent: BGH NJW 1994, 512.

not generate a reversal of the burden of proof, but only a presumption that a person would have heeded a very clear warning had it been provided.[116]

The reasoning relied upon to justify a reversal of the burden of proof for the breach of the duty to inform in these contractual situations is similar to that employed in the case law on destruction of proof.[117] The basic argument is that the purpose of duties 'to inform, to warn, or to advise' consists also in 'maintaining *clarity* over whether the other party, if he were fully aware of full nature of the risk, will stick to the course actually undertaken or whether he will distance himself from it'.[118] More precisely, part of the purpose of the duty to inform is to protect the right-holder from the 'frequently arising difficulty of proof' that arises in determining with sufficient precision how a person would have decided had they been properly informed of certain risks.[119]

In making this claim about the purpose of the duty, the courts are clearly influenced by the perceived need to deter breaches of the duty to inform. In one case, the BGH observed that those who breach duties to inform would have 'little to fear' if the burden of proof were on the other party, as such proof would frequently be impossible.[120] Indeed, the argument for the reversal of the burden of proof is sometimes put simply – without reference to the proof-preserving purpose of the duty – in terms of the need to provide incentives for conformity to the duty to inform, lest that duty become a 'blunt weapon'.[121] This is particularly so in the most important recent statement by the BGH of the law in this area, where the court stated that the purpose of the duty to inform, understood simply as ensuring that the claimant has the opportunity to make an informed decision, would not be achieved if the burden of proof were upon the claimant.[122] The implicit premise is that the defendants would not conform to the duty without the incentive provided by the reverse burden of proof. The need for a reversal of the burden of proof on this deterrence-based ground has been particularly emphasised in situations where the defendant had a duty to disclose a conflict of interest.[123]

---

[116] See H. Ahrens, 'Die Verteilung der Beweislast', 49.   [117] See p. 207.

[118] BGHZ 61, 118, 119 (emphasis added). The reasoning is repeated in, for example, BGHZ 89, 95, 103; BGH NJW-RR 1989, 1102, 1103.

[119] BGHZ 61, 118, 121. The court cites H. Stoll, 'Die Beweislastverteilung bei positive Vertragsverletzungen', which supported this idea.

[120] Ibid.   [121] See V. Wahrendorf, *Die Prinzipien der Beweislast im Haftungsrecht*, 109, 112.

[122] See BGH NJW 2012, 2427, 2430.   [123] LG Dusseldorf, 11.5.2012, 8 O 77/11.

Altering the standard of proof

Prima facie proof

The BGH has sometimes distinguished full proof under §286 ZPO and proof by virtue of prima facie proof (*Anscheinsbeweis*).[124] It is plausible that while the rules of *Anscheinsbeweis* do not necessarily lead to causation being found on the basis of a lower standard of proof, this is possible.[125]

It is suggested that the doctrine allows the claimant to prove causation by means of a probability that has less weight than may normally be insisted upon.[126] This is because, by virtue of this doctrine, the claimant need only demonstrate an abstract causal generalisation between c and e to the effect that c typically causes e whereupon it falls to the defendant to provide *case-specific* evidence that casts doubt upon the applicability of that generalisation to the facts at hand. For example, in cases of the breach of a duty by a lawyer to advise of a particular course of action, a presumption will be generated in favour of the claimant that it would have taken that option, if that option would have been the only reasonable option available.[127] Here the claimant may rely upon the generalisation that 'people normally follow the only reasonable course of action if they are aware of it'. It may then become difficult for the defendant to prove a concrete circumstance to rebut this presumption in cases where case-specific evidence is scarce.

Another way of putting this point is that the rule allows the claimant to avoid the difficulty of proving a negative proposition to the effect that 'alternative risk sources did not cause my injury'. For example, in a case where the claimant developed syphilis after a blood transfusion, the court held that an *Anscheinsbeweis* spoke for the proposition that the transfusion caused the syphilis.[128] It then fell to the defendant to show that this rather occurred due to another cause – principally, sexual intercourse with an infected person. The defendant could not present

---

[124] It is described as a *Beweiserleichterung* (proof-lightener) in BGH NJW 2010, 1072.

[125] In support of similar claims: G. Mäsch, *Chance und Schaden*, 31; A. Spickhoff, *Folgenzurechnung*, 81.

[126] On the concept of 'weight', see Chapter 2, 98–100.

[127] In the professional advice context: BGH NJW 1993, 3259; BGH NJW 2008, 2647. In the product warning context (for cases of 'deutlicher Gefahrenhinweise'): BGH NJW 1992, 560, 562.

[128] BGH NJW 1954, 718. On this case, see G. Kegel, 'Der Individualanscheinsbeweis und die Verteilung der Beweislast nach überwiegender Wahrscheinlichkeit', 328ff; V. Wahrendorf, *Die Prinzipien der Beweislast im Zivilprozeß*, 34 ('exceptional').

such evidence and so the claimant succeeded on this issue.[129] Here it is likely to be difficult for the defendant to produce case-specific evidence that the claimant had intercourse with an infected person.

England

English law does not conceptualise its primary departures from the general proof rules in relation to the cases discussed in this chapter as reversals in the burden of proof or reductions in the standard of proof. Rather, the law has created *distinct liability rules*, based around modifications to the substantive law's concept of causation in particular circumstances, which impose liability upon the defendant in situations where the general burden of proof would require the claimant to fail on the causal issue. These rules, so far as they create full liability, are functionally equivalent to burden of proof rules, however. To assist in transparent comparison between English law and the other systems, which do conceptualise their departures from the general rules simply as alterations in the proof rules, it will be helpful to classify them as such.

If the central context of German law's reversals of the burden of proof has been medical negligence, the central source of comparable rules in English law has been cases involving industrial diseases – an area dealt with almost entirely by employers' liability legislation in Germany.[130] These cases have given rise to the following complex rules. A rule functionally equivalent to a reversal of the burden of proof applies, first, in cases involving a particular kind of asbestos-caused cancer.[131] A rule functionally equivalent to a reversal of the burden also applies in cases in which the defendant has been shown to have materially contributed to the claimant's injury, but it is impossible due to the limits of scientific knowledge to determine whether the injury would have occurred in any event.[132] A rule of proportional liability applies – probably – in certain other cases where a defendant's wrongful conduct may have caused the claimant's personal injury where it is impossible to determine whether the defendant was a cause of the injury due to the limits of scientific knowledge, and harmful agents which operate in substantially similar ways have been a cause of the claimant's injury on the balance of probability.

The law on reductions in the standard of proof is simpler. Here, the law has flirted with allowing the claimant leniency once proof of

---

[129] More recently, in the context of HIV infected blood: BGH NJW 2005, 2614.
[130] See p. 280.   [131] See p. 231ff.   [132] See p. 239ff.

negligence and increased risk has been established, and has also relaxed the standard of proof, in much the same way as German law, in cases where the defendant's breach of duty to maintain evidence has deprived the claimant of evidence over causation.

Reversing the burden of proof on causation

Liability based upon material increase in risk when proof on the balance of probability is impossible

The law can be expressed in the following propositions:

(1) The claimant is exceptionally relieved of proving that the defendant caused his injury on the balance of probability where the claimant suffers from mesothelioma (a cancer caused by asbestos exposure) and it is impossible, due to limitations in scientific knowledge, to determine on the balance of probability whether or not the defendant's wrongful conduct was a cause of the claimant's mesothelioma, and either (a) all potential causes of the claimant's mesothelioma would operate to cause mesothelioma in a substantially similar way or (b) an agent which operates in a substantially similar way to the agent which the defendant has exposed the claimant has been a cause of the claimant's injury on the balance of probability. In such circumstances, C may establish that D is liable in damages for C's mesothelioma simply by showing that D's wrongful conduct has materially increased the risk of C contracting mesothelioma. At common law, D's liability is in proportion to the abstract probability that D's wrongful conduct was a cause of C's injury.

(2) It is likely that the rule in (1) also applies, more generally, in two situations. The first is where D wrongfully exposes C to a harmful agent, which conduct materially increases C's risk of suffering a disease, C suffers the disease, and it is impossible due to limitations in scientific knowledge, to determine on the balance of probability whether or not D's wrongful conduct was a cause of C's disease where either (a) all potential causes of the claimant's mesothelioma would operate to cause mesothelioma in a substantially similar way or (b) an agent which operates in a substantially similar way to the agent which the defendant has exposed the claimant has been a cause of the claimant's injury on the balance of probability and D's wrongful conduct did not occur in the course of D's providing medical treatment to C. The second is where one of conditions (a) and (b) hold and it is impossible to determine (perhaps not necessarily due to scientific uncertainty) whether D's wrongful conduct was a cause of C's injury, where D's wrongful conduct materially increased the risk of C's injury and D is one of a number of persons, each of whom may have been a wrongful cause of C's injury and at least one has been. This is a defendant indeterminacy situation discussed in Chapter 4. In both situations, D's liability is in proportion to the abstract probability that D's wrongful conduct was a cause of C's injury.

The aim of this section is to describe the prolix development of these complex rules and to assess the reasoning used to justify their current scope. First, the origins and then initial rejection of a rule recognising full liability where the defendant has materially increased the risk of the claimant's injury, but it is impossible to prove causation on the balance of probability, are traced. Second, the modern resurrection of such an exceptional rule, achieved in the House of Lords' decision in *Fairchild* v. *Glenhaven Funeral Services Ltd*[133] and its subsequent re-conceptualisation in *Barker* v. *Corus (UK) Ltd* is analysed. Third, the bifurcation, effected by legislation, of the exceptional rule created into a rule creating full liability (1) and a rule creating proportional liability (2), and the legal consequences of this, is explained. Fourth, it is argued that the justifications offered for the rule do not justify the limitations currently placed upon it.

Origins

From the 1940s, the courts began to develop a reversal of the burden of proof in cases involving breaches of statutory duties which were geared towards protecting the physical safety of employees. In *Vyner* v. *Waldenburg Bros Ltd*, Scott LJ stated that:

> If there is a definite breach of a safety provision imposed on the occupier of a factory, and a workman is injured in a way which could result from the breach, the onus of proof shifts on to the employer to show that the breach was not the cause. We think that that principle lies at the very basis of statutory rules of absolute duty.[134]

Scott LJ later explains that this principle underlies such duties because Parliament intended that the risk of uncertainty over causation be borne by the employer, since this risk is one which 'as Parliament realized, by the practice of insurance is distributed over the cost of the articles supplied and thus enters into the consumer's price'.[135]

In *Roberts* v. *Dorman Long & Co. Ltd*, the court of appeal suggested that this rule also applied to claims at common law in negligence for the failure by an employer to provide a safety harness to an employee, and made the further radical suggestion that a person in breach of duty 'cannot be heard to say' that the employee would not have worn

---

[133] [2003] 1 AC 32.
[134] *Vyner* v. *Waldenburg Bros Ltd* [1946] KB 50, 55. The only authority cited was *Lee* v. *Nursery Furnishing* [1945] 1 All ER 387, 390, where Lord Goddard had made remarks which could be interpreted as reversing the burden of proof where a breach of a safety regulation had been found.
[135] *Vyner*, 55.

the harness had it been provided.[136] According to a later case, such a plea simply 'does not lie in the defendants' mouth'.[137] Soon after, however, the House of Lords in *Bonnington Castings Ltd* v. *Wardlaw* and then in *McWilliams* v. *Arrol & Co.* expressly rejected both the reversal of the burden of proof in *Vyner* and the more radical rule in *Roberts* as simply inconsistent with the basic principle that the claimant must prove a causal connection between the breach of duty and the injury suffered on the balance of probability.[138]

Despite the clear affirmation of the general rule that the claimant bears the burden of proof on causation in *Bonnington* and *McWilliams*, the House of Lords nonetheless went on to recognise an exceptional rule allowing the claimant to succeed in full where the defendant's wrongful conduct had not been shown to have been a cause on the balance of probability, but had only materially increased the risk of the claimant's injury in the Scots case, *McGhee* v. *National Coal Board*.[139] The pursuer contracted dermatitis from working in hot and dusty brick kilns. The exposure to dust the claimant experienced in the kilns was not itself a breach of his employer's duty of care. The breach of duty rather consisted in the failure to provide showers to wash off the dust after work in the kiln. The causal issue was whether the pursuer would not have contracted dermatitis had showers been provided.

According to Lord Reid, the medical evidence suggested two different possible causal mechanisms for the contraction of dermatitis by brick dust:[140]

It may be that an accumulation of minor abrasions of the horny layer of the skin is a necessary precondition for the onset of the disease. Or it may be that the disease starts at one particular abrasion and then spreads, so that multiplication of abrasions merely increase the number of places where the disease can start and in that way increases the risk of its occurrence.

---

[136] [1953] 1 WLR 942, 946 (Lord Goddard CJ); 949 (Birkett LJ); 951 (Hodson LJ). Hodson LJ stated that 'it cannot lie in the mouth of the defendants to say that this was not the cause of the accident on the ground that the probabilities are that the deceased would never have elected to use a belt'. The only reasoning was offered by Lord Goddard CJ, who somewhat unpersuasively cited a case concerning defences to conversion under section 82 of the Bills of Exchange Act 1882.

[137] *Drummond* v. *British Building Cleaners Ltd* [1954] 1 WLR 1434, 1438.

[138] *Bonnington Castings Ltd* v. *Wardlaw* [1956] AC 613, 619–20; *McWilliams* v. *Sir William Arrol & Co. Ltd* [1962] SC (HL) 70, 82–3.

[139] *McGhee* v. *National Coal Board* [1973] 1 WLR 1. The literature on *McGhee* is voluminous. See, for example, E. Weinrib, 'A Step Forward in Factual Causation', 519, 523–9; Lord Hope, 'James McGhee – a Second Mrs. Donoghue?'; L. Khoury, *Uncertain Causation in Medical Liability*, 148–52.

[140] *McGhee*, 4.

It could not be determined which mechanism was more probable than the other. In these circumstances, reversing the decision of the court of Session, which had rejected the claim on the basis that 'the fact that the risk of contracting the disease might have been lessened to some unknown and unspecified extent, cannot mean that, on the probabilities, he would have escaped the disease',[141] the House of Lords held the defendant liable in full.

The original basis of the decision is unclear. The 'inference interpretation', as we may call it, is that McGhee adopted a 'robust and pragmatic approach' leading to a 'legitimate inference of fact that the defenders' negligence had materially contributed to the pursuer's injury'.[142] It cannot be denied that some passages in the judgments support this interpretation. Thus, Lord Kilbrandon firmly stated that the pursuer's 'injury was more probably than not, caused by, or contributed to by, the defenders' failure to provide a shower-bath'.[143]

However, there are convincing arguments against the inference interpretation of McGhee. First, the inference of causation simply could not be made on the balance of probabilities, given the medical evidence.[144] Let us assume, with Lord Reid, that there were two possibilities: either the dermatitis was caused by an accumulation of abrasions or the dermatitis was caused by one abrasion. If the 'one abrasion' view were correct, then to prove causation on the balance of probability, it would be necessary, at least, to show that the pursuer suffered more abrasions after work than during work (assuming a linear relationship between the number of abrasions and the risk). No such evidence was, however, adduced in McGhee. If the 'accumulation' view were correct, it is not obvious, as is sometimes assumed,[145] that the defendant would have been shown to be a cause on the balance of probability. If only a small number of abrasions were necessary for the threshold to be reached, then the dermatitis may still have been caused entirely by the brick dust exposure in the kiln alone. It may have been possible to argue that the brick dust on the skin after work contributed to the mechanism, even if not as a necessary condition, but this is not clear on the medical evidence as Lord Reid presents it. So, on either view of the mechanism, causation was not established on the balance of probability by the evidence.

---

[141] See 1973 SC (HL) 37, 39 (Lord Kissen).

[142] Wilsher v. Essex Area Health Authority [1988] AC 1074, 1090 (Lord Bridge). This interpretation has been carefully defended by A. Beever, Rediscovering the Law of Negligence, 466–72.

[143] McGhee, 10.   [144] J. Stapleton, 'The Gist of Negligence: Part 2', 404, n. 33.

[145] Cf. A. Beever, Rediscovering, 469–70.

Second, Lord Wilberforce's speech is clearly influenced by the consequentialist policy of ensuring that employers comply with their duties of care; if proof of causation against them is impossible, employers have little incentive to comply with their legal duty of care.[146] This policy consideration is also mentioned by Lord Simon.[147]

Third, some statements in the judgments appear to adopt the radical position of equating – at the level of substantive law – the concept of causation with the concept of material increase in risk. For example, Lord Reid described the result as reached by 'taking a broader view of causation'.[148] Lord Salmon considered that '[e]verything in the present case depends upon what constitutes a cause' and that the decision of the court of Session against the pursuer 'confuse[d] the balance of probability test with the nature of causation'.[149]

Despite the ambiguity in the basis of *McGhee*, Mustill LJ had interpreted the case in the court of appeal decision in *Wilsher* v. *Essex Health Authority* as indeed embodying a rule of law, based upon 'policy rather than a chain of direct reasoning'.[150] If the claimant's injury occurred within the risk created by the defendant's negligence then 'the [defendant] is taken to have caused the injury by his breach of duty even though the existence and extent of the contribution made by the breach cannot be ascertained'.[151]

In *Wilsher* the claimant baby suffered retrolental fibroplasia causing blindness. One possible cause of his condition was the defendant doctor's negligence over-administration of oxygen. However, a number of other possible (non-wrongful) conditions from which he likely suffered may have caused it. The *McGhee* doctrine, as Mustill LJ interpreted it, allowed the claimant to escape the conclusion that he had failed to show causation on the balance of probability.[152]

This approach was also applied in *Fitzgerald* v. *Lane*.[153] The causal uncertainty arose in that case since it was not possible to say whether one car collision or another alone caused the claimant's neck injury or whether both contributed. The court of appeal rejected the proposition that there was a satisfactory distinction between evidential gaps due to the imperfect state of medical knowledge and the factual inability of

---

[146] *McGhee*, 6ff.   [147] Ibid., 8.   [148] Ibid., 4.   [149] Ibid., 12.
[150] *Wilsher* v. *Essex Area Health Authority* [1987] QB 730. Similarly: *Clark* v. *MacLennan* [1983] 1 All ER 416 (QB); *Bagley* v. *North Herts Health Authority* (1986) NLJ 1014 (QB).
[151] Ibid., 771–2.   [152] Ibid.   [153] [1987] 1 QB 781.

medical experts to tell which collision was causal.[154] Thus, the defendant was held liable to the claimant for his tetraplegia on the basis of the interpretation of McGhee adopted in Wilsher.

The view that McGhee established a distinctive 'principle' was thoroughly rejected when Wilsher reached the House of Lords.[155] This followed primarily from close analysis of the speeches in McGhee, with Lord Wilberforce's speech being relegated to a 'minority opinion'.[156] Underlying this claim, however, was Lord Bridge's view that 'the law…requires proof of fault causing damage as the basis of liability in tort' and that alteration of the general rules of proof in the face of what 'may seem hard cases' would make 'the forensic process still more unpredictable and hazardous'.[157]

The revitalisation of an exceptional rule

The proof orthodoxy restored by Wilsher was disrupted once again by Fairchild.[158] Fairchild involved three claims, in each of which an employee had been wrongfully exposed to asbestos dust by successive employers and had either died or suffered from mesothelioma. Each employee had, on the balance of probability, contracted mesothelioma as a result of wrongful conduct, but was unable to prove on the balance of probability which employer's or employers' wrongful conduct had been causative because of limitations of scientific knowledge over the mechanism by which mesothelioma is caused. As Lord Bingham described the evidence:

[T]he condition may be caused by a single fibre, or a few fibres, or many fibres: medical opinion holds none of these possibilities to be more probable than any other, and the condition once caused is not aggravated by further exposure[159]

Consequently, each defendant could argue that the claimant's disease had been caused by a small number of fibres for which another negligent

---

[154] Ibid. 799; also 810–11 (Slade LJ). The result would have been different in German law, see Chapter 4, 148–150.

[155] [1987] AC 1074.   [156] Ibid., 1087.   [157] Ibid., 1092.

[158] [2003] 1 AC 32. For case notes on the decision, see J. Morgan, 'Lost Causes in the House of Lords'; J. Scherpe, 'Ausnahmen vom Erfordernis eines strikten Kausalitätsnachweis im englischen Deliktsrecht'; J. Stapleton, 'Lords a'Leaping Evidentiary Gaps'; T. Weir, 'Making it More Likely Versus Making it Happen'.

[159] Fairchild, 43. The precise mechanism by which asbestos fibres cause mesothelioma remains unclear. The single fibre theory seems unlikely, however, as the development of the mesothelioma seems to involve multiple stages, with each stage involving asbestos fibres. See M. Carbone and H. Yang, 'Molecular Pathways: Targeting Mechanisms of Asbestos and Erionite Carcinogenesis in Mesothelioma', 599–600; J. Thompson, et al., 'Malignant Mesothelioma: Development to Therapy', 1, 'the molecular pathogenesis of MM [malignant mesothelioma] is still an elusive multifactorial event involving multiple mechanisms'.

defendant was alone responsible. The House of Lords allowed the estates of the deceased employees and the only living employee to succeed against each defendant, allowing proof that each defendant had materially increased the risk of injury to suffice in lieu of proof on the balance of probability. Liability was assumed to be joint and several, although the defendants expressly reserved the right to raise the issue of apportionment at a later point.[160]

The route to liability was to recognise that McGhee[161] did indeed decide a point of law; each of their Lordships, apart from Lord Hutton, rejected the inference interpretation of McGhee. The claimant could, then, succeed where it had proven that the defendant had materially increased the risk of injury in breach of duty, but it could not be shown, due to the limits of scientific knowledge, that the breach was a cause of the injury. Some extension of McGhee, which concerned only one employer, exercising control over all possible causal sources of the injury, and where it could be said that the employer caused the injury, even if not through the negligent aspect of its conduct, was necessary.

Wilsher was distinguished on the ground not uniformly expressed by each judge that the McGhee rule does not apply where there is a non-minimal probability that the injury may have eventuated entirely from a risk of a different kind to the risk which the defendant has imposed. Thus, Lord Bingham observed that: 'it is one thing to treat an increase in risk as equivalent to the making of a material contribution where a single noxious agent is involved, but quite another where any one of a number of noxious agents may equally probably have caused the damage'.[162] Similarly, Lord Hutton approved the expansion of McGhee to multiple persons in breach of duty 'where there is only one causative agent (in this case asbestos dust)'.[163] Less exigent was Lord Rodger's formulation the injury must at least be caused 'by an agency that operated in substantially the same way' as the agent used by the defendant.[164] The bounds of this requirement are unclear: within it explicitly are different types of asbestos[165] and brick dust, possibly nearly simultaneous car collisions,[166] outside it are cancers

---

[160] E. Peel, 'Lost Chances and Proportional Recovery', 292 conjectures that this was a strategic move made by the defendants in order to create a stark choice between full liability or none at all.

[161] As Lord Mance, discussing Fairchild, observes in Durham v. BAI (Run Off) Ltd [2012] UKSC 14: 'McGhee was seen as a precursor of the decision there reached', [56].

[162] Fairchild, 57.   [163] Ibid. 95.

[164] Ibid. 118–19; Lord Hoffmann did not approve the single agent requirement in Fairchild, but later recanted: Barker v. Corus Ltd [2006] 2 AC 572, 587.

[165] Barker, 1049 (Lord Scott).

[166] Lord Rodger inclined to the view that the Fairchild/McGhee rule was properly applied in Fitzgerald v. Lane [1987] 1 QB 781: Fairchild 119.

possibly caused by exposure to asbestos or by smoking, at least where it is not proven on the balance of probability that asbestos contributed to the cancer.[167]

The *nature* of the rule by which the defendants were being held liable in *Fairchild* was variously expressed in the judgments. Lord Bingham at one point[168] expressly located the result as an alteration in the rules of proof: 'the ordinary approach to proof of causation is varied'.[169] It would be conceptually clear to understand this as a reversal of the burden of proof since, normally, if it is impossible to demonstrate a fact on the balance of probability, the claimant loses by virtue of the burden of proof. The liability in *Fairchild* arises precisely (subject to the single agent requirement) in situations where proof is impossible on the balance of probability. By contrast, Lord Nicholls stated that the increased risk of mesothelioma 'should be regarded as a sufficient degree of causal connection'.[170] Similarly, Lord Hoffmann stated that a material increase in risk was being 'treated. . .as sufficient in the circumstances to satisfy the causal requirements for liability'.[171] As others had in *McGhee*, these statements purport to alter the substantive law's concept of causation by replacing the but-for test or the test of material contribution to damage with the concept of material increase in risk. Analytically, this is unfortunate: increasing the risk of an outcome is simply not itself a kind of causation, no matter the context; the fact that x has increased the risk of y leaves it an open question whether x was a cause of y.[172] The simpler analysis is that the claimant is exceptionally held to have proven but-for or material contribution causation when a material increase in risk is demonstrated.

The shift to proportional liability: risks as legal injuries

The appropriate conceptualisation of the liability in *Fairchild* was addressed subsequently in *Barker* v. *Corus Ltd*.[173] This issue arose as a

---

[167] *Barker*, 587 (Lord Hoffmann). If tobacco smoking operates in a substantially similar way to cause the cancer as the defendant's wrongful conduct, then the rule will probably be satisfied: *Novartis Grimsby Ltd* v. *Cookson* [2007] EWCA Civ 1261 at [72]. It also appears, more generally, to be enough if the claimant proves that its injury was caused by the same or similar agent to the defendant's agent, even if there is a non-minimal probability that it was also caused by another, different, agent: see *Heneghan* v. *Manchester Dry Docks Ltd* [2014] EWHC 4190. For an argument that the single agent requirement should not apply to defendant indeterminacy cases, see S. Steel, 'On When *Fairchild* Applies'.

[168] Compare the quotation from Lord Bingham, see Note 159.   [169] *Fairchild*, 68.

[170] Ibid., 70.   [171] Ibid., 75.

[172] An analogous point has been made, for example, by J. Stapleton, 'Choosing what we Mean by "Causation" in the Law' in relation to unfortunate expression of normative conclusions about responsibility in the language of causation.

[173] [2006] 2 AC 576.

backdrop to the question of whether *Fairchild* had established joint and several liability. The distinguishing feature of *Barker* was that, in one case, not all of the exposures which could have caused the mesothelioma involved breaches of duty to the claimant by his employer.[174] For one period the claimant was self-employed as a plasterer: his exposure then amounted to a failure to take reasonable care for his own safety.[175] By a majority, the House of Lords held that each defendant was liable under *Fairchild*, but only in proportion to the extent it had increased the risk of the claimant contracting mesothelioma.

The majority moved from the premise that the inference interpretation of *McGhee* had been rejected in *Fairchild* to the proposition that the basis of liability in *McGhee/Fairchild* was 'the wrongful creation of a risk or chance of causing the disease' such that 'the damage which the defendant should be regarded as having caused is the creation of such a risk or chance'.[176] Since the basis of the liability in *McGhee* was materially increasing the risk of injury, '[c]onsistency of approach'[177] and 'fairness'[178] suggested that characterising the actionable injury as 'increased risk' was appropriate. The fairness of this characterisation resided in the smoothing of the 'rough justice' of a rule of joint and several liability where it had not been shown on the balance of probabilities that the defendant caused the harm. Further, since the damage for which the defendant is being held liable is its contribution to the total risk, and since it is only liable for *that* damage, the question of the claimant's contributory negligence does not arise directly: the defendant is only liable for *its* contribution to the total risk.

Baroness Hale rejected the conceptualisation of the legal injury as an increase in risk. In her view, the damage forming the gist of the actions *was* the mesothelioma, not the risk of contracting the mesothelioma.[179] Proportional liability was justified simply as a trade-off for the departure from proof that each defendant was a cause of the claimant's injury on the balance of probability.[180] That the defendants materially increased

---

[174] Again, background exposure was ignored.
[175] Their Lordships were patently aware of the insolvency of some of the negligent employers: 581 (Lord Hoffmann); 607 (Lord Rodger – though rejecting its relevance); 612 (Lord Walker – considering it as affecting the equities).
[176] 589–90 (Lord Hoffmann); [53], [59] (Lord Scott); [113] (Lord Walker).
[177] 589 (Lord Hoffmann).   [178] 591 (Lord Hoffmann).
[179] 615; as did Lord Rodger, though he did not agree that apportionment was appropriate.
[180] 617.

the risk of injury was not the conceptual root of apportioning liability but was only 'a sensible basis for doing so'.[181]

The reasoning in the sections of the majority judgments[182] which suggests that the damage in respect of which the defendant is liable is the *risk* of mesothelioma is, with respect, flawed. There are four reasons for this. First, from the fact that *McGhee* was not based upon an inference of natural causation on the balance of probability, it hardly follows that the *damage* for which the defendant is held liable is the risk of mesothelioma. This is so either because it is perfectly possible to conceptualise *McGhee*, and *Fairchild*, as reversing the burden of proof on causation, or because even if *McGhee* loosened the substantive law concept of *causation*, it hardly follows that the *damage* which the defendant should be said to have caused is different.

Second, section 1(1) of the Fatal Accidents Act 1976 provides that:

> If death is caused by any wrongful act, neglect or default which is such as would (if death had not ensued) have entitled the person injured to maintain an action and recover damages in respect thereof, the person who would have been liable if death had not ensued shall be liable to an action for damages, notwithstanding the death of the person injured.

If *McGhee* (and *Fairchild*) did not create a rule that allows one to say that the employer's negligence caused the employee's mesothelioma, as opposed to the *risk* of mesothelioma, then the employee's dependants would not be able to establish that the employer's negligence had caused his death for the purpose of bringing a claim against the employer under the 1976 Act. But it is known that *Fairchild* does apply to allow dependants to bring claims against negligent employers under the 1976 Act. Two of the three claimants in *Fairchild* were bringing claims under the 1976 Act for damages in respect of the deaths of their husbands, who had died from contracting mesothelioma after having been exposed to excessive quantities of asbestos dust by the defendants.

Third, the claimant must have actually suffered the mesothelioma in order to claim.[183] This is difficult to explain if the legal injury is the risk of mesothelioma.

---

[181] Ibid. The basis for the apportionment would have been: duration of exposure compared with total duration; intensity; type of agent: 614–15 (Lord Walker); 594 (Lord Hoffmann).

[182] Even Lord Hoffmann's speech in *Barker* at 585 also refers to *Fairchild* as allowing the claimant to satisfy 'the requirement of a sufficient causal link between the defendant's conduct and the claimant's injury'.

[183] *Barker*, 594 (Lord Hoffmann); 598 (Lord Scott); 613 (Lord Walker). See also J. Lee, 'Fidelity in Interpretation: Lord Hoffmann and the Adventure of the Empty House', 12.

Fourth, damages under *Barker* are calculated on the basis of probability of causation, not ex-ante increase in risk. The extent to which each defendant's negligence increased the risk of mesothelioma depends only on the extent to which it increased the background risk of mesothelioma. By contrast, the probability that a particular defendant's negligent exposure was a cause of the mesothelioma depends upon the extent of that exposure in relation to other exposures. If the legal injury were the risk, however, it would be difficult to justify calculating damages to reflect the probability of causation.[184]

In short, nothing explanatory is added to the proposition that the rules of proof of causation in *Barker* are being relaxed in the face of insuperable uncertainty, but that, as a trade-off to the defendant, the quantum of liability is discounted to reflect the uncertainty over an essential element of the cause of action, by treating the risk as itself constituting the damage.

A rule of full liability and a rule of proportional liability

In respect of cases of mesothelioma caused by asbestos, Parliament enacted legislation within three months of *Barker* intended retrospectively to reverse the apportionment of liability achieved therein.[185] Section 3(2) of the Compensation Act 2006 makes persons to whom section 3(1) applies liable in full, jointly and severally with any other defendants.

The effect of the legislation was explained by the Supreme court in *Sienkiewicz v. Greif (UK) Ltd.*[186] The Justices accepted that section 3(2) is parasitic upon liability existing at common law,[187] as section 3(1)(d)

---

[184] For clear statements of the distinction between liability tailored to ex-ante risk and liability based on probability of causation, see A. Porat and A. Stein, 'Indeterminate Causation and Apportionment of Damages', 682–4; G. Turton, 'Risk and the Damage Requirement in Negligence Liability' 9–11. It is sometimes claimed that it is impossible to say of any defendant in *Fairchild* that it, in fact, exposed the claimant to a risk of suffering mesothelioma, since it may have been that the claimant had already contracted mesothelioma at the time of the negligent exposure. See J. Scherpe, 'A New Gist?', 489; D. Nolan, 'Causation and the Goals of Tort Law', 177–8. The criticism is only valid if one construes risk in real-world, propensity-based terms (see ch 2, 64). It is not valid if risk is construed as a purely epistemic concept, since it is possible to say that from the limited epistemic perspective of each defendant, its conduct increased the probability of mesothelioma occurring to the claimant.

[185] The retrospective effect is achieved by s 16(3). For an extensive discussion of the Compensation Act, see J. Morgan, 'Causation, Politics and Law', 77–82.

[186] [2011] UKSC 10 (*Sienkiewicz*).

[187] [70] (Lord Phillips); [131] (Lord Rodger); [183] (Lord Brown). That the Act leaves the proportional liability at common law untouched is further confirmed by *Zurich Insurance Plc v. International Energy Group Ltd* [2015] UKSC 33, especially at [27]–[31].

requires that the 'responsible person is liable in tort'. Victims of mesothelioma may, then, receive full damages from a defendant who has wrongfully materially increased their risk of suffering injury, subject to the single agent rule and the requirement that proof on the balance of probability be impossible.

It follows from the parasitic nature of section 3 of the Compensation Act that it must leave the proportional liability established at common law by *Barker* untouched in relation to any other cases to which the exceptional rule established by *Fairchild* applies. Are there any such cases? There is reason to believe that *Fairchild* continues to apply, in proportional liability form, to some other cases.

First, *McGhee*, upon whose reinterpretation *Fairchild* was premised, concerned dermatitis, not mesothelioma. So *Fairchild* should apply to dermatitis claims in negligence against at least some defendants, on the assumption that medical understanding has not advanced since *McGhee*.[188] Second, the court of appeal applied *Fairchild*, albeit unnecessarily, since a finding of but-for causation could probably have been made, in a case involving Vibration White Finger condition.[189] Third, in *Sienkiewicz*, Lord Phillips and Lord Rodger, with whom the other Justices agreed, considered that the *Fairchild* decision was justified by the 'rock of uncertainty' faced by mesothelioma claimants, given the available scientific evidence over the aetiology of the disease.[190] This tends to

---

[188] *McGhee* was criticised in *obiter* remarks in *Sienkiewcz* ([92], Lord Phillips, [177], Lord Brown). These *obiter* remarks cannot undo the centrality of *McGhee* to the decision in *Fairchild*.

[189] *Brown v. Corus (UK) Ltd* [2004] PIQR P30, [2004] EWCA Civ 374. See also the earlier *obiter dicta* in *Transco v. Griggs* [2003] EWCA 564 at [35] (Hale LJ) that *Fairchild* applied in a Vibratory White Finger case and the view of Smith LJ in *Novartis (Grimsby) Ltd v. Cookson* [2007] EWCA Civ 1261 that *Fairchild* could not be applied to bladder cancer because it was not 'analogous to mesothelioma' [70] (implicitly accepting, then, that an analogy could be made to mesothelioma in cases of other diseases). It is true that *Fairchild* has also *not* been applied in cases which do not involve mesothelioma. But these cases are readily explicable in that *Fairchild* was not applicable for some reason other than simply that the disease was not mesothelioma. This is true of: *Sanderson v. Hull* [2008] EWCA Civ 1211 (the uncertainty over causation was not due to the lack of scientific knowledge); *Clough v. First Choice Holidays and Flights Ltd* [2006] EWCA Civ 15 (the same as *Sanderson*); *AB v. Ministry of Defence* [2012] UKSC 9 (there were multiple *different* possible causative agents).

[190] Admittedly, Lord Brown in *Sienkiewicz* attempted to restrict *Fairchild* to mesothelioma cases. His Lordship said that 'Save only for mesothelioma cases, claimants should henceforth expect little flexibility from the courts in their approach to causation': *Sienkiewicz*, [187]. None of the other Justices spoke in these very restrictive terms, however. Cf. Lord Phillips at [105]. See now *Zurich v. International Energy Group* [2015] UKSC 33: the *Fairchild* exception is not 'coterminous with liability for mesothelioma' [109] (Lord Hodge); 'the legal issue was not necessarily peculiar to mesothelioma' [127] (Lord Sumption).

suggest that if similar impenetrable uncertainty surrounded the aetiology of another disease then the Fairchild decision could apply to it. Fourth, as Chapter 4 suggested, Fairchild is likely to continue to apply to the normatively distinctive defendant indeterminacy situation, whose normatively distinctive feature lies in the fact that the claimant has suffered injury due to a tort and not the kind of injury suffered. These claims are vindicated by the recent decision in Heneghan which applies the proportional liability rule to a case of adenocarcinoma of the lung.[191]

The requirement that proof of causation be impossible on the balance of probability

In addition to proving that the defendant's wrongful conduct materially increased the risk of the claimant's injury, and that the injury could only have resulted from a 'single agent', the only other requirement under either the full liability or proportional liability rule is that proof of causation on the balance of probability is 'impossible'.[192]

This requirement has been explored in three decisions since Fairchild. The first is Sanderson v. Hull.[193] The causal issue was whether the claimant turkey-plucker would have heeded a warning by her employer to wear gloves that would probably have prevented the transfer of bacteria from her hands to her mouth. The court of appeal held that the trial judge was not faced with a situation where proof was impossible, but only one in which there were 'difficulties of proof'.[194] Smith LJ held that proof must be impossible 'because of the current state of scientific knowledge'; the earlier authority of Fitzgerald, which had rejected a distinction between purely scientific and other uncertainty over causation was not considered.[195] The decisions can be reconciled if it is assumed that, due to the normative peculiarity that the claimant has provably been the victim of a wrong, the requirement of distinctively 'scientific' uncertainty is not necessary in defendant indeterminacy cases such as Fitzgerald.

The second decision is Sienkiewicz v. Greif (UK) Ltd. Mrs Costello died of mesothelioma. She had been wrongfully exposed to asbestos while working for the defendants, but also, non-tortiously, to asbestos in the general atmosphere. The statistical evidence appeared to suggest that the background asbestos would lead to some 24 cases of mesothelioma

---

[191] Heneghan v. Manchester Dry Docks Ltd [2014] EWHC 4190.
[192] Fairchild, [2] (Lord Bingham), [47] [61] (Lord Hoffmann); Barker [17] (Lord Hoffmann), [53] (Lord Scott), [109] (Lord Walker).
[193] [2008] EWCA Civ 1211.   [194] Ibid., [63].
[195] Ibid., [53]. In Fairchild, Lord Rodger 'incline[d]' to the view that Fitzgerald v. Lane was correct: Fairchild, [170].

per million persons, and that the exposure by the defendant had increased this by approximately 18 per cent. Accepting for a moment the statistical evidence, the probability that Mrs Costello had died from a non-tortious cause was at least 85 per cent.[196] The Supreme court unanimously upheld the court of appeal in holding the defendant liable in full to Mrs Costello's estate.

The crucial issue in *Sienkiewicz* was whether the statistical evidence, which *purported* to show that there was approximately an 85 per cent chance that environmental exposure caused the mesothelioma, precluded the exception applying, on the grounds that the defendant had successfully shown itself on the balance of probabilities not to be a cause and thus that proof on the balance of probability was not impossible. Lord Dyson is particularly clear:

It is implicit in *Fairchild* and *Barker* that, if it were possible for a victim of mesothelioma to establish causation on the balance of probability in the conventional way, then the rationale for the *Fairchild* exception would disappear.[197]

That is to say, if the statistics really are probative, then proof on the balance of probabilities would not be impossible and *Fairchild* ought not to apply. For different reasons, the statistical evidence was rejected and so the exception did apply.[198]

The requirement of 'impossibility of proof' was liberally interpreted in *Heneghan*.[199] The deceased victim had been wrongfully exposed to

---

[196] The 85 per cent probability is generated by the fraction of risk attributable to the wrongful exposure compared to the total exposure: $1 - ((28.32 - 24)/28.32)$. For reasons discussed in Chapter 2, this should be expressed as an inequality, see p. 89 n 213.

[197] *Sienkiewicz*, [213]. The notion of 'impossibility of proof' cannot be restricted, however, to situations where it is *never* possible to establish causation on the balance of probability between a defendant's conduct and a particular kind of disease. This is because it will sometimes be possible to reason even in mesothelioma cases that *whatever the nature of the mechanism*, the defendant's breach has contributed to it. For instance, suppose we have an exposure by D1 lasting 35 years and an exposure from D2 lasting one day and occupational exposure of the same level as that one day of exposure. It is highly likely that whatever the nature of the causal mechanism in mesothelioma cases, D1's breach has contributed to it. In fact, there is an argument that we have already reached the position where causation is generally provable on the balance of probability in mesothelioma cases. If (as is now likely) the mechanism involves a large number of fibres, it will often be possible to construct an argument that the defendant's negligence contributed to it on the balance of probability.

[198] Cf. [135] (Lord Rodger); [45], [52] (Lord Phillips). See Chapter 2, 87–88.

[199] [2014] EWHC 4190. Despite the criticism in the text, the decision is consistent with that in *Fitzgerald* v. *Lane* [1987] 1 QB 781 where the existence of a valid claim against one defendant did not preclude the application of *McGhee* to the other.

asbestos dust sequentially by the six defendant employers and had died from an adenocarcinoma of the lung caused by asbestos exposure. The aggregate exposure due to the six defendants' breaches of duty was agreed to comprise 35.2 per cent of the victim's total occupational exposure to asbestos and thus, risk being proportional to exposure, each defendant was not proven to be a cause on the balance of probability. Applying *Fairchild* and *Barker*, Jay J nonetheless held each defendant liable in proportion to its share of the wrongful exposure. Had the victim's earlier employer, who was responsible for 56 per cent of the total exposure, been sued, Jay J stated he would have found this exposure to have been causative on the balance of probability. Assuming, then, that this earlier exposure was in breach of duty, the victim would have had a valid claim against the earlier employer. On this assumption, and if the argument of Chapter 4 is correct, the decision in *Heneghan* is problematic. Assuming a valid claim on the balance of probability against the earlier employer, the effect of the later defendants' conduct was not to deprive the claimant of a right of action nor would the defendants' reliance upon the wrongful conduct of the earlier employer to avoid liability have the effect of depriving the victim of a *right* to compensation.

The exclusion of medical negligence from the proportional liability rule

The proportional liability rule, which continues to exist at common law, and which applies to some, non-mesothelioma, personal injury cases, most probably does not apply to claims arising out negligent medical treatment. The issue was considered by the House of Lords in *Gregg v. Scott*. The claimant sought to recover for the less than 50 per cent chance that the defendant doctor's negligence had precluded his being cured of cancer. His claim was rejected by a 3–2 majority. The majority consisted of Lord Hoffmann, Lady Hale, and Lord Phillips. Lord Hoffmann stated that:

> wholesale adoption of possible rather than probable causation as the criterion of liability would be so radical a change in our law as to amount to a legislative act. It would have enormous consequences for insurance companies and the National Health Service.[200]

Lady Hale made three main points. First, doctors and health care professionals 'are not solely, or even mainly, motivated by fear of adverse legal

---

[200] *Gregg* v. *Scott* [2005] 2 AC 176, [90].

consequences'.[201] If true, the deterrence-based, 'empty duty' argument, which was found persuasive in *Fairchild*, does not apply with the same force in the medical context. Second, allowing claimants to recover in proportion to the less than evens chance that the defendant caused their injury would require limitation of damages awards to the probability of causation, even where it is greater than evens. Thus, claimants who recover in full at present under the balance of probability rule would receive less than full compensation. This would be 'a case of two steps forward, three steps back for the great majority of straightforward personal injury cases'.[202] Third, her Ladyship seemed to be generally concerned with the extent of the increase in liability likely to arise from permitting claimants to recover for the less than evens chance that the defendant caused their injuries.[203] Lord Phillips pointed to the increased complexity of introducing proportional liability in medical negligence claims: 'It is always likely to be much easier to resolve issues of causation on balance of probabilities than to identify in terms of percentage the effect that clinical negligence had on the chances of a favourable outcome'.[204]

Almost all of these arguments point against proportional liability *in general* rather than specifically against proportional liability in medical negligence claims. However, the *judicial* acceptance of proportional liability in mesothelioma claims in *Barker* v. *Corus* shows that no such general argument has been accepted.

The exceptional rule reconceived once more

The conceptual understanding of the rule in *Fairchild*, seemingly altered in *Barker*, was once more reconceived in *Durham* v. *BAI (Run off)*.[205] This case raised an issue as to the interpretation of employers' insurance policies which covered them against liabilities arising out of diseases 'sustained' or 'contracted' during the employment period.[206] The majority accepted that 'contracted' meant 'caused' and so the question arose whether, in respect of mesothelioma claims, the *Fairchild* doctrine could be relied upon to establish that an employer who had negligently exposed an employee to asbestos dust had 'caused' the mesothelioma during the insured period.

Lord Mance argued that, even as a matter of interpretation of the common law *as stated in Barker*, the cause of action created by *Fairchild*

---

[201] Ibid., [217].   [202] Ibid., [225]. For discussion of this argument, see Chapter 6, 353f.
[203] See especially, ibid., [215], [224].   [204] Ibid., [170].   [205] [2012] UKSC 14.
[206] For further detail, see N. McBride and S. Steel, 'The *Trigger* Litigation'. and see generally, R. Merkin and J. Steele, *Insurance and the Law of Obligations*, ch 12.

is one 'for' or 'in respect of' mesothelioma[207] and emphasised that it would be 'over-simple' to describe *Barker* as creating a cause of action simply for the risk of mesothelioma.[208] Moreover, his Lordship thought it apt to describe this liability as 'responsibility for the mesothelioma, based on a "weak" or "broad" view of the "causal requirements" or "causal link" appropriate in the particular context to ground liability for the mesothelioma'.[209] Lord Clarke claimed that *Fairchild* and *Barker* held liable 'the employer who can fairly be said to have caused the disease'.[210]

These statements meet the difficulties raised above as to the 'risk-as-damage' reasoning.[211] Nonetheless, the regrettable tendency, which runs through English law, to express an exception to the proof rules of causation as if it were a modification to the substantive concept of causation remains.[212]

The justifiability of the exceptional rule in *Fairchild*

The state of the current law cannot be justified.[213] This is so both in relation to the single agent requirement and the requirement that proof be impossible for reasons of scientific uncertainty.

The idea of a 'single agent' formally distinguishes the facts in *Fairchild* and *McGhee* from *Wilsher*, and the requirement of 'scientific uncertainty', despite its uncertain content, distinguishes *Sanderson v. Hull* from *McGhee*. Why, however, should liability where proof of causation is impossible on the balance of probability be restricted to situations where the claimant's injury may only have been caused by one or more of a number of agents which would, if causative, operate in the same way, and the uncertainty over which did is due to the limits of scientific knowledge?

Recall that the reasons given for the exception were that the defendant's duty of care would be empty of content if there were no liability, that the balance of justice favoured the claimant, and that it was unfair that a claimant who has been the victim of multiple acts of wrongdoing should be worse off in virtue of that fact.[214] None of these reasons implies that the exception should be limited to single agent cases

---

[207] Ibid. [65].   [208] Ibid. [66].   [209] Ibid.   [210] [84].   [211] See pp. 228–231.
[212] See further, on this tendency, p. 239ff.
[213] See, generally, S. Steel, 'Causation in English Tort Law', 247–50. For similar arguments, see K. Wellington, 'Beyond Single Causative Agents'.
[214] See Chapter 4, 169.

involving scientific uncertainty.[215] The defendants' duty of care would equally be without content where proof is recurrently impossible for reasons independent of the absence of scientific knowledge and there are multiple *different* agents or agents which operated in substantially different ways. If the concern addressed by the 'empty duty' argument is that defendants are not incentivised to adhere to their duties of care – that they are able to ignore them without fear of sanction – the concern applies wherever there is a recurrent evidential uncertainty over causation which is reasonably predictable *ex-ante* by defendants.

It may be correct that a defendant can readily predict severe difficulty in proving causation against it where the claimant has been, or will likely be, exposed to similar risk sources and there is impenetrable scientific uncertainty surrounding the mechanism by which a risk source operates. In such circumstances it may be rational to believe that because of the existence of multiple *similar* risk sources, it will be difficult to pinpoint the causative source.[216] But even if the idea of a similar risk source and absence of scientific knowledge over the mechanism of injury picks out a relatively sound rule of thumb for *one* situation in which a defendant's duty will be empty of content,[217] it cannot provide a necessary condition for such situations. There are many sources of recurrent, and so, predictable, uncertainty over causation. For example, lengthy latency periods between exposure to a toxic agent and disease manifestation give rise to substantial difficulties of causal attribution because of the diminution of evidence over long periods of time. This has nothing to do with the lack of scientific knowledge. Indeed, even if scientific knowledge advanced to the point where a refined understanding of the mechanism of mesothelioma were available, it would often still be impossible, due to the long latency period, to determine

---

[215] For similar views on the single agent requirement, see C. Miller, 'Causation in Personal Injury: Legal or Epidemiological Common Sense', 560–3; R. Stevens, *Torts and Rights*, 51; A. Beever, *Rediscovering*, 475; J. Morgan, 'The English and Scottish Asbestos Saga', 61–2.

[216] Another example outside of the mesothelioma context is the mass manufacture of generic defective drugs.

[217] Even this is doubtful. The defendant's duty will not be empty of content if, for example, (enforced) criminal sanctions for its mere breach are in place, or if the defendant's breach of duty could cause other injuries in respect of which causation can be proved. This is so in mesothelioma cases, where there are alternative criminal sanctions under Sections 2 and 3 of the Health and Safety at Work Act 1974, and where the negligent exposure to asbestos dust may cause asbestosis, in respect of which claimants can normally establish causation on the balance of probability. See *Holtby* v. *Brigham & Cowan (Hull) Ltd* [2000] 3 All ER 421.

the level of asbestos dust to which a person was exposed, which may be crucial in determining causation on the balance of probability.

The intuitive unfairness in the idea that the claimant's legal position becomes worse the more the claimant is the victim of wrongful conduct by successive persons – that is, the less the claimant's' chances of being able to sue for damages – is also, obviously, independent of the kinds of causal agents used by those wrongfully subjecting the claimant to risks of injury or the kind of uncertainty at stake. And, finally, it is obscure how the relative *injustices* of the situation change by reference to the types of causal agents used by wrongfully acting defendants or the type of uncertainty in question.

If the single agent and scientific uncertainty requirements were set aside, the result would be a rule which said that the defendant should be liable whenever proof of causation is impossible (i.e. a burden of proof situation), and the defendant materially increased the risk of the injury suffered. This would mean proportional liability in every case in which the burden of proof would normally require the claimant to lose.

If the empty duty argument were taken seriously as the normative basis for the exception, it would be consistent to restrict such a rule to situations where proof of causation is recurrently and predictably impossible *ex-ante* by defendants. This would, however, raise extremely difficult empirical questions as to the extent to which proof of causation is predictably impossible in particular domains.

English law is caught, here, in a dilemma. If the restrictions on *Fairchild* are lifted, the result is either an annihilation of the general burden of proof on causation or an unwieldy rule based upon the concept of 'predictable impossibility of proof'. If the restrictions are maintained, the law faces the charge of incoherence. If the argument of Chapter 4 is correct, this dilemma could have been avoided if *Fairchild* had been restricted to the defendant indeterminacy situation.[218]

Full liability where a material contribution to injury is shown

English law also recognises an exceptional rule, which creates full liability where the defendant has 'materially contributed' to the claimant's injury, but it cannot be shown, due to the limits of scientific knowledge, whether that injury would have occurred anyway. This rule is essentially

---

[218] J. Morgan, 'Causation, Politics and Law', 90–1, suggests the 'problem' would have better been dealt with by legislation which could avoid the hard-edged, unprincipled quality of the rules in *Fairchild/Barker/Sienkiewicz*. If the argument of ch 4 is correct, however, then a principled limitation could have been placed on *Fairchild*.

the same as the German reversal of the burden of proof for hypothetical causation, though it is not rationalised in the same way – indeed it is not rationalised at all – and it only applies where the uncertainty over what would have happened is due to the limits of scientific knowledge.

The law on 'material contribution' is deeply confused.[219] This is because the language of material contribution is used to achieve a number of different purposes. It will be helpful at the outset to distinguish them:

(1) The expression *c materially contributed to e* is often used simply to mean that *e* would not have occurred without *c*. This usage is obfuscating. It is clearer simply to say that *c* satisfies the but-for test.

(2) The expression *c materially contributed to e* is also used in circumstances where *some part of e* would not have occurred without *c*, but it is difficult to determine *how much of e* would not have occurred without *c*. That is: *c* has been a but-for cause of some part of a person's total injuries, but that part is difficult to isolate. In these circumstances, the courts have taken a liberal approach to assessing this part. This could be called the 'liberal *extent-of-liability* material contribution rule'.

(3) The expression *c materially contributed to e* is also used, it is suggested, in circumstances where *c* is a cause of *e* on the balance of probability, but this is determined without it being necessary to inquire whether *c* was a but-for cause of *e*. In these circumstances, the law accepts – *without any fiction* – that *c* is known to be a cause of *e* although the but-for test is not satisfied. This rule is not the same as the rule that the defendant is liable in certain circumstances merely for increasing the risk of injury. Here it is known that the defendant's wrongful conduct actually played a physical role in the mechanism by which the claimant's injury came about. In these circumstances, the law has developed a rule allowing C to succeed without proving that its injury would not have occurred had the defendant not behaved wrongfully.

This section is about (3). However, the evolution of (3) is intimately connected to the evolution of (2). The confusion in the current law stems partly from a failure to disaggregate (2) and (3).

Historical origins[220]

The language of 'material contribution' is generally sourced in the Scottish case, *Wardlaw* v. *Bonnington Castings*.[221] The pursuer, an industrial

---

[219] See S. Bailey, 'Causation in Negligence: What is a Material Contribution?', 167.
[220] This section draws partly upon S. Steel and D. Ibbetson, 'More Grief on Uncertain Causation in Tort'.
[221] 1955 SC 320; [1956] AC 613. *Bonnington* is formally accepted by Australia and Canada: *Athey* v. *Leonati* [1996] 3 SCR 458 [15]–[20]; *Cottrelle* v. *Gerrard* (2003) OJ No 4194 [28]; *March*

worker, contracted pneumoconiosis in the course of his work as a result of the inhalation of silica dust. The causal question raised was whether the dust which was in the atmosphere of the plant as a result of breach of duty was a cause of the pursuer's injury or whether the disease had been entirely caused by dust which was there without breach of duty on the defenders' part. It was probable that 'much the greater proportion of the noxious dust...came from the swing grinders [the non-tortious source]'.[222]

In the court of Session it was said that the defenders should be liable provided that the negligent dust had made a 'material contribution' to the injury. Lords Carmont and Russell held that once it was accepted that there had been a breach of duty by the defenders the burden of proof was on them to show that this was not a cause of the disease, and on this basis liability was established. Lord President Clyde dissented, denying that the burden of proof was reversed and holding that on the facts it had not been proved that the dust in the workshop in breach of duty had been shown to have made a material contribution. The decision was upheld in the House of Lords;[223] although the approach of Lords Carmont and Russell that the burden of proof should be reversed was rejected, it was held that on the true reading of the evidence the pursuer had in fact shown that the negligent dust had made a material contribution to the pneumoconiosis. Lord Reid said that 'the disease is caused by the whole of the noxious material inhaled and that if that material comes from two sources, it cannot be wholly attributed to material from one source or the other'.[224]

The genetic source of this manner of framing the causal question appears to have lain in the nineteenth-century Scots law of nuisance, where the claim related to the cumulation of pollutants from different sources.[225] The language of 'material contribution' was repeated in later

---

v. *Stramare (E & MH) Pty Ltd* (1991) 171 CLR 506, 514 (Mason CJ); 532 (McHugh J); *Bennett* v. *Minister of Community Welfare* (1993) 176 CLR 408, 419 (Gaudron J), 428 (McHugh J).

[222] *Bonnington*, 617 (Lord Reid).

[223] So far as one can judge from case notes, contemporaries did not see it as marking any major breach with orthodoxy: (1956) 72 L.Q.R. 306; (1956) 19 M.L.R. 530 (C. Grunfeld); (1956) 1 Jurist (N.S.) 177 (D. M. Walker).

[224] Some interpret this to mean that each source of dust was a but-for cause of the *contraction* of the disease but this is not entailed by any of the speeches and doubted by Lord Keith's remarks. See, however, for that view: V. Black and D. Klimchuk, 'Comment on *Athey* v *Leonati*'; G. Turton, 'A Case for Clarity in Causation?', 143.

[225] See *Duke of Buccleuch* v. *Cowan* (1866) 5 M. 214, 216 (Lord Justice-Clerk), 223–4, 227–9 (Lord Cowan), 232–3 (Lord Benholme), 234–7 (Lord Neave). Cf. *Strong* v. *Woolworths* [2012] HCA 5, at n 25 (Gummow J).

Scots cases on the same topic.[226] Although the nuisance cases were not cited, the situation in *Bonnington Castings* as analysed by the House of Lords was structurally identical to them.[227] The pursuer's illness was the result of the progressive build-up of silica dust in the lungs, so that all the dust – negligent and non-negligent – played its part in it, in exactly the same way as each bit of effluent in the rivers played its part in the totality of the pollution.

On this view the decision can be regarded as an application of the general proof rules in respect of causation, but with a possible alteration of the *substantive concept* of causation: the defendant can be said to be a NESS cause of the pneumoconiosis on the balance of probability. It may have been that the presence of the other non-tortious dust prevented the court from holding that the negligent production of dust was a but-for cause of any part of the disease – and yet, nonetheless, it *contributed*. Alternatively, it could be said that D's negligence was a but-for cause of the total injury happening *when* it did.[228]

However, on either interpretation, the *extent* of the defendant's liability in damages ought to have been determined by reference to what would have happened without the breach of duty. It would follow from the general proof rule that if the defendant could not be said to have made the claimant worse off on the balance of probability, then no damages should have been awarded or, at least, that the damages should have reflected the extent to which the claimant had been made worse off. However, the pursuer in *Bonnington* appears to have received damages reflecting the judgment that it would not otherwise have contracted the pneumoconiosis despite the fact that Lord Keith was only willing to say that: 'had it not been for the cumulative effect [of both sources of dust], the respondent would not have developed pneumoconiosis when he did, and *might* not have developed it at all'.[229] 'Might not' is not equivalent to 'probably not'.

Since the only issue before the House of Lords was whether the defendant was *liable*, it cannot be claimed that *Bonnington* stands as a

---

[226] *Countess Dowager of Seafield v. Kemp* (1899) 1 F 402, 406 n 3; *Fleming v. Gemmill* 1908 SC 340, 347, 350; *Brownlie & Son v. Magistrates of Barrhead* 1923 SC 915, 927, 933, 935. Note too its use by the Scottish Lord Watson in *Wakelin v. London & South Western Railway Co.* (1886) 12 App Cas 41, 47. Cf. H.L.A. Hart and T. Honoré, *Causation in the Law*, 1st edition, 211, citing American nuisance cases.

[227] See in particular the summary of Lord Reid, [1956] AC 613, 621.

[228] For this latter interpretation, see S. Bailey, 'Causation in Negligence: What is a Material Contribution?'

[229] *Bonnington*, 622.

matter of law for any kind of exceptional proof rule applying where there is uncertainty over the question of whether the injury would have occurred anyway or as to the extent of the damage caused by the defendant. Nonetheless, an incautious reading of the case could take one of two views. It could be said to have held that the defendant's breach of duty was an NESS cause of the pneumoconiosis and that, having shown natural causation in this sense, the claimant then only needs to show the possibility that the damage would not otherwise have occurred in order to obtain full damages. Or it could be said to have established that where it is clear on the balance of probability that the defendant has caused damage in the sense that it has accelerated the onset of the disease, but the claimant has not established the extent of that accelerated onset, uncertainty as to the extent of the acceleration is borne by the defendant. On this last view, the case could stand for the proposition that where there is no viable method of apportionment between what the defendant caused and what would have happened in any event, so long as the claimant can prove *some* damage (*non de minimis*) resulted from the defendant's conduct, then the latter is liable for all of the claimant's injuries.[230] On this interpretation the case stands for a proof rule that the risk of being unable to apportion the damage rests with the defendant. (This may in some cases already be inherent in the decision to class an injury as indivisible.)[231]

The modern law of material contribution

Subsequent authority in English law (and Australian law[232]) rejected both of these claimant-friendly interpretations of *Bonnington*. In *Holtby v. Brigham & Cowan (Hull) Ltd.*,[233] which concerned a claimant who had been exposed to asbestos dust by a number of defendants and had contracted asbestosis, it was held that while the legal burden of proving causation of the whole injury in respect of which damages are claimed is on the claimant, if the claimant shows that the defendant made a material contribution to her total injury (i.e. was a but-for cause of some part of it), and if the defendant does not *plead* the issue of apportionment, then the defendant may be held liable for the whole injury. That, according to *Holtby*, is what happened in *Bonnington*.

---

[230] J. Stapleton, 'Cause-in-Fact and the Scope of Liability for Consequences', 395.

[231] D. Dobbs, *The Law of Torts*, 425, puts this well: 'The thrust of the indivisible injury principle is that tortfeasors, not victims, should bear the burdens of uncertainty imposed by their tortious behaviour'.

[232] *Seltsam v. Ghaleb* [2005] NSWCA 208 follows *Holtby*.   [233] [2000] 3 All ER 421.

However: 'strictly speaking, the defendant is liable only to the extent of [its] contribution'.[234]

The proposition here is that if the claimant has only proved a *non de minimis* contribution to its total injuries and apportionment is impossible, the risk of not being able to show a means of apportionment is on the claimant (this is an effect of the burden of proof). However, the position *in practice* according to all the judges in *Holtby* is that issues as to the extent of the damage caused by a particular defendant should not be determined by the legal burden of proof, rather 'the question should be whether... on consideration of all the evidence, the claimant has proved that the defendants are responsible for the whole or quantifiable part of his disability...the court has to do the best it can using its common sense'.[235] The position is the same whether all the possible causes are wrongful, or where non-wrongful causes have also operated.[236]

Holtby thus conceives of *Bonnington* as a largely orthodox rule according to which D is only liable for the approximate extent of the damage it has caused on the balance of probability. Thus, *Holtby* established rule (2) as the appropriate interpretation of *Bonnington*. This rule should be considered as belonging to the rules on quantification, which attract the same liberal approach to assessment.[237]

In spite of *Holtby*, it is suggested that the first incautious interpretation of *Bonnington* developed above has *also* been adopted subsequently. That is, the case established a rule permitting the claimant who can show a contribution of a defendant's breach of duty to its injury to establish liability in full against the defendant without proof on the balance of probability that the defendant's breach of duty made the claimant worse off.

This interpretation is implicit in the court of appeal decision *Bailey v. Ministry of Defence*.[238] The claimant underwent an operation for a

---

[234] *Holtby*, 428 (Stuart-Smith LJ, with whom Clarke LJ agreed).

[235] Ibid. 429; Clarke LJ agreed that 'in reality these cases should not be determined by onus of proof', 433, though he would have held that the defendants had an evidential (or legal) onus to show that they did not cause all the damage once the claimant showed material contribution to some.

[236] *Allen & Others* v. *British Rail Engineering Ltd* [2001] ICR 942; *Rice* v. *Secretary of State for Business* [2008] EWHC 3216 (QB) (esp [165]).

[237] See Chapter 2, 52.

[238] [2008] EWCA Civ 883. An analogous subsequent case is *Canning-Kishver* v. *Sandwell & West Birmingham Hospitals NHS Trust* [2008] EWHC 2384 (QB). See also *Boustead* v. *North Western Strategic Health Authority* [2008] EWHC 2375 (QB) [69]–[70]; *Leigh* v. *London Ambulance Service NHS Trust* [2014] EWHC 286.

suspected gallstone at a hospital run by the defendant. Subsequent complications (substantial internal bleeding and pancreatitis) occurred as a result of the operation, and her post-operative care was negligently inadequate. She deteriorated, with her bleeding and pancreatitis continuing. Later when she seemed to be recuperating, she aspirated her vomit, resulting in a cardiac arrest and brain damage. This was due to her weakened condition. The claimant's causal theory was that, though it could not be said that she would not have aspirated her vomit without the negligence (the pancreatitis and bleeding might alone have caused the choking) the negligence had materially contributed to her overall weakened state and thus to her ultimate brain damage. It was held that the defendant had materially contributed to the brain damage.[239] Waller LJ considered that: 'in cumulative cause cases such as *Wardlaw's* case the "but for" test is modified'.[240]

In the case before him, cumulative causes acted 'so as to create a weakness' and the contribution of the defendant's negligence to the weakness was sufficiently material. The intuitive notion of contribution here is the idea of a NESS cause: if some of the weakness from the non-tortious conditions is disaggregated so that a sufficient set of conditions can be formed which includes the defendant's negligence, then its causal status is established. The defendant's negligent post-operative care was causal 'by forming part of an undifferentiated whole that operates to bring about the existence of the [damage]'.[241] The undifferentiated whole was the claimant's overall state of weakness.

The effect of demonstrating this kind of contribution is that: '[i]n a case where medical science cannot establish the probability that "but for" an act of negligence the injury would not have happened but can establish that the contribution of the negligent cause was more than negligible, the "but for" test is modified, and the claimant will succeed'.[242]

The case is deeply radical.[243] As we have seen, the progenitor *Wardlaw* can hardly be taken as authority for this view; and if it were taken to establish an exceptional rule, that rule could have been taken only to apply where there was uncertainty as to the *extent* of the defendant's

---

[239] Ibid., 1069.   [240] Ibid., 1068.   [241] J. Stapleton, 'Factual Cause in Australia', 476.
[242] *Bailey*, 1069.
[243] A similar conclusion was reached, however, in the tort of deceit where D's fraud had been shown to have been a cause of the collapse of certain points of C's sub-sea pipe line, but alleged that these would have occurred in any event. See *BHP Billiton Petroleum v. Dalmine SpA* [2003] EWCA 170, [36].

contribution to the total injury, where it was clear that at least some of that injury represented damage not entirely overdetermined by non-tortious conditions. By contrast, in *Bailey* there is uncertainty as to whether the injury may have been overdetermined *entirely* by non-tortious conditions.[244] Since a burden of proof rule determines which party succeeds where the facts are impossible to establish, the effect of *Bailey* is to reverse the burden of proof on the issue of whether the injury would have happened anyway.[245]

Analysis

The law on material contribution in English law is unsatisfactory. The most fundamental criticism is that the law inadequately distinguishes between substantive concepts of causation and the proof rules applicable to the causal inquiry. *Bailey* runs together a substantive exception to the but-for test with an evidential exception to the rule that one must prove that one is worse off as a result of the defendant's negligence.

Second, to locate the legal foundation of the *evidential* aspect of the *Bailey* exception in *Bonnington* is unsound. *Bonnington* simply did not decide that the burden of proof should be reversed. Consequently, since the court in *Bailey* was significantly expanding upon previous authority, reasoned justifications needed to be offered. None is found in *Bailey*.[246]

Third, the relationship between the interpretations of *Bonnington* in *Holtby* (rule (2)) and *Bailey* (rule (3)) is not well understood. It seems to be the case that *Holtby* will apply to cases where the injury is at least theoretically divisible and it is known that the defendant cannot have caused *all* of the claimant's damage, but has caused some part, whereas *Bailey* applies where the injury is not theoretically divisible, a material contribution to it is shown, and it is impossible, due to scientific uncertainty, to determine whether the injury would have happened anyway. This also seems to entail, as a matter of consistency with *Bailey*, that if the defendant's wrongful conduct has been a cause of some damage and *may* have caused the entirety, but it is scientifically impossible to determine this, that the claimant should receive full compensation.

---

[244] This understanding of *Bailey* is also reflected in earlier decisions. *Ministry of Defence* v. *AB & Ors* [2010] EWCA Civ 1317 [134]; *Ingram* v. *Williams* [2010] EWHC 758 (QB) at [83].

[245] A similar understanding of *Bonnington* is found in *Amaca Pty Ltd* v. *Ellis* [2008] WASCA 200 [309]. The *Ellis* decision has been reversed by the High court, but without undermining the point made here: *Amaca Pty Ltd* v. *Ellis* (2010) 240 CLR 111. Cf. Allsop P in *Evans* v. *Queanbeyan City Council* [2011] NSWCA 230, [32].

[246] Cf. M. Lunney and K. Oliphant, *Tort Law* 4th edition, 229 who seem to support the interpretation of *Bonnington* given in *Bailey*.

A reversal of the burden of proof where the defendant has caused the claimant's injury

In *Phethean-Coles* v. *Hubble*, the defendant driver collided with the claimant cyclist while driving negligently.[247] The causal issue was whether, had the defendant driven non-negligently, at a speed of 26mph or 27mph, instead of his actual speed of 35mph, this would have avoided the accident or lessened its severity. The court of appeal upheld the trial judge's finding of fact that it would have.[248] Both Longmore LJ and Tomlinson LJ added that, in any event, the burden of proof was on the defendant to establish that the injury would have occurred in any event.[249] Longmore LJ said:

> The injury which occurred was injury of a kind likely to have been caused by that breach...In these circumstances I do not consider that it is necessary for the claimant to prove positively the negative proposition that the accident would not have occurred if the defendant had been going at a safe speed; realistically it should be for the defendant (who has already been found to be in breach of duty) to show that even if he had been driving at a non-negligent speed, the accident would still have occurred.[250]

Longmore LJ's statement may be construed either as involving merely an inference of causation, where an 'evidential' burden falls upon the defendant to rebut the claimant's *prima facie* case, or as a true reversal of the legal burden of proof.[251]

The inference interpretation seems more likely, as Longmore LJ's language echoes the language used by him in an earlier court of appeal case where an inference of causation was drawn.[252] Moreover, there is no direct authority for such a reversal. Structurally, the case is similar to *McGhee*, where the defendant had caused the dermatitis, though it was not known whether the defendant's *negligence* had caused it, but the dimension of scientific uncertainty is absent, and *McGhee*, according to *Barker*, should lead to proportional liability, not a reversal of the burden of proof.[253]

Reductions in the standard of proof on causation

There are no clear rules of law establishing a lower standard of proof in particular types of causal case in English law. However, there are certain

---

[247] [2012] EWCA Civ 349.   [248] Ibid., [70], [88], [90].   [249] Ibid., [89], [90].
[250] Ibid., [90].
[251] *Phethean* was interpreted as reversing the legal burden of proof at first instance in *Robbins* v. *London Borough of Bexley* [2012] EWHC 2257, but the court of appeal in that case found that it was unnecessary to decide whether that was appropriate, [2013] EWHC 1333, [60], [73].
[252] See p.248.   [253] See p.231.

factors which seem to result in less scrutiny being applied to the claimant's causal claim. These are the increase in risk of injury posed by the defendant's wrongful conduct and the causation of uncertainty over causation.

Increase in risk

As Chapter 2 described, the mere fact that the defendant's wrongful conduct has increased the risk of the injury suffered by the claimant does not per se legitimate an inference of causation. Nonetheless, there is a lurking sense that the courts sometimes attach a significance to the fact that the defendant's conduct has wrongfully increased the risk of injury, which, in purely epistemic terms, it does not merit. In such cases, the courts do make a finding of causation on the balance of probability, yet the evidential basis of this finding is weak.

Consider, for example, *Vaile* v. *Havering LBC*.[254] The claimant, a teacher in a special needs school, was stabbed in the hand with a pencil by a child who showed signs of autism. This was on 4 July 2003. The child had also bitten the claimant on 10 June 2003, an incident that she reported to her employer. She sued the latter alleging that they had negligently failed to provide a safe system of work, specifically through failing to advise her that the child had autistic spectrum disorder when the child had been officially diagnosed as such, and through failing to advise her of appropriate (highly structured) teaching techniques for such a child. The court of appeal reversed the trial judge's finding that the claimant had failed to prove that this breach was causative.

Longmore LJ cited reasoning from the earlier decision in *Drake* v. *Harbour*:

> where a claimant proves both that a defendant was negligent and that loss ensued which was of a kind likely to have resulted from such negligence, this will ordinarily be enough to enable a court to infer that it was probably so caused, even if the claimant is unable to prove positively the precise mechanism[255]

The trial judge had found that if action had been taken once the July 4 incident had been reported, this would have led to an analysis of the child's situation, which would have taken some two to three weeks.[256] This would leave two to three weeks during which some – indeterminate – measure would have been taken in respect of the child, perhaps one-to-one

---

[254] [2011] EWCA Civ 246,
[255] Ibid., [32], citing from *Drake* v. *Harbour* [2008] EWCA Civ 25, [28] (Toulson LJ).
[256] Ibid., [34].

teaching sessions (but certainly not removal from the school). There was expert evidence at first instance that some measure would have been successful in preventing the pencil incident.[257] This was rejected by the trial judge on the ground that the expert did not identify *which* measure would have been successful. Given the short time period during which any measure would have been operative, and the lack of precision in identifying that measure, it seems legitimate to say that the claimant's causal claim was looked upon with some measure of generosity.[258]

Causing uncertainty over causation

If the defendant's breach of duty has deprived the claimant of evidence of causation, the court may lower the standard of proof on causation. In *Roadrunner Properties Ltd* v. *Dean*,[259] the defendant had carried out work on a party wall with an unsuitably large drill, which the claimant alleged, bringing a claim in both negligence and nuisance, had caused dislocation of floor tiles in his property. The damage to the tiles appeared within four or five weeks of the drilling, after a period of 13 years during which the tiles had remained undamaged. The defendant advanced the alternative theory that the damage was caused by exceptional climactic conditions in that time period, but adduced no evidence of such conditions. The trial judge had rejected the claim for want of proof of causation. The court of appeal disagreed, finding causation established on the balance of probability.

A central aspect of its reasoning was that under the Party Walls Act 1996, the defendant had a duty to serve notice to the claimant that works were being carried out on the party wall, which would have allowed the claimant to instruct a surveyor to monitor such works, as envisaged by section 10 of the Act.[260] Although the claim was not for breach of statutory duty, the fact that the defendant had breached a duty which might fairly be said to be in place partly to avoid disputes over causation, nonetheless influenced the claim at common law. Chadwick LJ said that a 'reasonably robust' approach to proof of causation was appropriate:

If it can be shown that the damage which has occurred is the sort of damage which one might expect to occur from the nature of the works that have been carried out, the court must recognise that the inability to provide any greater

---

[257] Ibid, [33], [38].

[258] For a similar generosity in moving from increased risk to an inference of causation, see *Mountford* v. *Newlands School* [2007] EWCA Civ 21.

[259] [2003] EWCA Civ 1816.   [260] Ibid., [6]–[7].

proof of the necessary causative link is an inability which results from the building owner's failure to comply with its statutory obligations.[261]

This approach was also applied, primarily to justify an inference of negligence, rather than causation, in *Keefe* v. *The Isle of Man Steam Packet Company*.[262] The defendant had breached its common law duty of care to monitor noise levels on its ships. The estate of a deceased former employee of the defendant alleged that the defendant's failure to monitor and take steps to reduce the noise levels caused the deceased to be exposed to excessive noise levels, leading to hearing loss. The trial judge rejected the claim for want of proof that the claimant had been repeatedly exposed to excess levels of noise. The court of appeal once more disagreed, finding that the hearing loss had been caused by exposure to excessive noise levels. According to Longmore LJ, the judge had not given weight to the 'potent additional consideration that any difficulty of proof for the claimant has been caused by the defendant's breach of duty in failing to take any measurements'.[263] In such circumstances, 'the court should judge a claimant's evidence benevolently and the defendant's evidence critically'.[264]

Finally, the *Keefe* reasoning was accepted to apply in principle in medical negligence in relation to causation in *Shawe-Lincoln* v. *Neelakandan*.[265] The 75-year-old claimant, who already suffered from ankylosing spondylitis, fell at home on 17 November 2002. He spent the next nine days in bed in considerable pain, and was visited by his GPs, who during that time considered the only injury to be to soft tissue. At 23:58 on November 26, due to the increased severity of the claimant's condition, the claimant's family telephoned an out-of-hours medical service, which was answered by the defendant GP. The defendant recorded that the claimant's legs had gone numb but decided to wait to see how his condition developed rather than to visit him at home. It was accepted that this was a negligent breach of duty and that the claimant should have been immediately referred to hospital, and would have been admitted by 05:30 on 27 November, had the defendant behaved non-negligently. As it was, the claimant was not admitted to

---

[261] Ibid., [29].   [262] [2010] EWCA Civ 683.   [263] Ibid., [18].

[264] Ibid., [19]. For further instances of this reasoning, citing *Keefe*, see *Mickelwright* v. *Surrey County Council*, [2011] EWCA Civ 922 (D, local council negligently failed to inspect trees, one tree fell, killing the victim; here *Keefe* was held to be relevant in relation to the council's failure to inspect the tree to determine the reason why it fell); *Robinson* v. *Bristol NHS Trust*, 4 June 2013, Bristol County court (unreported).

[265] [2012] EWHC 1150 (QB).

hospital until 18:24 on 28 November. He subsequently suffered neurological deterioration and increased paralysis. Ultimately, his claim for compensation was rejected.

The causal issue was whether earlier admission would have lessened the extent of the claimant's paralysis. This turned on whether, upon earlier admission, the claimant would have been revealed by various neurological observations by hospital doctors to have been in a deteriorating neurological condition, which condition would have received emergency treatment. The claimant argued that the defendant's negligence had deprived him of the evidence critical to proving this.[266] As a result of the defendant's negligent failure to refer, there were no records of what the claimant's condition would have been upon earlier admission.

The judge accepted that *Keefe* was relevant in principle to issue of causation in medical negligence.[267] Its effect was not to reverse the burden of proof but rather 'it is concerned with the weight which is to be attached to evidence and the circumstances in which the court may draw inferences'.[268] A 'benevolent' approach is to be applied. However, the reasoning in *Keefe* applied only with diminished force in the present case. First, because it was not the defendant's personal duty to maintain the evidence in question – the only duty of the defendant was to visit and to refer the claimant to hospital, the hospital doctors would have owed a duty to carry out tests on the claimant – and second, because the claimant had himself contributed to uncertainty over causation by failing to call the doctors who did treat him on the 28 November as witnesses on the state of his condition then.[269] The judge found that it was more probable on the evidence that the clamant was not in a deteriorating condition and so would not have received emergency treatment.

United States

American courts have generally held firm to the general burden of proof on causation. Yet sporadic departures have been made. On the one hand, a particular concern has been evinced in certain contexts – products liability, and breach of statutory regulations protecting against physical injuries – to reinforce incentives to conform to legal duties by a reversal

---

[266] Ibid., [12].   [267] Ibid., [83].   [268] Ibid., [81].
[269] Ibid., [83]. This would likely have been relevant to the state of his condition at the earlier time.

in the burden of proof. On the other hand, the courts have created a special liability rule, functionally equivalent to a reversal in the burden of proof, in asbestos cancer cases, which seems to be carved out simply as a response to the enormous numbers of asbestos victims who would otherwise go without compensation. As to the standard of proof, this section concludes by examining the 'liberal impulse'[270] to the assessment of a claimant's case on causation, principally by reference to the medical negligence context.

Reversal of the burden of proof

Sporadic reversal of the burden

A reversal of the legal burden of proof, beyond the *Summers* indeterminate wrongdoer situation, has not generally been accepted.[271] There are, however, exceptional cases in which various normative considerations trigger the reversal.

At the heart of this jurisprudence is the Californian case *Haft* v. *Lone Palm Hotel*.[272] The claimant brought an action in respect of the death of her husband and son who drowned in the defendant's hotel swimming pool, relying upon the hotel's negligent breach of safety regulations. The court framed the causal question by asking whether the absence of a lifeguard caused their drowning.[273] Tobriner J reasoned that modifying the normal burden of proof was appropriate because the defendant's failure 'greatly enhanced the chances' of the drowning and also because 'the evidentiary void in the instant action results primarily from defendants' failure to provide a lifeguard to observe occurrences within the pool area'.[274] Thus, the defendants could be considered to be 'culpably responsible for the uncertainty of proof'. Indeed, the case was considered stronger than *Summers* in this regard since the evidential uncertainty there had resulted from a 'coincidence', whereas in *Haft* this uncertainty was a 'direct and foreseeable result' of the negligence.[275]

---

[270] D. Dobbs, *The Law of Torts*, 421; similarly, D. Robertson, 'The Common Sense of Cause-in-Fact', 1774–5.

[271] Comment g to §28 of the Third Restatement states that courts 'do not ordinarily shift the burden of proof' in cases involving potential non-wrongful causes: *Restatement (Third) Torts* §28, 418. There are exceptions: *Anderson* v. *Somberg* 338 A 2d 1 (NJ 1975); *Chin* v. *St. Barnabas Med. Ctr*, 734 A 2d 778 (NJ 1999). The Reporters do at another point give the impression that the reverse burden is not infrequent, however. This is because they class certain 'presumptions' as reversals in the burden of proof: *Restatement (Third) Torts*, 428–9.

[272] 478 P 2d 465, 474–5 (1970 California). Cf BGH NJW 1962, 959, discussed on p. 202.

[273] Ibid. 472–3.   [274] 476.   [275] Ibid. Cf. *Ybarra* v. *Spangard* (1944) 25 Cal 2d 486.

The court was further influenced by the level of the defendant's culpability: the hotel had breached numerous safety standards;[276] and by the desire to impose a strong incentive to prevent future breaches of the statutory regulations: '[w]ithout such a shift in the burden of proof in the instant case, the promise of substantial protection held out by our statutory lifeguard requirement will be effectively nullified in a substantial number of cases'.[277] Finally, citing the work of Calabresi, the court noted that the result was supported by considerations of fair loss distribution: better to allow the hotel to spread its liability to other hotel customers than for the loss to be borne by the individual claimant.[278]

Subsequent Californian decisions have seized upon different aspects of this reasoning as normatively important. Sometimes *Haft* is located within a more widely accepted jurisprudence, which allows a presumption or inference of causation in cases where the defendant's negligence consists in the breach of a statute (negligence *per se*).[279] At other times, the focus is upon the supposed responsibility of the defendant for the impossibility of proof or simply the impossibility of proof *tout court*.[280] Yet other cases point to the vulnerability of the decedents in *Haft*.[281]

It is notable that the case has not been applied in cases involving purely economic interests, such as legal malpractice, except where the defendant has assumed a responsibility to retain items of evidence.[282] This is consonant, for example, with the almost universal American position in cases of legal malpractice, where the legal burden of proof remains with the claimant.[283] Other states have not displayed such an overtly policy-based approach to the legal burden of proof.[284]

---

[276] *Haft*, 468.   [277] Ibid. 477.   [278] *Haft*, at n. 20.

[279] *Rudelson v. United States* 431 F Supp 1101, 1107 (Cal Dist Ct 1977); *National Council Against Health Fraud* v. *King Bio Pharmaceuticals* 107 Cal App 4th 1336, 1347 (Cal CA 2003); *Ramirez* v. *Nelson* 42 Cal Rptr 3d 86 at [12] (Cal Dist CA 2006).

[280] The former: *Ramirez* above; *In re Agent Orange* 597 F Supp 740, 828 (NY 1984). The latter: *Fletcher* v. *Able Corp* 110 Cal App 4th 1658, 1670 (Cal CA 2003).

[281] *Blecher & Collins* v. *Northwest Airlines* 858 F Supp 1442, 1457 (Cal Dist Ct 1994).

[282] For its *general* rejection in legal malpractice: *Blecher*, 1457; *Thomas* v. *Lusk* 27 Cal App 4th 1709, 1717 (1994). Cf. *Galanek* v. *Wismar* 68 Cal App 4th 1417 (Cal CA 1999) (D meaningfully responsible for evidential deficit).

[283] J. Boysen, 'Shifting the Burden of Proof on Causation in Legal Malpractice Actions', 309 n 1; G. Mahaffey, 'Cause-in-Fact and the Plaintiff's Burden of Proof with Regard to Causation and Damages in Transactional Legal Malpractice Matters: The Necessity of Demonstrating the Better Deal', 397.

[284] See Note 271.

Reversals of the burden of proof (special liability rules) in asbestos litigation

An exceptional liability rule exists in asbestos-cancer cases brought either in negligence or under a strict product liability tort. Many US states allow the claimant to succeed on causation simply by showing that they were in close proximity to the defendant's asbestos product on a regular basis over some extended time period.[285] If the claimant shows this, then the exposure is deemed to be a 'substantial factor' in the production of the damage.[286] In cases where the mechanism of the disease from which the claimant suffers is not cumulative, or not proven to be cumulative, as in mesothelioma cases, the consequence of this doctrine is that claimants may often succeed without proof on the balance of probability that the defendant was a cause of their damage.[287]

In many cases, causal proof issues have gone largely unanalysed since courts have accepted scientific evidence that the physical mechanism by which asbestos-related cancers are contracted is cumulative, such that each and *every* non de minimis exposure is a cause of its contraction.[288] *Rutherford* v. *Owens-Illinois Inc.*, by contrast, acknowledged the inherent scientific uncertainty in relation to the causal mechanism. It recognised that while asbestos exposure increases the risk of cancer occurring, scientific uncertainty over the causal mechanism meant in that case that it was impossible to attribute the genesis of the claimant's cancer to any particular defendant's exposure.[289]

In *Rutherford*, the claimant smoker had contracted lung cancer, which he alleged had been caused by his exposure to asbestos products during a long career at a shipyard. He sued multiple asbestos manufacturers. Despite his inability to pinpoint which manufacturer's product caused his illness, the court held that the claimant could 'bridge this gap in the humanly knowable' by showing that the defendant's product:

---

[285] *Lohrmann* v. *Pittsburgh Corning Corp.* 782 F 2d 1156 (4th Cir 1986). courts generally refer to the 'Lohrmann test'. It was described in *Slaughter* v. *S Talc Co*, 949 F 2d 167, 171 (5th Cir 1991) as 'the most frequently used test for causation in asbestos cases'. 'The origins of this jurisprudence are traceable to *Borel* v. *Fibreboard Paper Products* (1973) 439 F 2d 1076'.

[286] Ibid.   [287] *Restatement (Third) Torts* §28 459.

[288] J. Stapleton, 'The Two Explosive Proof-of-causation Doctrines Central to Asbestos Claims', 1011. There is a recent growing trend of decisions rejecting this: for example, *Gregg* v. *VJ Auto-Parts Inc.* 943 A 2d 216 (Pa 2007); *Flores* v. *Borg-Warner Corp.* 232 SW 3d 765 (Tex 2007); *Moeller* v. *Garlock Sealing Technologies* 2011 US App Lexis 19987 (6th Cir 2011). See further the cases cited in S. Steel, *Sienkiewicz v Greif (UK) Ltd* and Exceptional Doctrines of Natural Causation at n. 26.

[289] 941 P 2d 1203, 1209 (Cal 1997).

in reasonable medical probability was a substantial factor in contributing to the aggregate dose of asbestos ... inhaled or ingested, and hence to the *risk* of developing asbestos-related cancer, without the need to demonstrate that fibers from the defendant's particular product were the ones, or among the ones, that actually produced the malignant growth.[290]

If contribution to the risk of developing cancer by the defendant is shown to be substantial then the defendant's exposure is 'deemed to be a substantial factor in bringing about the injury'.[291]

By way of justification, the court briskly stated that '[p]laintiffs cannot be expected to prove the scientifically unknown details of carcinogenesis'.[292] It is striking that the court felt little need to give extended justification. Rather, its principal concern was to distinguish the *Summers* v. *Tice* rule, which had been applied by the trial judge. The court reasoned that the alternative liability rule is an exception to general causation principles and thus needed justification. Having rejected its application partly on the grounds that not all defendants were joined and because different levels of risk were posed by different asbestos products,[293] logically, the next step in the reasoning should have been to consider why *nonetheless* the inability to prove which defendant's (or defendants') fibres caused the cancer was not fatal to the claim, despite non-fit with the exceptional *Summers* doctrine. Yet the court simply rested upon the 'fundamental reason' that in an 'asbestos-related cancer latent injury case'[294] the claimant's burden of proof should not be understood as requiring identification of specific fibres in light of the scientific impossibility of showing whose fibres contributed.[295]

Stapleton concludes that *Rutherford*'s reasoning proceeds 'on the idea (a fiction) that every asbestos fiber was involved in the cancer mechanism: and this would only be the case in an indivisible disease such as cancer if that were a threshold mechanism'.[296] This is supported by the court's language of 'deeming' a defendant's products increasing

---

[290] Ibid.   [291] Ibid., 1219.

[292] *Rutherford*, 1219. Cf. *Morin* v. *Autozone Northeast Inc.* 943 NE 2d 495 (Mass CA 2011) referring to the difficulty of proof as a justification. The *Restatement (third) torts* is equally glib: Reporter's Note to §27 comment g states: 'courts have not required plaintiffs to prove the unprovable': (citing *Rutherford*) 392.

[293] Ibid., 1215–16. The fact that the claimant was a smoker should also have justified a distinction.

[294] Ibid., 1218.

[295] *Rutherford* is approved by later California decisions: *McGonnell* v. *Kaiser Gypsum Co., Inc.* 98 Cal App 4th 1098, 1103 (Cal 2002); *Jones* v. *John Crane, Inc.* 132 Cal App 4th 990 (2005).

[296] J. Stapleton, 'Two Explosive Proof-of-causation Doctrines', 1029.

the risk of developing cancer a substantial factor[297], and the court did not deny the claimant's assertion that the defendant was jointly and severally liable for the entire cancer.[298] Another way of expressing this result would be to say that a reversal of the burden of proof applies in such cases: the defendant, not the claimant, bears the risk of proving causation being impossible. This at least has the advantage of avoiding an unnecessary fiction over the nature of the disease mechanism.

The limits of this risk-contribution-deemed-substantial-factor doctrine are largely untested.[299] The court in *Rutherford* described its holding as applying 'in an asbestos-related cancer case'.[300] In other strict liability product actions, the courts apply the orthodox burden of proof.[301] The uniqueness of the rule is illustrated by the existence of distinct jury instructions on causation for asbestos cases.[302] Subsequently, the issue of delimiting *Rutherford* has been avoided or its application has simply been excluded (without principled explanation) in other contexts like legal malpractice.[303]

Rutherford has justly been described as recognising a 'radical doctrine'.[304] The impression should be avoided, however, that US asbestos jurisprudence, as a whole, has been a radical departure from orthodox causal proof.[305] Many cases have simply proceeded under erroneous medical evidence that mesothelioma is caused by a cumulative mechanism and thus that significant exposure can be said to be a but-for cause of the entire disease on the preponderance of the evidence.[306] Although, this is radical *in effect*, whether it is in *intention* is less obvious. It should also be noted that, while the application of *Summers* v. *Tice* is generally rejected (correctly, in the context of truly cumulative diseases), a

---

[297] M. Green, W. Powers, and J. Sanders, 'The Insubstantiality of the "Substantial Factor" Test for Causation', 424ff.

[298] M. Green, 'Second Thoughts about Apportionment in Asbestos Litigation', 543, observes that even in indivisible cancer cases 'the courts have proceeded conceptually as if all defendants to whose asbestos plaintiff was exposed are a cause of the harm'.

[299] Cf. J. Sanders, 'Risky Business: Causation in Asbestos Cases (and Beyond?)', 21–2.

[300] *Rutherford*, 1223.

[301] For example, *In re Baycol Products Litigation* 596 F 3d 884 (2010, 8th Cir).

[302] See §435: http://www.courts.ca.gov/partners/documents/caci_2015_edition.pdf

[303] *Bockrath* v. *Aldrich Chemical Company* (1999) 21 Cal 4th 71; *Viner* v. *Sweet* 70 3 Pd 1046 (2004, Cal Sup Ct).

[304] J. Stapleton, 'Two Explosive Proof-of-causation Doctrines', 1023. Similarly: M. Green, 'Second Thoughts about Apportionment', 543.

[305] Cf. D. Gifford, 'The Challenge to the Individual Causation Requirement in Mass Products Torts'.

[306] Cf. J. Stapleton, 'Two Explosive Proof-of-causation Doctrines', 1026–7. For a recent case: *Smith* v. *Kelly-Moore Paint Co.*, 307 SW 3d 829, 834 (Texas CA 2010).

substantial number of claimants will at least be able to show that they have been the victim of a tort. Moreover, it is also possible to say that major asbestos manufacturers certainly will wrongfully have caused damage to many claimants.[307] These considerations at least give some asbestos claims normative distinctiveness.[308]

Reversal of the burden of proof in relation to failures to warn or to inform

Some states have developed *presumptions* of natural causation in cases involving defective products, whether based upon strict liability or negligence, where the product's defect consists in the inadequacy or absence of a warning of the risks of its use.[309] The causal question arises as to whether the presence or adequacy of a warning would have made any difference – that is, whether the claimant would have heeded the warning. Although the effect of the presumption is formally denoted by most jurisdictions as a shift in the burden of *production* on causation, with the persuasive burden remaining on the claimant, in reality, the result of the presumption is that, where it cannot be determined how the claimant would have responded to the warning, the defendant will be held liable. Indeed, sometimes the courts display considerable stringency in the proof required to rebut the presumption, with the result that the defendant may be held liable where causation is in fact improbable.[310]

Consider *Liriano* v. *Hobart Corp.*[311] The seventeen-year-old claimant immigrant who spoke little English was injured when feeding meat into a meat grinder, while employed as a butcher's assistant. This resulted in the amputation of his right fore-arm. The grinder was fitted with a

---

[307] Tort theorists have read into the doctrinal black hole different normative theories: cf. G. Keating, 'The Heroic Enterprise of the Asbestos Cases'; A. Bagchi, 'Distributive Justice and Private Law', 141 (distributive justice).

[308] Cf A. Bernstein, 'Asbestos Achievements', 691–2.

[309] *Technical Chemical Co.* v. *Jacobs* 480 SW 2d 602 (Tex 1972); *Nissen Trampoline* v. *Terre Haute First National Bank* 332 NE 2d 820 (Indiana CA, 1975); *Seley* v. *GD Searle & Co.* 423 NE 2d 831, 838 (Ohio, 1981); *Cunningham* v. *Charles Pfizer & Co.*, 523 P 2d 1377 (Okla 1975); *Coffman* v. *Keene Corp.* 628 A 2d 710 (NJ 1993). See generally, D. Fischer, 'Causation in Fact in Products Failure to Warn Cases'; M. Geistfeld, 'Inadequate Product Warnings and Causation'.

[310] See, for example, *Coffman*.

[311] 170 F 3d 264 (2nd Cir 1999). Calabresi used the same reasoning in *Zuchowicz* v. *United States* 140 F 3d 381, 388 (2nd Cir 1998). The analysis is clearly influenced by his economistic view of causation. See G. Calabresi, 'Concerning Cause and the Law of Torts'.

safety guard, which would have prevented the injury, but this had been sawn off by another employee. The basis of the claim was that the manufacturer Hobart had failed to provide a warning as to the danger of operating the grinder without a safety guard and that this would have prevented him or his employer from operating the grinder without the guard. Calabresi J upheld the jury verdict in favour of the employee, stating that:

> [w]hen a defendant's negligent act is deemed wrongful precisely because it has a strong propensity to cause the type of injury that ensued, that very causal tendency is evidence enough to establish a prima facie case of cause-in-fact. The burden then shifts to the defendant to come forward with evidence that its negligence was not such a but-for cause.[312]

It is true that the failure to warn increases the probability of injury *generally* – more injuries occur without warnings than otherwise. However, on the facts its heeding was improbable: it is inherently unlikely that any warning would have been heeded by the employee who poorly understood English or that his employer, which exploited cheap immigrant labour, would have prevented the grinder's use without a guard.[313] Nevertheless, the presumption of causation was not rebutted. Twerski and Cohen put the point strongly: 'though formally denominated as rebuttable [the presumption] was absolute'.[314]

The explicit motivation of a number of these decisions is the objective of reinforcing manufacturers' duties to warn. As one court reasoned: '[t]he use of the heeding presumption provides a powerful incentive for manufacturers to abide by their duty to provide adequate warnings'.[315] There is also a concern that, without a presumption, the claimant is often faced with a causation question which is purely speculative and upon which its evidence will be (considered to be) self-serving.[316]

The same justifications have not, however, generally been accepted in the context of medical failures to inform. The widely accepted decision in *Canterbury* v. *Spence*[317] held that the claimant must show that a 'prudent person' in her position would not have gone ahead with an operation if properly informed of the risks. Since most prudent persons

---

[312] *Liriano*, 271–2. A similar case to *Liriano* is *DeRienzo* v. *Trek Bicycle Corp.* 376 F Supp 2d 537 (SDNY 2005).

[313] Cf. A. Twerksi and N. Cohen, 'Informed Decision Making and the Law of Torts: The Myth of Justiciable Causation', 139.

[314] Ibid., 140.   [315] *Coffman*, 720.   [316] Ibid.

[317] 464 F 2d 772 (DC Cir 1972). For an overview: M. Berger and A. Twerski, 'Uncertainty and Informed Choice: Unmasking *Daubert*', 270–2.

follow the reasonable advice of their doctor, the incentives to inform are diminished by the inherent unlikelihood of proving causation.[318] Even some states which accept the heeding presumption in products liability do not follow the same approach to the causation inquiry in the medical context.[319]

Reversal of the burden of proof as to the extent of injury caused by wrongful conduct

If the claimant establishes that the defendant's wrongful conduct or defective product was a cause of some part of its total injuries, even if some part of those total injuries has been caused non-tortiously, the burden of proof to produce a viable means of apportioning the injuries between those caused by the defendant's wrongful conduct and the other causes is, in many states, upon the defendant.[320] The basic argument for this is one of relative injustice: denying the victim of a wrongfully caused injury claimant all compensation is more unjust than holding the defendant who has wrongfully caused some part of that injury liable for too much.

Reduction in the standard of proof

In contexts where claimants have been faced with recurrent difficulties of proof of causation, and people's bodily integrity has been at stake, US courts have sometimes relaxed the standard of proof. The most striking example is in the medical negligence context. The origin of a relaxed standard of proof approach is often traced to *Hicks v. United States*.[321] The defendant doctor negligently diagnosed the claimant's intestinal condition as gastroenteritis. The claimant suffered severe haemorrhaging and died. The court stated that: '[I]t does not lie in the defendant's mouth to raise conjectures as to the measure of chances that he has put beyond the possibility of realization. If there was any substantial

---

[318] Cf. A. Tweski and N. Cohen, 'Informed Decision Making and the Law of Torts: The Myth of Justiciable Causation'.

[319] For example, *Scott v. Bradford* 606 P 2d 554 (Okla 1979). M. Berger and A. Twerski, 'Uncertainty and Informed Choice', 272 suggests that claimants almost never lose on this issue *as a matter of law*, however.

[320] See, for example, *Newbury v. Vogel* (1963) 379 P 2d 811, 813, and generally, D. Robertson, 'Causation in the Restatement (Third) of Torts: Three Arguable Mistakes', 1016ff. See also *Restatement (Third) Torts: Products Liability*, §16: *Restatement (Third) Torts* §28(b) comment *d*.

[321] 368 F 2d 626 (4th Cir. 1966). Cf. C. Allen, 'Note: Loss of Chance in Wyoming', 535 ('first landmark case').

possibility of survival and the defendant has destroyed it, he is answerable'.[322] This dictum did indeed form a strand in the reasoning of courts which recognised a reduced standard of proof.[323]

The *Hicks* court cited *Gardner* v. *National Bulk Carriers* as an 'apt analogy'. [324] This case concerned whether the failure to change the course of a vessel to look for a seaman who had fallen overboard possibly some four hours prior to his being noticed missing was causally connected with his death. The court held that 'causation is proved if the master's omission destroys the reasonable possibility of rescue. Therefore, proximate cause here is implicit in the breach of duty...Once the evidence sustains the reasonable possibility of rescue, ample or narrow...total disregard of the duty, refusal to make even a try, as was the case here, imposes liability'.[325]

Gardner reflected a line of cases, drawn attention to by Malone, in which courts had taken a liberal approach to sending cause-in-fact questions to the jury or as fact finder.[326] In these cases, an emphasis was placed upon the affirmative nature of the duty to attempt to rescue: the duty itself was in place to maximise the claimant's chances of survival.[327] As Malone put it: '[t]he ever-present chance that the rescue might fail is part of the risk against which the rule protects'.[328] Moreover, to hold otherwise would have allowed defendants to escape liability by benefiting from the uncertainty inherent in the rescue operation.

By alluding to *Gardner*, then, the *Hicks* court drew attention to two structural features of the medical malpractice situation: first that the doctor's duty was akin to that of a rescuer, a positive duty to prevent the operation of some other non-tortious cause; and second that, as in the seaman cases, the claimant faces a difficult proof burden on causation due to the inherent background risks in the situation.[329] Subsequent courts, drawing upon these two considerations, have applied

---

[322] *Hicks*, 632.

[323] For example, *Jeanes* v. *Milner* 428 F 2d 598, 604 (8th Cir 1970); *Thomas* v. *Curso* 265 Md. 84, 101 (1972).

[324] 310 F 2d 284 (1962, 4th Cir).   [325] Ibid. 287.

[326] W. Malone, 'Ruminations on Cause-in-Fact', 75–7; J. Goldberg and B. Zipursky, 'Unrealized Torts', 1656–9.

[327] W. Malone, 'Ruminations', 75.   [328] Ibid., 77.

[329] Note, however, that the Fourth Circuit repudiated interpretations of *Hicks* which suggested it gave rise to a relaxed standard of proof of causation: *Hurley* v. *United States* 923 F 2d 1091, 1093–5 (4th 1991). Indeed, *Hicks* was a problematic authority since the preponderance test was potentially satisfied in it: cf. *Hicks*, 632. This point is made in *Cooper* v. *Sisters of Charity of Cincinnati* 272 Ohio St 2d 242, 251–3 (1971).

the relaxed standard of proof to cases where the claimant's chances of survival prior to the doctor's negligence are less than 50 per cent.[330]

The idea that the defendant's duty itself protects against the risk of failing to establish causation is strained – certainly in the *Gardner* situation – in the same way that the part of the purpose of the lifeguard statute in *Haft* was to provide eye-witnesses to establish causal proof. The incantation of the nature of the defendant's duty – without the premise that the part of that duty was to preserve causal evidence and that such evidence has been destroyed – is empty. Without this duty argument, the relaxed standard of proof approach has no clear boundaries: whenever there are recurrent inherent difficulties in proving causation, there is little reason not to apply this approach. Given the emptiness of the duty-based argument, it is not surprising that some courts justify the application of the reduced standard of proof *simply* by reference to the difficulty of proving causation in medical malpractice.[331]

France

As the next chapter details, French law has created a wide-ranging exceptional doctrine – liability for the loss of a chance – which applies in cases of potential non-tortious causation by modifying its substantive law, resulting in a form of probabilistic liability. This section discusses a more limited body of specifically evidential jurisprudence on causation that establishes full liability.

The central concept in this evidential jurisprudence is that of a 'presumption' of causation.[332] In French law, presumptions are either 'factual' (*présomptions du fait de l'homme*) or 'legal' (*présomptions légales*). In both cases, what is presumed is the existence of certain facts [d,e,f] from the existence of certain proven facts [a,b,c].[333]

In theory, a presumption of fact involves an *inference*, according to the standard of proof, from [a,b,c] to [d,e,f].[334] Such an inference is made

---

[330] *Kallenberg* v. *Beth Israel Hospital* 357 NY S 2d 508 (1974); *Beswick* v. *City of Philadelphia* 185 F Supp 2d 418, 433 (Penn 2001); *Thompson* v. *Sun City Community Hospital* (1984) 688 P2d 605, 616 (Ariz).

[331] Cf. *Evers* v. *Dollinger* 471 A 2d 405, 413 (NJ 1984) (noting more flexible standard than in 'conventional' tort claims due to difficulty of proof); *Reynolds* v. *Gonzalez*, 798 A 2d 67, 75–6 (NJ 2002). See, further, A. Stein, 'Towards a Theory of Medical Malpractice', 1218ff.

[332] For an overview: L. Khoury, *Uncertain Causation in Medical Liability*, 186–98.

[333] Cf. Art 1349 CC: 'des conséquences que la loi ou le magistrat tire d'un fait connu à un fait inconnu'.

[334] S. Galand-Carval, 'Country Report for France', 154–5.

on the basis that the existence of facts [a,b,c] genuinely make the existence of facts [d,e,f] highly probable.[335] A fact or facts may be presumed according to Article 1353 of the Code Civil where the indicators of that fact are 'serious, precise and convergent' (*graves, précises et concordantes*).

The meaning of the concept of a *legal* presumption is not always explained with precision in legal writing. Two usages may be identified. First, a presumption of causation may be denoted 'legal' where the Cour de Cassation or legislation has defined the circumstances in which an inference of causation may or should be drawn.[336] In this way, the designation of a presumption as a 'legal' presumption is simply an authoritative signal to lower courts that certain facts make an inference of causation highly probable. This is a means of constraining lower courts' fact-finding discretion and ensuring uniformity in factual findings. Second, a presumption of causation may be denoted 'legal' where the law is not claiming that the presumption of causation is justified as a matter of inference. Rather, the presumption is justified primarily on normative grounds. Such a presumption may be rebuttable or irrebuttable. The effect of a rebuttable legal presumption in this sense is normally a reversal of the burden of proof.[337]

Legal presumptions of causation

The situations in which legal presumptions of causation have been recognised are diverse. A theory of why legal presumptions of causation arise in particular contexts is difficult to excavate either from legal decisions themselves or from doctrinal understanding. The reasoning given by some[338] – that causation is by its nature particularly difficult to prove – would suggest a general legal presumption of causation, which is not the law. The following situations have given rise to legal presumptions.

---

[335] L. Grynbaum, JCP G.II.10131, citing J. Ghestin, G. Goubeaux, and M. Fabre-Magnan *Traité de droit civil, Introduction générale*, 4th edition 1994, [717]; J. Mouralis, *Dalloz Civil: Preuve*, [665]; G. Viney, P. Jourdain, and S. Carval, *Les Conditions de la Responsabilité*, 4th edition 274; C. Quézel-Ambrunaz, *Essai sur la causalité en droit de la responsabilité civile*, 255.

[336] For this usage, see, for example, P. Jourdain, 'Imputablité d'une contamination virale à une transfusion sanguine: la preuve par exclusion du lien de causalité érigée en présomption du droit'; G. Julia, 'La réception juridique de l'incertitude médicale', 132.

[337] G. Viney, P. Jourdain, and S. Carval, *Les Conditions de la Responsabilité*, 271. The effect is not always as strong, however. Some legal presumptions can be rebutted by pointing to the serious possibility (rather than full proof) that the potential wrongful cause did not cause the injury.

[338] See G. Viney, P. Jourdain, and S. Carval, *Les Conditions de la Responsabilité*, 280.

Traffic accidents

The second civil chamber of the Cour de Cassation has recognised a presumption of causation under the law of 5 July 1985 (the *loi Badinter*) which imposes strict liability, *inter alia*, where the defendant's driving a motor vehicle has caused the claimant's injuries.[339] Thus, in a decision of 19 February 1997, that court struck down a decision of the Lyon court of appeal, which had insisted that the claimant prove that the victim's heart attack, which occurred after a car accident, had been caused by the stress of the accident.[340] This was a violation of the law since it 'could not be excluded that the stress provoked by the accident played a role'.[341] More recent decisions of the second chamber have not applied the presumption, however.[342] It may be that what initially was recognised as a legal presumption is now being reduced to a *factual* presumption, with the result that the claimant needs to prove facts which support an inference of causation.[343]

Defective blood products

The courts have developed a presumption that a person's Hepatitis C was caused by a blood transfusion where the claimant demonstrates that he became infected after blood transfusion, and that he is not a member of any particular risk group for the hepatitis C.[344] In those circumstances, it is incumbent upon the blood transfusion centre to prove that its products were free of any defect and so could not be causal.[345]

---

[339] See, Cass Civ 2e, 28 June 1989, Bull civ II, no 41, Gaz Pal, 1989, 2 (note F Chabas); Cass Civ 2e, 8 November 1989, Bull civ II, no 200.

[340] Cass Civ 2e, 19 February 1997, Bull civ II, no 41, 24.   [341] Ibid.

[342] See Cass Civ 2e, 13 June 2013, no 11-28015 (presumption not applied where C suffered amyotrophic lateral sclerosis which was not diagnosed until over two years after the accident); Cass Civ 2e, 9 February 2012, Bull civ II, no 25 (presumption not applied where C suffered from fatigue, memory loss, problems of concentration, arising one year after the accident).

[343] This is suggested by G. Viney, P. Jourdain, and S. Carval, *Les conditions*, 274.

[344] The basis of liability is generally a contractual *obligation de securité* (obligation to secure a certain result) on the part of the blood transfusion centre. See L. Khoury, *Uncertain Causation*, 190. The claim could also be brought in tort under article 1386–1.

[345] Cass Civ 1e, 9 May 2001, D.2001, 2149 (rapp Sargos); Cass Civ 1e, 18 June 2002, Gaz Pal 2003.572.n.207 (Chabas); Cass Civ 1e, 2 July 2002, JCP G 2002, IV, 2476; Cass Civ 1e, 10 July 2002, JCP G 2003, I, 152, no 27. See, further, S. Galand-Carval, 'Country report on France', 155.

This judicially created presumption could be rationalised as a merely factual presumption involving an inference of causation to a very high probability.[346] However, the presumption created by the courts was then placed on a legislative basis by article 102, *loi no 2002–303* of 4 March 2002.[347] This provides that the presumption applies where it can be presumed that the infection had a transfusional origin, but states that 'the claimant has the benefit of doubt' (*le doute profite au demandeur*).

The Cour de Cassation has affirmed that, under this provision, it is enough for the claimant to establish simply the *possibility* of causation as opposed to probability.[348] Thus, even if the defendant shows that there was a serious possibility of infection of Hepatitis C due to unhygienic equipment used during a surgical procedure, the claimant should nonetheless succeed.[349]

The recognition of this presumption seems to have been influenced by the fact that HIV sufferers, who may have contracted the virus from a blood transfusion, had been granted access, from 1991, to a State compensation fund which operates by means of a legal presumption of causation arising where the claimant shows that they became infected after a blood transfusion.[350]

Factual presumptions

In theory, factual presumptions of causation are based upon an inference of causation in accordance with the general standard of proof. In practice, one sometimes finds that the facts upon which the inference is based do not support a finding of causation to a very high probability. In short, the application of factual presumptions sometimes effects a reduction in the standard of proof.

---

[346] See Cass Civ 2e, 2 July 2002, Bull Civ I 2002, no 182, where the court noted that the conditions for the application of the presumption made a finding of causation a 'quasi-certitude'.

[347] This provision applies to infections occurring before the law's entry into force – before 5 September 2001. It is not clear whether the common law will apply the rule that the claimant has the benefit of the doubt in cases after that date. See G. Viney, P. Jourdain, and S. Carval, *Les conditions*, 279–80.

[348] Cass Civ 1e, 12 July 2007, Bull civ I, no 272, cited by S. Galand-Carval, 'Case Report on France', 155. See also, perhaps more stringently, requiring that the claimant show that the hepatitis C had a transfusional origin to 'a sufficient degree of probability': Cass Civ 1e, 16 October 2013, no-12-26299. Interestingly, this presumption also extends to indeterminacy over *which* defendant supplied the defective blood: Cass Civ 1e, 7 Feb 2006, No-04–20.256; RCA 2006, no 117.

[349] Cass Civ 1e 12 July 2007, Bull civ I, no 272.

[350] Article 47, *loi no-91–1406*, 31 December 1991.

Presumptions by exclusion

French courts have frequently relied upon Sherlock Holmes' dictum that if one rules out the impossible, one must be left with the truth.[351] If alternative causes of an injury other than the defendant's responsible conduct are ruled out, causation is 'presumed'. The typical example given of this reasoning is the inference drawn that an HIV infection was caused by a blood transfusion.[352] Here the courts rely upon a series of indirect, positive indications of causation – the number of transfusions, the appearance of the HIV infection within the normal time-frame after transfusion, if possible, proof that at least one blood donor was in a risk group for infection.[353] Then the claimant must establish the absence of alternative causes by excluding that their sexual behaviour put them at risk, that their previous medical history placed them in a risk group for infection, and that they did not expose themselves to the risk of infection by travel in foreign countries with high infection rates for HIV.[354] The court may also make inquiries into the serology of the claimant's family.[355]

The liberalism of decisions relying upon this reasoning should not be overstated. Once the alternative risk sources have been ruled out, it is highly probable that the infection was caused by transfusion. This is because the means by which HIV can be transmitted are relatively well understood and a limited number of possible modes have been identified.[356] Ruling out the alternatives thus genuinely makes the transfusion a highly probable cause. The liberal tendency is, however, evident in the application of such reasoning to Hepatitis C infections, where there is more uncertainty as to the possible mechanisms by which the disease can be transmitted.[357]

Presumption based upon increase in risk

There are a number of cases in which the Cour de Cassation has upheld findings of causation which do not seem to be based upon a very high probability of causation. For example, in a decision of 3 October 1974, the court upheld the judgment of a court of appeal, which had failed to explain in its reasoning how it was proved that the defendant hotelier's negligence – in allowing the rooms to be occupied by a large number of

---

[351] See generally, L. Khoury, *Uncertain Causation*, 186–97. Cf. *Platter* v. *Sonatrach* (2004) CILL 2073 [98] (referring to 'Holmes' dicta').
[352] L. Khoury, *Uncertain Causation*, 190–1.   [353] Ibid., 191.   [354] Ibid.   [355] Ibid.
[356] Ibid., 189.   [357] See, for example, Cass Civ 1e, 9 July 1996, Bull Civ I 306.

guests when there was only a small lift and narrow staircase, and in failing to warn that a fire had broken out earlier – had been a cause of a hotel guest jumping, in what the court of appeal described as an 'impulsive and irrational action', from a first floor window to escape a fire in the hotel, in circumstances where other guests, who had listened to the instructions of the attending fire brigade, had escaped uninjured.[358]

The Cour de Cassation stated that the court of appeal could validly reach a finding of causation on the basis that there were a large number of guests in the hotel, the hotel lift was small, the corridor was narrow, and the guests had not been made aware of the existence of the fire until they heard the sirens of the fire engines. Undoubtedly, these circumstances increased the probability that a guest might panic in the wake of a fire and take impulsive action. However, it is doubtful whether the court could have been confident to a very high probability that such an action, by its nature unpredictable, would have been avoided.

On the basis of this and similar cases,[359] Viney and Jourdain suggest that one can identify a strand of case law which operates a presumption that, where a person has wrongfully increased the risk of an injury suffered by the claimant, it is presumed that the risk created has materialised in that injury, where the injury is the 'normal and foreseeable' consequence of the risk created.[360]

Many of the cases relied upon by these authors for this proposition do not themselves explicitly formulate such a rule, however.[361] The hotel-fire case, for example, does not mention 'risk'. Rather there are occasional explicit references to the fact that a person's wrongful conduct has increased the risk of injury. Even then, however, this is usually simply part of a broader inferential process.[362] For example, in a decision of 24 January 2006, the claimant had been prescribed Isomeride, a drug

---

[358] Cass Civ 1e, 3 Oct 1974, JCP 1975.II.18156 (note Rabut); Bull Civ I, 251.

[359] Cass Civ 2e, 4 March, 1966, Bull civ II, 309 (seemingly generous approach taken to whether instructions would have stopped employees and their guests throwing fireworks from a building during a party); Civ 2e, 5 March 1975, Bull Civ II, 75 (D's failure to press the horn upon approach to a junction held to be a cause of collision with a motorcyclist travelling towards the junction at a high speed with a noisy engine); Cass Civ 2e, 20 June 2002, RCA 2002, comm 279, pourvoi 99-19782 (D's serving more alcohol to an already very drunk C was a cause of C's choking on his food and dying); Cass Civ 1e, 24 April 2006, Bull civ I, 34.

[360] G. Viney, P. Jourdain, and S. Carval, *Les Conditions de la Responsabilité*, 281–4.

[361] None of the cases in Note 359, each cited by the authors, mentions the concept.

[362] See, for example, Cass Civ 1e, 23 May 1973 (second decision), Bull civ I, 1973 no 181, JCP 1975.G.II.17955 (Savatier).

given to treat obesity, for her becoming overweight after her pregnancy. She took the drug for two months. One year later she was diagnosed with pulmonary hypertension, necessitating heart surgery. She sued the manufacturer of the drug under article 1386–1, and 1382 and succeeded. The defendant sought the decision to be struck down on the ground that the court of appeal had reached a decision on 'probability', based upon epidemiological studies which had shown merely 'coincidences' between the drug and the illness. This was rejected because the court of appeal had properly concluded on the basis of epidemiological studies that one of the substances in the drugs (dexfenfluramine) was a risk factor (*facteur favorisant*) for pulmonary hypertension. This sufficed to prove causation *in addition to the facts that* the claimant had enjoyed good health prior to 1993, and the expert evidence had ruled out other possible causes of hypertension.

Presumptions without proof of increase in risk

The most striking loosening of the orthodox standard of proof has occurred in the acceptance of claims of those suffering from multiple sclerosis, which they attribute to vaccinations against Hepatitis B. Initially such claims were rejected.[363] This was the holding of the 23 September 2003 decision of the Cour de Cassation, where the claimant, previously in good health, had received three injections of an anti-Hepatitis B vaccination, and one month after the last was diagnosed with multiple sclerosis. At the time of that decision, there were no scientific studies supportive of a causal association between the vaccine and the illness, albeit that such a possibility could not be certainly excluded.[364]

Subsequently, however, the Cour de Cassation,[365] following the lead of the administrative courts,[366] upheld findings of causation in civil

---

[363] Cass Civ 1e, 23 Sept 2003, D.2004.898 (obs Yves Marie Serinet, Mislawski); JCP 2003 E&A II. 1749, JCP 2003, G.II.10179 (note Jonquet, Maillols, Mainguy, Terrier); D.2004.1344 (obs Mazeaud); RTDC 2004, 101 (obs Jourdain). Followed by: Cass Civ 1e, 27 February 2007, RCA 2007.comm.165 (obs A Gouttenoire, C Rade), D.2007.somm.2899 (Ph Brun).

[364] In 2003, the main studies were: A. Ascherio, et al., 'Hepatitis B Vaccination and the Risk of Multiple Sclerosis'; F. DeStefano, et al., 'Vaccinations and Hepatitis B Vaccine Central Nervous System Demyelinating Disease in Adults'. Most studies at this time pointed only to a very weak statistical association with relative risks ~1.0.

[365] Cass Civ 1e, 22 May 2008 (no.06–14.952P; no.06–10.967P; no.06–18.848; no.05-10593), JCP.G.II.10131 (Grynbaum), RTDC.2008, 492 (obs Jourdain), D.2008.1544 (obs Gallmeister).

[366] CE, 9 March 2007, D.2007.2204 (note L Neyret), JCP.G.2007.II.10142 (note A Laude), JCP.AC.no.43.2277 (comm Carpi-Petit).

claims against the vaccine manufacturer under Article 1386–1 CC.[367] In one decision, the court observed that, despite the lack of scientific evidence showing a significant increased risk from the vaccine, the absence of positive scientific evidence did not *exclude* the possibility of a causal link.[368] Proof of causation was upheld on the basis that the first manifestations of the MS were two months after the last injection and neither the claimant nor her family had a history of neurological problems.[369] Since very little is known of the potential causes of MS, the absence of family neurological problems hardly rules out the possibility of alternative causes. Thus, significant uncertainty is being tolerated here.[370] The motivation is the simple one of compensating the victims of terrible illnesses.[371]

Justifications for full liability beyond defendant indeterminacy

The different justifications adduced in each system either for a reversal in the burden of proof, a reduction in the standard of proof, or a presumption of causation can be grouped in three categories. First, some arguments appeal to the need to incentivise defendants to conform to their legal duties, particularly in situations of recurrent uncertainty over causation. Second, some arguments appeal to the defendant's responsibility for the existence of uncertainty over causation. Third, some appeal to a relative injustice or fairness argument. The latter category comprises appeals to the idea that causation is 'impossible' to prove or is particularly difficult to prove in a certain domain, to the idea that the defendant has behaved with a high level of fault, or to the idea that a false positive on causation is not as unjust, or otherwise regrettable, as a false negative where the defendant has been proven to have behaved with fault. Each category is considered in turn.

---

[367] Articles 1386–1 to 1386–18 transpose Directive 85/374.

[368] Cass Civ 1e, 19 July 2009: No.08–11.073, JCP.G, no.41.13 (note Sargos).

[369] In two other decisions of 22 May 2008, the Cour de Cassation upheld CA decisions which had rejected findings of causation: *Kister*: no.06–18.848; *Signeron*: no.05–10.593. As Jourdain notes: 'C'est donc vers une appréciation souveraine et au cas par cas du lien de causalité que l'on s'oriente' RTDC 2008, 492.

[370] Two recent decisions have upheld lower courts' finding of no causal link: Cass Civ 1e, 25 November 2010, Bull Civ 1 no 245, JCP G 2011.79 (Borghetti); Cass Civ 1e 26 Jan 2012, no 10-28195. Cf. the rejection of a claim in the different context of animals becoming ill near an electricity cable: Cass Civ 3e, 18 May 2011, no 10-17645, RTDC 2011, 542.

[371] J. Borghetti, 'Note under Cass Civ 1e, 25 Nov 2010'.

Deterrence

English, German, and US courts have appealed to the need to incentivise defendants to conform to their legal duties as a justification for either a reversal in the burden of proof or a reduction in the standard of proof.[372] In English law, this appeal takes the form of the 'empty duty' argument made initially in *McGhee* and then in *Fairchild*. In German law, the same argument is made in cases of breaches of duties to inform. In the US, the argument is found in the law on failures to warn of the dangers of products, in *Haft*, in order to incentivise adherence to statutory duties protecting people's bodily integrity, and in the *Gardner* line of cases where the victim's activity involves a recurrent background risk of injury.[373]

The incentives argument seems to be accepted most typically in situations where there is (a) recurrent causal uncertainty and (b) where a particularly valuable interest is at stake. The evidence for (a) is that in *McGhee* and *Fairchild* emphasis was placed on the fact that employers would very rarely, if ever, be liable due to the limits of scientific knowledge – the causal uncertainty was recurrent. Similarly, the German courts have drawn attention to the fact that in cases involving hypothetical human decisions (as in the breach of duty to inform cases), it is *rarely* possible to obtain the theoretically required certainty over the person's hypothetical decision.[374] Finally, the heeding presumption in products liability cases has been justified by the recurrent inability to determine whether a person would have heeded the warning on the preponderance of the evidence.[375] As to (b) – all of these situations involve physical injuries to the person or (autonomy) interests in control over how one's body is treated. The only exception to the latter is the expansive German reversal of the burden of proof, which also applies in certain cases involving purely economic interests.

Should we accept such deterrence-based arguments either for a reversal of the burden of proof or reduction in the standard of proof on causation (in a particular context)? These arguments need to be assessed in empirical terms and in normative terms. The empirical question can be formulated as follows:

Does the reduced or non-existent threat of liability, due to the impossibility or difficulty of proving causation in some context, lead persons to fail to behave in ways which would lead to fewer overall injuries being caused?

---

[372] See pp. 218–219; 237–238; 252–253.   [373] See pp. 259–261.   [374] See p. 218.
[375] See pp. 257–8.

If the answer is affirmative, this implies that the reduced or non-existent threat of liability, due to the impossibility or difficulty of proving causation, affects people's behaviour in a way which leads to more injuries being caused than if the threat existed. Notice that even if the answer is negative, this does not imply that tort liability does not affect behaviour nor that tort law does not affect behaviour in injury-reducing ways. It may be that tort law's setting legal standards of conduct even absent the threat of liability has beneficial effects.[376] And it may be that the reduced threat of liability for one reason (say, being judgment-proof) affects behaviour in a way that the reduced threat of liability for another reason (say, difficulty of causal proof) does not.

There is, to my knowledge, no existing empirical study comparing the effects on the occurrence of injuries of traditional causal proof rules with liability regimes which apply exceptional departures from those rules, such as a reversal of the burden of proof. Consequently, given its complexity, answers to the empirical question are currently at best reasoned conjecture. One basis for such conjectures might be general data on the effects of tort liability. If tort liability, in a certain context, leads to a reduction in injuries, then it might be argued that this reduction is contingent upon defendants not being able to count on causal proof being impossible. There are two problems with such an argument, however. First, the general data which exist on the injury-reducing effects of tort liability in a range of contexts are in any event equivocal.[377] Second, even if a reduction of injuries could be attributed to the threat of tort liability in a certain context, there may be a number of causal mechanisms by which tort liability achieves this reduction. It could not straightforwardly be inferred that defendants' awareness of the availability of causal proof is a necessary condition for these effects.

Economic models of liability provide another basis for reasoned conjecture. Legal economists often claim that the existence of difficulties of causal proof is likely to lead to underdeterrence.[378] On the simple model described in Chapter 3, the reason for this is simply that rational self-interested agents will not be incentivised to take injury-preventing

---

[376] For reasons why this might be so, see S. Smith, 'The Normativity of Private Law', 223–5.

[377] For a summary of relevant studies, see N. Jansen, *Die Struktur des Haftungsrechts*, 168–78.

[378] See, for example, M. Faure, 'The Complementary Roles of Liability, Regulation and Insurance in Safety Management: Theory and Practice', 2, 8; S. Shavell, 'Uncertainty over Causation and the Determination of Civil Liability', 588.

precautions where they can predict that liability will not attach due to the impossibility of causal proof.[379] In so far as we accept (1) the predictive utility of the model of individual rational self-interest in such models, and in so far as we accept that (2) the incentives provided by tort liability still exist where liability insurance is in place, and (3) in so far as we consider these incentives to be the only considerations affecting behaviour, and (4) so long as people can reasonably predict that causal proof will be difficult or impossible in a certain context, then we would probably expect more injuries to occur.

Each of these assumptions raises difficulties for the predictive utility of the economic model in relation to the effect of causal uncertainty. As to (1), there are two particular problems. First, there is the familiar concern that, particularly in the medical context, agents will take excessive care, with the possible result that the overall number of injuries does not decrease.[380] This may be a particular concern if the burden of proof on causation were reversed. Agents may tend to equate failures to take care with near inevitable liability in damages, possibly leading them to be excessively cautious.[381] Second, economic models typically ignore the moral emotions which may also affect individual agents' decision-making procedures.[382] A doctor's decision whether to give a patient who has a poor chance of survival from cancer a certain treatment (which is in some sense not cost-effective) is likely to be influenced by the significant moral cost to the doctor of not doing so.

The assumption in (3) will frequently not be realistic. Tort norms will often only be part of the relevant set of incentives for an agent. There may often be incentives provided by regulatory norms, the criminal law, the market, and moral norms. Indeed, as in mesothelioma cases where the defendant's conduct may also cause asbestosis, it may even be that *tort law* itself continues to have incentive effects in a certain domain because the wrongful conduct at issue could provably have caused other harms, even if the negligence cannot be proven to have caused the injury in question. It is too simple to move from the fact that

---

[379] Chapter 3, 135–6.

[380] P. Cane, *Atiyah's Accidents, Compensation and the Law*, 8th edition, 425.

[381] C. Ehlgen, *Probabilistiche Proportionalhaftung*, 303.

[382] B. Deffains and C. Fluet, 'Legal Liability when Individuals have Moral Concerns', 930: 'Most people exercise some care out of intrinsic concerns about hurting others'. They provide a model of liability which takes into account moral concerns: 934–8. They note that this departs from 'conventional' models (933). This problem is probably less important in relation to behaviour within firms: S. Shavell, 'Law versus Morality as Regulators of Conduct', 242–3.

tort law incentives are (arguably) diminished to the conclusion that agents have no incentives whatsoever to take injury-reducing precautions in a particular domain.[383]

The assumption in (4) can be questioned on at least two grounds. The first is that ordinary agents' assessments of probability are afflicted with a variety of biases and do not typically conform to the expected utility theory relied upon by standard economic models.[384] Though some models of liability rules attempt to incorporate different, more realistic, models of individual decision-making, it is unclear what the implications of these models are for situations of recurrent causal uncertainty.[385] For example, if doctors are overly optimistic about the extent to which certain precautions can improve the probability of better health outcomes, they also might overestimate the ex-post probability that their actions would have made a difference to patient's health. In that event, the effects of recurrent causal uncertainty would be significantly reduced by an optimistic bias. Or it may be that a pessimistic bias which weights low probabilities too highly may mean that even in situations of recurrent causal uncertainty, a small probability that the claimant will be able to bring proof of causation leads to efficient precautions being taken nonetheless. Or it may be that for individual doctors or individual employees in a firm the cognitive difficulty of estimating the ex-post probability of causation in the event that they decide to behave negligently leads to a general attitude of risk aversion in these individuals, perhaps because such decisions are effectively treated by individuals as decisions made without knowledge of the probabilities of causation. In short, there are several uncertainties as to the effect of recurrent causal uncertainty on individual behaviour due to the existence of cognitive biases in the perception and calculation of probabilities.

It might be objected that the effect of cognitive biases can be set aside or discounted when the focus is shifted from the individual behaviour of particular doctors or employees, to institutional decisions about

---

[383] See, further, S. Steel, 'Causation in English Tort Law', 252–6.

[384] See A. Tversky and D. Kahneman, 'Probabilistic Reasoning'.

[385] See generally, for example, E. Posner, 'Probability Errors' (Considering the Effects of Different Forms of Optimism/Pessimism in Perceptions of Probability); J. Teitelbaum, 'A Unilateral Accident Model under Ambiguity', 437–41. As noted by Y. Halbersberg and E. Guttel, 'Behavioural Economics and Tort Law', 414, existing models typically only model the effects of one type of bias, rendering their external validity when multiple biases are in play questionable.

precautions taken by experienced expert managers or directors.[386] While we would not expect an individual doctor in an accident and emergency ward to be deciding whether to be negligent because it will later be difficult for the already ill patient to prove that this negligence was causative of injury, let alone to maximise expected utility, we can expect such consequentialist calculations, undertaken more in line with expected utility theory, by the management of large companies or hospitals. Suppose that this is true – there remains a second doubt about (4). The doubt concerns how often the available evidence is of the kind that such actors can reliably predict the ex-post impossibility of proof of causation under the BPR. It is far from clear that there are situations where managers could *ex-ante* identify some systematic measure (demanded by a cost-benefit analysis), the failure to impose which would *never* be proven to be a cause of an injury. Perhaps, however, there are certain precautions (e.g. treatments for certain cancers) whose effects on patients can only be measured by very general statistics – say, to the effect that 20 per cent of patients enjoy longer periods of remission when treated by a certain drug. In that event, it might be rational from a cost-benefit perspective (again, assuming (1)–(3)) to discourage treatment by the drug, since, if only that general statistical evidence were available, no individual patient could satisfy the BPR if it were deemed negligent not to provide the drug. But how often certain situations are describable only at a very general statistical level, with individual characteristics of claimants not leading to a revision of the statistics in an individual case (potentially pushing the probability of causation to a BPR-satisfying level), is unclear.

Finally, it should also be observed that, even granting these assumptions, a reversal in the burden of proof or a reduction in the standard of proof would not provide an incentive in cases where the probability of causation can reliably be estimated at less than 51 per cent. Here defendants could satisfy the reversed burden of proof.[387] The greater the willingness to accept statistical evidence in such cases, the fewer incentives would be provided by a reversal in the burden of proof. The reversal of the burden of proof would only bite where no assessment of the probability of causation could be made – a situation of total impossibility of proof.

---

[386] Cf. M. Rabin, 'Psychology and Economics', 31: '...such factors [experience, expertise, and learning] probably do on average moderate biases. But the conjectures [that they do] do not appear to be nearly as valid as economists imagine'.

[387] This is sometimes used as an argument for proportional liability, see Chapter 6, 362.

As far as the empirical question goes, the most that can be said, then, is that there is some chance that overall injuries would be reduced to some extent in certain, very specific, contexts (e.g. the treatment of particular illnesses) were the burden of proof reversed in situations of recurrent causal uncertainty. The *normative* question can then be asked in two ways. First, given the conjectural state of the empirical case for altering the burden or standard of proof on causation, ought we nonetheless to do so? Second, if the empirical evidence *were* convincing that in some context altering the general burden or standard of proof prevented a certain number of (serious) injuries, ought we to do so?

The first normative question seems to have only one answer as stated. The normative starting point in a liberal society, as Chapter 3 argued, is that others are not presumed to be individually responsible for one's injuries and that such responsibility is essential to liability to compensate. To invade a person's general right to be free on the ground that there is a speculative chance that it might do others some good seems unjustifiable.[388] Second, the acceptance of the deterrence argument will lead to a highly dappled law of tort. Since predictable causal uncertainty will plausibly only exist in relation to very particular kinds of injury in particular contexts, the law would need to adopt highly specific rules – one could have a reversal of the burden of proof for one type of cancer, the orthodox burden governing another type. The point is not that this flouts some intrinsically valuable notion of coherence. Rather it is likely to lead to a sense of injustice among litigants, some of whom will succeed simply because of the impoverished state of knowledge about the causes of their injury. Third, there is a subsidiary point that it is difficult to believe that courts are the best institutions for resolving these complex empirical questions. The development of such rules, even if the rules can be justified, ought not to be done judicially.

The more difficult question is whether, were the empirical evidence *reasonably credible* (which is not to demand the impossible of *certainty*) that a reversal of the burden of proof or reduction in the standard of proof would improve safety, we should depart from the minimum requirement that a defendant be proven to have caused the claimant's injury on the balance of probability.[389] Much would ultimately depend on the details of such evidence. One would want to know whether

---

[388] See Chapter 3, 115–116.
[389] Cf. N.J. McBride, 'Rights and the Basis of Tort Law', 355, for one view on the evidential threshold necessary to ground recognition of new legal duties in tort law.

the improvements in safety were contingent upon the existence of *tort* liability (perhaps due to the benefits of private enforcement) or whether some form of regulation would be even better. If it had similar improvements in safety, some form of regulation may be more just in so far as it need not involve holding defendants liable for, and in the amount of, losses which they have not been proven to have caused. One would also want to know or to estimate how much of the injuries occurring under the regime without an alteration in the burden of proof on causation are down to highly culpable conduct. If many were, criminal offences of reckless endangerment might be more appropriate.[390]

Responsibility for causal uncertainty

English, French, German, and US law have each cited the defendant's responsibility – in some sense – for the existence of uncertainty over causation as a justification for altering their general proof rules in favour of the claimant. Two conditions are generally insisted upon for such responsibility to obtain:

(1) *More than wrongful conduct condition*. The case law in England, France, and Germany has not generally altered its proof rules simply on the ground that, had the defendant not behaved wrongfully, we would know how matters would have turned out had the defendant not behaved wrongfully. Even if it is true that, absent the defendant's wrongful conduct, there would have been more information on the hypothetical course of events, because those hypothetical events would have been the *actual* course of events, this alone does not suffice to trigger an exception to the general proof rules. Something more is required.

The law in each system generally requires the destruction, diminution in the probative value of, or failure to preserve an information-storing item: for instance, destruction of documentation, failure to record test results, failure to make measurements of the toxicity of a water supply, failure to record noise levels, failure to secure the presence of an eye-witness (for example, the lifeguard in *Haft*).

The requirement of 'something more' is, admittedly, not universal. In the German cases on breach of duty to inform, the claim is made that the breach of the duty to inform is itself a cause of uncertainty over how the claimant would have decided and that this is a reason for reversing the burden of proof.

---

[390] For a recent proposal to introduce a new criminal offence of wilful neglect in the medical context, based in part on the supposed reduced deterrent effects of tort law due to causal uncertainty, see K. Yeung and J. Horder, 'How Can the Criminal Law Support the Provision of Quality in Healthcare?', 2.

(2) *Nature of the duty condition.* Each system has insisted that the legal
duty, the breach of which has been a cause of less information
over causation, exist at least partly to serve the purpose of securing
information. Thus, the German cases all involve the breach of duties
to maintain documentation or test results which serve to secure
information. The English cases all concern duties to record information
or breach of a duty whose purpose has been held to be to suppress
disputes over evidence.

The German cases imply that a more stringent condition be met: the
defendant's duty must exist partly to serve the purpose of preserving
information for the purposes of future civil litigation. This condition is
interpreted liberally, however. It is surely rather strained to hold that
the duty to take tests for the purposes of a diagnosis exists partly to assist
the claimant in future litigation against the doctor.

English, German, and French law broadly converge on the legal
response to a situation where the defendant is responsible under these
two conditions. No system currently recognises a reversal of the burden
of proof on causation in such circumstances. The legal response is to
presume that the missing evidence would have been favourable to the
claimant or to assess the claimant's evidence in a favourable light.

The conditions of responsibility for diminishing evidence of causation

Are the conditions pursuant to which the law holds people accountable –
by way of relaxing the general proof rules – for causing uncertainty over
causation appropriate?

Causing evidential damage and causal uncertainty

The most considered analysis of the conditions under which such
responsibility is appropriate has been given by Porat and Stein. They
suggest that in some cases 'accuracy in fact-finding is undermined by
circumstances for which no person can be blamed' but that 'in other
cases...the existing uncertainty and the consequent inability of the
court to determine the facts accurately result from a person's wrongful
conduct'.[391] In such cases, they say that the defendant has inflicted
'evidential damage' upon the claimant. Evidential damage is inflicted
whenever the defendant 'impair[s] the plaintiff's ability or reduce[s] his
chances to establish the facts necessary for prevailing in a...lawsuit'.[392]

---

[391] A. Porat and A. Stein, *Tort Liability under Uncertainty*, 160.   [392] Ibid., 161.

They provide no general analysis, however, of exactly what it is to inflict evidential damage, but instead proceed by evocative examples. Thus, in their discussion of *Haft* v. *Lone Pine Hotel*,[393] they claim that the negligent failure to provide a lifeguard in that case was a cause of evidential damage to the claimant.[394] Similarly, in cases like *Hotson* v. *East Berkshire Health Authority*,[395] where it was unclear whether a doctor's negligent failure to diagnose the claimant timeously had caused his avascular necrosis, their claim is that the doctor's negligence inflicted evidential damage.[396] It seems clear that the authors would also hold that the defendant in *Sienkiewicz* inflicted evidential damage upon the claimant.[397]

Porat and Stein's view appears to be considerably broader than the core of the current law in each system. The doctor's negligent failure to diagnose the claimant earlier in *Hotson* seems to have been a cause of evidential damage on their view simply in virtue of the fact that the defendant's negligence deprived us of knowledge of what would have occurred had he behaved non-negligently. Though they do not say so, this seems to entail that *in every case* where the defendant has behaved wrongfully and there is less than certainty over what would have happened had the defendant not behaved wrongfully, the defendant will have inflicted evidential damage.

This might be considered to be a *reductio* of their view.[398] However, Porat and Stein might respond that, indeed, in every case where a defendant has behaved wrongfully and there is uncertainty over causation, the defendant's wrongful conduct will have inflicted evidential damage. In support of this, they might claim that it provides an explanation of the liberal impulse one sometimes finds in the assessment of the claimant's case on causation.[399]

Is it convincing to say that in every case involving wrongful conduct and uncertainty over causation that the defendant has been a cause of 'evidential damage'? It is suggested that three objections can be made to it. The first is a conceptual problem. To hold that someone is evidentially damaged in relation to proof of causation presumably means that

---

[393] Cf. p. 252.   [394] A. Porat and A. Stein, *Tort Liability under Uncertainty*, 163.

[395] [1987] 1 AC 750, discussed in Chapter 4.

[396] A. Porat and A. Stein, *Tort Liability Under Uncertainty*, 195. (described as a 'paradigmatic' instance of the infliction of evidential damage).

[397] See ibid., 175–7.

[398] This seems to be Wright's view of their position. See R. Wright, 'Liability for Possible Wrongs', 1306, n 43.

[399] See pp. 259–60.

they are worse off, evidentially speaking, in relation to their ability to prove causation. That means that a comparison can be made between their current evidential situation and a hypothetical situation in which the defendant did not behave wrongfully and that comparison shows that there is less (or worse) evidence concerning whether the defendant's wrongful conduct was a cause of the claimant's injury in the actual world compared to the hypothetical world. The problem is that this comparison is often unintelligible. Consider, for example, *McGhee*. Had the defendant employer not been negligent, would the claimant have been in a better evidential position to prove that the defendant's negligence was a cause of its injury? But *ex-hypothesi*, the defendant has *not* behaved negligently – so what sense can be made of the question of whether, in the world in which the defendant was not negligent, the claimant would be better able to prove that the defendant's negligence was a cause of the claimant's injury?

The second objection is that, if one avoids the conceptual problem, it will often be unclear whether, simply by dint of behaving wrongfully and our being uncertain whether that wrongful conduct was a cause of the claimant's injury, the defendant made the claimant evidentially worse off. Consider, again, *McGhee*. Suppose that the claimant's injury would not have occurred had the defendant not been negligent. What one can meaningfully ask now is whether the claimant would have had more information in that hypothetical world which would have assisted in determining whether the defendant's *not* behaving negligently was a cause of its *not* suffering injury. Only that information would be helpful in assisting the claimant to prove a causal connection between negligence and injury. But if the defendant was not negligent in *McGhee* and the injury did not occur, what would we know in the hypothetical world? We would not necessarily know whether the defendant's behaving carefully was a cause of the non-occurrence of the injury. In short, we would not necessarily be in a better evidential position to prove a causal connection between the absence of negligence and the absence of injury.

The third problem is a normative one. Even if one can establish that the claimant would have had more information about something had the defendant not behaved wrongfully, why should we think this normatively significant? Suppose that if the defendant had not behaved negligently in *McGhee*, the claimant would not have suffered an injury. What value is the information that 'my employer did not treat me negligently and I did not suffer an injury' to the claimant? Even if the information is 'my employer did not treat me negligently and that seems to have been crucial to my not suffering any injury' – what value does this information have? If the defendant has not behaved negligently and no injury has been suffered, what does it matter? Suppose, however, that if the defendant in *McGhee* had not behaved negligently, the injury would still have occurred. Then, in the hypothetical world, the claimant would (probably) know 'my employer took all reasonable care and I still suffered injury, so I know that no negligence caused my injury'. Perhaps there is some value to this information – it provides a sense of relief that everything was done which should have been – but it is hard to believe that the *possibility* that the defendant has deprived the claimant of this information could justify a reversal of the burden of proof or a reduction in the standard of proof against the defendant.

The current law generally avoids the first, conceptual, problem by focusing not simply on the fact that the defendant's wrongful conduct prevented the occurrence of the non-negligent series of events, but on the destruction or failure to maintain some information-storing item like a test result, a document containing details of treatment, or an eye-witness report of an accident. In these cases, it is possible intelligibly to ask whether the claimant would have been in a better position in relation *to its case against the defendant* if the evidence had been maintained.

It seems that the most we can say that defendants' wrongful conduct *generally* causes in relation to evidence and uncertainty are the following (putting aside cases where an information-storing item is destroyed or not maintained). First, one can say that the defendant's wrongful conduct is a but-for cause of the claimant being *uncertain* as to how things would have gone had the defendant not behaved wrongfully. But causing people to be uncertain about how their lives might have gone is surely not enough to justify imposing the significant costs of liability on defendants arising out of unresolvable issues of causation. Second, one can say that the defendant's wrongful conduct has been a but-for cause of the claimant's being in a position where it is difficult to prove that the defendant's negligence was a cause of its injury. The defendant does this, not by depriving the claimant of evidence, but by virtue of the fact that causation is simply difficult to prove.

The normative significance of causing uncertainty over causation

What normative significance should one attach to the fact that the defendant's wrongful conduct has been a but-for cause of the claimant's being in a position where it is difficult to prove that the defendant's wrongful conduct was a cause of its injury? In itself, probably none at all. For the claimant's conduct (for instance, in *McGhee*, in going to work) is also a but-for cause of its being in the position where it is difficult to prove causation against the defendant.

But can we not say that the defendant's wrongful conduct (unlike the claimant's conduct) is more than a mere but-for cause of the difficulty of proof of causation? It might be argued that it is reasonably foreseeable that if one behaves wrongfully that it may be difficult to prove that the wrongful conduct in question caused a person's injury. Reasonable people ought to know (especially in contexts involving recurrent causal uncertainty) that it will often be difficult to determine whether there were any causal consequences of their wrongful conduct. Moreover, it is normally easier for those who behave wrongfully to avoid bringing about the situation where proof of causation is impossible or difficult than it is for those injured without any culpable conduct on their part to avoid this situation. Given this, we might say that persons who behave wrongfully are outcome responsible for the fact that claimants are faced with a difficult question of proof in order to claim compensation from them. That outcome responsibility for the claimant's position, it might be claimed, justifies defendants bearing the risk of proof being impossible.

The claimant's basic argument here is this: 'You have put me in the position where I cannot prove whether your wrongful conduct caused my loss. You knew or should have known that this would happen. So you should be liable despite my inability to prove it.' But against this the defendant can say three things. First, although the defendant could have avoided bringing about this situation (by not behaving wrongfully), there is normally no way in which he could have behaved wrongfully and made causal proof any easier. So, while the wrongful conduct is avoidable, the defendant cannot alter the fact that causal proof is impossible or difficult in certain situations. The defendant is responsible for the fact *that* the claimant faces a difficult proof situation, but not for the *difficulty* of the situation itself. Second, the defendant is not plausibly under a *duty* not to place the claimant in this situation. It does not seem plausible that we owe others duties *to make sure* that if we behave wrongfully towards them, it is not impossible to prove whether that wrongful conduct caused them injury.[400] Even if the defendant wronged

---

[400] This is not to deny the plausibility of duties to take care not to *increase* the difficulty of proof here; but in situations where the defendant could make no difference to the

the claimant by, say, negligently exposing him to risk, the defendant did not wrong the claimant in some further way by doing so in circumstances where it is impossible to prove that the risk caused injury. Although the defendant owed the claimant a duty not to behave wrongfully, in most cases the purpose of that duty was not to protect the claimant from the inability to prove that the breach of duty caused loss. Third, the claim that 'you have put me in the position where I cannot prove whether your wrongful conduct caused my loss' overplays the defendant's responsibility for this situation. Other factors will often also be causes of it, such as the failure of scientific research programmes to identify the mechanisms of diseases.

A general duty not to cause reasonably foreseeable evidential damage is not appealing in the same way that a general duty to take care not to cause reasonably foreseeable economic loss is not appealing. There is, however, a plausible case for the existence of duties to take care not to inflict evidential damage (by destroying information-storing items) in situations where one party can be said to have assumed a responsibility to preserve evidence or where the parties are in a fiduciary relationship, and where it is reasonably foreseeable that the failure to take care will lead to evidential difficulties for the other.

The appropriate response to the breach of such a duty is a difficult question. The default response in tort to a breach of duty is compensation. So the default response is to put the claimant in the evidential position it would have been in had the breach not occurred. The difficulty, of course, is that it will generally be impossible to determine what the probative effect of the destroyed evidence would have been. English and French law could respond to this by allowing recovery for the extent to which the defendant has reduced the claimant's chance of winning the case against him.[401] Given the argument of the next chapter, however, the better response is the current one – a presumption that the missing evidence would have been favourable to the claimant or put consideration of the rest of the claimant's evidence in a favourable light. Although this cannot be justified strictly in compensatory terms – since we do not know that the evidence would have been favourable – it is the best that can be done in the circumstances.

---

difficulty of proof, such a duty would not suffice to show that the defendant wronged the claimant by putting them in a difficult proof situation. Cf. H.L.A. Hart and T. Honoré, *Causation in the Law*, 2nd edition 425 (describing liability for creation of difficulty of proof as 'an arbitrary form of strict liability').

[401] See Chapter 6, 292ff.

Fairness

Impossibility or difficulty of proof

Courts have sometimes appeared to claim that the justification, at least in part, for departing from the general proof rules is that, in some situations, proof of causation is 'impossible' or particularly difficult – putting aside any question of the defendant's *responsibility* for this impossibility. We have already discussed the way in which recurrent difficulties of proof may be relevant in terms of incentives. But there also seems to be an idea of fairness in the appeal to the impossibility of proof. The implicit idea is that it is unreasonable to insist that claimants prove causation where it is impossible to do so. Thus, in *Rutherford*, the court stated that '[p]laintiffs cannot be expected to prove the scientifically unknown details of carcinogenesis'.[402]

This claim gives rise to a puzzle. The general burden of proof rule decides who loses when it is impossible to prove what occurred according to the standard of proof.[403] If it is impossible to prove causation, the claimant loses – that is the essence of the legal burden of proof. It is odd, therefore, to assert as a justification for altering the burden of proof the fact that it is impossible to ascertain what happened according to the standard of proof.[404] The very situation to which the burden of proof should apply is being adduced as a justification for why it should not apply.

One way of resolving the puzzle is to interpret the claim made by courts invoking impossibility of proof as follows: while the legal burden of proof governs certain kinds of impossibility of proof, it does not govern others. For example, the orthodox burden of proof could be said to apply to situations where there is a perfect equipoise of probability between the parties' factual claims, whereas the exceptional rule applies to situations where the relevant probabilities are unknown or unknowable. If there is no special kind of impossibility of proof, distinct from that normally governed by the burden of proof, then the courts must be taken as making the radical claim that the ordinary burden of proof is not justified at all.

What, however, could this special notion of impossibility of proof be, and why would it be normatively significant so as to take such situations outside the general burden of proof? In appealing to the 'impossibility

---

[402] See p. 255.   [403] Chapter 2, 48.

[404] Cf. L. Röckrath, *Kausalität*, 183: 'Die Beweisnot des Geschädigten selbst kann die Regulung des §830 I 2 BGB nicht begründen'.

of proof as a justification for departing from the general rules, courts have spoken with bewildering divergence of meaning as to what impossibility of proof is. It has been appealed to where the causal issue involves asking what would have happened in the future;[405] where the causal issue involves asking how a third party, who is not before the court, would have behaved;[406] where only inadequate and unreliable statistical evidence is available;[407] where there is an absence of scientific understanding over the mechanism by which a disease can be caused.[408] Similarly, if one looks beyond judicial reasoning, commentators have used the notion of impossibility of proof where a causal process is indeterministic;[409] where causation depends upon the answer to a hypothetical question;[410] where there is only statistical evidence.[411]

It is difficult to understand why any of these kinds of 'impossibility' of proof (if they can really be so described) should receive special treatment (unless one accepts the incentives-based argument already rejected). If the claimant cannot prove her case on causation on the balance of probability, what does the reason for this matter, unless that reason is the defendant's responsibility? Subject to the defendant indeterminacy exceptions, it is difficult to understand why the defendant should lose its entitlement that a case be proved against it on the balance of probability, simply because of the different nature of the uncertainty at stake.

Fairness and recurrent uncertainty

Might not the *recurrent* nature of the impossibility of proving causation be a distinguishing feature of certain situations which has fairness implications? For example, suppose that nearly all mesothelioma sufferers who have been wrongfully exposed to asbestos dust will not be able to prove causation in relation to a wrongful risk imposition. If a judge applies the general burden of proof in any such case, he or she can be certain that a large number of false negatives will follow: a large number

[405] *Davies* v. *Taylor* [1974] AC 207, 212–13 (Lord Reid).
[406] *Henderson* v. *Hagblom* (2003) 232 Sask R 81 [203]; *Walker Estate* v. *York Finch General Hospital* [2001] 1 SCR 647 [88]; *Allied Maples* v. *Simmons and Simmons* [1995] 1 WLR 1602.
[407] *Sienkiewicz* v. *Greif (UK) Ltd* [2011] UKSC 10, [96] and *passim*.   [408] Ibid, [133], [142].
[409] I. Puppe, 'Zurechnung und Wahrscheinlichkeit – Zur Analyse des Risikoerhöhungsprinzip', 299; H. Reece, 'Losses of Chances in the Law', 192–4, 204–6; G. Mäsch, *Chance und Schaden*, 19–20; M. Hogg, 'Developing Causal Doctrine', 49ff.
[410] R. Strassfeld, 'If…Counterfactuals in the Law', 348–52 (where the author discusses judicial 'counterfactual dread').
[411] R. Wright, 'Proving Causation: Probability versus Belief', 216.

of tort victims will go without compensation. In the usual case, it might be argued, the judge cannot usually be certain that the application of the burden of proof will give rise to false negatives. Clearly, however, this is untrue. The operation of the general burden of proof in any context will certainly give rise to false negatives, on the assumption that, if the facts were known, claimants ought to succeed in some burden of proof situations.

Another argument might be that the application of the burden of proof is fair so long as we can assume that roughly 50 per cent of the time claimants deserve to win and 50 per cent of the time defendants deserve to win. The background distribution of deserving and undeserving claims is equal. The burden of proof is fair here since it reflects the normative position that, in general, a false negative on causation is to be preferred to a false positive where proof is impossible.[412] Consequently, if we thought that roughly 50 per cent of injuries in a certain domain were caused by wrongful conduct of defendants, and 50 per cent entirely through natural causes, the logic of the burden of proof would require that the claimant lose. (Merely because there are large numbers of claimants and defendants does not alter this logic.)

Suppose, however, we knew that, at a general level, in, say, asbestos mesothelioma cases, 80 per cent of injuries are caused by wrongful conduct, and only 20 per cent by natural causes, though we cannot say on the balance of probability (with a probability of sufficient weight) that an individual defendant's wrongful conduct was a cause of any injury at all. This would be a *claimant and defendant indeterminacy* case.[413] If those were the facts, then 80 per cent of all mesothelioma victims ought to be compensated by *some* wrongful injurer. In this instance, it might be argued, the application of the burden of proof reaches the result not mandated by the facts *most* of the time. By contrast, in the usual situation, assuming a 50:50 background distribution of deserving to undeserving claims, the general burden of proof gets it right half of the time.

There is a problem with this argument. The notion of a 'deserving' claimant is ambiguous. It could mean: this claimant deserves to be compensated because it has suffered wrongful injury at someone's hands. It could also mean: this claimant deserves to be compensated by *this* defendant because *this* defendant wrongfully injured the claimant. The only plausible way of framing the asbestos example is to say that

---

[412] See Chapter 3, 122ff.   [413] See p. 198.

80 per cent of all claimants deserve to be compensated by *someone*. This uses 'deserving' in the first sense. But the fact that the claimant deserves to be compensated by someone does not, by itself, justify altering the burden of proof in relation to a particular defendant. In situations where the defendant *has* wrongfully caused injury to someone, and that person may have been the claimant – *claimant indeterminacy* or *claimant and defendant indeterminacy, causative variant* – the defendant, as someone actually under a secondary duty to pay compensation to someone, has far less complaint to pay damages in some amount. As the next chapter explains, this might provide an appropriate justification for proportional liability.[414]

Relative injustice and culpability arguments

A relative injustice argument, in this context, claims either that a false positive is not as regrettable as a false negative in respect of causation, where fault has been established or simply that those who have behaved with fault or with a particular level of fault should bear the risk of evidential uncertainty over causation. The typical form of this argument runs: '*as between* the victim of an injury and a person whose wrongful conduct *may* have caused it, it is preferable that the latter bear the loss'. Such an argument can be adduced either to support a reversal in the burden of proof or reduction of the standard of proof. This kind of consideration underlies the German *grobe Behandlungsfehler* doctrine and probably strands of the US and English jurisprudence which lower the standard of proof.[415]

Such arguments seem strongest when the following conditions hold: the defendant has liability insurance; the defendant can easily pass on the cost of liability through the cost of its products or services; the defendant is a public body which has culpably breached a duty to protect the claimant from a risk of serious injury;[416] the defendant has behaved with gross fault. When one or more of these is the case, there is some plausibility in saying that a false positive on causation is not as regrettable as a false negative.

Yet the more that false positives are preferred to false negatives, the less effect is given to the normatively essential substantive law requirement that the defendant be causally responsible for the claimant's

---

[414] Chapter 6, 357–9.   [415] See e.g. p. 202.

[416] South African law has recognised in effect an exceptional material increase in risk rule in a case involving breach of constitutional rights protecting life: *Lee* v. *Minister of Correctional Services* [2012] ZACC 30.

injury. For example, if *any* doubt over causation goes in the claimant's favour, the situation approximates to a localised fault pool where a judgment of *distributive* (or, perhaps, retributive) justice allocates the loss to the at fault defendant.[417] Such a system is cause-based as a matter of substantive law, but the much greater weight given to false negatives at the evidential level stands in tension to this since the greater weight given to false negatives is hard to justify except by some *distributive* consideration (e.g. ability to bear the loss), which is theoretically irrelevant in a system based substantively upon individual responsibility. In general terms, the normative comparison of false positives and false negatives has a tendency to invite an overall distributive comparison between the two parties which undermines the normative basis of the substantive law.[418] Moreover, defendants might legitimately complain that they are already fulfilling their obligations of distributive justice through contributing to taxation. The distributive position of the claimant (say, its relative poverty compared to the defendant) is not the responsibility of any particular individual defendant. Finally, apart from the inconsistency a distributive comparison of the parties' ability to bear the cost of judicial errors on causation generates with an emphasis upon individual responsibility at the level of the substantive law, it also leads logically to the intolerable position of variable burdens and standards of proof in every case, depending upon each party's ability to bear the loss.

Nonetheless, it must be normatively possible to hold that some departures from the substantive law's ideal of only causally responsible defendants being liable are worse than others without engaging in an (impossible) overall comparison of the parties' wealth (or other attributes) in the same way that punishing an innocent is straightforwardly more unjust than letting the guilty go free.[419] We have suggested the defendant indeterminacy situation as one example where the risk of a false positive is preferable.

German law would add cases of gross breach of duties to take care to protect life and health. The best two arguments for the German position seem to me as follows.[420] First, a false negative on causation would mean

---

[417] On the idea of fault pools, see Chapter 3, 116.

[418] Cf. R. Seifert, *Ärztlicher Behandlungsfehler und schicksalhafter Verlauf*, 79.

[419] Cf. T. Keren-Paz, 'Risks and Wrongs' Account of Corrective Justice', 104.

[420] It may also be approved as a rough compromise in the absence of other means to soften the harsh §286 ZPO standard of proof. German law is not alone in using gross breaches of duty to reverse the burden of proof. Cf. for Danish and Norwegian law: V. Ulfbeck and M. Holle, 'Tort Law and Burden of Proof – Comparative Aspects', 38.

that a defendant who should be sanctioned will not be sanctioned (assuming the criminal law will not address the defendant's conduct) and an injustice will go uncorrected. Neither corrective nor retributive justice will be served. By contrast, if there is a false positive, a defendant will be justly sanctioned and there will only be a corrective injustice. The problem with this argument is that if one really believes that gross negligence should be sanctioned, there is no reason why this should result in a reversal of the burden of proof. Rather, the claimant should simply be entitled to exemplary damages.[421] Reversing the burden of proof leaves it up to chance whether the defendant will in fact be punished, since in some cases the defendant may be able to satisfy the reverse burden.[422] The second argument claims that the defendant's high culpability changes his normative position in such a way that we should be less concerned to avoid an erroneous assignment of liability against him. Somehow, the defendant's culpability forfeits his right to our solicitude over whether we correctly assign liability. But some explanation is due as to why the defendant only forfeits *that* right (why not some other right or all his rights?) It is not clear what that explanation could be.[423] It also seems simply unjust that the worse one behaves the less a case needs to be proven against one.[424]

---

[421] Even if one believes that the legal wrong in the tort of negligence occurs only when injury is caused, such that exemplary damages could be awarded only on proof of causation (if at all, in negligence), it would be unprincipled to subvert that rule by reversing the burden of proof on causation simply in order to give effect to the view that the grossly negligent defendant deserves punishment.

[422] A possible response to this is that even if we do not want to make it our business to punish people through tort law for gross negligence (because then we would be intentionally inflicting harm), we can still better live with the *possibility* that the grossly negligent are made to bear the costs of injuries for which they are not responsible than the possibility that those injured by the grossly negligent are not compensated by them.

[423] Here is one flawed possibility. The grossly negligent defendant imposes a serious risk of harm to the claimant. Retributive justice demands that a similar risk be imposed upon the defendant. A reversal of the burden of proof imposes such a risk in that there is a risk the defendant will not be able to discharge it. But why not impose other kinds of risk of harm on the defendant (why not toss a coin to decide whether the defendant should pay some third party compensation)?

[424] If the argument in the text is to be resisted in common law jurisdictions, appeal may be made to the more expansive scope of responsibility rules in the tort of deceit: *Standard Chartered Bank* v. *Pakistan National Shipping Corporation (nos 2 and 4)* [2003] 1 AC 959, on which see, R. Stevens, *Torts and Rights*, 140. Such punitive responses could be 'mirrored' at the evidential level. See also the more expansive substantive factual causation rules applied in duress to the person compared to economic duress in contract: *Barton* v. *Armstrong* [1973] UKPC 2.

Conclusions

The normative conclusion of this chapter is that the imposition of full liability beyond the defendant indeterminacy situation, where the defendant is not proven to have wrongfully caused injury, and the defendant is not meaningfully responsible for the causal uncertainty, is unjustifiable. Existing exceptional rules which go beyond this should either be abolished or confined as far as possible. From a comparative perspective, in contrast to defendant indeterminacy, the concrete outcomes in cases of potential non-wrongful causation leading to full liability vary significantly. Four examples can be given: the exceptional proof treatment of informed consent claims in German medical liability compared to the absence of such treatment in England; the powerful presumptions recognised by some US states in cases of failures to warn in product torts compared to the relatively orthodox approach of other systems; the reduction of the standard of proof in medical liability in US states compared to an orthodox standard elsewhere or a reversal of the burden in cases of gross error in Germany; the existence of a *de facto* reversal of the burden of proof in certain cases of industrial disease (England, United States) compared to the absence of such a doctrine elsewhere.

If we look beyond these concrete divergences, however, common strands of reasoning motivating exceptional doctrines emerge. A unifying thread is a concern with *systematic* causal uncertainty.[425] This is visible in the American medical and failure-to-warn jurisprudence; the treatment of informed consent in Germany; the notion of 'impossibility of proof' in English law; and arguably in the French legal presumptions. The appeal to recurrent uncertainty may be overtly consequentialist by referring to decreased incentives to conform to a duty as in US, English and German law, or it can be based in the intuitive unfairness of claimants being faced with *recurrent* or *systematic* uncertainty.

Concrete disagreements can be explained in part as concerning *which* situations bear this systematic feature, and in part, upon the need to limit the recognition of such situations at an ostensibly arbitrary point in order to avoid departing from the general proof rules *in every case*. This point varies in each system and is in part explained by the factual settings with which the courts have been faced. In this regard the absence of significant asbestos compensation schemes in the US and

---

[425] Particularly in cases where C's interest is close to the top of the hierarchy of protected interests: for example, physical injury.

England differentiates France and Germany.[426] However, we can observe that while asbestos has driven English and American law, it was at most the re-ignition of a broader reaction to the recurrent causal uncertainty present in other domains: after all, *Fairchild* was pre-dated by *McGhee*.

---

[426] For Germany: G. Wagner, 'Asbestschäden – Bismarck was Right: Anmerkung zu Englisch House of Lords, Entsch v 3.5.2006'; for France: A. Guégan-Lécuyer, *Dommages de Masse et Responsabilité Civile,* 169ff. Compare the relatively meagre lump sums awarded under the Pneumoconiosis etc. (Workers' Compensation) Act 1979 (on average £18,000 in respect of mesothelioma). Post-*Fairchild*, see Part 4 of the Child Maintenance and Other Payments Act 2008 (on average £20,000) and, in respect of victims unable to trace an employer or insurer of an employer responsible in tort, the considerably larger awards under regulations implemented pursuant to the Mesothelioma Act 2014. For these figures, see: www.gov.uk/government/news/asbestos-victims-to-get-123000-in-compensation (last accessed January 2015).

6   Probabilistic liability

This chapter is concerned with exceptions to the general proof rules which can collectively be referred to as doctrines of 'probabilistic liability'. A probabilistic liability is a liability to pay loss measured by reference to a probabilistic fraction of a damage which a person may have suffered at the hands of the defendant or may suffer in the future. Species of this form of liability may be differentiated as follows:[1]

Loss of chance liability: the loss of a chance as loss (CL)

If CL is recognised, the law claims that to suffer the loss of a chance of avoiding certain losses is itself to be caused loss, that persons who inflict such losses may be subject to legal liabilities to compensate their victims in virtue of that fact, and that liability to compensate in respect of the destruction of an x per cent chance of avoiding some loss amounts to x per cent of the (non-chance-based) loss suffered by the victim.

Increased risk liability: the increase of risk as loss (IR)

If IR is recognised, the law claims that to have been exposed to a risk of injury (either fleetingly, or for some extended time period) is itself to have been caused loss. The difference between IR and CL, by stipulation, is that a loss is described as an 'increased risk' if the bad outcome risked by the relevant conduct has not occurred, whereas a loss is described as a 'loss of chance' if there is now no chance of obtaining the outcome

---

[1] Sometimes probabilistic liability is treated as a unified category: for example, L. Khoury, *Uncertain Causation in Medical Liability*, 91–3. Cf. drawing similar distinctions to those in the text, G. Wagner, '*Schadensersatz: Zwecke, Inhalte, Grenzen*, 80–87'; L. Bieri and P. Marty, 'The Discontinuous Nature of the Loss of a Chance System', 23–6; I. Gilead, M. Green and B. Koch, 'General Report: Causal Uncertainty and Proportional Liability: Analytical and Comparative Report', 10–17.

which there was, or would have been, a chance of obtaining absent the wrongful conduct, or no chance of avoiding the outcome which has occurred. A 'pure' increased risk claim is one in respect *only* of an increased risk of loss. The purpose of differentiating between CL and IR is not (yet) a normative one – it is helpful simply in understanding the legal position in each system.

Probabilistic causal liability (PC)

If PC is recognised, the defendant is liable to pay a fraction of the loss the claimant has suffered or may suffer in the future, where the fraction is either:

(1) the probability that the defendant's wrongful conduct has been a cause of that loss.
(2) the lost chance or increased risk of which the defendant's wrongful conduct has been a cause.

For example, suppose that D negligently reduces C's chance of avoiding cancer from 75 per cent to 25 per cent and C suffers the cancer. Under certain assumptions concerning the disease aetiology,[2] the probability that D has been a cause of C's cancer is at least 66.6 per cent. The recoverable damages under (1) would be 66.6 per cent of the total loss due to the cancer. Under (2) the recoverable damages would be 50 per cent of the total loss.

Why is (2) different from CL or IR? The reason is that CL and IR crucially claim that to lose a chance or to be, or have been, at an increased risk is itself to suffer a loss. This claim is not made by PC(2). The reasons for holding persons liable under PC(2) do not include the fact that the defendant has been a cause of genuine loss constituted by the loss of a chance or increased risk.

It should be relatively clear that PC involves an exceptional departure from the standard of proof on wrong-constituting causation: the claimant establishes liability at least *in some cases* (where the probability of causation is less than or equal to 0.5, in the common law, or is less than a high probability, in France and Germany) without proof that the defendant caused its injury on the balance of probability or to a high probability.

Strictly, CL is not an exception to the general proof rules if we restrict that category to cases where liability in damages is established without

---

[2] On why this proviso is necessary, see Chapter 2, 89 n 213.

proof of causation (to the general standard of proof) between the defendant's legally relevant conduct and some *legally recognised* loss or injury. If the law insists upon the normal burden and standard of proof with respect to the legally recognised loss of a lost chance, then no exception is being applied. However, CL merits inclusion here since the legitimacy of treating lost chances as forms of loss is disputed.

The chapter is structured in three overarching parts. The first is concerned with the evolution of probabilistic liability in the systems which recognise it, namely, England and France. The second part analyses the cogency of the justifications for the CL/IR doctrine. Two central arguments will be pursued across these first two sections. The first is an argument about consistency. The claim is that *if* a legal system recognises CL/IR, it cannot rationally restrict their application to the lost chance of avoiding or increased risk of suffering purely economic losses. The second argument is an argument of substantive principle. The claim is that while a broad version of CL, encompassing chances of avoiding physical injuries and chances of avoiding economic losses, is justifiable in so far as it claims that to lose such chances can itself be a form of loss, the weakness of our interest in protection from such losses renders CL, in particular its measure of damages, undesirable all things considered. The third part discusses the justifications for PC. It argues that PC is generally undesirable, but briefly defends a principle ('the proven causation principle') according to which people may justly be held proportionally liable where they are known to have caused harm in circumstances where their proportionate liability will track the total harm they have caused.

The law on probabilistic liability

English law

This section first describes the development of probabilistic liabilities in English law.[3] Second, we explain the justificatory problems which arise when one tries to explain why this chance or risk-based recovery is limited to its present boundaries. Finally, we argue that no single principle or combination of principles can explain the law in its present form, with the result that the law is fraught with justificatory inconsistency.

The development of the law on probabilistic liability has been labyrinthine. Before entering the labyrinth, it may be helpful for the reader to see the endpoint of this development at the outset. The current law can be summarised in two parts: situations in which the causation of the

---

[3] This section draws partly upon S. Steel, 'Rationalising Loss of a Chance in Tort', 235-47.

loss of chance or increase in risk is what constitutes the wrong or is what makes the wrong actionable; situations in which the loss of chance or increase in risk is recovered once an actionable wrong has been established.

Loss of chance or increase in risk as establishing the wrong or the actionability of the wrong

Assuming that D satisfies all of the other requirements of a particular tort except the requirement of actionable 'injury':

(1)   C may successfully sue D for the lost chance of avoiding some economic loss or making some economic gain in so far as answering the question – would C have suffered that economic loss or made that economic gain without D's wrongful conduct? – requires us to determine what a third party, T, would have done. C may sue D for the chance that T would have behaved in such a way that C would not have suffered its economic loss or would have made its economic gain, even if that chance is below 50 per cent.

(2)   C may not sue D for the lost chance of avoiding some economic loss or of making some economic gain in so far as answering the question – would C have suffered that loss or made that gain without D's wrongful conduct? – requires us only to determine what C would have done. C must show on the balance of probability that it would have acted in such a way that the financial loss would not have occurred or that the financial gain would have been made.

   (a)   If answering the question – would C have suffered financial loss or made a financial gain without D's wrongful conduct? – requires us to determine both what C would have done and what a third party, T, would have done, then C must prove on the balance of probability how C would have acted. If C, having proven how C would have acted, can also show there was a chance that T would have acted in such a way that C would have avoided the financial loss or made the financial gain, C may recover for that chance, even if the chance is below 50 per cent.

(3)   C may not sue D for the lost chance of avoiding some physical loss or making some physical gain, but may recover damages in proportion to the probability that the defendant was a cause of its physical injury where the PC rule in *Barker* v. *Corus (UK) Ltd* applies.

(4)   C may not sue D for the pure increased risk of suffering some physical loss or the pure increased risk of suffering some economic loss

(5)   If C successfully sues D for the loss of a chance under rule (1), C's damages are calculated by multiplying the magnitude of the chance lost by C's total loss. This is the case regardless of whether C's chance is greater or less than 50 per cent.

These rules have developed principally in relation to the tort of negligence. In this tort, the requirements of liability, apart from injury, include the existence of a duty of care. Duties to take care not to cause chances to be lost are limited. The existence of such duties normally requires that there exist a special relationship between the defendant and victim, where the defendant has assumed responsibility to the victim.[4]

Loss of chance and increase in risk where liability in damages for a tort has been established ('quantification')

The principle can be stated as follows:

> C may recover damages for lost chances and increased risks of avoiding pecuniary or non-pecuniary losses or of making pecuniary or non-pecuniary gains whenever (1) D has committed a tort against C on the balance of probability, (2) that tort has caused C some loss on the balance of probability, (3) there is uncertainty as to the extent of that loss, and (4) determining the extent of C's loss involves asking what would have happened in the future had the tort not occurred or what will happen in the future. Moreover, where this principle applies, the balance of probabilities rule is fully replaced and the claimant is *restricted* to probabilistic recovery: the loss of a 70% chance results only in 70% damages.

The development of the law on probabilistic liability

It is helpful to consider the development of the law in three stages. The origins of the probabilistic liability lie in contract – the first stage. The second stage, chronologically, involves the crystallisation of the rules (of 'quantification') concerning chance- and risk-based recovery once liability in damages has been established. The third stage concerns the shift of the rules in contract, and in quantification, to wrong-constituting causation in tort.

Contractual origins of loss of chance

The first case clearly to award damages for the lost chance of a favourable outcome was a contract case: *Chaplin* v. *Hicks*.[5] The claimant had

---

[4] See further pp. 302–305.

[5] [1911] 2 KB 786. The earlier cases of *Richardson* v. *Mellish* (1824) 2 Bing 229 and *Watson* v. *Ambergate Railway Co.* (1851) 15 Jur 448 are largely uninformative. G. Washington, 'Damages in Contract at Common Law' (1932), 105 observes that '[t]he problem of certainty ... was not adequately dealt with until 1911'. For a brief history of English law

entered a competition, organised by the defendant theatrical manager, for which the prize was engagement as an actress. In breach of contract, the defendant did not give the claimant adequate notice of her selection interview, such that the selection process of twelve winners from the fifty contestants occurred without her having been interviewed. Damages were awarded to reflect the chance that the claimant might have been one of the twelve winners despite it not being shown on the balance of probabilities that she would have been one.

Vaughan Williams and Fletcher Moulton LJ focussed upon the idea that the defendant's breach had deprived the claimant of some thing of value. The 'thing' in question was the right to be considered for a prize within a narrowed class of individuals. Even though this right could not be assigned 'a jury might well take the view that such a right, *if it could have been transferred*, would have been of such a value that every one would recognize that a good price could be obtained for it'.[6]

The next significant case awarding loss of chance damages was another contractual one involving the negligence of a solicitor: *Kitchen v. Royal Air Force*.[7] The defendant solicitors negligently failed to issue proceedings within the limitation period. The defendant argued that the court had to determine whether the claimant in fact had a good claim by trying the original claim within the present proceedings. This was unanimously rejected, though Lord Evershed MR observed that it was the 'most difficult' point in a difficult case.[8] His Lordship stated that the court should instead determine whether the claimant had 'some right of value, some chose in action of reality and substance'[9] which the court would do its best to value by reference to its probability of success.[10] Although *Chaplin* is not cited in the judgments, Lord Evershed's reference to a 'right of value' clearly recalls the analysis of Vaughan Williams LJ and Fletcher Moulton LJ therein.[11]

His Lordship also offered a *further* analysis of why a chance-based approach is taken. He began by noting that in some simple cases it would be 'plain' that the claimant would have succeeded or failed in the lost claim. In a *third category* of case, however, it is:

---

here, see H. McGregor, 'Loss of Chance: Where has it Come from and Where is it Going?', 2–3; Lord Neuberger, 'Loss of Chance and Causation', 206–8.

[6] *Chaplin*, 793.

[7] [1958] 1 WLR 563. The earlier cases: *Otter* v. *Church, Adams, Tatham & Co.* [1953] 1 WLR 156; *Hall* v. *Meyrick* [1957] 2 WLR 458 are not clearly reasoned.

[8] [1958] 1 WLR 563, 574.   [9] Ibid. 575.   [10] Ibid.; also 576 (Parker LJ).

[11] This understanding is still reflected in modern interpretations of the case: for example, H. Evans, 'Lost Litigation and Later Knowledge', 204.

... quite impossible to try the "action within the action"... It may be that for one reason or another the action for negligence is not brought till, say, twenty years after the event and in the process of time the material witnesses or many of them may have died or become quite out of reach for the purpose of being called to give evidence.[12]

On this analysis, the chance-based approach is merited where it is impossible to try the action within the action.[13]

The primary rationale, however, for the award in *Chaplin* and *Kitchen* seems to be the fact that the claimant had something of value, and that thing's value is to be assessed, as it would be in a market, by reference to the full range of uncertainty over its chances of bearing monetary fruit. It should be noted that neither *Chaplin* nor *Kitchen* seems directly to treat the *chance* in itself as the loss in respect of which damages are being awarded. The issue is whether the claimant had a *thing* of value and this is conceptualised in *Chaplin* as the claimant's primary contractual *right* to participate in the competition. The 'thing' is the claimant's primary right. In *Kitchen*, the thing is the claimant's right to sue the defendant. It is notable in this regard that the tendency to look only to the exchange value of a thing at the time wrongful conduct destroys it is a general feature of the treatment of wrongful interference with *property* in English law.[14]

Kitchen has been followed many times.[15] Moreover, it has been interpreted expansively in two significant ways. First, it could have been argued that the chance-based approach approved by the case only applied in Lord Evershed's 'third category' of case, namely, those cases where a trial within a trial is impossible due to the passage of time and the inability to locate witnesses. Further, it could have been said that *Kitchen* was a special case in that the defendants had substantially hindered the claimant's ability to prove whether its case would have

---

[12] *Kitchen*, 575.

[13] This is slightly puzzling since the appropriate question on the face of it is the hypothetical one of how the court would have adjudicated C's claim, not whether, were the action tried now, C would win. Note, however, the latter view is taken in German law: G. Mäsch, *Chance und Schaden*, 76ff. Cf. the view of the court in *Henderson* v. *Hagblom* 2003 SKCA 40 that a trial within a trial *did* occur in *Kitchen*: [194].

[14] Cf. H. Street, 'Supervening Events and the Quantum of Damages', 70–1; S. Douglas, *Liability for Wrongful Interference with Chattels*, 193ff.

[15] For example, *Mount* v. *Barker Austin (a firm)* [1998] PNLR 493. For an extensive overview of subsequent developments: *Jackson and Powell on Professional Liability* 6th edition with 4th supplement, 824–46.

been successful: the defendant had, among other things, failed to obtain an expert witness report as to the cause of the claimant's husband's death.[16] More generally, allowing the limitation period to run out is highly likely to have had a deleterious effect upon the quality of the evidential base of the original claim. That is one reason for having limitation periods.[17]

While a restriction to cases of 'impossibility' is taken in one line of Canadian authority, this limitation upon the scope of *Kitchen* is clearly not accepted in English law.[18] In *Hanif* v. *Middleweeks (a firm)*,[19] the claimant's action against their insurer, who had failed to pay out in respect of fire damage to the claimant's night club, was struck out for negligent want of prosecution by the defendant. A crucial issue in that original claim was whether the claimant had intentionally set fire to the club. The trial judge in the action against the solicitors had found that there was only a 25 per cent chance that the claimant would have succeeded in showing that he was not an arsonist. The defendant argued on appeal that this was a finding on the balance of probability that the claimant had committed arson. The submission was that the judge had substantially the same evidence before him as the judge would have had in the claim against the insurer. Consequently, the argument runs, a trial within the trial was not impossible, and so *Kitchen* did not apply. This was rejected. Mance LJ explicitly rejected the interpretation given to *Kitchen* by the Canadian case of *Fisher* v. *Knibbe*.[20] His Lordship further stated that the evidence considered by the trial judge in the claim against the solicitors was in fact quite different to that available in the original action: for example, there had been no forensic evidence presented as to the cause of the fire and no cross-examination of key witnesses; this undermined the reliability of the evidence.[21]

---

[16] Cf. the Californian case *Galanek*. See Note p.253 n 282.

[17] Cf. J. Boysen, 'Shifting the Burden of Proof on Causation In Legal Malpractice Actions', 329. The fact that the defendant contributed to the uncertainty over causation has been adduced in support of a loose approach to the *quantification* of the chance in English law: *Sharif* v. *Garrett* [2002] 1 WLR 3118, [27], [39] referring to *Armory* v. *Delamirie* (1722) 93 ER 664.

[18] *Fisher* v. *Knibbe* 1992 ABCA 121; see, subsequently, *Stealth Enterprises* v. *Hoffmann Dorchik* 2003 ABCA 58. The same approach is applied in British Columbia: *Nichols* v. *Warner, Scarborough, Herman & Harvey* 2009 BCCA 277, and New Brunswick: *Stewart* v. *Ryan* 2002 CanLII 20503. *Fisher* is not followed in Saskatchewan, where a general chance-based approach is applied in *Kitchen*-type situations: *Henderson* v. *Hagblom* 2003 SKCA 40. The Supreme Court has noted the existence of the lost chance approach in *Athey* v. *Leonati* [1996] 3 SCR 458 but has left open its availability.

[19] [2000] Lloyd's Rep PN 920.   [20] Ibid. [17].

[21] [18]–[21]. See too: *Dixon* v. *Clement Jones Solicitors* [2005] PNLR 6, [27] per Rix LJ: 'There is no requirement in such a loss of a chance case to fight out a trial within a trial'.

The second way in which *Kitchen* has been interpreted expansively relates to the rationale of the chance-based assessment. In *Chaplin* and in *Kitchen* there is some plausibility to the idea that the claimant's primary legal right to participate and the claimant's right to sue had financial value since it is reasonably possible to estimate a hypothetical exchange value for such rights even if the rights could not in law be exchanged. This could not be said in relation to the expansive[22] application of chance-based recovery in *Acton* v. *Pearce & Co.* This case involved the negligent failure to present important evidence at a criminal trial, with the alleged result that the claimant was convicted of fraud offences. His conviction was later quashed on appeal, when this evidence was presented.[23] The judge awarded damages amounting to 50 per cent of the losses suffered due to the conviction. This reflected the 50 per cent chance that the jury would not have convicted him had the important evidence been presented at trial. This is an expansion of *Kitchen* since it is not plausible to treat the claimant's primary contractual right that the defendant solicitor submit evidence to the court as a right with an economic value that would reflect the 50 per cent chance of being acquitted. To the extent the right had economic value, its value consisted in the provision of careful legal services. Indeed, the justification offered for the chance-approach in *Acton* places no emphasis upon the idea of a valuable right at all. Rather, assessing the chances of avoiding a conviction 'enables the court to avoid a rehearing of the criminal trial'.[24]

Interestingly, *Acton* was not followed in *Folland* v. *Reardon*, a decision of the Ontario Court of Appeal, which involved similar facts. The court noted that the chance of acquittal had no 'settlement value' for the claimant, unlike the civil litigant. This is consonant with the valuable right idea. Further, echoing the approach of some Canadian courts in the context of negligent pursuit of civil litigation, the court considered that a chance-based approach was only appropriate where 'because of the complexity of the variables involved or the unavailability of crucial

---

[22] The chose in action idea has also been subject to *restriction* by other principles. Cf. *Whitehead* v. *Searle* [2009] 1 WLR 549; *Dudarec* v. *Andrews* [2006] 1 WLR 3002.

[23] [1997] 3 All ER 909. Earlier cases had suggested a balance of probability approach to such questions: *Rondel* v. *Worsley* [1967] 3 All ER 993, 1000 (Lord Reid), 1012 (Lord Morris).

[24] *Acton*, 931.

evidence, it will be impossible to realistically assess what would have happened but for the defendant's misconduct'.[25] This was not so on the facts. Finally, the court rejected the proposition that the lost chance approach allows one to avoid a re-hearing of the criminal trial: assessing the probability that the conviction would have been quashed also involves, to some extent, imagining the notional trial.[26]

In these contract cases, then, the primary line of reasoning is that the claimant has lost a thing of value. In *Chaplin* and *Kitchen*, this is conceptualised as a legal right. Alongside this primary line of reasoning are two others: that the defendant has created a situation where there is unreliable evidence to assess what would have happened had the defendant not been negligent (*Kitchen*) and that there are institutional reasons for not assessing what would have happened had the defendant not been negligent (*Acton*).

Recovery in respect of lost chances and increased risk as a matter of quantification of the extent of loss suffered

The law recognises that in assessing the *extent* of the defendant's liability for a tort (or breach of contract) which has been proven to have caused loss it is possible to take into account the chance that the claimant would have obtained a benefit or avoided a detriment, and the risk of future deterioration of an existing injury, in quantifying the extent of that loss. A classic formulation[27] is given by Lord Diplock in *Mallett* v. *McMonagle*:

But in assessing damages which depend upon its view as to what will happen in the future or would have happened in the future if something had not happened in the past, the court must make an estimate as to what are the chances that a particular thing will or would have happened and reflect those chances, whether they are more or less than even, in the amount of damages which it awards.[28]

---

[25] *Folland* v. *Reardon* (2005) 249 DLR (4th) 167. Cf. K. Barker, 'Unfamiliar Waters: Negligent Advocates, Egregious Errors and Lost Chances of Acquittal'.

[26] *Folland*, at [86]. The disvalue of re-hearing the case was also questioned.

[27] Under the heading, 'The quantification argument', Lord Hoffmann referred firstly to this passage from *Mallett* in his discussion in *Gregg* v. *Scott* [2005] 2 AC 176 at [67].
H. McGregor, *McGregor on Damages*, 19th edition, [10–045] also considers this to express a principle relating to the 'quantification of loss'.

[28] [1970] AC 166, 176. Cf. *Malec* v. *JC Hutton Pty* [1990] HCA 20, at [7]: 'But questions as to the future or hypothetical effect of physical injury or degeneration are not commonly susceptible of scientific demonstration or proof. If the law is to take account of future or hypothetical events in assessing damages, it can only do so in terms of the degree of probability of those events occurring'.

We can call this the 'quantification principle'. It follows from the quantification principle that the chance that the claimant would have advanced to a more lucrative career or gained some other financial benefit in the future may be taken into account in assessing damages.[29] Similarly, the risk that the victim of a tort may suffer some physical injury in the future as a result of the tort may also be taken into account – for example a risk of arthritis materialising in an injured arm or leg.[30] Although Lord Diplock spoke only of future and future-hypothetical propositions, the principle is also sometimes taken to apply to *past* hypothetical questions. Thus, following discussion of *Mallett*, Lord Hoffmann stated in *Gregg v. Scott* that: '[t]his principle applies when the extent of the loss depends upon what will happen after the trial or upon what might hypothetically have happened (*either before or after the trial*) if the claimant had not been injured'.[31]

Lord Hoffmann further refined the quantification principle in *Gregg*. The facts in *Gregg* were that D negligently failed to diagnose C's tumour with the alleged result that his tumour enlarged. C sought to convince the court that the physical enlargement had caused him to lose a 17 per cent chance of being cured from cancer and that this lost chance could be recovered under the quantification principle because the spread of the tumour constituted a tort, which had caused the increased risk of not being cured from cancer. C argued that damages were recoverable in respect of this risk in the same way as the increased risk of arthritis was recoverable as a tort that had caused a physical injury which increased the risk of arthritis. The majority of the House of Lords rejected this analysis; Lord Hoffmann and Lady Hale did so as a matter of law, whereas Lord Phillips rejected the factual claim that the increased risk was caused by the enlargement of the tumour.

In Lord Hoffmann's view, if the tort, established on the balance of probability, caused an x per cent increased risk of physical injury,

---

[29] Lost chances of financial gain: *Mulvaine v. Joseph* (1968) 112 Sol. Jo. 927; *Doyle v. Wallace* [1998] PIQR Q146; *Langford v. Hebran* [2001] PIQR Q13; *Collett v. Smith* [2009] EWCA Civ 583; *XYZ v. Portsmouth Hospital NHS Trust* [2011] EWHC 243. Increased risks of financial loss: *Moeliker v. A Reyrolle & Co. Ltd* [1977] 1 WLR 132 (risk of losing employment after personal injury); *Morgan v. UPS Ltd* [2008] EWCA Civ 375.

[30] *Hawkins v. New Mendip Engineering* [1966] 1 WLR 1341 (50 per cent risk of epilepsy); *Cook v. JL Kier & Co.* [1970] 1 WLR 774; *Malec v. JC Hutton Pty Ltd* (1990) 169 CLR 638, 642–3; *Kovats et al v. Ogilvy et al* [1971] 1 WWR 561 (BCCA); *Janiak v. Ippolito* [1985] 1 SCR 146. Cf. generally: K. Cooper, 'Assessing Possibilities in Damages Awards: the Loss of a Chance or the Chance of a Loss'.

[31] *Gregg*, [67] (emphasis added). Cf. *Malec*, at the pages cited in Note 30 and *Doyle*, above Note 29.

damages in respect of that increased risk could only be recovered if, were the risk to materialise, the physical injury would be 'attributable' to the wrong on the balance of probability. Thus, where C is the victim of a tort which increases C's risk of suffering epilepsy by 10 per cent, but C was already subject to a 60 per cent chance of contracting the illness, C cannot recover for the increased risk of 10 per cent. The reason for this is that:

> The rule against recovery of uncertain damages is directed against uncertainty as to cause rather than as to extent or measure.[32]

Baroness Hale seemed to agree with this analysis.[33] Lord Phillips did not express a considered view on this question.

At first sight, Lord Hoffmann's restriction seems inconsistent with previous authority. For example, in *Doyle* v. *Wallace*, the claimant recovered in respect of the 50 per cent chance that she may have qualified as a drama teacher had she not been caused brain damage by the defendant in a car accident.[34] There was no need to show that she would, on the balance of probability, have become a drama teacher. This could be viewed as uncertainty pertaining either to the extent of the claimant's losses (some loss of earnings was clearly shown on the balance of probability) *or* uncertainty over whether the tort caused the losses associated with not becoming a drama teacher (given her brain damage, it was certain that she would not become a drama teacher).

Lord Hoffmann approved of *Doyle* in *Gregg*, so the question would seem to be one of 'extent'. Yet if it was only 50 per cent probable that the claimant would have become a drama teacher, and thus the loss attributable to 'not becoming a drama teacher' was not attributable to the tort on the balance of probability, why does *Doyle* not fall within his restriction? The answer might be that the tort had been proven in *Doyle* to have made it certain that the claimant would not become a drama teacher. So causation of 'not becoming a drama teacher' was shown on the balance of probability. The issue was then one of the *extent* of loss caused by the fact that the claimant would not become a drama teacher. In more general terms, if the claimant is to recover in respect of the loss of less than a 50 per cent chance of a benefit, it must be shown on the

---

[32] *Gregg* [69], quoting from *Kranz* v. *McCutcheon* (1920) 18 Ontario WN 395 (Master J). This quotation was also approved in *Kenyon* v. *Bell* (1953) SC 125.

[33] *Gregg* [200].

[34] [1998] PIQR Q146 CA. H. McGregor, *McGregor on Damages*, 19th edition [10–081] views *Doyle* as a quantification case.

balance of probability that the tort foreclosed the possibility of this benefit being realised.

It is perhaps safest to conclude that the quantification principle is unlikely to apply *simply* because a tort has been established on the balance of probability. The question likely also needs to be framed as one relating to the *extent* of established loss and, in respect of risks of injury occurring in the future, it needs to be shown that, if the risk materialised, the injury would be attributable to the tort on the balance of probability.

Loss of a chance and increase of risk as establishing liability *in tort*

Lost chances of avoiding an economic loss or of making an economic gain

That the destruction of a chance of avoiding an *economic* loss could *establish* liability in tort was first clearly recognised in *Allied Maples* v. *Simmons & Simmons*.[35] In that case, the defendant solicitors negligently failed to advise their client, the claimant, as to the extent of the claimant's potential liabilities under a contract into which it was entering. Having incurred these liabilities, the claimant sued the defendant. The claimant argued that the defendant was liable for negligently depriving it of the chance of avoiding these liabilities by negotiating a better deal. The defendant argued that the only thing the claimant could sue for was the loss it had suffered as a result of being held liable under the contract, and to do that it would have to show that had the claimant been properly advised, it was more probable than not that the claimant would have been allowed to negotiate a better deal and escape those liabilities. The court held that the claimant had to demonstrate on the balance of probability that it would have attempted to renegotiate the terms of the contract for better protection but that it was only necessary to show 'as a matter of causation that [the claimant had] a real or substantial chance as opposed to a speculative one'[36] that the third party would have acceded to the more protective term.[37]

---

[35] [1995] 1 WLR 1602. See, generally, on *Allied*: M, Lunney, 'Chances of Recovery in Tort'; A. Burrows, 'Uncertainty about Uncertainty: Damages for Loss of a Chance', 36–7.

[36] *Allied Maples*, 1614.

[37] For arguments against distinguishing third parties' past hypothetical conduct: J. Stapleton, 'Cause-in-Fact and the Scope of Liability for Consequences', 407–11. Cf. H. McGregor, *McGregor on Damages*, 19th edition [10–060], for the problematic argument that the claimant need only show as part of its burden of proof facts relating to its own conduct. This is false: the claimant needs to show causation, and that can require showing third party conduct.

Stuart-Smith LJ provided a novel analysis of the availability of chance-based recovery:

(i) If the wrongful conduct is a *misfeasance*, then whether it caused the claimant's damage is a question of *past fact* whose truth is assessed on the balance of probability.

(ii) If the wrongful conduct is *omissive*, then (in contrast to the first category) a *hypothetical* question is a necessary part of the causal inquiry.

    (a) Hypothetical inquiries as to how the *claimant* would have behaved are assessed on the balance of probability.

    (b) Hypothetical inquiries as to how a *third party* would have behaved are assessed on a chance basis. Consequently, whether, in *Allied*, the third party would have acceded to the claimant's requests for a different contractual term could be assessed on a chance basis.

(iii) *Future* questions and *future hypothetical* questions are assessed on a chance basis where the issue is the quantification of the extent of loss.

Although there clearly was a contract between the parties in *Allied*, this analysis makes no explicit distinctions between claims in contract and tort. That none was intended is supported by the approving citation of *Spring* v. *Guardian Assurance Plc*,[38] where Lord Lowry stated *obiter* that if an employer negligently prepared a reference for a former employee, the latter only had to show that a non-negligent reference would have given him a 'reasonable chance of employment ... He does not have to prove that, but for the negligent reference [the firm to whom he had applied] would have employed him'.[39] This dictum envisages a successful chance-based claim where a *former* employer negligently prepares a reference: any claim would have to be in tort.

Alongside the absence of a distinction between contract and tort, a further result of Stuart-Smith LJ's analysis is a clear differentiation between the hypothetical conduct of third parties and hypothetical conduct of the claimant. It is now a necessary condition of establishing liability in tort in respect of a loss of chance that the chance relate to how a third party would have behaved.[40]

---

[38] [1995] 2 AC 296.   [39] Ibid. 375–6.

[40] Citing *Allied Maples*, courts in Australia, Canada, and New Zealand have come to accept this position. New Zealand: *MacLean* v. *Annan & Co.* HC Tauranga [2011] NZHC 1733 at [86]; *McLeish* v. *Rock Hill Ltd* [2010] NZHC 1938; *Benton* v. *Miller & Poulgrain (a firm)* [2005] 1 NZLR 66 at [48]–[49]. Most recent Australian authorities approve or apply the *Allied* distinction: *NIGAM* v. *HARM (no.2)* [2011] WASCA 221, at [203]; *Hammond Worthington* v. *Da Silva* [2006] WASCA 180, at [118]; *Ng* v. *Chong* [2005] NSWSC 270, at [51]; *Smith* v. *Moloney* [2005] SASC 305; *Sellars* v. *Adelaide Petroleum NL* (1994) 179 CLR 332, 353. H. Luntz, 'Loss of a Chance in Medical Negligence' also suggests that *Allied* represents the law: ibid. text at fns 153–4.

What reasons were given for this distinction? The distinction seems to be offered by Stuart-Smith LJ primarily as a way of reconciling previous authorities. On the one hand, some cases (to which his Lordship refers) had assessed the question of how the claimant would have behaved on the balance of probabilities. Thus, in *McWilliams* v. *Sir William Arrol & Co*, the causal issue of whether the defendant employer's negligent failure to provide a safety harness had been a cause of its employee's injury depended upon whether the claimant would have worn the harness. The House of Lords held that the claimant had to prove that the employee would have worn the harness.[41] On the other hand, there were cases such as *Chaplin* v. *Hicks* and *Kitchen*, which had assessed whether the claimant would have won the competition or the litigation by reference to the chances of success.[42] The difference between these cases seized upon by Stuart-Smith LJ was that *McWilliams* concerned how the claimant would have decided, whereas *Chaplin* and *Kitchen* concerned how a third party (the competition officials, the court) would have decided. His Lordship also relied, in this regard, upon the House of Lords decision in *Davies* v. *Taylor*.[42(a)] In that case, the claimant widow had separated from her husband prior to his being tortiously killed. The defendant submitted that it had to be shown on the balance of probability that she would have reconciled with him and thereby received financial benefit. This was rejected: the issue was whether there was a substantial *chance* that they would have been reconciled. Once more, this case could be said to concern how a third party would have behaved.

This reasoning is problematic. Neither strand of authority laid any emphasis upon particular problems of hypotheticals relating to *third parties*. The focus was on the loss of a thing of value in *Chaplin* and *Kitchen*,

However, in *Bak* v. *Glenleigh Homes Pty* [2006] NSWCA 10, a contract case, the majority applied a loss of chance approach to whether the claimant would have noticed a termite infestation of his property and avoided consequent loss. Hodgson JA is equivocal as to whether this is a rule particular to contract. That it is suggested by the fact that the same judge in *Rufo* v. *Hosking* [2004] NSWCA 391 accepted the *Allied* distinction in the tort context, at [9]. Canada: *Ristimaki* v. *Cooper* 2004 CanLII 16074, at [154].

[41] *McWilliams* v. *Sir William Arrol & Co* [1962] 1 WLR 295. See also: *Sykes* v. *Midland Bank Executor and Trustee Co. Ltd* [1971] QB 113; *Norwest Refrigeration Services Pty. Ltd.* v. *Bain Dawes (W.A.) Pty. Ltd.* [1984] HCA 59; *Hall* v. *Foony* (1995) 65 SASR 281, 301.

[42] Note, however, that *Chaplin* is not a case where the claimant's loss depended upon the hypothetical decision of a third party – it depended, at least in part, upon how the defendant would have decided. But note Farwell LJ in *Chaplin*, at 799. Cf. V. Black, 'Decision Causation', 320.

[42(a)] *Davies* v. *Taylor* [1974] AC 207.

while Lord Reid's reasoning in *Davies* pointed to the impossibility of proving propositions about the future. According to Lord Reid:

> You can prove that a past event happened, but you cannot prove that a future event will happen and I do not think that the law is so foolish as to suppose that you can. All that you can do is to evaluate the chance.[43]

In addition, some earlier first instance cases had seemed to assume that the question of how the claimant would have behaved could be assessed on a chance basis, citing *Chaplin* as authority for this.[44] Equally, it could be said that *McWilliams* v. *Arrol* simply did not address the issue of loss of chance since the claim was in respect of the physical injury – not the loss of chance of avoiding a physical injury. The issue is considered as a matter of principle later in this section.

Part of the explanation for Stuart-Smith LJ's grouping is perhaps that Lord Reid's dicta in *Davies* referred broadly to the inherent impossibility in proving certain types of proposition.[45] It could have been thought that proof of past hypotheticals relating to the conduct of third parties displayed a similar type of inherent difficulty of proof and therefore a chance-based approach was to be applied to them, too.[46]

As a result of *Allied*, then, the law arrived at the position that the negligent destruction of a chance of avoiding an economic loss could establish liability in tort – so long as the question of whether the claimant would have avoided an economic loss depends upon how a third party would have behaved.

Lost chances of avoiding physical injury

What of lost chances of avoiding a physical injury – be it personal injury or property damage? Suppose that D, a shop owner, negligently fails to place a warning beside a broken step in D's shop. C, a blind child, trips on the step and breaks an arm. C argues that he or she should recover for the chance that his parent, T, would have stopped him or her

---

[43] *Davies* v. *Taylor* [1974] AC 207, 213.
[44] *Otter* v. *Church, Adams, Tatham & Co.* [1953] 1 WLR 156, 164. *Otter* concerned a claim brought by the estate of the victim of a breach of contract, alleging that the victim, if properly advised by his solicitor, would have completed a disentailing will and that the estate would have received property. The estate seems to have received damages for the (greater than 50 per cent) chance that this would have been the case. See also *Hall* v. *Meyrick* [1957] 2 WLR 458.
[45] Cf. J. Stapleton, 'Cause in Fact and the Scope of Liability for Consequences, 406–10' for other explanations.
[46] A similar suggestion is made by Mance LJ in the Court of Appeal in *Gregg* v. *Scott* [2002] EWCA 1471 [71].

from mounting the step had a warning been provided. The basic position is that lost chances of avoiding a physical injury cannot establish liability in tort unless *Barker* v. *Corus (UK) Ltd* applies. This would seem to require at least that (1) it is impossible, due to the limits of scientific knowledge, to prove causation; (2) the single agent requirement is met; (3) the defendant is not providing medical care. Consequently, C's claim would fail.

The general position is illustrated by *Vaile* v. *Havering London Borough Council*.[47] C, who taught at a school for children with learning difficulties, was stabbed in class by an autistic pupil with a pencil. D, C's employer, negligently failed to provide C with appropriate training for teaching autistic children. The Court of Appeal determined on the balance of probability that C's injury would not have occurred without D's negligence. There was no suggestion that C's claim could have been assessed on a loss of chance basis – even though the causal question depended upon how a third party (the autistic child) would have behaved. The *Allied Maples* rule that a chance-based approach is taken to assessing how a third party would have behaved does not seem to apply.

That lost chances of avoiding a physical injury cannot establish liability in tort is also supported by a complex line of authority involving medical negligence claims. The starting point is *Hotson* v. *East Berkshire Area Health Authority*.[48] The claimant child fell from a tree. When treated at hospital, his doctor negligently failed to diagnose the nature of his injury. Some days later he was appropriately treated but nonetheless suffered avascular necrosis in his hip, leading to a crippling injury. He sought to recover in respect of the 25 per cent chance that he would have avoided the hip injury had the defendant doctor timeously diagnosed his condition. His claim succeeded at first instance and in the Court of Appeal but was unanimously rejected by the House of Lords.[49]

---

[47] *Vaile* v. *Havering London Borough Council* [2011] EWCA Civ 246, [2011] ELR 274. Cf. the *obiter dicta* at first instance suggesting otherwise in *J Sainsbury* v. *Broadway Malyan* [1999] PNLR 286, especially at [325]–[328].

[48] *Hotson* v. *East Berkshire Area Health Authority* [1988] UKHL 1, [1987] AC 750 [*Hotson*].

[49] *Hotson* has been followed in Australia and Canada. The Australian position is largely settled by *Tabet* v. *Gett* [2010] HCA 12. See H. Luntz, 'Loss of a Chance in Medical Negligence'. For the earlier cases: L. Khoury, *Uncertain Causation*, 104–8. For the Canadian common law position, rejecting CL in physical injury cases: *Cottrelle* v. *Gerrard* (2003) 233 DLR (4th) 45 at [25], [36] (citing *Hotson*); *O'Grady* v. *Stokes* (2005) ABQB 247 (Alberta) [200].

At first instance, Simon Brown J held the doctor liable in respect of that 25 per cent chance.[50] The judge was primarily convinced by an analogy with the *Kitchen* line of cases. If a client goes to his lawyer with a legal claim with a 25 per cent chance of success and the lawyer negligently destroys that claim, the client succeeds to recover 25 per cent of the value of the claim if it were successful. The doctor–patient relationship could not, in his view, be rationally distinguished. If the distinction were that *Kitchen* was a contractual claim, then the consequence would be that private patients could recover for loss of chance but not those treated by the National Health Service.[51] This analogy provided strong reason to say that the case was one of 'quantification' rather than causation.[52]

This analysis is problematic. Whether a question is one of quantification depends upon whether liability was established on the balance of probability: that is true of *Kitchen* but not of *Hotson*.[53] If this results in undesirable consequences, then, if these ought to be avoided, the appropriate response is to say that the quantification principle is not engaged where liability is not established on the balance of probability, but *nonetheless* chance-based recovery ought to be granted. In other words, it is confusing to use the label 'quantification' to denote all situations in which the court ought to allow chance-based recovery. Rather one should say that *Kitchen* was a case explicable by the quantification principle (liability was established), but that the principle does not exhaust the situations in which chance-based recovery should apply.

In the Court of Appeal, Sir John Donaldson MR and Dillon LJ avoided manipulation of the quantification principle by clearly accepting that the injury forming the gist of Hotson's action was the 25 per cent chance of avoiding the necrosis, causation of such injury having to be proved on the balance of probabilities.[54] The Court therefore placed less emphasis on the arguments from quantification and openly considered whether the 'categories of loss should be closed' to loss of chance as a distinct injury. A foothold in answering this question was given by an analogy with the contract cases allowing recovery for loss of a chance.[55] But the main argument of both Sir John Donaldson MR and Dillon LJ was that

---

[50] Ibid., 1044.   [51] Ibid., 1044.   [52] Ibid.

[53] It could have been argued that the issue was one of quantification because the claimant had actually established a NESS causal contribution: R. Wright, 'Liability for Possible Wrongs: Causation, Statistical Probability and the Burden of Proof', 1321ff.

[54] [1987] AC 750, 760–1 (Donaldson MR); 764 (Dillon LJ).

[55] Ibid 760; 763 (citing *Chaplin* v. *Hicks*).

it was contrary to 'common sense' that those whose less than 50 per cent chance of avoiding a better medical outcome is destroyed by negligence could be without remedy.[56]

The House of Lords allowed the defendant's appeal. In essence their Lordships considered that the question of what caused the claimant's injury was a question of historical fact to be determined on the balance of probabilities: either the claimant had sufficient blood vessels to avoid the injury or he did not. The trial judge's finding that there was a 75 per cent chance that the necrosis would have occurred regardless of the negligence amounted to the proposition that the cause of the necrosis was the fall, since past facts are treated as certain once shown to have greater than 50 per cent probability.[57] Thus, Lord Ackner thought that recovery for a lost chance was excluded 'where there has been a positive finding that before the duty arose the damage complained of has already been sustained or become inevitable'.[58] In matters of whether an event occurred or did not occur, or whether a state of affairs obtained or did not obtain, a finding is to be made on the balance of probability.

The principal distinction made between situations where a loss of chance approach is applicable and those where it is not, then, is that such an approach may be applied to *hypothetical* or *future* questions, not to questions of whether a certain state of affairs obtained or did not. So Lord Ackner allowed the possibility of assessing the claimant's loss in probabilistic terms in a future-question case where the risked injury had not materialised, giving the example of the risk of epilepsy consequent upon a tortiously caused head trauma.[59]

The difficulty with this analysis is that the question in *Hotson* can readily be framed as a hypothetical: would the claimant have avoided the necrosis had the defendant behaved non-negligently? Perhaps the pragmatic response to this is that a causal question will be treated as one of *past fact* rather than a hypothetical question unless it depends upon the hypothetical conduct of a third party.[60] However, as we have seen, even where the question of whether the defendant has been a cause

---

[56] Ibid 759–60; 764. Criticised by G. Mäsch, *Chance und Schaden*, 236.
[57] [1987] 1 AC 750, 782 (Lord Bridge); 784 (Lord Mackay); 791 (Lord Ackner).
[58] Ibid., 792.   [59] Ibid., 794.
[60] Of course, it is right to point out that the CL issue was not formally decided in *Hotson* (e.g. T. Hill, 'A Lost Chance for Compensation', 519), but the reasoning makes it difficult to imagine cases in the medical negligence context where a CL approach could be applied (unless the physical injury depended upon the hypothetical conduct of a third party – but see Note 61). Cf. J. Stapleton, 'The Gist of Negligence', 393–4.

of the claimant's physical injury depends upon the hypothetical conduct of a third party, the lost chance of avoiding the physical injury is still irrecoverable.[61]

That C cannot sue for the loss of a chance of a physical injury was subsequently confirmed by *Gregg* v. *Scott*.[62] As we have seen, in *Gregg*, Dr Scott negligently failed to diagnose Mr Gregg's tumour with the alleged result that the tumour's enlargement led to the loss of a 17 per cent chance of being cured from cancer, though he had not in fact suffered the loss of a cure (defined in terms of 10 years of remission). By a majority of three to two, the House of Lords held that Gregg could not recover for what their Lordships termed a loss of a chance.[63]

The majority comprised Lord Hoffmann, Lord Phillips and Baroness Hale. Lord Hoffmann said: 'Everything is determined by causality. What we lack is knowledge and the law deals with lack of knowledge by the concept of the burden of proof.'[64] He qualified this statement in cases where whether the claimant would have suffered his or her loss requires determination of how a human being would have decided. In those contexts, it is possible to speak of genuine chance, but not so in cases involving purely physical processes because 'chance' simply does not exist in this context.[65]

Baroness Hale rejected Gregg's claim principally because she thought that allowing claimants to recover for less than even chances of avoiding a physical injury required defendants only to be liable to the extent of the chance lost in cases where the destroyed chance was greater than even; as a result, claimants who would currently be able to prove causation of their traditional physical injury on the

---

[61] See *Vaile*, Note 47. See also *Wright* v. *Cambridge Medical Group* [2011] EWCA Civ 669, [2011] Med LR 496. In *Wright*, D, a doctor, argued that had he conformed to his duty of care and referred C to hospital earlier, C would have been treated negligently by X hospital with the result that C's physical injury would have occurred in any event. This plea was rejected (correctly) as a matter of law because D was seeking to rely upon the hypothetical wrongdoing of X However, even if D had argued that X would have treated C non-negligently and that C's injury would have occurred anyway on the balance of probability, it would not have been open to C to argue that a lost chance approach should be applied because X's hypothetical actions were at stake. See ibid., [84].

[62] [2005] 2 AC 176; see A. Beever, 'Gregg v Scott and Loss of a Chance'; E. Peel, 'Loss of a Chance in Medical Negligence'; J. Stapleton, 'Loss of the Chance of Cure from Cancer'; G. Mäsch, 'Gregg v Scott: much ado about Nothing?'. In the earlier *Tahir* v. *Haringey HA* [1998] Lloyds Rep Med 105, Otton LJ interpreted *Hotson* as ruling out loss of chance claims.

[63] In our terms, it was a case of increase in risk.   [64] *Gregg*, [79].   [65] *Gregg*, [83].

balance of probability would be worse off.[66] Lord Phillips decided the case on a point of fact.

Although, then, there is no overall majority in *Gregg* against the recovery of the loss of a chance of physical injury, anyone seeking to generate such liability would need to ignore the core reasoning of both Lord Hoffmann and Baroness Hale.[67] Moreover, Lord Hoffmann's reasoning applies equally to cases where the injury which there was a lost chance of avoiding has materialised and those where it has not.[68] If 'everything is determined by causality' (except human action) then it does not matter whether the injury has materialised or not – it is determined whether this is so.

The decision in *Barker v. Corus (UK) Plc* would seem to stand in the way of the proposition that lost chances of physical injury cannot establish liability in tort.[69]

In *Barker*, it will be remembered, the claimant contracted mesothelioma caused by asbestos exposure. The House of Lords held that the claimant could rely upon the rule in *Fairchild* to establish liability despite the impossibility of proving that the defendant employer's negligence had been a cause of the injury. By a majority, it held that this liability should be in proportion to the defendant's contribution to the overall risk of mesothelioma. As we saw in Chapter 5, Lord Hoffmann seemed to hold that the injury in respect of which the defendant was being held liable was the risk to which the defendant had exposed the claimant. *Barker* might then be seen as an example of a physical process case where the claimant recovered for an increase in risk, which could be thought to entail liability for the loss of a chance.[70]

But, as we also saw in Chapter 5, it is now clear that the injury for which the defendant was liable in *Barker* was not the risk of mesothelioma.[71] Although liability at common law is in proportion to the risk, the reason for this is not that the damage is the risk, but that it is unfair to hold the defendant liable in full without causation of the mesothelioma being proven against it at least on the balance of probability.

---

[66] Ibid., [225].

[67] Cf. the different view of Jones in M. Jones and A. Dugdale (eds), *Clerk and Lindsell on Torts*, 21th edition (London, Sweet & Maxwell, 2010) [2–92].

[68] This distinction was favoured by Lord Nicholls: *Gregg*, [35]–[42].

[69] *Barker v. Corus (UK) Plc* [2006] UKHL 20, [2006] 2 AC 572 [*Barker*].

[70] As stated by Lord Walker in *Barker* itself: [2006] 2 AC 572 at [114]. See also Lord Mackay's remark in *Hotson* at 786: 'Material increase of the risk of contraction of dermatitis is equivalent to material decrease in the chance of escaping dermatitis'.

[71] See Chapter 5, 236–7.

Damages are for the chance of causation, not causation of a lost chance. The rule is thus one of PC species, not CL or IR.

Increased risk of economic loss

The basic position is that being exposed to the pure increased risk of suffering an economic loss cannot serve as a loss which establishes liability in tort. This is illustrated by *Law Society v. Sephton & Co. (a firm)*.[72] The Law Society had made compensation payments to persons who had suffered loss as a result of a fraud conducted by Payne, a solicitor. The Society sued the defendant firm of accountants on the basis that the Society had refrained from investigating the fraudulent solicitor as a result of the accountants' negligently certifying the solicitor's accounts as satisfactory. The defendant argued that the claim was barred as 'damage' had occurred more than six years before when the Society was exposed to the risk of having to make a compensation payment in respect of the solicitor's fraud. The House of Lords rejected this argument: a 'contingent liability is not as such damage until the contingency occurs... the possibility of an obligation to pay money in the future is not in itself damage'.[73]

This is subject to three provisos. First, if the claimant can show that the defendant's wrongfully increasing the risk of economic loss has diminished the value of an existing asset of the claimant's, then *that* may constitute an actionable injury. This is illustrated by *Forster v. Outred & Co.*[74] The claimant, Mrs Forster, executed a mortgage deed in February 1973 charging her farm as security for a loan being made to her son for the purchase of a hotel. The hotel was a failure and in January 1975 the mortgagee demanded payment of about £70,000, which she paid in August 1975. In March 1980 she issued a writ against the solicitors who had advised her in the mortgage transaction, alleging that they had negligently failed to explain its import. The issue was whether the action against the solicitors was barred as it was outside the limitation period of six years, the period running from the date upon which the cause of action accrued.[75] Her contractual claim arose because the cause of action in contract accrues upon the date of breach – that is, in 1973. Whether her concurrent claim in tort was also out of time depended

---

[72] *Law Society v. Sephton & Co (a firm)* [2006] UKHL 22, [2006] 2 AC 543 [*Sephton*].
[73] Ibid., [30]–[31] (Lord Hoffmann). For a helpful discussion of *Sephton*, see J. O'Sullivan, 'The Meaning of Damage in Pure Financial Loss Cases – Contract and Tort Collide'.
[74] *Forster v. Outred & Co.* [1982] 1 WLR 86.
[75] Limitation Act 1980, section 2 (contract), section 5 (tort).

upon whether she had suffered injury when she executed the deed or only later when the demand to pay was made. The Court of Appeal held the former and thus the claim was unsuccessful. In *Sephton*, the House of Lords interpreted *Forster* as involving the crucial feature that the execution of the mortgage had immediately depressed the value of the claimant's farm.[76]

Second, if the claimant can demonstrate that, as a result of the defendant's breach of an undertaking, it is exposed to an increased risk of economic loss and this is because it received a legal right or set of legal rights less economically valuable than the legal right that it would have received had the defendant not breached, this will constitute an actionable injury in tort. Here the loss is constituted by the fact that the claimant has received a less valuable right than that bargained for – not by the increase in risk itself. For example, in *DW Moore & Co.* v. *Ferrier*,[77] the claimant company was held to have suffered loss immediately upon entering into an employment contract with its director, which, as a result of negligent drafting, contained an ineffective restrictive covenant against competition in the event that the employee left the company. At this point, the company was exposed to the risk that the director would leave and compete with their business. According to Bingham LJ, 'instead of receiving a potentially valuable chose in action they received one that was valueless'.[78]

Third, and most expansively, if the defendant undertook to provide the claimant with protection from a risk of economic loss, the claimant relies upon the undertaking and the defendant negligently fails to provide that protection, it seems that the claimant will have suffered injury in this situation. *Shore* v. *Sedgwick Financial Services Ltd* is an example.[79] On the defendant financial advisor's advice, his client, the claimant, shifted accrued benefits under a pension scheme to another pension scheme in 1997. By 1999, annuity rates had gone down, and by May 2000, it was clear that the claimant would receive less income from the fund than if he had not shifted to the other scheme. The claimant brought proceedings in 2005, arguing that he did not suffer any injury until October

---

[76] See *Sephton*, [14]–[18] (Lord Hoffmann); [44]–[45] (Lord Walker). The reasoning in *Forster* itself seems broader. In *Forster* Stephenson LJ accepted, at 93, the following definition of 'actual damage' suggested by counsel: 'any detriment, liability or loss capable of assessment in money terms and it includes liabilities which may arise on a contingency, particularly a contingency over which the plaintiff has no control; things like loss of earning capacity, loss of a chance or bargain'.

[77] [1988] 1 WLR 267.   [78] Ibid,, 279.

[79] [2008] EWCA Civ 863; [2009] Bus LR 42. See also *Axa Insurance* v. *Akther & Darby & others* [2010] PNLR 10, [73].

2000, when he turned sixty – so that the claim would not be barred for limitation. The Court of Appeal disagreed, holding that the claimant suffered injury upon shifting into the other scheme. According to Dyson LJ, this was because:

[The second scheme] was inferior because Mr Shore wanted a secure scheme: he did not want to take risks. In other words, from Mr Shore's point of view, it was less advantageous and caused him detriment. If he had wanted a more insecure income than that provided by the Avesta scheme [the first scheme], then he would have got what he wanted and would have suffered no detriment. In the event, however, he made a risky investment with an uncertain income stream instead of a safe investment with a fixed and certain income stream which is what he wanted.[80]

The 'injury' seems to consist here of 'not receiving what one bargained for even if one received something of equal financial value to what one bargained for'. This reasoning sits in tension with the law on lost chances of avoiding physical injury. Since the cause of action in *Shore* is in tort, it is not clear what the relevance of the fact that the claimant *bargained* for the security from risk could be. It is a short step from saying that 'not receiving what one bargained for' is a loss to 'not receiving what someone undertook to provide' is a loss. If a doctor undertakes not negligently to deprive one of a chance of avoiding a physical injury, then the rejection of liability in *Hotson* is inconsistent with the reasoning in cases like *Shore*.

Increased risk of physical injury

That the exposure to increased risk of physical injury could not itself establish liability in tort was affirmed by their Lordships in *Grieves* v. *FT Everard*.[81] The claimants had been exposed by their employers, in breach of duty, to asbestos dust, which had resulted in the development of pleural plaques: fibrous thickening of the pleural membrane surrounding the lungs. These plaques do not cause any symptoms or any asbestos-related disease but are indicators of the presence of asbestos fibres in the lungs and pleura, which might independently bring about asbestos-related diseases like mesothelioma in the future. The claimants argued that the plaques, alongside the anxiety occasioned by what the plaques indicated, and the risk[82] of future grave diseases constituted, each independently or in combination, a cause of action against the negligent employers. Their Lordships refused the claims based upon each

---

[80] *Shore*, [37].   [81] [2008] 1 AC 281.
[82] There was said to be a 5 per cent risk of contracting an asbestos-related disease at [62].

individual head of loss and on an 'aggregation theory': mere physical change without making a person more than trivially worse off was not actionable damage;[83] nor was anxiety per se; and, on the authority of *Gregg*, nor was increase in risk of future disease.[84]

Rationalising the law on probabilistic liability
Can the law be rationally explained? The matter can be considered in two stages: loss of a chance and increase in risk as establishing liability and loss of a chance and increase in risk as recoverable once liability has been established.

Loss of chance and increase in risk as establishing liability
There are three kinds of principle worth assessing as potential explanations of the law on when loss of a chance and increase in risk can establish liability in tort.

The loss of a chance or exposure to a risk is only a loss under certain conditions
The first kind of explanation says that losing a chance or being exposed to a risk is only to suffer a genuine loss under certain conditions. Consider (for convenience, I refer only to loss of chance – each applies *mutatis mutandis* to increase in risk):

> LP1 A loss of chance constitutes a 'loss' if and only if the lost chance was a chance of avoiding a financial loss or making a financial gain.
> LP2 A loss of chance constitutes a 'loss' if and only if the lost chance was a chance of avoiding an injury or making a gain (whether financial in nature or otherwise), and was an objective chance.
> LP3 A loss of chance constitutes a 'loss' if and only if the lost chance was a chance of avoiding an injury or making a gain (whether financial in nature or otherwise), and regardless of whether it was an epistemic or objective chance.

Some explanation of the distinction between 'objective' and 'epistemic' chances in LP2 and LP3 is necessary. Roughly speaking, epistemic chance is a measure of our ignorance over some fully-determined state of the world. By contrast, objective chances exist as a result of the indeterminism in a certain real-world process. To illustrate the distinction,

---

[83] The plaques had 'no effect upon [the claimants'] health at all' (Lord Hoffmann); [47] (Lord Hope); [71] (Lord Scott).
[84] [14] (Lord Hoffmann); [41] (Lord Hope); [67] (Lord Scott); [88] (Lord Rodger).

suppose that you are asked what the chance is that the next card chosen from the top of a well-shuffled deck will be the ace of spades. You will (probably) correctly say '1/52'. It turns out that the ace of spades is actually in the middle of the deck. The state of the world prior to the unveiling of the top card has determined that it will not be the ace of spades. Given this it would be perfectly legitimate to say that, in one sense, there was no chance that the top card would be the ace of spades. For this reason, the 1/52 chance is a measure of our ignorance about which card is at the top: it is an epistemic chance.[85] Objective chances, by contrast, exist, if they do exist at all,[86] despite all possible facts being known. Suppose that having decided you would like an ice cream, you go to the ice cream shop, where there are a variety of ice creams from which to choose. You choose strawberry flavour. Imagine that we could 'roll back' the world to the moment just prior to your choice. If it were the case that sometimes you choose strawberry, and sometimes banana, despite all antecedent conditions being the same prior to the choice, it could be said there was an objective chance that you would choose other than you did.[87] Ex hypothesi, there was no fact which could explain your different choices and so the chance does not reflect our ignorance over some fact: it is an objective chance.[88]

Fit with the current law

The simple, compelling, case for *some version* of the loss principle – as an explanation of the law – is that the courts routinely refer to lost chances as forms of loss or as forming 'actionable damage'.[89]

---

[85] See J. Schaffer, 'Deterministic Chance', 138.

[86] It is not assumed that there are any actual objective chances in the world. It is unclear whether this is so, even at the level of quantum mechanics. The Bohmian interpretation of quantum mechanics denies that it provides evidence of objective chance. For an overview, see T. Handfield, *A Philosophical Guide to Chance*, chs 9–10.

[87] On the idea of 'rolling back', see P. van Inwagen, 'Free Will Remains a Mystery', 13–18.

[88] Some philosophers only grant the status of 'chance' to objective chances in the sense of 'objective' as explained above: for example, Schaffer, Note 85. However, not all philosophers would agree with my description of an 'objective' chance. Some allow that there can be objective chances in deterministic systems, whereas my definition is tied to indeterminism. See, for example, C. Hoefer, 'The Third Way on Objective Probability: a Sceptic's Guide to Objective Chance'. It is important to realise that merely because a chance is 'epistemic', this does not mean it is 'subjective' in the sense of 'irreducibly personal or without rational basis'. Some sciences use epistemic probabilities (again, see Schaffer at 138).

[89] See, for example, *Parabola Investments Ltd* v. *Browallia Cal Ltd* [2010] EWCA Civ 486, [2010] 3 WLR 1266, [23]; *Vasiliou* v. *Hajigeorgiou* [2010] EWCA Civ 1475, at [21].

That losing a chance can be a 'loss' is clear not only in tort but also in contract and in equity.[90]

LP1 is the strongest fit with the current law. Only the lost chances either of avoiding some financial loss or of obtaining some financial gain may currently serve to establish liability. However, LP1 cannot, of itself, explain the distinction embodied by rules (1) and (2), namely, that the lost chance approach is applied to determine how a third party would have behaved without the defendant's wrongful conduct but not to how the claimant would have behaved without the defendant's wrongful conduct.

However, the distinction can be defended in a way consonant with LP1. First, if the claimant in *Allied Maples* were allowed to recover on the ground that there was a chance that it would have renegotiated and there was a chance that the renegotiation would have been successful, it would be recovering for the lost chance of a chance of avoiding loss. Losing a chance and losing the chance of a chance are different. The latter may be more speculative than the former. The interpretation of the distinction as based upon precluding recovery for speculative chances does imply, however, that if there were, say, a 40 per cent chance that the claimant would have acted differently, whereupon there would have been a 90 per cent chance that a third party would have prevented the claimant's loss from occurring, the claimant should recover. The current law inflexibly applies the balance of probability standard to all claimant-related hypotheticals, however. In addition, this view cannot explain why recovery is made contingent upon the hypothetical conduct of a third *person* rather than how some natural occurrence would have developed.

Even if the distinction can be defended as a rough *general* rule, LP1 is not consistent with the *obiter* suggestions that if the third party gives evidence to the court this would preclude recovery in respect of a lost chance.[91] This explanatory problem is faced by all versions of the loss principle.

Why may we not say that LP2 better fits the law? The case for LP2 rests upon the idea that objective chances exist in indeterministic processes, and human action is such a process, because human beings have 'free

---

[90] See, for example, *Giedo van der Garde BV* v. *Force India Formula One Team Ltd* [2010] EWHC 2373 (QB); *Aerostar Maintenance International Ltd* v. *Wilson* [2010] EWHC 2032 (Ch), [216].

[91] See p. 319.

will'.[92] This could partly explain why people can recover for lost chances in cases where we need to determine how a human being would have behaved had the defendant not behaved wrongfully, if we think that how a human being would have behaved is a matter of objective chance. It might also explain why one cannot recover for lost chances in cases where the question of whether the victim would have suffered an injury depends entirely upon how some physical process would have developed. LP2 explains this on the basis that such processes are not subject to true chance: they are governed by deterministic causal laws. This explains the result in *Hotson*. There the claimant plausibly only lost an epistemic, not an objective, chance.

What makes LP2 fit less with the law than LP1, however, is that lost chances of avoiding physical losses are not recoverable even where we need to determine how a human being would have behaved without the defendant's wrongful conduct (as in the blind child example above[93]). But if how a human being would have behaved is a matter of objective chance, then LP2 would tell us that such a lost chance of avoiding a physical loss should be recoverable.

Justifiability of a loss principle

If LP1 best fits the law – is it the best justified of LP1–LP3? The main issue here is whether one can justify a distinction between losing a chance of avoiding an economic loss and losing a chance of avoiding a physical injury, such that only the former constitute losses. This is a fundamental issue which merits extended treatment after we have considered the position in other systems. However, we may note that the prospects of the viability of such a distinction in English law seem bleak.

---

[92] This suggestion was made by H. Reece, 'Losses of Chance in the Law'. The idea that indeterminism is a necessary condition of free will (and that human beings have it) is an extremely controversial philosophical claim. For the claim that it is not, see famously H. Frankfurt, 'Alternate Possibilities and Moral Responsibility'.

[93] See p. 305. S. Green, *Causation in Negligence*, 152–72, proposes that the existing law can be explained by reference to a different loss principle. On her account, the existing pattern of recovery is explained by the fact that the claimant in reality is recovering for an interference with its autonomy. A breach of duty deprives a person of autonomy on her account where it prevents the person availing itself of an opportunity which existed 'independently of the breach of duty' (152). In *Hotson*, Green claims, no such opportunity was lost since Hotson's chance only existed if the defendant behaved non-negligently. The dependence of the existence of the chance on the absence of a breach of duty on the part of the defendant seems to be true of both *Hotson* and *Allied Maples*, however (see further, p. 331). As Green concedes, the language of autonomy is entirely absent from the judicial reasoning in these authorities. However, her account has some normative force: see, p. 345.

We can bring this out by asking – what *could* be the significance of a distinction between these types of chance? There are, it seems, two possibilities. The first is that it is easier to assign a value to the lost chance of an economic benefit compared to the lost chance of avoiding a physical injury. Burrows writes: 'it is straightforward and natural to assign a present value to uncertainties as to what the plaintiff's financial position might have been compared to what it actually is, because, as Baroness Hale stressed in *Gregg v Scott*, "it is all money"'.[94] This is unconvincing. The law is already willing to assign a value to the chance of avoiding an adverse verdict in a criminal prosecution – this is neither straightforward nor natural[95]. It would not be a significant leap to assign a value to the chance of avoiding, say, cancer. In any event, difficulties of measurement are not usually a reason for denying a claim, so long as the claimant has indeed suffered a legally recognised loss.[96]

The other possible distinction is that the chance of avoiding a physical injury is a 'nothing' – it is simply an expression of our uncertainty over how things would have been had the defendant not behaved wrongfully – whereas the chance of avoiding an economic loss is itself like having an economically valuable asset or, at any rate, is something of *economic* value. Thus, Lord Hoffmann claimed in *Gregg v. Scott* that many lost chance cases could be explained on the basis that the chance could 'plausibly be characterised as an item of property, like a lottery ticket'.[97] But it is difficult to understand how the chance of renegotiating the terms of the contract in the leading case – *Allied Maples* – involved anything like an item of property.[98] The same is also true of the lost chance of avoiding an adverse verdict in a criminal prosecution.

---

[94] A. Burrows, 'Comparing Compensatory Damages in Contract and Tort: Some Problematic Issues', text at n. 89–n. 92.

[95] See p. 298.

[96] For a similar view: N. Jansen, 'The Idea of a Lost Chance', 288ff. For a quite different argument that by *contracting* for medical treatment by giving valuable consideration one transforms the chance of a cure into an economic loss: G. Mäsch, *Chance und Schaden*, 290ff. For Mäsch, the breach of a contract geared towards preserving a chance in itself constitutes an economic loss. Cf. G. Wagner, *Neue Perspektiven im Schadensersatzrecht – Kommerzialisierung, Strafschadensersatz, Kolletivschaden Gutachten A für den 66 Deutschen Juristentag*, 57.

[97] *Gregg*, [83].

[98] Cf. G. Reid, 'Gregg v Scott and Lost Chances', 90: 'in *Allied Maples*, and similar cases, the claimant could not demonstrate identifiable harm in the form of deprivation of an asset or harm to an existing one'. J. Stapleton, 'Cause in Fact and the Scope of Liability for Consequences', 410. considers that an informed market actor would pay less for C's business in *Allied* at the point at which the defendant was negligent.

Moreover, even if one accepts that these are not proprietary assets, but only things with 'economic value', the sense in which the chance of avoiding a criminal prosecution can be said to have economic value but not the chance of avoiding cancer is not obvious.[99]

Impossibility of proof

A structurally different kind of consideration is what we can call the 'impossibility of proof principle'. This principle states that the court should apply a probabilistic approach to recovery wherever the question of whether the defendant's wrongful conduct caused the claimant's traditional injury is insusceptible of proof on the balance of probability. This principle will likely appear unfamiliar, yet it seems to underpin at least some judicial thought in this area.

Fit with the current law

This principle at least suggests why a distinction between determining how a third party would have behaved without the defendant's wrongful conduct and how the claimant would have behaved could be considered justifiable. It may generally be true that third parties will not be before the court with the result that an assessment of how they would have behaved is particularly difficult, compared to assessing how the claimant, whose evidence has been heard, would have behaved.[100] This explanation was offered at first instance in *Feltham v. Bouskell*:

> the logic justifying the difference [between hypotheticals concerning claimant conduct and hypotheticals concerning third party conduct] is between matters which should be, in principle, within the knowledge of the claimant, and therefore capable of proof by the claimant, and matters which depend on the act of a third party, where the basis of the hypothesis is more uncertain and not capable of proof in the same way.[101]

---

[99] For a similar point, see J. Edelman, 'Loss of a Chance', 10.

[100] As suggested by Mance LJ in the Court of Appeal in *Gregg v. Scott* [2002] EWCA Civ 1471, [2002] All ER (D) 418. See similarly, J. Poole, 'Loss of Chance and the Evaluation of Hypotheticals in Contract Claims' 66ff; K. Barker, P. Cane, M. Lunney, and F. Trindade, *Law of Torts in Australia*, 4th edition 544. However, one might challenge this on the basis that assessing how the claimant would have behaved is often very difficult in virtue of self-serving or hindsight-biased evidence: See, for example, *Chubb Fire Ltd v. The Vicar of Spalding* [2010] EWCA Civ 981, [2010] 2 CLC 277, [40] where the court rejected evidence for the claimant on how it would have acted had the defendant not behaved negligently on the ground that it 'smacks of hindsight'.

[101] [2013] EWHC 1952 (Ch), [111].

The principle also gains support from *obiter* suggestions recently made by some judges that the chance-based approach should not apply where the third party is before the court. The claim made by these judges is that where the third party is before the court there is sufficient evidence to determine on the balance of probability how the third party would have behaved had the defendant not behaved wrongfully.[102]

However, this principle is ultimately untenable as a 'fit' with the current law. First, it does not explain why a decision is taken on the balance of probability where the *victim* of the tort, being dead, is not before the court.[103] Second, it cannot be maintained that uncertainty concerning how third parties would have behaved is generally more impenetrable than, say, how claimants' medical conditions would have developed without, for instance, negligently late diagnosis. Perhaps one can see *Barker* as an example of the principle going beyond the human decision-making context: the extreme evidential uncertainty in mesothelioma cases engages the principle.[104] Ultimately, however, the principle cannot explain the absence of wider chance-based recovery in physical injury cases.

Justifiability of the impossibility of proof principle

As we argued in the last chapter, the appeal to the 'impossibility of proof' in itself as a justification for departing from general proof rules is problematic.[105] Even if we construed the appeal to that idea as an incentives-based argument, it is far from clear how this incentives-based argument would map on to the distinction between lost economic chances and lost chances of physical injury. That is: it is not clear that the need for incentives is particularly strong in relation to contexts involving economic losses compared to those involving physical injuries.

---

[102] *Stone Heritage Developments Ltd* v. *Davis Blank Furniss*, unreported, 31 May 2006; *Dayman* v. *Lawrence Graham (a firm)* [2008] EWHC 2036 (Ch), [2008] Lloyd's Rep PN 22, [83]. But cf. *Tom Hoskins Plc* v. *EMW (a firm)* [2010] EWHC 479 (Ch), [2010] ECC 20, [126] (Floyd J): 'The loss of a chance principle is not, as it seems to me, simply a judicial tool to aid with difficult questions of causation or assessment of damages. The principle has a very significant effect on both the recoverability of and assessment of damages. In principle, therefore, its application ought to depend on the nature of the loss claimed rather than the evidence which happens to be called.'

[103] For example, *McWilliams* v. *Sir William Arrol & Co. Ltd* [1961] UKHL 8, 1962 SC (HL) 70.

[104] See pp. 228–31.   [105] See p. 282ff.

A loss principle qualified by competing fairness or consequentialist considerations
The law could also be explained on the following basis that, though either LP2 or LP3 is correct, and thus the loss of the chance of a physical injury is (sometimes) a loss, there are competing considerations which justify barring recovery for such losses. Such considerations include:

(1) Permitting recovery would necessitate that if a person lost a 60 per cent chance of avoiding a physical injury, they would only receive 60 per cent damages. The undesirable result would be that victims of personal injuries would not receive full compensation if they proved that the defendant caused their injury on the balance of probability.

(2) The increased length and complexity of litigation which requires the quantification of a chance through expert evidence.

(3) The possibility of a large increase in the number of claims, particularly against the NHS.

Each of these competing considerations was advanced in *Gregg v. Scott.*[106] As to (1), in essence, the claim is that, if the law recognised the recovery of loss of chance in physical injury cases, this would necessitate the abandonment of the balance of probability rule in cases where that rule would generate full recovery. This competing consideration is undermined by two points. First, if lost chances of physical injury were recognised to establish liability in tort, this could plausibly be restricted to cases where the defendant's duty was to take care to protect the claimant's chances. It would therefore not entail that *in every case* where a defendant's carelessness was a cause of the lost chance of a physical injury that this chance would establish liability. Just as pure economic losses may only establish liability where the defendant owes a special legal duty, so too, the law might only impose chance-protecting duties in special situations. This also blunts the force of (3). Second, more fundamentally, it is not clear that the claimant should not be able to *elect* whether to sue for the lost chance of avoiding a physical injury *or* the physical injury itself. We return to this issue later.

Summary

The justifiability of English law depends crucially upon the validity of two distinctions: (1) that between lost chances of physical injury and lost chances of economic loss and (2) that between hypothetical questions relating to how a third party would have behaved and hypothetical questions relating to how the victim of the tort would have behaved.

---

[106] See Chapter 4, 235–236.

In short, this section has suggested that (1) is difficult to justify, but (2) can be justified *in so far as* it is (re-)interpreted as a rule precluding the recovery of highly speculative chances.

Loss of chance and increase in risk once liability is established

Once liability in tort in respect of some loss is established, there is a relative liberalism (compared to the wrong-constituting stage) in allowing probabilistic liability. The main aspect of this is that, under the quantification principle, it is possible to recover in respect of the increased risk of physical injury, as well as the increased risk of economic loss and lost chances of avoiding economic loss. There are, again, three main potential explanations of the current law.

Impossibility of proof
The justification for the quantification principle has not often been the subject of judicial consideration. However, as we saw above, in *Davies* v. *Taylor*, Lord Reid explained that:

> You can prove that a past event happened, but you cannot prove that a future event will happen and I do not think that the law is so foolish as to suppose that you can. All that you can do is to evaluate the chance.[107]

Similarly, in *Poseidon Ltd & Sellars* v. *Adelaide Petroleum NL*, the High Court of Australia stated:

> The principle recognized in *Malec* [the quantification principle] was based on a consideration of the peculiar difficulties associated with the proof and evaluation of future possibilities and past hypothetical fact situations, as contrasted with proof of historical facts.[108]

It seems to emerge from this that the basis of the quantification principle is not that the loss of a chance of obtaining some benefit or of avoiding some loss in the future is itself a distinct form of loss.[109] The idea is that some kinds of proposition are insusceptible of *proof*.

---

[107] *Davies* v. *Taylor* [1974] AC 207, 213.
[108] (1994) 179 CLR 332, 355. See also, ibid., at [22]: 'this court [draws] a distinction between, on the one hand, proof of historical facts – what has happened – and, on the other hand, proof of future possibilities and past hypothetical situations. The civil standard of proof applies to the first category but not to the second, particularly when it is necessary to determine future possibilities and past hypothetical situations for the purpose of assessing damages'.
[109] This is convincingly shown by H. McGregor, *McGregor on Damages*, 19th edition, [10–45]–[10–49].

Consequential losses

The dominant view in the cases understands the quantification principle simply as a method of assessing damages which responds to the difficulty in determining what would have happened in the future absent the tort and what will happen, and *not* as redefining the nature of the loss which C has suffered.[110] The idea of quantification as a *method* of assessing an established loss is indeed implicit in the phrase 'quantification of loss': the phrase implies the pre-existence of the concept of loss, in the same way that quantifying the bricks making up a building first requires the identification of what counts as a brick. For this reason Lord Justice Patten in *Vasiliou v. Hajigeorgiou* said that the quantification principle 'has nothing to do with loss of chance as such. It is simply the judge making a realistic and reasoned assessment of a variety of circumstances in order to determine what the level of loss has been'.[111]

Yet, on the other hand, sometimes judges do conceive of the quantification principle as generating recovery for the lost chance of some benefit, where the lost chance is itself a form of consequential loss. Thus, Spencer J in *XYZ v. Portsmouth Hospitals NHS Trust* speaks of 'the principle in *Davies v Taylor*' as permitting 'damages for lost chance'.[112]

If one accepts the reasoning of Lord Hoffmann and Lady Hale in *Gregg* as the most authoritative statement of the boundaries of the quantification principle, the consequential loss view cannot be accepted as an explanation of the current law. On the evidence accepted by those judges, the increased risk of losing a cure from cancer *was* consequential upon the spread of the tumour. The absence of recovery for this loss would then be very difficult to explain if the quantification principle were about recovery for consequential lost chances and increased risks, themselves conceived of as distinctive losses.

In short, if the quantification principle were simply about allowing recovery for consequential lost chances and increased risks as consequential losses, it is difficult to understand why there must be an issue as to the 'extent' of the loss suffered by the victim of the tort in order for the principle to apply.

---

[110] This view is endorsed by H. McGregor, *McGregor on Damages*, 19th edition, [10–49].
[111] *Vasiliou v. Hajigeorgiou* [2010] EWCA Civ 1475, [25] [*Vasiliou*].
[112] *XYZ v. Portsmouth Hospitals NHS Trust* [2011] EWHC 243 (QB), (2011) 121 BMLR 13, [55].

Relative injustice and litigation economy

The judicial reliance upon the impossibility of proof of future hypothe-ticals and questions about the future as a justification for the quanti-fication principle is, in itself, problematic. It proves too much. If the rationale of the principle is the 'impossibility' of proving the answer to certain types of question, this should also apply to causal questions concerning the *establishing* of liability.

A better justification of the principle begins from the simple fact that, for the quantification principle to apply, the victim has to have been the victim of a wrong that has caused some loss. Unlike the situation where it is impossible to determine on the balance of probability whether the defendant's wrongful conduct was a cause of the claimant's injury, the quantification principle applies where the defendant has been proven tortiously to have caused loss. The fact that the defendant has been proven wrongfully to have caused loss at least opens up the possibility that, as a matter of fairness, there could be reason to adopt a different approach once liability has been established.

Even if we accept the plausibility of operating a different proof regime at the quantification stage compared to the liability stage, the puzzle still remains why this different approach should take the form of prob-abilistic liability. Why not simply require the claimant to prove the *approximate* amount of loss it has suffered *on the balance of probability*? This seems to be the position in Germany.[113] For instance, one might require the claimant to prove an approximate range of loss it has suffered on the balance of probability and then, as a matter of fairness, assume that the claimant suffered an amount towards the higher end of this range. Under this approach, if the claimant could prove that there was a 60 per cent chance that its earnings would have increased by £10,000 in five years it would recover that £10,000 for the relevant period, rather than the chance-discounted amount of £6,000.

So the puzzle remains why a probabilistic approach is taken. Perhaps the best answer is that the restriction of claimant's recovery to 60 per cent in the above example can, contrary to appearances, be justified on the basis that it gives the claimant an advantage it would not have if the balance of probability rule were applied. If the 60 per cent chance represents an abstract, low-weight probability, then it would not satisfy the balance of probability rule. Consequently, allowing the claimant to

[113] See p. 56ff.

recover in respect of such a chance gives the claimant a benefit it would not otherwise receive under the balance of probability rule. In this way, the proportionate liability under the quantification principle can be justified as part of a general liberal approach applied once liability has been established.

The recovery of increased risks of physical injury and of economic loss under the quantification principle can arguably be justified by a policy of economy of litigation. If the court awards damages for the increased risk of physical injury, this serves to settle as many issues as possible at once.[114] This argument only applies once it has been proven that the claimant has been the victim of a wrong and there could be a possibility of future litigation over the extent of that loss.

French law

If one looked to the state of French law shortly after *Kitchen* v. *Royal Air Force* was decided in England, there were similarities between the two systems: chance-based recovery had so far developed in both systems in cases involving the lost chance of an economic gain. The comparison would be entirely superficial, however. Unlike English law, the loss of a chance of a gain or of avoiding a loss had already by that point crystallised in French doctrinal writing and jurisprudence as a form of loss in itself. In principle, the loss of any valuable chance was recoverable. When the doctrine expanded in the 1960s to the medical context, it was a natural development: the lost chance of a cure was valuable, and so recoverable. Nonetheless, the legitimacy of this shift was soon contested. Yet doctrinal attempts to derail the expansion have (so far) failed. The result has been the continued existence of a doctrine of very broad scope: in principle, if valuable, the lost chance of any gain or avoidance of any loss is recoverable.

The first section explains this legal development with reference to the doctrinal disputes which underlay it, in particular the later attempts to distinguish lost economic chances from other cases. It then briefly outlines the current law as it relates to the recovery of lost chances and increased risks. Importantly, given the expansive scope of the lost chance doctrine, many of the justificatory problems discussed in relation to

---

[114] See A. Burrows, 'Comparing Compensatory Damages in Contract and Tort', at n. 89–n. 92; E. Voyiakis, 'The Great Illusion: Tort Law and Exposure to Danger of Physical Harm', 914, for this explanation. This policy also underlies the statutory power to assess the extent of damages which might occur in the future in the original litigation under section 32A, Supreme Court Act 1981.

English law do not directly arise. Nonetheless, the second section identifies some justificatory problems in the current law.

Emergence of the doctrine of *perte d'une chance*

A decision of the Chambre des Rêquetes of 17 July 1889 is generally, though erroneously, cited as the first to recognise recovery for the loss of a chance.[115] The case concerned a legal official (a *huissier*) who had wrongfully rendered an appeal document void, thereby preventing the claimant's appeal being heard by the court of appeal. According to the Chambre des Rêquetes, the official's liability depended upon whether the original judgment would have been affirmed by the court of appeal and this involved 'l'examen du mérite de cet appel'.[116] It affirmed the lower court's decision that the appeal would not have been successful. There is no suggestion that whether the appeal would have been successful could have been assessed on a chance basis. Indeed, the contrary is assumed: '[it is necessary to] rechercher si, sur un appel valable, le jugement eut été ou non confirmé'.[117] Unsurprisingly, then, early commentators understood the decision as establishing that the official is not liable unless the appeal was proven by the claimant to be well-founded.[118]

Nonetheless, there was, undeniably, some early doctrinal support for allowing chance to play a role in the assessment of loss suffered in cases requiring the assessment of the result of a hypothetical trial or appeal. Thus, Bouvier criticised a later decision which applied an all-or-nothing approach on the same facts as the 1889 Chambre des Requêtes case.[119] His argument was not, however, that the loss of a chance was a real loss. It was that the defendant *huissier* had compromised the claimant's ability to prove whether the appeal would have been successful and this itself was *dommage*. In the measurement of *this* loss, he argued that the court ought to take into account the chances of success of the lost appeal: '[o]n pourrait, en s'appuyant sur la constation que les chances de gain du procès arrêté par la faute de l'huissier étaient très faibles, réduire le

---

[115] S.1891.1.399. It is cited thus by Y. Chartier, *La réparation du préjudice*, 33; J. Borghetti, 'La reparation de la perte d'une chance en droit Suisse et en droit français', 1074.

[116] S.1891.1.399, 400.   [117] Ibid.

[118] R. Demogue, *Traité des Obligations en Général Tomes III–IV*, 1924, 26. The all-or-nothing approach is clearly reflective of the 19th-century decisions: CA Chambéry 1 May 1868, D.1868.2.111; CA Grenoble 25 June 1875, D.1880.2.225; CA Bourges, 15 April 1889, D.1891.2.43.

[119] Req 30 June 1902, S.1907.1.434, note Bouvier D.1903.1.569.

chiffre de l'indemnité'.[120] Similarly, Demogue, in 1924, analysed an early (and isolated) case where the damages seem to have been reduced to reflect uncertainty over the occurrence of loss as recognising a 'responsabilité partielle', where the *loss* was uncertain, describing this as 'une voie nouvelle'.[121] There is not yet, then, indication in this early jurisprudence or doctrinal writing of the later idea that the loss of a chance itself is a loss.[122]

The first edition of Savatier's *Traité de la Responsabilité Civile* in 1939 had made the suggestion that, in cases involving *competitions*, the courts should recognise that 'la chance de gagner la course...représentait elle-même une valeur qu'il n'est pas impossible...d'apprécier', though the author only cited two decisions which had in fact rejected claims for damages in such cases as too uncertain.[123] Savatier did not extend this analysis to the legal context, however, on the ground that the legal system ought not to allow the result of a legal process to appear to be based upon 'chance'. Perhaps more important in the development of the doctrine was the insistence of the influential Mazeaud brothers in numerous notes in the *Revue Trimestrielle de Droit Civil*, and in their treatise, that:[124]

Whoever causes you to lose a chance of making a gain or avoiding a loss does not cause you a possible, hypothetical loss, but a certain one.[125]

This explicitly dealt with the point made in the cases cited by Savatier that the damage was 'uncertain' and therefore irrecoverable: the chance itself was the loss, and the claimant had certainly suffered it. These authors repeatedly emphasised that to lose a chance was itself to suffer a loss – be it the lost chance of winning a legal proceeding; the lost chance to receive benefits from one's wrongfully killed fiancé; or the lost

---

[120] Ibid. (Bouvier), 569. Bouvier also made the interesting point that the loss of the ability to appeal was itself a 'dommage moral' which deserved at least nominal damages of 1 Franc.

[121] R. Demogue, *Traité des obligations*, 29.

[122] Nor is there evidence to suggest that the position was different in the administrative courts: see C. Chatelain, *La Théorie de la Perte de Chance en Droit Hospitalier*, 347.

[123] R. Savatier, *Traité de la Responsabilité Civile en Droit Français Tomes I–II* (1939), 12, [436]: Limoges, 24 March 1896, D.1898.2.259; Rouen, 8 August 1903, S.1904.2.282, D.1904.2.175.

[124] H. Mazeaud and L. Mazeaud, *Traité théorique et pratique de la responsabilité civile délictuelle et contractuelle*, 149 and RTDC 1940, 269; RTDC 1951, 70; RTDC 1956, 519; RTDC 1959, 91; RTDC 1960, 300.

[125] RTDC 1951, 70.

chance to sell a property at higher value.[126] By the middle of the 1950s, there was doctrinal consensus that the loss of a chance either of obtaining a gain or of avoiding a loss was a distinct, compensable loss.[127] There seem to be two important features of this consensus. First, the view was held that losing a chance was itself losing something valuable and was therefore a loss which merited compensation: 'une chance de gain a une valuer *en soi*'.[128] Strikingly, according to these writers, so long as the lost chance could be said to have *value*, it was recoverable. The fact that the value might be difficult to assess was not, on this view, a convincing reason to refuse compensation since the courts are familiar with such difficulties in assessing damages for non-pecuniary losses (*dommages moraux*).[129] Second, all of these authors drew attention to the fact that it is impossible to say *with certainty* (i.e. according to the theoretically governing standard of proof) how a hypothetical world would have turned out: the language of chance becomes necessary.[130] It may then be possible to say that the development of the lost chance doctrine was partly influenced by the theoretical strictness of the French standard of proof.[131]

It is difficult to find clear reception of this idea *in the courts* earlier than the 1950s.[132] When it does appear, it arises in various contexts: and this is what one would expect, given the breadth of the principle proposed by *la doctrine*. Thus, LeSourd, an avocat at the Cour de Cassation, writing in 1963, identified four situations in which the courts had recognised the loss of a chance as recoverable:[133] the lost chance of becoming an air-hostess due to a traffic accident;[134] the lost chance of obtaining a licence to open a pharmacy;[135] the lost chance of winning a sculpture

---

[126] See references above Note 124.

[127] M. Planiol and G. Ripert, *Traité Pratique de Droit Civil Français Tome VI Obligations* 2nd edition, 747; C. Aubry, C. Rau, and P. Esmein (eds), *Droit Civil Français VI* 6th edition (1951), 422–4; H. Mazeaud, L. Mazeaud, A. Tunc, *Traité Théorique et Pratique de la Responsabilité Civile Délictuelle et Contractuelle Tome I* 6th edition, 219.

[128] C. Aubry, C. Rau, and P. Esmein (ed), *Droit civil*, 424. See also M. Planiol and G. Ripert, *Traité pratique de droit civil français*, 748: 'cette chance avait une valeur; les hommes montrent qu'ils le pensent en faisant des paris'.

[129] See, for example, N. LeSourd, 'La Perte d'une Chance', 51, making this point.

[130] C. Aubry, C. Rau, and P. Esmein (ed), *Droit Civil*, 424.

[131] A claim made by K. Oliphant, 'Proportional Liability' 179.

[132] Req 26 May 1932, S.1932.1.387 *might* be an early example, though it is very briefly reasoned indeed and does not mention the word 'chance'.

[133] In an article entitled: 'La Perte d'une Chance'.

[134] Cass Civ 1e, 17 February 1961, RTDC 1962, 99.

[135] TGI Corbeil-Essonnes, RTDC 1959, 62.

competition;[136] and the lost chance of winning an appeal.[137] There appears to have been some resistance to the lost chance idea in this last context of claims against legal professionals for failure to bring proceedings within a time limit. Some courts, even into the 1960s, held to Savatier's early position that one ought not to consider the hypothetical course of legal proceedings to be a matter of chance since the court could always declare the 'legal truth' of the matter.[138] This resistance was soon defeated: 'aucune decision de justice ne saurait être considérée comme échappant à toute possibilité de réformation'.[139] The dominant position, achieved at the latest by the early 1970s, and reflecting the current state of the law in the civil courts[140] clearly approves of lost chance reasoning in cases of the negligence of a legal professional.[141]

None of these cases had suggested any limiting feature of the lost chance doctrine. The basic proposition was that the lost chance of a gain or of avoiding a loss was itself a loss. Consequently, if that loss was caused by another's fault, it should be recoverable.[142] In particular, nothing hinged upon the nature of the lost gain or avoided loss, so long as losing the chance could be said to losing something *valuable*. Against this background, it is not at all surprising that the doctrine came to be accepted in the early 1960s in cases of medical negligence. The first decision is from the Cour de Grenoble in 1961.[143] The defendant doctor negligently failed to diagnose the claimant's shoulder injury: he misread an X-Ray of the shoulder. The court stated that the failure to diagnose '...certainly deprived the claimant of a chance of a cure' and that 'the certain and directly caused damage...is constituted exclusively by this lost chance of a cure'. LeSourd discusses this case and treats it

---

[136] Lyon, 1e Chambre, 17 November 1958, Gaz Pal 1959.1.195. See, later: Cass Civ 2e, 4 May 1972, D.1972.596 (note Ph Le Tourneau); Cass Civ 2e, 25 January 1973, D.1974.320 (note Porchier); JCP 1974 II 17641, (note A Bénabent).

[137] TGI Amiens, 1 October 1959, RTDC, 301 (Mazeaud/Mazeaud).

[138] Cour de Paris, 30 October 1956, D.1956.782; TI Nice, 22 December 1959, JCP 1960, 11410, RTDC 1960, 299 (obs Mazeaud/Mazeaud); CA Paris, 13 November 1962, JCP 1963 II. 13061; Cass Civ 1e, 29 April 1963, JCP 1963 II.13226, RTDC 1963, 607 (Hebraud).

[139] Trib de GI d'Amiens, 1 October 1959, RTDC 1960, 301 (Mazeaud/Mazeaud).

[140] It seems that if the chance of the more favourable result lost is sufficiently serious that the Conseil d'État grants full, rather than limited to the chance, liability: CE, 5 July 2006, JCP 2006, act.350.

[141] CA Paris, 5 March 1985, D.1987.somm.104; Cass Civ 1e, 8 July 1997, Bull Civ. I (1997) no 236; Cass Civ 1e, 4 April 2001, JCP 2001 II 10640 (obs Noblot); Cass Civ 1e, 2 April 2009, no 08-12848 Juris Data no 2009-047654, JCP G 2009.IV.1777, JCP 2009 chronique, 248.38, 41 (Stoffel-Munck).

[142] Art 1382 CC.   [143] CA Grenoble, 24 October 1961, RTDC 1963, 334 (note Tunc).

(alongside the other cases mentioned above) as a straightforward application of the principle that 'the loss of a chance can. . .constitute a loss meriting compensation'.[144] This reasoning was accepted by the Cour de Cassation from 1965.[145] Thus, in a case where a person died after the administration of local anaesthetic, the court rejected the surgeon's appeal, holding that though uncertainty persisted as to the link between the fault and the final damage (the death), there was sufficient certainty over the causal link between the fault and the lost chance which constituted itself a type of damage: 'un préjudice peut être invoqué du seul fait qu'une chance existait et qu'elle a été perdue'.[146]

The doctrinal dispute

The expansion of loss of chance to cases involving negligent treatment by doctors gave rise to doctrinal dispute over the legitimacy of this expansion.[147] In a series of articles,[148] Savatier, later supported by Penneau,[149] criticised this shift. The position of the Cour de Cassation was defended by Durry.[150] The critique was essentially that the application of the lost chance doctrine in the medical context involved a confusion between questions of causation and questions of damage or loss.[151] The claim was that the lost chance could not be conceived of as a distinct form of loss in the medical cases. Therefore, the only question was whether the materialised injury was caused by the doctor's negligence.

---

[144] N. LeSourd, 'La perte d'une chance', 51.

[145] Cass Civ 1e, 14 December 1965; 10 March 1966: JCP 1966 G.II.14753 (Savatier); Cass Civ 2e, 2 May 1978, JCP 1978.II.18966 (Savatier), D.1978.IR.408 (obs Larroumet). For calculation of the damages, see for example, Cass Civ 1e, 24 January 2006, pourvoi no.02-12260, Bull Civ No 30: 'une fraction des différents chefs de préjudice resultant du handicap'. The calculation exercise is particularly clearly illustrated by: Cass Civ 1e, 7 June 1989, Bull Civ I no.230, D.1991.158 (note Couturier); D.1991.Somm.323 (obs Aubert).

[146] Cass Civ 1e, 27 January 1970, JCP 1970.G.II.16422 (note Rabut). See also Cass Civ 1e, 18 March 1969 in the same note. Consistently, the criminal chamber of the Court of Cassation may award loss of chance damages while denying the causal link between the fault and the actual death for the purposes of criminal liability: Cass Crim 18 June 2002, pourvoi no. 01–86.503.

[147] Cf. L. Khoury, *Uncertain Causation*, 111; G. Mäsch, *Chance und Schaden*, 171–4 for discussion of the debate.

[148] R. Savatier, 'Commentary on Decision of 14 December 1965'; 'Commentary on Decision of 1 June 1976'; 'Commentary on Decision of 2 May 1978'.

[149] J. Penneau, D.1973.895.

[150] G. Durry, 'La faute du médecin diminuant les "chances de guérison" du malade'; 'Faute médicale et perte de chances de survie'.

[151] G. Durry, 'Faute médicale et perte de chances de survie', 409 notes that Savatier's critique consisted 'à reprocher à la Cour de cassation de confondre un problème de préjudice et un problème de causalité'.

The main argument for this was that the previous cases could be rationalised on the basis that the claimant's chance of gain or of avoiding loss was 'une sorte de propriéte antérieure'.[152] This was so because these chances were *distinct* from the defendant's fault. The horse has a certain chance of winning the race – calculated by the betting odds. The appellant has a certain chance of winning the appeal, given by assessing the merits of their case. The examinee has a certain chance of passing. These chances can be assessed without any reference to the defendant's fault. In the medical cases, by contrast, the claimant's chance of survival is *dependent* upon, and can only be assessed by, reference to the non-negligent conduct of the doctor. The claimant's chance of avoiding a negative outcome is dependent upon, and calculable only with reference to, the situation where the doctor is not at fault. As such, it is not a distinct asset of the claimant's which exists prior to the doctor's fault. Consequently, its destruction cannot be treated as causing a loss to the claimant. The only question is one of certainty over the causal link between the negligent treatment and the materialised injury.

This is not a convincing distinction.[153] In both cases, the odds assigned to the claimant's chance of gaining are actually dependent upon considering the position where the defendant was not at fault: the horse only has the chance assigned to it by the bookmaker if it is not prevented from turning up to the race. The fundamental thread linking both types of case is that it is unclear whether the claimant would have obtained the hoped-for benefit: be it avoidance of cancer or winning the horse-race. In both types of case it is not clear whether the claimant would have won the race or survived the cancer without the defendant's negligence. In any event, there had been no suggestion in the previous cases that one could only lose a chance of value where one had a 'kind of asset'.

The Cour de Cassation has largely rejected or ignored this criticism. Thus, the court explicitly stated that there is no contradiction in holding that damages can be awarded for the loss of a *chance* of avoiding an injury where it is uncertain whether the doctor has actually caused the injury to become incurable: this is because causation is established with

---

[152] R. Savatier, 'Commentary on Decision of 14 December 1965, Cour de Cassation'.
[153] For a different view: R. Mislawski, *La causalité dans la Responsabilité Civile: Recherches sur ses Rapports Avec la Causalité Scientifique*, 260. S. Green, *Causation in Negligence*, 152ff. The distinctions are rightly rejected by G. Durry, 'Faute médicale et perte de chances de survie', 410; F. Descorps-Declere, 'La Cohérence de la jurisprudence de la Cour de Cassation sur la perte de chance consécutive à la faute du médecin', 746.

regard to the autonomous loss of chance.[154] At one point, it seemed, however, that the Cour de Cassation had accepted some version of Savatier's criticism in its decision of 17 November 1982.[155] In that case the defendant doctor negligently continued to inject air into the claimant's sinus, despite the appearance of a haemorrhage. An embolism occurred. The issue was whether the embolism was caused by the negligent addition of air or by the air already (non-tortiously) present in the sinus. The court of appeal held the defendant liable in respect of the lost chance of avoiding the embolism, while (consistently) observing that it was unclear whether the negligence had caused the embolism itself. The decision was struck down by the Cour de Cassation on the cryptic (though Savatier-esque) basis that loss of a chance relates to the assessment of damage, not to the existence of causation. Dorsner-Dolivet suggested the interpretation that the Court accepted Savatier's view that in the extra-medical cases 'la chance s'isole comme une sorte de propriété antérieure de la victime'.[156] Others made the less radical suggestion the court was objecting to the fact that causation had not been established with respect to the *lost chance*.[157] Whatever the court actually intended, the Cour de Cassation has subsequently consistently applied the lost chance doctrine in the medical context.[158]

The current law on lost chance and exposure to risk

The claimant must show that the defendant's wrongful conduct was causative of the loss of a substantial probability of a favourable result, where the possibility of achieving that favourable result is now foreclosed.[159] In a recent formulation of the Cour de Cassation: 'seule

---

[154] For similar statements: Cass Civ 1e, 18 March 1969, JCP.1970.II.16422 (note Rabut); Cass Civ 1e, 24 March 1981, D.1981.545 (obs Penneau); Cass Civ 1e, 8 January 1985, D.1986.390 (obs Penneau); Cass Civ 1e, 10 January 1990, D.1991.somm.358 (obs Penneau); Cass Civ 1e, 4 November 2003, D.2004.601 (obs Penneau).

[155] D.1984.Jur.305 (obs Dorsner-Dolivet); D.1983.IR.380 (obs Penneau); JCP. 1983.G.IV.41, JCP.1983.G.II.20056 (obs Saluden).

[156] D.1984.Jur.305.

[157] For example, M. Saluden, 'Commentary on Cass Civ 1e 17 November 1982'.

[158] For an overview of some post-1983 decisions: H. Großerichter, *Hypothetischer Geschehensverlauf und Schadensfestellung* 137ff; F. Descorps-Declère, 'La cohérence de la jurisprudence de la Cour de Cassation sur la perte de chance consécutive à la faute du médecin'.

[159] G. Viney, P. Jourdain, and S. Carval, *Les conditions*, 97; X. Pradel, *Le préjudice dans le droit civil de la responsabilité*, 239–40; Y. Chartier, *La réparation du préjudice*, 51–2; S. Hocquet-Berg, JCP.2007.II.1005; P. Stoffel-Munck, 'Confirmation de la définition de la perte de chance' (interpreting 'certaine' in cited formula above as meaning the chance is definitely foreclosed).

constitue une perte de chance réparable, la disparition actuelle et certaine d'une éventualité favorable'.[160] This is subject to the limitation that the chance has to be a 'substantial' one, but the court has refused to strike down decisions allowing damages for as low as a 5 per cent chance.[161] Beyond this, as Chartier observes: 'there are no limits to the principle, no precluded domain'.[162] As a result, none of the common law distinctions between medical liability and other cases or between claimant hypotheticals and third party hypotheticals plays a role.[163]

There is little support for pure increased risk claims in French law. The situation comes to be analysed as a question of *certainty of loss*.[164] There is no bar to the recovery of a future loss, so long as that loss is certain to occur.[165] The certainty required is relative in that it also applies to losses of *chances* of future gains,[166] the chance conceived here, too, as a distinct loss. However, the *definition* of what constitutes a lost chance itself excludes recovery in respect of a pure increased risk.[167] There must be a 'disparition actuelle et certaine d'une éventualité

---

[160] Cass Civ 1e, 4 June 2007, Juris-data no 2007-039205, JCP 2007.I.185, no.2 (obs Stoffel-Munck); O. Moréteau, 'Case Report on France', 276. This is not new: Cass Crim 18 March 1975, Bull Crim No 79, 223; C. Quézel-Ambrunaz, note under Cass Civ 1e, 11 March 2010, pourvoi no 09-11270, in Gaz Pal, nos 83–4, 24–5 March 2010.

[161] Cass Civ 2e, 1 July 2010, no 09–15.594, RDC 2011, 83. Compare Cass Civ 1e, 7 May 2008, no 06–14.836, JurisData no 2008-043816, striking down a decision which awarded damages for loss of a chance while noting that the chance was 'très faible'. The quantification of the chance is a matter under the sovereign appraisal of the *juge du fond*: Cass Civ 1e, 28 January 2010, pourvoi no 08-20755;-8-21692.

[162] Y. Chartier, *La réparation du préjudice*, 50.

[163] Interestingly, in one case, the Cour de Cassation did draw a distinction between claimant and third-party hypotheticals: Cass Cass 1e, 2 October 1984, JCP.1984.IV.338, Bull Civ.I.no 245. This was almost immediately denounced as arbitrary: Cf. J. Huet, 'Perte d'une chance: du plus ou moins classique'. The courts now clearly draw no distinction: cf. G. Viney, P. Jourdain, and S. Carval, *Les conditions*, 227; and: Cass Civ 1e, 7 February 1990, RTDC 1991, 121 (obs Jourdain); Cass Civ 1e, 16 July 1991, Bull Civ 1 1991 no 248; Cass Civ 1e, 20 June 2000, no 98-23046, Bull Civ 2000 I, no 193, D.2000.471 (somm Jourdain); Cass Civ 1e, 7 December 2004, no 02-10957, Juris-data no 2004-026046, JCP.G.2005.IV.1154.

[164] X. Pradel, *Le préjudice dans le droit civil de la responsabilité*, 213; P. LeTourneau, *Droit de la responsabilité et des contrats*, 7th edition, 431.

[165] Ibid. The 'leading case' is: Req 1 June 1932, D.1933.1.102; S.1933.1.49 (note H. Mazeaud).

[166] P. LeTourneau, *Droit de la responsabilité*, 442–3; C. Müller, *La perte d'une chance*, 69ff.

[167] P. LeBrun, *Responsabilité civile extra-contractuelle* 2nd edition, no.182; L. Raschel, 'La délicate distinction de la perte de chance et du risque de dommage'.

favorable'.[168] This is interpreted to mean that it must no longer be possible for the benefit to accrue to the claimant or for the loss to be avoided.[169] Thus, to be exposed to a 20 per cent increased risk of cancer, where the cancer has not occurred, is not to suffer a lost chance.[170]

Some cases might seem, however, to give support to the possibility of recovery for pure increased risk. In these cases the claimant is awarded damages where it has been wrongfully exposed to a risk of X and X has not occurred. Yet the impression is misleading since, in each case, the claimant has suffered some other damage brought about by the risk, in respect of which damages are awarded. Consider the holding of the Cour de Cassation of 11 May 2010.[171] The claimants had been wrongfully exposed to asbestos dust by their employers. They had not suffered any asbestos-related illness but were subject to an increased risk of suffering such illnesses. The Court upheld the Court of Appeal's decision to award 7,500 euro to reflect the *préjudice moral* suffered by each employee. This was a 'préjudice spécifique d'anxiété' constituted by their 'permanent situation of worry faced with the risk at any moment of being told they have an illness linked to asbestos and consequently their being led to have various tests which re-ignite this anxiety'.[172] The award of damages is, therefore, in respect of the anxiety occasioned by the risk-exposure and the need for medical monitoring.[173] Without anxiety, there is no award of damages.[174] Further examples of analytically similar awards involving financial expenditure taken out to prevent some loss could be given.[175] Again, the damage here is not the risk, but the expenditure.[176]

---

[168] See Note 160.   [169] C. Bloch, 'Exposition à un risque et perte de chance', 1915.

[170] As in English law, there is a procedure whereby damages can be assessed in respect of the future loss and then collected later: Cass Civ 2e, 20 July 1993, D.1993.526 (note Chartier); RTDC 1994, 107 (obs Jourdain). Cf. X. Pradel, *Le préjudice dans le droit civil de la responsabilité*, 221.

[171] Cass Soc 11 May 2010, JCP G no 41, 11 October 2010, 1015 (obs Bloch).   [172] Ibid.

[173] Cf. *Grieves* v. *FT Everard* [2008] 1 AC 281.

[174] For the same result in cases of possibly defective pacemakers causing anxiety: Cass Civ 1e, 19 December 2006, no 05–15.721; JCP G 2007 II 10052 (note Hocquet-Berg). Affirmed by the CA Paris after cassation: CA Paris 1e, 12 September 2008, JCP E 2008, 2253 (note Bandon-Tourret and Gorny).

[175] Cass Civ 2e, 15 May 2008, Bull Civ II, no 112; RTDC 2008, 679 (Jourdain); JCP 2008, I, 186, n1 – Stoffel-Munck; D.2008, 2900. See, generally, P. Jourdain, 'Comment traiter le dommage potentiel'.

[176] Cf. possibly in favour of pure risk: Cass Civ 1e, 14 January 2010, no 08–16.760; RTDC 2010, 330 (obs Jourdain). The case is rightly described as equivocal, however, by C. Bloch, 'Exposition à un risque et perte de chance', 1915.

Justificatory problems in the current law

The exclusion of recovery for pure increased risk
What justifies the expansive recovery for lost chances but the non-existent recovery for increased risks? The exclusion of recovery for pure increased risk is usually defended by reference to the Cour de Cassation's definition of a lost chance as 'la disparition actuelle et certaine d'une éventualité favorable': the present and certain disappearance of a beneficial possibility.[177] The idea is that a person has not lost the chance of obtaining a benefit unless that the possibility of obtaining that benefit has been foreclosed entirely. If D exposes C to the risk of suffering injury, but C has not yet suffered it, the possibility of avoiding the injury has not 'disappeared' or been foreclosed.[178]

Loss of a chance and mere causal uncertainty
A significant strand of doctrinal writing holds the view that the loss of a chance doctrine is only applicable where a specific form of uncertainty exists: a distinction should hold between cases of (what we can call) *simple* causal uncertainty and cases of loss of a chance.[179] The claim is that in certain factual situations it is only possible to speak of there being a probability that the defendant caused the claimant's damage, and not, additionally, that the defendant has caused the loss of a chance, even in situations where the probability of causation is significant. For example, the DES cases – or defendant indeterminacy cases more generally – are treated in French law as cases of *simple* causal uncertainty, and not lost chance. The result is that under the reversal of the burden of proof each DES defendant is liable *in solidum*, whereas their liability would be less if lost chance were applicable.[180]

To illustrate this view further, consider the facts of Cour de Cassation, 28 January 2010.[181] A child was born with a severe brain injury due to insufficient oxygen reaching his brain. The medical evidence stated that of children with similar injuries, 69 per cent were due to *antepartum* factors – and the presence of these or the failure to control them constituted negligence by the defendants. There was approximately a 25 per cent

---

[177] See pp. 332–3.
[178] R. Stevens, *Torts and Rights*, 43ff, also thinks there is an important conceptual (and normative) distinction. See further, pp.350–1.
[179] F. Chabas, 'La perte d'une chance en droit français', 139–140.
[180] On the DES cases in French law, see Chapter 4, 158–160. Cf., however, R. Savatier, 'Commentary on Decision of 14 December 1965, Cour de Cassation' drawing the conclusion that recognition of the lost chance in medical cases meant that liability could be apportioned in a *Summers* v. *Tice* situation.
[181] Cass Civ 1e, 28 January 2010, JCP no 17 474 (note Hocquet-Berg).

chance that the brain injury had a congenital, incurable origin. The court upheld the decision of the Court of Appeal which held the defendant doctors liable for a 75 per cent loss of the chance of avoiding the brain injury.

Hocquet-Berg argues that this is a misapplication of the *perte d'une chance* doctrine since it was not shown that the child had a 'chance' of avoiding the injury – for the reason that the injury was *either* due to the congenital problem *or* the negligent factors. The fact that there was a chance that the defendants' negligence *caused* the brain injury is not to be equated with the proposition that the claimant had a chance of avoiding the injury pre-negligence. For this to be case, it has to be shown that the fault has 'played a causal role in the damaging *process*, by compromising the chances which the claimant had to avoid the final damage which has realised'.[182] This comes close to saying that the negligence has to be a NESS contribution to the final injury or that it must have accelerated it (even marginally), even if it remains unclear whether the injury would have happened or not.[183]

The main problem with this distinction is that it leads to *prima facie* anomalous results. Suppose that the claimant has negligently been given medicine by a doctor at hospital A and has been given the same medicine non-wrongfully by hospital B. The medicine causes C injury. There is no possibility of the doses acting cumulatively: either hospital A caused the injury or hospital B but it is impossible to tell which. The claim against hospital A would likely fail in French law because A would not be said to have caused C the loss of the chance of avoiding the injury. Yet if C had been suffering from a pre-existing condition, which A negligently omitted to treat, and some chance that C would have been cured was destroyed by A, A would be liable for that lost chance. Given that in both cases there is uncertainty over whether a non-wrongful cause or a wrongful cause brought about the injury, this may be hard to sustain. This is especially so if one adopts a capacious, epistemic, notion of chance: if such a conception is adopted, it becomes extremely difficult to avoid the re-formulation of any causal uncertainty into chance terms.

---

[182] S. Hocquet-Berg, 'La perte d'une chance pour fixer la réparation à la mesure statistique du lien causal entre les fautes et le dommage' citing from F. Chabas, above Note 179, 131, who first developed this view. See also the similar evidential situation in Cass Civ 1e, 14 October 2010, D.2010.2682 (note Sargos), RTDC 2011, 128 (Jourdain). Jourdain cites the same phrase from F. Chabas, 131. The distinction is also accepted by J. Borghetti, 'La réparation de la perte d'une chance en droit Suisse et en droit français', 1080.

[183] It may be that many lost chance cases could be re-analysed as NESS contribution cases: the shift from an n per cent chance of a cure to a 0 per cent chance of a cure will often be the result of some role being played in the mechanism of the injury by the defendant's wrongful conduct. Cf. E. Johnson, 'Criminal Liability for Loss of a Chance', 86–106.

All-or-nothing tendencies

A further tension arises from a current of jurisprudence which applies a lower standard of proof in respect of causation, thereby achieving full liability when only a lost chance has been shown. For example, in one decision the Cour de Cassation upheld a lower court, which had found causation of a child's entire brain injury to be established on the basis of expert testimony that 'normalement' non-negligent treatment would have avoided it.[184] In another, recent, decision the Cour de Cassation (upholding the Court of Appeal) struck down an award of lost chance damages in respect of a (75 per cent) lost chance of avoiding blindness, had a doctor properly diagnosed the claimant, instead observing that there was a 'certain' causal link with the blindness.[185] This approach is particularly visible in cases of breaches of a duty to inform of the risks of medical treatment where courts have sometimes been content to rely upon broad generalisations about how a reasonable patient would have decided if informed to award either full or no damages.[186] The product liability cases discussed in the last chapter also fall within this all-or-nothing category.[187]

The sceptical understanding of loss of a chance

A prevalent view among doctrinal writers is that, in some cases at least, the lost chance doctrine involves a fiction. The fiction is that the loss

---

[184] Cass Civ 1e, 1 June 1976, JCP G.II.18483 (comm Savatier). See also Cass Civ 1e, 29 May 1979, Bull Civ I no 156; Cass Civ 1e 23 May 1973, Bull Civ I no 180; CA Bourges, 27 March 1984, D.1985.IR.112 (100 per cent liability of avocat); Cass Crim, 18 March 1986, JCP 1986. IV.154 (loss of employment after a criminally inflicted injury is not to be equated with a simple loss of chance); CA Paris, 29 October 1993, D.1995.somm.97 (Penneau).

[185] Cass Civ 1e, 13 November 2008, no 07–18.008; JCP.G.II.10030 (2009) (note Sargos).

[186] CA Admin, Paris, 31 December 2009, No 08PA00574 (claimant not informed of 'highly exceptional' risk of serious complication: 'une patiente se déterminant de manière raisonnable' and who was hoping for fertility success and in the absence of other treatment would still have gone ahead: no loss of chance); Cass Civ 1e, 6 December 2007, Bull Civ I, no 380, D.2008.192 (note Sargos), JCP.2008.II.125 no.3 (obs Stoffel-Munck); CA Bordeaux, Chambre 1 (Admin), 4 March 2010, No 09BX01189; CA Versailles, Chambre 4 (Admin), 2 March 2010, No.08VE01096; Cass Civ 1e, 13 November 2002, No.01-.00.377. Cf. the personalised approach of: CA Paris (Admin) 30 December 2009, No.08PA04468; Cass Civ 1e, 8 July 2008, no 07–12.159, Juris-data no 2008-044756, JCP.G.2008.II.10166 (note Sargos).

[187] In some cases loss of chance has also been used to recognise the violation of C's autonomy where D has failed to inform C despite it being largely clear that D has caused C no loss: cf. CA Paris (Admin) Ch8, 2 November 2009, No 07PA02234 (30 per cent lost chance awarded where a hip operation was undertaken without advising of risk of invalidity; despite C being in pain and the only other option being a course of drugs involving significant pain, the patient had been deprived of the opportunity to differ 'for reasons personal or otherwise').

of a chance of a gain or of avoiding a loss is itself a loss. The claim is not necessarily that the outcomes generated by the doctrine are not justified in these cases, only that the legal reasons offered for its justification do not hold.

Thus, Viney and Jourdain title their section on loss of chance in medical liability: '[l]'utilisation de la notion de la perte d'une chance pour pallier l'incertitude sur le lien de causalité'.[188] Similarly a recent report of the Cour de Cassation considers that the doctrine rests upon the concern to avoid systematic rejection of liability in damages wherever certainty over causation is unobtainable.[189] This understanding is expressed well by Quézel-Ambrunaz: 'the supposed autonomy of the loss of a chance is sometimes but a helpful expedient used to mask the integration of probabilistic reasoning in the field of causation...The loss of a chance to avoid the realisation of a risk approximates to...a proportional liability'.[190]

Justifications of this re-distribution of the risk of uncertainty over causation are, however, little worked out in the literature. It is often asserted that it is fairer to apportion liability by reference to the probability of a benefit lost because it is *impossible* to know what would have happened absent the defendant's wrongful conduct.[191] In view of this impossibility of proof, and in view of the proven fault of the defendant,[192] it is considered preferable to award probabilistically-measured damages rather than systematically to deny liability or to award liability in full where significant uncertainty remains.[193] Loss of a chance is a fairer middle-ground between these two extremes.[194]

---

[188] G. Viney, P. Jourdain, and S. Carval, Les conditions, 4th edition 229. Similarly: P. Jourdain, 'Usage et abus de la notion de perte d'une chance', 85, 'Sur la perte d'une chance', 109ff.

[189] Cour de Cassation, Rapport annuel, 268. Similarly: X. Pradel, Le préjudice dans le droit civil de la responsabilité, no 190; C. Quézel-Ambrunaz, Essai, 164, n 7.

[190] C. Quézel-Ambrunaz, 'Note under Cass Civ 1e, 11 Mars 2010', 834. This understanding is also implicit in P. Sargos, 'La causalité en matière de responsabilité ou le "droit Schtroumpf"', 1940.

[191] P. Jourdain, 'Usage et abus de la notion de perte d'une chance', 85; F. Descorps-Declere, 'La Cohérence de la jurisprudence de la Cour de Cassation sur la perte de chance', 746.

[192] See the remark of P. Esmein in C. Aubry, C. Rau, and P. Esmein, Droit civil that loss of a chance forms part of a modern tendency not to allow negligent defendants to profit from uncertainty over causation, 423, n. 47.

[193] G. Durry, 'La faute du médecin diminuant les "chances de guérison" du malade' 798; G. Durry, 'Faute médicale et perte de chances de survie', 408.

[194] G. Durry, 'La faute du médecin diminuant les "chances de guérison" du malade', 798 also makes a deterrence-based argument that without loss of a chance in the medical context, there would be an 'irresponsabilité automatique' of medical professionals.

Justifying probabilistic liability: lost chances and increased risks as loss

For the English and French law on when the loss of a chance can establish liability in tort to be justified, it must be the case that:

(1) To lose a chance of avoiding injury or to be exposed to a risk of an injury is itself in certain circumstances to suffer a loss;

(2) People ought to enjoy legal rights that others – in certain circumstances – do not cause them to lose such a chance or to be exposed to such a risk;

(3) The measure of damages should be a probabilistic proportion of the loss suffered by the victim.

OR

(4) People sometimes ought to enjoy legal rights that others – in certain circumstances – not cause them to lose such a chance or to be exposed to such a risk and substantial damages can be awarded on the ground that this right has been infringed, with the chance or risk being taken into account as a measure of the value of right infringed.

In this section, I will argue that (1) and (2) are true, but that (3) is problematic. I will suggest, in outline, that (4) is the most plausible basis for the recovery of substantial damages in direct proportion to the probability of the loss suffered in respect of lost chances. Less abstractly, it will be argued first that losing a chance of avoiding a physical injury and losing a chance of avoiding a chance of an economic loss can be to suffer a loss – regardless of whether these are objective or epistemic chances. Second, it will be argued that people ought to enjoy legal rights that others not negligently destroy such chances principally in situations where the person who destroyed the chance undertook to take care of the victim's chance of avoiding a physical injury. Third, it will be argued that the weakness of our interest in having a chance in itself is such that the measure of damages for lost chances of avoiding physical injuries should not be a probabilistic fraction of the underlying loss which has been suffered in so far as these damages aim to reflect the loss suffered by the claimant. Finally, the relationship between damages for loss of chance of avoiding an injury and damages for the injury itself is explained.

The value of chance

Everyone agrees that for a person to suffer a loss minimally involves that person being 'worse off' in some sense, or, at the very least, involves that person being in some bad state.[195] If so we need an account of what it is that makes it the case that a person is worse off. What makes a person worse off is whatever negatively affects that person's interests. What is in a person's interests depends upon what is good or valuable for that person. And so, as McBride has written, we cannot know whether someone is better or worse off 'unless we can construct some sort of line of value' for that person.[196] The best theory of loss requires us to have some theory about what is good or valuable for a person.

Why losing a chance can be a loss

It should be straightforward to see the intuitive normative force of the idea that losses of chance can be losses. We speak and act as if chances of good things matter to us.[197] We care whether we have chances and we care whether the people we care about have chances. And, across many cases, all of this seems perfectly reasonable.[198] The person who cares whether they have a chance of avoiding cancer is right to care about this. Does anyone deny that it is reasonable to value having opportunities or chances of good things? From these facts, it seems justified to infer that losing a chance of something can be a loss.

Explaining why lost chances are losses: attitudinal accounts

The reason why the inference seems justified can potentially be explained by the following general accounts of when a person will have suffered a loss. Consider Edelman's sufficient condition of what it is to suffer loss: 'Were the consequences of the infringement undesired by the claimant? If so, he will have suffered a loss.'[199] Similarly, Webb has written: 'We suffer a loss every time something happens ... which we value less than the state of affairs which existed before or which would otherwise have come about.'[200] And Stevens writes that being exposed to an increased risk of harm by the leak of a toxic chemical is a loss

---

[195] It is possible to deny the 'worse off' idea by thinking that there is no need to conceive of loss in comparative terms. Being worse off is always a matter of comparison. It could be thought, for example, that X causes Y 'loss' if X causes Y to be in a state of severe pain even if, had X not acted, Y would have been in even greater pain. See E. Harman, 'Harming as Causing Harm', 137.

[196] N. McBride, 'Tort Law and Human Flourishing' 20.

[197] N. Jansen, 'The Idea of a Lost Chance', 293: 'the law has to protect chances because people apparently regard their protection as very important'.

[198] C. Finkelstein, 'Is Risk a Harm?', 971–73.

[199] J. Edelman, 'The Meaning of Loss and Enrichment', 213.

[200] C. Webb, 'Justifying Damages', 160.

because, 'We would all prefer not to be in the vicinity of the leak.'[201] According to him, that the child in *Hotson* lost something 'can be demonstrated by contemplating what a parent would be prepared to pay to go back in time and have the child given careful treatment'.[202] We can call these 'attitudinal conceptions of loss' by virtue of their focusing upon people's 'attitudes' – understood broadly as including desires, preferences and valuations – in determining what constitutes a loss.

It is natural to analyse a person's good in terms of that particular person's desires or preferences. One major reason for this simply is that it makes a person's good depend upon his or her attitudes. Never being allowed to see a Shakespeare play again is no loss (one might think) if you detest Shakespeare. This seems to provide a bulwark against overly paternalistic views of what is good for a person.

Yet we can see why we need to focus upon a subset of a person's desires or preferences if the attitudinal account is to be at all plausible as an account of what makes a person's life go well. If one focuses simply upon the actual preferences or desires of a person, the attitudinal account is obviously false. People often actually prefer or desire what is not in their interest, as when I prefer to eat a chocolate bar which, unbeknown to me, is laced with poison. This is why it becomes necessary, in a preference- or desire-based account of good for a person, to insist not upon actual preferences or desires, but well-informed preferences or desires.

If, however, we look not to a person's actual preferences but to his or her well-informed preferences, we cause problems for the idea that losing a chance in itself makes a person's life go worse in cases where the chance is purely epistemic.[203] Once well informed and so aware of all the facts, Stephen Hotson would no longer have had a preference or desire that he not lose his 25 per cent chance of avoiding a hip injury. Rather, on the assumption that the relevant physical processes were deterministic, he would know whether there were enough blood vessels in his leg necessary to make any treatment effective and prefer either to have the treatment or not. Since he would be aware of all the facts, his preferences would simply not have chances as their object. If what is in one's interests is defined by what one would prefer when one is well informed, then losing a chance cannot be a setback to one's

---

[201] R. Stevens, *Torts and Rights*, 43.   [202] Ibid., 50.
[203] This problem was raised by S. Perry, 'Risk, Harm, Interests, and Rights', 190.

interests, since what one prefers when well informed does not relate to one's chances, but only the valuable matters to which the chance relates.

While this critique does not apply to objective chances, because even a well-informed person would still prefer to have an objective chance of some good, we still have good reason to doubt that a theory of loss based upon the idea of preference or desire-satisfaction can give much support to the claim that losing objective chances is to suffer a loss. This is because there is a fundamental general objection to any such account.

The idea that preference or desire-satisfaction contributes to a person's good probably works for certain things: tasting the flavour of ice cream you prefer rather than the one you do not makes life go better. But beyond matters of this kind (matters of 'mere' preference or 'taste'), preference or desire-satisfaction provides a poor account of what makes a person's life go better. Many things are good, without their being good being wholly dependent upon our preferring them; we prefer them because they are good.[204] It is odd to say that friendship is good because it is preferable. This gets the order of explanation the wrong way around.[205]

Perhaps some purely preference-based account can be rescued by limiting the extent to which the agent must be 'well informed'. One possibility is that a chance of avoiding an injury counts as good for a person if that person prefers that chance in full knowledge of the facts consistent with that chance existing. The issue would then arise as to when tort law should protect a person's preferences.[206]

Why chances are valuable

A different account of what makes a person's life go well can better justify the intuition that losing a chance can sometimes be to suffer a loss in a stronger sense. Purely desire- and preference-based accounts of the good are often rejected in favour of objective list accounts.[207] On such views, there are certain valuable things whose value is not wholly determined by our preferring or desiring them. For example, Scanlon lists: (1) having pleasurable experiences; (2) success in or achievement

---

[204] For this objection see, for example, T. Scanlon, *What we Owe to Each Other*, ch 3.

[205] For other problems with it, see D. Parfit, *Reasons and Persons*, 494.

[206] For the claim that preference can be protected as an element of a person's interest in autonomy, see p. 344.

[207] See, for example, the movement of the discussion in Scanlon, referenced in Note 204, ch 3. Scanlon calls 'objective list' accounts 'substantive good' theories.

of one's rational aims; (3) friendship, other personal relations and (4) achievements of excellence.[208]

I will discuss three accounts of why chances of good things are valuable. The first draws connections between chances and interests in autonomy. The second connects chances and interests in security. The third suggests that chances of good things have a value distinct from their contribution to autonomy or security. Each of these accounts can lend support to the claim that the loss of a chance of avoiding an injury can itself constitute a loss, but only the third establishes a non-contingent connection between the loss of a chance and the suffering of loss.

The autonomy account of the value of chance

Living an autonomous life is valuable. There are different aspects to autonomous life, each of which can support to some extent the claim that having chances of good things makes one's life go better.

Autonomy and valuable options.

According to Raz's plausible account, an autonomous life requires that we have an adequate range of valuable options available to us so that we have a meaningful choice as to what sort of life we will lead.[209] An option is an ability do something, exercisable by a choice. As Oberdiek has argued, exposure to risk of injury (which always entails the reduced chance of avoiding some injury) can foreclose a person's valuable options.[210] Suppose A increases B's risk of suffering cancer by 40 per cent. B may now need regular medical checks, which, putting aside their potential financial cost, require B to forego other valuable activities B might have otherwise pursued. In short, risks can prevent one from exercising valuable options.

This account can sometimes explain why a person suffers a loss in loss of chance cases. Consider again *Hotson*. As a result of D's negligence, C is not given a 25 per cent chance of avoiding a physical injury. What valuable option(s) of C's does this foreclose? The most obvious possibility is 'the option of receiving non-negligent medical treatment'. Alternatively, if C would have gone to another doctor who would have treated C non-negligently, had D not represent that D would take care of C,

---

[208] T. Scanlon, *What we Owe to Each Other*, 124–5; see also J. Finnis, *Natural Law and Natural Rights*, ch 2.

[209] Raz, *The Morality of Freedom*, 369–99.

[210] J. Oberdiek, 'The Moral Significance of Risking', 350-4.

we might say that D has foreclosed C's option of receiving non-negligent treatment from that other doctor. We could say that D has caused C to lose the option of non-negligent medical treatment by inducing C to rely upon D's representation that D will take reasonable care.[211]

Why is this unprovided option *valuable*? We cannot say it is valuable because it provides a chance of avoiding the injury on pain of circularity. This will not be an explanation of the value of chance in terms of the value of autonomy. If we say the option is valuable because it provides a chance, this account tells us nothing about *why* the chance is valuable. Here Perry asserts that 'it is clearly preferable to be treated competently rather than incompetently'.[212] There remains a concern of circularity with this suggestion – namely, that the option of competent treatment is valuable only in virtue of its providing a chance of a better outcome. To avoid this, it is necessary to claim that the option of acting upon a reasonable preference is itself valuable so far as one's autonomy is concerned. If we accept this plausible claim, then we have identified a genuine loss suffered by Hotson in relying upon the doctor's (implied) representation that reasonable care would be taken of him.

Autonomy as informed decision-making

If a person makes a decision of some importance to them under conditions where they do not fully understand the nature or implications of the decision, it may be said their autonomy has been set back. If a doctor fails to inform a patient of a significant risk attached to an operation, it might be said that the decision to have the procedure is not fully autonomous. In such cases, however, the lost chance is a lost chance *to decide under better conditions*. The loss of such a chance may or may not also lead to lost chances of avoiding an injury. The distinctiveness of this kind of chance from the chance of avoiding an injury is supported by the fact that in French law distinct awards have been made in medical negligence cases against doctors for the interference with autonomy and the loss of a chance on the same facts. If a doctor negligently fails

---

[211] This suggestion is made by S. Perry, 'Protected Interests and Undertakings in the Law of Tort', 308-11. See also S. Green, *Causation in Negligence*, 152-66, who relies upon the idea of autonomy to explain the existing English law, but argues interestingly that an interest in autonomy does not support a claim in *Hotson*. Cf. for legal recognition of autonomy-constituting importance of valuable options: *Rees* v. *Darlington Memorial NHS Trust* [2004] AC 309, [123]: 'the parents have lost the opportunity to live their lives in the way that they wished and planned to do'.

[212] S. Perry, 'Protected Interests and Undertakings in the Law of Tort', 309.

to inform a patient of the risk of some injury occurring in a operation and the patient suffers the injury as a result of the operation, the patient could obtain a conventional sum for the loss of autonomy *and* damages to reflect the x per cent chance that it would not have had the operation, and thereby avoided an injury suffered in the operation, if properly informed of the risks.[213]

The security account of the value of chance

Security is valuable. It is good to be in a position where one can expect that one's important interests will be preserved from attack or diminishment. One reason is that if one fears that one's interests will be attacked – that what is important to one will be taken away – it will be difficult to live a fulfilling life. The more risk one faces the less one can plan ahead for the future. One's present attachment to one's life dwindles.

Can this idea explain the sense in which the claimant in *Hotson* lost something valuable? If the defendant had not been negligent in *Hotson*, the claimant would have had a greater expectation that his health would not deteriorate significantly. Therefore, he would have had more security if the defendant had not behaved negligently. Of course, there would still have been a much *greater* expectation that his health would deteriorate (a 75 per cent chance), but security is plausibly a matter of degree. To a very small extent, his interest in security from injury would have been improved.

But is it the *sense* of security or peace of mind which matters or does *actually* being secure in itself contribute to a person's well-being? If *feeling* secure is what matters, then the claimant in *Hotson* would only have been better off if he actually felt more secure. The issue is not clear. On balance, it seems that actual security is of some value. One's life is going better if there are no bombs under one's house which might explode at any moment – even if one does not know of it. Or suppose that a computer system accidentally signs up one to an insurance policy validly insuring one, at no cost, against personal injury for the next ten years.

---

[213] See V. Vioujas, 'La reconnaissance d'un préjudice, distinct de la perte de chance, en cas de manquement du médecin à son obligation d'information : le Conseil d'État suit l'impulsion de la Cour de cassation'. It recently seems to have been established, however, that the mere interference with autonomy is not actionable in itself – rather the damage (still distinct from the lost chance of avoiding an injury) consists in having an operation when one was not prepared to have an operation (*dommage d'impréparation*): Cass Civ 1e, 23 January 2014 (12-22.123).

Even if one never claims during the ten years, it seems that it is still better for one to be insured than not.[214]

The derivative value account of the value of chance

It is plausible that chances of good things are also valuable simply in virtue of the goodness of the objects to which they relate. Chances of avoiding cancer are good because cancer is bad. The value of chance is therefore a kind of 'derivative', not intrinsic, value. Chances obtain this value by being facilitators of the good states of affairs to which they relate.[215] But 'derivative' value is still value. If the object to which the chance relates is intrinsically valuable, the chance has a derivative, non-financial value. In the same way that there is a value in not having a broken leg that is not simply constituted by any economic losses which having a broken leg might bring, there is a (not purely financial) value in having a chance of not having a broken leg. It does not follow from the fact that such a chance cannot straightforwardly be bought and sold that it does not have value. If that were true, many things – children, autonomy, avoiding pain, life – would not have value.

The weakness of our interest in chances of goods and freedom from risk

If we allow that conferring the chance of avoiding an injury upon someone itself benefits them, even if they are unaware of it, we must also accept that our interest in having such chances *per se* is a very weak interest. This is for two reasons.

First, consider again this example:

> *Ticking bomb.* Deep under A's house, unbeknown to A, there is a bomb which has either an epistemic or an objective 20 per cent chance of exploding at some time during a period of 50 years and killing A.

Suppose that A reaches the end of his life completely unscathed and the period of risk is over. Only now does A discover that he has been at risk for the past 50 years. Suppose A is asked how much money he would pay to have lived exactly the same life, but free of the risk which he never knew about and which never materialised. It seems unlikely that

---

[214] For a helpful discussion of this, see M. Otsuka, 'The Fairness of Equal Chances' (unpublished manuscript; cited with permission of the author).

[215] For a general analysis of 'derivative' value, see J. Raz, *From Normativity to Responsibility*, ch 8.

A would be willing to pay anything at all. This tends to suggest that we care mainly about risks because we care about the harms they may bring about and how we may avoid those harms, not because of the risks in themselves.

Second, suppose that determinism is true. If determinism is true,[216] there are no objective chances *in the sense that* all events would have a chance of 1 or 0 if we had all possible information at the time of assessing the chance.[217] If so, all chances are only ever epistemic. To see why this poses a problem for the claim that chances have significant value, consider:

> *Snake bite.* A arrives at hospital two hours after being bitten by a snake. The snake's venom can cause blindness if untreated. B, doctor, negligently fails to give A an antidote and A becomes blind. It is known that 20 per cent of people when treated with the antidote will definitely avoid blindness, but for 80 per cent it is definitely ineffective. A test can determine whether A falls within the 20 per cent or not but only if the test is performed within one hour of being bitten. After that point, it is impossible to say whether the person would have avoided blindness. The test is not performed on A.

This case involves a deterministic situation: if A receives the antidote, the result will always be the same – it will not sometimes be the case that A recovers and sometimes A does not. A's hypothetical destiny is fixed, but we do not know which way. A has lost an epistemic chance of 20 per cent of avoiding blindness. Suppose that A would have become blind even if the antidote had been administered. If that is the case, then the reason why we are saying that A has been caused loss is because a test result, which would have shown A to be untreatable, has not been performed. But how could whether A has suffered a loss depend *entirely* upon whether a test result is available or not? If A has been caused a loss here – by virtue of having less of a rational expectation of safety for a period of time – the loss is very insignificant.

---

[216] 'Determinism requires a world that (a) has a well-defined state or description, at any given time, and (b) laws of nature that are true at all places and times. If we have all these, then if (a) and (b) together logically entail the state of the world at all other times (or, at least, all times later than that given in (b)), the world is deterministic...' C. Hoefer, 'Causal Determinism'.

[217] Here I set aside the possibility of chance claims continuing to exist because of the course-grained nature of our descriptions of certain phenomena. For such an account of chance, see C. List and M. Pivato, 'Emergent Chance'.

Or consider:

Scratchcard. A machine in Brazil has been mistakenly purchasing lottery scratchcards for C in the UK. C never finds this out. Whether each card is a winner or loser is printed under an opaque covering, which one must scratch off. Whether one will win is therefore determined by the card's printing. Thirty per cent of the cards printed by the machine are winners, but all of the cards printed for C are losers, though this cannot be determined except by scratching off the surface of the cards.

Has C been benefitted by these losing scratchcards, which provide some epistemic chance of winning the lottery, of which he never learns? If C has, the benefit is very small.[218]

Legal rights that others not destroy chances or increase risks

The case for the conferral of *freestanding* legal rights that others not intentionally or negligently deprive one of a chance of avoiding an injury or increase one's risk of injury is weak. By 'freestanding' I mean a right (a) whose sole justificatory ground lies in an individual's well-being interest in not suffering such a deprivation or (b) whose justificatory ground does not lie in some special relationship, such as an undertaking to preserve a chance, between the parties.

This is true regardless of whether one considers the value of chance to lie in its provision of valuable options, in security, or simply in its derivative value. As we have seen, on the derivative value account of the value of chance, an individual's well-being interest in having a chance or not being exposed to a risk is itself very weak. It is therefore implausible to claim that other individuals should be under legal duties to protect such interests *simply* on the ground of the value of those interests. This leaves open the possibility that there should be legal rights that others not unreasonably deprive one of a chance or expose one to a risk whose sole justificatory ground is our interest in not suffering the injury risked, rather than the risk itself. But if the sole justificatory ground for the right were the actual injury, rather than

---

[218] For a slightly different view, see S. Perry, 'Risk, Harm and Responsibility' 321, 334–6. Perry has slightly qualified his view: see S. Perry, 'Risk, Harm, Interests, and Rights', 199–202. For a view similar to mine, see M. Adler, 'Risk, Death and Harm: the Normative Foundations of Risk Regulation', 1388.

the risk of injury, then we should say, in cases where only pure risk exposure is suffered, that no actionable injury has been suffered.

Even if the autonomy-based account of the value of chance provides a stronger well-being-based reason than the other accounts for the imposition of duties not to interfere with chances in certain ways, it is highly implausible that the deprivation of valuable options should be generally legally wrongful. This follows from the common law's general approach to pure economic loss. To lose wealth is to lose valuable options (to do things with that wealth). Yet nonetheless there is no general right in the common law to protection from purely economic loss. So to the extent that one holds that there should be no general right to protection from purely economic loss, this also rules out protection of valuable options *tout court*. This analogy between economic loss and the loss of valuable options is weaker where the valuable option relates directly to one's bodily integrity, since it might be said that options which may preserve one's bodily integrity deserve special treatment.[219] Nonetheless, it is difficult to accept that the deprivation of a single valuable option, even where that option relates to the preservation of one's health, should be treated in precisely the same way as liability in respect of bodily injury. Possession of valuable options in relation to the preservation of one's health is a weaker, second-order, interest than one's interest in one's bodily integrity itself.

These observations suggest that the pattern of legal protection of valuable options and derivative interests in chance might justifiably approximate the legal protection of purely economic loss.[220] If so, wrong-constituting liability in respect of the deprivation of a chance or valuable option should *only* exist in cases of undertakings to protect a person's chance of avoiding an injury, deliberately induced reliance upon a representation, and in other situations where intentional infliction of economic loss is unlawful. Liability existing where an individual has relied to his or her detriment on another's undertaking to take reasonable care of one's chance of avoiding provides reasonable limits on liability. Moreover, this limitation has a plausible moral underpinning: the moral basis of this liability, as Perry explains, lies in the fact that

---

[219] See Chapter 4, 180ff. For a test case, suppose D negligently causes a road accident, with the result that C's ambulance cannot reach hospital, C suffers a physical injury, and had D not behaved negligently, C would have had a 30 per cent chance of avoiding this injury.

[220] For a convincing analogy between the scope of liability for pure economic loss and for lost chances, see R. Stevens, *Torts and Rights*, 49–50.

the individual has been induced to rely (reasonably) upon the other's undertaking to take reasonable care.[221]

It might be objected that this limited right that others not deprive one of a chance of avoiding an injury, limited to situations of undertakings to protect a chance, nonetheless has an implausible consequence. The implausible consequence is that wherever D undertakes to take care to protect C's chance of avoiding injury from diminution, whereupon C relies upon that undertaking, D ought to be liable to C not only where D deprives C of the chance of avoiding an injury but also wherever D merely increases the risk that C will suffer the injury in the future. For instance, if a doctor negligently momentarily increases a patient's risk of suffering an injury, it might be suggested that this liability formula would demand that D pay C damages in respect of the risk imposition, even if C has suffered no material injury whatsoever.

There are three convincing responses to this objection. First, if a doctor momentarily negligently increases the risk of an injury (and only does this), the patient has not been deprived of the option of non-negligent treatment of its condition. If the injury has not yet occurred, and is still preventable, that option remains open. That is not so in cases like *Hotson* where the option of non-negligent treatment is forever foreclosed. Second, it is not clear that, objectively interpreted, doctors, lawyers and others whose duties in tort are based upon assumed responsibilities, typically undertake to take care to protect persons from momentary risk impositions. Even if the patient suffers a momentary set-back to its security, it is not clear that doctors assume responsibility in respect of this form of loss.[222] Third, where a person is exposed to a risk of injury

---

[221] See p. 344.

[222] A different approach draws a strong conceptual distinction between lost chances and increased risks, with the latter being perhaps *de minimis*. Cf. R. Stevens, *Torts and Rights*, 47–50. This is difficult to sustain. If A imposes a risk of injury on B, B faces an increased probability of injury. If B fails to provide A with a chance of avoiding an injury, what A would have had is an increased probability of avoiding injury. It cannot be maintained that there is a radical asymmetry in the loss-constituting features of increased probabilities of injury compared to increased probabilities of avoiding injury, if we simply look to what each of these things *are*. In fact, many typical lost chance cases are structurally identical to cases of *momentary* risk impositions, such as where B's negligent driving momentarily imposes a risk upon A. In most cases of lost chance, it is true that, had the defendant not behaved negligently, the claimant would have had a chance of avoiding an injury *for a fleeting period*, after which the injury would either have been avoided or not. For example, if the doctor in *Hotson* had behaved non-negligently, Stephen Hotson would not necessarily have been *physically* better off. He may not have been in less pain and his crippling injury may still have occurred. Rather, he would simply have had, for some short period of time, a chance of avoiding necrosis

occurring in the future, and there is a reasonable probability that the risk could be reduced (without unreasonable cost), for instance, by receiving further treatment, then the claimant who claims damages simply for the increased risk without taking available steps to alleviate the risk, will have failed to mitigate its loss.

The assessment of damages

It should be clear that losing a chance of avoiding a physical injury is nothing like suffering a physical injury. It is an immaterial loss. Consequently, losing a 20 per cent chance of avoiding a painful physical injury is nothing like suffering 20 per cent of the pain involved in that injury. If damages for the loss of a chance *in itself* are to be awarded, this has significance for the level of compensation which ought to be payable in respect of such a loss. Suppose that a person who suffers a painful leg injury resulting from a tort may recover £10,000 to compensate for the year of painful aching in the leg. It is hard to accept that the person who has suffered the loss of a 20 per cent chance of avoiding such an injury should be entitled even to £2,000. Not having the immaterial benefit of the chance is nothing like suffering two months of pain. It is a far less serious loss. The same is true of not being able to exercise a valuable option which may have produced a better medical outcome. The interest in question here is one's interest in autonomy; the gist of the claim is not being able to run one's life in accordance with one's choices, not the suffering of physical injury itself.[223]

Thus, if we are to have damages for lost chances or the interferences with autonomy constituted by the deprivation of a valuable option, it would be preferable to operate a system whereby alongside the tariffs for pain and suffering and loss of amenity there are significantly scaled-down equivalent tariffs for losing the chance of these non-pecuniary losses.[224] So if the loss of a leg is valued at £5,000. The 90 per cent lost chance of avoiding the loss of a leg could be valued at, say, £1,000, with proportional reductions down to lower levels of

---

in his hip. This itself provides an additional argument for the claim that the damages in respect of lost chances should be minimal.

[223] Compare the award in *Rees v. Darlington Memorial NHS Trust* [2004] 1 AC 309.

[224] Should those who have lost objective rather than only epistemic chances receive greater compensation? Probably. But in practice the courts cannot determine whether an objective chance has been lost and so must proceed as if only an epistemic chance has been lost. See M. Balaguer, 'Why There are no Good Arguments for Any Interesting Version of Determinism', 8; A. Beever, *Rediscovering*, 499ff.

chance. The exercise is no more arbitrary than the initial assignment of financial values to the loss of a leg.

Losing a chance of avoiding an economic loss can be akin to suffering an economic loss. If a company is exposed to a 20 per cent risk of a significant liability in the future, the value of the company may be presently depressed. Similarly, if the bailee of one's antique vase exposes it to moisture with the result that it is subject to a 20 per cent increased risk of cracking in the next year, the financial value of the vase is immediately depressed (for, at least, the next year).

In cases where the depression in value resulting from a risk exposure is unlikely to be of limited duration, it might be that a sensible way of calculating damages is simply the difference between the pre-tort value and the present value. It is not clear, however, whether this will always capture the nature of the loss suffered. In cases where the asset is unlikely to have been sold had the risk imposition not occurred, the nature of the loss is simply having less security as to the physical integrity of one's corporeal asset. In such cases it may be too generous to award the difference in value for the next year. A better measure would be the loss of the use value of an object of reduced financial value or the extent to which the lease value of the object is reduced during the period of the risk exposure.

Similarly, in cases like *Allied Maples* it also seems inappropriate to award a fraction of the total economic loss suffered. Had the defendant solicitor not been negligent, the claimant would have had a chance of renegotiating its contract with a third party for better protection against contingent liabilities. What is the value of this chance? It has two components. It has a non-financial value: the value of having good prospects in relation to one's assets. But this is an extremely weak second-order value. The main value of the chance consists in its financial value. What is this financial value? If the claimant had been given a chance of re-negotiation, this would temporarily have increased the market value of the claimant company. A person would rationally pay more for a company with some chance of avoiding a contingent liability than one without it. On the balance of probability, however, this swell in the value of the company was likely to be temporary – on the balance of probability the company would not have been able to negotiate protection against the liabilities. The fact that the claimant would have had a temporary swell in the value of its assets is quite unlike standard economic losses, which involve some more than purely fleeting diminution in wealth. It is doubtful whether any damages at all are merited on loss-based grounds.

The relationship between damages for CL, IR, and damages in respect of the injury itself

Suppose that a doctor negligently destroys a patient's 60 per cent chance of avoiding a permanent brain injury and that this 60 per cent chance would entitle the judge to find on the balance of probability that the patient's brain injury would not have occurred had the doctor not been negligent. Can the claimant recover damages both for the lost 60 per cent chance *and* full damages for the brain injury?

If the BPR operates as follows, then the answer is negative. If the BPR requires the judge to find or accept that *p*, then whenever the judge believes that *more probably than not p*, then the finding that *p* would be inconsistent with the proposition that the claimant lost a chance. In the brain injury case, if the 60 per cent chance means that the judge must find, not that *more probably than not* the brain injury would not have occurred, but that *the brain injury would not have occurred*, then this finding would be logically inconsistent with saying that there was a chance it would not have occurred. The law treats as certain what is only probable. If this understanding of the BPR is correct, it also rules out any recovery for lost chances, since if the chance is less than 51 per cent, this requires the finding that the injury would have happened anyway. This appears to be the dominant understanding of the BPR.[225] Thus, damages for lost chances require an exception to this rule to be made.

If the BPR simply required a finding *that probably this is what happened*, then there is no inconsistency between making this finding *and* awarding damages for the loss of a chance. But this understanding of the rule gives rise to the possibility that in cases of chances greater than 50 per cent, the claimant could argue that he should recover full damages for his injury, because he has satisfied the BPR, *and* damages for the lost chance. If the damages for lost chances were as minimal as they ought to be, this might not be entirely unappealing. However, there is a strong argument for saying that if one is exposed to a risk of harm that compensation for the harm itself also *ipso facto* compensates for the risk. The reason is that one's interest in protection from risk is itself derivative of one's interest in avoiding the risked injury.[226] On the

---

[225] See J. Coleman, 'Mistakes, Misunderstandings, and Misalignments', 562–3: '. . .[the BPR] holds that in the context of a tort action, one should accept a proposition as true (that is, believe it) only if the evidence renders it more likely than not to be true'. Though one might doubt Coleman's equation of acceptance and belief here.

[226] For such an 'absorption' thesis, see C. Finkelstein, 'Is Risk a Harm?' 993–5. Some French authors argue that when a risked injury occurs that it absorbs the 'intermediary' damage of loss of chance, see L. Khoury, 'Causation and Risk', 126.

derivative value account of the value of chance, one's reasons for caring about not being exposed to risks are derivative of the disvalue of the outcomes are actually risked. Thus, if one is compensated for the outcome itself, there is some plausibility in thinking that this also addresses the loss due to the risk exposure considered alone.[227] In short, the better view is that the claimant can only recover *either* in respect of the traditional loss or in respect of the lost chance, where the BPR is satisfied: they must elect.

Rights-based damages in cases involving lost chances

Suppose that D sells a lottery ticket to C on Monday for £1,000. The lottery is drawn on Friday afternoon. In breach of contract, D fails to deliver the ticket on Friday morning. Suppose that, had the ticket been delivered, it would have had a 1/3 chance of winning £50,000, by virtue of being entered into a draw of three tickets. It cannot now be determined whether the ticket would have won or lost. To what remedies is C entitled in English law?

C could claim restitution of the £1,000. On the account offered above, it is doubtful whether C should, alternatively, recover substantial compensatory damages. Had D not breached the contract, C would have had a 1/3 chance of £50,000 for a few hours. Unless C would have sold this chance or otherwise profited from it, C has lost something very minor. If we (generously) say the chance has an approximate financial value of £17,000 during that period – the loss is like not having the use of £17,000 for few hours.

It could alternatively be argued that C should recover substantial damages simply to reflect that C did not obtain the benefit of its bargain. This award would enforce C's 'performance interest' or serve as a 'substitute' for performance.[228] Such an award could either be quantified by reference to an estimate of the market value of performance or what a reasonable person would have accepted to release the D from his obligation at the

---

[227] A different explanation may be needed on the valuable options theory of the value of chance, since one's interest in autonomy is distinct from the value of the option of which one has been deprived. Yet it may be that by putting the victim in the position it would have been in had the wrongful conduct not occurred (by awarding full damages) that this also at least partly addresses the interference with autonomy: it gives the victim the next-best substitute to how it would have exercised its choice.

[228] On awards substituting for performance generally, see D. Winterton, 'Money Awards Substituting for Performance'.

time of breach.[229] Neither award would likely benefit the claimant in this example, compared to a claim for restitution of the £1,000, unless the market value could indeed be shown to be higher than the contract price. It is doubtful whether such an award is available in English *tort* law, beyond cases involving the wrongful use of property.[230] Furthermore, on normative grounds, in cases where what is at issue is not simply an obligation to provide a chance but an obligation to take reasonable care to provide a chance of avoiding physical injury, it may be that it is morally inappropriate or futile for the court to engage in the exercise of determining what a reasonable person would accept to allow the other person not to conform to their obligation to take reasonable care of their chances. This is especially true where the chance is of avoiding a physical injury. However, to the extent that the 'performance interest' in a promise can be enforced in tort law, this is the most plausible ground for substantial damages in proportion to the probability of the loss actually suffered – since this probability would enter into a calculation of the value of the right infringed.[231]

Justifying probabilistic liability: beyond lost chances and increased risks as loss

The last part suggested that chances of obtaining benefits contribute, in themselves, so little to well-being that requiring people to pay substantial compensation in respect of their deprivation alone is undesirable. It remains an open question whether persons should *for reasons other than the genuine loss suffered in losing a chance* obtain damages in proportion to the probability that the defendant caused their injury. Under a PC rule, damages should be recoverable in proportion to the probability that the defendant's wrongful conduct was a cause of the claimant's injury.[232]

Eight arguments for some version of PC are discussed. It is argued that only one of these arguments is persuasive; this argument applies only where the defendant's wrongful conduct is known to have caused injury.

---

[229] Cf. *Giedo van der Garde BV* v. *Force India Formula One Team Ltd* [2010] EWHC 2373, [437]–[438], [499]–[560].

[230] See C. Rotherham, 'Gain-based Relief in Tort after *Attorney General v Blake*', 107–115 .

[231] For the claim that 'substitutive' damages are and should be widely available in tort, see R. Stevens, *Torts and Rights*, 59–88. This reasoning is already found in inchoate form in some of the English contract authorities discussed at p.296ff, where the central concern seems to be to value the lost right to performance.

[232] See p. 291.

Proven causal wrongs

Recall the following kinds of case:

Claimant indeterminacy: D has behaved wrongfully in relation to C1, C2 ... Cn. It is known according to the standard of proof that D has wrongfully injured at least one of C1–Cn, each of whom has suffered similar injuries, but it is not known which. The claimants not injured by D have suffered injury non-wrongfully.

Claimant and defendant indeterminacy, causative variant: D1, D2 ... Dn have each wrongfully caused injury to at least one of C1–Cn, where some number of C1–Cn have also suffered injuries non-wrongfully, but it cannot be determined which D has caused which C's injury.

Intuitively, the important normative features of these cases are that (1) each defendant has wrongfully caused injury to someone, (2) there is some probability that each defendant may have wrongfully caused each claimant's injury, (3) at least some of those for whom there is a probability that the defendant caused their injury have in fact been caused injury by the defendants' wrongdoing (4) if no liability is imposed upon any defendant, a defendant which is liable to *a* claimant will not be required to pay compensation; (5) if each defendant is held liable in full to each claimant, each defendant will pay more compensation than it ought to pay.

These are the strongest cases for holding that D should pay damages to each claimant in proportion to the statistical probability that the defendant's wrongful conduct was a cause of the claimant's injury. There are two reasons for this. First, each defendant cannot complain that it is being held liable for more damage than it caused: it is only being held liable in the same amount as it would have been held liable had the evidence been available. For instance, consider:

Scarce antidote. An ambulance negligently fails to turn up to an incident where three people have each been bitten by a snake. Had the ambulance turned up, it would only have had enough antidote to treat one of the three people.[233] The ambulance crew would have decided which person would have received the antidote by lot, giving each person a 1/3 chance of avoiding serious injuries. Each person suffers an injury of the same extent due to the absence of an antidote.

---

[233] Let us assume it would not have been negligent only to carry such a small amount of antidote.

In this case, no individual can prove that its injury would have been prevented on the balance of probability had the ambulance service not behaved negligently. If the defendant is held liable to each claimant for 1/3 of its injuries, the defendant will pay the same as if it were clear which claimant would have been saved.

Second, if all claimants who may have been wrongfully caused injury by the defendant sue, the defendant knows that it will be wholly satisfying its compensatory obligation. There are two possible reasons why this is true. First, if all claimants enter into an agreement whereby they each agree to share damages awarded by the court, then the defendant knows that the person to whom it is (as a matter of substantive law) under a legal liability wants that liability to be satisfied by sharing the damages with the other potential victims. By paying the damages to each member of the group, the liable defendant is simply following the instruction of the person to whom it is liable.

The moral power correlative to the defendant's liability can surely be satisfied in this way – by the defendant acting on the claimant's direction. If claimants do not agree in this way, then, subject to the second argument, there is a still a plausible, if highly controversial, argument in favour of liability where all claimants are, on the balance of probability, before the court. In this situation, in *Scarce antidote*, requiring the defendant to pay a proportionate sum to each claimant would ensure that it partly fulfilled its compensatory duty to its victim, whilst also enforcing a further secondary duty which arguably arises from the fact that it has causally wronged someone. If a person wrongfully causes injury to an individual who cannot possibly be compensated, the wrongful injurer is surely still morally required to make the world as if his wrongdoing never occurred. On the hypothesis that the injured victim cannot be found, the best way of ensuring this is to contribute to the relief of suffering of similar victims. It is this moral duty which would be enforced in *Scarce antidote* in the event that the claimants did not agree on the proportionate disbursement of the liability.

Second, in some cases the 'duty to authorise' argument developed in Chapter 4 will apply where there are multiple defendants. This argument applies regardless of the agreement of the claimants. Suppose there are two defendants, D1 and D2, who together have caused 100 injuries, but because of the background risks of such injuries it cannot be determined which 100 injuries were tortiously caused out of a total of 150 injuries. Suppose that D1 is responsible for 40 per cent of the 100 injuries, while D2 is also responsible for 40 per cent. If D1 and D2 agree to authorise each other to compensate the other's victims, they will substantially increase their chance of compensating their own victims.

The following principle therefore seems justifiable:

> *Proven causation principle.* If statistical or other evidence shows that D has wrongfully caused x per cent of the injuries within a group of persons, each of whom has suffered an injury which may have been caused by D, but none of whom can establish on the balance of probability that D's wrongful conduct was a cause of their injury, D should be liable either (a) to each member for x per cent of each member's losses or (b) to contribute in the entirety of the amount of loss it has caused to a court held fund from which members may claim proportionate shares, to the extent that this does not more likely than not require D to pay for more loss than D has wrongfully caused.

Minimising expected injustice

It was shown in Chapter 3 that the BPR generally leads to a lesser expected amount of injustice compared to a PC rule.[234] It might be questioned whether this result holds when there is a cluster of cases at one end of the probability distribution that is not matched by a similar large cluster at the opposite end of the probability distribution.[235] Suppose that in a particular context there are 100 cases of uncertain causation and that in all of those cases (each against a different defendant by a different claimant) the probability of causation is 0.3. Let us say the damages in each case should be 100. Thirty cases should succeed, but under the BPR none will. Consequently, the total expected injustice under the BPR is 3,000. By contrast under the PC rule, if each defendant pays 1/3 of each claimant's damages, then there is no expected injustice *where defendants and claimants are considered as groups.* Defendants as a group should transfer 3,000 to claimants as a group; the PC rule achieves this. The problem with this argument, however, is that there is no justification for treating the claimants or defendants as groups. If we consider the total amount of expected injustice considered on a case-by-case basis, the PC rule leads to much greater expected injustice than the BPR. If there are 100 cases, in each case there is an expected injustice of the following amount if a PC rule is adopted: $0.3(70) + (0.7)(30) = 42$. Therefore, the total amount of expected injustice is 4,200. Nor will the

---

[234] See pp. 134–5.
[235] Cf. D.H. Kaye, 'The Limits of the Preponderance of the Evidence Standard', 503ff.

proven causation principle apply since each defendant has not been proven to have caused an injury.[236]

Minimising expected error due to large injustices

Suppose we thought that *large* errors are particularly problematic in the sense that delivering, for example, £500 less compensation than is due is more than twice as bad as delivering £250 less compensation than is due. In short, suppose that departures from the true situation become worse in a non-linear fashion. If so, we find that the PC rule is superior to the BPR in minimising the expected amount of error.[237] In intuitive terms, the reason for this is that whenever we make an error under the BPR, we are always totally incorrect: the difference between the amount awarded and the defendant's actual liability is always as large as it could be. By contrast, under the PC rule the difference between the defendant's actual liability and the mistaken amount awarded is always smaller than under the BPR. For example, if the probability that D caused C injury is 0.8, but in fact D did not cause C injury, and the size of C's injury is 100, the BPR awards C 100 too much, while the PC rule awards only 80 too much.

Why would we place much greater (non-linear) weight on large errors? Orloff and Stedinger observe that 'small losses can often be paid "out-of-pocket" or from savings, and impose little hardship. Large losses can force a person to sell his residence, reduce his standard-of-living, or cause bankruptcy, and, accordingly, involve substantial hardship'.[238] This is one way of making precise the claim that the BPR is a *harsh* or extreme rule; this kind of harshness is exacerbated in German law by the very high possibility that a large error will be inflicted.[239] Notice that the PC rule does not, of course, *prevent* crushing errors from occurring. At the

---

[236] Even if one were attracted to the minimising expected injustice across groups argument, it is unclear what real-world contexts actually have asymmetrical bias in the probability distribution of cases. The relative distribution of cases at the p<0.5 level as opposed to the p>0.5 level is unknown. It could be that for every case of p=0.2, there is a case of p=0.8. In this way any under-compensation would be cancelled out by the equivalent over-compensation.

[237] For the proof of this as a general proposition, see N. Orloff and J. Stedinger, 'A Framework for Evaluating the Preponderance-of-the-Evidence Standard', 1165–8, where large errors are given extra weight by squaring the difference between the true liability position and the mistaken divergence from that position under each rule.

[238] Ibid., 1167.

[239] Cf. G. Mäsch, *Chance und Schaden*, 143, noting the harshness of all-or-nothing rules in German law. See also J. Taupitz, 'Proportionalhaftung zur Lösung von Kausalitätsproblemen insbesondere in der Arzthaftung', 1232.

upper end and lower end of the probability spectrum, the PC rule can impose errors similar in size to the BPR. For instance, if the probability of causation is 0.9, but in fact the defendant did not cause the injury, the defendant will pay full damages under the BPR and 90 per cent damages under the PC rule. Where the PC rule performs significantly better, from this perspective, is towards the centre of the probability distribution, between, say, 0.4 – 0.6. Suppose C is entitled to 100 in damages, but C's case only has 0.4 probability. Under the BPR, C receives nothing, while under the PC rule, C still receives 40 (an error of 60 compared to an error of 100). So if we were particularly concerned to avoid imposing significant risks of large errors on individuals, it seems that the PC rule is (to that extent) superior.

Suppose we did have this concern. Whether it should lead us to adopt PC would still depend upon a number of further issues. First, if the concern is to avoid the crushing effects of large mistakes, the resources of each party must surely be relevant. If one party could easily absorb a large error, but a significant (albeit less large) error would still cause serious hardship to the other party, then the reason for adopting PC would be significantly reduced. So if the defendant is a large company and the claimant is an uninsured individual, capping the claimant's damages at 51 per cent where the probability of the case is 51 per cent in order to protect the company from a large error would be misguided. In such cases, it might be that claimants' interest in full compensation far outweighs the risk of a large error upon insured corporate defendants, given that failure to achieve full compensation will harm claimants more than slightly larger payments of compensation will harm such defendants.[240] In such contexts, an asymmetric application of the PC rule would better meet the large error concern: that is where p < 0.51, PC applies, but where p >0.5, the BPR applies. So, whether the large error concern points towards PC would depend at least upon (a) whether, in a certain context, defendants are better able as a group to bear the costs of large errors than claimants[241] and (b) the legitimacy of taking (a) into account.

Consider *simple uncertainty* or *claimant and defendant indeterminacy* industrial disease cases brought by employees against negligent employers in English law. Let us suppose it is plausible that employers as a group can better absorb the costs of large errors than employees

---

[240] This may be a more precise rendering of one concern expressed in *Gregg* v. *Scott*, see p. 309.

[241] On the assumption that working out the parties relative capacities to bear the loss in every individual case would be problematic for all sorts of reasons.

and thus that the large errors concern would support an asymmetric PC rule. There are still several significant arguments against creating such a rule. First, it remains the case that this joint PC-BPR system would not minimise total expected error (without weighting for large errors). Second, in every case where the $p < 0.5$ the court will arrive at the incorrect amount of liability. Since the claimant is in fact entitled either to full damages or none, every award will be incorrect. Third, most significantly, the defendant can complain that it has a moral right to be free of the state's coercing it to give up its property unless it is under a moral liability to compensate to the individual claimant. Such a liability is dependent on its outcome responsibility for the claimant's injury. The actual basis of the defendant's liability is that it caused the claimant's injury. Where the claimant can only show a 30 per cent chance that this is so, it simply cannot be said that the case for interfering with the defendant's right has been made out. Fourth, the defendant can complain that *everyone* (or those who could justly be taxed) should contribute to mollify the greater costs of errors in civil litigation to the worst off; the tort system singles out individual defendants as the bearers of this cost when everyone should be liable to it.

Deterrence and incentives

Much of the law and economics literature, as we have observed,[242] draws a distinction between occasional or haphazard uncertainty over causation and recurring, predictable, causal uncertainty. Porat illustrates systematic uncertainty with the example of hospital unit which only treats very ill patients whose average chances of recovery are 30 per cent.[243] In such situations, there is a 'downward bias'[244] in the distribution of the probabilities of causation.

The effect of this bias, according to Porat, is that the rational self-interested defendant no longer has incentive to take efficient care: if all patients have only a 30 per cent chance of survival, none will be able to prove causation on the BPR. (The converse point – concerning overdeterrence – can be made where there is *upward* bias[245]). All of the objections to this argument made in the last chapter continue to

---

[242] Chapter 3, 136–7, Chapter 5, 269ff.   [243] A. Porat, 'Misalignments in Tort Law', 108.
[244] Ibid.
[245] However, the *upward bias* point is less clear. If the standard of care is set correctly, there is no need to be concerned with upward bias, since defendants can simply take efficient care to avoid liability.

apply here.[246] We might add, however, that it seems unrealistic that there will be situations where *every* patient out of a set of 100 has a 30 per cent chance of avoiding injury. Porat in fact speaks of *average* chances. But the fact that the average chance of recovery in a group of 100 is 30 per cent is consistent with 50 having a chance of recovery of 55 per cent and 50 having a chance of 5 per cent. The incentive effects of this would theoretically depend upon whether it is possible and cheaper to operate a system which could reliably determine the chance of survival in each case and make care contingent upon that determination or whether a system requiring care in each case. The issue is less straightforward than Porat's framing might suggest.

The analogy with contributory negligence

It has been argued that proportional liability can be justified by an analogy with the apportionment of liability for contributory negligence.[247] The argument is that, in the same way that the claimant's fault should not serve as a total bar to the recovery of damages, but only a proportionate reduction in the amount of recovery, the reduced probability of the claim should not be a total bar, but lead to proportionate recovery.

There are at least two problems with this analogy. First, contributory negligence rules function so as to reduce an already existing liability in damages. This doctrine only comes into operation once the claimant has already established liability. Since the claimant has established liability, it would be unjust to deny the claim entirely. Second, contributory negligence is underpinned by a substantive judgement about responsibility: the defendant's responsibility for the injury is only partial, given the claimant's culpable contribution to its injury. But to say that there is a 20% probability that the defendant wrongfully injured the claimant is not plausibly to make a substantive judgement of responsibility: it merely expresses the uncertainty over whether the defendant is indeed responsible.[248]

The argument from quantification

English and German law are both characterised by operating dual systems of proof: one rule applying to questions of liability and one applying to questions concerning the extent of liability. The difference

---

[246] Chapter 5, 269–75.

[247] See F. Bydlinski, *Probleme der Schadensverursachung*, 77ff, 113, building on W. Wilburg, *Die Elemente des Schadensrechts*, 74ff.

[248] Cf. N. Jansen, *Die Struktur*, 597; A. Kletecka, 'Alternative Verursachungskonkurrenz mit dem Zufall – Die Wahrscheinlichkeit als Haftungsgrund'.

is that German law applies all-or-nothing rules at both stages, with a reduction in the standard of proof at the extent-of-liability stage. By contrast, English law operates a proportional liability system once liability is established and the extent of liability is in issue.[249]

The existence of proportional liability once liability has been established naturally raises the question of whether it is inconsistent to apply an all-or-nothing rule to liability questions and may form the basis of an argument for doing so. May proportional liability be justified as a matter of quantification but not as a matter of liability? It is suggested that it may be.

The basic argument is this. Although courts can estimate the probability that a certain event would have occurred in, say, 10 years had the claimant not been the victim of a tort, the probability arrived at will typically be lacking in weight. It will be based on general facts about, for example, the employment market and so on. The more distant the event in the future, the more conjectural the probability (other things being equal). Consequently, although courts can say there is a 60 per cent probability that x would have occurred 10 years from now, this is typically not the kind of probability which would satisfy the BPR. Therefore, if the BPR were applied to such questions, claimants would almost always lose, despite it being known that they have suffered *some* future loss due to the defendant's tort. Applying the PC rule would avoid the manifestly unjust result that claimants who are known to have suffered some future loss as a result of the defendant's tort cannot recover in respect of it. As Sedley LJ has observed in this context: 'The court cannot know: it can only make an educated guess which is bound to result in either over or under compensation; but to make no award at all for this reason would be a greater injustice to the claimant than a speculative award is to the defendant'.[250]

This justification for the PC approach to quantification is, however, a contingent one. The more that we can come to firm judgements about future events and future hypothetical questions, the less reason there is to apply the PC rule. Indeed, if in a rare case a claimant could prove

---

[249] Strictly, the issue must additionally concern a future or future-hypothetical question, see Chapter 2, 52.

[250] *Morgan* v. *UPS* [2008] EWCA 275 at [33]. The less stringent standard of proof under §287 ZPO is justified by some German authors on a similar ground that because the defendant has actually been shown to have committed a wrong causing loss against the claimant, this justifies placing more of the risk of uncertainty upon him at the quantification stage: P. Arens, 'Dogmatik und Praxis der Schadensschätzung', 20; H. Stoll, 'Haftungsverlagerung durch beweisrechtliche Mittel', 183ff.

on the BPR that it would have not suffered a certain loss in the distant future, there seems to be no reason not to allow the claimant to recover in full for that loss. The fact that German law applies a BPR rule to some quantification questions suggests there is reason to doubt whether English law's approach can be fully vindicated. Finally, to the extent that English law switches to a PC rule *as soon as* liability is established, as opposed to when liability *and some amount of loss caused by the tort* is established, it is difficult to justify.

Other fairness-based objections to the standard of proof

A frequently made claim is that the balance of probability standard is arbitrary.[251] The arbitrariness is said to consist in the fact that a small change in the probability of causation (from 50 per cent to 51 per cent) results in large differences in outcome for litigants. The response to this is twofold. First, this kind of argument can be made against virtually any legal rule. Second, in any legal system concerned to hold defendants liable for what they are *actually* liable for – a system which is concerned to match its attributions of liability with the true state of affairs – there is a need to set some threshold at which propositions will be taken as true, with some claims falling just below the threshold and others just above.

A different argument is that the BPR is unfair because it distributes the risk of error unequally and thus unfairly. In cases where the probability of causation is greater than 0.5, all of the risk of error is borne by the defendant, and none by the claimant.[252] In cases where the probability is below 0.5, all of the risk of error is borne by the claimant, and none by the defendant. Four responses may be made. First, as we have argued, some inequality in the distribution of the risk of error may be justified on the ground that the court is inflicting injustice with false positives as opposed to merely failing to alleviate it. Second, the rule is fair as between claimants as a group and defendants as a group since each group is equally benefited and burdened by the rule, even if not in the individual case. Third, most importantly, this argument fails to take seriously the fact that the defendant has a right not to be held liable in damages unless it is proven to have caused the claimant's injury. It is

---

[251] Cf. Lord Phillips in *Sienkiewicz* at [26]: '[t]he balance of probabilities test is one that is inherently capable of producing capricious results', criticised by R. Wright, 'Proving Causation: Probability versus Belief', 216, n. 94. Note also the reference to 'unbillige Extremlösungen' by the Austrian OGH, which accepts proportional liability: 4 Ob 445/95.

[252] This may be what Porat and Stein have in mind with their 'equality' argument, see Chapter 3, 129ff.

hardly to respect this right to reason thus to the defendant: 'although it is more likely true than not that you did not cause this person's injury, and thus, although it is more likely true than not that an essential ground for your responsibility to this person is missing, nonetheless, we hold you liable in damages'. Fourth, the argument proves too much, since it would equally apply to cases where there is some less than 51 per cent probability that the defendant had behaved negligently (or generally, where fault is uncertain in fault-based causes of action), yet it seems deeply unfair to apply PC to uncertainty over fault.[253]

Aggregation

Let us return to Porat's hospital, and assume that there are 100 patients each of whom has a 30 per cent chance of survival negligently destroyed by 100 different doctors, each employed by the hospital, and that none could prove on the BPR that the doctor was a cause of their injury. It follows, then, that 30 patients ought to have recovered, but none will. Now, if these 100 patients simply sued the 100 doctors, their claims should fail, because there is no basis for grouping together the 100 doctors. But suppose these claimants were permitted to aggregate their claims against *the hospital*. We know that there are 30 tort victims among the 100 and therefore that the hospital is, as a matter of substantive law, vicariously liable for 30 torts.[254] The *proven causation principle* would apply to this case. Some might object to this on the ground that vicarious liability presupposes the personal liability of the individual doctors. In a sense, this objection is correct: vicarious liability presupposes that as a matter of substantive law an employee is liable. But it is not true that the claimant must be able to *prove* a case against an individual employee; it suffices if the claimant can prove that *some one* or number of employees committed a tort.[255] The procedural vehicle for such a claim is a complex issue, but as a matter of substantive principle, it can be justified.

Conclusions

This conclusion falls in two parts. The first part sets out the normative conclusions of this chapter on the scope of compensatory liability for lost

---

[253] See Chapter 3, 124–5.
[254] This argument is made by A. Porat and E. Posner, 'Aggregation and Law', 13–18.
[255] See *Cassidy* v. *Ministry of Health* [1951] 2 KB 343, 355–6.

chances and proportional liability. The second makes some comparative observations on these doctrines.

Normative conclusions on loss of chance and proportional liability

The loss of a chance of avoiding either a physical injury or an economic loss can constitute a setback to a person's interests. Whether this setback is construed as the deprivation of a valuable option, the interference with security, or as the deprivation of an item with derivative value, the gravity of the setback, considered in itself, is relatively minor. The case for the imposition of legal duties to protect against the deprivation of chances is strongest where those chances relate to a person's physical integrity, and in circumstances where the duty-bearer would owe a duty to protect against a purely economic loss. This will be true wherever D induces C to rely upon D's undertaking to behave with reasonable care, with the effect that C does not pursue an alternative course of action, which may have prevented C's injury, and which C would otherwise have pursued. This would justify liability in respect of this interference with autonomy in medical negligence cases against doctors who, in breach of duty, fail to take reasonable care of a patient, with the result that their chance of avoiding a physical injury is destroyed. The argument is weaker, but possibly still weighty enough, in relation to chances relating to one's property and economic interests.

There is no compelling reason to value the deprivation of chance in the current way, namely, as the lost probability of avoiding the loss multiplied by the extent of the loss. The ideal situation would be a distinct award for the deprivation of the chance qua derivatively valuable interest or qua interference with autonomy.[256] This approach is, however, unlikely to be accepted in English or French law, both of which have long valued lost chances as a probabilistic proportion of the underlying loss. The most that can said for the current approach to valuation is that it follows from the general probabilistic approach to quantification of the *extent* of loss already taken in English law – the probability of avoiding the loss would enter, under this approach, as part of the quantification of the *extent* of the loss caused by the interference with autonomy.[257] Yet there are two problems with this justification. First, it seems

---

[256] In the manner described at pp. 351–2.
[257] This is how Green justifies the probabilistic approach where an interference with autonomy is proven: S. Green, *Causation in Negligence*, 153. See also S. Perry, 'Protected Interests and Undertakings in the Law of Tort', 308–11.

that the quantification principle is only justified in relation to questions concerning the distant hypothetical future or the distant future.[258] Second, there seems to be little reason to *restrict* the claimant's recovery to a probabilistic fraction where it can prove that the defendant's wrongful conduct was indeed a cause of its underlying injury on the balance of probability.[259]

Finally, it was argued that the case for proportional liability is only compelling in situations where the defendant has been proven to have wrongfully caused injury on the balance of probability.

Comparative observations on loss of chance and proportional liability

France and England recognise CL in some contexts, whereas in Germany CL (and other forms of probabilistic liability) is not recognised. Two things, then, call for discussion: Germany's divergence and the different contexts in which CL is recognised. A number of considerations partly explain the former. First, as to the absence of CL as a matter of liability, the lost chance of some gain or avoiding some loss is simply not one of the protected interests in §823 I BGB.[260] Second, both §287 ZPO[261] and §252 2 BGB, a provision dealing with consequential losses (*entgangene Gewinn*), had been interpreted by doctrinal writing, soon after the Code's entry into force, as imposing a reduced standard of proof in respect of such losses.[262] This has been taken to endorse an all-or-nothing solution to uncertainty in such matters.[263] It is noteworthy, however, that recently some authors have begun to suggest a re-interpretation or avoidance of §287 ZPO/§252 2 BGB with the result that CL or PC should be available *de lege lata* in matters of quantification of loss (*Haftungsausfüllung*).[264] A third *partial* explanation is the evolution of

---

[258] See p. 364.

[259] This restriction is mandated by the quantification principle: Chapter 2, 53.

[260] H. Koziol, 'Schadenersatz für den Verlust einer Chance', 233; J. Taupitz, 'Proportionalhaftung zur Lösung von Kausalitätsproblemen insbesondere in der Arzthaftung', 1234.

[261] See Chapter 2, 56ff.

[262] On §252 2 BGB: N. Jansen, 'Historical Commentary on §249 and § 252 BGB', n. 470, noting also that this was 'im Anschluss an das gemeine Recht'. The author also notes at n. 296 that, despite other unclarity over §252 2 BGB: 'Fest stand aber jedenfalls, dass Gewinnaussichten *nicht nach ihrer Wahrscheinlichkeit bewertet* und als verlorene Gewinnchancen ersetzt werden sollten'.

[263] Recently, this has become an object of some dispute, however, by those who would allow PC: see, for example, G. Wagner, 'Proportionalhaftung für ärztliche Behandlungsfehler de lege lata'.

other doctrines which have dealt with causal uncertainty, most notably the *grobe Behandlungsfehler* doctrine, the reversal of the burden of proof in cases of *hypothetische Kausalität*, and *Anscheinsbeweis*.[265]

The expansive French position is partly explained by the generality of Article 1382 CC. Unlike the BGB, the Code Civil provides no explicit legal limits on what types of interest can be protected by the law of tort. Damage is left undefined. Similarly, without legislative provisions like §287 ZPO or §252 2 BGB, which regulate the proof of damages, there was more legal room for innovation. This allowed the doctrinal writing's emphasis upon the loss-constituting nature of lost chances to take root, as well as the theoretically high standard of proof of causation to be *de facto* subverted. Moreover, the commonsensical notion of 'value' with which doctrinal writers operated precluded any clear distinction between lost economic chances and others. The English position can be seen to be a kind of mid-point between the French and German positions. However, the English position is characterised by an appeal to technical rules concerning quantification and the nature of the uncertainty at issue; the normative basis of these rules is not particularly clear.[266]

The comparative development of probabilistic liability (PC rules) more generally is now considered. It is possible to construe the English law on quantification as doctrines of proportional liability, since the quantification principle generally makes no claim that chances are losses. The French system can also be construed, at least theoretically, as a form of proportional liability in so far as the sceptical understanding of the lost chance doctrine is adopted; on this understanding the courts are in effect imposing proportional liability in respect of the ultimate harm, rather than aiming to compensate for a distinct interest in chances of avoiding that harm.

If these re-configurations are made, the comparative picture becomes interesting and complex. A striking feature of English doctrine is that, on the face of it, it *generally* applies a proportional chance-based liability regime at the stage of quantification and – *generally* – an all-or-nothing

---

[264] J. Taupitz, 'Proportionalhaftung zur Lösung von Kausalitätsproblemen insbesondere in der Arzthaftung'; G. Wagner, 'Proportionalhaftung', (even more expansive). Cf. W. Müller-Stoy, *Schadensersatz für verlorene Chancen – Eine rechtsvergleichende Untersuchung*, 219.

[265] A fourth speculation is that Mommsen's conception of financial loss does not sit easily with CL. Cf. T. Mommsen, *Zur Lehre vom Interesse*, 3. For this history: M. Gebauer, *Hypothetische Kausalität*, 74; N. Jansen, 'Historical Commentary', text at n. 728.

[266] For a suggestion of how this may be achieved, But see pp.364–5.

regime at the stage of liability. French and German law are in agreement that a less strict proof regime is necessary at the stage of quantification, but in German law this remains an all-or-nothing, reduced standard of proof approach (§287 ZPO; §252 2 BGB).

Beyond the general agreement that it is normatively acceptable to apply different proof rules once liability has been established, it is also clear that probabilistic liability has appeared especially attractive where proof of causation is perceived to be particularly difficult. English law frequently makes the claim that certain kinds of proposition are inherently difficult or impossible to prove and for that reason should attract proportional liability – third party and future hypotheticals being the main examples. French doctrinal writers justified CL partly on the ground that it is impossible to assess counterfactual questions definitively.[267] Finally, the pervasive nature of uncertainty over causal questions has been emphasised in some German literature.[268] Equally clearly, however, while there could be said to be some abstract consensus on the (at least partial) normative appeal of probabilistic liability in such situations, there is considerable *disagreement* on the situations in which proof of causation is inherently impossible to prove. English law treats hypotheticals relating to third parties specially, while some French writers explain the wide-ranging scope of the lost chance doctrine on the basis that hypothetical questions are generally impossible to prove to the governing standard of proof.[269]

---

[267] See p. 328.   [268] G. Mäsch, *Chance und Schaden*, 17–20.   [269] See p. 328.

7   Conclusion

This conclusion falls in two parts. The first provides a brief comparative summary of the exceptions made to proof of causation in each system. The second returns to the three sets of problems raised in the introduction – the conceptual, consistency, and normative problems – and outlines the answers at which we have arrived.[1]

Comparative conclusions

Table 1 illustrates the current law in each system. The most striking aspects of the law are its divergence across systems beyond the defendant indeterminacy situation and the internally inconsistent approach adopted by each system. English law is exemplary in its inconsistency: full liability in mesothelioma (and only mesothelioma) cases where a material increase in risk is shown, the single agent and *scientific* uncertainty requirements, such wide-ranging liability for lost economic chances but none for lost chances of avoiding physical injury,[2] and an unexplained reversal of the burden of proof leading to full liability in cases of material contribution to damage involving scientific uncertainty. Both French and German law are afflicted by inconsistency, too, but of a less extensive kind. German law attaches a reversal of the burden of proof to gross breaches of duty to protect persons from physical injury, but

---

[1] See Introduction, 1–3.
[2] Even if, as Chapter 6 argued, the award of substantial compensatory damages simply in respect of the loss of a chance is always undesirable, it remains the case that accepting such liability simply in respect of economic chances is inconsistent. On all accounts of the value of chance described in Chapter 6, no strict distinction can be drawn between these categories of chance and all accounts would suggest that the loss of a chance of a physical injury is a more serious matter.

limits this largely to the medical context. French law applies generous presumptions of causation, especially in the product liability context, without this approach being fully replicated elsewhere.

Several explanations for the divergence and the inconsistent approaches may be given. First, the relationship between tort law and other sources of compensation in each system is of importance. In situations where the compensation provided by alternative sources is relatively minimal or at least significantly less generous, and the number of injured people is significant – in England, in asbestos cases, and France, in HIV, Hepatitis C, and multiple sclerosis cases – judges have dispensed with the orthodox causal proof rules. In both England and France, this has led to *ad hoc* statutory interventions in the general law of tort regulating special situations often involving mass injuries.[3] Second, the inherent difficulty of identifying the normatively distinctive features of certain cases has led to inconsistent development in the law. Thus, in English law, the normatively distinctive features of *Fairchild* – that the claimant was proven to be the victim of a tort, that the causative defendant's avoidance of liability depended upon relying upon another's wrongful conduct, and that each defendant fell within the *prevented claim principle* – were not identified.[4] This led to problems in rationally restricting the doctrine, with the single agent rule seized upon to achieve this purpose.[5] Third, the expansive notion of damage in French law and the stringency of the standard of proof provided favourable conditions for the development of a more extensive lost chance doctrine.[6] Fourth, where judges have relied upon incentive-based, deterrence arguments, there has been disagreement as to the force of these arguments in particular contexts. For instance, German judges have made reference to the need to incentivise doctors to conform to their duties to inform to justify reversing the burden of proof on causation, but have not done so in the context of the obligation of manufacturers to provide product warnings.[7] Similarly, English judges have selectively relied upon incentives-based reasoning in cases involving dermatitis and mesothelioma, but not elsewhere.[8] It may be that the scarcity of empirical evidence in relation to the effects of exceptional causal rules inevitably leads to conflicting speculations.

---

[3] See Chapter 5, 231–2; 264–5.   [4] See Chapter 4, 168–169; 174ff; Introduction, 3–4.
[5] See Chapter 5, 227–8; 237–9.   [6] See Chapter 6, 328ff.   [7] Chapter 5, 202–203.
[8] Chapter 5, 225ff. Such reasoning has also been employed to justify an exception to rules of legal causation in relation to doctors' duties to inform: *Chester* v. *Afshar* [2005] 1 AC 134. However, the point that this reasoning is relied upon only sporadically still holds.

Table 1 *Comparative overview of exceptional causal rules*

	(1) Defendant indeterminacy	(2) Defendant indeterminacy, causative variant	(3) Claimant indeterminacy	(4) Claimant and defendant indeterminacy	(5) Claimant and defendant indeterminacy, causative variant	(6) Simple uncertainty
England	a. Full liability in negligence and for breach of statutory duty in asbestos mesothelioma cases involving single agents by virtue of a weaker risk-based concept of causation. b. Proportional liability in negligence and for breach of statutory duty in other defendant indeterminacy situations involving single agency by virtue of a weaker risk-based concept of causation.	Unclear, but, as a matter of principle, it would be inconsistent to accept defendant indeterminacy liability and not liability here.	Proportional liability, probably, if uncertainty due to limits of scientific knowledge, involves single agency, by virtue of a weaker risk-based concept of causation.	a. Full liability in negligence in asbestos mesothelioma cases involving single agents by virtue of a weaker risk-based concept of causation (*Fairchild*, Compensation Act 2006, section 3). b. Proportional liability in negligence (and breach of statutory duty) in other cases involving scientific uncertainty by virtue of a weaker risk-based concept of causation.	Unclear, but, as a matter of principle, it would be inconsistent to accept liability in (1) and (4) but not in (5).	a. Full liability in negligence in asbestos mesothelioma cases involving single agents by virtue of a weaker risk-based concept of causation. b. Full liability in negligence where a material contribution to damage is proven and the issue of whether the claimant is worse off cannot be determined due to scientific uncertainty. c. Proportional liability in negligence in other situations

involving single agency, scientific uncertainty, and not concerning medical negligence, by virtue of a weaker risk-based concept of causation.

d. Liability for lost chances of avoiding economic losses/making economic gains in negligence, where a duty of care owed, and in other torts, where chance is dependent on hypothetical action of a third party.

a. Full liability in cases of gross

Germany	Full liability in all tort causes of	Full liability under §830 I 2	No liability, since §830 I 2 BGB	No liability, unless C has been the	Full liability under §830 I 2 BGB,

Table 1 (cont.)

(1) Defendant indeterminacy	(2) Defendant indeterminacy, causative variant	(3) Claimant indeterminacy	(4) Claimant and defendant indeterminacy	(5) Claimant and defendant indeterminacy, causative variant	(6) Simple uncertainty
action in defendant indeterminacy situations under §830 1 2 BGB, generally conceived as reversal of burden of proof.	BGB, possibly, if *concrete endangerment* is proven.	requires that C be proven to be the victim of a tort.	victim of gross fault in the medical negligence context, whereupon a reverse burden applies.	possibly, if *concrete endangerment* is proven.	fault by doctors where reverse burden of proof not discharged. b. Full liability in cases where a contribution is proven, and the issue of whether the claimant is worse off cannot be proven, as a result of a reversal of the burden of proof on that issue. c. Full liability in cases for breaches of duty to inform arising in special relationships where a reverse burden of proof is not satisfied, which applies against

374

France	Full liability by virtue of reverse burden or presumption of causation.	Full liability by virtue of reverse burden or presumption of causation.	Probably no liability unless C can prove that D's conduct deprived C of a *chance of* avoiding the injury (of whatever nature).	Probably no liability unless C can prove that D's conduct deprived C of a *chance of* avoiding the injury (of whatever nature).	Probably no liability unless C can prove that D's conduct deprived C of a *chance of* avoiding the injury (of whatever nature).	various professional service providers, but (probably) not against doctors. a. Full liability where a generous presumption of causation applies – for instance in cases of defective products. b. Liability for lost chances of avoiding physical or other loss under Art 1382 CC.

Three recurring problems

The book began by introducing three kinds of problem – the conceptual, consistency, and normative problems – posed by causal uncertainty. Each is considered in turn.

Conceptual problems

The two conceptual problems concerned the nature of the standard of proof and the nature of exceptional departures from the burden or standard of proof. Chapter 2 argued that the BPR requires the judge to believe that the evidential support for believing the claimant's case on causation to be true is stronger than the evidential support for believing that case to be false. The notion of probability is thus understood in terms of evidential support for belief in a proposition. It was argued that while evidential support is not to be equated with the statistical probability of truth, the statistical probability of truth can affect the evidential support for a proposition sufficiently so as to satisfy the BPR where the probabilities in question have sufficient weight. Weight was understood in terms of the extent to which the evidential is specific to the case at hand and rules out alternative explanations of the situation which could significantly alter the statistical probability of causation.

The second conceptual problem concerned the nature of exceptions to the burden and standard of proof. Straightforwardly, the exceptional rules in French and German law are simply reversals of the legal burden of proof or reductions in the standard of proof.[9] Less straightforwardly, English law conceptualises its material increase in risk rule – in both its full and proportional liability forms – as an alteration in the *concept* of causation in a particular context, where increasing the risk of an outcome is a *kind* of causing.[10] Since increasing the risk of an outcome is in no sense to be a cause of it (rather risk only enters as *evidence* of causation), this is undesirable. The better view is that this rule should either be treated as a reversal of the burden of proof on but-for causation in the particular circumstances, with liability being quantified, under the proportional liability rule, in proportion to the probability of causation as a trade-off for the alteration in the normal proof requirements or as a *sui generis* liability rule – in either case, the risk imposed by each defendant enters into the quantification of the liability, rather than as characterising the damage suffered by the

---

[9] See Chapter 4, 143–161; Chapter 5, 199–220; 261–268. In some cases, the reduction in the standard of proof is achieved by the loose requirements for a presumption of causation.

[10] See Chapter 5, 236–237.

claimant.[11] Finally, English and US law's proportional liability rules – under *Barker* v. *Corus*, market share liability, and, in English law, when the court is quantifying the extent of liability– function as exceptions to the burden of proof. This is because a condition for the application of these rules is that proof on the balance of probability is impossible.[12] In effect, these rules generate liability in proportion to probabilities which are lacking in sufficient weight to prove an individual case to the balance of probability standard.[13]

A simple, but important, point is that no system has explicitly altered its *substantive* law commitment to the requirement of natural causation (even if, as in English law, the concept of causation has been construed to include increases in risk) in response to evidential uncertainty. Rather, even in their differently conceptualised departures from the proof of causation, systems demonstrate their allegiance to it. Thus, French and English law have reformulated the concept of damage in a way which allows uncertainty to obtain between wrongful conduct and morally significant loss, but the responsibility-based normative framework is maintained by requiring a causal connection to the lost chance. The fact that no damages can be awarded in any system in situations of evidential uncertainty without there being *some* probability of causation also shows that systems remain fundamentally cause-based. Finally, although one version of the US market share doctrine purports to impose liability based solely upon *culpability*, this itself is to ensure that defendants pay for the harm they have caused.[14]

If the normative arguments of this book were accepted – namely, that each defendant ought to be liable in defendant indeterminacy situations, causative claimant and defendant indeterminacy situations, and claimant indeterminacy situations – the issue arises as to how such liability should be conceptualised. Consider first the defendant indeterminacy situation. To the extent that the prevented claim theory applies, this liability does not arise in virtue of any exceptional proof of causation rule: each defendant has provably wrongfully injured the claimant. However, given the problems in applying the prevented claim theory in the event of one defendant's insolvency, liability in that event must be

---

[11] See Chapter 4, 193; Chapter 5, 228–231.
[12] See Chapter 4, 139; Chapter 5, 322; and for the connection between impossibility of proof and burden of proof rules, see Chapter 2, 48–49.
[13] On the idea of a probability lacking weight sufficient to satisfy the BPR: Chapter 2, 98ff.
[14] See Chapter 4, 167.

conceptualised as a departure from the general burden of proof.[15] In those situations, it can either be considered a reversal in the burden of proof or as a *sui generis* rule which allows the causal element of the claim to be satisfied by proof of a material increase in risk.[16]

Consider next the causative defendant indeterminacy situation.[17] To the extent that the prevented claim theory applies in this situation, full liability follows and again the liability is not premised on the application of an exceptional rule. However, the grant of a freestanding claim to each claimant against each defendant for full damages has normatively problematic consequences. If all claimants sue only one defendant, that defendant will be held liable for a greater amount of loss than it could possibly have caused. Holding each defendant proportionally liable to each claimant avoids this problem, but is not straightforwardly consistent with the normative bases of liability in these situations.[18] The ideal solution, given that the liability enforces the defendant's secondary duty to pay compensation to *a* victim, is some form of coordination of the claims – for instance, a class action requiring payment of damages into a fund such that the defendant can be assured that its own victim is being compensated by its participation.[19] In that event, the liability is, strictly, not exceptional, if the general rule is that in order to have a right to obtain damages from a particular defendant, the claimant must prove causation against that defendant. This is because the claimant is *not* given such a right *against a particular defendant* where the damages are paid into a court fund. However, the liability is still exceptional in the weaker sense that each defendant is being held liable to pay damages without proof on the part of any individual that the defendant wrongfully injured that individual. The same remarks apply to the causative claimant indeterminacy and claimant indeterminacy situations.

Problems of consistency

The basic problem of consistency is whether one can rationally recognise an exception to the orthodox causal proof rules of limited scope. Table 2 illustrates the results of the book's arguments to this question. It ranks

---

[15] For the problem, see Chapter 4, 178.

[16] The degree of risk or probability of causation could be taken into account in quantifying liability if proportional liability is thought to be more appropriate.

[17] See the discussion of *Two Cars* in Chapter 4, 184–185 and Chapter 6, 357–359.

[18] For these normative bases, see ibid.

[19] For a more comprehensive discussion of this see S. Steel, 'Justifying Exceptions to Proof of Causation in Tort Law'.

Table 2 *Justificatory support for different exceptional causal rules*

Exceptional rule	Justificatory support
(1) Defendant indeterminacy, causative variant.	Secondary duty to authorise argument, secondary duty arising where claimants agree to share damages, prevention principle, relative injustice argument, reliance on another's wrong argument.
(2) Claimant and defendant indeterminacy, causative variant.	Secondary duty to authorise argument, secondary duty arising where claimants agree to share damages, prevention principle, relative injustice argument.
(3) Defendant indeterminacy.	Prevention principle, relative injustice argument, reliance on another's wrong argument.
(4) Claimant indeterminacy.	Secondary duty arising where claimants agree to share damages, relative injustice argument.
(5) Simple uncertainty.	
a. Culpability-based exception (where D has behaved with gross fault).	False negative worse than false positive since a false negative involves both a corrective and retributive injustice, while a false positive only involves a corrective injustice; defendant forfeits right to have case proven to the same degree of stringency.
b. Incentives-based exception (where Ds can readily predict causal uncertainty arising in litigation against them).	Reduces overall occurrence of harms/wrongs.
c. Responsibility-for-evidential-uncertainty-based exception (where D can reasonably foresee that causal proof will be impossible or difficult).	The burden and standard of proof distribute the risk of error on the assumption that neither the claimant nor defendant is responsible for the existence of uncertainty; that assumption no longer applies if it can truly be said that the defendant is responsible for such uncertainty.
d. Egalitarian or prioritarian argument for proportional liability (perhaps this should only apply in situations where Ds	Where a large error will harm the claimant much more than the defendant, an asymmetric application of proportional liability

Table 2 (*cont.*)

Exceptional rule	Justificatory support
as a group must have insurance, where Cs cannot reasonably be expected to insure, and where Cs are an economically disadvantaged group).	will minimise the risk of this occurring.
e. Risk-sharing-based proportional liability (implies rejection of orthodox burden and standard of proof in all cases).	A proportionate distribution of the risk of error in individual cases is fairer than one which places all risk on one party above or below a certain probability threshold.

A related rule	
f. Proportional liability as a matter of quantification of damages.	A relative injustice argument of this form: where the claimant has been wrongfully caused loss of some extent by the defendant, it would be unfair if the claimant could not recover in respect of that future loss because it could not satisfy the BPR.

each exceptional rule in terms of its overall justificatory support (but it does not rank rules within category [5]) and shows that it is rationally possible to recognise exceptional rules without eliminating the general rule.

The argument has been that (1)–(4) can be justified.[20] Of these we can see that (1) is the most powerfully supported. There may be some dispute as to whether there is a more powerful case for either (3) or (4). At any rate, each of (1)–(4) enjoy several justifications which do not apply to simple uncertainty situations (5).[21] Therefore, it would be consistent to adopt (1)–(4) without intruding upon the orthodox burden and standard of proof in (5).

---

[20] A narrower version of (5)(c), leading to a presumption that missing evidence would have been favourable to the claimant, was also defended in Chapter 5, 279–281.

[21] The relative injustice argument relied upon in (1)–(4), however, does provide an argument for (5)(e) since the argument relies on the idea that it is fairer to share the risk of error *across* individuals, rather than for that risk to be centered on one particular individual. See Chapter 4, 279–281. This is not, however, the only argument for (1)–(4), whose other justifications do not support extension into category (5).

Even if one holds the view that (5)(a)–(e) cannot ultimately be justified, it remains true that the justifications for some of these rules, if they were valid, do not undermine the rationality of the orthodox burden and standard of proof in all cases. Thus, the arguments for a culpability-based exception ((5)(a)) to the burden or reduction in the standard of proof need not apply to all cases since it is implausible to think that every wrongful act – even one of minor negligence – merits a retributive response; nor, of course, would it apply to strict liability causes of action. While what constitutes 'gross' fault is naturally open-textured, legal systems mandate similar inquiries as to the relative grossness of fault, in other contexts, notably in contribution actions between tortfeasors.[22] Although we have argued against this rule as a matter of principle, it at least appeals to a normatively distinctive feature of certain cases of simple uncertainty. Nor would the adoption of (5)(d) imply a total rejection of the orthodox rules, albeit that isolating its precise ambit would be an extremely difficult exercise.

Would the adoption of an incentives-based exception imply the abandonment of the general burden and standard of proof in all cases? Economic analysis suggests that an exception to the general rules is only required where there is predictable *ex-post* causal uncertainty such that potential injurers can predict that the potentially injured will not be able to prove their causal claim.[23] Predictability of such uncertainty comes in degrees. This much is already recognised by the fact that the law distinguishes between the burden of proof (which governs an *impossibility* of proof situation) and the standard of proof situation (which governs findings in cases where the probabilities allow a finding to be made). For example, a fully rational defendant who considers such matters would presumably consider that it is likely to be possible to determine the causal facts in (most) cases of negligent driving, since the large, observable, causal processes at stake are well understood and the background risk of similar injury to the claimant may not be particularly high. A reversal of the burden of proof on causation or proportional liability in relation to traffic accidents would therefore not be supported by an incentives-based argument. The predictability of a probability of causation less than that required to satisfy the standard of proof becomes more plausible in cases where the claimant is already faced

---

[22] For a defence of the possibility of adopting gross negligence standards in certain contexts in English law, see D. Nolan, 'Varying the Standard of Care in Negligence'.
[23] See Chapter 3, 136–137 and Chapter 5, 269ff.

with a significant probability of being injured, which the defendant's negligence would fail to alleviate. Such features are present in some medical negligence cases, professional negligence cases (for instance, involving lawyers dealing claims with a low probability of success), and employers' liability cases (for instance, where employers are permitted to expose employees to significant risks where safety precautions are taken, such that there are significant background risks of injury, as in *McGhee*). So, while acceptance of an incentives-based exception would likely require significant inroads to be made to the general rules, it would not imply a wholesale rejection of them since not all contexts involve predictable causal uncertainty favouring the defendant.

Whether the same can be said of (5)(c) depends on the degree of foresight which such a doctrine would require before a defendant could be said to be (outcome) responsible for the claimant's facing a situation of impossibility of proof. If only foresight of the *risk* that it would be impossible to prove causation were required, such a rule would require an exception to be made in every case. If one believes simply that a proportionate sharing of the risk of error is fairer ((5)(e)), this implies a general rejection of the general proof rules. As to (5)(f), it has been argued that it does not imply a rejection of an all-or-nothing approach as a matter of establishing liability.[24]

The answer to the consistency problem, then, is that it can be consistent to adopt a limited exception to the general rules: not every rationale for an exception implies that the general rules are never justified. More importantly, not every valid rationale has this implication.

Normative problems

It was argued that the common law's general rule that the claimant bears the burden of proving causation on the balance of probability is generally justified.[25] The further normative question was whether any exception to this rule can be justified. It has been argued that an exception of some form can be justified in situations (1)–(4). The basic unifying feature of (1)–(4) is that, in almost all cases, the imposition of legal liability to compensate provides a mechanism by which the defendant's moral liability to compensate the claimant, arising out of the defendant's having wrongfully caused injury to the claimant, can be enforced, even if the identity of the injurer and/or the person injured cannot be established. Although an exception is made in (2)–(4) in the sense that each

---

[24] See Chapter 6, 364–365.   [25] Chapter 3, 127–135.

claimant succeeds without proof that a particular defendant caused its injury, nonetheless liability is premised on the fact that the defendant's liability will ultimately contribute to compensating the person it has wrongfully injured. Liability in situations (1)–(4), then, is consistent with the importance of assigning liability on the basis of the defendant's responsibility for the claimant's injury.[26]

The central normative problem with (5)(a), (b), (d), (e) is that the justifications for departing from the general proof rules do not further implicate the defendant's responsibility for the claimant's injury (or for the difficulty of proof). Even if we granted the empirical premises of the incentives-based argument, the fact that imposing liability would (with some significant degree of probability) prevent a greater amount of harm occurring is not to add to the case for saying that the defendant is outcome responsible for the injury. This is not a conclusive argument against imposing such liability.[27] If, however, we think that the defendant has a right that a case be proven that he is responsible for the injury, then this right does serve to give the defendant some protection against the argument that his liability without proof of causation would produce better consequences.

The attraction of the argument of (5)(c) is that it does seek to implicate the defendant's responsibility for the evidential difficulty faced by the claimant in proving causation. It has been argued that the boundaries of this responsibility are not so wide as to encompass any situation where the defendant behaves wrongfully and proof of causation is impossible or particularly difficult. It must minimally depend upon the defendant having *worsened* the claimant's evidential position.[28] It may merit further consideration whether there is a case for reversing the burden of proof in situations where the defendant is proven to have caused injury to the claimant by his wrongful positive action (and is outcome responsible for that injury) on the issue of whether the injury was caused by the wrongful aspect of the defendant's conduct.[29] Such an exceptional rule would at least be consistent with the importance of responsibility for the assignment of liability.

---

[26] See Chapter 3, 109ff.

[27] It is certainly not enough to say that tort law would become less like tort law if such arguments were accepted.

[28] Chapter 5, 278–288.

[29] This is the position in German law: Chapter 5, 214–216. Once the claimant has proven that the injury would not have occurred but for the defendant's wrongful act (for instance, driving negligently), we might reasonably think there is a *pro tanto* case for compensation in respect of the injury, with the legal burden of proving that the wrongful *aspect* of the act was not causative falling on the defendant.

Although holding people liable only for outcomes for which they bear responsibility is important, it is not everything. If this were held to be of supreme importance, then the standard of proof on causation would need to be set closer to requiring a strong outright belief that the defendant was a cause of the claimant's injury – a position to which French and German law, in theory, approximate. Rather, the injustice in a false positive on causation needs to be weighed against the injustice in a false negative. It seems to me that here is the most fertile territory for those seeking to challenge the insistence that claimants prove causation on the balance of probability in category (5) cases.[30]

The reason is that in balancing these injustices, it can seem irrational to ignore the tangible *effects* of these injustices on each party. It can seem that in distributing the risks of error over our determinations of corrective justice, we should have regard to the relative abilities of the parties to bear those errors. The case for not doing so is that wrongly taking £x from a wealthy, insured, defendant violates their rights just as much as wrongly failing to compensate a claimant for £x of injuries,[31] even if the effects on the claimant's welfare are greater than the effects on the defendant's welfare. Another part of the case is that, to the extent the claimant's relative inability to bear the costs of error is due to an unfair distribution of goods in society as a whole, this injustice is not solely or possibly even partly the defendant's responsibility. Another part of the case is that the right to have a case proved against one may enjoy some independence from the relative weighting given to false positives and false negatives. Even if false negatives had a greater effect on claimants' welfare than false positives on defendants', it would still surely violate the defendant's entitlement to have a case proven against them if liability were imposed when there was only a small chance they should be liable.[32] The justificatory burden, then, for departing from the general rules of proof of causation, beyond the situations described in this book, is not easily discharged.

---

[30] The approximate equality of false positives and false negatives seems most challengeable in cases where the normative basis of the substantive law does not assume a normative equality between the parties: see Chapter 3, 123. An example might be the liability of public authorities for breaches of fundamental rights.

[31] Strictly, the injustice is slightly worse as against D, see Chapter 3, 122–123.

[32] The point is particularly clear with proof of fault. If my liability justly depends on my being at fault, the fact that you have much riding on the outcome of my being found to be at fault should surely only have *limited* relevance to the standard of proof for such a finding.

Bibliography

Books and theses

Anderson, T., Schum, D., and Twining, W. *Analysis of Evidence* 2nd edition (Cambridge University Press, 2005)

Aubry, C. and Rau, C. *Droit Civil Français Book Six* 6th edition (Esmein, P. (ed.)) (Paris: Librairies Techniques Juris-Classeurs, 1951)

Balkin, R.P. and Davis, J.L.R. *Law of Torts* 4th edition (London: Butterworths, 2008)

Ballot-Léna, A. *La Responsabilité Civile en Droit Des Affaires Des Régimes Spéciaux Vers Un Droit Commun* (Paris: LGDJ, 2008)

Barker, K., Cane, P., Lunney, M., and Trindade, F. *The Law of Torts in Australia* 5th edition (Oxford University Press, 2011)

Beever, A. *Rediscovering the Law of Negligence* (Oxford: Hart, 2007)

Bénabent, A. *Droit Civil: Les Obligations* 12th edition (Paris: Montchrestien, 2010) *La Chance et Le Droit* (Paris: LGDJ, 1973)

Bennett, J. *Events and Their Names* (Oxford University Press, 1988)

Brinkmann, M. *Das Beweismaß im Zivilprozess aus rechtsvergleichender Sicht* (Cologne: Heymanns, 2005)

Broome, J. *Weighing Goods: Equality, Uncertainty and Time* (Oxford: Basil Blackwell Press, 1991)

Burrows, A. *The Law of Restitution* 3rd edition (Oxford University Press, 2011)

Buxbaum, W. *Solidarische Schadenshaftung bei ungeklärter Verursachung im deutsche, französichen und anglo-amerikanischen Recht* (Karlsruhe: CF Müller, 1965)

Bydlinski, F. *Probleme der Schadensverursachung nach deutschem und österreichischem Recht* (Stuttgart: F Enke, 1964)

Cane, P. *Atiyah's Accidents, Compensation and the Law* 8th edition (Cambridge University Press, 2013) *Responsibility in Law and Morality* (Oxford: Hart, 2002) *The Anatomy of Tort Law* (Oxford: Hart, 1997)

Cane, P., Lunney, M., and Trindade, F. *The Law of Torts in Australia* 4th edition (Oxford University Press, 2007)

Chabas, F. *L'influence de la pluralité de causes sur le droit à la réparation* (Paris: LGDJ, 1967)

Chartier, Y. *La réparation du préjudice* (Paris: Dalloz 1983)

Chatelain, C. *La Théorie de la Perte de Chance en Droit Hospitalier* (Thesis, Lille, 2002)

Clerk, J.F. (Jones, M. ed.) *Clerk & Lindsell on Torts* 19th edition (London: Sweet & Maxwell, 2007)

   Clerk & Lindsell on Torts 20th edition (London: Sweet & Maxwell, 2010)

   Clerk & Lindsell on Torts 21st edition (London: Sweet & Maxwell, 2014)

Cohen, L.J. *The Probable and the Provable* (Oxford: Clarendon Press, 1977)

Coleman, J. *Risks and Wrongs* (Cambridge University Press, 1992)

   The Practice of Principle: In Defence of a Pragmatist Approach to Legal Theory (Oxford University Press, 2001)

Cooter, R. and Porat, A. *Getting Incentives Right Improving Torts, Contracts, and Restitution* (Princeton University Press, 2014)

Cranor, C.F. *Toxic Torts: Science, Law and the Possibility of Justice* (Cambridge University Press, 2006)

Cross, R. and Tapper, C. *Cross & Tapper on Evidence* 12th edition (Oxford University Press, 2010)

Darwall, S. *Welfare and Rational Care* (Princeton University Press, 2002)

Deakin, S., Johnston, A., and Markesinis, B. *Markesinis and Deakin's Tort Law* 7th edition (Oxford University Press, 2013)

Demarez, J. *L'indemnisation du dommage occasionné par un member inconnu d'un groupe determine* (Paris: LGDJ, 1967)

Demogue, R. *Traité des Obligations en Général Tomes III-IV* (Paris: Librairie Arthur Rousseau, 1924)

Descheemaeker, E. *The Division of Wrongs* (Oxford University Press, 2009)

Deutsch, E. *Haftungsrecht: Erster Band: Allgemeine Lehren* (Cologne, Germany: Carl Heymanns, 1976)

Deutsch, E. and Spickhoff, A. *Medizinrecht* 6th edition (Berlin: Springer, 2008)

Dobbs, D. *The Law of Torts* (St. Paul, MN: West, 2000)

Douglas, S. *Liability for Wrongful Interference with Chattels* (Oxford: Hart, 2011)

Dowe, P. 'A Counterfactual Theory of Prevention and "Causation" By Omission', *Australasian Journal of Philosophy*, 79 (2001), 216

Dressler, J. *Understanding Criminal Law* 4th edition (New York: Bender & Co, 2006)

Dworkin, R.M. *Justice for Hedgehogs* (Cambridge, MA: Harvard University Press, 2011)

   Law's Empire (Cambridge, MA: Harvard University Press, 1986)

Dwyer, D. *The Judicial Assessment of Expert Evidence* (Cambridge University Press, 2008)

Ehlgen, C. *Probabilistische Proportionalhaftung und Haftung für den Verlust von Chancen* (Tübingen: Mohr Siebeck, 2013)

Emson, R. *Evidence* 4th edition (Basingstoke: Palgrave Macmillan, 2008)

Epstein, R. *Cases and Materials on Torts* 9th edition (New York: Aspen, 2009)

Fabre-Magnan, M. *Droit des Obligations: Tome 2* 2nd edition (Paris: Presses Universitaires de France, 2010)

Feinberg, J. *Harm to Others* (New York: Oxford University Press, 1984)

Finnis, J. *Natural Law and Natural Rights* (Oxford: Clarendon, 1980)

Fleming, J.G. *The Law of Torts* 9th edition (Sydney: LBC, 1999)

Fletcher, G. *Rethinking Criminal Law* (Boston: Little Brown & Co, 1978)

Franzki, D. *Die Beweisregeln im Arzthaftungsprozeß* (Berlin: Duncker & Humblot, 1982)

Fröhlich, D. *Die Beweisvereitelung im Zivilprozess* (Thesis submitted at Julius Maximilian University Würzburg: opus.bibliothek.uni-wuerzburg.de/files/ 2990/dissFroehlich.pdf, 2008)

Fuchs, M. *Deliktsrecht* 6th edition (Berlin: Springer, 2006) *Deliktsrecht* 7th edition (Berlin: Springer, 2009)

Gardner, J. *Offences and Defences* (Oxford University Press, 2007)

Gebauer, M. *Hypothetische Kausalität* (Tübingen: Mohr, 2007)

Ghestin, J., Goubeaux, G., and Fabre-Magnan, M. *Traité de droit civil, Introduction générale* 4th edition (Paris: LGDJ, 1994)

Gilead, I., Green, M., and Koch, B. (eds.) *Proportional Liability: Analytical and Comparative Perspectives* (Berlin: De Gruyter, 2013)

Gillies, D. *Philosophical Theories of Probability* (Oxford: Routledge, 2000)

Goldberg, J. and Zipursky, B. *Torts: Oxford Introductions to US Law* (New York: Oxford University Press, 2010)

Goldberg, R. *Causation and Risk in the Law of Torts: Scientific Evidence and Medicinal Product Liability* (Oxford: Hart, 1999)

(ed.) *Perspectives on Causation* (Oxford: Hart, 2011)

Green, S. *Causation in Negligence* (Oxford: Hart, 2014)

Großerichter, H. *Hypothetischer Geschehensverlauf und Schadensfestellung – Eine rechtsvergleichende Untersuchung vor dem Hintergrund der perte d'une chance* (Munich: Beck, 2001)

Guégan-Lécuyer, A. *Dommages de Masse et Responsabilité Civile* (Paris: LGDJ, 2006)

Hald, A. *A History of Probability and Statistics and Their Applications before 1750* (New Jersey: Wiley, 1990)

Hanau, P. *Die Kausalität der Pflichtwidrigkeit* (Göttingen: Schwartz & Co, 1971)

Harder, Y. *Die Beweisfigur des Befunderhebungs-und Befundsicherungsfehlers im Arzthaftungsprozess nach der Rechtsprechung des BGH und der Instanzgerichte* (Thesis, Regensburg, 2009)

Hart, H.L.A. *Punishment and Responsibility* (Oxford University Press, 2008)

Hart, H.L.A. and Honoré, T. *Causation in the Law* 1st edition (Oxford: Clarendon, 1959)

Causation in the Law 2nd edition (Oxford: Clarendon, 1985)

Handfield, T. *A Philosophical Guide to Chance* (Cambridge University Press, 2012)

Hausch, A. *Der grobe Behandlungsfehler in der gerichtlichen Praxis: Eine kritische Bestandsaufnahme* (Karlsruhe: Verlag Versicherungswirtschaft, 2007)

Häusler, M. *Haftung ohne Kausalitätsnachweis* (Dissertation, Universität Wien, 2010)

Hawthorne, J. *Knowledge and Lotteries* (Oxford University Press, 2005)

Heck, P. *Grundriß des Schuldrechts* (Tübingen: Mohr, 1929)

Heinrich, E. *Haftung bei alternative Kausalität mit Zufall* (Vienna: Verlag Osterreich, 2010)

Helbron, H. *Entwicklungen und Fehlentwicklungen im Arzthaftungsrecht* (Munich: Herbert Utz, 2001)

Hensler, D.R. and Carroll, S. *Asbestos Litigation* (Cambridge: Rand Institute, 2005)

Hernan, M. and Robins, J. *Causal Inference* (Online book draft: www.hsph.harvard. edu/miguel-hernan/causal-inference-book/)

Ho, H.L. *Philosophy of Evidence Law* (Oxford University Press, 2008)

Hofmann, E. *Die Umkehr der Beweislast in der Kausalfrage* (Karlsruhe: Verlag Verisicherungswirtschaft, 1972)

Howarth, D. *Textbook on Tort* (London: Butterworths, 1995)

Hurley, P. *Beyond Consequentialism* (Oxford University Press, 2010)

Jackson, R. and Powell, J. (and Stewart, R.) *Jackson and Powell on Professional Liability* 6th edition with 4th supplement (London: Sweet & Maxwell, 2010)

Jansen, N. *Die Struktur des Haftungsrechts* (Tübingen: Mohr, 2003)

Kasche, M. *Verlust von Heilungschancen – Eine rechtsvergleichende Untersuchung* (Frankfurt: Peter Lang, 1999)

Katzenmeier, C. *Arzthaftung* (Tübingen: Mohr Siebeck, 2002)

Keeton, R, Dobbs, D., and Owen, D. *Prosser & Keeton on Torts*, 5th edition (St. Paul, Mn: West, 1984)

Keren-Paz, T. *Torts, Egalitarianism and Distributive Justice* (Aldershot: Ashgate, 2007)

Keynes, J. *A Treatise on Probability* (London: Macmillan & Co, 1921)

Khoury, L. *Uncertain Causation in Medical Liability* (Oxford: Hart, 2006)

Klar, L. *Tort Law* 3rd edition (Canada: Thomson, 2003)

  Tort Law 4th edition (Canada: Thomson, 2008)

Knight, F.H. *Risk, Uncertainty and Profit* (Boston: Houghton Mifflin Co., 1921)

Kötz, H. and Wagner, G. *Deliktsrecht*, 11th edition (Munich: Vahlen, 2010)

Koziol, H. *Grundfragen des Schadenersatzrechts* (Vienna: Jan Sremak Verlag, 2010)

Krüse, C. *Alternative Kausalität* (Munich: LIT, 2006)

Kyburg, H. *Probability and the Logic of Rational Belief* (Middletown, Conn.: Wesleyan University Press, 1961)

Lambert-Faivre, Y. and Porchy-Simon, S. *Droit du dommage corporel* 7th edition (Paris: Dalloz, 2012)

Lange, H. and Schiemann, G. *Schadensersatz (Handbuch des Schuldrechts)* 3rd edition (Tübingen: Mohr, 2003)

Larenz, K. and Canaris, CW. *Lehrbuch des Schuldrechts Band II/2: Besonderer Teil* 13th edition (Munich: Beck, 1994)

Laudan, L. *Truth, Error and Criminal Law* (Cambridge University Press, 2006)

Laufs, A., Katzenmeier, C., and Lipp, V. *Arztrecht* (Munich: Beck, 2009)

LeBrun, P. *Responsabilité civile extra-contractuelle* 2nd edition (LexisNexis, Litec: Paris, 2009)

Lepa, M. *Die Verteilung der Beweislast im Privatrecht und ihre rationelle Begründung* (Dissertation, Cologne, 1963)

LeTourneau, P. *Droit de la responsabilité et des contrats* 7th edition (Paris: Dalloz, 2008)

Linden, A.M. *Canadian Tort Law*, 7th edition (London: Butterworths, 2002)

Lipton, P. *Inference to Best Explanation* (London: Routledge, 1993)

Lord, R.A. *Williston on Contracts* vol 24 4th edition. (Thomson West, 2002)

Lunney, M. and Oliphant, K. *Tort Law: Text Cases and Materials* 4th edition (Oxford University Press, 2010)

  Tort Law: Text Cases and Materials 5th edition (Oxford University Press, 2013)

Mackie, J.L. *The Cement of the Universe: A Study of Causation* (Oxford University Press, 1990)

Maassen, B. *Beweismaßprobleme im Schadensersatzprozeß* (Carl Heymanns Verlag: Cologne, 1975)

Mäsch, G. *Chance und Schaden* (Tübingen: Mohr, 2004)

Markesinis, B.S. and Unberath, H. *The German Law of Torts* (Oxford University Press, 2002)

Markesinis, B.S., Unberath, H., and Johnston, A. *The German Law of Contract* 2nd edition (Oxford University Press, 2006)

Mazeaud, H. and Mazeaud, L. *Traité Théorique et Pratique de la Responsabilité Civile Délictuelle et Contractuelle* 3rd edition (Paris: Sirey, 1939)

Mazeaud, H., Mazeaud, L., and Mazeaud, J. *Traité Théorique et Pratique de la Responsabilité Civile Délictuelle et Contractuelle Tome II* 6th edn (Paris: Montchrestien, 1970)

Mazeaud, H., Mazeaud, L., and Tunc, A. *Traité Théorique et Pratique de la Responsabilité Civile Délictuelle et Contractuelle Tome I* 6th edition (Paris: Montchrestien, 1965)

McCormick, C.T. *McCormick on Evidence* 5th edition (Strong, J.W., Broun, K.S., Dix, G.E., Inmwinkelried, E.J., Kaye D.H., Mosteller, R.P. and Roberts, E.F. Contributors) (St. Paul, Mn: West, 1999)

McBride, N. and Bagshaw, R. *Tort Law* 3rd edition (London: Pearson, 2008) *Tort Law* 4th edition (London: Pearson, 2012)

McGregor, H. *McGregor on Damages* 18th edition (London: Sweet & Maxwell, 2009) *McGregor on Damages* 19th edition (London: Sweet and Maxwell, 2014)

Mehring, T. *Beteiligung und Rechtswidrigkeit bei 830 I 2 BGB* (Berlin: Duncker & Humblot, 2003)

Merkin, R. and Steele, J. *Insurance and the Law of Obligations* (Oxford University Press, 2013)

Mislawski, R. *La Causalité dans la Responsabilité Civile: Recherches sur ses Rapports Avec la Causalité Scientifique* (Thesis: University Cergy-Pontoise, 2006)

Mommsen, T. *Zur Lehre vom Interesse* (Braunschweig: Schwetschke, 1855)

Moore, M. *Causation and Responsibility: Essays in Law, Metaphysics and Morals* (Oxford University Press, 2009)

Motsch, R. *Vom rechtsgenügenden Beweis* (Berlin: Duncker & Humblot, 1983)

Mouralis, J.L. *Dalloz Civil: Preuve* (Paris: Dalloz, 2002)

Müller, C. *La Perte d'une Chance* (Bern: Staempfli, 2002)

Müller-Stoy, W. *Schadensersatz für verlorene Chancen – Eine rechtsvergleichende Untersuchung* (Freiburg, Thesis, 1973)

Murphy, J. and Witting, C. *Street on Torts*, 13th edition (Oxford University Press, 2007)

Neyers J. and Chamberlain, E. (eds.) *Emerging Issues in Tort Law* (Oxford: Hart, 2007)

O'Malley, F., et al. (eds.) *Federal Jury Practice and Instructions* 6th edition (Thomson West, 2009)

Osborne, P.H. *The Law of Torts*, 2nd edition (Toronto: Carswell, 2003)

Otsuka, M. *Libertarianism without Inequality* (Oxford University Press, 2003)

Owen, D (ed) *Philosophical Foundations of the Law of Tort* (Oxford University Press, 1995)

Parfit, D. *On What Matters Volumes I & II* (Oxford University Press, 2011) *Reasons and Persons* (Oxford University Press, 1984)

Paul, L.A. and Hall, N. *Causation: A User's Guide* (Oxford University Press, 2013)

Phipson, S.L. (co-contributors: Howard, M.N. and Bagshaw, R.) *Phipson on Evidence*, 5th edition (London: Sweet & Maxwell, 2005)

Planiol, M. and Ripert, G. *Traité Pratique de Droit Civil Français Tome VI Obligations* 2nd edition, Esmein, P. (ed.) (Paris: LGDJ, 1952)

Porat, A. and Stein, A. *Tort Liability under Uncertainty* (Oxford University Press, 2001)

Posner, R. and Landes, W. *Economic Structure of Tort Law* (Cambridge, MA: Harvard University Press, 1987)

Posner, R. *Economic Analysis of Law* (Aspen Publishers, 2007)

Pradel, X. *Le Préjudice dans le droit civil de la responsabilité* (Paris: LGDJ, 2004)

Prütting, H. *Gegenwartsprobleme der Beweislast* (Munich: CH Beck, 1983)

Quentin, A. *Kausalität und deliktische Haftungsbegründung* (Berlin: Duncker & Humblot, 1994)

Quézel-Ambrunaz, C. *Essai sur la causalité en droit de la responsabilité civile* (Paris: Dalloz, 2010)

Rawls, J. *A Theory of Justice* (Cambridge, MA: Harvard University Press, 1971)
Justice as Fairness: A Restatement (Cambridge, MA: Belknap Press, 2001)

Raz, J. *From Normativity to Responsibility* (Oxford University Press, 2011)
The Practice of Value (Oxford University Press, 2001)
The Morality of Freedom (Oxford: Clarendon Press, 1988)

Reimann, M. and Zimmermann, R. *The Oxford Handbook of Comparative Law* (Paperback Edition) (Oxford University Press, 2008)

Restatements (1931–2010 published by the American Law Institute)
Restatement of Contracts (1931)
Restatement (Second) Contracts (1981)
Restatement (Second) Torts (1965–1979)
Restatement (Third) Torts (1998): *Products Liability*
Restatement (Third) Torts (2010): *Liability for Physical and Emotional Harm*, Volume 1

Riegger, T. *Die historische Entwicklung der Arzthaftung* (Thesis, Regensburg University, 2007)

Ripstein, A. *Equality, Responsibility and the Law* (Cambridge University Press, 1999)
Force and Freedom (Cambridge, MA: Harvard University Press, 2009)

Röckrath, L. *Kausalität, Wahrscheinlichkeit und Haftung* (Munich: Beck, 2004)

Rogers, W.V.H. *Winfield & Jolowicz on Tort*, 17th edition (London: Sweet & Maxwell, 2007)
Winfield & Jolowicz on Tort, 18th edition (London: Sweet & Maxwell, 2011)

Romerio, F. *Toxische Kausalität. Eine rechtsvergleichende und interdisziplinäre Studie* (Basel: Helbing & Lichtenhahn, 1996)

Rothman, K. *Epidemiology: An Introduction*, 2nd edition (New York: Oxford University Press, 2012)

Rothman, K., Greenland, S., and Lash, T. *Modern Epidemiology* 3rd edition (Philadelphia: Lippincott, Williams & Wilkins, 2008)

Sappideen, C. and Vines, P. (eds.) *Flemming's Law of Torts*, 10th edition. (Prymont: Thomson Reuters (Professional) Australia, 2010)

Savatier, R. *Traité de la Responsabilité Civile en Droit Français Tomes I-II* (Paris : LGDJ, 1939)

Scanlon, T.M. *What We Owe to Each Other* (Cambridge, MA: Belknap Press, 2000)

Schäfer, H. and Ott, C. *Lehruch der ökonomischen Analyse des Zivilrechts* (Berlin: Springer, 2000)

Schauer, F. *Profiles, Probabilities and Stereotypes* (Cambridge, MA: Harvard University Press, 2006)

Seifert, R. *Ärztlicher Behandlungsfehler und schicksalhafter Verlauf: Zur haftungsrechtlichen Bewältigung eines Kausalitätsdilemmas* (Baden: Nomos, 2008)

Sen, A. *The Idea of Justice* (London: Penguin, 2010)

Seyfert, C. *Mass Toxic Torts: Zum Problem der kausalen Unaufklärbarkeit toxischer Massenschäden* (Berlin: Duncker & Humblot, 2004)

Sick, J. *Beweisrecht im Arzthaftungsprozeß* (Bern: Peter Lang, 1987)

Spickhoff, A. *Folgenzurechnung in Schadensersatzrecht: Gründe und Grenzen* (ed. Lorenz, E.) (Karlsruher Forum 2007; Munich: Beck, 2008)

Stapleton, J. *Disease and the Compensation Debate* (Oxford: Clarendon, 1986)

Stauch, M. *The Law of Medical Negligence in England and Germany* (Oxford: Hart, 2008)

Steele, J. *Risks and Legal Theory* (Oxford: Hart, 2004)

Stein, A. *Foundations of Evidence Law* (Oxford University Press, 2005)

Sträter, J. *Grober Behandlungsfehler und Kausalitätsvermutung. Beweislastumkehr ohne medizinwissenschaftliche Basis?* (Baden: Nomos, 2006)

Stevens, R. *Torts and Rights* (Oxford University Press, 2007)

Strong, J.W., Roberts E.F., Kaye D.H., and Broun, K.S. (eds.) *McCormick on Evidence*, 5th edition (St Paul, MN: West, 1999)

Tadros, V. *The Ends of Harm* (paperback edition) (Oxford University Press, 2013)

Tillers, P, and Green, E. *Probability and Inference in the Law of Evidence: The Uses and Limits of Bayesianism* (Dordrecht: Springer, 1988)

Todd, S., et al. *The Law of Torts in New Zealand*, 5th edition (London: Thomson Reuters, 2009)

Traeger, L. *Der Kausalbegriff im Straf-und Zivilrecht* (Marburg: Elwert, 1904)

van Dam, C. *European Tort Law*, 1st edition (Oxford University Press, 2006)

Viney, G. and Jourdain, P. *Les Conditions de la Responsabilité* 3rd edition (Paris: LGDJ, 2006)

(with Carval, S.) *Les Conditions de la Responsabilité* (4th edition, Paris: LGDJ, 2013)

Von Bar, C. *The Common European Law of Torts* Volume 1 (Oxford: Clarendon Press, 2000)

The Common European Law of Torts Volume 2 (Oxford: Clarendon Press, 2000)

Verkehrspflichten (Cologne: Heymanns, 1980)

Wagner, G. *Neue Perspektiven im Schadensersatzrecht – Kommerzialisierung, Strafschadensersatz, Kolletivschaden Gutachten A für den 66 Deutschen Juristentag* (Munich: Beck, 2006)

Schadensersatz: Zwecke, Inhalte, Grenzen (Karlsrüher Forum 2006, 2006)

Wahrendorf, V. *Die Prinzipien der Beweislast im Haftungsrecht* (Köln: Heymann, 1976)

Weber, H. *Der Kausalitätsbeweis im Zivilprozeß* (Tübingen: Mohr, 1997)

Weinrib, E. *The Idea of Private Law* (Cambridge, MA: Harvard University Press, 1995)

Corrective Justice 1st edition (Oxford University Press, 2012)

Weir, T. *Tort Law* (Oxford: Clarendon Press, 2002)

Tort Law 2nd edition (Oxford: Clarendon Press, 2006)
Wilburg, W. *Die Elemente des Schadensrechts* (Marburg: Elwert, 1941)
Wilhelmi, R. *Risikoschutz durch Privatrecht* (Tubingen: Mohr, 2009)
Williams, B. *Moral Luck* (Cambridge University Press, 1981)
  Shame and Necessity (California: University of California Press, 1994)
Williamson, T.W. *Knowledge and its Limits* (Oxford University Press, 2002)
Winiger, B., Koziol, H., Koch, B., Zimmermann, R. (eds.) *Digest of European Tort
  Law: vol 1: Essential Cases on Natural Causation* (Vienna: Springer, 2007)
Winiger, B., Koziol, H., Koch, B., Zimmermann, R. (eds.) *Digest of European Tort
  Law: vol 2: Essential Cases on Damage* (Berlin: de Gruyter, 2011)
Zuckermann, A. *The Principles of Criminal Evidence* (Oxford University Press, 1989)

Articles, etc.

Aberkane, H. 'Du dommage causé par une personne indéterminée dans un
  groupe déterminé de personnes' *Revue Trimestrielle de Droit Civil* (1958)
Aboodi, R., Borer, A., and Enoch, D. 'Deontology, Individualism, and Uncertainty,
  a Reply to Jackson and Smith' *Journal of Philosophy*, 105 (2008)
Abraham, K.S. 'Self-Proving Causation' *Virginia Law Review*, 99 (2013): 1811
Adler, M.D. 'Risk, Death and Harm: The Normative Foundations of Risk
  Regulation', *Minnesota Law Review*, 87 (2003): 1293
Ahrens, H. 'Die Verteilung der Beweislast' in Lorenz, E. (ed.) *Karlsruher Forum
  2008* (2009)
Alexander, L. and Moore, M. 'Deontological Theories of Morality', Zalta, E. (ed)
  Stanford Online Encyclopedia of Philosophy (2007)
Allen, C. 'Note: Loss of Chance in Wyoming' *Wyoming Law Review*, 6 (2006): 533
Allen, R.J. 'Rationality, Algorithms, and Juridical Proof: A Preliminary Enquiry',
  The International Journal of Evidence and Proof, (1996–7): 254
Allen, R.J. and Stein, A. 'Evidence, Probability and the Burden of Proof' *Arizona
  Law Review*, 55 (2013): 557
Amirthalingam, K. 'Causation and the Gist of Negligence' *Cambridge Law Journal*,
  64 (2004): 32
  'Causation, Risk and Damage' *Law Quarterly Review*, 126 (2010): 162
Anscombe, G.E.M. 'Causality and Determination' in *Metaphysics and the Philosophy
  of Mind (The Collected Philosophical Papers of G. E. M. Anscombe, Volume 2)*
  (Minneapolis: University of Minnesota Press, 1981)
Ashworth, A. 'A Change of Normative Position: Determining the Contours of
  Culpability in Criminal Law' *New Criminal Law Review*, 11 (2008): 232
Arens, P. 'Dogmatik und Praxis der Schadensschätzung' *Zeitschrift für Zivilprozess*,
  88 (1975): 1
Bacher, K. Entry on Beweisvereitelung in §284 ZPO in Vorwerk, V. and Wolf, C.
  (eds.) *Beck'scher Online-Kommentar ZPO* (2012)
Bagchi, A. 'Distributive Injustice and Private Law' *Hastings Law Journal* 60 (2008) 105
Bagshaw, R. 'Causing the Behaviour of Others and Other Causal Mixtures' in
  Goldberg, R. (ed). *Perspectives on Causation* (Oxford: Hart, 2011).

Bailey, S.H. 'Causation in Negligence: What is a Material Contribution?' *Legal Studies*, 30 (2010): 167

Balaguer, M. 'Why There are No Good Arguments for any Interesting Version of Determinism' *Synthese*, 168 (2009): 1

Ballhausen, B. 'Anwendung der Beweislastumkehr nach den für die Arzthaftung entwickelten Grundsätzen bei einem groben Behandlungsfehler im Rahmen der Arzneimittelhaftung' *Medizinrecht*, 29 (2011): 575

Barker, K. 'Unfamiliar Waters: Negligent Advocates, Egregious Errors and Lost Chances of Acquittal' *University of Queensland Law Journal*, 24 (2005): 469

Barker, S. 'Counterfactuals, Probabilistic Counterfactuals and Causation' *Mind*, 108 (1999): 427

Bauer, M. 'Die Problematik gesamtschuldnerischer Haftung trotz ungeklärter Verursachung' *Juristenzeitung*, (1971): 4

Baumgartner, M. 'A Regularity Theoretic Approach to Actual Causation' *Erkenntnis*, 78 (2013): 85

Beebee, H. 'Does Anything Hold the Universe Together?' *Synthese*, 149 (2006): 509

Beever, A. 'Cause-in-Fact: Two Steps Out of the Mire' *University of Toronto Law Journal*, 51 (2001): 327

'Gregg v Scott and Loss of a Chance' *University of Queensland Law Journal*, 24 (2005): 201

'Policy in Private Law: An Admission of Failure' *University of Queensland Law Journal*, 25 (2006): 287

Ben-Shahar, O. 'Causation and Foreseeability' in Faure, M. (ed.) *Tort Law and Economic: Volume 1: Encyclopedia of Law and Economics* 2nd edition (Cheltenham: Edward Elgar, 2009)

Béraud, R. 'Les Mythes de la Responsabilité Civile' *Semaine Juridique* 1964.I.1837

'Quelques difficultés de preuve de la responsabilité délictuelle' *Semaine Juridique* 1950.I.870

Berger, M.A. 'Eliminating General Causation: Notes Toward a New Theory of Justice and Toxic Torts' *Columbia Law Review*, 97 (1997): 2117

Berger, M.A. and Twerski, A.D. 'Uncertainty and Informed Choice: Unmasking *Daubert*' *Michigan Law Review*, 104 (2005): 257

Bernstein, A. 'Asbestos Achievements' *Southwestern University Law Review*, 37 (2008): 691

'Hymowitz v. Eli Lilly & Co.: Markets of Mothers', in Rabin and Sugarman (eds). *Torts Stories* (New York: Foundation Press, 2003)

'Keep it Simple: An Explanation of the Rule of No Recovery for Pure Economic Loss' *Arizona Law Review*, 48 (2006): 773

Berryman, J. 'The Compensation Principle in Private Law', *Loyola of Los Angeles Law Review*, 42 (2008): 91

Bernstein, D. 'Getting to Causation in Toxic Tort Cases' *Brooklyn Law Review*, 74 (2008): 51

Bieri, L. and Marty, P. 'The Discontinuous Nature of the Loss of a Chance System' *Journal of European Tort Law*, 2 (2011): 23

Birks, P. 'The Concept of Civil Wrong' in Owen, D. (ed.) *Philosophical Foundations of Tort Law* (Oxford: Oxford University Press, 1995)

Black, V. 'Decision Causation: Pandora's Tool-Box', in Chamberlain, Neyers, Pitel (eds). *Emerging Issues in Tort Law* (Oxford: Hart, 2007)

Black, V. and Klimchuk, D. 'Comment on Athey v. Leonati: Causation, Damages, and Thin Skulls', *University of British Columbia Law Review*, 31 (1997): 163

Bloch, C. 'Exposition à un risque et perte de chance' *Semiane Juridique* 2010. III.1914–1915

'Exposition à un risque et préjudice moral d'anxiété' *Semaine Juridique* 2010. III.1914

Bodewig, T. 'Probleme Alternative Kausalität bei Massanschaden' *Archiv für civilistische Praxis*, 185 (1985): 505

Boivin, D. 'Factual Causation in the Law of Manufacturer Failure to Warn' *Ottawa Law Review*, 30 (1998): 47

Boon, A. 'Causation and the Increase of Risk' *Modern Law Review*, 51 (1988): 508

Boré, J. 'L'indemisation pour les chances perdues: une forme d'appréciation quantative de la causalité d'un fait dommageable' *La Semaine Juridique* 1974. I.2620

Borghetti, J-S. 'La reparation de la perte d'une chance en droit Suisse et en droit français' *European Review of Private Law*, (2008): 1072

'Note under Cass Civ 1e, 25 Nov 2010' *Semaine Juridique* G.2011.79

Boston, G. 'A Mass-Exposure Model of Toxic Causation: The Content of Scientific Proof and the Regulatory Experience" *Columbia Journal of Environmental Law*, 18 (1993): 181

'Apportionment of Harm in Tort Law: A Proposed Restatement' *University of Dayton Law Review*, 21 (1995): 268

Botterell, A. and Essert, C. 'Normativity, Fairness, and the Problem of Factual Uncertainty' *Osgoode Hall Law Journal*, 47 (2009): 663

Boysen, J. 'Shifting the Burden of Proof on Causation in Legal Malpractice Actions' *St Mary's Journal on Legal Malpractice & Ethics*, 1 (2011): 308

Braun, J. 'Zur schadensersatzrechtlichen Problematik des hypothetischen Inzidentprozesses bei Regreßklagen gegen den Anwalt' *Zeitschrift für Zivilprozessrecht*, 96 (1983): 89

Brehm, W. 'Zur Haftung bei alternativer Kausalität' *Juristenzeitung*, (1980): 585

Brennan, T.A. 'Causal Chains and Statistical Links' *Cornell Law Review*, 73 (1987–8): 469

'Environmental Torts' *Vanderbilt Law Review*, 46 (1993): 1

Broadbent, A. 'Epidemiological Evidence in Proof of Specific Causation' *Legal Theory*, 17 (2011): 237

Brown, C. 'Consequentialize This' *Ethics*, 121 (2011): 749.

Brown, R. 'Material Contribution's Expanding Hegemony: Factual Causation After Hanke v. Resurfice Corp.' *Canadian Business Law Journal*, 45 (2007): 432

'The Possibility of "Inference Causation": Inferring Cause-in-Fact and the Nature of Legal Fact Finding' *McGill Law Journal*, 55 (2010): 1

Buchak, L. 'Belief, Credence and Norms' *Philosophical Studies*, 169 (2014): 285

Buchberger, M. 'Le role de l'article 1315 du code civil en cas d'inexécution d'un contrat' *Dalloz Doctrine*, (2011): 465

Burrows, A. 'Comparing Compensatory Damages in Tort and Contract' in Degeling, S., Edelman, J., and Goudkamp, J. *Torts in Commercial Law* (Law Book Co., 2011)

'Uncertainty about Uncertainty: Damages for Loss of a Chance' *Journal of Personal Injury Law*, 1 (2008): 31

Bush, RAB. 'Between Two Worlds: The Shift from Individual to Group Responsibility in the Law of Causation of Injury' *University of California Los Angeles Law Review*, 33 (1985–6): 1473

Bydlinski, F. 'Aktuelle Streitfragen um die alternative Kausalität' in Sandrock, O. (ed.) *Festschrift Beitzke* (Berlin: de Gruyter, 1979)

'Causation as a Legal Phenomenon' in Tichy, L. (ed.) *Causation in Law* (Prague: Univerzita Carlova, 2007)

'Haftung bei alternativer Kausalität' *Juristische Blätter*, (1959): 1

'Haftungsgrund und Zufall als alternative mögliche Schadensursachen' in Enziger M., et al. (eds.) *Festschrift Frotz* (Vienna: Manz, 1993)

Calabresi, G. 'Concerning Cause and the Law of Torts: An Essay for Harry Kalven, Jr.', *University of Chicago Law Review*, 43 (1975): 69

Campbell, D. 'The End of Posnerian Law and Economics' *The Modern Law Review*, 73 (2010): 305

Canaris, C.W. 'Die Vermutung "aufklärungsrichtigen Verhaltens" und ihre grundlagen' in *Festschrift für Hadding* (Berlin: De Gruyter,2004)

Cane, P. 'Corrective Justice and Correlativity in Private Law' *Oxford Journal of Legal Studies*, 16 (1996): 471

'Distributive Justice and Tort Law' *New Zealand Law Review*, (2001): 401

'The Anatomy of Private Law Theory: A 25th Anniversary Essay' *Oxford Journal of Legal Studies*, 25 (2005): 203

'The General/Special Distinction in Criminal Law, Tort Law, and Legal Theory', *Law and Philosophy*, 26 (2007): 465

Carbone, M. and Yang, H. 'Molecular Pathways: Targeting Mechanisms of Asbestos and Erionite Carcinogenesis in Mesothelioma' *Clinical Cancer Research*, 18 (2012): 598

Cartwright, N. 'Are RCTs the Gold Standard?' *Biosocieties*, 2 (2007): 11

Chabas, F. 'La perte d'une chance en droit français' in Guillod, O. (ed.) *Colloque Développements récents du droit de la responsabilité civile* (Zurich: Schulthess, 1991)

Cheifitz, D. 'Materially Increasing the Risk of Injury as Factual Cause of Injury' *The Advocates' Quarterly*, 29 (2004): 253

'Not Clarifying Causation' (unpublished, 2011)

Cheifitz, D. and Black, V. 'Through the Looking Glass, Darkly: Resurfice v. Hanke' *Alberta Law Review*, 45 (2007–8): 241

Chignell, A. 'Belief in Kant' *Philosophical Review*, 116 (2007): 323

Clermont, K. 'Standards of Proof Revisited' *Vermont Law Review*, 43 (2009): 469

Clermont, K. and Sherwin, E. 'A Comparative View of Standards of Proof' *American Journal of Comparative Law*, 50 (2002): 243

Cohen, L.J. 'Subjective Probability and the Paradox of the Gatecrasher' *Arizona State Law Journal*, (1981): 627

Coleman, J. 'Doing Away with Tort' *Loyola of Los Angeles Law Review*, 41 (2008): 1149
  'Mistakes, Misunderstanding, and Misalignments' *Yale Law Journal Online*, 121 (2012): 541
  'On the Moral Argument for the Fault System' *The Journal of Philosophy*, 71 (1974): 473
  'Property, Wrongfulness and the Duty to Compensate' *Chicago-Kent Law Review*, 63 (1987): 451
  'Tort Law and Tort Theory: Preliminary Reflections on Method' in Postema, G. *Philosophy and the Law of Torts* (Cambridge University Press, 2001)
Collins, J. 'Pre-emptive Pre-emption' in Collins, J., et al. (eds.) *Causation and Counterfactuals* (Cambridge, MA: Massachusetts Institute of Technology Press, 2004)
Coons, J.E. 'Approaches to Court Imposed Compromise–The Uses of Doubt and Reason' *North Western University Law Review*, 58 (1964): 750
  'Compromise as Precise Justice' *California Law Review*, 68 (1980): 250
Cooper, K. 'Assessing Possibilities in Damages Awards: The Loss of a Chance or the Chance of a Loss' *Saskatchewan Law Review*, 37 (1973): 193
Cour de Cassation. *Annual Report* (2007)
Dan-Cohen, M. 'Luck and Identity' *Theoretical Inquiries in Law*, 9 (2008): 1
Daniels, N. 'Reflective Equilibrium' in Zalta, E. (ed.) *Stanford Online Encyclopedia of Philosophy* (2011)
Dannemann, G. 'Comparative Law: Study of Similarities or Differences' in Reimann, M. and Zimmermann, R. (eds.) *Oxford Handbook of Comparative Law* (Oxford University Press, 2008)
Davies, P. 'Complicity' in Dyson, M. (ed.) *Unravelling Tort and Crime* (Cambridge University Press, 2014)
Dawid, A.P. 'The Difficulty about Conjunction' *The Statistician*, 36 (1987): 91
  'The Role of Scientific and Statistical Evidence in Assessing Causality' in Goldberg, R. (ed.) *Perspectives on Causation* (Oxford: Hart Publishing, 2011)
Deffains, B. and Fluet, C. 'Legal Liability when Individuals have Moral Concerns' *Journal of Law, Economics and Organization*, 29 (2013): 930
Déjean de la Batie, N. 'Note under Cass Civ 3e, 19 May 1976 (3 decisions)' *Semaine Juridique* 1978.II.18773 (1978)
Delgado, R. 'Beyond Sindell: Relaxation of Cause-in-Fact Rules for Indeterminate Plaintiffs', *California Law Review*, 70 (1982): 881
Demougin, D. and Fluet, C. 'Preponderance of Evidence' *European Economic Review*, 50 (2006): 963
Department for Work and Pensions. 'Asbestos-Related Diseases' (London: Crown Copyright, 2005)
Descorps-Declère, F. 'La Cohérence de la jurisprudence de la Cour de Cassation sur la perte de chance consécutive à la faute du médecin' *Dalloz*, 2005.742
Deutsch, E. 'Die dem Geschädigten nachteilige Adäquanz: Zur einschränkenden Auslegung des §830 I 2 BGB durch den BGB' *Neue juristische Wochenschrift* (1981): 2731
Dewes, D. and Trebilcock, M. 'The Efficacy of the Tort System and its Alternatives: A Review of Empirical Evidence' *Osgoode Hall Law Journal*, 30 (1992): 57

Dowe, P. 'Absences, Possible Causation, and the Problem of Non-locality' *The Monist*, 92 (2009): 23

Durry, G. 'Faute médicale et perte de chances de survie' *Revue Trimestrielle de Droit Civil*, (1972): 408

'Jurisprudence française en matière de droit civil' *Revue Trimestrielle de Droit Civil*, (1971): 377

'La faute du médecin diminuant les "chances de guérison" du malade' *Revue Trimestrielle de Droit Civil*, (1967): 181

'La faute du médecin diminuant les "chances de guérison" du malade' *Revue Trimestrielle de Droit Civil*, (1969): 797

'Note on Cass Civ 2e, 19 May 1976' in *Revue Trimestrielle de Droit Civil* (1977): 129

Dworkin, G. 'Risk and Remoteness. Causation Worse Confounded' *The Modern Law Review*, 27 (1964): 344

Dworkin, R.M. 'Hart's Postscript and the Character of Political Philosophy' *Oxford Journal of Legal Studies*, 24 (2004): 1

'Is Wealth a Value?' *The Journal of Legal Studies*, 9 (1980): 191

'Principle, Policy, Procedure' in Dworkin, R.M. *A Matter of Principle* (Cambridge, MA: Harvard University Press, 1985)

Eberl-Borges, C. '§830 BGB und die Gefährdungshaftung' *Archiv für civilistische Praxis*, 196 (1996): 491

Commentary in *J von Staudingers Kommentar zum Bürgerlichen Gesetzbuch: §830 BGB* (2008)

Edelman, J. 'The Meaning of Loss and Enrichment' in Chambers, R., Mitchell, C., and Penner, J. *Philosophical Foundations of Unjust Enrichment* (Oxford University Press, 2009)

'Loss of a Chance' *Torts Law Journal* 21 (2013). 1

Eisenberg, M.A. 'Probability and Chance in Contract Law' *UCLA Law Review* 45 (1998): 1005

Ellis, L. 'Note, Loss of Chance as Technique: Toeing the Line at Fifty Percent' *Texas Law Review*, 72 (1993): 369

Engel, C. 'Preponderance of the Evidence Versus *Intime Conviction*' *Vermont Law Review*, 33 (2008–9): 435

Enoch, D. and Fisher, T. "'Sense and Sensitivity': Epistemic and Instrumental Approaches to Statistical Evidence" *Stanford Law Review* 67 (2015): 557

Enoch, D., Spectre, L., and Fisher, T. 'Statistical Evidence, Sensitivity, and the Legal Value of Knowledge' *Philosophy & Public Affairs*, 40 (2012): 197

Esmein, P. 'Note under Cour d'Appel Riom, 5 February 1964' *Semaine Juridique* 1964.II.13640

Evans, H. 'Lost Litigation and Later Knowledge' *Professional Negligence*, 23 (2007): 204

'The Scope of Sephton: Limitation Where You Don't Get what You Ought' *Professional Negligence*, 25 (2009): 15

Evatt, P.L. 'A Closer Look at Loss of Chance under Nebraska Medical Law' *Nebraska Law Review*, 76 (1997): 979

Faure, M.G. and Bruggeman, V. 'Causal Uncertainty and Proportional Liability' in Tichy, L. (ed.) *Causation in Law* (Prague: Univerzita Carlova, 2007)

Faure, M.G. 'The Complementary Roles of Liability, Regulation and Insurance in Safety Management: Theory and Practice' *Journal of Risk Research*, 17 (2014): 689

Ferrante, M. 'Causation in Criminal Responsibility' New Criminal Law Review, 11 (2008): 470

Finkelstein, C. 'Is Risk a Harm?' University of Pennsylvania Law Review, 151 (2003): 963

Finnis, J. 'Allocating Risks and Suffering: Some Hidden Traps' Cleveland State Law Review, 38 (1990): 193

Finn, M. 'Anmerkung zu BGH, Urt v.19.6.2012 – VI ZR 77/11', Medizinrecht, 31 (2013): 367

Fischer, D.A. 'Causation in Fact in Omission Cases' Utah Law Review, (1992): 1335
  'Causation in Fact in Products. Liability Failure to Warn Cases' Journal of Products & Toxic Liability, 17 (1995): 271
  'Insufficient Causes' Kentucky Law Journal, 94 (2005–6): 277
  'Products Liability – An Analysis of Market Share' Vanderbilt Law Review, 34 (1981): 1623
  'Proportional Liability, Statistical Evidence, and the Probability Paradox' Vanderbilt Law Review, 46 (1993): 1201
  'Successive Causes and the Enigma of Duplicated Harm' Tennessee Law Review, 66 (1998–9): 1127
  'Tort Recovery for Loss of a Chance' Wake Forest Law Review, 36 (2001): 605

Fischer, J.M. '"Ought-Implies-Can" Causal Determinism and Moral Responsibility' Analysis, 63 (2003): 244

Fischer, J.M. and Ennis, R.H. 'Causation and Liability' Philosophy and Public Affairs, 15 (1986): 33

Fisher, T. 'Conviction without Conviction' Minnesota Law Review, 96 (2012): 833

Fleischer, H. 'Schadensersatz für verlorene Chancen im Vertrags-und Deliktsrecht' Juristenzeitung, (1999): 766

Fleming, J. 'Probabilistic Causation in Tort Law' Canadian Bar Review, 68 (1989): 661

Fletcher, G.P. 'Fairness and Utility in Tort Theory' Harvard Law Review, 85 (1972): 537

Foerste, U. Commentary to §§286–287 ZPO in Musielak, H. (ed.) Kommentar zur Zivilprozessordnung 9th edition (Munich: Beck, 2009)
  Commentary on §§286–287 ZPO in Musielak, H. (ed.) Kommentar zur Zivilprozessordnung 10th edition (Munich: Beck, 2013)

Fossier, T. and Lévêque, F. 'Le "presque vrai" et le "pas tout à fait faux": probabilities et decision juridictionnelle' JCP no. 14, doctr. 427 (2012)

Frankfurt, H. 'Alternative Possibilities and Moral Responsibility' Journal of Philosophy, 23 (1969): 829

Frasca, R. 'Loss of Chance Rules and the Valuation of Loss of Chance Damages' Journal of Legal Economics, 15 (2008–9): 91

Fraser, J.D. and Howarth D.R. 'More Concern for Cause', Legal Studies, 4 (1984): 131

Fumerton, R. and Kress, K. 'Causation and the Law: Preemption, Lawful Sufficiency and Causal Sufficiency' Law and Contemporary Problems, 64 (2001): 83

Galand-Carval, S. 'Causation under French Law' in Spier, J. (ed.) Unification of Tort Law: Causation (Hague: Kluwer, 2000)
  'Country Report for France' in Oliphant, K. (ed.) Aggregation and Divisibility of Damage (Vienna: Springer, 2009)

Galia-Beauchesne, A. 'Note under Cass Crim. 19 May 1978' Dalloz, (1980): 3

Gardner, J. 'Corrective Justice, Corrected' Diritto & Questioni Pubbliche, 12 (2012): 9

'Law's Aim in Law's Empire' in Scott Hershovitz (ed.) *Exploring Law's Empire* (Oxford: Oxford University Press, 2006)

'Obligations and Outcomes in the Law of Torts' in Cane, P. and Gardner, J. (eds.) *Relating to Responsibility: Essays for Tony Honoré* (Oxford: Hart, 2001)

'Some Rule-of-Law Anxieties about Strict Liability in Private Law' in Austin, L. and Klimchuk, D. (eds.) *Private Law and the Rule of Law* (Oxford University Press, 2014)

'The Mark of Responsibility' *Oxford Journal of Legal Studies*, 23 (2003): 157

'The Wrongdoing That Gets Results' *Philosophical Perspectives:* 18 (2004): 53

'Torts and Other Wrongs' *Florida State University Law Review*, 39 (2011): 43

'What is Tort Law For? Part 1: The Place of Corrective Justice' *Law and Philosophy*, 30 (2011): 1

'What is Tort Law For? Part 2: The Place of Distributive Justice' in Oberdiek, J. (ed.) *Philosophical Foundations of Tort Law* (Oxford University Press, 2014)

'Wrongs and Faults' *The Review of Metaphysics*, 59 (2005): 95

Geiger, S. and Kruse, C. 'House of Lords 3 May 2006, Barker v. Corus Neue Impulse für das Europäische Deliktsrecht vom House of Lords' *European Review of Private Law*, (2008): 339

Geistfeld, M. 'Inadequate Product Warnings and Causation' *University of Michigan Journal of Law Reform*, 30 (1996–7): 309

'Scientific Uncertainty and Causation in Tort Law' *Vanderbilt Law Review*, 54 (2001): 1011

'Social Value as a Policy-Based Limitation on the Ordinary Duty to Exercise Reasonable Care' *Wake Forest law Review*, 44 (2009): 899

'The Analytics of Duty: Medical Monitoring and Related Forms of Economic Loss' *Vanderbilt Law Review*, 88 (2002): 1921

'The Doctrinal Unity of Alternative Liability and Market Share Liability' *University of Pennsylvania Law Review*, 155 (2006): 447

Gernhuber, J. 'Haftung bei alternativer Kausalität' *Juristenzeitung* (1961): 152

Giesen, I. 'The reversal of the burden of proof in the Principles of European Tort Law A comparison with Dutch tort law and civil procedure rules' *Utrecht Law Review*, 6 (2010): 22

Gifford, D. 'The Challenge to the Individual Causation Requirement in Mass Products Torts' *Washington & Lee Law Review*, 62 (2005): 873

Gilead, I., Green, M. and Koch, B., 'General Report: Causal Uncertainty and Proportional Liability: Analytical and Comparative Report' in Gilead, I., Green, M., and Koch, B. (eds.) *Proportional Liability: Analytical and Comparative Perspectives* (Berlin: de Gruyter, 2013)

Gold, S. 'Causation in Toxic Torts: Burdens of Proof, Standards of Persuasion, and Statistical Evidence' *Yale Law Journal*, 96 (1986–7): 376

Gold, S.C. 'Causation in Toxic Torts: Burdens of Proof, Standards of Persuasion, and Statistical Evidence' *Yale Law Journal*, 96 (1986): 376

'The More We Know, The Less Intelligent We Are? – How Genomic Information Should and Should Not, Change Toxic Tort Doctrine' *Harvard Environmental Law Review*, 34 (2010): 369

'The "Reshapement" of the False Negative Asymmetry Doctrine in Toxic Tort Causation' *William Mitchell Law Review*, 37 (2011): 1507

Goldberg, J.C.P. 'What Clients Are Owed: Cautionary Observations on Lawyers and Loss of a Chance' *Emory Law Journal*, 52 (2003): 1201

Goldberg, J.C.P and Zipursky, B. 'Rights and Responsibility' in Nolan, D. and Robertson, A. *Rights and Private Law* (Oxford: Hart, 2012)

'Torts as Wrongs' *Texas Law Review*, 88 (2010): 917

'Unrealized Torts' *Virginia Law Review*, 88 (2002): 1625

Goldberg, R. 'Using Scientific Evidence to Resolve Causation Problems in Product Liability: UK, US and French Perspectives' in Goldberg, R. (ed.) *Perspectives on Causation* (Oxford: Hart, 2011)

Goldstein, B. and Henifin, M. 'Reference Guide on Toxology' in *Reference Manual on Scientific Evidence* 3rd edition (Washington DC: National Academies Press, 2011)

Graßhoff, G. and May, M. 'Causal Regularities' in Spohn, W., Ledwig, M., and Esfeld, M. (eds.) in *Current Issues in Causation* (Paderborn, Mentis, 2001)

Grechenig, C. and Stremitzer, A. 'Der Einwand rechtmäßigen Alternativverhaltens – Rechtsvergleich, ökonomische Analyse und Implicationen für die Proportionalhaftung' *Rabel Journal of Comparative and International Private Law*, 73 (2009): 336

Green, M.D. 'Pessimism About Milward' *Wake Forest Journal of Law and Policy*, 3 (2005): 41

'Second Thoughts about Apportionment in Asbestos Litigation' *Southwestern University Law Review*, 37 (2008): 531

'The Future of Proportional Liability: The Lessons of Toxic Substances Causation' in Madden, S. (ed.) *Exploring Tort Law* (Cambridge University Press, 2005)

'The Intersection of Factual Causation and Damages' *De Paul Law Review*, 55 (2006): 571

Green, M.D., Freedman, M., and Gordis, L. 'Reference Guide on Epidemiology' in *Reference Manual on Scientific Evidence* 3rd edition (Washington DC: National Academies Press, 2011)

Green, M.D., Powers, W., and Sanders, J. 'The Insubstantiality of the 'Substantial Factor' Test for Causation' *Missouri Law Review*, 73 (2008): 399

Green, S. 'The Risk Pricing Principle: a Pragmatic Approach to Causation and Apportionment of Damages' *Law, Probability and Risk*, 4 (2005): 159

Grey, B. 'The Plague of Causation in National Childhood Vaccine Injury Act' *Harvard Journal of Legislation*, 48 (2011): 343

Griffin, L. '"Which one of you did it?" Criminal Liability for "Causing or Allowing" the Death of a Child' *Indiana International & Comparative Law Review*, 15 (2004–5): 89

Grodsky, J. 'Genomics and Toxic Torts: Dismantling the Risk-Injury Divide' *Stanford Law Review*, 59 (2007): 1671

Gunson, J. 'Turbulent Causal Waters: The High Court, Causation and Medical Negligence' *Tort Law Review*, 9 (2000): 53

Haack, S. 'Proving Causation: The Holism of Warrant and the Atomism of Daubert' *Journal of Health and Biomedical Law*, 4 (2009): 253

'Risky Business: Statistical Proof of Individual Causation' in Ferrer, J. (ed.) *Causalidad y Atribución de Responsibilidad* (Madrid: Marcial Pons, 2012)

Häger, J. 'Die Kausalität bei Massenschäden' in *Festschrift für Canaris* (Munich: Beck, 2007)

Hajek, A. 'Interpretations of Probability' in *Stanford Online Encyclopedia of Philosophy* (2011)
    'Mises Redux' – Redux: Fifteen Arguments Against Finite Frequentism" *Erkenntnis*, 45 (1996): 209
Halbersberg, Y. and Guttel, E. 'Behavioural Economics and Tort Law' in Zamir, E. and Teichman, D. *The Oxford Handbook of Behavioral Economics and the Law* (Oxford University Press, 2014)
Hall, N. 'Two Concepts of Causation' in Collins, J. et al. (eds.) *Causation and Counterfactuals* (Cambridge, MA: MIT Press, 2004)
Halpérin, J. 'French Legal Doctrine' in Jansen, N. (ed.) *The Development and Making of Legal Doctrine* (Cambridge University Press, 2010)
Hamer, D. 'Before the High Court - Mind the Evidential Gap: Causation and Proof in *Amaca Pty Ltd* v *Ellis*' *Sydney Law Review*, 31 (2009): 465
    'Chance would be a fine thing: Proof of Causation and Quantum in an Unpredictable World' *Melbourne University Law Review*, 23 (1999): 24
    'Probabilistic Standards of Proof: Their Complements and the Errors that Are Expected to Flow from Them' *University of New England Law Journal*, 1 (2004): 71
    'The Civil Standard of Proof Uncertainty: Probability, Belief and Justice' *Sydney Law Review*, 16 (1994): 506
Hanau, P. 'Anmerkung zum Urteil des BGH vom 11.6.1968 (VI ZR 116/67)' *Neue Juristische Wochenschrift*,(1968): 2291
Handfield, T. and Wilson, A. 'Chance and Context' in Wilson, A. (ed.) *Chance and Temporal Asymmetry* (Oxford University Press, 2014)
Handfield, T. and Pisciotta, T. 'Is Risk-Liability Theory Compatible with Negligence Law?' *Legal Theory*, 11 (2005): 387
Harel, A. and Porat, A. 'Aggregating Probabilities Across Cases: Criminal Responsibility for Unspecified Offenses' *Minnesota Law Review*, 94 (2009): 261
Harman, E. 'Harming as Causing Harm' in Roberts, M. and Wasserman, D. (eds.) *Harming Future Persons* (Dordrecht: Springer, 2009)
Hausch, A. 'Vom therapierenden zum dokumentierenden Arzt – Über die zunehmende haftungsrechtliche Bedeutung der ärztlichen Dokumentation' *VersR*, (2006): 612
Heinemann, K. 'Baustein anwaltlicher Berufshaftung: die Beweislast' *Neue Juristische Wochenschrift*, (1990): 2345
Henckel, W. 'Grenzen richterlicher Schadensschätzung' *JuS*, (1975): 221
Hensler D.R. 'Has the Fat Lady Sung? The Future of Mass Toxic Torts' *Review of Litigation*, 26 (2007): 883
Hernán, M. and Jick, S.S. 'Hepatitis B vaccination and multiple sclerosis: the jury is still out' *Pharmacoepidemiology and Drug Safety*, 15 (2006): 653
Hill, A.B. 'The Environment and Disease: Association or Causation?' *Proceedings of the Royal Society of Medicine*, 58 (1965): 295
Hill, J., Reiter, J., and Zanutto, E. 'A Comparison of Experimental and Observational Data Analyses' in Gelman, A. and Weng, X. (eds.) *Applied Bayesian Modelling and Causal Inference from Incomplete-Data Perspectives* (New York: Wiley, 2004)

Hill, T. 'A Lost Chance for Compensation in the Tort of Negligence by the House of Lords', *Modern Law Review*, 4 (1991): 511

Hocquet-Berg, S. 10052 'La perte d'une chance pour fixer la réparation à la mesure statistique du lien causal entre les fautes et le dommage' *Semaine Juridique* 2010.II.878

'Note' in *Semaine Juridique* 2007.II.

Hoefer, C. 'Causal Determinism' in Zalta, E. (ed.) *Stanford Encyclopedia of Philosophy* (2010)

'The Third Way on Objective Probability: A Sceptic's Guide to Objective Probability' *Mind*, 116 (2007): 549

Hoffmann, L. 'Causation' *Law Quarterly Review*, 121 (2005): 421

'*Fairchild and After*' in Burrows, A., Johnston, D., and Zimmermann, R. (eds.) *Judge and Jurist: Essays in Memory of Lord Rodger* (Oxford University Press, 2013)

'Common Sense and Causing Loss' (*Lecture to the Chancery Bar Association*, 1999)

Hogan, T.B. 'Cook v. Lewis Re-examined' *Modern Law Review*, 24 (1961): 331

Hogg, M. 'Developing Causal Doctrine' in Goldberg, R. (ed.) *Perspectives on Causation* (Oxford: Hart, 2011)

Hohfeld, W.N. 'Some Fundamental Legal Conceptions as Applied in Judicial Reasoning' *Yale Law Journal*, 23 (1913–14): 15

Honoré, A.M. 'Necessary and Sufficient Conditions in Tort Law' in Owen, D. (ed.) *Philosophical Foundations of Tort Law* (Oxford University Press, 1995)

'Review: Legal Cause in the Law of Torts by Robert E. Keeton' *Harvard Law Review*, 77 (1964): 495

'Responsibility and Luck: The Moral Basis of Strict Liability', *Law Quarterly Review*, 104 (1988): 530

'The Morality of Tort Law – Questions and Answers' in Owen, D. (ed.) *Philosophical Foundations of Tort Law* (Oxford University Press, 1995)

Lord Hope of Craighead. 'James McGhee – A Second Mrs. Donoghue?' *Cambridge Law Journal*, 62 (2003): 587

Howarth, D.H. 'Three Forms of Responsibility: On the Relationship between Tort Law and The Welfare State' *Cambridge Law Journal*, 60 (2001): 553

'Libel: Its Purpose and Reform' *Modern Law Review*, 74 (2011): 845

Huet, J. 'Perte d'une Chance: du plus ou moins classique?' *Revue Trimestrielle de Droit Civil*, (1986): 117

Hylton, K. 'Causation in Tort Law: A Reconsideration' in Arlen, J. (ed.) *Research Handbook on the Economics of Torts* (Cheltenham: Edward Elgar, 2013)

Ibbetson, D.J. 'Harmonisation of the Law of Tort and Delict' in Zimmermann, R. (ed.) *Grundstrukturen des Europäischen Deliktsrechts* (Baden: Nomos, 2003)

IIAC. 'Laryngeal Cancer and Asbestos Exposure' www.iiac.org.uk (*Position Paper 22*) (2008)

Illari, P. and Williamson, J. 'What is a Mechanism? Thinking About Mechanisms Across the Sciences' *European Journal for Philosophy of Science*, 2 (2012): 119

Jakubowitz, D. '"Help I've Fallen and Can't Get Up!" New York's Application of the Substantial Factor Test' *St John's Journal of Legal Commentary*, 18 (2003–4): 593

Jansen, N. Entry on §249 and § 252 BGB in Schmoeckel, M., Rückert, J., and Zimmermann, R. (eds.) *Historisch-kritischer Kommentar zum BGB Band II:*

Schuldrecht. Allgemeiner Teil. 1. Teilband: §§ 241–304. 2. Teilband: §§ 305–432 (Tübingen: Mohr, 2007)

'The Concept of Non-Contractual Obligations: Rethinking the Divisions of Tort, Unjustified Enrichment, and Contract Law' *Journal of European Tort Law*, 1 (2010): 16

'The Idea of a Lost Chance' *Oxford Journal of Legal Studies*, 19 (1999): 271

Johnson, E. 'Criminal Liability for Loss of a Chance' *Iowa Law Review*, 91 (2005): 59

Jourdain, P. 'Comment traiter le dommage potentiel?' *Responsabilité Civile et Assurances n° 3*, March 2010, dossier 11

'Sur la perte d'une chance' *Revue Trimestrielle de Droit Civil*, (1992): 109

'Un recul de la responsabilité "in solidum" des members d'un groupe de personnes dont l'un d'entre eux est l'auteur non identifié du dommage' *Revue Trimestrielle de Droit Civil*, (1988): 769

'Usage et abus de la notion de perte d'une chance' *Revue Trimestrielle de Droit Civil*, (1989): 85

Julia, G. 'La réception juridique de l'incertitude médicale' *Medicine et Droit*, (2009): 127

Jungk, A. 'Grundsätze und manche Ausnahme: Beweislastfragen im Regressprozess' *Anwaltsblatt*, (2013): 142

Kadner-Graziano, T. 'Alles oder nichts oder anteilige Haftung bei Verursachungszweifeln? – Zur Haftung für perte d'une chance/loss of a chance-Entscheidungen des schweizerischen Bundesgerichts vom 13. Juni 2007, des belg. Hof van Cassatie vom 5. Juni 2008 u.a.' *Zeitschrift für europäisches Privatrecht*, (2011): 171

'Loss of a Chance in European Private Law "All or Nothing" or Partial Liability in Cases of Uncertain Causation' *European Review of Private Law*, 6 (2008): 1009

Kahan, M. 'Causation and the Incentives to Take Care under the Negligence Rule', *Journal of Legal Studies*, 18 (1989): 427

Kagan, S. 'Causation, Liability, and Internalism' *Philosophy and Public Affairs*, 15 (1986): 41

Karner, E. 'The Function of the Burden of Proof in Tort Law' in Koziol, H. and Steininger, B. (eds.) *European Tort Law 2008* (Springer: Vienna, 2008)

Katz, L. 'Proximate Cause in Michael Moore's *Act and Crime*' *University of Pennsylvania Law Review*, 142 (1993–4): 1513

Katzenmeier, C. 'Beweismaßreduzierung und probabilistische Proportionalhaftung' *Zeitschrift für Zivilprozessrecht*, 117 (2004): 187

'Haftung für HIV-kontaminierte Blutprodukte' *Neue Juristische Wochenschrift*, (2005): 3391

'Verschärfung der Berufshaftung durch Beweisrecht – der grobe Behandlungsfehler' in *Humaniora: Medizin, Recht, Geschichte 2006, Part 4* (Berlin: Springer, 2006)

Kaye, D.H. 'The Error of Equal Rates' *Law Probability and Risk*, 1 (2002): 3

'Statistical Significance and the Burden of Persuasion' *Law and Contemporary Problems*, 46 (1983): 13

'The Limits of the Preponderance of Evidence Standard: Justifiably Naked Statistics and Multiple Causation', *American Bar Foundation Research Journal*, (1982): 487.

'The Paradox of the Gatecrasher and Other Stories' *Arizona State Law Journal*, (1979): 101

Keating, G.C. 'The Heroic Enterprise of the Asbestos Cases' *Southwestern University Law Review*, 38 (2008): 623

Keeler, J. 'Increased Risk, causation and Speeding: Van den H'euvel v Tucker' *Torts Law Journal*, 12 (2004): 1

Kegel, G. 'Der Individualanscheinsbeweis und die Verteilung der Beweislast nach überwiegender Wahrscheinlichkeit' in *Festgabe für Kronstein* (Karlsruhe: C F Mueller, 1967)

Keren-Paz, T. 'Risks and Wrongs' Account of Corrective Justice in Tort Law: Too Much or Too Little?' *Diritto e questioni publiche*, 12 (2012): 75

Kerkorian, P.G. 'Negligent Spoliation of Evidence: Skirting the "Suit Within a Suit" Requirement of Legal Malpractice Actions' *The Hastings Law Journal*, 41 (1989–90): 1077

Kessler, L.W. 'Alternative Liability in Litigation Malpractice Actions' *San Diego Law Review*, 37 (2000): 401

Khoury, L. 'Causation and Risk in the Highest Courts of Canada, England and France' *Law Quarterly Review*, 124 (2008): 103

King, J.H. 'Causation, Valuation and Chance in Personal Injury Torts Involving Preexisting Conditions and Future Consequences' *Yale Law Journal*, 90 (1981): 1353

'"Reduction of Likelihood" Reformulation and Other Retrofitting of the Loss-of-a-Chance Doctrine' *University of Memphis Law Review*, 28 (1997–8): 491

Klein, A. 'A Model for Enhanced Risk Recovery in Tort', *Washington & Lee Law Review*, 56 (1999): 1173

'Beyond DES: Rejecting the Application of Market Share Liability in Blood Products Litigation' *Tulane Law Review*, 66 (1993–4): 883

'Causation and Uncertainty: Making Connections in a Time of Change' *Jurimetrics Journal*, 49 (2008): 5

'Fear of Disease and the Puzzle of Future Cases in Tort' *University of California, Davis Law Review*, 35 (2001–2): 965

'Rethinking Medical Monitoring' *Brooklyn Law Review*, 64 (1998): 1

Kleinschmidt, J. 'Kausalität' in *Handwörterbuch des europäischen Privatrechts* (Tübingen: Mohr, 2009)

Kletecka, A. 'Alternative Verursachungskonkurrenz mit dem Zufall – Die Wahrscheinlichkeit als Haftungsgrund?' *Juristische Blätter*, (2009): 137

Klöhn, L. 'Wertende Kausalität im Spiegel von Rechtsvergleichung, Rechtsdogmatik und Rechtsökonomik' *Zeitschrift für vergleichende Rechtswissenschaft*, 105 (2006): 455

Koehler, J. 'When do Courts Think Base Rae Statistics are Relevant?' *Jurimetrics Journal*, 42 (2002): 373

(with Meixner, J.) 'Decision Making and the Law: Truth Barriers' (on SSRN) (2013)

Koziol, H. 'Schadenersatz für den Verlust einer Chance?' in *Festschrift für Hans Stoll zum 75. Geburtstag* (Tübingen: Mohr, 2001)

Kraus, J. 'A Non-Solution to a Non-Problem: A Comment on Alan Strudler's "Mass Torts and Moral Principles' *Law & Philosophy*, 16 (1997): 91

Kriebel, D. 'How Much Evidence is Enough? Conventions of Causal Inference' *Law and Contemporary Problems*, 72 (2009): 121

Knutsen E.S. 'Ambiguous Cause-in-Fact and Structured Causation: A Multi-Jurisdictional Approach' *Texas International Law Journal*, 38 (2003): 249

Kortmann, J.S. 'Ab alio ictu(s): Misconceptions about Julian's View on Causation' *Journal of Legal History*, 20 (1999): 95

Laleng, P. 'Sienkiewicz v Grief (UK) Ltd. and Willmore v Knowsley Metropolitan Borough Council: A Material Contribution to Uncertainty' *Modern Law Review*, 74 (2012): 777

Laudan, L. 'Strange Bedfellows: Inference to the Best Explanation and the Criminal Standard of Proof' *The International Journal of Evidence and Proof*, 11 (2007): 292

Lee, J. 'Fidelity in Interpretation: Lord Hoffmann and the Adventure of the Empty House' *Legal Studies*, 28 (2008): 1

Leipold, D. Commentary to §§286–287 ZPO in Stein, F. & Jonas, M. *Kommentar zur Zivilprozeßordnung* Band 3 §§253–299a 22nd edition (Tübingen, 2008)

Leshem, S. and Miller, G. 'All-or-Nothing versus Proportionate Damages' *Journal of Legal Studies*, 38 (2009): 345

LeSourd, N. 'La Perte d'une Chance' *Gazette du Palais* 1963 2.doct.49

Levmore, S. 'Probabilistic Recoveries, Restitution, and Recurring Wrongs' *Journal of Legal Studies*, 19 (1990): 691

Lewis, D. 'Causation' *Journal of Philosophy*, 70 (1973): 556

Lin, A.C. 'Beyond Tort: Compensating Victims of Environmental Toxic Injury' *South California Law Review*, 78 (2004–5): 1439

List, C. and Pivato, M. 'Emergent Chance' (ms on file with the author, 2014)

Lord, P.A. 'Loss of Chance in Legal Malpractice' *Washington Law Review*, 61 (1986): 1479

Lunney, M. 'Chances of Recovery in Tort' *King's College Law Journal*, 7 (1996)
'What Price a Chance?' *Legal Studies*, 15 (1995): 1

Luntz, H. 'A View from Abroad' *New Zealand Law Review*, (2008): 92
'Loss of a Chance in Medical Negligence' *University of Melbourne Law Research Series*, (2010): 14
'Loss of Chance' in Freckelton and Mendelson (eds.) *Causation in Law and Medicine* (Surrey: Ashgate, 2002)

Madden, M.S. and Holian, J. 'Defendant Indeterminacy: New Wine into Old Skins' *Louisiana Law Review*, 67 (2006–7): 785

Magnus, U. 'Why is US Tort Law so Different?' *Journal of European Tort Law*, 1 (2010): 102

Mahaffey, G.S. 'Cause-In-Fact and the Plaintiff's Burden of Proof with Regard to Causation and Damages in Transactional Legal Malpractice Matters: The Necessity of Demonstrating the Better Deal' *Suffolk University Law Review*, 37 (2004): 393

Malone, W. 'Ruminations on Cause-in-Fact', *Stanford Law Review*, 9 (1956): 60

Mansfield, J.H. 'Hart and Honoré, Causation in the Law-A Comment' *Vanderbilt Law Review*, 17 (1963–4): 487

Markovits, R. 'On the Economic Inefficiency of a Libera-Corrective-Justice Securing Law of Torts' *2006 Illinois Law Review*, (2006): 525

Mäsch, G. 'Der Fußballtrainer und die Anwaltshaftung, oder: Meine objektive Meinung' *Anwaltsblatt*, 12 (2009): 855

'Gregg v Scott: Much Ado about Nothing? Entscheidung des House of Lords vom 27. Januar 2005 mit Anmerkung von Gerald Mäsch' *Zeitschrift für europäisches Privatrecht* (2006)

Matthies, K. 'Anmerkung zu BGH, Urt. v. 21.9. 1982, Az. VI ZR 302/80' *Neue Juristische Wochenschrift*, (1983): 335

Mautner, M. 'Luck in the Courts' *Theoretical Inquiries in Law*, 9 (2008): 217

Mayer, D. 'La 'Garde' en Commun' *Revue Trimestrielle de Droit Civil*, (1975): 197

Mazeaud, H. & Mazeaud, L. 'Impossibilité d'identifier parmi les members d'un groupe l'auteur de la faute dommageable' *Revue Trimestrielle de Droit Civil*, (1942): 60

'Impossibilité de determiner, parmi des fautes simultanément commises par plusiers personnes, celle qui a cause le dommage' *Revue Trimestrielle de Droit Civil*, (1950): 60

'Tir simultané par plusiers chasseurs; blessure par plusiers projectiles; garde collective des armes' *Revue Trimestrielle de Droit Civil*, (1960): 479

McBride, N.J. 'Duties of Care: Do They Really Exist?' *Oxford Journal of Legal Studies*, 24 (2004): 417

'Rights and the Basis of Tort Law' in Nolan, D. and Robertson, A. (eds). *Rights and Private Law* (Oxford: Hart, 2011)

'Duties of Care in Negligence' (unpublished, 2011)

'Tort Law and Human Flourishing' in Pitel, S.A., Neyers, J., and Chamberlain, E. *Challenging Orthodoxy in Tort Law* (Oxford: Hart Publishing, 2013)

McBride, N. and Steel, S. 'Suing for the Loss of the Right to Sue: Why Wright is Wrong' *Professional Negligence*, 28 (2012): 27

McCarthy, D. 'Liability and Risk' *Philosophy and Public Affairs*, 25 (1996): 238

McIvor, C. 'The Use of Epidemiological Evidence in UK Tort Law' in Loue, S. (ed.) *Forensic Epidemiology in the Global Context* (New York: Springer, 2013)

McGovern, F.E. 'The Tragedy of the Asbestos Commons' *Vanderbilt Law Review*, 88 (2002): 1721

McGregor, H. 'Loss of Chance: Where Has it Come from and Where Is it Going?' *Professional Negligence*, 24 (2008): 2

McInnes, M. 'Causation in Tort Law: A Decade in the Supreme Court of Canada' *Saskatchewan Law Review*, 63 (2000): 445

McLachlin, B. 'Negligence Law – Proving the Connection' in Mullany and Linden (eds.) *Torts Tomorrow: A Tribute to John Fleming* (London: LBC, 1998)

McLaughlin, G.A. 'Proximate Cause' *Harvard Law Review*, 39 (1925–6): 149

Miller, C. 'Causation in Personal Injury after (and before) *Sienkiewicz*' *Legal Studies* 32 (2012): 396

'Causation in Personal Injury: Legal or Epidemiological Common Sense' *Legal Studies*, 26 (2006): 533

'Gregg v. Scott: Loss of Chance Revisited' *Law, Probability and Risk* 4 (2005): 227

'Liability for Negligently Increased Risk: The Repercussions of Barker v Corus UK (plc)' *Law Probability and Risk*, 8 (2009): 39

'Loss of Chance in Personal Injury: A Review of Recent Developments' *Law Probability and Risk*, 5 (2006): 63

'NESS for Beginners' in Goldberg, R. (ed). *Perspectives on Causation* (Oxford: Hart, 2011)

Mislawski, R. 'La Causalité Dans La Responsibilité Civile' (Unpublished Thesis, 2006)

'Vaccin contre l'hépatite B et sclérose en plaques; retour sur la causalité' *Medicine & Droit*, 102 (2010): 105

Mitchell, P. 'Loss of a Chance in Deceit' *Law Quarterly Review*, 125 (2009): 12

Moreteau, O. 'Case Report on France' in Koziol, H. and Steininger, B. (eds.) *European Tort Law 2005* (Vienna: Springer, 2005)

Morgan, J. 'Lost Causes in the House of Lords' *Modern Law Review*, 66 (2003): 277

'Causation, Politics and Law: The English - and Scottish - Asbestos Saga' in Goldberg, R. (ed). *Perspectives on Causation* (Oxford: Hart, 2011)

Mullany, N.J. 'Common Sense Causation – An Australian View' *Oxford Journal of Legal Studies*, 12 (1992): 431

Nace, A.B. 'Market Share Liability: A Current Assessment of a Decade Old Doctrine' *Vanderbilt Law Review*, 44 (1991): 395

Nance, D. 'A Comment on the Supposed Paradoxes of a Mathematical Interpretation of the Logic of Trials' *Boston University Law Review*, 66 (1986): 947

'Civility and the Burden of Proof' *Harvard Journal of Law and Public Policy*, 17 (1994): 647

Neuberger, Lord. 'Loss of Chance and Causation', *Professional Negligence*, 24 (2008): 206

Nichols, S. '*Jorgenson v Vener*: The South Dakota Supreme Court Declares Loss-of-Chance Doctrine as Part of Our Common Law in Medical Malpractice Torts' *South Dakota Law Review*, 46 (2001): 618

Noah, L. 'An Inventory of Mathematical Blunders in Applying the Loss-of-a-Chance Doctrine', *Review of Litigation*, 24 (2006): 369

Nolan, D. 'Causation and the Goals of Tort Law' in Robertson, A. and Tang Hang Wu (eds.) *The Goals of Private Law* (Oxford: Hart, 2009)

Note. 'Latent Harms and Risk-Based Damages' *Harvard Law Review*, 111 (1997–8): 1505

Harvard Law Review, 122 (2009): 1247

Harvard Law Review, 123 (2010): 1771

Oberdiek, J. 'Philosophical Issues in Tort Law' *Philosophy Compass*, 3 (2008): 734

'The Moral Significance of Risking' *Legal Theory*, 18 (2011): 339

'Towards a Right Against Risking' *Law and Philosophy*, 28 (2009): 367

Oetker, H. Commentary to §249 BGB in *Münchener Kommentar zum BGB: Band 2: Schuldrecht, Allgemeiner Teil (§241–432)* 6th edition (2012)

5th edition (2007)

Offerman, J. '"The Dose Makes the Poison": Specific Causation is Texas Asbestos Cases after *Borg-Warner*' *Texas Tech Law Review*, 41 (2009): 709

Oliphant, K. 'Alternative Causation: A Comparative Analysis of Austrian and English Law' in *Festschrift für Helmut Koziol* (Vienna: Jan Sramek Verlag, 2010)

'Proportional Liability' in Verschraegen, B. (ed.) *Interdisciplinary Studies of Comparative and Private International Law* (Vol. 1) (Vienna: Jan Sramek Verlag, 2010, 179)

O'Mealley, Hon J.L. 'Asbestos Litigation in New South Wales' *Journal of Law and Policy*, (2007): 1209

Orloff, N. and Stedinger, J. 'A Framework for Evaluating the Preponderance-of-the-Evidence Standard' *University of Pennsylvania Law Review*, 131 (1983): 1159

Otsuka, M. (unpublished). 'The Fairness of Equal Chances' (on file with the author)

Overvold, M. 'Self-interest and the Concept of Self-Sacrifice' *Canadian Journal of Philosophy*, 10 (1980): 105

Pardo, M.S. 'Second Order Proof Rules' *Florida Law Review*, 61 (2009): 1083

Pardo, M.S. and Allen, R. 'Juridical Proof and the Best Explanation' *Law and Philosophy*, 27 (2008): 223

Paul, L.A. 'Keeping Track of the Time: Emending the Counterfactual Analysis of Causation' *Analysis*, 58 (1998): 191

Peel, W.E. 'Loss of a Chance in Medical Negligence' *Law Quarterly Review*, 121 2005: 364

'Lost Chances and Proportionate Recovery' *Lloyd's Maritime and Commercial Law Quarterly*, (2006): 289

Penneau, J.L. 'Note under Cass Civ 1e, 27 March 1973' *Dalloz* 1973.895

'Note under Cass Civ 1e, 17 November 1982' *Dalloz*, (1982) *Info Rapides* 380

Perry, S.H. 'Protected Interests and Undertakings in the Law of Negligence' *University of Toronto Law Journal*, 42 (1992): 247

'Risk, Harm and Responsibility' in *Philosophical Foundations of Tort Law* Owen, D. (ed.) (Oxford: Clarendon, 1995)

'Risk, Harm, Interests, and Rights', in *Risk: Philosophical Perspectives* Lewens, T. (ed.) (London: Routledge, 2007, 190)

'The Moral Foundations of Tort Law' *Iowa Law Review*, 77 (1992): 449

Phegan, C. 'The Limits of Compensation: An Australian Perspective on Public Policy, Causation, and Mitigation' *International and Comparative Law Quarterly*, 34 (1985): 470

Pizzirusso, J. 'Increased Risk, Fear of Disease, and Medical Monitoring: Are Novel Damage Claims Enough to Overcome Causation Difficulties in Toxic Torts' *The Environmental Lawyer*, 7 (2000–1): 183

Poisson-Drocourt, E. 'Note under Cass Civ 2e 15 December 1980' *Dalloz*, (1981): 455

Poole, J. 'Loss of Chance and the Evaluation of Hypotheticals in Contract Claims' *Lloyds Maritime and Commercial Law Quarterly*, (2007): 63

Porat, A. 'Misalignments in Tort Law' *Yale Law Journal*, 121 (2011): 82

Porat, A. and Posner, E. 'Aggregation and Law' *Yale Law Journal*, 122 (2012): 2

Porat, A. and Stein, A. 'Indeterminate Causation and Apportionment of Damages: An Essay on Holtby, Allen and Fairchild' *Oxford Journal of Legal Studies*, 23 (2003): 667

'Liability for Future Harm' in Goldberg, R. (ed). *Perspectives on Causation* (Oxford: Hart, 2011)

'Liability for Uncertainty: Making Evidential Damage Actionable' *Cardozo Law Review*, 18 (1996–7): 1891

Posner, E. 'Probability Errors: Some Positive and Normative Implications for Tort and Contract Law' *Supreme Court Economic Review*, 11 (2003): 125

Posner, R.A. 'A Theory of Negligence' *Journal of Legal Studies*, 1 (1972): 29

'The Concept of Corrective Justice In Recent Theories of Tort Law' *Journal of Legal Studies*, 10 (1981): 187

'Wealth Maximization and Tort Law: A Philosophical Inquiry' in Owens, D. (ed.) *Philosophical Foundations of Tort Law* (Oxford: Clarendon Press, 1995)

Postacioglu, I.E. 'Les faits simultanés et le problème de la responabilité' *Revue Trimestrielle de Droit Civil*, (1954): 438

Pryor, E.S. 'After the Judgment' *Vanderbilt Law Review*, 88 (2002): 1757

Pryor, R. 'Lost Profit or Lost Chance Reconsidering the Measure of Recovery for Lost Profits in Breach of Contract Actions' *Regent University Law Review*, 19 (2007): 561

Prütting, H. Commentary on §286, §287 ZPO in *Münchener Kommentar zum Zivilprozessordnung* 3rd edition (Munich: Beck, 2008)

Commentary on §§286 – 287 ZPO, 4th edition (2013)

Psillos, S. 'Causal Explanation and Manipulation' in Persson, J., and Ylikoski, P. (eds.) *Rethinking Explanation* (New York: Springer, 2007)

'Regularity Theories' in Menzies, P. and Hitchcock, C. (eds.) *The Oxford Handbook of Causation* (Oxford University Press, 2009)

Pundik, A. 'Epistemology and the Law of Evidence: Four Doubts about Alex Stein's *Foundations of Evidence Law*' *Civil Justice Quarterly*, 25 (2006): 504

'Statistical Evidence and Individual Litigants' *International Journal of Evidence and Proof*, 12 (2008a): 303

'The Epistemology of Statistical Evidence' *Evidence & Proof*, 15 (2011): 117

'What is Wrong with Statistical Evidence? Attempts to Establish an Epistemic Deficiency' *Civil Justice Quarterly*, 27 (2008b): 461

Puppe, I. Commentary on §13 StGB in Kindhäuser, U., Neumann, U., and Paeffgen, H. (eds.) *Strafgesetzbuch* 3rd edition (Baden: Nomos, 2010)

'Zurechnung und Wahrscheinlichkeit – Zur Analyse des Riskoerhöhungsprinzips' *Zeitschrift für die gesamte Strafrechtswissenschaft*, 95 (1983): 287

Quézel-Ambrunaz, C. 'La fiction de la causalité alternative' *Dalloz* 2010.1162 (2010)

'Note under Cass Civ 1e, 11 Mars 2010' 2010 *Gazette du Palais* II.833 (2010)

Rabin, M. 'Psychology and Economics' *Journal of Economic Literature*, 36 (1998): 11

Rabin, R.L. 'Enabling Torts' *DePaul Law Review*, 49 (1999–2000): 345

'Harms from Exposure to Toxic Substances: The Limits of Liability Law' *Pepperdine Law Review*, 38 (2010–11): 419

'Indeterminate Future Harm in the Context of September 11' *Vanderbilt Law Review*, 88 (2002): 1831

'Some Thoughts on the Efficacy of a Mass Toxics Administrative Compensation Scheme' *Maryland Law Review*, 52 (1993): 951

Raschel, L. 'La delicate disintinction de la perte de chance et du risque de
    dommage', *Semaine Juridique* G.No.15, 763, note under Cass Civ 1e, 14 Jan
    2010, no.08–16.760 (2010)
Redmayne, M. 'Exploring the Proof Paradoxes' *Legal Theory*, 14 (2008): 281
    'Objective Probability and the Assessment of Evidence' *Law, Probability and
    Risk*, 2 (2003): 275
    'Standards of Proof in Civil Litigation' *Modern Law Review*, 62 (1999): 167
Reece, H. 'Losses of Chances in the Law' *Modern Law Review*, 59 (1996): 188
Reid, G. 'Gregg v Scott and Lost Chances' *Professional Negligence*, 21 (2005): 78
Rescher, N. 'Leibniz, Keynes, and the Rabbis on a Problem of Distributive Justice'
    Journal of Philosophy, 86 (1989): 337
Rhee, R. 'Application of Finance Theory to Increased Risk Harms', *Virginia
    Environmental Law Journal*, 23 (2004): 111
    'Probability, Policy and the Problem of Reference Class' *International Journal
    of Evidence and Proof*, 11 (2007): 286
Ripert, G. 'Note under Cour d'Orléans (17 January 1949)' *Dalloz 1949 Jurisprudence*,
    (1949). 502
Ripstein, A. 'Mischief and Misfortune' *McGill Law Journal*, 41 (1995): 91
    'As If It Had Never Happened' *William and Mary Law Review*, 48 (2007): 1957
    'Closing the gap', *Theoretical Inquiries in Law*, 9 (2008): 61
    'Justice and Responsibility' *Canadian Journal of Law and Jurisprudence*, 17 (2004):
    361
    'Private Law and Private Narratives' *Oxford Journal of Legal Studies*, 20 (2000):
    683
    'Tort Law in a Liberal State' *Journal of Tort Law*, 1 (2007): 1
Ripstein, A. and Zipursky, B. 'Corrective Justice in an Age of Mass Torts' in
    Postema, (ed.) *Philosophy and the Law of Torts*, (Cambridge University Press,
    2001)
Riss, O. 'Hypothetische Kausalität, objective Berchnung bloßer Vermögensschäden
    und Ersatz verlorner Prozesschancen' *Juristische Blätter*, (2004): 440
Robertson, A. 'Justice, Community Welfare and the Duty of Care' *Law Quarterly
    Review*, 127 (2011): 370
Robertson, D.W. 'Causation in the Restatement (Third) of Torts: Three Arguable
    Mistakes' *Wake Forest Law Review*, 44 (2009): 1007
    'The Common Sense of Cause-in-Fact' *Texas Law Review*, 75 (1997): 1765
Robinson, G. 'Multiple Causation in Tort Law: Reflections on the DES Cases'
    Virginia Law Review, 68 (1982): 713
    'Probabilistic Causation and Compensation for Tortious Risk' *Journal of Legal
    Studies*, 14 (1985): 779
Rosenberg, D. 'Decoupling Deterrence and Compensation Functions in Mass Tort
    Class Actions for Future Loss' *Vanderbilt Law Review*, 88 (2002): 1871
    'Individual Justice and Collectivizing Risk-Based Claims in Mass Exposure
    Cases' *New York University Law Review*, 71 (1997): 210
    'Mass Torts and Class Actions: What Defendants Have and Plaintiffs Don't'
    Harvard Journal on Legislation, 37 (2000): 393

'The Causal Connection in Mass Exposure Cases: A Public Law Vision of the Tort System' *Harvard Law Review*, 97 (1985): 851

Rostron, A. 'Beyond Market Share Liability: A Theory of Proportionate Share Liability for Non-Fungible Products', *University of California Los Angeles Law Review*, 52 (2004): 151

Rotherham, C. 'Gain-Based Relief in Tort after *Attorney General v Blake*' *Law Quarterly Review*, 126 (2011): 102

Rothman, K. and Greenland, S. 'Causation and Causal Inference in Epidemiology' *American Journal of Public Health*, 95 (2005): 144

Rue, J.D. 'Returning to the Roots of the Bramble Bush: The 'But-For Test Regains Primacy in Causal Analysis in the American Law Institute's Proposed Restatement (Third) of Torts' *Fordham Law Review*, 71 (2002–3): 2679

Saluden, M. 'Commentary on Cass Civ 1e 17 November 1982' *Semaine Juridique* II 20056

Sanchiricho, C. 'Evidence Tampering' *Duke Law Journal*, 53 (2004): 1215

Sanders, J. 'Risky Business: Causation in Asbestos Cases (and beyond?)' in Goldberg, R. (ed). *Perspectives on Causation* (Oxford: Hart, 2011)

Sanders, J., Green, M., and Powers, W. 'The Insubstantiality of the "Substantial Factor" Test for Causation' *Missouri Law Review*, 73 (2008): 399

Sargos, P. 'Faute et perte de chance dans l'organisation du diagnostic et l'organisation d'une clinique' *Semaine Juridique* 2009.II.10030 (2009)

'La causalité en matière de responsabilité ou le "droit Schtroumpf" 2008 *Dalloz* (2008): 1935

Sartorio, C. 'How to be Responsible for Something Without Causing it' *Philosophical Perspectives*, 18 (2004): 315

'Moral Inertia' *Philosophical Studies*, 140 (2008): 117

Savatier, R. 'Commentary on decision of 14 December 1965, Cour de Cassation' *Semaine Juridique* 1966.G.II.14753 (1966)

'Commentary on decision of 1 June 1976, Cour de Cassation' *Semaine Juridique* 1976.G.II.18483 (1976)

'Commentary on decision of 2 May 1978, Cour de Cassation' *Semaine Juridique* 1978.II.18966 (1978)

'Une faute peut-elle engendrer la responsabilité d'un damage sans l'avoir cause?' *Dalloz* 1970.chron.123 (1970)

Schaffer, J. 'Contrastive Causation in the Law' *Legal Theory*, 16 (2010): 259

'Counterfactuals, Causal Independence and Conceptual Circularity' *Analysis*, 64 (2004): 299

'Deterministic Chance' *British Journal Philosophy of Science*, 58 (2007): 113

Scheines, R. 'Causation, Statistics, and the Law' *Journal of Law and Policy*, 16 (2007–8): 135

'Causation, Truth, and the Law' *Brooklyn Law Review*, 73 (2009): 959

Scherpe, J. 'A New Gist?' *Cambridge Law Journal*, 65 (2006): 487

'Ausnahmen vom Erfordernis eines strikten Kausalitätsnachweises im englischen Deliktsrecht' *Zeitschrift für Europäisches Privatrecht*, (2004): 164

Scheuerman, S. 'Against Liability for Private Risk Exposure' *Harvard Journal of Law and Public Policy*, 35 (2012): 681

Schiemann, G. Entry in *J von Staudingers Kommentar zum Bürgerlichen Gesetzbuch*: *Buch 2: Recht der Schuldverhältnisse §249–254 (Schadensersatzrecht)* (2005)
  'Kausalitätsprobleme bei der Arzthaftung' in *Festschrift für Canaris* (Tubingen, 2007)

Schmelk, R. 'Note under Cass Civ 2e, 11 February 1966' *Dalloz* 1966.229 (1966)

Schmueli, B. and Sinai, Y. 'Liability under Uncertain Causation? Four Talmudic Answers to a Contemporary Tort Dilemma' *Boston University International Law Journal* (forthcoming)

Schroeder, C. 'Corrective Justice and Liability for Increasing Risks' *University of California Los Angeles*, 37 (1990): 439

Schubert, C. Commentary on §249 BGB in *Bamberger/Roth-Schubert, Beck' scher Online-Kommentar* (2012)

Schwartz, G. 'Mixed Theories of Tort Law: Affirming both Deterrence and Corrective Justice', *Texas Law Review*, 75 (1996–7): 1801

Seavey, W. 'Tabula in Naufragio' *Harvard Law Review*, 63 (1949–50): 643

Shavell, S. 'An Analysis of Causation and the Scope of Liability in the Law of Torts' *Journal of Legal Studies*, 9 (1980): 463
  'Causation and Tort Liability' in *The New Palgrave Dictionary of Economics and the Law* (New York: Stockton Press, 1998)
  'Economic Analysis of Accident Law' (2003) (Working Paper on National Bureau of Economics Website, www.nber.org/papers/w9694.pdf)
  'Liability for Accidents' in *The New Palgrave Dictionary of Economics Online* www. dictionaryofeconomics.com/article?id=pde2008_E000215 (2008)
  'Liability for Accidents' in Shavell, S. and Polinsky, A.M. (eds.) *Handbook of Law and Economics* (Oxford: Elsevier, 2007)
  'Uncertainty over Causation and the Determination of Civil Liability' *The Journal of Law and Economics*, 28 (1985): 587

Sheiner, N. 'DES and a Proposed Theory of Enterprise Liability' *Fordham Law Review*, 46 (1997): 1007

Simmonds, N.E. 'Epstein's Theory of Strict Tort Liability' *Cambridge Law Journal*, 51 (1992): 113

Sirks, B. 'The Delictual Origin, Penal Nature and Reipersecutory Object of the *Action Damni Iniuriae Legis Aquiliae*' *Tijdschrift voor Rechtsgeschiedenis*, 77 (2009): 303

Slim, H. 'Les intérêts protégés par la responsabilité civile': available at grerca. univ-rennes1.fr, 2009 (accessed 1 June 2015)

Smith, Janet. 'Causation in Tort: The Search for Principle' *Munkman Lecture* (2009)

Smith, J. 'Legal Cause in Actions of Tort' *Harvard Law Review* 25 (1911–12): 103

Smith, M. and Jackson, F. 'Absolutist Moral Theories and Uncertainty' *Journal of Philosophy*, 103 (2006): 267

Smith, S. 'The Normativity of Private Law' *Oxford Journal of Legal Studies*, 31 (2011): 215

Solum, L. 'Presumptions and Transcendentalism: You Prove It! Why Should I?' *Harvard Journal of Law and Public Policy*, 17 (1994): 691
  'Procedural Justice' *Southern California Law Review*, 78 (2004): 181

'Uncertainty, Risk and Ignorance' (2011) at Legal Theory Lexicon: 070 at http:// lsolum.typepad.com/legal_theory_lexicon

Solum, L. and Marzen, S. 'Truth and Uncertainty: Legal Control of the Destruction of Evidence' *Emory Law Journal*, 36 (1987): 1085

Souplet, I. 'La Perte De Chances Dans La Droit De La Responsabilite Medical' (Unpublished Thesis, 2002)

Spector, H. 'The MMTS Analysis of Causation' in Goldberg, R. (ed.) *Perspectives on Causation* (Oxford: Hart, 2011)

Spellman, B.A. and Kincannon, A. 'The Relation Between Counterfactual ('But For') and Causal Reasoning' *Law and Contemporary Problems*, 64 (2001): 241

Spickhoff, A. 'Grober Behandlungsfehler und Beweislastumkehr' *Neue juristische Wochenschrift*, (2004): 2345

Spindler, G. 'Kausalität im Zivil-und Wirtschaftsrecht' *Archiv für civilistische Praxis*, 208 (2008): 283

'Commentary on §830 I 2 BGB' in Bamberger and Roth (eds). *Beck'scher Online-Kommentar BGB* (2013)

Stapleton, J. 'Benefits of Comparative Tort Reasoning: Lost in Translation' *Journal of Tort Law*, 1 (2007): 1 – 'Cause-in-Fact and the Scope of Liability for Consequences' Law Quarterly Review, 119 (2003): 388

'Choosing What We Mean by "Causation" in the Law' *Missouri Law Review*, 73 (2008): 433

'Duty of Care and Economic Loss: A Wider Agenda' *Law Quarterly Review*, 107 (1991): 389

'Evaluating Goldberg and Zipursky's Civil Recourse Theory' *Fordham Law Review*, 75 (2006): 1529

'Factual Causation' *Federal Law Review*, 38 (2010): 467

'Factual Causation and Asbestos Cancers' *Law Quarterly Review*, 126 (2010): 351

'Factual Causation, Mesothelioma and Statistical Validity' *Law Quarterly Review*, 128 (2012): 221

'Legal Cause, Cause-in-Fact and the Scope of Liability for Consequences' *Vanderbilt Law Review*, 54 (2001): 941

'Lords a'Leaping Evidentiary Gaps' *Torts Law Journal*, 10 (2002): 1

'Loss of the Chance of Cure from Cancer' *Modern Law Review*, 68 (2005): 996

'Occam's Razor Reveals an Orthodox Basis for Chester v Afshar' *Law Quarterly Review*, 122 (2006): 426

'Review of Porat and Stein, Tort Law under Uncertainty' *Modern Law Review*, 66 (2003): 308

'The Gist of Negligence: Part 2 the Relationship between "Damage" and Causation' *Law Quarterly Review*, 104 (1988): 389

'The Two Explosive Proof-of-Causation Doctrines Central to Asbestos Claims' *Brooklyn Law Review*, 74 (2009): 1011

'Two Causal Fictions at the Heart of US Asbestos Doctrine' *Law Quarterly Review*, 122 (2006): 189

'Unnecessary Causes' *Law Quarterly Review*, 129 (2013): 39

'An 'Extended But-for Test' for the Causal Relation in the Law of Obligations', *Oxford Journal of Legal Studies*, (2015): forthcoming

Stauch, M. 'Causation, Risk and Loss of Chance in Medical Negligence' *Oxford Journal of Legal Studies*, 17 (1996): 205
  '"Material Contribution" as a Response to Causal Uncertainty: Time for a Rethink' *Cambridge Law Journal*, 68 (2009): 27
Stein, A. 'The Refoundation of Evidence Law' *Canadian Journal of Law & Jurisprudence*, 9 (1996): 279
  'Towards a Theory of Medical Malpractice' *Iowa Law Review*, 97 (2012): 1201
Steel, S. and Ibbetson, D.J. 'More Grief Over Uncertain Causation in Tort' *Cambridge Law Journal*, 70 (2011): 451
Steel, S. 'Causation in English Tort Law: Still Wrong After All These Years' *University of Queensland Law Journal*, 31 (2012): 243
  'Causation in Tort and Crime: Unity or Divergence?' in Dyson, M.N. *Unravelling Tort and Crime* (Cambridge University Press, 2014)
  'Defining Causal Counterfactuals in Negligence' *Law Quarterly Review*, 130 (2014): 564
  'False Imprisonment and the Fetch of Hypothetical Warrant' *Law Quarterly Review*, 127 (2011): 527
  'Justifying Exceptions to Proof of Causation in Tort' *Modern Law Review*, Forthcoming
  'On when *Fairchild* Applies' *Law Quarterly Review*, 131 (2015): 363
  'Rationalising Loss of a Chance in Tort' in Pitel, S.A., Neyers, J., and Chamberlain E. *Challenging Orthodoxy in Tort Law* (Oxford: Hart Publishing, 2013)
  '*Sienkiewicz v Greif (UK) Ltd* and Exceptional Doctrines of Natural Causation' *Journal of European Tort Law*, 2 (2011): 294
  'Suing for the Loss of the Right to Sue: Why Wright is Wrong' *Professional Negligence*, 28 (2012): 27
  'Uncertainty over Causal Uncertainty (Karen Sienkiewicz (Administratrix of the Estate of Enid Costello) v Greif (UK) Ltd)' *Modern Law Review*, 73 (2010): 646
Steffey, D.L., Fienberg, S.E., and Sturgess, R.H. 'Statistical Assessment of Damages in Breach of Contract Litigation' *Jurimetrics*, 46 (2005–6): 129
Steiner, T. 'Der grobe ärztliche Behandlungsfehler in der Praxis' *Versicherungsrecht*, (2009): 474
Stevens, R. 'Rights and Other Things' in Robertson, A. and Nolan, D. (eds.) *Rights in Private Law* (Oxford: Hart, 2011)
Stiggelbout, M. 'The Case of Losses in Any Event' *Legal Studies*, 30 (2010): 558
Stoffel-Munck, P. 'Confirmation de la définition de la perte de chance' *Semaine Juridique* 2007.I.185
  Note in *Dalloz* 2009.2817
Stoll, H. 'Die Beweislastverteilung bei positiven Vertragsverletzungen' in *Festschrift für Hippel* (Tubingen: Mohr, 1967)
  'Haftungsverlagerung durch beweisrechtliche Mittel' *Archiv für civilistische Praxis*, 176 (1976): 145
  'Schadensersatz für verlorene Heilungschancen vor englischen Gerichten in rechtsvergleichender Sicht' in *Festschrift für Hippel* (1995)
Stone, J. 'Burden of Proof and the Judicial Process' *Law Quarterly Review*, 60 (1944): 262
Strachan, D.M.A. 'Variations on an Enigma' *Modern Law Review*, 33 (1970): 378

Strassfield, R.N. 'If. . .: Counterfactuals in the Law' *The George Washington Law Review*, 60 (1992): 339

Stremitzer, A. 'Negligence-Based Proportional Liability: How More Lenient Sanctions Lead to Higher Compliance' (unpublished, available on SSRN: http://papers.ssrn.com/sol3/papers.cfm?abstract_id=2088977)

Street, H. 'Supervening Events and the Quantum of Damages' *Law Quarterly Review*, 78 (1962): 70

Strevens, M. 'Mackie Remixed' in Campbell, O'Rourke, Silverstein (eds.) *Causation and Explanation*, vol. 4 of *Topics in Contemporary Philosophy* (Cambridge, MA: MIT, 2007)

Tabbach, A. 'Causation, Discontinuity and Incentives to Choose Levels of Care and Activity Under the Negligence Rule' *Review of Law and Economics*, (2008): 133.

Tadros, V. 'Obligations and Outcomes' in Cruft, R., Kramer, M.H., and Reiff, M. (eds.) *Crime, Punishment, and Responsibility: The Jurisprudence of Antony Duff* (Oxford University Press, 2011)

Taruffo, M. 'Rethinking the Standards of Proof' *The American Journal of Comparative Law*, 51 (2003): 659

Taupitz, J. 'Proportionalhaftung zur Lösung von Kausalitätsproblemen insbesondere in der Arzthaftung' in *Festschrift für CW Canaris* (Tübingen, 2007)

Teitelbaum, J.C. 'A Unilateral Accident Model Under Ambiguity' *Journal of Legal Studies*, 36 (2007): 431

Teske, W. 'Anmerkung to BGH 9.6.1994' *Juristenzeitung* , (1995): 472

Tettenborn, A. 'Personal Injury Claims and Assignment: Interesting Times?' *Professional Negligence*, 28 (2012): 61

'What is a Loss?' in Neyers, J., Chamberlain, E., and Pitel, S. *Emerging Issues in Tort Law* (Oxford: Hart, 2007)

'What It's Worth to Do Your Best' *Pace Law Review*, 28 (2007): 297

Thompson, J. et al. 'Malignant Mesothelioma: Development to Therapy' *Journal of Cell Biochemistry*, 115 (2014): 1

Thomson, J.J. 'Liability and Individualized Evidence' *Law and Contemporary Problems*, 49 (1986): 199

'Remarks on Causation and Liability' *Philosophy & Public Affairs*, 13 (1984): 101

'Some Reflections on Hart and Honoré, Causation in the Law' in Kramer, M.H. et al. (eds.) *The Legacy of HLA Hart: Legal, Political and Moral Philosophy* (Oxford University Press, 2008)

'The Decline of Cause' *The Georgetown Law Review*, 76 (1987–8): 137

'The Trolley Problem' *The Yale Law Journal*, 94 (1985): 1395

Tribe, L.H. 'Trial by Mathematics: Precision and Ritual in the Legal Process' *Harvard Law Review*, 84 (1971): 1329

Tse, M.H. 'Tests for Factual Causation: Unravelling the Mystery of Material Contribution, Contribution to Risk, the Robust and Pragmatic Approach and the Inference of Causation' *Torts Law Journal*, 16 (2008): 249

Turton, G. 'A Case for Clarity in Causation?' *Medical Law Review*, 17 (2009): 140

'Risk and the Damage Requirement in Negligence Liability' *Legal Studies*, 35 (2014): 75

Tversky, A. and Kahneman, D. 'Judgment Under Uncertainty: Heuristics and Biases' *Science*, 185 (1974): 1121

Twerski, A.D. 'Market Share – A Tale of Two Centuries' *Brooklyn Law Review*, 55 (1989–90): 869

Twerski, A.D. and Cohen, N.B. 'Informed Decision Making and the Law of Torts: The Myth of Justiciable Causation' *University of Illinois Law Review*, (1988): 607
'Resolving the Dilemma of Non-Justiciable Causation in Failure-to-Warn Litigation' *Southern California Law Review*, 84 (2010): 125

Ulfbeck, V. and Holle, M. 'Tort Law and Burden of Proof – Comparative Aspects. A Special Case for Enterprise Liability' in Koziol, H. and Steininger, B. (eds.) *European Tort Law 2008* (Springer: Vienna, 2008)

Unberath, H. Entry on §259 BGB in Bamberger/Roth *Beck'scher Online-Kommentar BGB* (2011)

Van Inwagen, P. 'Free Will Remains a Mystery' *Philosophical Perspectives*, 14 (2000): 1

Veitch, E. 'The Many Facets of Cook v Lewis' 34 *Manitoba Law Journal*, (2010): 287

Viney, G. 'La responsabilité des fabricants de medicaments et de vaccines: les affres de la prevue' *Dalloz*, (2010): 391

Vioujas, V. 'La reconnaissance d'un préjudice, distinct de la perte de chance, en cas de manquement du médecin à son obligation d'information : le Conseil d'État suit l'impulsion de la Cour de cassation' *JCP*, 46 (2012): 2369

Voyiakis, E. 'The Great Illusion: Tort Law and Exposure to Danger of Physical Harm' *Modern Law Review*, 72 (2009): 909

Waddams, S.M. 'Damages: Assessment of Uncertainties' *Journal of Contract Law*, 13 (1998): 1

Wagner, G. 'Asbestschäden – Bismarck was Right: Anmerkung zu Englisch House of Lords, Entsch v 3.5.2006' *Zeitschrift für europäische Privatrecht*, (2007): 1122
Commentary to §§823 – 840 BGB in *Münchener Kommentar zum BGB Band 3: Schuldrecht, Besonderer Teil III §705–853 BGB* 5th edition (Munich: Beck, 2009)
'Comparative Tort Law' in Reimann, M. and Zimmermann, R. (eds.) *Oxford Handbook on Comparative Law* (Paperback Edition) (Oxford University Press, 2008)
'Proportionalhaftung für ärztliche Behandlungsfehler de lege lata' in: *Festschrift für G. Hirsch* 2008

Waldron, J. 'Moments of Carelessness and Massive Loss' in Owen, D. (ed). *Philosophical Foundations of Tort Law* (Oxford University Press, 1995)

Washington, G.T. 'Damages in Contract at Common Law' *Law Quarterly Review*, 48 (1932): 90

Wasserman, D. 'The Morality of Statistical Proof and the Risk of Mistaken Liability' *Cardozo Law Review*, 13 (1991): 935

Webb, C. 'Justifying Damages' in Neyers, J. and Pitel, S. (eds). *Exploring Contract Law* (Oxford: Hart, 2009)

Wedgwood, R. 'Outright Belief' *Dialectica*, 66 (2012): 309

Weigand, T. 'Loss of Chance in Medical Malpractice: Recent Developments' *Defense Counsel Law Journal*, 70 (2003): 301
'Lost Chances, Felt Necessities, and the Tale of Two Cities' *Suffolk University Law Review*, 43 (2010): 327

Weinrib, E. 'A Step Forward in Factual Causation' *Modern Law Review*, 38 (1975): 518
'Causation and Wrongdoing' *Chicago-Kent Law Review*, 63 (1987): 407; 2

'Causal Uncertainty' *Oxford Journal of Legal Studies*, Forthcoming

'Correlativity, Personality and The Emerging Consensus on Corrective Justice' *Theoretical Inquiries in Law*, 2 (2001): 107

'Poverty and Property in Kant's System of Rights' *Notre Dame Law Review*, 78 (2003): 795

'The Passing of Palsgraf?' *Vanderbilt Law Review*, 54 (2001): 803

Weir, T. 'Loss of a Chance: Compensable in Tort? The Common Law' in Guillod, O. (ed.) *Colloque Développements récents du droit de la responsabilité civile* (Zürich : Schulthess, 1991)

'Making it More Likely Versus Making it Happen' *Cambridge Law Journal*, 61 (2002): 519

Wellington, K. 'Beyond Single Causative Agents: the Scope of the *Fairchild* Exception *Post-Sienkiewicz*' *Torts Law Journal*, 20 (2013): 208

Wellman, C. 'The Rights Forfeiture Theory of Punishment' *Ethics*, 122 (2012): 371

Werro, F. 'Liability for Harm Caused by Things' (2010) (available on Social Science Research Network: accessed 1 June 2015)

Williams, B. 'Moral Luck' in Williams, B. *Moral Luck* (Cambridge University Press, 1981)

Williams, G. 'Case Comment on Cook v Lewis' *Canadian Bar Review*, 31 (1953): 315

'Which of You Did It?' *Modern Law Review*, 52 (1989): 179

Williamson, T.W. 'Armchair Philosophy, Metaphysical Modality and Counterfactual Thinking' (Presidential Address to Aristotelian Society, 2004)

'Philosophical Knowledge and Knowledge of Counterfactuals' in Christian Beyer and Alex Burri (eds.) *Philosophical Knowledge — Its Possibility and Scope* (Amsterdam: Rodopi, 2007)

Winterton, D. 'Money Awards Substituting for Performance' *Lloyd's Maritime and Commercial Law Quarterly*, (2012): 626

Wright, Lord. 'Notes on Causation and Responsibility in English Law' *Cambridge Law Journal*, (1955): 163

Wright, R.W. 'Acts and Omissions as Positive and Negative Causes' in Neyers, J.W. et al. (eds.) *Emerging Issues in Tort Law* (Oxford: Hart, 2007)

'Actual Causation vs. Probabilistic Linkage: The Bane of Economic Analysis' *Journal of Legal Studies*, 14 (1985): 435

'Allocating Liability Among Multiple Responsible Causes' *University of California, Davis Law Review*, 21 (1987–8): 1141

'Causation in Tort Law' *California Law Review*, 73 (1985): 1737

'Causation, Responsibility, Risk, Probability, Naked Statistics, and Proof: Pruning the Bramble Bush by Clarifying the Concepts' *Iowa Law Review*, 73 (1989): 1001

'Hand, Posner, and the Myth of the "Hand Formula"' *Theoretical Enquiries in Law*, 4 (2003): 145

'Liability for Possible Wrongs: Causation, Statistical Probability and the Burden of Proof', *Loyola of Los Angeles Law Review*, 41 (2009): 1295

'Once More into the Bramble Bush: Duty, Causal Contribution, and the Extent of Legal Responsibility' *Vanderbilt Law Review*, 54 (2001): 1071

'Proving Causation: Probability versus Belief' in Goldberg, R. (ed.) *Perspectives on Causation* (Oxford: Hart, 2011)

'Substantive Corrective Justice' *Iowa Law Review*, 77 (1992): 625

'The Grounds and Extent of Legal Responsibility' *San Diego Law Review*, 40 (2003): 1425

'The NESS Account of Natural Causation: A Response to Criticisms' in Goldberg, R. (ed.) *Perspectives on Causation* (Oxford: Hart, 2011)

Yeung, K. and Horder, J. 'How Can the Criminal Law Support the Provision of Quality in Healthcare' *BMJ Quality Safety* (2014) (Online first: 5 March, 2014)

Zamir, E. and Ritov, I. 'Loss Aversion, Omission Bias, and the Burden of Proof' *The Journal of Legal Studies*, 41 (2012): 165

Zardini, E. 'Luminosity and Vagueness' *Dialectica*, 66 (2012): 375

Zilich, G. 'Cutting through the Confusion of the Loss-of-Chance Doctrine: A New Cause of Action or a New Standard of Proof?' *Cleveland State Law Journal*, 50 (2002–3): 273

Zipursky, B.C. 'Civil Recourse, not Corrective Justice', *Georgetown Law Journal*, 91 (2003): 695

'Evidence, Unfairness and Market-Share Liability: A Comment on Geistfeld' *University of Pennsylvania Law Review PENNumbra*, 156 (2007): 126

'Two Dimensions of Responsibility in Crime, Tort and Moral Luck' *Theoretical Inquiries In Law*, 9 (2008): 97

Index

CAMBRIDGE STUDIES IN INTERNATIONAL AND COMPARATIVE LAW

Books in the series

Proof of Causation in Tort Law
SANDY STEEL

Taking Economic, Social and Cultural Rights Seriously in International Criminal Law
EVELYNE SCHMID

Climate Change Litigation: Regulatory Pathways to Cleaner Energy?
JACQUELINE PEEL AND
HARI OSOFSKY

Mestizo International Law: A global intellectual history 1842–1933
ARNULF BECKER LORCA

Sugar and the Making of International Trade Law
MICHAEL FAKHRI

Strategically-Created Treaty Conflicts and the Politics of International Law
SURABHI RANGANATHAN

Investment Treaty Arbitration as Public International Law: Procedural Aspects and Implications
ERIC DE BRABANDERE

The New Entrants Problem in International Fisheries Law
ANDREW SERDY

Substantive Protection under Investment Treaties: A Legal and Economic Analysis
JONATHAN BONNITCHA

Popular Governance of Post-Conflict Reconstruction: The Role of International Law
MATTHEW SAUL

Evolution of International Environmental Regimes: The Case of Climate Change
SIMONE SCHIELE

Judges, Law and War: The Judicial Development of International Humanitarian Law
SHANE DARCY

Religious Offence and Human Rights: The Implications of Defamation of Religions
LORENZ LANGER

Forum Shopping in International Adjudication: The Role of Preliminary Objections
LUIZ EDUARDO RIBEIRO SALLES

International Law and the Arctic
MICHAEL BYERS

Cooperation in the Law of Transboundary Water Resources
CHRISTINA LEB

International Organizations Before National Courts
AUGUST REINISCH

The Changing International Law of High Seas Fisheries
FRANCISCO ORREGO VICUÑA

Trade and the Environment: A Comparative Study of EC and US Law
DAMIEN GERADIN

Unjust Enrichment: A Study of Private Law and Public Values
HANOCH DAGAN

Religious Liberty and International Law in Europe
MALCOLM D. EVANS

Ethics and Authority in International Law
ALFRED P. RUBIN

Sovereignty Over Natural Resources: Balancing Rights and Duties
NICO SCHRIJVER

The Polar Regions and the Development of International Law
DONALD R. ROTHWELL

Fragmentation and the International Relations of Micro-States: Self-determination and Statehood
JORRI DUURSMA

Principles of the Institutional Law of International Organizations
C. F. AMERASINGHE

42671347R00260

Printed in Poland
by Amazon Fulfillment
Poland Sp. z o.o., Wrocław